Praise for Thomas Erl's Books

"Service Oriented Architecture is a hot, but often misunderstood topic in IT today. Thomas articulately describes the concepts, specifications, and standards behind service orientation and Web Services. For enterprises adopting SOA, there is detailed advice for service-oriented analysis, planning, and design. This book is a must read!"

—Alex Lynch, Principal Consultant, Microsoft Enterprise Services

"One primary objective of applying SOA in design is to provide business value to the solutions we build. Understanding the right approach to analyzing, designing, and developing service-oriented solutions is critical. Thomas has done a great job of demystifying SOA in practical terms with his book."

—Rick Weaver, IBM Senior Consulting Certified SW I/T Specialist

"A pragmatic guide to SOA principles, strategy, and best practices that distills the hype into a general framework for approaching SOA adoption in complex enterprise environments."

—Sameer Tyagi, Senior Staff Engineer, Sun Microsystems

"A very timely and much needed contribution to a rapidly emerging field. Through clarifying the principles and nuances of this space, the author provides a comprehensive treatment of critical key aspects of SOA from analysis and planning to standards ranging from WS-specifications to BPEL. I'll be recommending this book to both clients and peers who are planning on embracing SOA principles."

—Ravi Palepu, Senior Field Architect, Rogue Wave Software

"Finally, an SOA book based on real implementation experience in production environments. Too many SOA books get lost in the technical details of Web Services standards, or simply repeat vendor hype. This book covers the really hard parts: the complex process of planning, designing and implementing service-oriented architectures that meet organizational goals. It is an essential companion to any software developer, architect, or project manager implementing—or thinking about implementing—a service-oriented architecture."

—Priscilla Walmsley, Managing Director of Datypic

Service-Oriented Architecture

Service-Oriented Architecture

Concepts, Technology, and Design

Thomas Erl

PRENTICE HALL PROFESSIONAL TECHNICAL REFERENCE

UPPER SADDLE RIVER, NJ • BOSTON • INDIANAPOLIS • SAN FRANCISCO

NEW YORK • TORONTO • MONTREAL • LONDON • MUNICH • PARIS • MADRID

CAPE TOWN • SYDNEY • TOKYO • SINGAPORE • MEXICO CITY

The publisher offers excellent discounts on this book when ordered in quantity for bulk purchases or special sales, which may include electronic versions and/or custom covers and content particular to your business, training goals, marketing focus, and branding interests. For more information, please contact:

U. S. Corporate and Government Sales
(800) 382-3419
corpsales@pearsontechgroup.com

For sales outside the U. S., please contact:

International Sales
international@pearsoned.com

Visit us on the Web: informit.com/ph

Library of Congress Number: 2005925019

ISBN-10   0-13-185858-0
ISBN-13   978-0-13-185858-9

Text printed in the United States on recycled paper at R.R. Donnelley in Crawfordsville, Indiana.
Thirteenth Printing: January 2014

Contents

Chapter 4

The Evolution of SOA   71

Part III

SOA and Service-Orientation   277

Chapter 8

Principles of Service-Orientation   279

Chapter 9

Service Layers

Part IV

Building SOA (Planning and Analysis)   355

Chapter 10

SOA Delivery Strategies   357

Part V

Building SOA (Technology and Design)   445

Chapter 13

Service-Oriented Design (Part I: Introduction)   447

Chapter 14

Service-Oriented Design (Part II: SOA Composition Guidelines)   475

Chapter 18

SOA Platforms   651

Appendix A

Case Studies: Conclusion   707

Appendix B

Service Models Reference   717

Glossary   721

About the Author   723

About the Photographs   725

Index   727

Preface

Authoring this book involved nearly a year of writing, research, and staying on top of a subject matter that is constantly expanding its reach and importance. Although the majority of the chapters focus on service-oriented architecture from a vendor-neutral perspective, achieving an accurate representation of this perspective required that I spend a great deal of time evaluating SOA support in all primary vendor platforms. As part of this research stage I spoke with more than a hundred senior IT professionals, either through interviews or through my work as an awards judge evaluating platform submissions.

One of the most interesting facets of this project has been in defining service-orientation within the context of Web services. While studying the individual parts of what constitutes service-orientation as a paradigm, I came to realize just how many of its roots lie in past innovations. Yet at the same time, it is distinct, blending traditional and new concepts in support of a unique architectural model.

Despite its apparent "newness," SOA, on a fundamental level, is based on a very old and established school of thought. Service-orientation, as a means of separating things into independent and logical units, is a very common concept. As I progressed through these chapters, I began to notice this more often in everyday life. Items, people, organizations we come into contact with either offer some form of service or participate in performing a service. Once applied to technology architecture, though, service-orientation is concerned with a specific part of our service-oriented world: business automation.

Competitive business climates demand that corporations minimize redundant effort and maximize the expediency with which strategic goals can be achieved. Inefficient organizations that consistently waste resources are bound to fall behind. The manner in which an organization automates its business is a critical factor in determining the level of efficiency at which it operates and, ultimately, the extent of success it attains in its ventures.

This is what makes SOA so valuable. By shaping automation logic through service-orientation, existing investments can be leveraged, business intelligence can be accurately expressed, and inherent automation agility can be achieved. When coupled with the Web services technology platform, SOA offers a significant and real benefit potential that can transform the technology and outlook of an organization. My goal for this book is to help you explore, understand, and realize this potential.

Acknowledgments

While writing this book I was blessed with a strong team of technical reviewers and superior editorial, production, and marketing professionals. My thanks to all of you for your tireless efforts. A special thanks to my family for their patience and unwavering support.

Chapter 1

Introduction

1.1 Why this book is important

One of my favorite quotes came from an exchange I overheard while preparing to speak at a conference. Two IT professionals were discussing their respective environments, when one asked the other if his team was building a service-oriented architecture. The individual responded by saying "My architect thinks it's service-oriented, my developers insist it's object-oriented, and my analysts wish it would be more business-oriented. All I can tell you is that it isn't what it was before we started building Web services."

This candid statement is a sign of the times. Service-oriented architecture (SOA) has become the focal point of the IT industry, yet few fully understand it. This book aims to fill this knowledge gap by helping you accomplish the following goals:

- understand SOA, service-orientation, and Web services
- learn how to build SOA with Web services

Let's begin by identifying the most common obstacle to adopting SOA.

1.1.1 The false SOA

I cannot recall any one term causing as much confusion as "service-oriented." Its apparent ambiguity has led vendors, IT professionals, and the media to claim their own interpretations. This, of course, makes grasping the meaning of a technical architecture labeled as "service-oriented" all the more difficult.

SOA, as an abstract paradigm, has traditionally represented a baseline distributed architecture with no reference to implementation. While relevant to us, this model represents only a subset of SOA in its most common and contemporary form.

Coupled with the Web services platform and a set of commonly accepted service-orientation principles, SOA has emerged as an architectural platform explicitly distinct from its predecessors. It introduces new concepts supported by select technologies that significantly augment characteristics of traditional distributed computing platforms—so much so that service-oriented environments often end up redefining IT infrastructure.

This contemporary variety of SOA has received its share of attention. It has been promoted as a platform capable of revolutionizing enterprise environments by leveraging advancements in Web services technology and injecting organizations with hopes of federation, agility, and cross-platform harmony.

Many have been led to the notion that a technical architecture deemed service-oriented is simply one comprised of Web services. This is a common but dangerous assumption that leads to the number one mistake made by organizations intending to adopt SOA— the perception that the benefits promised by current mainstream SOA are attainable solely through a deeper investment in the Web services platform.

The reason this is happening is understandable. It is difficult for an organization to measure the extent of service-orientation possessed by its automation solutions when it is not clear what it actually means for automation logic to be truly service-oriented. What is needed is an ideal organizations can use as a target model.

1.1.2   The ideal SOA

We all have ideals that we aspire to attain. Ideals represent a state of excellence that motivate us to accomplish things beyond what we may have been able to without the ideal to look up to.

Service-orientation presents an ideal vision of a world in which resources are cleanly partitioned and consistently represented. When applied to IT architecture, service-orientation establishes a universal model in which automation logic and even business logic conform to this vision. This model applies equally to a task, a solution, an enterprise, a community, and beyond.

By adhering to this vision, past technical and philosophical disparities are blanketed by layers of abstraction that introduce a globally accepted standard for representing logic and information. This level of standardization offers an enormous benefit potential for organizations, as many of the traditional challenges faced by ever-changing IT environments can be directly addressed through the application of these standardized layers.

The service-orientation ideal has sparked a movement that has positioned SOA as the next phase in the evolution of business automation. In the same manner in which mainframe systems were succeeded by client-server applications, and client-server environments then evolved into distributed solutions based on Web technologies, the contemporary, Web services-driven SOA is succeeding traditional distributed architecture on a global scale.

All major software manufacturers and vendors are promoting support for SOA—some even through direct involvement in the development of open standards. As a result, every major development platform now officially supports the creation of service-oriented solutions. It would appear as though the realization of the SOA ideal is well underway. Why, then, is the false SOA so common?

1.1.3   The real SOA

The reality is that the rise of the false SOA has distorted the vision of the ideal SOA. Not only is the false SOA divergent from the "true path of service-orientation," it reinforces SOA anti-patterns by extending and further entrenching the traditional distributed computing model to which SOA offers an alternative. The eventual realization that initial expectations will not be fulfilled can be further compounded once the costs, effort, and overall ugliness of a retro-fitting effort are calculated.

All of this can be avoided. What is required is an understanding of service-orientation, how it shapes technical architecture into SOA, and concrete, step-by-step processes for realizing SOA in a contemporary form.

Be forewarned, though, that SOA makes some impositions. A change in mindset is required, as business logic now needs to be viewed within a service-oriented context. Applying this context also requires a change in automation logic, as solutions now need to be built in support of service-orientation. Finally, a technical architecture capable of hosting service-oriented automation logic further introduces new technology and infrastructure requirements.

Real SOAs demand that an organization undergo this form of top-down transformation. However, the ideal an organization works toward during this process is not necessarily part of a universal vision of global service-orientation. It is an ideal based on how the concept of service-orientation, the architectural model provided by contemporary SOA, and the feature set offered by supporting technologies can benefit the vision and goals of your organization.

A real SOA requires real change, real foresight, and real commitment. Most of all, though, it requires guidance. This last requirement is what this book intends to assist you with.

1.2   Objectives of this book

Let's revisit the two primary goals we established earlier and elaborate on each.

1.2.1 Understanding SOA, service-orientation, and Web services

This book is not solely focused on architecture. Service-oriented architecture is a core part of the service-oriented computing platform that brings with it new concepts, technologies, and challenges. This book explores key parts of this platform to provide well-rounded coverage of the multi-faceted world of building service-oriented automation solutions.

Specifically, the following aspects of the SOA platform are explained:

- Primitive and contemporary variations of SOA are described and defined, establishing a set of nearly 20 common characteristics that can be fulfilled by current Web services technologies and design techniques explained in the step-by-step "how to" processes.

- Fundamental Web services theory is covered, along with a study of how the emergence of XML and Web services, coupled with the dynamics between standards organizations and software vendors, have all influenced and contributed to the evolution of SOA.

- The principles of service-orientation are described in detail. Their influence on Web service design is explained, and they are further incorporated into the step-by-step design processes.

- Over 10 WS-* specifications are described in detail. Separate parts of this book are dedicated to explaining concepts in plain English and then covering the technical details with code samples.

- Advanced SOA concepts and design issues are discussed, including the creation of specialized service layers. These allow for the abstraction of business and technology domains within the enterprise and form the basis for business and application-centric service designs.

1.2.2 Learning how to build SOA with Web services

A large portion of this book is dedicated to providing step-by-step instructions on how to accomplish the following tasks:

- perform a service-oriented analysis
- model service candidates derived from existing business documentation
- design the composition of an SOA

- design application services for technology abstraction
- design business services for business logic abstraction
- design service-oriented business processes
- assess SOA support provided by J2EE and .NET platforms

1.3   Who this book is for

SOA is a broad subject matter. It represents a new generation architectural platform that encompasses a series of contemporary technologies (both proprietary and vendor-neutral).

This book will therefore be useful to various IT professionals who are interested in learning more about the following:

- how to build SOA
- service-orientation principles
- designing different types of services for SOA
- service-oriented business modeling
- features provided by key WS-* specifications
- orchestration with WS-BPEL
- SOA support in J2EE and .NET platforms
- modeling business-centric services
- creating design standards for SOA-based solutions
- Web services technology within the context of SOA

1.4   What this book does not cover

While issues relating to integration and interoperability are referenced and discussed throughout this book, service-oriented integration as a specific topic is not covered. This is to prevent overlap with *Service-Oriented Architecture: A Field Guide to Integrating XML and Web Services*, this book's companion guide. The *Field Guide* is dedicated to matters of integration and explores numerous service-oriented integration architectures, strategies, and best practices.

Also though this book will be useful to developers who want to understand how to build services for SOA and how different technology platforms support the SOA model, this is not a book that explains how to program Web services using any particular programming language. The step-by-step instructions provided focus on building and orchestrating service endpoints—not the underlying component logic. We therefore supply tutorials and/or code examples for the following open Web services languages: WSDL, SOAP, XML Schema, WS-BPEL, WS-Coordination, WS-Policy, WS-Metadata-Exchange, WS-Security, WS-Addressing, and WS-ReliableMessaging.

> **NOTE**
>
> A knowledge of XML is recommended prior to reading this book. Suggested reading materials are listed at www.soabooks.com, and a collection of introductory papers can be found at www.xmltechnologyexpert.com.

1.5 How this book is organized

The next 17 chapters contain a mountain of information. Some serious thought was given to organization so that this book would be easy to read, while maintaining a logical structure.

Content was finally divided into the following primary parts:

- Part I: SOA and Web Services Fundamentals
- Part II: SOA and WS-* Extensions
- Part III: SOA and Service-Orientation
- Part IV: Building SOA (Planning and Analysis)
- Part V: Building SOA (Technology and Design)

Essentially, Parts I, II, and III cover basic and advanced SOA concepts and theory that prepare you for Parts IV and V, which supply a series of step-by-step "how to" instructions for building SOA. Part V further contains coverage of WS-* technologies and SOA platform support provided by J2EE and .NET.

A common thread across all parts of the book is the consistent use of case studies. Over 125 individual case study examples are interspersed throughout the chapters to provide constant real-life reference points that further demonstrate key topics. Case studies are introduced in Chapter 2, which establishes background information for two fictional organizations.

Let's now take a closer look at what's covered in the remaining chapters.

1.5.1   Part I: SOA and Web Services Fundamentals

Key SOA concepts are explained, a look at how SOA has evolved from past platforms follows, and then a description of the Web services framework wraps up this first part of the book.

Introducing SOA (Chapter 3)

We start off with a chapter dedicated to nailing down a clear definition of what SOA actually is and is not. We accomplish this by first studying the core characteristics of what constitutes a fundamental or "primitive SOA." We supplement this by introducing the principles of service-orientation, and then look at the many influences that are elevating the primitive service-oriented architecture into a broader, enterprise-level platform.

As part of this exercise, we identify and explain 20 key characteristics associated with what we term as "contemporary SOA." After we progress through individual descriptions of these characteristics, we provide detailed and generic definitions of what constitutes an SOA.

To further clarify what SOA is *not*, we proceed to address a series of common myths and misperceptions. These sections help cut through some of the confusion surrounding SOA and set the groundwork for the many SOA-related topics we discuss in subsequent chapters.

We then move on to identifying and explaining the key benefits behind adopting SOA. Although these benefits are discussed throughout this book, it is important to separate them ahead of time so that we can form a clear vision of what it is we are accomplishing by transitioning to this architectural model.

Finally, we conclude this chapter with a look at the most common pitfalls facing any organization on the path toward SOA. Understanding these "worst practices" is important not only to avoiding a whole lot of problems, but also to better appreciate the reasoning behind some of the analysis and design processes provided in later chapters.

The Evolution of SOA (Chapter 4)

This chapter continues with an exploration of how SOA came to be. Specifically, we follow a timeline that looks at the following:

- Past architectural platforms from which SOA has evolved and inherited traits and qualities.

- Current influences (as fueled by XML and Web services technology platforms) that have shaped SOA into what it is now.
- The ongoing activity of standards organizations and contributing vendors that are further extending the breadth of the SOA platform.

We begin with a brief historical account of XML and Web services and discuss how these now established technologies have shaped SOA and are, to a large extent, responsible for its success. Subsequently, we turn the tables and discuss how the resulting popularity of SOA has changed the manner in which some XML and Web services technologies have been traditionally positioned and utilized.

We then dive into the current world of SOA as we discuss who and what is making SOA happen. Organizations and software vendors involved with developing contemporary SOA specifications and products are discussed. Most notably, the roles played by the following organizations are explained:

- World Wide Web Consortium (W3C)
- Web Services Interoperability Organization (WS-I)
- Organization for the Advancement of Structured Information Standards (OASIS)

The unique dynamics between standards organizations and software manufacturers are explored, with an emphasis on how vendors have influenced and contributed to the development of Web services specifications.

Next, we provide definitions for the terms "application architecture" and "enterprise architecture" and then define the architectural scope of SOA as it relates to these types of architectures. We subsequently dig up the roots of service-orientation by describing each of the following traditional platforms for the purpose of contrasting them with SOA:

- client-server architecture
- distributed Internet architecture
- distributed architectures that use Web services peripherally

For each of these architectural models, we explore the following aspects: application logic, application processing, technology, security, and administration. This part of the chapter is rounded out by a preliminary comparison of service-orientation and object-orientation.

Web Services and Primitive SOA (Chapter 5)

In Chapter 3 we formally defined the characteristics of primitive SOA. This chapter now explains how these characteristics are fulfilled by first-generation Web services technologies.

Note that this chapter introduces a new feature of the book called *In Plain English*. Even though all sections in this chapter are supplemented with examples that are part of our continuing case studies, they are further outfitted with these intentionally simplistic, non-technical analogies.

We begin with a review of the fundamental mechanics behind the Web services communications framework.

Topics covered include the following:

- basic Web services messaging
- service providers and service requestors
- service descriptions, service contracts, and metadata
- active and passive intermediaries
- message paths and service compositions
- common service models

Next, we move on to primitive SOA specifics, as we describe how service descriptions accomplish the core quality of loose coupling that contractually binds services within an SOA. Concepts specific to abstract and concrete WSDL definitions are explained and then supplemented with an introduction to UDDI and service registries.

We follow this section with an explanation of how SOAP is being used to address the messaging needs of SOA. The standardized messaging format provided by SOAP is discussed, along with a look at the SOAP message structure and the runtime roles played by SOAP processing nodes.

1.5.2   Part II: SOA and WS-* Extensions

The next set of chapters tackle advanced issues related to a multitude of contemporary SOA extensions.

Web Services and Contemporary SOA—Part I: Activity Management and Composition (Chapter 6)

This chapter picks up the tempo by venturing into the WS-* landscape. This is the first of two chapters dedicated to exploring how SOA can be extended using features provided by WS-* specifications.

The following parts of contemporary SOA are explored:

- message exchange patterns
- activities
- coordination
- atomic transactions
- business activities
- orchestration
- choreography

The sequence of these topics is intentional, as each establishes a layer of functionality upon which the next builds.

Concepts relating to the latter five items in the above list are derived from the following WS-* specifications:

- WS-Coordination
- WS-AtomicTransaction
- WS-BusinessActivity
- WS-BPEL (formerly known as BPEL4WS)
- WS-CDL (formerly known as WS-Choreography)

Because this book intentionally separates concepts from technology, the actual language and syntax-level details for these WS-* extensions are covered in *Part V: Building SOA (Technology and Design)*.

Further, this chapter explains how these specifications and their associated concepts inter-relate, as well as how they individually tie into and fulfill the predefined characteristics of contemporary SOA. Finally, it is also worth mentioning that this chapter continues providing *In Plain English* sections to help clarify concepts using non-technical analogies.

Web Services and Contemporary SOA—Part II: Advanced Messaging, Metadata, and Security (Chapter 7)
This chapter dives even more deeply into the world of SOA extensions, as we study and explain another series of concepts related to additional WS-* specifications.

The following topics are covered:

- addressing
- reliable Messaging
- correlation
- policies
- metadata Exchange
- security
- notification and Eventing

The concepts behind each of these topics are derived from the following WS-* specifications:

- WS-Addressing
- WS-ReliableMessaging
- WS-Policy Framework (including WS-PolicyAttachments and WS-PolicyAssertions)
- WS-MetadataExchange
- WS-Security (including XML-Encryption and XML-Signature)
- WS-Notification Framework (including WS-BaseNotification, WS-Topics, and WS-BrokeredNotification)
- WS-Eventing

As with Chapter 6, only concepts are discussed at this stage. The respective languages of the first five specifications in the above list are explained later in Chapter 17.

Also as with the previous chapter, how the individual extensions inter-relate and address specific characteristics of contemporary SOA is explained and supplemented with additional *In Plain English* sections.

1.5.3 Part III: SOA and Service-Orientation

Service-orientation, as a design paradigm, is explored in this part of the book. These chapters establish crucial concepts that form the basis for service and architecture-level design approaches described in later chapters.

Principles of Service-Orientation (Chapter 8)

We now turn our attention to the fundamental principles of service-orientation. It is these principles that form the basis for SOA and shape and standardize the individual services from which SOA is comprised.

This chapter introduces a view of the enterprise referenced throughout subsequent parts of this book, establishing a model that separates an enterprise into business and application logic domains. We then go on to discuss how SOA promotes service-orientation throughout both of these domains.

Next, we dissect a logical SOA and study its most fundamental parts. We begin this process with an examination of the core components of the Web services framework and then illustrate how these are positioned and augmented within SOA. We continue this exercise by examining how the components of an SOA inter relate.

We then move on to a detailed review of the eight most common principles of service-orientation. Each is explained individually and each is accompanied by a case study example. These principles are then revisited as we explore how they inter-relate. In these sections we discover how some principles support or rely on others.

The subsequent section provides a mini-study of how common object-orientation (OO) principles relate to or influence the service-orientation principles we just discussed. This is an interesting analysis for those familiar with object-orientation.

The chapter concludes with an important revelation. After explaining the principles of service-orientation, we compare them with the feature set supplied by the first-generation Web services platform. This then tells us which of the service-orientation principles are provided automatically by the mere use of Web services and which require explicit effort to realize. This is an important piece of knowledge, as it gives us a checklist of design issues that we later incorporate in the step-by-step design processes.

Service Layers (Chapter 9)

Advanced service-orientation issues are addressed in this chapter, as we set our sights on realizing further characteristics of *contemporary* SOA. We first examine the primary influences that are shaping and broadening the reach of SOA. We then study which of these influences are responsible for realizing certain characteristics. Through deduction we end up with a list of contemporary SOA characteristics that require explicit design effort. Key among these are service-oriented business modeling and organizational agility.

We then move on to defining an approach to designing SOA in support of these characteristics wherein a series of specialized service layers abstract key parts of generic and application-specific logic. This fosters SOA throughout the enterprise and facilitates the realization of many important benefits.

The following three service layers are defined at this stage:

- application service layer
- business service layer
- orchestration service layer

These layers establish the basis for a series of standardized services that are discussed and further explained in subsequent chapters. Next, we raise some issues in relation to the creation of solution-agnostic services and then conclude this chapter with an exploration of eight different service layer configuration scenarios that illustrate a range of possible SOA designs.

1.5.4   Part IV: Building SOA (Planning and Analysis)

All of the previous chapters provide a knowledge of concepts and theory that can now be applied to the real world. These next two chapters structure an SOA delivery project around the creation of a contemporary SOA and then supply detailed guidance as to how business and application logic can be defined and modeled into service candidates.

SOA Delivery Strategies (Chapter 10)
SOA is now viewed from a project delivery perspective by identifying and describing the typical phases that comprise an SOA delivery lifecycle. These phases are then assembled into the following three delivery strategies:

- top-down strategy
- bottom-up strategy
- agile strategy

The pros and cons of each are contrasted, and an emphasis is placed on the agile strategy, which attempts to blend the benefits and requirements of the top-down and bottom-up approaches.

Service-Oriented Analysis—Part I: Introduction (Chapter 11)

At this point we have covered fundamental and advanced concepts relating to SOA, service-orientation, and the many facets of the supporting Web services framework. This chapter now takes the first step of applying this knowledge by establishing the service-oriented analysis phase.

The overall objectives of service-oriented analysis are defined, followed by a list of steps required to complete this stage. The last of these steps is a service modeling process that is described in Chapter 12.

This chapter then examines what constitutes a business-centric SOA. It explains the key benefits of investing in the creation of business service layers and highlights the various ways business services can be derived from existing business models.

For the most part, the sections in this chapter assist you in preparing for the step-by-step service modeling process described in the following chapter.

Service-Oriented Analysis—Part II: Service Modeling (Chapter 12)

We now embark on a twelve-step analysis process wherein we apply service-orientation to an existing business workflow and derive business and application service candidates.

This important part of building SOA allows us to create service candidates that become a primary input for the ultimate SOA design we finalize as part of the service-oriented design processes described in upcoming chapters. Our service modeling process is supplemented with detailed case study examples that demonstrate the execution of individual process steps.

Following the process description are a dozen service modeling guidelines, providing advice, recommended analysis standards, and further insights into how best to approach and complete an SOA analysis.

Next, we provide an optional classification system that can be applied to further enhance the analysis process. This approach breaks down and labels units of logic, which can improve the clarity of documentation and the identification of potential reuse opportunities.

Finally, we complete this chapter with another detailed case study example wherein the second of our two fictional companies takes us through the service modeling process again, this time applying the aforementioned classification system. Additionally, this example results in the creation of three different service candidate combinations for the purpose of contrasting approaches.

1.5.5   Part V: Building SOA (Technology and Design)

This, the largest part in the book, provides step-by-step processes for designing specialized SOA services and creating a service-oriented business process. Numerous technology tutorials are supplied to help understand the code examples used throughout these chapters. This part concludes with an overview of what constitutes an SOA technology platform, including a review of current SOA support provided by the .NET framework and the J2EE platform.

Service-Oriented Design—Part I: Introduction (Chapter 13)

This chapter continues where we left off when we completed the service-oriented analysis phase. We now prepare to move our service candidates into service-oriented design.

The first step is an SOA composition exercise that helps identify the architectural boundary of our planned solution (this step is detailed in Chapter 14). The remaining steps consist of the following individual design processes:

- entity-centric business service design
- application service design
- task-centric business service design
- service-oriented business process design

Step-by-step descriptions for each of these design processes are provided in Chapters 15 and 16. These exercises result in the creation of WSDL definitions that implement service candidates (which originated from the service-oriented analysis process). The purpose of this chapter is to help us prepare for these processes by providing short tutorials for the following key language elements:

- WSDL
- WSDL-related XML Schema elements
- SOAP message structure elements

(Note that the language elements described are limited to those used in the case study code samples.)

This chapter ends with a discussion of service interface modeling approaches, during which modeling tools are contrasted with hand coding techniques.

Service-Oriented Design—Part II: SOA Composition Guidelines (Chapter 14)

Chapter 14 kicks off the service-oriented design process by providing guidance for composing a service-oriented architecture based on known functional requirements and technical limitations. As part of this procedure, we provide guidelines for choosing service layers and positioning identified standards and SOA extensions.

Specifically, we raise design issues related to incorporating XML, WSDL, XML Schema, SOAP, UDDI, and the WS-I Basic Profile into SOA. We then conclude this chapter with a set of considerations and guidelines for choosing WS-* specifications, with an emphasis on the use of WS-BPEL.

Service-Oriented Design—Part III: Service Design (Chapter 15)

This chapter, the longest in this book, contains three detailed, step-by-step process descriptions for designing services that correspond to two of the three service layers we established in Chapter 9.

The following design processes are described:

- entity-centric business service design
- application service design
- task-centric business service design

Each process description is supplemented with extensive case study examples that demonstrate the application of individual process steps in real-world scenarios. This important chapter is then concluded with a set of service design guidelines applicable to the previously described processes.

Service-Oriented Design—Part IV: Business Process Design (Chapter 16)

Step-by-step instructions for building a service-oriented business process are provided in this chapter. A WS-BPEL process definition is created as part of the case study examples to orchestrate services that were modeled and designed in previous chapters.

Before we get into the service-oriented business process design, we provide a tutorial describing key WS-BPEL language elements used in the detailed examples that supplement the process description steps. (A brief look at the contents of WS-Coordination SOAP headers is also included.)

Fundamental WS-* Extensions (Chapter 17)

Our SOA so far consists of a set of services that establish up to three levels of abstraction, along with a service-oriented business process responsible for orchestrating them. This next chapter provides technical insight into how the feature set of SOA can be extended with the WS-* specifications we introduced in Chapter 7.

Key elements and constructs for the following specifications are covered:

- WS-Addressing
- WS-ReliableMessaging
- WS-Policy
- WS-MetadataExchange
- WS-Security

Each language description is supplemented with case study examples containing the code used to implement the corresponding conceptual examples provided in Chapter 7.

SOA Platforms (Chapter 18)

Our final chapter takes a close look at what constitutes an implementation platform for SOA. The individual parts that comprise the development and runtime environments required to build and host a service-oriented solution are explained, along with an "under the hood" look at the implementation logic behind a typical Web service.

This is followed by two identically structured sections that supply an overview of SOA support provided by the J2EE and .NET platforms. Each of these sections begins with a high-level introduction of the respective platforms and then continues to revisit the following aspects of SOA established in earlier chapters:

- characteristics of primitive SOA
- principles of service-orientation
- characteristics of contemporary SOA

Case Studies: Conclusion (Appendix A)

Appendix A acts as a bookend to the case study storylines that began in Chapter 2. The progress of each organization is reviewed, and the resulting solution environments are studied. The original objectives established at the beginning of the book are revisited to ensure that all have been met.

Service Models Reference (Appendix B)

This appendix provides a quick reference table for all of the service models described in this book.

1.5.6 Conventions

- *Summary of Key Points*— Each primary section within a chapter ends with a summary that recaps and highlights the main topics or conclusions covered. These summaries are provided to allow readers to confirm that a given subject matter was fully understood.

- *Figures*—This book contains over 300 diagrams, which are referred to as "figures." A legend for the symbols used in these figures is provided by the book's Web site at www.soabooks.com.

- *Code examples*—On several occasions code used in this book contains examples with long lines. This happens most often when some of the larger URLs are used for namespace references. To avoid these lines from wrapping, hard line breaks are sometimes inserted. While this is done intentionally to improve clarity, it can also result in invalid XML. If you are trying out any of these examples, rejoin these lines before validating the code.

1.6 Additional information

1.6.1 The XML & Web Services Integration Framework (XWIF)

Some of the contents in this book originated from research I performed for SOA Systems Inc. (formerly XMLTC Consulting Inc.), as part of the XML & Web Services Integration Framework (XWIF) project. For more information, visit www.soasystems.com or www.xwif.com.

1.6.2   www.soabooks.com

Updates, source code, and various other supporting resources can be found at `www.soa-books.com`. I am interested in your feedback. Any experiences you'd like to share or suggestions you may have as to how I can continue to improve this book would be much appreciated.

1.6.3   Contact the Author

To contact me directly, visit my bio site at `www.thomaserl.com/technology`.

Chapter 2

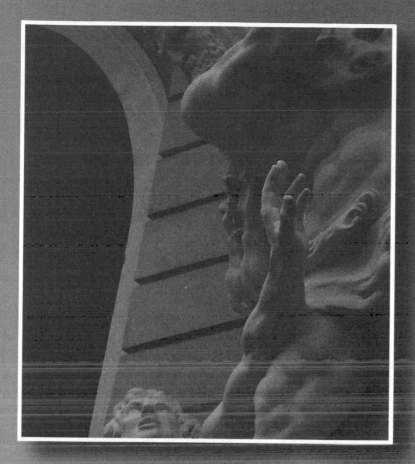

Case Studies

D ue to the distinctive nature of modern-day service-oriented architectures, using case studies is an effective way of conveying the topics covered by this book. Though purely fictional, the examples derived from these case studies raise common issues and problems faced by typical IT departments.

This chapter provides background information for two separate organizations. The first is RailCo Ltd., a mid-size company with a modest IT staff. The second, Transit Line Systems Inc. (TLS), is a larger corporation with multiple IT departments managing enterprise-level solutions. Though treated as separate case studies, these companies also have a business relationship.

2.1 How case studies are used

This book weaves approximately 125 examples relating to these case studies throughout all subsequent chapters. This essentially establishes these two organizations as constant real-world reference points. Appendix A concludes this book by ending the storylines of both case studies and exploring the results of the organizations' respective transitions to SOA.

2.1.1 Style characteristics

To more easily identify these examples, a special style element has been incorporated. Any portion of the book (beyond Chapter 2) that discusses our case studies will contain a light gray background. Below is an example.

> ...Initially, there was no concern around this approach, as each application delivered its promised set of features and solved its corresponding business problems. However, because no strategy was used to ensure that XML and Web services were being applied in a standardized manner in support of SOA, there was nothing in place to prevent the resulting design disparity...

2.1.2 Relationship to abstract content

For those of you *not* interested in learning with case studies, you can consider these parts of the book as voluntary reading. None of the abstract descriptions reference or rely on the examples. They are provided only to further assist in communicating the purpose and meaning behind the concepts, technologies, and processes covered. Feel free to bypass shaded areas or perhaps only reference them when you need further elaboration on a given subject.

2.1.3 Code samples

The chapters that comprise *Part V: Building SOA (Technology and Design)* contain numerous case study examples with markup code. These code samples are used to demonstrate many of the technologies discussed.

This book has been designed so that the supplementary technology tutorials include descriptions of all of the language elements used in the case study code samples. (Note that there are three samples in Chapter 17 that introduce elements from languages that are not explained to demonstrate an aspect of a container element that is explained.)

Now, let's introduce RailCo and TLS.

2.2 Case #1 background: RailCo Ltd.

RailCo Ltd. is an established parts supplier for railways, specializing in air brakes and related installation tools. RailCo ships air brake parts internationally, but 90% of its sales are in North America. Though its primary line of business is product resale, RailCo also has a small group of specialized technicians that are hired out locally for installations and repairs.

2.2.1 History

Established in the early 90s, this company has gradually grown from a staff of 12 to 40. It started out as a brokerage for various railway wholesalers, but then came to specialize in air brakes. The narrowed business focus resulted in increased opportunities, as RailCo was able to become a wholesaler in its own right by dealing directly with air brake parts manufacturers.

2.2.2 Technical infrastructure

Five employees and one manager are dedicated to full-time IT duties, responsible primarily for maintaining client workstations and back-end servers. Custom development tasks have typically been outsourced to local consulting firms, whereas periodic upgrades and maintenance fixes have been the responsibility of in-house staff.

2.2.3   Automation solutions

RailCo's automated environment consists of the following applications:

- A two-tier client-server system governing all accounting and inventory control transactions. Two administrative clerks manually feed this solution with standard transaction document data (primarily incoming and outgoing purchase orders and invoices). Receipt and submission of these documents typically initiates corresponding inventory receiving and order shipping processes.

- A contact management system in which customer and business partner profile information is stored and maintained. This simple application consists of a database fronted by Web-based data entry and reporting user-interfaces. Users range from managers to administrative assistants and accounting personnel.

2.2.4   Business goals and obstacles

Profit margins have been noticeably declining over the past year. A recent review revealed that the overhead associated with RailCo's current business processes is limiting its ability to remain competitive. Clients have been switching to another company providing the same products in a more efficient manner and at a lower cost.

Further investigation led to the discovery that this competitor has implemented an extension to their existing accounting system, allowing them to perform various transactions online via B2B solutions provided by some of the larger clients. They have subsequently been able to reduce the staff required for processing orders, while increasing response time and lowering their overall price point. Another unpleasant revelation was that RailCo's primary client, Transit Line Systems, has started an online relationship with this competitor as well.

RailCo is a company with outdated technology automating inefficient business processes. It is looking to overhaul its technical environment to better respond to new business trends and automation requirements.

To remain competitive and minimize losses, RailCo must upgrade its automation environment as soon as possible. Its top priority is to participate in online transactions with TLS. Before our storyline begins, RailCo has already hurried to build a pair of Web services (Figure 2.1) that enable it to connect with the existing TLS B2B solution. These services are explained and referenced as we progress through chapters discussing Web services technology.

The design of this solution, though, is revisited and expanded in Part V. By that point RailCo runs into some limitations and decides to re-evaluate its environment in consideration of establishing an SOA. Further, RailCo realizes that it must also seek new clients to make up for the lost sales to TLS. This new requirement ends up also affecting the design of its SOA.

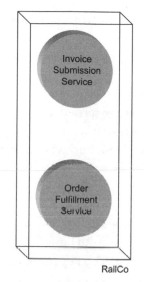
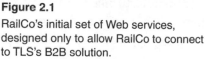

Figure 2.1

RailCo's initial set of Web services,
designed only to allow RailCo to connect
to TLS's B2B solution.

Note that though technically a Web service with its own WSDL, the Invoice Submission Service frequently acts as a service requestor, issuing invoice documents to a TLS Web service. It is important not to view this service as just a Web service client program. It begins to perform more of a provider role in later chapters where it evolves along with RailCo's SOA. Chapter 5 explains how services play both requestor and provider roles.

2.3   Case #2 background: Transit Line Systems Inc.

Transit Line Systems Inc. (TLS) is a prominent corporation in the private transit sector. It employs over 1,800 people and has offices in four cities. Though its primary line of business is providing private transit, it has a number of secondary business areas, including the following:

- A maintenance and repair branch that outsources TLS service technicians to public transit sectors.
- Parts manufacturing for other industries.
- A tourism branch that partners with airlines and hotels.

2.3.1 History

TLS existed as a mid-sized corporation centered around a single private railway for several years. However, the end of a long-term battle with a rival railway (which resulted in the bankruptcy of its competitor) sparked an era of growth. TLS enjoyed a successful period of expansion during which it established two further private railways in separate cities. Over the course of approximately ten years, TLS made a series of corporate acquisitions, including:

- G&R Tracks Ltd., a privately owned railway company (its original competitor) that provided TLS with enough rail assets to launch a new railway in a neighboring city. G&R had over 180 employees, but TLS kept only ten technical specialists.
- Sampson Steel Corp., a large manufacturing plant that produced various metal parts for clients in the automobile and airline industries. An economic downturn sent this company to the brink of liquidation until TLS stepped in. TLS formed a partnership with Sampson Steel, making TLS majority owners, but allowing the original Sampson management group to continue operational control of the factory. While Sampson Steel continues to service its existing clientele, its primary focus became the production and assembly of parts for TLS's railways. Though only generic parts can be produced by the factory, this arrangement allows TLS to acquire these parts at a fraction of the original supplier's prices.

2.3.2 Technical infrastructure

The TLS head office contains a sizable IT department. Of the 200 IT professionals that support TLS's automation solutions, approximately 50% are contractors, hired on a per-project basis.

The overall technical infrastructure is mixed. More contemporary eBusiness solutions are hosted in a clustered server environment, capable of high transaction volumes and with robust backup and disaster recovery mechanisms in place. Individual legacy systems are typically isolated in separate environments, depending on the nature of the system. Mainframes have their own space, and a series of Windows servers individually house older, specialized client-server applications and associated databases.

2.3.3 Automation solutions

Following is the subset of TLS's inventory of legacy systems that we will be referencing in case study examples:

- A distributed enterprise accounting solution, accommodating some 400 users. It replaced TLS's original accounting package during its expansion period, when accounting requirements grew along with the size of the company. This solution is partially custom developed but relies mostly on out-of-the-box accounting features. It provides sophisticated Web front-ends for intranet and remote access but also offers some desktop tools for analysis and reporting. The product vendor is relatively progressive and has offered a set of Web service adapters that plug into different modules of the overall system.

- A third-party time tracking system used by employees that are outsourced by TLS to record the time they spend at client sites. The information collected by this program is later manually entered into the accounts receivable module of the accounting system.

2.3.4 Business goals and obstacles

TLS is a corporation that has undergone a great deal of change over the past decade. The identity and structure of the company has been altered numerous times, mostly because of corporate acquisitions and the subsequent integration processes. Its IT department has had to deal with a volatile business model and regular additions to its supported set of technologies and automation solutions. TLS's technical environment therefore is riddled with custom developed applications and third-party products that were never intended to work together.

The cost of business automation has skyrocketed, as the effort required to integrate these many systems is increasingly complex and onerous. Not only has the maintenance of automation solutions become unreasonably expensive, their complexity and lack of flexibility have significantly slowed IT response time to business process changes.

Tired of having to continually invest in a non-functional technical environment, IT directors decided to adopt SOA as the standard architecture to be used for new applications and as the founding principle to unite existing legacy systems. The primary motivation behind this decision is a desperate need to introduce enterprise-wide standardization and increase organizational agility.

As the storyline begins, TLS has built its first service-oriented solution already (Figure 2.2). This is the B2B system to which RailCo and many other vendors connect to conduct transactions online. The services that comprise this solution are introduced in Chapter 5, and are then referenced throughout the chapters that discuss Web services technology. However in Part V, TLS embarks on its second SOA project. This shifts our focus to a new set of services, as well as the related adjustments TLS makes to its technology platform.

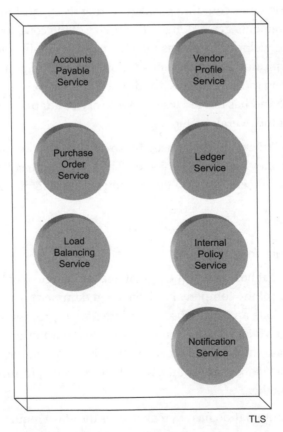

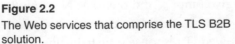

Figure 2.2
The Web services that comprise the TLS B2B
solution.

Part I

SOA and Web Services Fundamentals

This book fully acknowledges that SOA and service-orientation are implementation-agnostic paradigms that can be realized through any suitable technology platform. Perhaps one day Web services will be supplanted by a superior platform even more capable of bringing the world closer to pure service-orientation. For now, though, the Web services platform (and all that comes with it) is as good as it gets.

Much of this book is therefore focused on realizing SOA through and applying service-orientation principles to Web services technology. Conversely, our coverage of Web services concepts and technology is provided specifically within the context of SOA and service-orientation.

"The following three chapters lay the groundwork by establishing, on a high level, what SOA is, how it's come to be, and the basic Web services technologies most commonly used for its implementation."

Introducing SOA

efore we get into the many details of understanding and building service-oriented solutions, let's first introduce some basic concepts and establish a range of associated issues.

3.1 Fundamental SOA

Because the term "service-oriented" has existed for some time, it has been used in different contexts and for different purposes. One constant through its existence has been that it represents a distinct approach for separating concerns. What this means is that logic required to solve a large problem can be better constructed, carried out, and managed if it is decomposed into a collection of smaller, related pieces. Each of these pieces addresses a concern or a specific part of the problem.

This approach transcends technology and automation solutions. It is an established and generic theory that can be used to address a variety of problems. What distinguishes the service-oriented approach to separating concerns is the manner in which it achieves separation.

3.1.1 A service-oriented analogy

Let's take your average cosmopolitan city. It is already full of service-oriented businesses. Individual companies are service-oriented in that each provides a distinct service that can be used by multiple consumers. Collectively, these businesses comprise a business community. It makes sense for a business community not to be served by a single business outlet providing all services. By decomposing the community into specialized, individual outlets, we achieve an environment in which these outlets can be distributed.

When coupled with "architecture," service-orientation takes on a technical connotation. "Service-oriented architecture" is a term that represents a model in which automation logic is decomposed into smaller, distinct units of logic. Collectively, these units comprise a larger piece of business automation logic. Individually, these units can be distributed.

Distributing automation logic into separate units is nothing new. What is it then that makes *service-oriented* separation so different? Much of this book is dedicated to answering that question. However, let's take a preliminary look at some notable distinctions.

Even in a distributed business community, if we impose overbearing dependencies, we could inhibit the potential of individual businesses. Although we want to allow outlets to interact and leverage each other's services, we want to avoid a model in which outlets form tight connections that result in constrictive inter-dependencies. By empowering businesses to self-govern their individual services, we allow them to evolve and grow relatively independent from each other.

Though we encourage independence within our business outlets, we must still ensure that they agree to adhere to certain baseline conventions—for example, a common currency for the exchange of goods and services, a building code that requires signage to conform to certain parameters or perhaps a requirement that all employees speak the same language as the native consumers. These conventions standardize key aspects of each business for the benefit of the consumers without significantly imposing on the individual business's ability to exercise self-governance.

Similarly, service-oriented architecture (SOA) encourages individual units of logic to exist autonomously yet not isolated from each other. Units of logic are still required to conform to a set of principles that allow them to evolve independently, while still maintaining a sufficient amount of commonality and standardization. Within SOA, these units of logic are known as *services*.

3.1.2   How services encapsulate logic

To retain their independence, services encapsulate logic within a distinct context. This context can be specific to a business task, a business entity, or some other logical grouping.

The concern addressed by a service can be small or large. Therefore, the size and scope of the logic represented by the service can vary. Further, service logic can encompass the logic provided by other services. In this case, one or more services are composed into a collective.

For example, business automation solutions are typically an implementation of a business process. This process is comprised of logic that dictates the actions performed by the solution. The logic is decomposed into a series of steps that execute in predefined sequences according to business rules and runtime conditions.

As shown in Figure 3.1, when building an automation solution consisting of services, each service can encapsulate a task performed by an individual step or a sub-process comprised of a set of steps. A service can even encapsulate the entire process logic. In the latter two cases, the larger scope represented by the services may encompass the logic encapsulated by other services.

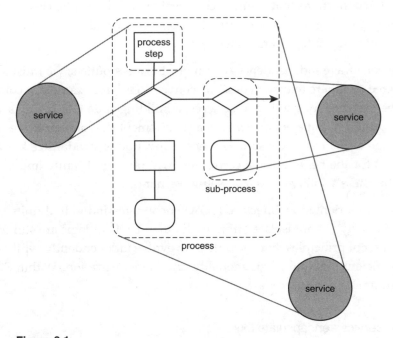

Figure 3.1
Services can encapsulate varying amounts of logic.

For services to use the logic they encapsulate they can participate in the execution of business activities. To do so, they must form distinct relationships with those that want to use them.

3.1.3   How services relate

Within SOA, services can be used by other services or other programs. Regardless, the relationship between services is based on an understanding that for services to interact, they must be aware of each other. This awareness is achieved through the use of *service descriptions*.

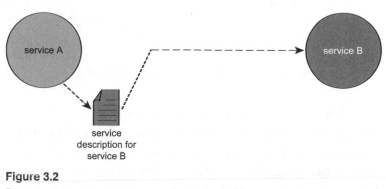

Figure 3.2

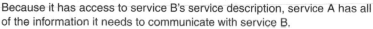

Because it has access to service B's service description, service A has all of the information it needs to communicate with service B.

A service description in its most basic form establishes the name and location of the service, as well as its data exchange requirements. The manner in which services use service descriptions results in a relationship classified as *loosely coupled*. For example, Figure 3.2 illustrates that service A is aware of service B because service A is in possession of service B's service description. (Loose coupling is explained in detail in Chapter 8.)

For services to interact and accomplish something meaningful, they must exchange information. A communications framework capable of preserving their loosely coupled relationship is therefore required. One such framework is *messaging*.

3.1.4   How services communicate

After a service sends a message on its way, it loses control of what happens to the message thereafter. That is why we require messages to exist as "independent units of communication." This means that messages, like services, should be autonomous. To that effect, messages can be outfitted with enough intelligence to self-govern their parts of the processing logic (Figure 3.3).

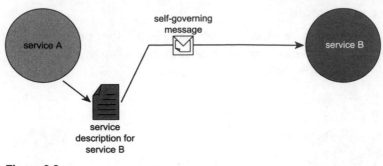

Figure 3.3
A message existing as an independent unit of communication.

Services that provide service descriptions and communicate via messages form a basic architecture. So far, this architecture appears similar to past distributed architectures that support messaging and a separation of interface from processing logic. What distinguishes ours is how its three core components (services, descriptions, and messages) are designed. This is where *service-orientation* comes in.

3.1.5   How services are designed

Much like object-orientation, service-orientation has become a distinct design approach which introduces commonly accepted principles that govern the positioning and design of our architectural components (Figure 3.4).

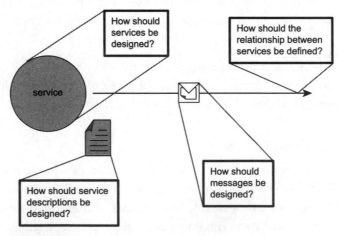

Figure 3.4
Service-orientation principles address design issues.

The application of service-orientation principles to processing logic results in standardized service-oriented processing logic. When a solution is comprised of units of service-oriented processing logic, it becomes what we refer to as a *service-oriented solution*.

The individual principles of service-orientation are fully explained later in this book. For the purpose of providing a preliminary introduction, let's highlight some of the key aspects of these principles here:

- *Loose coupling*—Services maintain a relationship that minimizes dependencies and only requires that they retain an awareness of each other.

- *Service contract*—Services adhere to a communications agreement, as defined collectively by one or more service descriptions and related documents.

- *Autonomy*—Services have control over the logic they encapsulate.

- *Abstraction*—Beyond what is described in the service contract, services hide logic from the outside world.

- *Reusability*—Logic is divided into services with the intention of promoting reuse.

- *Composability*—Collections of services can be coordinated and assembled to form composite services.

- *Statelessness*—Services minimize retaining information specific to an activity.

- *Discoverability*—Services are designed to be outwardly descriptive so that they can be found and assessed via available discovery mechanisms.

With a knowledge of the components that comprise our basic architecture and a set of design principles we can use to shape and standardize these components, all that is missing is an implementation platform that will allow us to pull these pieces together to build service-oriented automation solutions. The *Web services* technology set offers us such a platform.

3.1.6   How services are built

As we mentioned earlier, the term "service-oriented" and various abstract SOA models existed before the arrival of Web services. However, no one technology advancement has been so suitable and successful in manifesting SOA than Web services.

All major vendor platforms currently support the creation of service-oriented solutions, and most do so with the understanding that the SOA support provided is based on the use of Web services. Therefore, while we fully acknowledge that achieving SOA does not require Web services, this book's focus is on how SOA can and should be realized through the use of the Web services technology platform.

3.1.7 Primitive SOA

The past few sections have described the individual ingredients for what we call *primitive SOA*. It is labeled as such because it represents a baseline technology architecture that is supported by current major vendor platforms.

All forms of SOA we explore from here on are based on and extend this primitive model. Some of the extensions we discuss are attainable today through the application of advanced design techniques, while others rely on the availability of pre-defined Web services specifications and corresponding vendor support.

CASE STUDY

RailCo's accounting solution exists as a two-tier client-server application, where the bulk of application logic resides within an executable deployed on client workstations. The details of this application are described in the next chapter. For now, let's identify two of the primary tasks it can perform:

- Enter Customer Purchase Order
- Create Customer Order

The completion of each task involves a series of steps that constitute a business process. This process was originally modeled using standard workflow logic and then implemented as part of a packaged solution. Within the application, the process may or may not be separately represented by individual sets of programming routines. Regardless, it is compiled into a single executable that provides a fixed manner in which the process is automated.

Within a service-oriented business model, the logic behind each process would be partitioned into one or more services. If multiple services are used, the execution of the entire process would involve the composition of these services. In this case, each service may represent a sub-process or even a single step within the process that can be executed independently. For example, the Create Customer Order Process may consist of the following sub-processes:

- Retrieve Purchase Order Data
- Check Inventory Availability
- Generate Back Order
- Publish Customer Order

As we know, a process in its entirety can be viewed and modeled as a service. Additionally, one or more processes can be combined to represent an even larger service. For example, the Create Customer Order and Generate Customer Invoice Processes may be combined to form a single Order Processing Process.

Finally, we would also expect these processes to be flexible so that they can incorporate processes or resources that exist elsewhere in the enterprise. For instance, we may decide to extend the Order Processing Process to include a sub-process that automatically retrieves the customer's current accounts payable mailing address. This sub-process may already exist as part of a separate Customer Contact Reporting Process.

To implement such a model, we need a technical architecture capable of providing the following:

- The ability for business automation logic to be partitioned into units so as to properly represent services.
- The ability for these units of logic to be relatively independent of each other so as to support the requirement for them to participate in different compositions.
- The ability for these units of logic to communicate with each other in such a manner that their respective independence is preserved.

The fundamental characteristics of service encapsulation, loose-coupling, and messaging, as realized through service-orientation principles and the Web services technology set, collectively fulfill these requirements through the implementation of a primitive SOA.

SUMMARY OF KEY POINTS

- SOA and service-orientation are implementation-agnostic paradigms that can be realized with any suitable technology platform.
- Our primitive SOA model represents a mainstream variation of SOA based solely on Web services and common service-orientation principles.
- Throughout the remainder of this book, any reference to the term "SOA" implies the primitive SOA model.

3.2   Common characteristics of contemporary SOA

Numerous recent and ongoing industry trends and developments have shaped the real world look of SOA. Its founding principles remain, but many have been expanded primarily because the opportunity to do so has been readily acted upon.

Major software vendors are continually conceiving new Web services specifications and building increasingly powerful XML and Web services support into current technology platforms. The result is an extended variation of service-oriented architecture we refer to as *contemporary SOA.*

Contemporary SOA builds upon the primitive SOA model by leveraging industry and technology advancements to further its original ideals. Though the required implementation technology can vary, contemporary SOAs have evolved to a point where they can be associated with a set of common characteristics.

Specifically, we explore the following primary characteristics:

- Contemporary SOA is at the core of the service-oriented computing platform.
- Contemporary SOA increases quality of service.
- Contemporary SOA is fundamentally autonomous.
- Contemporary SOA is based on open standards.
- Contemporary SOA supports vendor diversity.
- Contemporary SOA fosters intrinsic interoperability.
- Contemporary SOA promotes discovery.
- Contemporary SOA promotes federation.
- Contemporary SOA promotes architectural composability.
- Contemporary SOA fosters inherent reusability.
- Contemporary SOA emphasizes extensibility.
- Contemporary SOA supports a service-oriented business modeling paradigm.
- Contemporary SOA implements layers of abstraction.
- Contemporary SOA promotes loose coupling throughout the enterprise.
- Contemporary SOA promotes organizational agility.
- Contemporary SOA is a building block.
- Contemporary SOA is an evolution.

- Contemporary SOA is still maturing.
- Contemporary SOA is an achievable ideal.

Note the absence of traditional architectural qualities such as "secure," "transactional," "reliable," and so on. These have been grouped into the "Contemporary SOA increases quality of service" characteristic. Chapters 6 and 7 explain how the evolving landscape of Web services specifications addresses typical quality of service (QoS) requirements.

As we step through the following sections we elaborate on each of the characteristics in our list and discuss their overall meaning to SOA. In doing so, we also build a formal definition of contemporary SOA.

3.2.1   Contemporary SOA is at the core of the service-oriented computing platform

Before we get into the actual meaning behind contemporary SOA, let's first discuss how the term "SOA" has been tossed about within the IT industry. Many argue that the manner in which SOA is used to qualify products, designs, and technologies elevates this term beyond one that simply relates to architecture. SOA, some believe, has become synonymous with an entire new world application computing platform.

Past terms used to identify distinct application computing platforms were often suffixed with the word "architecture" when the architecture was actually being referenced. The terms "client-server" or "n-tier," for example, can be used to classify a tool, an administration infrastructure, or an application architecture.

With SOA, however, the actual acronym has become a multi-purpose buzzword used frequently when discussing an application computing platform consisting of Web services technology and service-orientation principles. Because the acronym already represents the word "architecture" we are unfortunately subjected to statements that can be confusing.

Perhaps the best way to view it is that if a product, design, or technology is prefixed with "SOA," it is something that was (directly or indirectly) created in support of an architecture based on service-orientation principles. Along those same lines, this book, though partially titled "Service-Oriented Architecture," goes well beyond architectural boundaries to explore the contemporary service-oriented platform.

Because we positioned contemporary SOA as building upon and extending the primitive SOA model, we already have a starting point for our definition:

> *Contemporary SOA represents an architecture that promotes service-orientation through the use of Web services.*

3.2.2　Contemporary SOA increases quality of service

There is a definite need to bring SOA to a point where it can implement enterprise-level functionality as safely and reliably as the more established distributed architectures already do.

This relates to common quality of service requirements, such as:

- The ability for tasks to be carried out in a secure manner, protecting the contents of a message, as well as access to individual services.

- Allowing tasks to be carried out reliably so that message delivery or notification of failed delivery can be guaranteed.

- Performance requirements to ensure that the overhead imposed by SOAP message and XML content processing does not inhibit the execution of a task.

- Transactional capabilities to protect the integrity of specific business tasks with a guarantee that should the task fail, exception logic is executed.

Contemporary SOA is striving to fill the QoS gaps of the primitive SOA model. Many of the concepts and specifications we discuss in *Part II—SOA and WS-* Extensions* provide features that directly address quality of service requirements. For lack of a better term, we'll refer to an SOA that fulfills specific quality of service requirements as "QoS-capable."

3.2.3　Contemporary SOA is fundamentally autonomous

The service-orientation principle of autonomy requires that individual services be as independent and self-contained as possible with respect to the control they maintain over their underlying logic. This is further realized through message-level autonomy where messages passed between services are sufficiently intelligence-heavy that they can control the manner in which they are processed by recipient services.

SOA builds upon and expands this principle by promoting the concept of autonomy throughout solution environments and the enterprise. Applications comprised of autonomous services, for example, can themselves be viewed as composite, self-reliant services that exercise their own self-governance within service-oriented integration environments.

Later we explain how, by creating service abstraction layers, entire domains of solution logic can achieve control over their respective areas of governance. This establishes a level of autonomy that can cross solution boundaries.

3.2.4   Contemporary SOA is based on open standards

Perhaps the most significant characteristic of Web services is the fact that data exchange is governed by open standards. After a message is sent from one Web service to another it travels via a set of protocols that is globally standardized and accepted.

Further, the message itself is standardized, both in format and in how it represents its pay-load. The use of SOAP, WSDL, XML, and XML Schema allow for messages to be fully self-contained and support the underlying agreement that to communicate, services require nothing more than a knowledge of each other's service descriptions. The use of an open, standardized messaging model eliminates the need for underlying service logic to share dependencies (such as type systems) and supports the loosely coupled paradigm.

Contemporary SOAs fully leverage and reinforce this open, vendor-neutral communications framework (Figure 3.5). An SOA limits the role of proprietary technology to the implementation and hosting of the application logic encapsulated by a service. The opportunity for inter-service communication is therefore always an option.

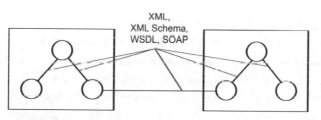

Figure 3.5
Standard open technologies are used within and outside of
solution boundaries.

3.2.5   Contemporary SOA supports vendor diversity

The open communications framework explained in the previous section not only has significant implications for bridging much of the heterogeneity within (and between) corporations, but it also allows organizations to choose best-of-breed environments for specific applications.

For example, regardless of how proprietary a development environment is, as long as it supports the creation of standard Web services, it can be used to create a non-proprietary service interface layer, opening up interoperability opportunities with other, service-capable applications (Figure 3.6). This, incidentally, has changed the face of integration architectures, which now can encapsulate legacy logic through service adapters, and leverage middleware advancements based on Web services.

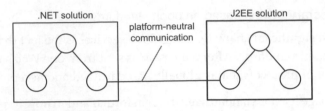

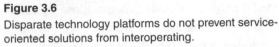

Figure 3.6
Disparate technology platforms do not prevent service-oriented solutions from interoperating.

Organizations can certainly continue building solutions with existing development tools and server products. In fact, it may make sense to do so, only to continue leveraging the skill sets of in-house resources. However, the choice to explore the offerings of new vendors is always there. This option is made possible by the open technology provided by the Web services framework and is made more attainable through the standardization and principles introduced by SOA.

3.2.6   Contemporary SOA promotes discovery

Even though the first generation of Web services standards included UDDI, few of the early implementations actually used service registries as part of their environments. This may have to do with the fact that not enough Web services were actually built to warrant a registry. However, another likely reason is that the concept of service discovery was simply not designed into the architecture. When utilized within traditional distributed architectures, Web services were more often employed to facilitate point-to-point solutions. Therefore, discovery was not a common concern.

SOA supports and encourages the advertisement and discovery of services throughout the enterprise and beyond. A serious SOA will likely rely on some form of service registry or directory to manage service descriptions (Figure 3.7).

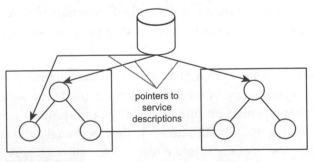

Figure 3.7
Registries enable a mechanism for the discovery of services.

3.2.7 Contemporary SOA fosters intrinsic interoperability

Further leveraging and supporting the required usage of open standards, a vendor diverse environment, and the availability of a discovery mechanism, is the concept of intrinsic interoperability. Regardless of whether an application actually has immediate integration requirements, design principles can be applied to outfit services with characteristics that naturally promote interoperability.

When building a service-oriented application from the ground up, services with intrinsic interoperability become potential integration endpoints (Figure 3.8). When properly standardized, this leads to service-oriented integration architectures wherein solutions themselves achieve a level of intrinsic interoperability. Fostering this characteristic can significantly alleviate the cost and effort of fulfilling future cross-application integration requirements, and evolves the enterprise into one where traditional application boundaries begin to disappear.

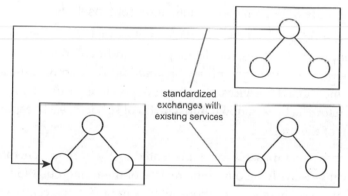

standardized exchanges with existing services

Figure 3.8
Intrinsically interoperable services enable unforeseen integration opportunities.

3.2.8 Contemporary SOA promotes federation

Establishing SOA within an enterprise does not necessarily require that you replace what you already have. One of the most attractive aspects of this architecture is its ability to introduce unity across previously non-federated environments. While Web services enable federation, SOA promotes this cause by establishing and standardizing the ability to encapsulate legacy and non-legacy application logic and by exposing it via a common, open, and standardized communications framework (also supported by an extensive adapter technology marketplace).

Obviously, the incorporation of SOA with previous platforms can lead to a variety of hybrid solutions. However, the key benefit is that the communication channels achieved by service-oriented integration are all uniform and standardized (Figure 3.9).

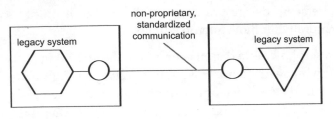

Figure 3.9
Services enable standardized federation of disparate legacy systems.

3.2.9   Contemporary SOA promotes architectural composability

Composability is a deep-rooted characteristic of SOA that can be realized on different levels. For example, by fostering the development and evolution of composable services, SOA supports the automation of flexible and highly adaptive business processes. As previously mentioned, services exist as independent units of logic. A business process can therefore be broken down into a series of services, each responsible for executing a portion of the process.

A broader example of composability is represented by the second-generation Web services framework that is evolving out of the release of the numerous WS-* specifications. The modular nature of these specifications allows an SOA to be composed of only the functional building blocks it requires.

What provides this flexibility is the fact that second-generation Web services specifications are being designed specifically to leverage the SOAP messaging model. Individual specifications consist of modular extensions that provide one or more specific features. As the offering of WS-* extensions supported by a given vendor platform grows, the flexibility to compose allows you to continue building solutions that only implement the features actually needed (Figure 3.10). In other words, the WS-* platform allows for the creation of streamlined and optimized service-oriented architectures, applications, services, and even messages.

With respect to our definition, let's represent this characteristic by describing the architecture as a whole as being composable. This represents both composable services, as well as the extensions that comprise individual SOA implementations.

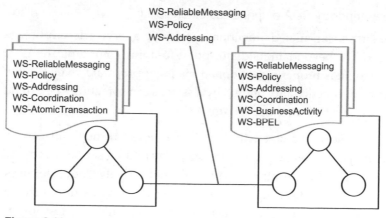

Figure 3.10

Different solutions can be composed of different extensions and can continue to interoperate as long as they support the common extensions required.

3.2.10 Contemporary SOA fosters inherent reusability

SOA establishes an environment that promotes reuse on many levels. For example, services designed according to service-orientation principles are encouraged to promote reuse, even if no immediate reuse requirements exist. Collections of services that form service compositions can themselves be reused by larger compositions.

The emphasis placed by SOA on the creation of services that are agnostic to both the business processes and the automation solutions that utilize them leads to an environment in which reuse is naturally realized as a side benefit to delivering services for a given project (Figure 3.11).

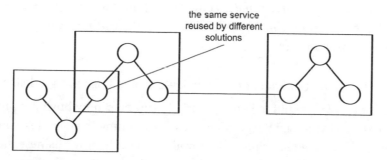

Figure 3.11

Inherent reuse accommodates unforeseen reuse opportunities.

3.2.11   Contemporary SOA emphasizes extensibility

When expressing encapsulated functionality through a service description, SOA encourages you to think beyond immediate, point-to-point communication requirements. When service logic is properly partitioned via an appropriate level of interface granularity, the scope of functionality offered by a service can sometimes be extended without breaking the established interface (Figure 3.12).

Extensibility is also a characteristic that is promoted throughout SOA as a whole. Extending entire solutions can be accomplished by adding services or by merging with other service-oriented applications (which also, effectively, "adds services"). Because the loosely coupled relationship fostered among all services minimizes inter-service dependencies, extending logic can be achieved with significantly less impact.

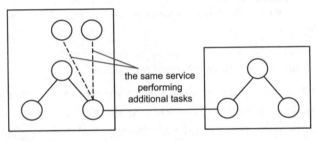

Figure 3.12
Extensible services can expand functionality with minimal impact.

Time to revisit our original definition to add a few adjectives that represent the characteristics we've covered.

> *Contemporary SOA represents an **open, extensible, federated, composable** architecture that promotes service-orientation and is **comprised of autonomous, QoS-capable, vendor diverse, interoperable, discoverable**, and **potentially reusable** services, implemented as Web services.*

3.2.12   Contemporary SOA supports a service-oriented business modeling paradigm

In our description of a primitive SOA, we briefly explored how business processes can be represented and expressed through services. Partitioning business logic into services that can then be composed has significant implications as to how business processes can be modeled (Figure 3.13). Analysts can leverage these features by incorporating an extent of service-orientation into business processes for implementation through SOAs.

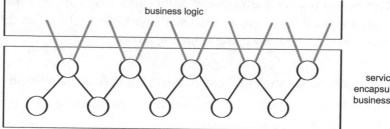

Figure 3.13
A collection (layer) of services encapsulating business process logic.

In other words, services can be designed to express business logic. BPM models, entity models, and other forms of business intelligence can be accurately represented through the coordinated composition of business-centric services. This is an area of SOA that is not yet widely accepted or understood. We therefore spend a significant portion of this book exploring the service-oriented business modeling paradigm.

3.2.13   Contemporary SOA implements layers of abstraction

One of the characteristics that tends to evolve naturally through the application of service-orientation design principles is that of abstraction. Typical SOAs can introduce layers of abstraction by positioning services as the sole access points to a variety of resources and processing logic.

When applied through proper design, abstraction can be targeted at business and application logic. For example, by establishing a layer of endpoints that represent entire solutions and technology platforms, all of the proprietary details associated with these environments disappear (Figure 3.14). The only remaining concern is the functionality offered via the service interfaces

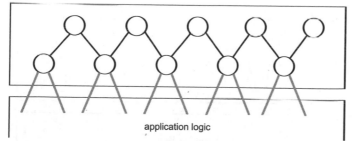

Figure 3.14
Application logic created with proprietary technology can be abstracted through a dedicated service layer.

It is the mutual abstraction of business and technology that supports the service-oriented business modeling paradigm we discussed and further establishes the loosely coupled enterprise model explained in the following section.

3.2.14   Contemporary SOA promotes loose coupling throughout the enterprise

As we've established, a core benefit to building a technical architecture with loosely coupled services is the resulting independence of service logic. Services only require an awareness of each other, allowing them to evolve independently.

Now, let's take a step back and look at the enterprise as a whole. Within an organization where service-orientation principles are applied to both business modeling and technical design, the concept of loose coupling is amplified.

By implementing standardized service abstraction layers, a loosely coupled relationship also can be achieved between the business and application technology domains of an enterprise (Figure 3.15). Each end only requires an awareness of the other, therefore allowing each domain to evolve more independently. The result is an environment that can better accommodate business and technology-related change—a quality known as organizational agility.

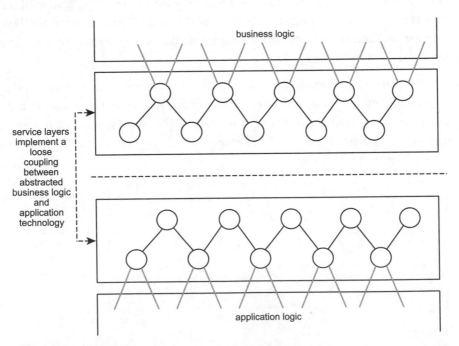

Figure 3.15
Through the implementation of service layers that abstract business and application logic, the loose coupling paradigm can be applied to the enterprise as a whole.

3.2.15   Contemporary SOA promotes organizational agility

Whether the result of an internal reorganization, a corporate merger, a change in an organization's business scope, or the replacement of an established technology platform, an organization's ability to accommodate change determines the efficiency with which it can respond to unplanned events.

Change in an organization's business logic can impact the application technology that automates it. Change in an organization's application technology infrastructure can impact the business logic automated by this technology. The more dependencies that exist between these two parts of an enterprise, the greater the extent to which change imposes disruption and expense.

By leveraging service business representation, service abstraction, and the loose coupling between business and application logic provided through the use of service layers, SOA offers the potential to increase organizational agility (Figure 3.16).

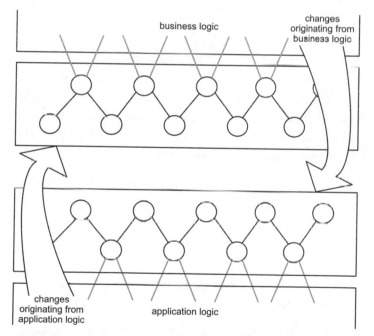

Figure 3.16

A loosely coupled relationship between business and application technology allows each end to more efficiently respond to changes in the other.

Other benefits realized through the standardization of SOA also contribute to minimizing dependencies and increasing overall responsiveness to change: notably, the intrinsic interoperability that can be built into services and the open communications framework established across integration architectures that enable interoperability between disparate platforms. Change imposed on any of these environments is more easily facilitated for the same reasons—a loosely coupled state between services representing either ends of the communication channel.

Organizational agility is perhaps the most significant benefit that can be realized with contemporary SOA.

3.2.16   Contemporary SOA is a building block

A service-oriented application architecture will likely be one of several within an organization committed to SOA as the standard architectural platform. Organizations standardizing on SOA work toward an ideal known as the service-oriented enterprise (SOE), where all business processes are composed of and exist as services, both logically and physically.

When viewed in the context of SOE, the functional boundary of an SOA represents a part of this future-state environment, either as a standalone unit of business automation or as a service encapsulating some or all of the business automation logic. In responding to business model-level changes, SOAs can be augmented to change the nature of their automation, or they can be pulled into service-oriented integration architectures that require the participation of multiple applications.

What this all boils down to is that an individual service-oriented application can, in its entirety, be represented by and modeled as a single service. As mentioned earlier, there are no limits to the scope of service encapsulation. An SOA consists of services within services within services, to the point that a solution based on SOA itself is one of many services within an SOE.

This past set of characteristics has further broadened our definition. Let's append the definition with the following:

> *SOA can establish an abstraction of business logic and technology, resulting in a loose coupling between these domains. These changes foster service-orientation in support of a service-oriented enterprise.*

3.2.17 Contemporary SOA is an evolution

SOA defines an architecture that is related to but still distinct from its predecessors. It differs from traditional client-server and distributed environments in that it is heavily influenced by the concepts and principles associated with service-orientation and Web services. It is similar to previous platforms in that it preserves the successful characteristics of its predecessors and builds upon them with distinct design patterns and a new technology set.

For example, SOA supports and promotes reuse and encapsulation, as well as the componentization and distribution of application logic. These and other established design principles that are commonplace in traditional distributed environments are still very much a part of SOA.

3.2.18 Contemporary SOA is still maturing

While the characteristics described so far are fundamental to contemporary SOA, this point is obviously more of a subjective statement of where SOA is at the moment. Even though SOA is being positioned as the next standard application computing platform, this transition is not yet complete. Despite the fact that Web services are being used to implement a great deal of application functionality, the support for a number of features necessary for enterprise-level computing is not yet fully available.

Standards organizations and major software vendors have produced many specifications to address a variety of supplementary extensions. Additionally, the next generation of development tools and application servers promises to support a great deal of these new technologies. When SOA platforms and tools reach an adequate level of maturity, the utilization of Web services can be extended to support the creation of enterprise solutions, making the ideal of a service-oriented enterprise attainable.

If you needed to provide an accurate definition of SOA today, you would not be out of line to mention the state of its underlying technology. Considering the rate at which the IT industry as a whole is adopting and evolving the SOA platform, though, it should not be too long before such a statement would no longer be required.

3.2.19 Contemporary SOA is an achievable ideal

A standardized enterprise-wide adoption of SOA is a state to which many organizations would like to fast-forward. The reality is that the process of transitioning to this state demands an enormous amount of effort, discipline, and, depending on the size of the organization, a good amount of time. Every technical environment will undergo changes during such a migration, and various parts of SOA will be phased in at differ-ent stages and to varying extents. This will likely result in countless hybrid architectures, consisting mostly of distributed environments that are part legacy and part service-oriented.

Further supporting this prediction is the evolving state of the technology set that is emerging to realize enterprise-level SOAs. As companies adopt SOA during this evolu-tion, many will need to retrofit their environments (and their standards) to accommo-date changes and innovations as SOA-related specifications, standards, and products continue to mature.

However, the majority of the contemporary SOA characteristics we just covered are attainable today. This book provides a series of tutorials and step-by-step process descriptions that explain how to manifest them.

3.2.20 Defining SOA

Now that we've finished covering characteristics, we can finalize our formal definition.

> *Contemporary SOA represents an open, agile, extensible, federated, composable architecture comprised of autonomous, QoS-capable, vendor diverse, interoperable, discoverable, and potentially reusable services, implemented as Web services.*

> *SOA can establish an abstraction of business logic and technology, resulting in a loose coupling between these domains.*

> *SOA is an evolution of past platforms, preserving successful characteristics of traditional architectures, and bringing with it distinct principles that foster service-orientation in support of a service-oriented enterprise.*

> *SOA is ideally standardized throughout an enterprise, but achieving this state requires a planned transition and the support of a still evolving technology set.*

Though accurate, this definition of contemporary SOA is quite detailed. For practical purposes, let's provide a supplementary definition that can be applied to both primitive and contemporary SOA.

> *SOA is a form of technology architecture that adheres to the principles of service-orientation. When realized through the Web services technology platform, SOA establishes the potential to support and promote these principles throughout the business process and automation domains of an enterprise.*

3.2.21   Separating concrete characteristics

Looking back at the list of characteristics we just covered, we can actually split them into two groups—characteristics that represent concrete qualities that can be realized as real extensions of SOA and those that can be categorized as commentary or observations. Collectively, these characteristics were useful for achieving our formal definition. From here on, though, we are more interested in exploring the concrete characteristics only.

Let's therefore remove the following items from our original list:

- Contemporary SOA is at the core of the service-oriented computing platform.
- Contemporary SOA is a building block.
- Contemporary SOA is an evolution.
- Contemporary SOA is still maturing.
- Contemporary SOA is an achievable ideal.

By trimming these items, along with some superfluous wording, we end up with the following set of concrete characteristics.

Contemporary SOA is generally:

- based on open standards
- architecturally composable
- capable of improving QoS

Contemporary SOA supports, fosters, or promotes:

- vendor diversity
- intrinsic interoperability
- discoverability
- federation
- inherent reusability
- extensibility
- service-oriented business modeling
- layers of abstraction
- enterprise-wide loose coupling
- organizational agility

It is these characteristics that, when realized, provide tangible, measurable benefits.

NOTE
Though we qualify these as "concrete" here, it is this set of characteristics that we refer to when we use the term "contemporary SOA characteristics" from here on.

SUMMARY OF KEY POINTS

- We distinguish contemporary SOA with a number of common characteristics that build upon and extend the original qualities and principles established by primitive SOA.

- The realization of contemporary SOA characteristics is explored in detail throughout this book.

3.3   Common misperceptions about SOA

You'll often hear about the shift in mindset required to fully adopt SOA. The myths we tackle here only scratch the surface of the change that's in store for those firmly entrenched with traditional architectural views. Our focus in this section is to dispel the most common points of confusion about SOA and the use of the term "service-oriented."

3.3.1   "An application that uses Web services is service-oriented."

This comes down to how SOA is defined. As we've established, there is a distinction between SOA as an abstract model and SOA based on Web services and service-orientation. Depending on which abstract model you use, almost any form of distributed architecture can be classified as being service-oriented.

To realize the benefit potential of the mainstream variation of SOA we've been discussing, you need to standardize how Web services are positioned and designed, according to service-orientation principles.

So whether this statement is a misperception or not actually depends on your expectations. A traditional distributed architecture can be called service-oriented as long as the benefits associated with primitive and contemporary SOA are not expected.

3.3.2 "SOA is just a marketing term used to re-brand Web services."

Certainly the term "SOA" has been (appropriately and otherwise) used excessively for marketing purposes. It has become a high-profile buzzword, riding the wave of hype brought on by the rise of Web services. The fact that contemporary SOAs are being implemented using Web services has led to some skepticism around the validity of the term itself. Some believe that "SOA support" is just a re-labeling of "Web services support."

SOA is not an invention of the media or some marketing department. SOA is a legitimate and relatively established technical term. It represents a distinct architecture based on a set of distinct principles. It just happens that contemporary SOA also implies the use of a distinct set of technology used to realize fundamental SOA principles. The technology platform of choice is currently Web services and all that comes with it.

3.3.3 "SOA is just a marketing term used to re-brand distributed computing with Web services."

There are many people who believe this, which has led to the "false SOA" syndrome explained in Chapter 1. The reasons behind this myth are understandable. Much of the hype surrounding SOA has overshadowed its actual meaning. Additionally, many of the migration paths laid out by product vendors blend traditional distributed computing with Web services, accompanied by advertised "SOA support." The results certainly can be confusing. Further, the validity of some promoted SOA support is questionable at best.

However, SOA is its own entity. It consists of a set of design principles that are related to, but differ significantly from, the distributed computing platforms of the past. We compare SOA characteristics to distributed computing in detail in the following chapter.

3.3.4 "SOA simplifies distributed computing."

The principles behind SOA are relatively simple in nature. However, applying these principles in real life can prove to be a complex task. Though SOA offers significant benefit potential, this can only be realized by investing in thorough analysis and adherence to the design principles of service-orientation.

Typical SOA implementations require more up-front research than solutions created under previous platform paradigms. This is in part due to the broad Web services technology platform imposed by contemporary SOA.

The quality of simplicity surfaces later, once service-orientation is established and stan-dardized within an IT environment. Then, when integration requirements emerge, when a sufficient number of composable services exist, and when service-orientation principles are well integrated into an organization, that's when SOA can simplify the delivery of automation requirements.

3.3.5 "An application with Web services that uses WS-* extensions is service-oriented."

While the entire second generation of Web services specifications are certainly driving SOA into the IT mainstream, simply making these extensions part of an architecture does not make it service-oriented. Regardless of the functionality with which Web serv-ices are outfitted, what makes them part of a service-oriented architecture is how the architecture itself is designed.

Having stated that, though, it is expected that most solutions that seriously employ the use of WS-* extensions will, in fact, be service-oriented. This is partially because the adoption rate of SOA is anticipated to roughly coincide with the availability of WS-* extension support in development and middleware products.

3.3.6 "If you understand Web services you won't have a problem building SOA."

A technical and conceptual knowledge of Web services is certainly helpful. However, as we established at the beginning of this chapter, fundamental service-orientation princi-ples are pretty much technology agnostic. Service-orientation requires a change in how business and application logic are viewed, partitioned, and automated. It therefore also requires that Web services be utilized and designed according to specific principles.

Web services are easily incorporated into existing traditional distributed architectures. There they can be centrally positioned and assigned significant processing responsibili-ties, or they can be appended as peripheral application endpoints.

The manner in which Web services are utilized in SOA is significantly different. The emphasis placed on business logic encapsulation and the creation of service abstraction layers often will require a blend of technology and business analysis expertise. It is best to assume that realizing contemporary SOA requires a separate skill set that goes beyond a knowledge of Web services technology.

3.3.7 "Once you go SOA, everything becomes interoperable."

The media attention and marketing push behind SOA has likely contributed to this myth. Many assume that by virtue of building service-oriented solutions, their technical environments will naturally transform into a united, federated enterprise.

Though this ultimate goal is attainable, it requires investment, analysis, and, above all, a high degree of standardization. By leveraging the open Web services communications framework, service-oriented architectures (and service-oriented integration architectures) naturally abstract and hide all that is proprietary about a particular solution, its platform, and its technology.

This establishes a predictable communications medium for all applications exposed via a Web service. However, it does not automatically standardize the representation of the information that is exchanged via this medium. Therefore, as SOAs become more common, there will be good and not so good implementations. A quality SOA requires that individual services conform to common design standards for federation, interoperability, reusability, and other benefits to be fully realized.

SUMMARY OF KEY POINTS

- Much of the confusion surrounding the meaning of SOA is caused by how this term has been used by the media and in marketing literature.

- The most common misperceptions relate to the use of Web services within distributed Internet architectures being mistaken as contemporary SOA.

- Some of the more dangerous assumptions about SOA are that service-oriented solutions are simple by nature, easy to build, and automatically interoperable.

3.4 Common tangible benefits of SOA

So far we've discussed what constitutes an SOA. Much of this book expands on this topic by providing details about the inner workings of service-oriented solutions. Provided in this section is a list of the reasons why the IT community is going through the trouble of changing so much of its philosophy and technology in an effort to adopt SOA.

The benefits described in this section focus on tangible returns on investment, related primarily to:

- how SOA leads to improvements in automated solution construction
- how the proliferation of service-orientation ends up benefiting the enterprise as a whole

> **NOTE**
>
> SOA will benefit organizations in different ways, depending on their respective goals and the manner in which SOA and its supporting cast of products and technologies is applied. This list of common benefits is generalized and certainly not complete. It is merely an indication of the potential this architectural platform has to offer.

3.4.1   Improved integration (and intrinsic interoperability)

SOA can result in the creation of solutions that consist of inherently interoperable services. Utilizing solutions based on interoperable services is part of service-oriented integration (SOI) and results in a service-oriented integration architecture.

Because of the vendor-neutral communications framework established by Web services-driven SOAs, the potential is there for enterprises to implement highly standardized service descriptions and message structures. The net result is intrinsic interoperability, which turns a cross-application integration project into less of a custom development effort, and more of a modeling exercise.

The bottom line: The cost and effort of cross-application integration is significantly lowered when applications being integrated are SOA-compliant.

3.4.2   Inherent reuse

Service-orientation promotes the design of services that are inherently reusable. Designing services to support reuse from the get-go opens the door to increased opportunities for leveraging existing automation logic.

Building service-oriented solutions in such a manner that services fulfill immediate application-level requirements while still supporting a degree of reuse by future potential requestors establishes an environment wherein investments into existing systems can potentially be leveraged and re-leveraged as new solutions are built.

The bottom line: Building services to be inherently reusable results in a moderately increased development effort and requires the use of design standards. Subsequently leveraging reuse within services lowers the cost and effort of building service-oriented solutions.

3.4.3 Streamlined architectures and solutions

The concept of composition is another fundamental part of SOA. It is not, however, limited to the assembly of service collections into aggregate services. The WS-* platform is based in its entirety on the principle of composability.

As described in the *Common characteristics of contemporary SOA* section, this aspect of service-oriented architecture can lead to highly optimized automation environments, where only the technologies required actually become part of the architecture.

The bottom line: Realizing this benefit requires adherence to design standards that govern allowable extensions within each application environment. Benefits of streamlined solutions and architectures include the potential for reduced processing overhead and reduced skill-set requirements (because technical resources require only the knowledge of a given application, service, or service extension).

NOTE

The reduced performance requirements mentioned previously only refer to the fact that SOA extensions are composable and therefore allow each application-level architecture to contain extensions only relevant to its solution requirements. Message-based communication in SOAs can, in fact, increase performance requirements when compared to RPC-style communication within traditional distributed architectures. See the *Not understanding SOA performance requirements* section later in this chapter for more information.

3.4.4 Leveraging the legacy investment

The industry-wide acceptance of the Web services technology set has spawned a large adapter market, enabling many legacy environments to participate in service-oriented integration architectures. This allows IT departments to work toward a state of federation, where previously isolated environments now can interoperate without requiring the development of expensive and sometimes fragile point-to-point integration channels.

Though still riddled with risks relating mostly to how legacy back-ends must cope with increased usage volumes, the ability to use what you already have with service-oriented solutions that you are building now and in the future is extremely attractive.

The bottom line: The cost and effort of integrating legacy and contemporary solutions is lowered. The need for legacy systems to be replaced is potentially lessened.

3.4.5   Establishing standardized XML data representation

On its most fundamental level, SOA is built upon and driven by XML. As a result, an adoption of SOA leads to the opportunity to fully leverage the XML data representation platform. A standardized data representation format (once fully established) can reduce the underlying complexity of all affected application environments.

Examples include:

- XML documents and accompanying XML Schemas (packaged within SOAP messages) passed between applications or application components fully standardize format and typing of all data communicated. The result is a predictable and therefore easily extensible and adaptable communications network.

- XML's self-descriptive nature enhances the ability for data to be readily interpreted by architects, analysts, and developers. The result is the potential for data within messages to be more easily maintained, traced, and understood.

- The standardization level of data representation lays the groundwork for intrinsic interoperability. Specifically, by promoting the use of standardized vocabularies, the need to translate discrepancies between how respective applications have interpreted corporate data models is reduced.

Past efforts to standardize XML technologies have resulted in limited success, as XML was either incorporated in an ad-hoc manner or on an "as required" basis. These approaches severely inhibited the potential benefits XML could introduce to an organization. With contemporary SOA, establishing an XML data representation architecture becomes a necessity, providing organizations the opportunity to achieve a broad level of standardization.

The bottom line: The cost and effort of application development is reduced after a proliferation of standardized XML data representation is achieved.

NOTE

The last two benefits (legacy integration and XML data representation within SOA) are covered in *Service-Oriented Architecture: A Field Guide to Integrating XML and Web Services*, the companion guide to this book.

3.4.6 Focused investment on communications infrastructure

Because Web services establish a common communications framework, SOA can centralize inter-application and intra-application communication as part of standard IT infrastructure. This allows organizations to evolve enterprise-wide infrastructure by investing in a single technology set responsible for communication.

The bottom line: The cost of scaling communications infrastructure is reduced, as only one communications technology is required to support the federated part of the enterprise.

3.4.7 "Best-of-breed" alternatives

Some of the harshest criticisms laid against IT departments are related to the restrictions imposed by a given technology platform on its ability to fulfill the automation requirements of an organization's business areas. This can be due to the expense and effort required to realize the requested automation, or it may be the result of limitations inherent within the technology itself. Either way, IT departments are frequently required to push back and limit or even reject requests to alter or expand upon existing automation solutions.

SOA won't solve these problems entirely, but it is expected to increase empowerment of both business and IT communities. A key feature of service-oriented enterprise environments is the support of "best-of-breed" technology. Because SOA establishes a vendor-neutral communications framework, it frees IT departments from being chained to a single proprietary development and/or middleware platform. For any given piece of automation that can expose an adequate service interface, you now have a choice as to how you want to build the service that implements it.

The bottom line: The potential scope of business requirement fulfillment increases, as does the quality of business automation.

3.4.8 Organizational agility

Agility is a quality inherent in just about any aspect of the enterprise. A simple algorithm, a software component, a solution, a platform, a process—all of these parts contain a measure of agility related to how they are constructed, positioned, and leveraged. How building blocks such as these can be realized and maintained within existing financial and cultural constraints ultimately determines the agility of the organization as a whole.

Much of service-orientation is based on the assumption that what you build today will evolve over time. One of the primary benefits of a well-designed SOA is to protect organizations from the impact of this evolution. When accommodating change becomes the norm in distributed solution design, qualities such as reuse and interoperability become commonplace. The predictability of these qualities within the enterprise leads to a reliable level of organizational agility. However, all of this is only attainable through proper design and standardization.

Change can be disruptive, expensive, and potentially damaging to inflexible IT environments. Building automation solutions and supporting infrastructure with the anticipation of change seems to make a great deal of sense. A standardized technical environment comprised of loosely coupled, composable, and interoperable and potentially reusable services establishes a more adaptive automation environment that empowers IT departments to more easily adjust to change.

Further, by abstracting business logic and technology into specialized service layers, SOA can establish a loosely coupled relationship between these two enterprise domains. This allows each domain to evolve independently and adapt to changes imposed by the other, as required. Regardless of what parts of service-oriented environments are leveraged, the increased agility with which IT can respond to business process or technology-related changes is significant.

The bottom line: The cost and effort to respond and adapt to business or technology-related change is reduced.

SUMMARY OF KEY POINTS

- When assessing the return on investment for an SOA there are several concrete benefits that can be taken into account.

- However, many of the benefits promised by SOA do not manifest themselves until the use of service-orientation principles becomes established within an enterprise. As a result, there are few short-term benefits.

3.5 Common pitfalls of adopting SOA

Having just covered the benefit potential of contemporary SOA, it's time for a reality check. As with any application design or architecture, quality can vary. SOA is no exception. In fact, considering the extent to which organizations need to shift technology and mindset to fully adopt SOA, it is actually probable that some will inadvertently build bad service-oriented architectures. Following are descriptions of some of the more common mistakes.

3.5.1   Building service-oriented architectures like traditional distributed architectures

Probably the number one obstacle organizations face in achieving SOA is building traditional distributed architectures under the pretense that they are building contemporary SOA. This is often the result of an acceptance of one or more of the misperceptions listed earlier in this chapter.

The danger with this scenario is that an organization can go quite far in terms of integrating the Web services technology set before realizing that they've been heading down the wrong path.

Examples of some of the problems this can introduce include:

- Proliferation of RPC-style service descriptions (leading to increased volumes of fine-grained message exchanges).
- Inhibiting the adoption of features provided by WS-* specifications.
- Improper partitioning of functional boundaries within services.
- Creation of non-composable (or semi-composable) services.
- Further entrenchment of synchronous communication patterns.
- Creation of hybrid or non-standardized services.

Understanding the fundamental differences between SOA and previous architectures is the key to avoiding this situation. (Part of Chapter 4 is dedicated to discussing this topic.)

3.5.2   Not standardizing SOA

In larger organizations where various IT projects occur concurrently, the need for custom standards is paramount. If different development projects result in the creation of differently designed applications, future integration efforts will be expensive and potentially fragile. This is a lesson many IT departments have already learned through past legacy nightmares.

The ability for SOA to achieve federation across disparate environments has been well promoted. The potential exists. However, it does not happen by simply purchasing the latest upgrades to a vendor's development tools and server software. SOA, like any other architecture, requires the creation and enforcement of design standards for its benefits to be truly realized. (See the *"Once you go SOA, everything becomes interoperable"* myth described earlier in this chapter.)

For example, if one project builds a service-oriented solution in isolation from others, key aspects of its solution will not be in alignment with the neighboring applications it may be required to interoperate with one day.

This can lead to many problems, including:

- Incompatible data representation that results in disparate schemas representing the same types of information.
- Service descriptions with irregular interface characteristics and semantics.
- Support for different extensions or extensions being implemented in different ways.

SOA promotes a development environment that abstracts back-end processing so that it can execute and evolve independently within each application. However, standardization is still required to ensure consistency in design and interaction of services that encapsulate this back-end logic. Design standards, such as the "WSDL first" approach explored throughout Parts IV and V of this book, are required to realize many of the key benefits provided by SOA.

3.5.3 Not creating a transition plan

The chances of a successful migration will be severely diminished without the use of a comprehensive transition plan. Because the extent to which service endpoints are positioned within an enterprise can lead to a redefinition of an IT environment's infrastructure, the repercussions of a poorly executed migration can be significant.

Transition plans allow you to coordinate a controlled phasing in of service-orientation and SOA characteristics so that the migration can be planned on a technological, architectural, and organizational level.

Examples of typical areas covered by a transition plan include:

- An impact analysis that predicts the extent of change SOA will impose on existing resources, processes, custom standards, and technology.
- The definition of transition architectures, where those environments identified as candidates for a migration to SOA evolve through a series of planned hybrid stages.

- A speculative analysis that takes into account the future growth of Web services and supporting technologies.

- Detailed design changes to centralized logic (such as a new security model).

Creating a transition plan avoids the many problems associated with an ad-hoc adoption of SOA. Each plan, though, will be unique to an organization's requirements, constraints, and goals.

3.5.4   Not starting with an XML foundation architecture

In the world of contemporary SOA, everything begins with Web services. That statement has become a mantra of sorts within some organizations, but it is not entirely true. In the world of contemporary SOA, everything, in fact, begins with XML. It is the standard from which multiple supplementary standards have evolved to form a de facto data representation architecture. It is this core set of standards that has fueled the creation of the many Web services specifications that are now driving SOA.

So much attention is given to how data is transported between services that the manner in which this same data is structured and validated behind service lines is often neglected. This oversight can lead to an improper implementation of a persistent XML data representation layer within SOAs. The results can severely affect the quality of data processing. For example, the same data may be unnecessarily validated multiple times, or redundant data processing can inadvertently be performed before and after a service transmits or receives a message.

Standardizing the manner in which core XML technologies are used to represent, validate, and process corporate data as it travels throughout application environments (both within and between services) lays the groundwork for a robust, optimized, and interoperable SOA.

3.5.5   Not understanding SOA performance requirements

When starting out small, it is easy to build service-oriented solutions that function and respond as expected. As the scope increases and more functionality is added, the volume of message-based communication predictably grows. This is when unprepared environments can begin experiencing significant processing latency.

Because contemporary SOA introduces layers of data processing, it is subject to the associated performance overhead imposed by these layers. Contemporary SOA's reliance on Web services deepens its dependence on XML data representation, which, in turn, can magnify XML processing-related performance challenges. For example, Web services security measures, such as encryption and digital signing, add new layers of processing to both the senders and recipients of messages.

Critical to building a successful service-oriented solution is understanding the performance requirements of your solution and the performance limitations of your infrastructure ahead of time.

This means:

- Testing the message processing capabilities of your environments prior to investing in Web services.
- Stress-testing the vendor supplied processors (for XML, XSLT, SOAP, etc.) you are planning to use.
- Exploring alternative processors, accelerators, or other types of supporting technology, if necessary. For example, the XML-binary Optimized Packaging (XOP) and SOAP Message Transmission Optimization Mechanism (MTOM) specifications developed by the W3C. (For more information, visit www.w3c.org.)

Performance is also one of the reasons coarse-grained service interfaces and asynchronous messaging are emphasized when building Web services. These and other design measures can be implemented to avoid potential processing bottlenecks.

3.5.6   Not understanding Web services security

The extent to which Web services technology grows within a given environment is typically related to the comfort level developers and architects have with the overall technology framework. Once it does expand it is easy to simply continue building on simplistic message exchanges, which usually rely on Secure Sockets Layer (SSL) encryption to implement a familiar measure of security.

While SSL can address many immediate security concerns, it is not the technology of choice for SOA. When services begin to take on greater amounts of processing responsibility, the need for message-level security begins to arise. The WS-Security framework establishes an accepted security model supported by a family of specifications that end up infiltrating service-oriented application and enterprise architectures on many levels.

One of the more significant design issues you may face when WS-Security hits your world is the potential introduction of centralized security. With this approach, the architecture abstracts a large portion of security logic and rules into a separate, central layer that is then relied upon by service-oriented applications.

Even if your vendor platform does not yet provide adequate support for WS-Security, and even if your current SSL-based implementation is meeting immediate requirements, it is also advisable to pay close attention to the changes that are ahead. Proceeding without taking WS-Security into account will inevitably lead to expensive retrofitting and redevelopment. This impact is amplified if you decide to implement a centralized security model, which would essentially become an extension of IT infrastructure. Acquiring a sound knowledge of the framework now will allow you to adjust your current architecture and application designs to better accommodate upcoming changes.

3.5.7   Not keeping in touch with product platforms and standards development

IT professionals used to working within the confines of a single development platform have become accustomed to focusing on industry trends as they apply to the product set they are currently working with. For example, .NET developers are generally not too concerned with what's happening in the Java world, and vice versa.

A transition to SOA opens up the arena of products and platforms that IT departments can choose from to build and/or host custom-developed application logic. While the tendency will be there to continue with what you know best, the option to look elsewhere is ever-present. As explained earlier, this is the result of establishing a vendor-neutral communications framework that allows solutions based on disparate technologies to become fully interoperable.

Another factor that can (and should) weigh in when comparing products is how product vendors relate to the WS-* specification development process that is currently underway. As different vendor alliances continue to produce competing extensions, how your vendors position themselves amidst this landscape will become increasingly important, especially once you begin to identify the extensions required to implement and execute key parts of your solutions' application logic.

In the meantime, specific aspects to look out for include:

- which specifications vendors choose to support
- the involvement vendors demonstrate with the standards development process itself

- which other organizations vendors choose to ally themselves with (for a given standard)
- roadmaps published by vendors explaining how their product or platform will support upcoming specifications and standards

Chapter 4 provides an overview of the standards development process, including descriptions of the primary standards organizations related to SOA.

SUMMARY OF KEY POINTS

- Many of the pitfalls relate to a limited understanding of what SOA is and what is required to fully incorporate and standardize service-orientation.

- A transition plan is the best weapon against the obstacles that tend to face organizations when migrating toward SOA.

- Staying in touch with commercial and standards-related developments is an important part of keeping an existing SOA aligned with future developments.

Chapter 4

The Evolution of SOA

O ne of the SOA characteristics we identified in Chapter 3 is that it is in a state of evolution. To fully appreciate this quality we need to take a look at what industry developments are influencing SOA today and the overall direction SOA is headed.

This chapter examines the relationship between XML, Web services, and SOA and explains how vendors and standards organizations have formed a strangely competitive and collaborative arena from which Web services specifications are continually surfacing. We then conclude by embarking on a short historical recount of application architecture over the past two decades.

> **NOTE**
>
> The sequence of topics in this chapter may seem a bit odd. We begin with recent and current developments and end with a look at past architectural platforms. This structure was chosen simply because the information in the last section of this chapter may not be of interest to everyone and is not considered required reading.

How case studies are used: This chapter provides us with an opportunity to better establish the existing environments within our two fictional companies. Upon the conclusion of each of the architectural comparisons, examples are provided describing details of legacy applications from RailCo and TLS.

4.1 An SOA timeline (from XML to Web services to SOA)

We begin our timeline by covering the history of key industry developments that have emerged to shape the current SOA platform. We then take a look at how the emancipation of SOA as a contemporary architectural platform in its own right has altered the roles of XML and Web services technologies.

4.1.1 XML: a brief history

Like HTML, the Extensible Markup Language (XML) was a W3C creation derived from the popular Standard Generalized Markup Language (SGML) that has existed since the late 60s. This widely used meta language allowed organizations to add intelligence to raw document data.

XML gained popularity during the eBusiness movement of the late 90s, where server-side scripting languages made conducting business via the Internet viable. Through the use of XML, developers were able to attach meaning and context to any piece of information transmitted across Internet protocols.

Not only was XML used to represent data in a standardized manner, the language itself was used as the basis for a series of additional specifications. The XML Schema Definition Language (XSD) and the XSL Transformation Language (XSLT) were both authored using XML. These specifications, in fact, have become key parts of the core XML technology set.

The XML data representation architecture represents the foundation layer of SOA. Within it, XML establishes the format and structure of messages traveling throughout services. XSD schemas preserve the integrity and validity of message data, and XSLT is employed to enable communication between disparate data representations through schema mapping. In other words, you cannot make a move within SOA without involving XML.

4.1.2   Web services: a brief history

In 2000, the W3C received a submission for the Simple Object Access Protocol (SOAP) specification. This specification was originally designed to unify (and in some cases replace) proprietary RPC communication. The idea was for parameter data transmitted between components to be serialized into XML, transported, and then deserialized back into its native format.

Soon, corporations and software vendors began to see an increasingly large potential for advancing the state of eBusiness technology by building upon the proprietary-free Internet communications framework. This ultimately led to the idea of creating a pure, Web-based, distributed technology—one that could leverage the concept of a standardized communications framework to bridge the enormous disparity that existed between and within organizations. This concept was called Web services.

The most important part of a Web service is its public interface. It is a central piece of information that assigns the service an identity and enables its invocation. Therefore, one of the first initiatives in support of Web services was the Web Service Description Language (WSDL). The W3C received the first submission of the WSDL language in 2001 and has since continued revising this specification.

To further the vision of open interoperability, Web services required an Internet-friendly and XML-compliant communications format that could establish a standardized messaging framework. Although alternatives, such as XML-RPC, were considered, SOAP won out as the industry favorite and remains the foremost messaging standard for use with Web services.

In support of SOAP's new role, the W3C responded by releasing newer versions of the specification to allow for both RPC-style and document-style message types. The latter are used more frequently within SOAs. Eventually, the word "SOAP" was no longer considered an acronym for "Simple Object Access Protocol." As of version 1.2 of the specification, it became a standalone term.

Completing the first generation of the Web services standards family was the UDDI specification. Originally developed by UDDI.org, it was submitted to OASIS, which continued its development in collaboration with UDDI.org. This specification allows for the creation of standardized service description registries both within and outside of organization boundaries. UDDI provides the potential for Web services to be registered in a central location, from where they can be discovered by service requestors. Unlike WSDL and SOAP, UDDI has not yet attained industry-wide acceptance, and remains an optional extension to SOA.

Custom Web services were developed to accommodate a variety of specialized business requirements, and a third-party marketplace emerged promoting various utility services for sale or lease. Existing messaging platforms, such as messaging-oriented middleware (MOM) products, incorporated Web services to support SOAP in addition to other message protocols. Some organizations were also able to immediately incorporate Web services to facilitate B2B data exchange requirements—often as an alternative to EDI (Electronic Data Interchange).

4.1.3 SOA: a brief history

It wasn't long before organizations began to realize that instead of just accommodating existing distributed applications, Web services could become the basis of a separate architectural platform—a platform that could leverage the benefits of the Web services technology set to realize the concept of services in the enterprise. Thus, service-oriented architecture entered the IT mainstream.

At this point an SOA was frequently classified in different ways, often depending on the implementation technology used to build services. An early model, mostly inspired by the initial set of Web services standards, defined SOA as an architecture modeled around three basic components: the service requestor, the service provider, and the service registry (Figure 4.1).

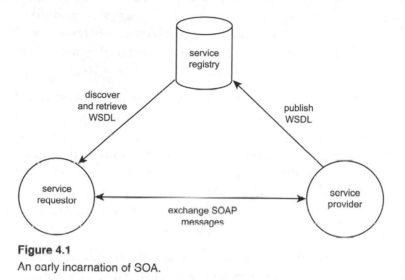

Figure 4.1
An early incarnation of SOA.

First-generation Web services standards fulfilled this model as follows:

- WSDL described the service.
- SOAP provided the messaging format used by the service and its requestor.
- UDDI provided the standardized service registry format.

From a physical architecture perspective, this first variation of a Web services-based SOA actually goes beyond the primitive SOA model we established in Chapter 3. You may recall that our primitive SOA did not require the use of a service registry. Instead, discoverability is classified as one of the contemporary SOA characteristics and is promoted, on a service-level, through service orientation priciples.

Our primitive SOA model is easily attained today, as it is supported by all major vendor development and runtime platforms. These same vendors have big plans for SOA, many of which are manifesting themselves right now. Numerous of the contemporary SOA characteristics we introduced in Chapter 3 are the result of aggressive development and collaborative initiatives which have produced a series of extensions to the first-generation Web services platform. Known as the "second-generation" or "WS-*" specifications, these extensions address specific areas of functionality with the overall goal of elevating the Web services technology platform to an enterprise level.

Complementing the WS-* landscape was also an interest in applying service-orientation concepts to the world of business analysis. Through service-orientation, business logic can be cleanly encapsulated and abstracted from the underlying automation technology. This vision has been further supported by the rise of business process definition languages, most notably WS-BPEL. These not only allowed for the decomposition of traditional Business Process Management (BPM) models into a series of services, they further bridged the gap between analysis and implementation by providing a language capable of fully expressing business logic in a concrete and executable format.

These and other industry influences have broadened the scope and potential of SOA. As more contemporary characteristics are added, it is likely that what we classify as a contemporary SOA today will form the basis for a primitive SOA in the future.

SOA is truly an evolution. Its prominence today is the result of numerous interrelated initiatives driven by a variety of standards organizations and software vendors. Through a volatile environment fueled by a mixture of collaboration and competition, extensions are being strategically positioned, each defining a specific part of what we are calling the contemporary SOA technology platform. In section 4.2 we take a closer look at the standards development processes.

4.1.4   How SOA is re-shaping XML and Web services

As with any architecture, SOA introduces boundaries and rules. Though contemporary SOA is made possible by the XML and Web services technology platforms, these platforms are required to undergo a number of changes in order for their respective technologies to be properly positioned and utilized within the confines of service-oriented architectures.

Traditional distributed application environments that use XML or Web services are therefore in for some rewiring as service-oriented design principles require a change in both technology and mindset. Following are some examples of potential issues you may be faced with when having to retrofit existing implementations.

> **NOTE**
>
> A number of these issues are explored in more detail in the *Considerations for positioning core SOA standards* section of Chapter 14.

- SOA requires that data representation and service modeling standards now be kept in alignment. This rather vague requirement has many implications and is fundamental to fostering intrinsic interoperability.

- SOA relies on SOAP messaging for all inter-service communication. As a result, any place that XML needs to go, SOAP messages are generally there, taking care of transportation, interim processing and routing, and the ultimate delivery. XML documents and associated XSD schemas now constantly need to be modeled with SOAP messaging in mind.

- SOA standardizes the use of a document-style messaging. The shift from RPC-style to document-style messages imposes change on the design of service descriptions. Specifically, interface characteristics need to be expressed in more generic terms, and the overall operation granularity increases.

- Due to this emphasis on document-style SOAP messages, SOA promotes a content and intelligence-heavy messaging model. This supports service statelessness and autonomy, and minimizes the frequency of message transmissions. Whereas previously RPC-style approaches supported the transmission of granular XML documents with targeted data, XML documents within SOAs often need to represent bundled data related to more than one data context.

- Until the advanced messaging capabilities of WS-* extensions become commonplace, many applications will need to be outfitted with custom SOAP headers to implement interim solutions to manage complex message exchanges. Some of the more pressing requirements include context management and correlation. These interim designs effectively establish transition models that need to be designed in such a manner that they are easily migrated to industry-standard implementations.

SUMMARY OF KEY POINTS

- The core XML technology set has become a common part of distributed Internet architecture. It now also provides a foundation data representation and data management layer for SOA.

- The first-generation Web services architecture grew out of the development of three key standards: WSDL, SOAP, and UDDI. While UDDI is still an optional discovery mechanism for most environments, WSDL and SOAP have become core technologies that build upon the XML layer to define the fundamental communications framework for SOA.

- SOA fully leverages the roads paved by the XML and Web services initiatives. Its marriage of proven concepts with progressive technology has been fully embraced by the global IT community.

- Though contemporary SOA has been shaped by the emergence and industry-wide acceptance of XML and Web services, the arrival of SOA introduces changes to the manner in which XML and Web services have been traditionally applied.

4.2   The continuing evolution of SOA (standards organizations and contributing vendors)

XML, as a language, is defined in a specification but is also used as the language through which practically all XML and Web services specifications are expressed. This common thread is a tribute to the fact that despite how vast the specifications landscape may grow, it continues to share a common root.

Whether or not you are required to directly work with these extensions, their existence and evolution will continue to affect any service-oriented solutions you build. Knowledge of how and why specifications and standards come to be is therefore relevant to acquiring a complete understanding of the world of SOA.

4.2.1   "Standards" vs. "Specifications" vs. "Extensions"

These terms are often used interchangeably, but many—especially those involved with standards organizations—make a clear distinction. A specification is a document that proposes a standard. It is not officially an industry standard until the specification is submitted to, accepted by, and released as such by a recognized standards organization.

Still, specifications released by vendors (especially collaborating vendors) and subsequently implemented by the vendors' platforms often go on to become unofficial industry standards simply because they become so commonplace.

To avoid confusion, this book defines these terms as follows:

- *Standard*—An accepted industry standard. All of the first-generation Web services specifications are considered standards, as are a number of XML specifications.

- *Specification*—A proposed or accepted standard, described in a specification. XML standards, first-generation Web services standards, and WS-* extensions all exist within specifications.

- *Extension*—An extension typically represents a WS-* specification or a feature provided by a WS-* specification.

4.2.2   Standards organizations that contribute to SOA

As we know, standards are what drive SOA. Previous architectural platforms were realized within vendor-specific boundaries; environments in which the only standards that mattered were proprietary. With the promise of a vendor-neutral communications framework comes the non-negotiable requirement that the standards defining this framework be vendor-neutral as well.

How exactly these standards are produced, though, is not always that clear. Internet standards organizations have existed for some time now, but their respective agendas are not always distinct and sometimes even overlap. Further complicating the issue is the fact that the primary contributors to these vendor-neutral standards are the vendors themselves. Microsoft, IBM, Sun Microsystems, and many others have played increasingly significant roles in not only formalizing Web services specifications, but also in accelerating the implementation of these specifications as industry standards.

How vendors contribute to and influence the standards development process is explained in the subsequent section. Let's first learn more about the three most prominent standards organizations. Collectively, they are responsible for seeing through the evolution of XML and Web services architectures.

The World Wide Web Consortium (W3C)

Originally founded by Tim Berners-Lee in 1994, the W3C has been hugely responsible for furthering the World Wide Web as a global, semantic medium for information sharing. It began with the release of HTML, one of the most popular technical languages the IT industry has ever produced. When the use of the Internet broadened to include eBusiness initiatives, the W3C responded by producing key foundation standards based on XML, such as XML Schema and XSLT.

Four separate working groups made significant contributions to W3C Web Services Activity projects, resulting in the development of important base standards for Web services. First-most are the SOAP and WSDL standards, which have now become the signature specifications associated with Web services. More recently, the W3C has produced the Web Services Choreography Description Language (WS-CDL), a specification that governs standardized inter-service exchange patterns. Also worth noting is the Web Services Architecture document itself. Though this document continues to undergo changes, it remains a reference point, and one of the few platform-neutral Web services architecture documents available.

The W3C is known for its formal and rigorous approach to standards development. Its process requires that specifications be subjected to numerous review and revision stages, with each new version being published to their public Web site. The thoroughness of its process comes at the cost of time. Standards can take two to three years to be completed.

Organization for the Advancement of Structured Information Standards (OASIS)

Originally established in 1993 as the SGML Open, OASIS changed its name five years later to represent a shift in focus from SGML to XML-related standards. With thousands of members from over 600 organizations, OASIS is a recognized international standards producing organization.

OASIS assumed ownership of the prominent WS-BPEL specification and is also known for its development of ebXML (a specification that aims to establish a standardized means of B2B data interchange) and its contributions to the UDDI specification, one of the core standards associated with the first-generation Web services platform.

The OASIS group has been instrumental in furthering the development of XML and Web services security extensions. Both the Security Assertion Markup Language (SAML) and the Extensible Access Control Markup Language (XACML) provide important features in the areas of single sign-on and authorization. However, the most important security-related project is being carried out by the Web Services Security (WSS) technical committee. This group is entrusted with further developing and realizing the important WS-Security framework.

Whereas the W3C focuses on establishing core, industry-agnostic standards, the OASIS group's primary interests lie in leveraging these standards to produce additional specifications that support various vertical industries. Further, the standards development processes used by OASIS are noticeably shorter.

The Web Services Interoperability Organization (WS-I)

The primary objective of the WS-I is not to create new standards, but to ensure that the ultimate goal of open interoperability is realized. Established in 2002, this consortium has rapidly grown to gain the support of nearly 200 organizations, including all major SOA vendors.

The WS-I is best known for releasing the Basic Profile, a recommendation-based document that establishes which of the available standards should be collectively used to form the most desirable interoperability architecture. By formally positioning specific versions of WSDL, SOAP, UDDI, XML, and XML Schema, the Basic Profile has become an important document within the IT community. Those organizations wanting to ensure that the SOAs they develop are fully interoperable with others can guarantee a high-level of acceptance with compliance to the Basic Profile.

More recently, the WS-I developed the Basic Security Profile. Essentially the same concept as the Basic Profile, this document establishes the most important collection of Web services and XML security technologies. The WS-I has announced that it plans to continue releasing Profiles for each major aspect of Web services-related interoperability, including reliable messaging, Web service management, and orchestration.

In addition to establishing a base interoperability architecture, Profiles are supplemented with sample implementations and best practices on how the standards are to be used together to achieve a quality level of interoperability. Further, the WS-I provides a series of testing tools that can be used to ensure compliance with Profiles. Many vendors also provide their own variation of these tools, such as validity checkers that use Basic Profile conformance as part of the validation criteria.

The WS-I strives to provide a level playing field when it comes to receiving contributions from its members. While its membership includes significant SOA vendors, no one company has more clout than another, regardless of its size or market share.

Although the W3C recently rejected an invitation to become an associate member of the WS-I, working group members from the WS-I continue to contribute to W3C and OASIS initiatives by directly participating in their respective working groups. The role of these WS-I representatives is to provide continual feedback relating to interoperability issues.

How they compare

Table 4.1 provides a summary-level overview of how the three organizations we discussed in this section compare to each other.

Table 4.1   A Comparison of Standards Organizations

	W3C	OASIS	WS-I
Established	1994	1993 as the SGML Open, 1998 as OASIS	2002
Approximate membership	400	600	200
Overall goal (as it relates to SOA)	To further the evolution of the Web, by providing fundamental standards that improve online business and information sharing.	To promote online trade and commerce via specialized Web services standards.	To foster standardized interoperability using Web services standards.
Prominent deliverables (related to SOA)	XML, XML Schema, XQuery, XML Encryption, XML Signature, XPath, XSLT, WSDL, SOAP, WS-CDL, WS-Addressing, Web Services Architecture	UDDI, ebXML, SAML, XACML, WS-BPEL, WS-Security	Basic Profile, Basic Security Profile

4.2.3   Major vendors that contribute to SOA

Though standards organizations have their own culture and philosophies around how standards should be developed, they are all heavily influenced by the commercial market. And so they should be, as that is what they are there to support. Even though these organizations exist as independent entities, their membership includes pretty much all major software vendors. And these same vendors supply a significant portion of the contributors that actually end up developing the standards.

Some of the companies that have participated in the standards development processes include Microsoft, IBM, BEA Systems, Sun Microsystems, Oracle, Tibco, Hewlett-Packard, Canon, Commerce One, Fujitsu, Software AG, Nortel, Verisign, and WebMethods. The dynamics resulting from the interaction between vendors, their various alliances, and the standards organizations is pretty interesting and worth discussing further.

Why standards are being developed in support of SOA

No one person or organization owns or controls SOA. Having evolved from proprietary platforms into an architecture that promotes and supports open standards and vendor-neutral protocols, SOA will likely remain an important architecture for as long as the major software vendors choose to support it.

That is because the benefits of SOA can only be realized as long as it continues to receive the global acceptance it does now. What would be the point of building interoperable applications if only a portion of the solutions out there supported the technology used for cross-application communication?

Regardless, SOA today is foremost on every major software organization's priority list. Non-compliance with SOA is not even being considered, as it would mean cutting yourself out of an ever-growing market. For now and the foreseeable future, SOA is it.

The vendor influence

Even though no one exclusively controls SOA, everyone has an opinion as to how its underlying technology platform should be shaped. To that end, the vendor's influence in the standards development process has turned the evolution of SOA into a battle of agendas.

Each vendor has its own vision as to how it plans to advance its line of products. IBM has laid out a technology path for increasing support of SOA within its WebSphere platform. Microsoft is not only increasing SOA features within the .NET technology framework, but is also building Web services technology directly into the Windows operating system.

Though Web services standards are meant to remain non-proprietary, a vendor who can help shape a standard might be motivated to do so with proprietary technology considerations in mind. This isn't necessarily devious or even manipulative. One could argue that since these standards are intended to support implementation by common products, they should be influenced by the requirements of the vendors that represent product lines with larger market shares. The challenge, however, is getting *all* vendors to agree on how one standard should be designed.

Vendor alliances

Past battles between the more established vendors have led to a great deal of distrust. Now, when asked to collaborate on specifications intended to foster interoperability between vendor platforms, these suspicions surface and turn into obstacles. This issue, coupled with how closely aligned some vendors' requirements are for the contents of a particular specification, has led to some companies forming loose alliances.

Forming an alliance allows vendors to join forces in order to attain common goals. Generally, the lifespan of an alliance is centered around the development cycle of a particular specification. However, the most noticeable team of repeat-collaborators (IBM, Microsoft, and BEA) have persisted their working relationship to push forward a series of WS-* extensions.

One of the more talked about examples of alliances playing a significant role in standards development is the creation of the WS-ReliableMessaging specification. Originally, the need for a reliable messaging mechanism was being addressed by an OASIS technical committee. Its contributors included Sun Microsystems and Oracle, and the specification was titled WS-Reliability. However, only weeks after its release, Microsoft, IBM, and others announced their own specification, called WS-ReliableMessaging.

The specifications are very similar and address the same overall requirements. However, even though it was released later and had not been developed through (or even submitted to) a standards organization, the WS-ReliableMessaging extension became an immediate contender. This is simply due to the fact that the vendors that developed it collectively held a larger market share of the Web services technology platform. Incidents such as this not only reflect the volatile state of the Web services industry, they also reveal a lack of authority held by standards organizations.

Choosing a standards organization

Generally, though, it is to a vendor's benefit to have specifications formalized through a standards organization. It officially establishes that the specification's purpose is to support an open standard and subjects it to a process that is generally open to the public.

However, sometimes the choice of standards organization can have implications. Another dynamic within the standards development arena is directly related to market demand. Vendors have market-driven goals fueled by pressures to deliver product releases that meet customer demands and match or outdo what the competition is offering (or planning to offer). Given that the W3C relies on a longer standards development process, it is tempting for vendors to submit their standards to OASIS instead.

Although having organizations develop similar specifications may seem redundant, one always seems to rise to the top. And despite the fact that opposing motives may seem counter-productive to fostering a collection of platform-neutral technology standards, the quality of what's been delivered so far has been adequate for furthering the cause of SOA.

Why you should care

In the *Common pitfalls of adopting SOA* section of Chapter 3 we discussed the importance of staying in tune with developments around product and standards releases. Let's conclude this section by reiterating this point and listing some specific reasons as to why you should keep an eye on what is happening in the standards development landscape.

- When planning a migration to SOA it is beneficial to take the maturation process of key extensions into account. These specifications will end up enabling the functionality you need this architecture to eventually support.

- Observing the standards development process allows you to form your own opinions as to which specifications are progressing and which are not. This is important for you to retain control of the direction in which you evolve your existing service-oriented solutions.

- Keeping in touch with how standards are developed and who is driving them will enable you to better understand SOA-related technology trends.

- Because SOA provides you with the choice to build different applications using different development platforms, you need to maintain a vendor-neutral perspective. This will empower you to better compare the features and SOA support of available product platforms.

SUMMARY OF KEY POINTS

- The W3C's contributions to advancing the World Wide Web cannot be understated. In the SOA arena, its role has been primarily as a standards body responsible for specifications that provide core and generic functionality.

- OASIS evolved from an SGML standards organization to one focused almost exclusively on eBusiness specifications. Its overall goal is to support the creation of standards targeted at specific industries and to foster trade and commerce between eBusiness-enabled enterprises.

- As a group dedicated to the interoperability concerns of disparate platforms, the WS-I does not produce technology standards. Instead, this organization provides profile documents that establish a proven and tested collection of standards. Compliance to these profiles guarantees organizations that their environments support a level of industry-standard interoperability.

- Though standards organizations exist as separate entities, all are supported by and receive contributions from vendor representatives. Vendor contributions are motivated by a mixture of self-interest and common good.

- It is important to stay on top of the standards development landscape because it will allow you to plan a more educated migration toward SOA.

4.3   The roots of SOA (comparing SOA to past architectures)

We now actually jump back in our timeline to take a look at the differences between past architectural platforms and SOA. This is an interesting study from which we can identify how SOA derived many of its current characteristics.

> **NOTE**
>
> A number of traditional architectures are explained and illustrated in this section. However, the architectural details of SOA itself are not covered until later in this book. Reading this section is therefore not required to proceed with subsequent chapters. If you are not interested in learning about how SOA differs from other architectures, then feel free to skip ahead to Chapter 5.

4.3.1   What is architecture?

For as long as there have been computerized automation solutions, technology architecture has existed. However, in older environments, the construction of the solution was so straight forward that the task of abstracting and defining its architecture was seldom performed.

With the rise of multi-tier applications, the variations with which applications could be delivered began to dramatically increase. IT departments started to recognize the need for a standardized definition of a baseline application that could act as a template for all others. This definition was abstract in nature, but specifically explained the technology, boundaries, rules, limitations, and design characteristics that apply to all solutions based on this template. This was the birth of the *application architecture*.

Application architecture

Application architecture is to an application development team what a blueprint is to a team of construction workers. Different organizations document different levels of application architecture. Some keep it high-level, providing abstract physical and logical representations of the technical blueprint. Others include more detail, such as common data models, communication flow diagrams, application-wide security requirements, and aspects of infrastructure.

It is not uncommon for an organization to have several application architectures. A single architecture document typically represents a distinct solution environment. For example, an organization that houses both .NET and J2EE solutions would very likely have separate application architecture specifications for each.

A key part of any application-level architecture is that it reflects immediate solution requirements, as well as long-term, strategic IT goals. It is for this reason that when multiple application architectures exist within an organization, they are almost always accompanied by and kept in alignment with a governing *enterprise architecture*.

Enterprise architecture

In larger IT environments, the need to control and direct IT infrastructure is critical. When numerous, disparate application architectures co-exist and sometimes even integrate, the demands on the underlying hosting platforms can be complex and onerous. Therefore, it is common for a master specification to be created, providing a high-level overview of all forms of heterogeneity that exist within an enterprise, as well as a definition of the supporting infrastructure.

Continuing our previous analogy, an enterprise architecture specification is to an organization what an urban plan is to a city. Therefore, the relationship between an urban plan and the blueprint of a building are comparable to that of enterprise and application architecture specifications.

Typically, changes to enterprise architectures directly affect application architectures, which is why architecture specifications often are maintained by the same group of individuals. Further, enterprise architectures often contain a long-term vision of how the organization plans to evolve its technology and environments. For example, the goal of phasing out an outdated technology platform may be established in this specification.

Finally, this document also may define the technology and policies behind enterprise-wide security measures. However, these often are isolated into a separate security architecture specification.

Service-oriented architecture

Put simply, service-oriented architecture spans both enterprise and application architecture domains. The benefit potential offered by SOA can only be truly realized when applied across multiple solution environments. This is where the investment in building reusable and interoperable services based on a vendor-neutral communications platform can fully be leveraged. This does not mean that the entire enterprise must become service-oriented. SOA belongs in those areas that have the most to gain from the features and characteristics it introduces.

Note that the term "SOA" does not necessarily imply a particular architectural scope. An SOA can refer to an application architecture or the approach used to standardize technical architecture across the enterprise. Because of the composable nature of SOA (meaning that individual application-level architectures can be comprised of different extensions and technologies), it is absolutely possible for an organization to have more than one SOA.

Note that, as explained in the previous chapter, the Web services platform offers one of a number of available forms of implementation for SOA. It is the approach exclusively explored by this book, but other approaches, such as those provided by traditional distributed platforms, also exist. An important aspect of the terminology used in the upcoming sections and throughout this book is that our use of the term "SOA" implies the contemporary SOA model (based on Web services and service-orientation principles) established in Chapter 3.

4.3.2   SOA vs. client-server architecture

Just about any environment in which one piece of software requests or receives information from another can be referred to as "client-server." Pretty much every variation of application architecture that ever existed (including SOA) has an element of client-server interaction in it. However, the industry term "client-server architecture" generally refers to a particular generation of early environments during which the client and the server played specific roles and had distinct implementation characteristics.

Client-server architecture: a brief history

The original monolithic mainframe systems that empowered organizations to get seriously computerized often are considered the first inception of client-server architecture. These environments, in which bulky mainframe back-ends served thin clients, are considered an implementation of the single-tier architecture (Figure 4.2).

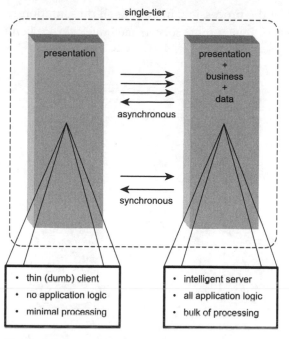

Figure 4.2
A typical single-tier architecture.

Mainframe systems natively supported both synchronous and asynchronous communication. The latter approach was used primarily to allow the server to continuously receive characters from the terminal in response to individual key-strokes. Only upon certain conditions would the server actually respond.

While its legacy still remains, the reign of the mainframe as the foremost computing platform began to decline when a two-tier variation of the client-server design emerged in the late 80s.

This new approach introduced the concept of delegating logic and processing duties onto individual workstations, resulting in the birth of the fat client. Further supported by the innovation of the graphical user-interface (GUI), two-tier client-server was considered a huge step forward and went on to dominate the IT world for years during the early 90s.

The common configuration of this architecture consisted of multiple fat clients, each with its own connection to a database on a central server. Client-side software performed the bulk of the processing, including all presentation-related and most data access logic (Figure 4.3). One or more servers facilitated these clients by hosting scalable RDBMSs.

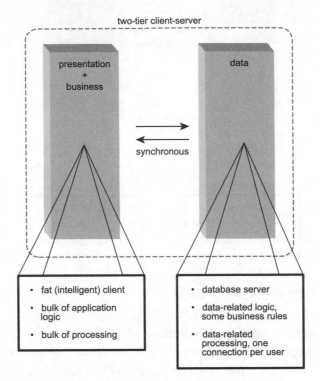

Figure 4.3
A typical two-tier client-server architecture.

Let's look at the primary characteristics of the two-tier client-server architecture individually and compare them to the corresponding parts of SOA.

Application logic
Client-server environments place the majority of application logic into the client software. This results in a monolithic executable that controls the user experience, as well as the back-end resources. One exception is the distribution of business rules. A popular trend was to embed and maintain business rules relating to data within stored procedures and triggers on the database. This somewhat abstracted a set of business logic from the client and simplified data access programming. Overall, though, the client ran the show.

The presentation layer within contemporary service-oriented solutions can vary. Any piece of software capable of exchanging SOAP messages according to required service contracts can be classified as a service requestor. While it is commonly expected for requestors to be services as well, presentation layer designs are completely open and specific to a solution's requirements.

Within the server environment, options exist as to where application logic can reside and how it can be distributed. These options do not preclude the use of database triggers or stored procedures. However, service-oriented design principles come into play, often dictating the partitioning of processing logic into autonomous units. This facilitates specific design qualities, such as service statelessness and interoperability, as well as future composability and reusability.

Additionally, it is more common within an SOA for these units of processing logic to be solution-agnostic. This supports the ultimate goal of promoting reuse and loose coupling across application boundaries.

Application processing

Because most client-server application logic resides in the client component, the client workstation is responsible for the bulk of the processing. The 80/20 ratio often is used as a rule of thumb, with the database server typically performing twenty percent of the work. Despite that, though, it is the database that frequently becomes the performance bottleneck in these environments.

A two-tier client-server solution with a large user-base generally requires that each client establish its own database connection. Communication is predictably synchronous, and these connections are often persistent (meaning that they are generated upon user login and kept active until the user exits the application). Proprietary database connections are expensive, and the resource demands sometimes overwhelm database servers, imposing processing latency on all users.

Additionally, given that the clients are assigned the majority of processing responsibilities, they too often demand significant resources. Client-side executables are fully stateful and consume a steady chunk of PC memory. User workstations therefore often are required to run client programs exclusively so that all available resources can be offered to the application.

Processing in SOA is highly distributed. Each service has an explicit functional boundary and related resource requirements. In modeling a technical service-oriented architecture, you have many choices as to how you can position and deploy services.

Enterprise solutions consist of multiple servers, each hosting sets of Web services and supporting middleware. There is, therefore, no fixed processing ratio for SOAs. Services can be distributed as required, and performance demands are one of several factors in determining the physical deployment configuration.

Communication between service and requestor can be synchronous or asynchronous. This flexibility allows processing to be further streamlined, especially when asynchronous message patterns are utilized. Additionally, by placing a large amount of intelligence into the messages, options for achieving message-level context management are provided. This promotes the stateless and autonomous nature of services and further alleviates processing by reducing the need for runtime caching of state information.

Technology

The emergence of client-server applications promoted the use of 4GL programming languages, such as Visual Basic and PowerBuilder. These development environments took better advantage of the Windows operating system by providing the ability to create aesthetically rich and more interactive user-interfaces. Regardless, traditional 3GL languages, such as C++, were also still used, especially for solutions that had more rigid performance requirements. On the back-end, major database vendors, such as Oracle, Informix, IBM, Sybase, and Microsoft, provided robust RDBMSs that could manage multiple connections, while providing flexible data storage and data management features.

The technology set used by SOA actually has not changed as much as it has expanded. Newer versions of older programming languages, such as Visual Basic, still can be used to create Web services, and the use of relational databases still is commonplace. The technology landscape of SOA, though, has become increasingly diverse. In addition to the standard set of Web technologies (HTML, CSS, HTTP, etc.) contemporary SOA brings with it the absolute requirement that an XML data representation architecture be established, along with a SOAP messaging framework, and a service architecture comprised of the ever-expanding Web services platform.

Security

Besides the storage and management of data and the business rules embedded in stored procedures and triggers, the one other part of client-server architecture that frequently is centralized at the server level is security. Databases are sufficiently sophisticated to manage user accounts and groups and to assign these to individual parts of the physical data model.

Security also can be controlled within the client executable, especially when it relates to specific business rules that dictate the execution of application logic (such as limiting access to a part of a user-interface to select users). Additionally, operating system-level security can be incorporated to achieve a single sign-on, where application clearance is derived from the user's operating system login account information.

Though one could boast about the advantages of SOA, most architects envy the simplicity of client-server security. Corporate data is protected via a single point of authentication, establishing a single connection between client and server. In the distributed world of SOA, this is not possible. Security becomes a significant complexity directly relational to the degree of security measures required. Multiple technologies are typically involved, many of which comprise the WS-Security framework (explained in Chapters 7 and 17).

Administration

One of the main reasons the client-server era ended was the increasingly large maintenance costs associated with the distribution and maintenance of application logic across user workstations. Because each client housed the application code, each update to the application required a redistribution of the client software to all workstations. In larger environments, this resulted in a highly burdensome administration process.

Maintenance issues spanned both client and server ends. Client workstations were subject to environment-specific problems because different workstations could have different software programs installed or may have been purchased from different hardware vendors. Further, there were increased server-side demands on databases, especially when a client-server application expanded to a larger user base.

Because service-oriented solutions can have a variety of requestors, they are not necessarily immune to client-side maintenance challenges. While their distributed back-end does accommodate scalability for application and database servers, new administration demands can be introduced. For example, once SOAs evolve to a state where services are reused and become part of multiple service compositions, the management of server resources and service interfaces can require powerful administration tools, including the use of a private registry.

RailCo's accounting system is a classic two-tier client-server application. Its GUI front-end consists of a single executable designed for deployment on old Windows workstations. It provides user-interfaces for looking up, editing, and adding various accounting records. It also offers a financial reporting facility that can produce a fixed amount of statements with detailed or summarized accounting data.

Considering it's only ever had two to three users, there have never really been performance problems on the database end. The now outdated RDBMS that has been in place for the past decade has been reliable and has required little attention.

However, problems with this application have surfaced:

- Operating system upgrades have introduced erratic behavior on some screens, resulting in unexplainable error messages. It is uncertain if these are caused by other programs that have been installed on the workstations.

- The workstations themselves have been rarely upgraded and have not kept pace with the hardware demands of recent software upgrades. After the accounting system launches, there is little more the user can do with the computer. As a result, employee productivity has been affected somewhat.

- Following a new records management policy and some billing procedure changes, a modification to the overall billing process was imposed on the accounting personnel. Because the accounting system was not designed to accommodate this change, employees are required to supplement the automated billing process by manually filling out supplementary forms.

Fundamentally, this accounting system has been getting the job done. However, the actual accounting tasks performed by the users have become increasingly convoluted and inefficient. This is due to the questionable stability of the workstation environments and also because the system itself is not easily adaptable to changes in the processes it automates.

SOA can address issues such as these, as follows:

- Service-oriented solutions eliminate dependencies on user workstation environments by delegating all processing to the server-side (as regular distributed Internet applications already have been doing).

> • SOA establishes an adaptable and extensible architectural model that allows
> solutions to be enhanced with minimal impact. Services can encapsulate exist-
> ing legacy logic providing a standardized API that can plug into larger inte-
> grated solutions. Further, when building custom service-oriented applications,
> extensibility can be built into the solution environment, supporting future
> enhancements, also with minimal impact.

4.3.3 SOA vs. distributed Internet architecture

This comparison may seem like a contradiction, given that SOA can be viewed as a form
of distributed Internet architecture and because we established earlier that previous
types of distributed architecture also could be designed as SOAs. Though possible, and
although there are distributed environments in existence that may have been heavily
influenced by service-oriented principles, this variation of SOA is still a rarity. Consider
the comparison provided here as one that contrasts *traditional* distributed Internet architecture in the manner it was most commonly designed.

Distributed Internet architecture: a brief history

In response to the costs and limitations associated with the two-tier client-server architecture, the concept of building component-based applications hit the mainstream. Multi-
tier client-server architectures surfaced, breaking up the monolithic client executable into
components designed to varying extents of compliance with object-orientation.

Distributing application logic among multiple components (some residing on the client,
others on the server) reduced deployment headaches by centralizing a greater amount
of the logic on servers. Server-side components, now located on dedicated application
servers, would then share and manage pools of database connections, alleviating the
burden of concurrent usage on the database server (Figure 4.4). A single connection
could easily facilitate multiple users.

These benefits came at the cost of increased complexity and ended up shifting expense
and effort from deployment issues to development and administration processes. Building components capable of processing multiple, concurrent requests was more difficult
and problem-ridden than developing a straight-forward executable intended for a
single user.

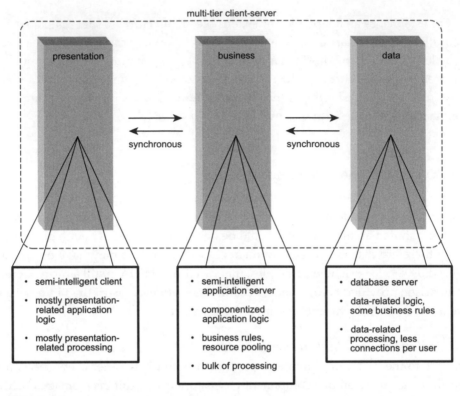

Figure 4.4
A typical multi-tier client-server architecture.

Additionally, replacing client-server database connections was the client-server remote procedure call (RPC) connection. RPC technologies such as CORBA and DCOM allowed for remote communication between components residing on client workstations and servers. Issues similar to the client-server architecture problems involving resources and persistent connections emerged. Adding to this was an increased maintenance effort resulting from the introduction of the middleware layer. For example, application servers and transaction monitors required significant attention in larger environments.

Upon the arrival of the World Wide Web as a viable medium for computing technology in the mid-to-late 90s, the multi-tiered client-server environments began incorporating Internet technology. Most significant was the replacement of the custom software client component with the browser. Not only did this change radically alter (and limit) user-interface design, it practically shifted 100% of application logic to the server (Figure 4.5).

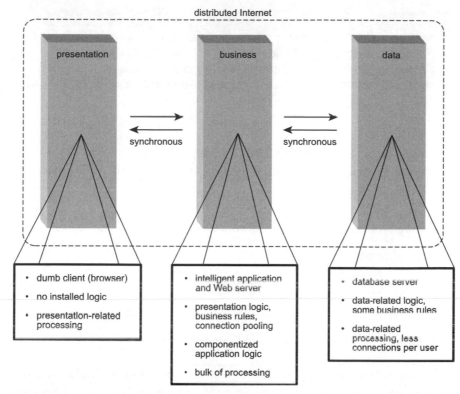

Figure 4.5
A typical distributed Internet architecture.

Distributed Internet architecture also introduced a new physical tier, the Web server. This resulted in HTTP replacing proprietary RPC protocols used to communicate between the user's workstation and the server. The role of RPC was limited to enabling communication between remote Web and application servers.

From the late 90s to the mid 2000s, distributed Internet architectures represented the de facto computing platform for custom developed enterprise solutions. The commoditization of component-based programming skills and the increasing sophistication of middleware eventually lessened some of the overall complexity.

How then, does this popular and familiar architecture compare with SOA? The following sections contrast distributed Internet architecture and SOA characteristics.

> **NOTE**
>
> Although multi-tier client-server is a distinct architecture in its own right, we do not provide a direct comparison between it and SOA. Most of the issues raised in the client-server and the distributed Internet architecture comparisons cover those that would be discussed in a comparison between multi-tier client-server and SOA.

Application logic

Except for some rare applications that embed proprietary extensions in browsers, distributed Internet applications place all of their application logic on the server side. Even client-side scripts intended to execute in response to events on a Web page are downloaded from the Web server upon the initial HTTP request. With none of the logic existing on the client workstation, the entire solution is centralized.

The emphasis is therefore on:

- how application logic should be partitioned
- where the partitioned units of processing logic should reside
- how the units of processing logic should interact

From a physical perspective, service-oriented architecture is very similar to distributed Internet architecture. Provider logic resides on the server end where it is broken down into separate units. The differences lie in the principles used to determine the three primary design considerations just listed.

Traditional distributed applications consist of a series of components that reside on one or more application servers. Components are designed with varying degrees of functional granularity, depending on the tasks they execute, and to what extent they are considered reusable by other tasks or applications. Components residing on the same server communicate via proprietary APIs, as per the public interfaces they expose. RPC protocols are used to accomplish the same communication across server boundaries. This is made possible through the use of local proxy stubs that represent components in remote locations (Figure 4.6).

At design time, the expected interaction components will have with others is taken into account—so much so that actual references to other physical components can be embedded within the programming code. This level of design-time dependence is a form of tight-coupling. It is efficient in that little processing is wasted in trying to locate a required component at runtime. However, the embedded coupling leads to a tightly bound component network that, once implemented, is not easily altered.

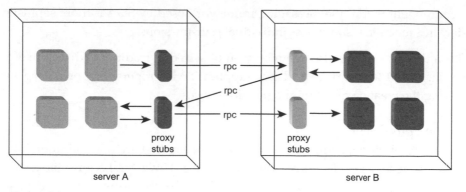

Figure 4.6
Components rely on proxy stubs for remote communication.

Contemporary SOAs still employ and rely on components. However, the entire model-ing approach now takes into consideration the creation of services that encapsulate some or all of these components. These services are designed according to service-orientation principles and are strategically positioned to expose specific sets of func-tionality. While this functionality can be provided by components, it also can originate from legacy systems and other sources, such as adapters interfacing with packaged soft-ware products, or even databases.

The purpose of wrapping functionality within a service is to expose that functionality via an open, standardized interface—irrespective of the technology used to implement the underlying logic. The standardized interface supports the open communications framework that sits at the core of SOA. Further, the use of Web services establishes a loosely coupled environment that runs contrary to many traditional distributed appli-cation designs. When properly designed, loosely coupled services support a composi-tion model, allowing individual services to participate in aggregate assemblies. This introduces continual opportunities for reuse and extensibility.

Another significant shift related to the design and behavior of distributed application logic is in how services exchange information. While traditional components provide methods that, once invoked, send and receive parameter data, Web services communi-cate with SOAP messages. Even though SOAP supports RPC-style message structures, the majority of *service-oriented* Web service designs rely on document-style messages. (This important distinction is explored in subsequent chapters.)

Also messages are structured to be as self-sufficient as possible. Through the use of SOAP headers, message contents can be accompanied by a wide range of meta infor-mation, processing instructions, and policy rules. In comparison to data exchange in the pure component world, the messaging framework used by SOA is more sophisticated, bulkier, and tends to result in less individual transmissions.

Finally, although reuse is also commonly emphasized in traditional distributed design approaches, SOA fosters reuse and cross-application interoperability on a deep level by promoting the creation of solution-agnostic services.

Application processing

Regardless of platform, components represent the lion's share of application logic and are therefore responsible for most of the processing. However, because the technology used for inter-component communication differs from the technology used to accomplish inter-service communication, so do the processing requirements.

Distributed Internet architecture promotes the use of proprietary communication protocols, such as DCOM and vendor implementations of CORBA for remote data exchange. While these technologies historically have had challenges, they are considered relatively efficient and reliable, especially once an active connection is made. They can support the creation of stateful and stateless components that primarily interact with synchronous data exchanges (asynchronous communication is supported by some platforms but not commonly used).

SOA, on the other hand, relies on message-based communication. This involves the serialization, transmission, and deserialization of SOAP messages containing XML document payloads. Processing steps can involve the conversion of relational data into an XML-compliant structure, the validation of the XML document prior and subsequent to transmission, and the parsing of the document and extraction of the data by the recipient. Although advancements, such as the use of enterprise parsers and hardware accelerators are on-going, most still rank RPC communication as being noticeably faster than SOAP.

Because a network of SOAP servers can effectively replace RPC-style communication channels within service-oriented application environments, the incurred processing overhead becomes a significant design issue. Document and message modeling conventions and the strategic placement of validation logic are important factors that shape the transport layer of service-oriented architecture.

This messaging framework promotes the creation of autonomous services that support a wide range of message exchange patterns. Though synchronous communication is fully supported, asynchronous patterns are encouraged, as they provide further opportunities to optimize processing by minimizing communication. Further supporting the statelessness of services are various context management options that can be employed, including the use of WS-* specifications, such as WS-Coordination and WS-BPEL, as well as custom solutions.

Technology

The technology behind distributed Internet architecture went through a number of stages over the past few years. Initial architectures consisted of components, server-side scripts, and raw Web technologies, such as HTML and HTTP. Improvements in middleware allowed for increased processing power and transaction control. The emergence of XML introduced sophisticated data representation that actually gave substance to content transmitted via Internet protocols. The subsequent availability of Web services allowed distributed Internet applications to cross proprietary platform boundaries.

Because many current distributed applications use XML and Web services, there may be little difference between the technology behind these solutions and those based on SOA. One clear distinction, though, is that a contemporary SOA will most likely be built upon XML data representation and the Web services technology platform. Beyond a core set of Internet technologies and the use of components, there is no governance of the technology used by traditional Internet applications. Thus XML and Web services are optional for distributed Internet architecture but not for contemporary SOA.

Security

When application logic is strewn across multiple physical boundaries, implementing fundamental security measures such as authentication and authorization becomes more difficult.

In a two-tiered client-server environment, an exclusive server-side connection easily facilitates the identification of users and the safe transportation of corporate data. However, when the exclusivity of that connection is removed, and when data is required to travel across different physical layers, new approaches to security are needed. To ensure the safe transportation of information and the recognition of user credentials, while preserving the original security context, traditional security architectures incorporate approaches such as delegation and impersonation. Encryption also is added to the otherwise wide open HTTP protocol to allow data to be protected during transmission beyond the Web server.

SOAs depart from this model by introducing wholesale changes to how security is incorporated and applied. Relying heavily on the extensions and concepts established by the WS-Security framework, the security models used within SOA emphasize the placement of security logic onto the messaging level. SOAP messages provide header blocks in which security logic can be stored. That way, wherever the message goes, so does its security information. This approach is required to preserve individual autonomy and loose coupling between services, as well as the extent to which a service can remain fully stateless.

Administration

Maintaining component-based applications involves keeping track of individual component instances, tracing local and remote communication problems, monitoring server resource demands, and, of course, the standard database administration tasks. Distributed Internet architecture further introduces the Web server and with it an additional physical environment that requires attention while solutions are in operation. Because clients, whether local or external to an organization, connect to these solutions using HTTP, the Web server becomes the official first point of contact. It must therefore be designed for scalability—a requirement that has led to the creation of Web server farms that pool resources.

Enterprise-level SOAs typically require additional runtime administration. Problems with messaging frameworks (especially when working with asynchronous exchange patterns) can more easily go undetected than with RPC-based data exchanges. This is because so many variations exist as to how messages can be interchanged. RPC communication generally requires a response from the initiating component, indicating success or failure. Upon encountering a failure condition, an exception handling routine kicks in. Exception handling with messaging frameworks can be more complex and less robust. Although WS-* extensions are being positioned to better deal with these situations, administration effort is still expected to remain high.

Other maintenance tasks, such as resource management (similar to component management), are also required. However, to best foster reuse and composability, a useful part of an administration infrastructure for enterprises building large amounts of Web services is a private registry. UDDI is one of the technologies used for standardizing this interface repository, which can be manually or programmatically accessed to discover service descriptions.

The TLS accounting system consists of a large, distributed component-based solution. Some 50 odd components host and execute various parts of the application logic. For performance and security reasons, some components have been deployed on separate application servers.

Overall, the execution of a typical accounting task will involve four to five physical layers consisting of:

- A Web server hosting server-side scripts that relay HTTP requests to components on application servers and then relay responses from those components back to the browser clients.

- An application server hosting a controller component that generates a transaction context and manages more specialized components.

- A possible second application server hosting two or more business components that enforce specific business rules and perform various functions related to a particular business context. This server also may host one or more data components that encapsulate the data access logic required to interact with application repositories.

- A database server hosting a complete RDBMS environment.

This enterprise solution has undergone many changes and enhancements over the past few years. Some of the primary issues that have arisen include:

- Initially, many components were custom developed to alter or extend existing functionality. Each redevelopment project has become increasingly expensive. This trend is being blamed on the overhead associated with the amount of testing and redeployment effort required to ensure that all pre-existing dependencies are not affected by any modification to a component's functionality.

- Because state management was never standardized, a design disparity has emerged. Some components manage state information by caching data in memory, while others use application server-deployed databases. This became an issue when XML was first introduced as a standard data format. Permanent state management designs already had a relational storage format in place that was incompatible with the required XML document structures.

Subsequent chapters explain how SOA addresses these types of problems as follows:

- SOA establishes a loosely coupled relationship between units of processing logic encapsulated as services. This allows the logic within each service boundary to be updated and evolved independently of existing service requestors, as long as the original service contract is preserved.

- SOA promotes the standardization of XML data representation throughout solution environments. Further, service statelessness is emphasized by deferring state management to the message level. This maximizes reuse, availability, and scalability of service logic but also provides a standardized state management approach.

4.3.4   SOA vs. hybrid Web service architecture

In the previous section we mentioned how more recent variations of the distributed Internet architecture have come to incorporate Web services. This topic is worth elaborating upon because it has been (and is expected to continue to be) at the root of some confusion surrounding SOA.

First, the use of Web services within traditional architectures is completely legitimate. Due to the development support for Web services in many established programming languages, they easily can be positioned to fit in with older application designs. And, for those legacy environments that do not support the custom development of Web services, adapters are often available.

NOTE
Although we are focusing on distributed Internet architecture here, there are no restrictions for two-tier client-server applications to be outfitted with Web services.

Web services as component wrappers

The primary role of Web services in this context has been to introduce an integration layer that consists of wrapper services that enable synchronous communication via SOAP-compliant integration channels (Figure 4.7). In fact, the initial release of the SOAP specification and the first generation of SOAP servers were specifically designed to duplicate RPC-style communication using messages.

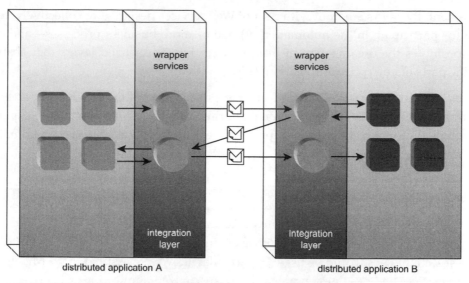

Figure 4.7
Wrapper services encapsulating components.

These integration channels are primarily utilized in integration architectures to facilitate communication with other applications or outside partners. They also are used to enable communication with other (more service-oriented) solutions and to take advantage of some of the features offered by third-party utility Web services. Regardless of their use or purpose within traditional architectures, it is important to clarify that a distributed Internet architecture that incorporates Web services in this manner does not qualify as a true SOA. It is simply a distributed Internet architecture that uses Web services.

Instead of mirroring component interfaces and establishing point-to-point connections with Web services, SOA provides strong support for a variety of messaging models (based on both synchronous and asynchronous exchanges). Additionally, Web services within SOAs are subject to specific design requirements, such as those provided by service-orientation principles. These and other characteristics support the pursuit of consistent loose coupling. Once achieved, a single service is never limited to point-to-point communication; it can accommodate any number of current and future requestors.

Web services within SOA

While SOAs can vary in size and quality, there are tangible characteristics that distinguish an SOA from other architectures that use Web services. Much of this book is dedicated to exploring these characteristics. For now it is sufficient to state that fundamentally, SOAs are built with a set of Web services designed to collectively auto-mate (or participate in the automation of) one or more business processes—and that SOA promotes the organization of these services into specialized layers that abstract specific parts of enterprise automation logic.

Also by standardizing on SOA across an enterprise, a natural interoperability emerges that transcends proprietary application platforms. This allows for previously disparate environments to be composed in support of new and evolving business automation processes.

CASE STUDY

TLS had the development of a group of custom eBusiness solutions outsourced to a number of consulting firms. With each project, TLS was guaranteed that the latest technologies would be used. In particular, they were assured that XML and Web services had been incorporated. These specialized applications were even referred to as "service-oriented."

Later, a requirement arose for one solution to integrate with another. A subse-quent analysis revealed an alarming degree of inconsistency with regard to how each application managed and represented corporate data and the messaging formats used to package this data. To achieve the level of required interoperabil-ity between these two systems, a complex and expensive integration project was needed. Many stakeholders wondered why, if both systems were based on com-mon technologies, sharing data between them was still such a monumental issue.

It turned out that each solution managed corporate data relevant to its applica-tion scope in a different way. Some used XML only to represent data in a unique context. Though promoted as service-oriented solutions, Web services were not actually a key part of the application architecture. These "token services" addressed some specific requirements but were not built with future interoper-ability in mind.

There was no initial concern around this approach, as each application delivered its promised set of features and solved its corresponding business problems. However, because no design principles were applied to ensure that XML and Web services were being implemented in a standardized manner in support of SOA, there was nothing in place to prevent the resulting design disparity.

4.3.5 Service-orientation and object-orientation (Part I)

Note that this section title is "Service-orientation *and* object-orientation," as opposed to "Service-orientation *vs.* object-orientation." That distinction was made to stress the fact that the relationship between these two schools of thought is not necessarily a competitive one.

In fact, object-oriented programming is commonly used to build the application logic encapsulated within Web services. However, how the object-oriented programming methodology differs fundamentally from service-orientation is worth exploring. An understanding of their differences will help you make them work together.

Below is a list comparing aspects of these design approaches. (Whereas service-orientation is based on the design of services, object-orientation is centered around the creation of objects. Because comparing services to objects can be confusing, the term "units of processing logic" is used.)

- Service-orientation emphasizes loose coupling between units of processing logic (services). Although object-orientation supports the creation of reusable, loosely coupled programming routines, much of it is based on predefined class dependencies, resulting in more tightly bound units of processing logic (objects).

- Service-orientation encourages coarse-grained interfaces (service descriptions) so that every unit of communication (message) contains as much information as possible for the completion of a given task. Object-oriented programming fully supports fine-grained interfaces (APIs) so that units of communication (RPC or local API calls) can perform various sized tasks.

- Service-orientation expects the scope of a unit of processing logic (service) to vary significantly. Object-oriented units of logic (objects) tend to be smaller and more specific in scope.

- Service-orientation promotes the creation of activity-agnostic units of processing logic (services) that are driven into action by intelligent units of communication (messages). Object-orientation encourages the binding of processing logic with data, resulting in highly intelligent units (objects).

- Service-orientation prefers that units of processing logic (services) be designed to remain as stateless as possible. Object-orientation promotes the binding of data and logic, resulting in the creation of more stateful units (objects). (However, more recent component-based design approaches deviate from this tendency.)

- Service-orientation supports the composition of loosely coupled units of processing logic (services). Object-orientation supports composition but also encourages inheritance among units of processing logic (objects), which can lead to tightly coupled dependencies.

You may have noticed that we avoided referencing specific object-orientation principles, such as encapsulation, inheritance, and aggregation. Because we have not yet fully described the principles of service-orientation, we cannot compare the respective paradigms on this level. Chapter 8 explains the individual service-orientation principles in detail and then continues this discussion in the *Service-orientation and object-orientation (Part II)* section.

SUMMARY OF KEY POINTS

- SOA is a radical departure from client-server architecture. Current SOAs still employ some of the technologies originally used to build client-server applications. Though more sophisticated, SOAs introduce complexity that sharply contrasts the simplicity of a two-tier client-server architecture.

- Distributed Internet architecture has much in common with SOA, including a significant amount of its technology. However, SOA has distinct characteristics relating to both technology and its underlying design principles. For example, SOA introduces processing and security requirements that differ from distributed Internet architecture, and SOA administration is typically more complex due to its reliance on messaging-based communication.

- Traditional architectures have and can continue to use Web services within their own design paradigms. It's important to not confuse these architectures with SOA. Non-SOA use of Web services is typically found within distributed Internet architectures, where Web services are employed to mirror RPC-style communication.

Web Services and Primitive SOA

Contemporary SOA is intrinsically reliant on Web services—so much so that Web services concepts and technology used to actualize service-orientation have influenced and contributed to a number of the common SOA characteristics we identified in Chapter 3. An understanding of SOA therefore begins with a close look at the overall framework that has been established by the first and second-generation Web services extensions.

We can categorize concepts provided to us by these specifications into the following two groups:

- Basic concepts that relate to primitive SOA and core Web services standards (covered in this chapter).
- Advanced concepts that extend the basic framework to support numerous supplementary features that relate to specific contemporary SOA characteristics (covered in Chapters 6 and 7).

This chapter kicks things off with an introductory overview of the concepts of the first-generation Web services framework as related to the realization of primitive SOA characteristics.

NOTE

The framework we've assembled here consists of terms and concepts derived from a number of open specifications, including WSDL, SOAP, and UDDI. If you are already comfortable with these technologies and concepts relating to Web services in general, you can skip ahead to Chapter 6.

In Plain English sections

For those not yet familiar with the topics covered by this chapter, we provide the *In Plain English* sections. Their purpose is to convey the most fundamental concepts behind specific topics by providing intentionally simplistic, non-technical analogies. If you are new to the world of Web services, these sections will hopefully provide some extra clarity.

How case studies are used: We introduce the Web services-enabled portions of the RailCo and TLS solution environments and highlight specific parts of these applications to demonstrate some key concepts.

5.1   The Web services framework

A technology framework is a collection of things. It can include one or more architectures, technologies, concepts, models, and even sub-frameworks. The framework established by Web services is comprised of all of these parts.

Specifically, this framework is characterized by:

- an abstract (vendor-neutral) existence defined by standards organizations and implemented by (proprietary) technology platforms
- core building blocks that include Web services, service descriptions, and messages
- a communications agreement centered around service descriptions based on WSDL
- a messaging framework comprised of SOAP technology and concepts
- a service description registration and discovery architecture sometimes realized through UDDI
- a well-defined architecture that supports messaging patterns and compositions (covered in Chapter 6)
- a second generation of Web services extensions (also known as the WS-* specifications) continually broadening its underlying feature-set (covered in Chapters 6 and 7)

Another recommended addition to this list is the WS-I Basic Profile (introduced in Chapter 4 and further explained in later chapters). It provides standards and best practices that govern the usage of WSDL, SOAP, and UDDI features. Therefore, much of what the Web services framework is comprised of can be standardized by the Basic Profile.

In its entirety this technology framework is conceptually in alignment with the principles of service-orientation. To further explore this synergy, the next three sections are intentionally labeled to mirror the three sub-sections from Chapter 3 in which we first defined the parts of primitive SOA (Figure 5.1).

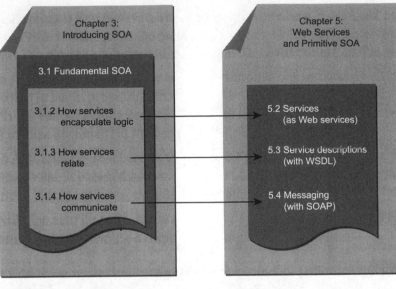

Figure 5.1
The structural relationship between sections in Chapters 3 and 5.

SUMMARY OF KEY POINTS

- First- and second-generation technologies, along with design-agnostic concepts and implementation-neutral architectures, form an abstract Web services framework.

- The fundamentals of this framework are in alignment with the core characteristics of primitive SOA.

5.2 Services (as Web services)

In Chapter 3 we introduced the concept of services and how they provide a means of encapsulating various extents of logic. Manifesting services in real world automation solutions requires the use of a technology capable of preserving fundamental service-orientation, while implementing real world business functionality.

Web services provide the potential of fulfilling these primitive requirements, but they need to be intentionally designed to do so. This is because the Web services framework is flexible and adaptable. Web services can be designed to duplicate the behavior and functionality found in proprietary distributed systems, or they can be designed to be fully SOA-compliant. This flexibility has allowed Web services to become part of many existing application environments and has been one of the reasons behind their popularity. It also reveals the fact that Web services are not necessarily inherently service-oriented.

NOTE

We use the terms "Web services" and "services" interchangeably throughout this book.

Let's start with an overview of the most basic Web services design concepts. Fundamentally, every Web service can be associated with:

- a temporary classification based on the roles it assumes during the runtime processing of a message
- a permanent classification based on the application logic it provides and the roles it assumes within a solution environment

We explore both of these design classifications in the following two sections:

- service roles (temporary classifications)
- service models (permanent classifications)

IN PLAIN ENGLISH

Bob and Jim are two old friends I occasionally meet. During our last get-together we talked about Chuck, another friend we used to hang out with, but with whom we lost touch several years ago. None of us know where he went off to, and we think it would be fun to see if we could contact him again. Bob says that he's heard of an agency called "Reconnect" that specializes in this particular type of service.

For us to make use of any of the services offered by Reconnect, we must:

1. Find out (discover) how we can contact this agency.
2. Compile the information about Chuck that the agency will require to perform the search (formulate a request).
3. Forward this information (issue the request) to the agency.

(These steps are explained individually in the subsequent *In Plain English* sections.)

Reconnect is providing a service and can therefore be seen as fulfilling the role of service provider. We are requesting a service and are therefore considered to be acting as service requestors.

5.2.1 Service roles

A Web service is capable of assuming different roles, depending on the context within which it is used. For example, a service can act as the initiator, relayer, or the recipient of a message. A service is therefore not labeled exclusively as a client or server, but instead as a unit of software capable of altering its role, depending on its processing responsibility in a given scenario.

It is not uncommon for a Web service to change its role more than once within a given business task. It is especially not uncommon for a Web service within an SOA to assume different roles in different business tasks.

Provided here are descriptions of the fundamental service roles.

Service provider

The *service provider* role is assumed by a Web service under the following conditions:

- The Web service is invoked via an external source, such as a service requestor (Figure 5.2).
- The Web service provides a published service description offering information about its features and behavior. (Service descriptions are explained later in this chapter.)

The service provider role is synonymous with the server role in the classic client-server architecture. Depending on the type of message exchange used when invoking a service provider, the service provider may reply to a request message with a response message. (Types of message exchanges are categorized as "message exchange patterns," which are explained in the next chapter.)

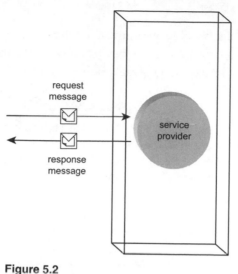

Figure 5.2

As the recipient of a request message, the
Web service is classified as a service
provider.

The term "service provider" also is used to identify the organization (or individual)
responsible for actually providing the Web service. To help distinguish the service role
from the service's actual provider, the following, more qualified terms are sometimes
used:

- *service provider entity* (the organization or individual providing the Web service)
- *service provider agent* (the Web service itself, acting as an agent on behalf of its
  owner)

It is, however, most common to simply refer to the service being invoked as the service
provider.

NOTE
A service provider agent is different from a service agent, which is a small run-time program used to perform generic processing tasks in support of Web services. Service agents are explained in Chapter 18.

Service requestor

Any unit of processing logic capable of issuing a request message that can be understood by the service provider is classified as a *service requestor*. A Web service is always a service provider but also can act as a service requestor.

> **NOTE**
>
> Almost all of the service requestors discussed in this book are classified as Web services and are referenced and depicted as such. Chapter 18 provides platform-specific details about how Web services are implemented and how the physical parts of a Web service interact in service provider and service requestor roles.

A Web service takes on the service requestor role under the following circumstances:

- The Web service invokes a service provider by sending it a message (Figure 5.3).
- The Web service searches for and assesses the most suitable service provider by studying available service descriptions. (Service descriptions and service registries are covered in the *Service descriptions (with WSDL)* section.)

The service requestor is the natural counterpart to the service provider, comparable to the client in a typical client-server environment. It is important to note that a service provider is not acting as a service requestor when it sends a message in response to a request message. A service requestor is best viewed as a software program that initiates a conversation with a service provider.

As with "service provider," this term is subject to some ambiguity. A service requestor can represent both the Web service itself as well as the Web service owner. Therefore, the following extended terms are available (but not really used that often):

- *service requestor entity* (the organization or individual requesting the Web service)
- *service requestor agent* (the Web service itself, acting as an agent on behalf of its owner)

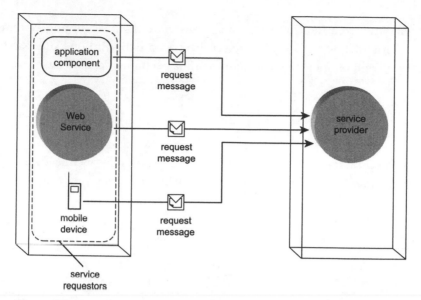

Figure 5.3

The sender of the request message is classified as a service requestor.

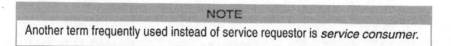

NOTE

Another term frequently used instead of service requestor is *service consumer.*

CASE STUDY

RailCo is one of many long-time vendors used by TLS. Historically, it was the primary air brake parts supplier TLS relied upon. Until recently, TLS had to order parts from RailCo via phone or fax. When a new air brake supplier surfaced, offering competitive prices and signing up with TLS's B2B solution, there was little need for TLS to continue exclusively with RailCo. In fact, TLS only contacted RailCo again when its new primary vendor could not supply a requested part.

For RailCo to join its competitor as an online partner of TLS, it had to conform to rules and specifications defined by TLS. Specifically, TLS dictates that every supplier must allow TLS to programmatically interface with their inventory control system to submit purchase orders. Additionally, the supplier must be able to connect to TLS's external accounting interface to submit invoices and back-order information.

These policies forced RailCo to build an extension to their accounting system, capable of interacting with TLS's Web service-based B2B solution. After RailCo's application went online, the most common data exchange scenarios were as follows:

- TLS's Purchase Order Service submits electronic POs that are received by RailCo's Order Fulfillment Service.

- Upon shipping the order, RailCo's Invoice Submission Service sends an electronic invoice to TLS's Accounts Payable Service.

Figure 5.4 illustrates these two message exchanges.

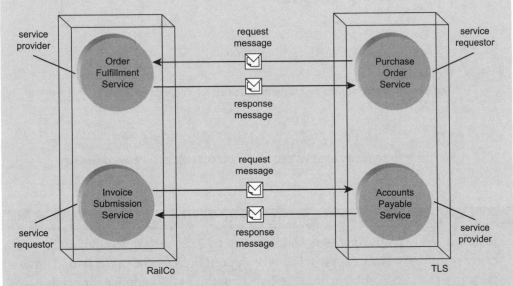

Figure 5.4
TLS and RailCo services swapping roles in different but related message exchanges.

In the first scenario, TLS acts as the service requestor entity. Its Purchase Order Service was the service requestor (or service requestor agent) that initiated the interaction. Being the recipient of the order request, the Order Fulfillment Service is classified as the service provider (or service provider agent). As the owner of this Web service, RailCo is the service provider entity.

The roles are reversed in the second scenario, where RailCo is the service requestor entity because its Invoice Submission Service acts as the service requestor. TLS's Accounts Payable Service receives the invoice message, making that Web service the service provider, and TLS the service provider entity.

IN PLAIN ENGLISH

Because we need to send a piece of mail to Reconnect for them to initiate the search, we also introduce an intermediary into this scenario. Although the letter is addressed to Reconnect, it is actually first sent to the Post Office. From there it is routed to a carrier that delivers it to the Reconnect office. In this scenario, the Post Office acts as an intermediary that provides a routing service.

Intermediaries

The communications framework established by Web services contrasts the predictable nature of traditional point-to-point communications channels. Though less flexible and less scalable, point-to-point communication was a great deal easier to design. Web services communication is based on the use of messaging paths, which can best be described as point-to-* paths. This is because once a service provider submits a message, it can be processed by multiple intermediate routing and processing agents before it arrives at its ultimate destination. (Message paths are explained at the end of this chapter.)

Web services and service agents that route and process a message after it is initially sent and before it arrives at its ultimate destination are referred to as *intermediaries* or *intermediary services*. Because an intermediary receives and submits messages, it always transitions through service provider and service requestor roles (Figure 5.5).

There are two types of intermediaries. The first, known as a *passive intermediary*, is typically responsible for routing messages to a subsequent location (Figure 5.6). It may use information in the SOAP message header to determine the routing path, or it may employ native routing logic to achieve some level of load balancing. Either way, what makes this type of intermediary passive is that it does not modify the message.

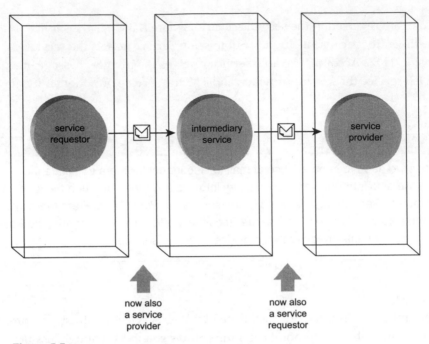

Figure 5.5

The intermediary service transitions through service provider and service
requestor roles while processing a message.

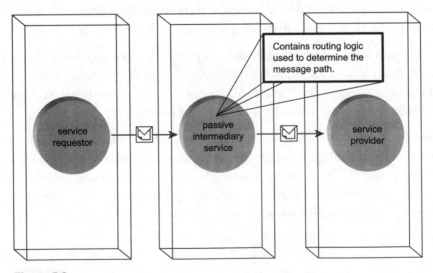

Figure 5.6

A passive intermediary service processing a message without altering its contents.

CASE STUDY

After shipping a TLS order, RailCo's Invoice Submission Service transmits a message containing an electronic invoice. The first TLS Web service to receive the message is a passive intermediary called the Load Balancing Service. Its purpose is to provide load balancing logic by checking the current processing statistics of available TLS servers. When the server with the lowest usage is identified, this passive intermediary routes the message accordingly.

Upon receiving the message from the Invoice Submission Service requestor, the passive Load Balancing intermediary acts as the service provider. After it has determined where the message is to be forwarded to, it changes its role to service requestor to forward the invoice document to the destination Accounts Payable Service provider.

NOTE

The Load Balancing Service (and the upcoming Internal Policy Service) is a form of intermediary that can be explicitly accessed as a Web service through a WSDL or it can act as a service agent. Service agents are intermediaries designed to intercept and process messages en route to their ultimate destinations and are explained further in Chapter 18. TLS opted to develop flexible intermediaries to fulfill requirements specific to their environments.

Like passive intermediary services, *active intermediaries* also route messages to a forwarding destination. Prior to transmitting a message, however, these services actively process and alter the message contents (Figure 5.7). Typically, active intermediaries will look for particular SOAP header blocks and perform some action in response to the information they find there. They almost always alter data in header blocks and may insert or even delete header blocks entirely. (Header blocks are explained later in this chapter.)

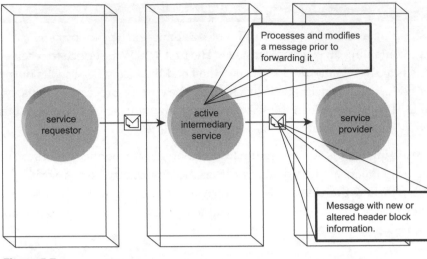

Figure 5.7
An active intermediary service.

CASE STUDY

TLS employs a number of active intermediaries. The Internal Policy Service, for example, examines the message to determine whether it is subject to any internal policy restrictions. If it is, the active intermediary inserts a new header block containing one or more policy rules used by subsequent service providers. As with the passive intermediary example, the active intermediary transitions through service provider and service requestor roles before finally forwarding the message to the appropriate TLS service provider.

Initial sender and ultimate receiver

Initial senders are simply service requestors that initiate the transmission of a message. Therefore, the initial sender is always the first Web service in a message path. The counterpart to this role is the *ultimate receiver*. This label identifies service providers that exist as the last Web service along a message's path (Figure 5.8).

Note that intermediary services can never be initial senders or ultimate receivers within the scope of a service activity.

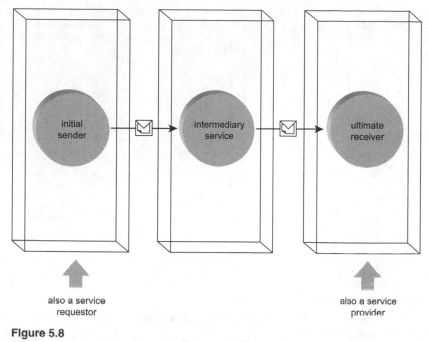

Figure 5.8
Web services acting as initial sender and ultimate receiver.

Expanding on the previous example that demonstrated the use of a passive intermediary, let's take a look at all the services involved in that message exchange. In this scenario, we had the RailCo Invoice Submission Service (acting as the service requestor) initiating the message transmission. By receiving the message, the Load Balancing intermediary acts as the service provider. Upon routing the message, the intermediary temporarily assumes the service requestor role and sends the message to the Accounts Payable Service, another service provider (Figure 5.9).

These three physical services created four logical roles to complete two service requestor-to-service provider transmissions. There was, however, only one Web service that initiated the transmission. This was the Invoice Submission Service, and it is therefore considered the initial sender. Similarly, there was only one Web service that ended the overall activity, which makes the Accounts Payable Service the ultimate receiver.

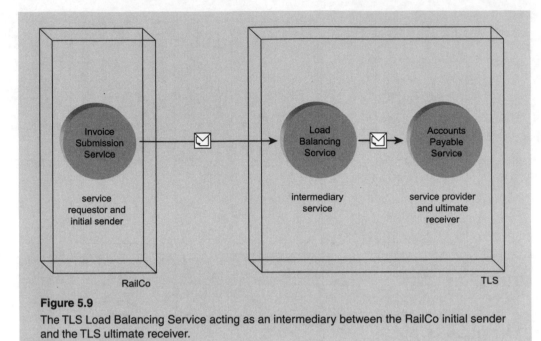

Figure 5.9
The TLS Load Balancing Service acting as an intermediary between the RailCo initial sender
and the TLS ultimate receiver.

Service compositions

As the name suggests, this particular term does not apply to a single Web service, but
to a composite relationship between a collection of services. Any service can enlist one
or more additional services to complete a given task. Further, any of the enlisted services can call other services to complete a given sub-task. Therefore, each service that
participates in a composition assumes an individual role of *service composition member*
(Figure 5.10).

Typically, Web services need to be designed with service composition in mind to be
effective composition members. Service-orientation principles place an emphasis on
composability, allowing some Web services to be designed in such a manner that they
can be pulled into future service compositions without a foreknowledge of how they
will be utilized.

The concept of service composability is very important to service-oriented environments (and is explained as a service-orientation principle in Chapter 8). In fact, service
composition is frequently governed by WS-* composition extensions, such as WS-BPEL
and WS-CDL, which introduce the related concepts of orchestration and choreography,
respectively (as explained in Chapter 6).

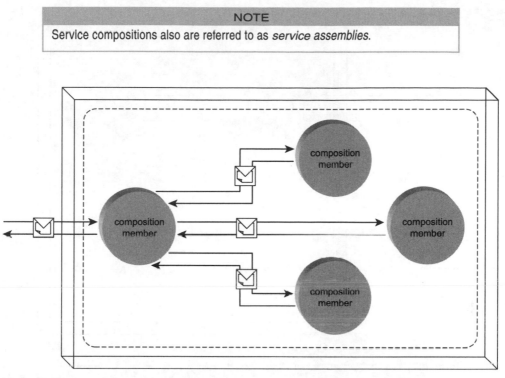

Figure 5.10
A service composition consisting of four members.

CASE STUDY

When the TLS Accounts Payable Service receives an invoice, it invokes a series of additional services to fully process the invoice contents:

1. It first uses the Vendor Profile Service to validate the invoice header data and link the invoice document to a vendor account.

2. Next, the Accounts Payable Service extracts taxes and shipping fees and directly logs all amounts into the appropriate A/P accounts.

3. Finally, the Accounts Payable Service passes the Ledger Service the invoice total, which it uses to update the General Ledger.

In this scenario our service composition consists of three composition members, spearheaded by the Accounts Payable Service (Figure 5.11).

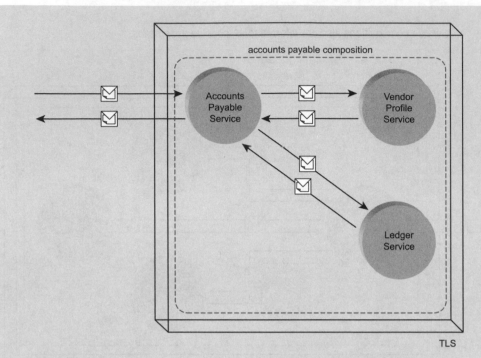

Figure 5.11
The Accounts Payable Service enlisting other TLS services in a service composition.

NOTE

A characteristic of this particular composition that is not discussed here is the fact that all three actions we described would very likely be wrapped in a transaction. Should one of them fail, all others would be rolled back. (Concepts relating to service transactions are covered in Chapter 6.)

5.2.2   Service models

The roles we've explored so far are agnostic to the nature of the functionality being provided by the Web service. They are generic states that a service can enter within a generic context. The manner in which services are being utilized in the real world, though, has led to a classification based on the nature of the application logic they provide, as well as their business-related roles within the overall solution. These classifications are known as *service models*.

The sections that follow describe the basic set of common service models. Additional service models are introduced in later chapters. Appendix B further provides a reference table listing all service models covered in this book. It is important to note that a service can and frequently does belong to more than one service model.

Business service model

Within an SOA, the *business service* represents the most fundamental building block. It encapsulates a distinct set of business logic within a well-defined functional boundary. It is ideally autonomous but still not limited to executing in isolation, as business services are frequently expected to participate in service compositions.

Business services are used within SOAs as follows:

- as fundamental building blocks for the representation of business logic
- to represent a corporate entity or information set
- to represent business process logic
- as service composition members

For future reference, when building an SOA around layers of abstraction, the business service model can correspond to the business service layer introduced in Chapter 9.

Utility service model

A service providing generic functionality usually not associated with business logic can be classified as a *utility service*.

Utility services are used within SOAs as follows:

- as services that enable the characteristic of reuse within SOA
- as solution-agnostic intermediary services
- as services that promote the intrinsic interoperability characteristic of SOA
- as the services with the highest degree of autonomy

When working with the service abstraction layers described in Chapter 9, a utility service is most commonly associated with the application service layer. As a result, a utility service can be referred to as a *utility application service*.

CASE STUDY

In the examples we've gone through so far in this chapter, we've described eight Web services. Six of these are business services, while the other two are utility services, as follows:

- Accounts Payable Service = business service
- Internal Policy Service = utility service
- Invoice Submission Service = business service
- Ledger Service = business service
- Load Balancing Service = utility service
- Order Fulfillment Service = business service
- Purchase Order Service = business service
- Vendor Profile Service = business service

The Load Balancing and Internal Policy Services are classified as utility services because they provide generic functionality that can be reused by different types of applications. The application logic of the remaining services is specific to a given business task or solution, which makes them business-centric services.

Controller service model

Service compositions are comprised of a set of independent services that each contribute to the execution of the overall business task. The assembly and coordination of these services is often a task in itself and one that can be assigned as the primary function of a dedicated service or as the secondary function of a service that is fully capable of executing a business task independently. The *controller service* fulfills this role, acting as the parent service to service composition members.

Controller services are used within SOAs as follows:

- to support and implement the principle of composability
- to leverage reuse opportunities

The controller service model represents a role a service assumes when one of its operations carries out logic that composes operations within other services.

Note that controller services themselves can become subordinate service composition members. In this case the composition coordinated by a controller is, in its entirety, composed into a larger composition. In this situation there may be a master controller service that acts as the parent to the entire service composition, as well as a sub-controller, responsible for coordinating a portion of the composition (Figure 5.12).

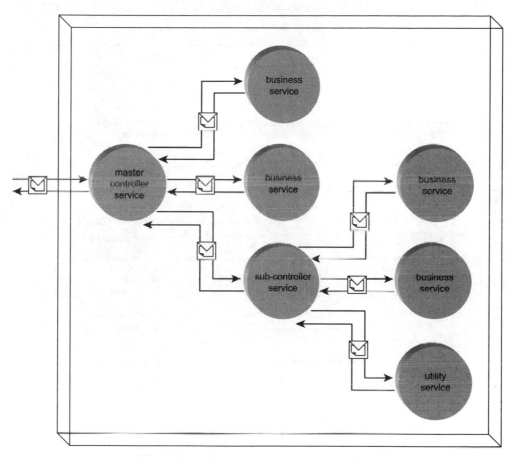

Figure 5.12
A service composition consisting of a master controller, a sub-controller, four business services, and one utility service.

The controller service model is used frequently when building SOA with specialized service abstraction layers, as explained later in Chapter 9.

In our previous example we demonstrated how the Accounts Payable Service initiated and coordinated a service composition consisting of two additional composition members. That would classify the Accounts Payable Service as a controller service. The fact that we already labeled this service as a business service does not conflict with this new classification; a single service can be classified as more than one service model (Figure 5.13).

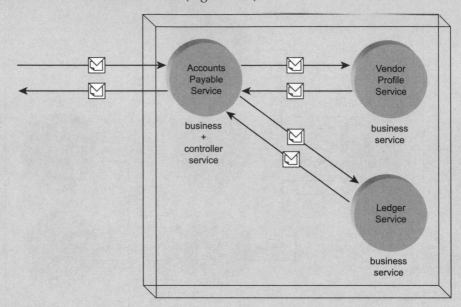

Figure 5.13
The Accounts Payable Service acting as a business and controller service, composing two other business services.

SUMMARY OF KEY POINTS

- Web services can be labeled using temporary and permanent classifications.

- Temporary classifications relate to roles assumed by a service at runtime. For example, an intermediary service can transition through different roles while processing a message.

- Service models refer to permanent classifications that represent the logic housed by the service, as well as its role within the overall solution. A service can belong to more than one service model.

5.3   Service descriptions (with WSDL)

When we covered loose coupling in Chapter 3 as part of our primitive SOA discussion, we introduced the essential need for service descriptions. This part of SOA provides the key ingredient to establishing a consistently loosely coupled form of communication between services implemented as Web services.

For this purpose, description documents are required to accompany any service wanting to act as an ultimate receiver. The primary service description document is the WSDL definition (Figure 5.14).

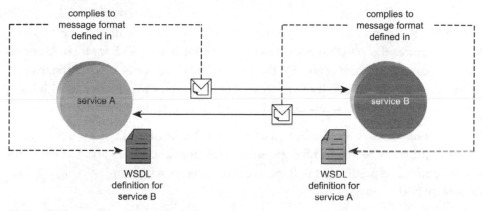

Figure 5.14
WSDL definitions enable loose coupling between services.

> **NOTE**
>
> Only WSDL concepts are discussed in this section. For WSDL language examples, see the *WSDL language basics* section in Chapter 13.

IN PLAIN ENGLISH

To provide Reconnect with the information it needs about Chuck, we are supplied with a brochure and a form. The brochure explains that:

1. The location service offered by Reconnect requires the completion of the form.
2. Once the form is received, the search will be performed.
3. Once the search has been completed, a response will be mailed out to us.

This form requires us to organize background details about Chuck into specific fields. We fill out the form and sign a disclaimer that states that though Reconnect will perform the search on our behalf, results cannot be guaranteed.

Collectively, the brochure and the form represent a service description vaguely similar to a WSDL definition. The WSDL establishes the terms of use for the service provider by defining exactly the information it requires to perform its service and also whether or not a response will be issued.

CASE STUDY

For RailCo to design its B2B Web services in full compliance with the TLS services, RailCo acquires the WSDL service description published by TLS for their Accounts Payable Service. This definition file then is used by developers to build the Invoice Submission Service so that it can process SOAP messages in accordance with the service interface requirements defined in the TLS service descriptions.

Further, RailCo provides TLS with a copy of the WSDL definition for the RailCo Order Fulfillment Service. TLS registers this service description and adds it to the list of vendor endpoints that will receive electronic purchase orders. (Figure 5.15 illustrates both scenarios.)

Note that because it is TLS that defines the terms of message exchange with other parties, RailCo developed both of its services to meet TLS's requirements.

The Invoice Submission Service was built as a service requestor that issues messages compliant with the Accounts Payable WSDL. The Order Fulfillment Service was designed as a service provider according to published specifications by TLS. This guarantees TLS that its Purchase Order Service (acting as a service requestor) can continue to issue messages in its current format and that all recipient endpoints will be able to receive and understand them.

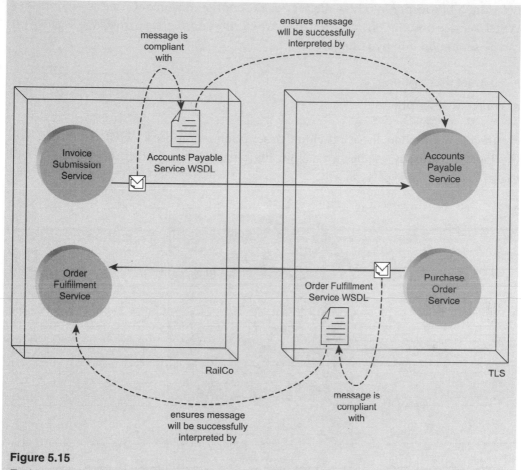

Figure 5.15

Each service requestor is using the WSDL of a service provider to ensure that messages sent will be understood and accepted.

5.3.1   Service endpoints and service descriptions

A WSDL describes the point of contact for a service provider, also known as the *service endpoint* or just *endpoint*. It provides a formal definition of the endpoint interface (so that requestors wishing to communicate with the service provider know exactly how to structure request messages) and also establishes the physical location (address) of the service.

Let's dig a bit deeper into how the service description document itself is organized. A WSDL service description (also known as *WSDL service definition* or just *WSDL definition*) can be separated into two categories:

- abstract description
- concrete description

Figure 5.16 shows how these individual descriptions comprise a WSDL definition. Note the logical hierarchy established within the parts of the abstract definition. We will explain each of these parts shortly.

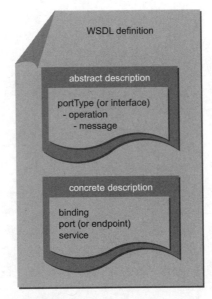

Figure 5.16
WSDL document consisting of abstract and concrete parts that collectively describe a service endpoint.

5.3.2   Abstract description

An *abstract description* establishes the interface characteristics of the Web service without any reference to the technology used to host or enable a Web service to transmit messages. By separating this information, the integrity of the service description can be preserved regardless of what changes might occur to the underlying technology platform.

Below is a description of the three main parts that comprise an abstract description.

portType, operation, and message

The parent *portType* section of an abstract description provides a high-level view of the service interface by sorting the messages a service can process into groups of functions known as *operations.*

Each operation represents a specific action performed by the service. A service operation is comparable to a public method used by components in traditional distributed applications. Much like component methods, operations also have input and output parameters. Because Web services rely exclusively on messaging-based communication, parameters are represented as messages. Therefore, an operation consists of a set of *input and output messages.*

Note that the transmission sequence of these messages can be governed by a predetermined message exchange pattern that also is associated with the operation. (Message exchange patterns are discussed in Chapter 6.)

NOTE
The term "portType" is being renamed to "interface" in version 2.0 of the WSDL specification.

5.3.3   Concrete description

For a Web service to be able to execute any of its logic, it needs for its abstract interface definition to be connected to some real, implemented technology. Because the execution of service application logic always involves communication, the abstract Web service interface needs to be connected to a physical transport protocol. This connection is defined in the *concrete description* portion of the WSDL file, which consists of three related parts:

binding, port, and service

A WSDL description's *binding* describes the requirements for a service to establish physical connections or for connections to be established with the service. In other words, a binding represents one possible transport technology the service can use to communicate. SOAP is the most common form of binding, but others also are supported. A binding can apply to an entire interface or just a specific operation.

Related to the binding is the *port,* which represents the physical address at which a service can be accessed with a specific protocol. This piece of physical implementation data exists separately to allow location information to be maintained independently from other aspects of the concrete description. Within the WSDL language, the term *service* is used to refer to a group of related endpoints.

NOTE

The term "port" is being renamed "endpoint" in version 2.0 of the WSDL specification. The WSDL endpoint should not be confused with the general term "endpoint" used to reference the point of contact for a Web service. Though related, the term "endpoint" is used in a much broader sense than the WSDL endpoint, which refers to a language element that only represents the physical address of the service.

CASE STUDY

The TLS Accounts Payable Service was created to receive invoices submitted by numerous vendors. Its associated service description therefore has a simple abstract description consisting of one interface definition that contains a single operation called SubmitInvoice.

Specified within the operation is one input and one output message. The input message is responsible for accepting the invoice document from a vendor service requestor (such as the RailCo Invoice Submission Service). The output message is used by the Accounts Payable Service to send a message of acknowledgement indicating that the submitted invoice document has been successfully received and that its contents are valid. The concrete part of this service description simply binds the operation to the SOAP protocol and provides a location address for the Accounts Payable Service.

5.3.4   Metadata and service contracts

So far we've established that the abstract and concrete descriptions provided by a WSDL definition express technical information as to how a service can be interfaced with and what type of data exchange it supports.

WSDL definitions frequently rely on XSD schemas to formalize the structure of incoming and outgoing messages. Another common supplemental service description document is a *policy*. Policies can provide rules, preferences, and processing details above and beyond what is expressed through the WSDL and XSD schema documents. (Policies are explained in Chapter 7.)

So now we have up to three separate documents that each describe an aspect of a service:

- WSDL definition
- XSD schema
- policy

Each of these three service description documents can be classified as service *metadata*, as each provides information about the service. Service description documents can be collectively viewed as establishing a *service contract*—a set of conditions that must be met and accepted by a potential service requestor to enable successful communication.

Note that a service contract can refer to additional documents or agreements not expressed by service descriptions. For example, a Service Level Agreement (SLA) agreed upon by the respective owners of a service provider and its requestor can be considered part of an overall service contract (Figure 5.17).

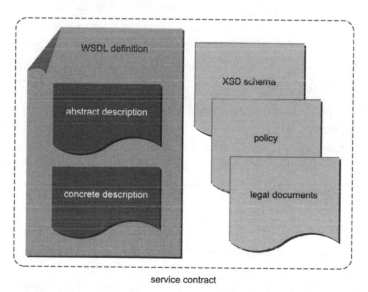

service contract

Figure 5.17

A service contract comprised of a collection of service descriptions and possibly additional documents.

5.3.5 Semantic descriptions

Most of the metadata currently provided by services focuses on expressing technical information related to data representation and processing requirements. However, these service description documents generally do not prove useful in explaining details about a service's behavioral characteristics. In fact, the most challenging part of providing a complete description of a Web service is in communicating its semantic qualities.

Examples of service semantics include:

- how a service behaves under certain conditions
- how a service will respond to a specific condition
- what specific tasks the service is most suited for

Most of the time service semantics are assessed by humans, either verbally by discussing the qualities of a service with its owner, or by reading supplementary documentation published alongside service descriptions. The ultimate goal is to provide sufficient semantic information in a structured manner so that, in some cases, service requestors can go as far as to evaluate and choose suitable service providers independently.

Semantic information is usually of greater importance when dealing with external service providers, where your knowledge of another party's service is limited to the information the service owner decides to publish. But even within organizational boundaries, semantic characteristics tend to take on greater relevance as the amount of internal Web services grows.

Although service policies can be designed to express preferences and assertions that communicate aspects of service behavior, efforts are currently underway (primarily by the W3C) to continually extend the semantic information provided by service description documents. For the time being, we must focus on the service description capabilities offered to us through WSDL definitions, XSD schemas, and policies.

5.3.6   Service description advertisement and discovery

As we've established, the sole requirement for one service to contact another is access to the other service's description. As the amount of services increases within and outside of organizations, mechanisms for advertising and discovering service descriptions may become necessary. For example, central directories and registries become an option to keep track of the many service descriptions that become available. These repositories allow humans (and even service requestors) to:

- locate the latest versions of known service descriptions
- discover new Web services that meet certain criteria

When the initial set of Web services standards emerged, this eventuality was taken into account. This is why UDDI formed part of the first generation of Web services standards. Though not yet commonly implemented, UDDI provides us with a registry model worth describing.

Private and public registries

UDDI specifies a relatively accepted standard for structuring registries that keep track of service descriptions (Figure 5.18). These registries can be searched manually and accessed programmatically via a standardized API.

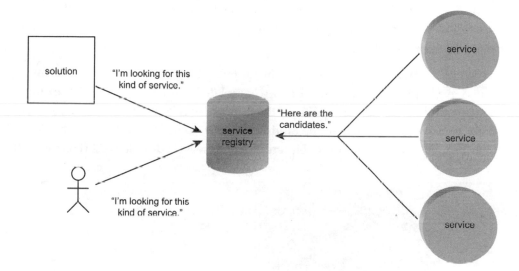

Figure 5.18
Service description locations centralized in a registry.

Public registries accept registrations from any organizations, regardless of whether they have Web services to offer. Once signed up, organizations acting as service provider entities can register their services.

Private registries can be implemented within organization boundaries to provide a central repository for descriptions of all services the organization develops, leases, or purchases.

Following are descriptions of the primary parts that comprise UDDI registry records.

Business entities and business services
Each public registry record consists of a *business entity* containing basic profile information about the organization (or service provider entity). Included in this record are one or more *business service* areas, each of which provides a description of the services offered by the business entity. Business services may or may not be related to the use of Web services.

Binding templates and tModels
You might recall that WSDL definitions stored implementation information separately from the actual interface design. This resulted in an interface definition that existed independently from the transport protocols to which it was eventually bound. Registry records follow the same logic in that they store binding information in a separate area, called the *binding template*.

Each business service can reference one or more binding templates. The information contained in a binding template may or may not relate to an actual service. For example, a binding template may simply point to the address of a Web site. However, if a Web service is being represented, then the binding template references a *tModel*. The tModel section of a UDDI record provides pointers to actual service descriptions (Figure 5.19).

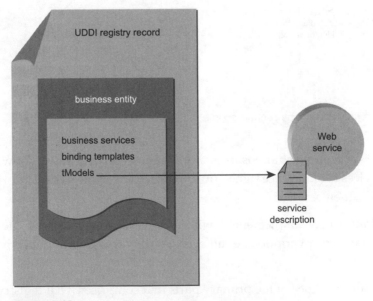

Figure 5.19
The basic structure of a UDDI business entity record.

CASE STUDY

At any given time there are several concurrent development and integration projects underway at TLS. Almost every project results in the creation of new services. Some are developed as part of service-oriented solutions, while others originate from legacy adapters and ancillary services appended to older distributed systems. The net result is a constantly growing pool of unmanaged services.

After a year-end review of past development initiatives, it was discovered that several project teams had inadvertently built Web services with very similar functionality. To avoid a recurrence of redundant effort, a private registry was created (Figure 5.20). Project teams responsible for any currently active service descriptions were required to register their services in the registry (and this registration process became part of the standard development lifecycle from there on).

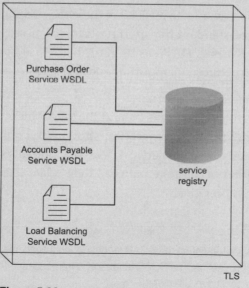

Figure 5.20

The TLS service registry containing pointers to current TLS WSDL definitions.

SUMMARY OF KEY POINTS

- The WSDL definition is divided into two parts: the abstract description that defines the service interface, and the concrete description that establishes the transport and location information.

- The two other primary service description documents are XSD schemas and policies.

- Service descriptions can be dynamically discovered by humans or applications, using private or public service registries.

5.4 Messaging (with SOAP)

Because all communication between services is message-based, the messaging framework chosen must be standardized so that all services, regardless of origin, use the same format and transport protocol. Additionally, within SOAs, so much emphasis is placed on a message-centric application design that an increasing amount of business and application logic is embedded into messages. In fact, the receipt of a message by a service is the most fundamental action within SOA and the sole action that initiates service-oriented automation. This further demands that the messaging framework be extremely flexible and highly extensible.

The SOAP specification was chosen to meet all of these requirements and has since been universally accepted as the standard transport protocol for messages processed by Web services. Since its initial release, SOAP has been further revised to accommodate more sophisticated message structures in support of enterprise distributed applications and enterprise SOAs.

Here we examine the high-level concepts behind the SOAP messaging framework. We begin with a look at how SOAP messages are structured, and then move on to an overview of SOAP's underlying node network. We conclude this section and this chapter with a brief explanation of message paths as they relate to SOAP messaging and other concepts we covered previously.

> **NOTE**
>
> The following is not a tutorial on the SOAP language; only concepts and terms are discussed in this section. The SOAP language is introduced in the *SOAP language basics* section in Chapter 13.

Now that we've completed the required application form, we need to figure out how to get this information to the agency. Because Bob only knew the name of the company, we need to look up its mailing address in the phone book. We add the mailing address to an envelope, place the application form inside, and throw it in a mailbox.

A phone book is commonly compared to a service registry, and a mailing address is the equivalent of a WSDL endpoint (or port). An envelope represents a standardized medium for transporting mail—much like SOAP represents a standardized format for transporting messages.

When we are ready to let our letter go, we place it in a mailbox, the same way service requestors hand over SOAP messages to SOAP nodes to perform the actual transmission.

Finally, the route traveled by the letter from us to the Reconnect agency is much like the message path a SOAP message follows from service requestor to service provider.

5.4.1   Messages

Even though it was originally named the Simple Object Access *Protocol*, the SOAP specification's main purpose is to define a standard message format. The structure of this format is quite simple, but its ability to be extended and customized has positioned SOAP messaging as the driving force behind many of the most significant features of contemporary SOAs. This section takes a closer look at the details of the SOAP message format.

NOTE

As of version 1.2 of the SOAP specification, the word "SOAP" is no longer an acronym that stands for "Simple Object Access Protocol." It is now considered a standalone term.

Envelope, header, and body

Every SOAP message is packaged into a container known as an *envelope*. Much like the metaphor this conjures up, the envelope is responsible for housing all parts of the message (Figure 5.21).

Each message can contain a *header*, an area dedicated to hosting meta information. In most service-oriented solutions, this header section is a vital part of the overall architecture, and though optional, it is rarely omitted. Its importance relates to the use of header blocks through which numerous extensions can be implemented (as described next).

The actual message contents are hosted by the message *body*, which typically consists of XML formatted data. The contents of a message body are often referred to as the message *payload*.

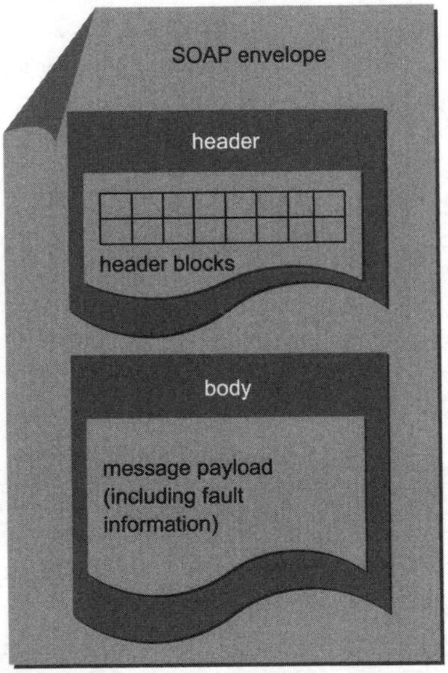

Figure 5.21
The basic structure of a SOAP message.

Header blocks
A primary characteristic of the SOAP communications framework used by SOAs is an emphasis on creating messages that are as intelligence-heavy and self-sufficient as possible. This results in SOAP messages achieving a level of independence that increases the robustness and extensibility of this messaging framework—qualities that are extremely important when relying on communication within the loosely coupled environment that Web services require.

Message independence is implemented through the use of *header blocks*, packets of supplementary meta information stored in the envelope's header area. Header blocks outfit a message with all of the information required for any services with which the message comes in contact to process and route the message in accordance with its accompanying rules, instructions, and properties. What this means is that through the use of header blocks, SOAP messages are capable of containing a large variety of supplemental information related to the delivery and processing of message contents.

This alleviates services from having to store and maintain message-specific logic. It further reinforces the characteristics of contemporary SOA related to fostering reuse, interoperability, and composability. Web services can be designed with generic processing functionality driven by various types of meta information the service locates in the header blocks of the messages it receives.

The use of header blocks has elevated the Web services framework to an extensible and composable enterprise-level computing platform. Practically all WS-* extensions are implemented using header blocks. (Chapter 17 provides various examples of what SOAP headers look like.)

Examples of the types of features a message can be outfitted with using header blocks include:

- processing instructions that may be executed by service intermediaries or the ultimate receiver
- routing or workflow information associated with the message
- security measures implemented in the message
- reliability rules related to the delivery of the message
- context and transaction management information
- correlation information (typically an identifier used to associate a request message with a response message)

These and many other features are available, and the selection is continually growing. Because header blocks can be based on the use of different supplementary extensions, SOAP allows the recognition and processing of header blocks to be marked as optional. This way messages can be safely outfitted with header blocks that implement non-critical features from newer extensions.

NOTE

Processing instructions provided in SOAP header blocks are different from the processing instructions natively supported by the XML language.

CASE STUDY

Invoices sent via SOAP messages to TLS are required to contain a number of standard header blocks for them to be accepted and processed by the TLS Accounts Payable Service.

Specifically, the required header blocks include:

- A correlation identifier that conforms to a standard format and is further extended with a value derived from the date and time of the message transmission. The correlation identifier therefore relates the original submission to the eventual response.

- Organization-level security credentials used for authentication purposes. Each vendor has a security account with the TLS B2B system, and the assigned credentials are required with every message transmission.

The Accounts Payable Service expects these pieces of meta information, and the gathered rules and instructions shape its subsequent processing of the message contents.

Message styles

The SOAP specification was originally designed to replace proprietary RPC protocols by allowing calls between distributed components to be serialized into XML documents, transported, and then deserialized into the native component format upon arrival. As a result, much in the original version of this specification centered around the structuring of messages to accommodate RPC data.

This *RPC-style* message runs contrary to the emphasis SOA places on independent, intelligence-heavy messages. SOA relies on *document-style* messages to enable larger payloads, coarser interface operations, and reduced message transmission volumes between services.

NOTE

Don't confuse document-style SOAP messages with *document-centric* XML documents. The latter term generally refers to published documents represented by XML and is used to distinguish these types of XML documents from those that contain application data (which are typically referred to as *data-centric* XML documents).

Traditionally, the submission of an invoice involved a number of interactions between RailCo and its customer, including:

- The generation and mailing of the invoice document.
- The generation and mailing of an account statement, showing all currently outstanding amounts owed by the customer.
- The generation and mailing of a quantity discount reminder, explaining RailCo's volume pricing policy, and showing how close the customer is to reaching a quantity discount based on parts ordered to date.

When forced to submit invoices electronically to TLS via the Invoice Submission Service, all three of these documents needed to be included in the same message. As a result, a single document-style message used by RailCo is capable of providing an invoice, an account statement, and volume discount pricing formulas (Figure 5.22).

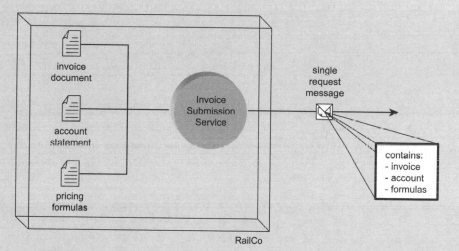

Figure 5.22
The RailCo Invoice Submission Service packaging the contents of three documents into one SOAP message.

Attachments

To facilitate requirements for the delivery of data not so easily formatted into an XML document, the use of *SOAP attachment* technologies exist. Each provides a different encoding mechanism used to bundle data in its native format with a SOAP message. SOAP attachments are commonly employed to transport binary files, such as images.

CASE STUDY

TLS accounting policy requires that all issued purchase orders in excess of $100,000 require the signature of a senior manager. Further, these purchase orders are not allowed to be issued in the standard electronic format, as the signature is required to be an ever-present part of the document. To accommodate this requirement, the Purchase Order Service was designed with an alternative operation.

The accounting system currently used by TLS offers the ability to scan any accounting-related documents. The scanned images are archived on a separate server and linked to the corresponding accounting records via the archive image path. When PO cost totals exceed the $100,000 limit, a custom-developed extension to the accounting system invokes the alternative Purchase Order Service operation and passes it a copy of the signed PO document image. The service, in turn, generates a SOAP message in which the PO document image exists as a SOAP attachment.

Faults

Finally, SOAP messages offer the ability to add exception handling logic by providing an optional *fault* section that can reside within the body area. The typical use for this section is to store a simple message used to deliver error condition information when an exception occurs.

CASE STUDY

The before mentioned SOAP message containing a SOAP attachment is also outfitted with a fault area housing exception information relating specifically to the attached data. Should the recipient of the SOAP message be unable to properly process the attachment or should the attachment encounter delivery problems, standard fault codes and descriptions are used to generate a response message that is returned to TLS.

5.4.2   Nodes

Although Web services exist as self-contained units of processing logic, they are reliant upon a physical communications infrastructure to process and manage the exchange of SOAP messages. Every major platform has its own implementation of a SOAP communications server, and as a result each vendor has labeled its own variation of this piece of software differently. In abstract, the programs that services use to transmit and receive SOAP messages are referred to as *SOAP nodes* (Figure 5.23).

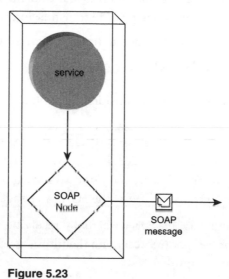

Figure 5.23
A SOAP node transmitting a SOAP
message received by the service logic.

Regardless of how they are implemented, SOAP nodes must conform to the processing standard set forth in the versions of the SOAP specification they support. This critical characteristic is what preserves the vendor-neutral communications framework upon which SOA is based. It is what guarantees that a SOAP message sent by the SOAP node from service A can be received and processed by a SOAP node (supporting the same version of the SOAP standard) from any other service.

Node types

As with the services that use them, the underlying *SOAP nodes* are given labels that identify their type, depending on what form of processing they are involved with in a given message processing scenario.

Below is a list of type labels associated with SOAP nodes (in accordance with the standard *SOAP Processing Model*). You'll notice that these names are very similar to the Web service roles we discussed at the beginning of this chapter. The SOAP specification has a different use for the term "role" and instead refers to these SOAP types or labels as *concepts*.

*   *SOAP sender*—a SOAP node that transmits a message
*   *SOAP receiver*—a SOAP node that receives a message
*   *SOAP intermediary*—a SOAP node that receives and transmits a message, and optionally processes the message prior to transmission
*   *initial SOAP sender*—the first SOAP node to transmit a message
*   *ultimate SOAP receiver*—the last SOAP node to receive a message

Figure 5.25 illustrates how SOAP nodes transition through these roles.

When the RailCo Invoice Submission Service sends a SOAP message containing an invoice, the underlying SOAP server software (representing the initial SOAP sender node) executes the transmission of the SOAP message via HTTP.

Prior to the TLS Accounts Payable Service actually receiving the invoice message, the TLS SOAP server or listener (representing the ultimate SOAP receiver node) receives the message first (Figure 5.24).

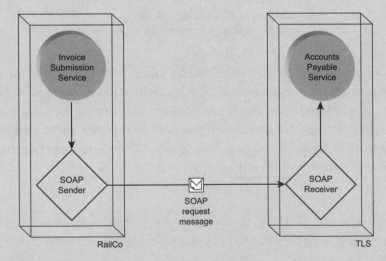

Figure 5.24
The positioning of SOAP nodes within a message transmission between RailCo and TLS.

SOAP intermediaries

The same way service intermediaries transition through service provider and service requestor roles, *SOAP intermediary* nodes move through SOAP receiver and SOAP sender types when processing a message (Figure 5.25).

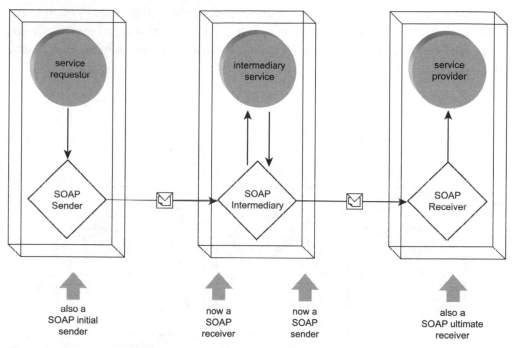

Figure 5.25

Different types of SOAP nodes involved with processing a message.

SOAP nodes acting as intermediaries can be classified as forwarding or active. When a SOAP node acts as a *forwarding intermediary*, it is responsible for relaying the contents of a message to a subsequent SOAP node. In doing so, the intermediary will often process and alter header block information relating to the forwarding logic it is executing. For example, it will remove a header block it has processed, as well as any header blocks that cannot be relayed any further.

Active intermediary nodes are distinguished by the type of processing they perform above and beyond forwarding-related functions. An active intermediary is not required to limit its processing logic to the rules and instructions provided in the header blocks of a message it receives. It can alter existing header blocks, insert new ones, and execute a variety of supporting actions.

5.4.3 Message paths

A *message path* refers to the route taken by a message from when it is first sent until it arrives at its ultimate destination. Therefore, a message path consists of at least one initial sender, one ultimate receiver, and zero or more intermediaries (Figure 5.26). Mapping and modeling message paths becomes an increasingly important exercise in SOAs, as the amount of intermediary services tends to grow along with the expansion of a service-oriented solution. Design considerations relating to the path a message is required to travel often center around performance, security, context management, and reliable messaging concerns.

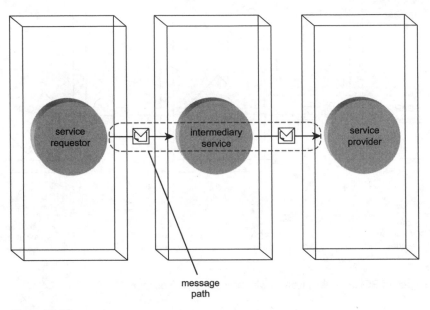

Figure 5.26
A message path consisting of three Web services.

Note also that a message path is sometimes not predetermined. The use of header blocks processed by intermediaries can dynamically determine the path of a message. This may be the result of routing logic, workflow logic, or environmental conditions (Figure 5.27).

When used within the context of SOAP nodes, this term is qualified and therefore referred to as a *SOAP message path*. While a message path in abstract can be purely logical, the SOAP node perspective is always focused on the actual physical transport route. A SOAP message path is comprised of a series of SOAP nodes, beginning with the initial SOAP sender and ending with the ultimate SOAP receiver. Every node refers to a physical installation of SOAP software, each with its own physical address.

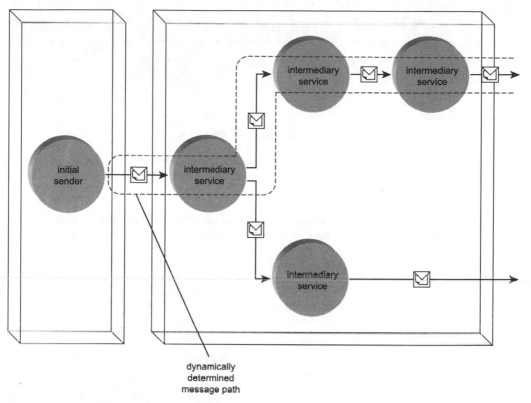

Figure 5.27
A message path determined at runtime.

CASE STUDY

Revisiting our invoice submission scenario one last time, we can establish both logical and physical views of the path along which the invoice SOAP message travels.

From a logical perspective, the message path is always the same. The RailCo Invoice Submission Service requestor acts as the initial sender and is therefore the starting point of the path. The first service provider the message encounters is the TLS Load Balancing intermediary. This service then becomes the next service requestor and forwards the message to the Accounts Payable Service provider. As the last service provider along the path, this Web service becomes the ultimate receiver. This establishes a logical message path consisting of three services.

The corresponding SOAP message path is not as predictable. Because the Load Balancing Service will only decide which physical server to route a message to when it actually receives and processes the message, the ultimate SOAP receiver is not determined until runtime.

SUMMARY OF KEY POINTS

- The SOAP messaging framework fulfills the need for SOA's reliance on "independent units of communication," by supporting the creation of intelligence-heavy, document-style, and highly extensible messages.

- SOAP messaging establishes a standard message structure that includes an extensible header section used by numerous WS-* extensions to implement enterprise-level features.

- The SOAP node view of the Web services framework abstracts the physical communications framework, which consists of a series of SOAP servers.

Part II

SOA and WS-* Extensions

One thing we learned in Part I of this book is that, though simple in concept, SOA in real life can quickly become a complex entity. Looking back at all of the characteristics we associated with contemporary SOA, we now need to roll up our sleeves and start figuring out exactly how we are going to go about realizing them.

A good place to start is by continuing our exploration of the Web services framework into the world of second-generation Web services specifications—or *WS-**. The most interesting and perhaps unnerving part of the contemporary SOA landscape is this ever-evolving family of Web services specifications. As we discussed in Chapter 4, there are different paths along which these documents can make their way into the IT mainstream. And, as with any form of evolution, some survive, and some don't.

Over the next two chapters we delve into detailed concepts introduced by a key collection of WS-* extensions. The majority of the specifications covered are relatively established. Some emerging specifications are also discussed to provide a glimpse of what's on the horizon.

The extensions or features offered by WS-* specifications have not only duplicated some of the traditional features associated with enterprise computing, they have also built upon and extended the fundamentals of service-orientation. As much as these extensions are enabling vendors to broaden the Web services-based feature-set of their proprietary platforms, they are also responsible for expanding the technology landscape that comprises SOA.

Sections covering concepts derived from WS-* specifications are ended with a study of how these extensions support a subset of the primitive and contemporary SOA characteristics we identified in Chapter 3.

Specifically, we look at the following:

- loose coupling
- composability
- interoperability
- reusability
- extensibility
- vendor diversity
- discoverability
- quality of service

How contemporary SOA characteristics are further supported by WS-* extensions and other SOA influences is explored in Chapter 9. Note also that considering our focus in this part of the book remains the conceptual side of SOA, we do not explain the language or syntax behind the specifications themselves. (Language details are covered in subsequent chapters.)

What is "WS-*"?

The term "WS-*" has become a commonly used abbreviation that refers to the second-generation Web services specifications. These are extensions to the basic Web services framework established by first-generation standards represented by WSDL, SOAP, and UDDI. The term "WS-*" became popular because the majority of titles given to second-generation Web services specifications have been prefixed with "WS-". (See www.soaspecs.com for examples of WS-* specifications.)

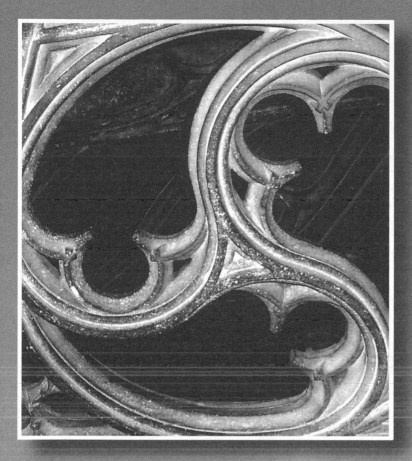

Chapter 6

Web Services and Contemporary SOA (Part I: Activity Management and Composition)

The messaging model used for inter-service communication is simple in nature. The challenge lies in implementing this model on an enterprise level while supporting SOA characteristics and preserving the principles of service-orientation.

To execute an automated business task with any substance, we need to be able to coordinate and compose a set of available services. To successfully perform this type of coordination requires that we have control over messaging that occurs between our composed services. Both conversational characteristics inherent in the Web services framework and specific features provided by key WS-* specifications provide a means to assert this control.

This chapter explains key concepts that define the messaging-based services activity model and also discusses the role and context of concepts derived from WS-* specifications that implement standardized activity management and composition mechanisms. Collectively, these concepts (and the specifications from which they are derived) contribute to a robust, coordinated, and transaction-capable service-oriented architecture that is characteristically composable and extensible. (Figure 6.1 illustrates the concepts discussed in this chapter and shows, on a high-level, how they can inter-relate.)

To demonstrate common concepts, this chapter uses terms provided by current specifications in various stages of industry acceptance. In particular:

- WS-Coordination (including WS-AtomicTransaction and WS-BusinessActivity coordination types)
- WS-BPEL (also known as BPEL4WS)
- WS-CDL (also known as WS-Choreography)

Because we are focused solely on concepts in this part of the book, we do not yet provide language examples. Sample mark-up code is provided in Chapter 16 for the WS-BPEL and WS-Coordination languages as part of an introductory tutorial.

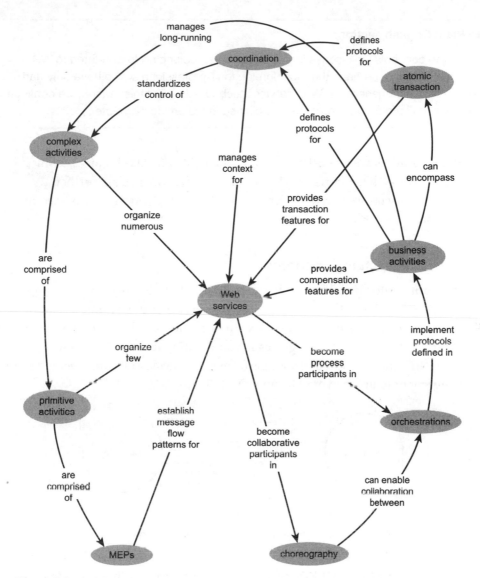

Figure 6.1
Specifications and concepts covered in this chapter.

NOTE
Choreography, as a concept, is explored at the end of this chapter, but the WS-CDL language is not covered in this book. Its source specification is not yet mature, and it is therefore more relevant to us on a conceptual level.

In Plain English sections

Of all the concepts we discuss in this guide, those belonging to or related to WS-*
specifications are perhaps the most foreign to IT professionals who have only had
exposure to first-generation Web services technologies. For this reason, we continue
with our *In Plain English* sections established in the previous chapter.

How case studies are used: The details of the RailCo-to-TLS Invoice Submission
and the TLS-to-RailCo Purchase Order Submission Processes are further
explained to identify specific aspects that pertain to the concepts discussed in
this chapter.

6.1   Message exchange patterns

Every task automated by a Web service can differ in both the nature of the application
logic being executed and the role played by the service in the overall execution of the
business task. Regardless of how complex a task is, almost all require the transmission
of multiple messages. The challenge lies in coordinating these messages in a particular
sequence so that the individual actions performed by the message are executed properly
and in alignment with the overall business task (Figure 6.2).

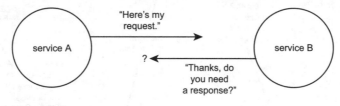
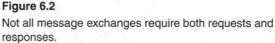

Figure 6.2
Not all message exchanges require both requests and
responses.

Message exchange patterns (MEPs) represent a set of templates that provide a group of
already mapped out sequences for the exchange of messages. The most common example is a request and response pattern. Here the MEP states that upon successful delivery
of a message from one service to another, the receiving service responds with a message
back to the initial requestor.

Many MEPs have been developed, each addressing a common message exchange
requirement. It is useful to have a basic understanding of some of the more important
MEPs, as you will no doubt be finding yourself applying MEPs to specific communication requirements when designing service-oriented solutions.

IN PLAIN ENGLISH

The Reconnect agency we discussed in the last chapter finally responds with good news. They have located and contacted Chuck. We subsequently arrange a meeting to catch up on old times.

During this reunion, I observe different types of conversations. For example, when Chuck asks Bob something, Bob typically responds back to Chuck with an answer. However, Chuck also says something to Bob after which Bob chooses not to say anything back. Then I notice Bob tell Chuck to only talk to him if Chuck has something to say that might actually interest Bob. (I begin to realize why Chuck lost touch with Bob in the first place.)

An MEP is like a type of conversation. It's not a long conversation; it actually only covers one exchange between two parties. Incidentally, each of these example scenarios represents actual message exchange patterns.

6.1.1 Primitive MEPs

Before the arrival of contemporary SOA, messaging frameworks were already well used by various messaging-oriented middleware products. As a result, a common set of *primitive MEPs* has been in existence for some time.

Request-response

This is the most popular MEP in use among distributed application environments and the one pattern that defines synchronous communication (although this pattern also can be applied asynchronously).

The *request-response* MEP (Figure 6.3) establishes a simple exchange in which a message is first transmitted from a source (service requestor) to a destination (service provider). Upon receiving the message, the destination (service provider) then responds with a message back to the source (service requestor).

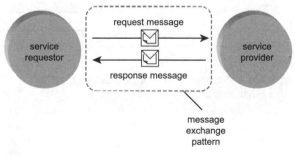

Figure 6.3
The request-response MEP.

Note that within this MEP, services typically require a means of associating the response message with the corresponding request message. This can be achieved through correlation, a concept explained in Chapter 7.

CASE STUDY

In the *Service compositions* section of Chapter 5, we provided an example where the TLS Accounts Payable Service, upon receiving an invoice submission from a vendor, enlists the TLS Vendor Profile Service to validate the invoice header information.

The MEP used in this situation is the standard request-response pattern, where a response from the Vendor Profile Service is expected once it receives and processes the original request. The Accounts Payable Service requires a response to ensure that the header details provided in the invoice submission are valid and current (Figure 6.4). Failure to validate this information terminates the Invoice Submission Process and results in the Accounts Payable Service responding to the vendor with a rejection message.

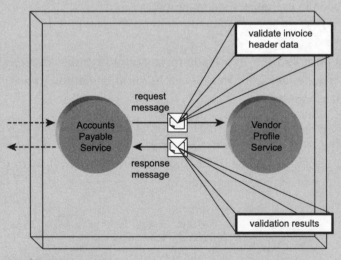

Figure 6.4

A sample request-response exchange between the TLS Accounts Payable and Vendor Profile Services.

Fire-and-forget

This simple asynchronous pattern is based on the unidirectional transmission of messages from a source to one or more destinations (Figure 6.5).

A number of variations of the *fire-and-forget* MEP exist, including:

- The *single-destination* pattern, where a source sends a message to one destination only.

- The *multi-cast* pattern, where a source sends messages to a predefined set of destinations.

- The *broadcast* pattern, which is similar to the multi-cast pattern, except that the message is sent out to a broader range of recipient destinations.

The fundamental characteristic of the fire-and-forget pattern is that a response to a transmitted message is not expected.

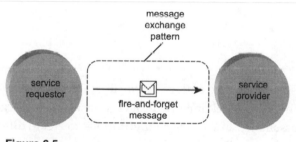

Figure 6.5
The fire-and-forget MEP.

CASE STUDY

The TLS Accounts Payable Service contains a rule that when an invoice header fails validation, an e-mail notification is generated. To execute this step, the Accounts Payable Service sends a message to the Notification Service. This utility service records the message details in a notification log database. (These records are used as the basis for e-mail notifications, as explained in the next example.) Because the message sent from the Accounts Payable Service to the Notification Service requires no response, it uses a single-destination fire-and-forget MEP (Figure 6.6).

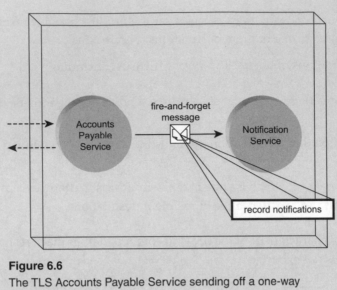

Figure 6.6
The TLS Accounts Payable Service sending off a one-way
notification message.

Complex MEPs

Even though a message exchange pattern can facilitate the execution of a simple task, it
is really more of a building block intended for composition into larger patterns. Primitive MEPs can be assembled in various configurations to create different types of messaging models, sometimes called *complex MEPs*.

A classic example is the *publish-and-subscribe* model. Although we explain publish-and-subscribe approaches in more detail in Chapter 7, let's briefly discuss it here as an example of a complex MEP.

The publish-and-subscribe pattern introduces new roles for the services involved with
the message exchange. They now become *publishers* and *subscribers*, and each may be
involved in the transmission and receipt of messages. This asynchronous MEP accommodates a requirement for a publisher to make its messages available to a number of
subscribers interested in receiving them.

The steps involved are generally similar to the following:

Step 1.   The subscriber sends a message to notify the publisher that it wants to receive
messages on a particular topic.

Step 2.   Upon the availability of the requested information, the publisher broadcasts messages on the particular topic to all of that topic's subscribers.

This pattern is a great example of how to aggregate primitive MEPs, as shown in Figure 6.7 and explained here:

- Step 1 in the publish-and-subscribe MEP could be implemented by a request-response MEP, where the subscriber's request message, indicating that it wants to subscribe to a topic, is responded to by a message from the publisher, confirming that the subscription succeeded or failed.

- Step 2 then could be supported by one of the fire-and-forget patterns, allowing the publisher to broadcast a series of unidirectional messages to subscribers.

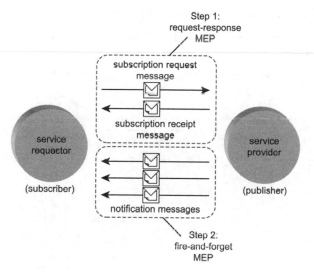

Figure 6.7
The publish-and-subscribe messaging model is a composite of two primitive MEPs.

WS-* specifications that incorporate this messaging model include:

- WS-BaseNotification
- WS-BrokeredNotification
- WS-Topics
- WS-Eventing

Concepts relating to these specifications are discussed in the next chapter as part of the *Notification and eventing* section.

The utility Notification Service periodically generates and distributes notification messages for a number of different topics. Messages from outside vendors that fail validation, for example, are first logged in a dedicated notification repository. At the end of every working day, the Notification Service queries this repository to retrieve all failed submissions.

It then summarizes specific pieces of information from the query results and uses this data to populate a broadcast notification message. This message is subsequently sent to a list of subscribers consisting primarily of specialized accounting services (Figure 6.8). These services record the notification data into various profile and account records. Some pass the notification on as an e-mail to select accounting personnel.

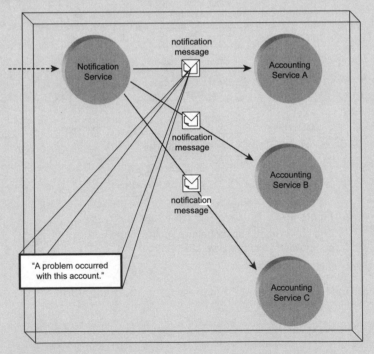

Figure 6.8
The TLS Notification Service notifying subscribers about a problem condition via a notification broadcast.

Several other applications that integrate with the TLS accounting system provide the means for subscribers (humans and services) to add or remove themselves from topic notification distribution lists.

6.1.2 MEPs and SOAP

On its own, the SOAP standard provides a messaging framework designed to support single-direction message transfer. The extensible nature of SOAP allows countless messaging characteristics and behaviors (MEP-related and otherwise) to be implemented via SOAP header blocks. The SOAP language also provides an optional parameter that can be set to identify the MEP associated with a message. (Note that SOAP MEPs also take SOAP message compliance into account.)

6.1.3 MEPs and WSDL

Operations defined within service descriptions are comprised, in part, of message definitions. The exchange of these messages constitutes the execution of a task represented by an operation. MEPs play a larger role in WSDL service descriptions as they can coordinate the input and output messages associated with an operation. The association of MEPs to WSDL operations thereby embeds expected conversational behavior into the interface definition.

WSDL operations support different configurations of incoming, outgoing, and fault messages. These configurations are equivalent to message exchange patterns, but within the WSDL specification, they often are referred to simply as *patterns*. It is important to note that WSDL definitions do not restrict an interface to these patterns; they are considered minimal conversational characteristics that can be extended.

Release 1.1 of the WSDL specification provides support for four message exchange patterns that roughly correspond to the MEPs we described in the previous section. These patterns are applied to service operations from the perspective of a service provider or endpoint. In WSDL 1.1 terms, they are represented as follows:

- *Request-response operation*—Upon receiving a message, the service must respond with a standard message or a fault message.
- *Solicit-response operation*—Upon submitting a message to a service requestor, the service expects a standard response message or a fault message.

- *One-way operation*—The service expects a single message and is not obligated to respond.

- *Notification operation*—The service sends a message and expects no response.

Of these four patterns (also illustrated in Figure 6.9), only the request-response operation and one-way operation MEPs are recommended by the WS-I Basic Profile.

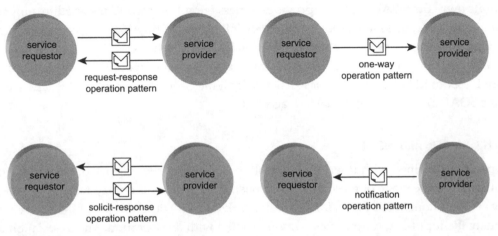

Figure 6.9
The four basic patterns supported by WSDL 1.1.

Not only does WSDL support most traditional MEPs, recent revisions of the specification have extended this support to include additional variations. Specifically, release 2.0 of the WSDL specification extends MEP support to eight patterns (and also changes the terminology) as follows.

- The *in-out pattern*, comparable to the request-response MEP (and equivalent to the WSDL 1.1 request-response operation).

- The *out-in pattern*, which is the reverse of the previous pattern—where the service provider initiates the exchange by transmitting the request. (Equivalent to the WSDL 1.1 solicit-response operation.)

- The *in-only pattern*, which essentially supports the standard fire-and-forget MEP. (Equivalent to the WSDL 1.1 one-way operation.)

- The *out-only pattern*, which is the reverse of the in-only pattern. It is used primarily in support of event notification. (Equivalent to the WSDL 1.1 notification operation.)

- The *robust in-only pattern*, a variation of the in-only pattern that provides the option of launching a fault response message as a result of a transmission or processing error.

- The *robust out-only pattern*, which, like the out-only pattern, has an outbound message initiating the transmission. The difference here is that a fault message can be issued in response to the receipt of this message.

- The *in-optional-out pattern*, which is similar to the in-out pattern—with one exception. This variation introduces a rule stating that the delivery of a response message is optional and should therefore not be expected by the service requestor that originated the communication. This pattern also supports the generation of a fault message.

- The *out-optional-in pattern* is the reverse of the in-optional-out pattern, where the incoming message is optional. Fault message generation is again supported.

Until version 2.0 of WSDL becomes commonplace, these new patterns will be of limited importance to SOA. Still, it is useful to know in what direction this core standard is heading.

> **NOTE**
>
> Version 2.0 of the WSDL specification was originally labeled 1.2. However, the working group responsible for the new specification decided that the revised feature set constituted a full new version number. Therefore, 1.2 was changed to 2.0. However, you still may find references to version 1.2 in some places. WSDL 2.0 is not yet widely used, and details regarding this version of the specification are provided here as they demonstrate the broadening applicability of MEPs.

6.1.4 MEPs and SOA

MEPs are highly generic and abstract in nature. Individually, they simply relate to an interaction between two services. Their relevance to SOA is equal to their relevance to the abstract Web services framework. They are therefore a fundamental and essential part of any Web services-based environment, including SOA.

6.2 Service activity

The completion of business tasks is an obvious function of any automated solution. Tasks are comprised of processing logic that executes to fulfill a number of business requirements. In service-oriented solutions, each task can involve any number of services. The interaction of a group of services working together to complete a task can be referred to as a *service activity* (Figure 6.10).

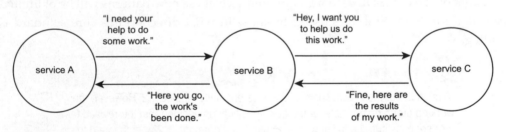

Figure 6.10
In an activity, multiple Web services collaborate to do a specific piece of work.

NOTE

Though there is no formal definition of the term "activity," it is used by several of the specifications we discuss in this book. It is a generic term that is most frequently associated with a logical unit of work completed by a collection of services.

IN PLAIN ENGLISH

Any type of task will consist of one or more steps. The task of turning on the TV is relatively simple, consisting of perhaps the following two steps:

1. Pick up the remote control.
2. Press the "Power" button.

The task of washing a car, on the other hand, can be a bit more complicated. It could exist of a series of steps, including:

1. Locate bucket.
2. Locate sponge.
3. Locate hose.
4. Fill bucket with warm water.
5. Add soap to water.
6. Soak sponge in water.
7. Rub sponge on car.

...and so on.

The steps that comprise this more complex task could be summarized into a series of simple (or primitive) tasks, as follows:

1. Gather required equipment.
2. Prepare water.
3. Wash car.

Each simple task consists of a smaller number of steps. Collectively these simple tasks represent a larger, logical unit of work. Individually, simple tasks do not accomplish anything of relevance, primarily because each subsequent task is dependent on the completion of the former. It is only when they are assembled into a complex task that they represent a useful unit of work.

Similarly, most business tasks automated by service-oriented applications consist of a complex activity that requires the involvement of multiple services that each complete a subset of the work.

6.2.1   Primitive and complex service activities

The scope of an activity can drastically vary. A simple or *primitive activity* is typified by synchronous communication and therefore often consists of two services exchanging information using a standard request-response MEP (Figure 6.11). Primitive activities are almost always short-lived; the execution of a single MEP generally constitutes the lifespan of a primitive activity.

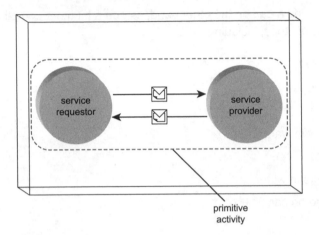

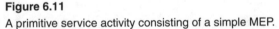

Figure 6.11
A primitive service activity consisting of a simple MEP.

Complex activities, on the other hand, can involve many services (and MEPs) that collaborate to complete multiple processing steps over a long period of time (Figure 6.12). These more elaborate types of activities are generally structured around extension-driven and composition-oriented concepts, such as choreography and orchestration. However, a business task automated by a series of custom-developed services and without the use of a composition extension can just as easily be classified a complex activity.

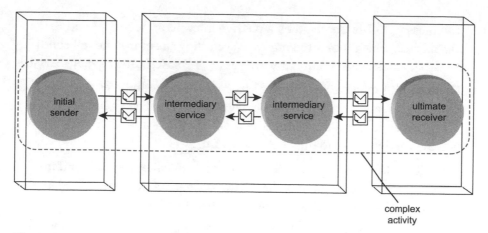

Figure 6.12
A complex activity involving four services.

6.2.2   Service activities and SOA

In SOAs, activities represent any service interaction required to complete business tasks. The scope of a service activity is primarily concerned with the processing and communication between services only. The underlying application logic of each Web service, whether it consists of a single component or an entire legacy system, is generally not mapped as part of a service activity. Complex activities are commonplace in larger service-oriented solutions and can involve numerous participating services.

> **NOTE**
>
> The term "Web services activity" also happens to represent the ongoing Web services-related work being performed by numerous W3C working groups.

CASE STUDY

The message path traveled by a RailCo invoice submission is a great example of a complex activity.

Here is a recap of the Invoice Submission Process we introduced in Chapter 5:

1. The initial sender, RailCo's Invoice Submission Service, transmits the invoice message.

2. The message is first received by a passive intermediary, TLS's Load Balancing Service, which routes the message according to environmental conditions. The message subsequently arrives at TLS's Accounts Payable Service.

3. The Accounts Payable Service acts as a controller and initiates a service composition to begin processing the message contents. It begins by interacting with the Vendor Profile Service to validate invoice header data and attaches the invoice document to the vendor account.

4. The Accounts Payable Service then extracts taxes, shipping fees, and the invoice total. It passes these values to the Ledger Service, which updates various ledger accounts, including the General Ledger.

5. Finally the activity ends, as the Accounts Payable Service completes its processing cycle by sending a response message back to RailCo.

Collectively, these processing steps constitute a complex activity involving five services (Figure 6.13).

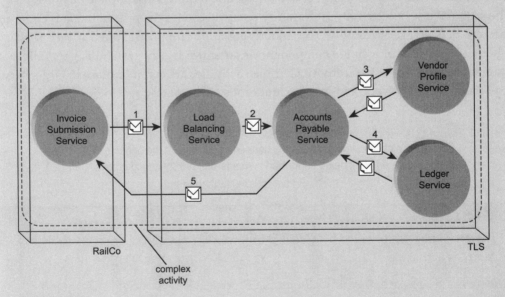

Figure 6.13

A sample complex activity spanning RailCo and TLS boundaries.

6.3 Coordination

Every activity introduces a level of context into an application runtime environment. Something that is happening or executing has meaning during its lifetime, and the description of its meaning (and other characteristics that relate to its existence) can be classified as context information.

The more complex an activity, the more context information it tends to bring with it. The complexity of an activity can relate to a number of factors, including:

- the amount of services that participate in the activity
- the duration of the activity
- the frequency with which the nature of the activity changes
- whether or not multiple instances of the activity can concurrently exist

A framework is required to provide a means for context information in complex activities to be managed, preserved and/or updated, and distributed to activity participants. *Coordination* establishes such a framework (Figure 6.14).

NOTE

This section derives concepts from the WS-Coordination specification. Some examples of WS-Coordination SOAP headers are provided in the *WS-Coordination overview* section of Chapter 16.

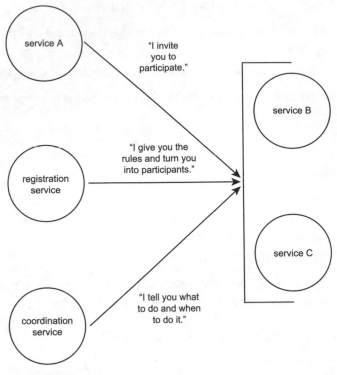

Figure 6.14
Coordination provides services that introduce controlled structure
into activities.

IN PLAIN ENGLISH

I decide to get Chuck, Bob, and Jim to wash my car. When we're all ready to go, I
assign each of them a simple task, as follows:

> Chuck—Gather equipment.
>
> Bob—Prepare the water.
>
> Jim—Wash the car.

You might recall each of these simple tasks consists of a series of steps. Chuck's
task, for instance, is comprised of the following steps:

1. Locate bucket.
2. Locate sponge.
3. Locate hose.

Completion of the first step is required before Bob can begin his task of preparing the water. Completion of Chuck's and Bob's tasks is required for Jim to start washing the car. However, allowing Bob to start on his task after Chuck completes only the first step of his task will allow both Chuck and Bob to complete their respective tasks at around the same time. The benefit here is that Jim can start his task sooner than if Bob had to wait for Chuck to fully complete all steps in his task.

To coordinate the complex activity of car washing in an efficient manner, Chuck needs to communicate to Bob when he has located the bucket. Because Bob may not be immediately available and because Chuck doesn't want to go looking for Bob to hand over the bucket, Chuck tells me that the bucket is ready. Chuck then continues with his other work, and when I see Bob next, I can relay the status of the bucket availability to him.

In this scenario, the bucket availability status is considered context information that I managed. Because a separate context manager (me) was in place, Chuck was alleviated of the responsibility of remembering and communicating the context information to Bob. This freed Chuck to continue with his other work. It also spared Bob from having to directly locate and communicate with Chuck to get the context information. Finally, my knowledge of who was doing what in this car washing process also would be classified as context information.

6.3.1 Coordinator composition

WS-Coordination establishes a framework that introduces a generic service based on the *coordinator service model* (Figure 6.15). This service controls a composition of three other services that each play a specific part in the management of context data.

The coordinator composition consists of the following services:

- *Activation service*—Responsible for the creation of a new context and for associating this context to a particular activity.

- *Registration service*—Allows participating services to use context information received from the activation service to register for a supported context protocol.

- *Protocol-specific services*—These services represent the protocols supported by the coordinator's coordination type. (This is further explained in the next sections.)

- *Coordinator*—The controller service of this composition, also known as the *coordination service*.

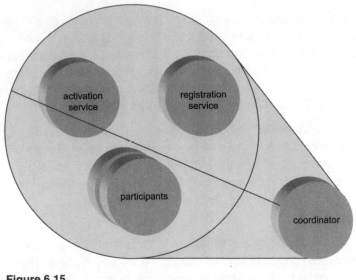

Figure 6.15
The coordinator service composition.

6.3.2 Coordination types and coordination protocols

Each coordinator is based on a *coordination type*, which specifies the nature and under-lying logic of an activity for which context information is being managed. Coordination types are specified in separate specifications. The WS-Coordination framework is exten-sible and can be utilized by different coordination types, including custom variations. However, the two coordination types most commonly associated with WS-Coordination are WS-AtomicTransaction and WS-BusinessActivity. (Concepts relating to these speci-fications are explained in the upcoming *Atomic transactions* and *Business activities* sections.)

Coordination type extensions provide a set of *coordination protocols*, which represent unique variations of coordination types and consist of a collection of specific behaviors and rules. A protocol is best viewed as a set of rules that are imposed on activities and which all registered participants must follow.

6.3.3 Coordination contexts and coordination participants

A context created by the activation service is referred to as a *coordination context*. It contains a collection of information that represents the activity and various supplemen-tary data.

Examples of the type of data held within a coordination context include:

- a unique identifier that represents the activity
- an expiration value
- coordination type information

A service that wants to take part in an activity managed by WS-Coordination must request the coordination context from the activation service. It then can use this context information to register for one or more coordination protocols. A service that has received a context and has completed registration is considered a *participant* in the coordinated activity.

6.3.5 The activation and registration process

The coordination service composition is instantiated when an application service contacts the activation service (Figure 6.16). Via a *CreateCoordinationContext* request message, it asks the activation service to generate a set of new context data. Once passed back with the *ReturnContext* message, the application service now can invite other services to participate in the coordination. This invitation consists of the context information the application service originally received from the activation service.

Any Web service in possession of this context information may issue a registration request to the registration service. This allows the service to enlist in a coordination based on a specific protocol. (Protocols are provided by separate specifications and are discussed later in this chapter as part of the *Atomic transaction* and *Business activities* sections.) Upon a successful registration, a service is officially a participant. The registration service passes the service the location of the coordinator service, with which all participants are required to interact. At this time, the coordination service is also sent the address of the new participant.

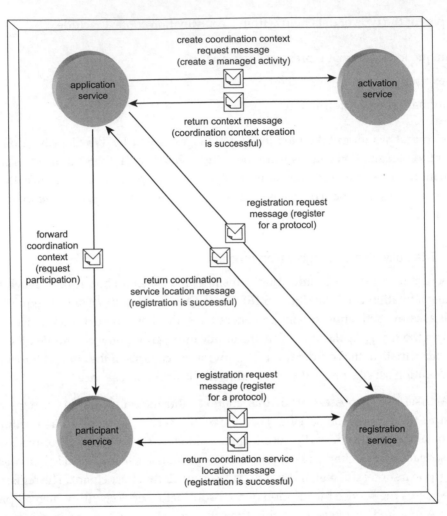

Figure 6.16
The WS-Coordination registration process.

6.3.5 The completion process

The application service can request that a coordination be completed by issuing a *completion request* message to the coordination service. The coordinator, in turn, then issues its own completion request messages to all coordination participants. Each participant service responds with a *completion acknowledgement* message (Figure 6.17).

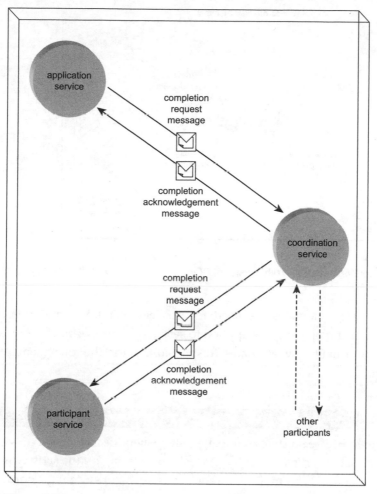

Figure 6.17
The WS-Coordination completion process.

6.3.6   Coordination and SOA

A coordinator-based context management framework, as provided by WS-Coordination and its supporting coordination types, introduces a layer of composition control to SOAs (Figure 6.18). It standardizes the management and interchange of context information within a variety of key business protocols.

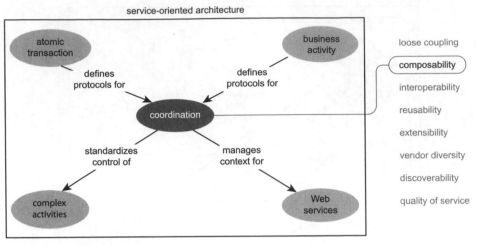

Figure 6.18
Coordination as it relates to other parts of SOA.

Coordination also alleviates the need for services to retain state. Statelessness is a key service-orientation principle applied to services for use within SOAs. Coordination reinforces this quality by assuming responsibility for the management of context information.

CASE STUDY

In the previous case study example, we established the individual process steps that comprised a complex activity. Once the processing of this activity enters the TLS environment, TLS employs a context management system to coordinate the flow of the message through its internal services.

As shown in Figure 6.19, coordination is applied to the following steps:

3. The Accounts Payable Service uses the Vendor Profile Service to validate the invoice header data. If the data is valid, the invoice document is attached to the vendor account.

4. The Accounts Payable Service extracts taxes and shipping fees from the invoice document. These values, along with the invoice total, are submitted to the Ledger Service. The Ledger Service is responsible for updating the General Ledger and numerous sub-ledgers, such as the Accounts Payable Ledger.

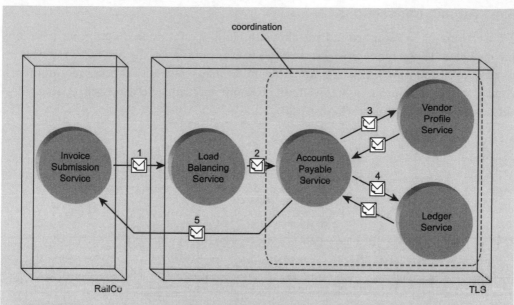

Figure 6.19

The TLS Accounts Payable, Vendor Profile, and Ledger Services being managed by a coordination.

The atomic transaction coordination type is used to coordinate these processing steps, as explained in the next two case studies.

SUMMARY OF KEY POINTS

- Complex activities tend to introduce the requirement for context data and the subsequent need for this data to be managed and coordinated at runtime.

- WS-Coordination provides a context management framework using a standardized service composition spearheaded by a coordinator service.

- Specialized implementations of this framework are realized through the use of coordination types, such as WS-AtomicTransaction and WS-BusinessActivity.

- By introducing an activity management layer to SOA, coordination promotes service statelessness and supports the controlled composition of complex activities.

6.4 Atomic transactions

Transactions have been around for almost as long as automated computer solutions have existed. When managing certain types of corporate data, the need to wrap a series of changes into a single action is fundamental to many business process requirements. *Atomic transactions* implement the familiar commit and rollback features to enable cross-service transaction support (Figure 6.20).

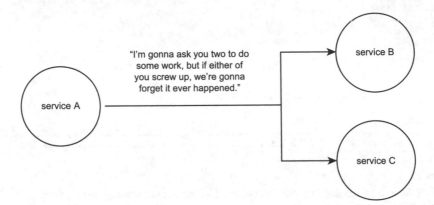

Figure 6.20
Atomic transactions apply an all-or-nothing requirement to work performed as part of an activity.

IN PLAIN ENGLISH

While we were washing my car, a neighbor stops by and offers us some money to wash his car. Having nothing else planned for the afternoon, we oblige and apply the same car washing process to the neighbor's car.

In the following weeks, word of our car washing abilities gets around, and others from the neighborhood start requesting our services. We soon find ourselves washing four or five cars every weekend.

We then come across a car with a special metallic finish. Not knowing any better, we proceed to apply our standard car washing process. When the car dries, though, we notice spots of discoloration throughout its exterior. A subsequent investigation leads us to find out that the soap we've been using is not suitable for some finishes (including metallic paint).

This turns into an expensive lesson, as we subsequently fund a new paint job. To prevent this from happening again, we decide to take measures. We proceed to purchase some specialized soaps for use in our water. The choice of soap is dependent on the finish of the car we are washing.

Sometimes the use of these new soaps requires us to carefully mix two or more cleaning solutions together. We determine a correct mixture by assessing the resulting color of the water. However, because we tend to eyeball this process, it can sometimes go wrong. We agree that if the correct color is not attained, we empty the contents of the bucket and start again.

This change to our process affects the following two steps:

4. Fill bucket with warm water.

5. Add soap to water.

Originally, these steps were simply performed in sequence as a continuation of the overall process. Now we have a requirement that dictates that should the resulting soap mixture be unacceptable, the bucket needs to be reset to its original state (empty). This requirement emulates an atomic transaction, where at the completion of Step 5, the process is either rolled back to the beginning of Step 4, or the quality of water is accepted (committed) so that it can be applied to washing the car.

6.4.1   ACID transactions

The protocols provided by the WS-AtomicTransaction specification enable cross-service transaction functionality comparable to the ACID-compliant transaction features found in most distributed application platforms.

For those of you who haven't yet worked with ACID transactions, let's quickly recap this important standard. The term "ACID" is an acronym representing the following four required characteristics of a traditional transaction:

- *Atomic*—Either all of the changes within the scope of the transaction succeed, or none of them succeed. This characteristic introduces the need for the rollback feature that is responsible for restoring any changes completed as part of a failed transaction to their original state.

- *Consistent*—None of the data changes made as a result of the transaction can violate the validity of any associated data models. Any violations result in a rollback of the transaction.

- *Isolated*—If multiple transactions occur concurrently, they may not interfere with each other. Each transaction must be guaranteed an isolated execution environment.

- *Durable*—Upon the completion of a successful transaction, changes made as a result of the transaction can survive subsequent failures.

6.4.2 Atomic transaction protocols

WS-AtomicTransaction is a coordination type, meaning that it is an extension created for use with the WS-Coordination context management framework we covered in the previous section. To participate in an atomic transaction, a service first receives a coordination context from the activation service. It can subsequently register for available atomic transaction protocols.

The following primary transaction protocols are provided:

- A *Completion* protocol, which is typically used to initiate the commit or abort states of the transaction.

- The *Durable 2PC* protocol for which services representing permanent data repositories should register.

- The *Volatile 2PC* protocol to be used by services managing non-persistent (temporary) data.

Most often these protocols are used to enable a two-phase commit (2PC) that manages an atomic transaction across multiple service participants.

6.4.3 The atomic transaction coordinator

When WS-AtomicTransaction protocols are used, the coordinator controller service can be referred to as an *atomic transaction coordinator*. This particular implementation of the WS-Coordination coordinator service represents a specific service model. The atomic transaction coordinator (Figure 6.21) plays a key role in managing the participants of the transaction process and in deciding the transaction's ultimate outcome.

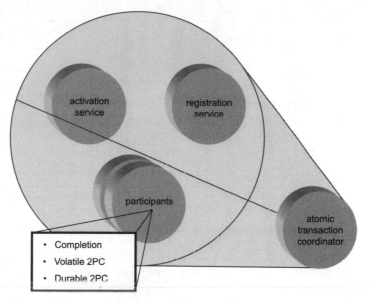

Figure 6.21

The atomic transaction coordinator service model.

6.4.4 The atomic transaction process

As previously mentioned, the atomic transaction coordinator is tasked with the responsibility of deciding the outcome of a transaction. It bases this decision on feedback it receives from all of the transaction participants.

The collection of this feedback is separated into two phases. During the *prepare* phase (Figure 6.22), all participants are notified by the coordinator, and each is asked to prepare and then issue a vote. Each participant's vote consists of either a "commit" or "abort" request (Figure 6.23).

After the votes are collected, the atomic transaction coordinator enters the *commit* phase. It now reviews all votes and decides whether to commit or rollback the transaction. The conditions of a commit decision are simple: if all votes are received and if all participants voted to commit, the coordinator declares the transaction successful, and the changes are committed. However, if any one vote requests an abort, or if any of the participants fail to respond, then the transaction is aborted, and all changes are rolled back (Figure 6.24).

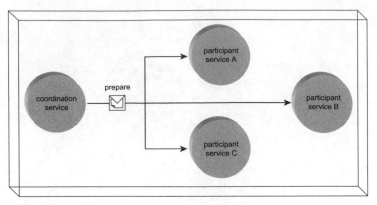

Figure 6.22
The coordinator requesting that transaction participants prepare to vote.

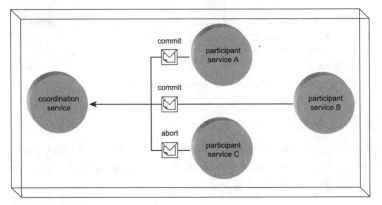

Figure 6.23
The transaction participants voting on the outcome of the atomic transaction.

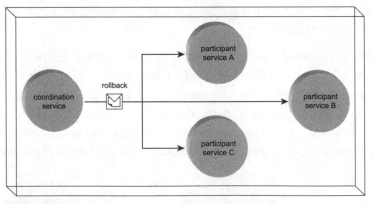

Figure 6.24
The coordinator aborting the transaction and notifying participants to rollback all changes.

6.4.5 Atomic transactions and SOA

Much of the transactional functionality implemented in service-oriented solutions is done so among the components that execute an activity on behalf of a single service. However, as more services emerge within an organization and as service compositions become more commonplace, the need to move transaction boundaries into cross-service interaction scenarios increases. Being able to guarantee an outcome of an activity is a key part of enterprise-level computing, and atomic transactions therefore play an important role in ensuring quality of service.

Not only do atomic transactional capabilities lead to a robust execution environment for SOA activities, they promote interoperability when extended into integrated environments. This allows the scope of an activity to span different solutions built with different vendor platforms, while still being assured a guaranteed all-or-nothing outcome. Assuming, of course, that WS-AtomicTransaction is supported by the affected applications, this option broadens the application of the two-phase commit protocol beyond traditional application boundaries (thus, supporting service interoperability). Figure 6.25 illustrates how atomic transactions support these aspects of SOA.

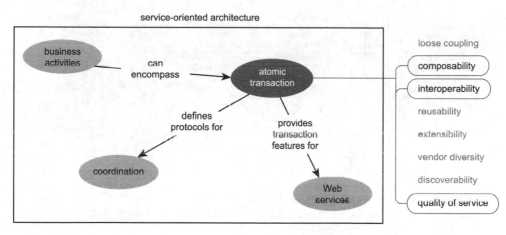

Figure 6.25
Atomic transaction relating to other parts of SOA.

Continuing with our previous case study example, a look under the hood reveals that TLS actually wraps Steps 3 and 4 into an atomic transaction. This guarantees that should any one update fail by any of the services involved in this composition, all previous updates performed (as of Step 3) will be rolled back (Figure 6.26).

To accomplish this, TLS relies on WS-Coordination, as implemented by the WS-AtomicTransaction coordination type. It utilizes the context coordinator along with the Complete transaction protocol to incorporate ACID-type transaction features into this complex activity.

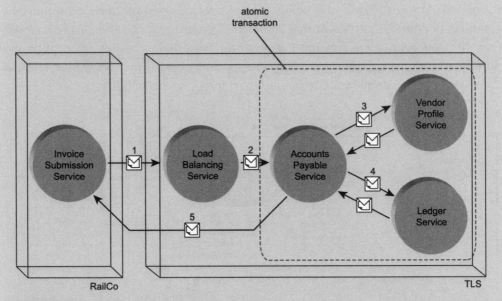

Figure 6.26

All changes made by the TLS Accounts Payable, Vendor Profile, and Ledger Services are under the control of an atomic transaction.

SUMMARY OF KEY POINTS

- WS-AtomicTransaction is a coordination type that supplies three coordination protocols that can be used to achieve two-phase commit transactions across multiple service participants.

- The atomic transaction coordinator makes the ultimate decision to commit or rollback a transaction. This decision is based on votes collected from participants.

- Contemporary SOAs can incorporate cross-service, ACID-type transaction features by using WS-AtomicTransaction.

6.5   Business activities

Business activities govern long-running, complex service activities. Hours, days, or even weeks can pass before a business activity is able to complete. During this period, the activity can perform numerous tasks that involve many participants.

What distinguishes a business activity from a regular complex activity is that its participants are required to follow specific rules defined by protocols. Business activities primarily differ from the also protocol-based atomic transactions in how they deal with exceptions and in the nature of the constraints introduced by the protocol rules.

For instance, business activity protocols do not offer rollback capabilities. Given the potential for business activities to be long-running, it would not be realistic to expect ACID-type transaction functionality. Instead, business activities provide an optional *compensation* process that, much like a "plan B," can be invoked when exception conditions are encountered (Figure 6.27).

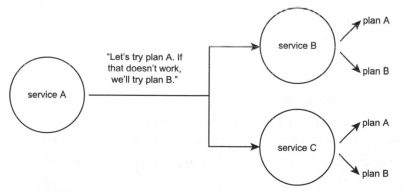

Figure 6.27
A business activity controls the integrity of a service activity by providing participants with a "plan B" (a compensation).

<table>
<tr><td>

NOTE

The concepts discussed in this section are derived from the WS-BusinessActivity specification, which (like WS-AtomicTransaction) provides protocols for use with WS-Coordination. The *WS-Coordination overview* section in Chapter 16 contains a brief example of how a coordination type referencing WS-BusinessActivity exists within a SOAP header.

</td></tr>
</table>

IN PLAIN ENGLISH

Over time, we find that as a result of poor weather conditions, we need to cancel a number of pre-scheduled car wash appointments. Every time this happens, though, confusion ensues, as we scramble to notify each other and the customer in time.

We agree that we need some sort of system to deal with this situation. Chuck comes up with an idea. Chuck owns a house with a large garage. He volunteers his house as a location to which we can take cars for washing when it rains. We all like Chuck's idea so much, we elect him as the person responsible for assessing the weather and then determining if a particular appointment will go ahead. If it doesn't, he must notify each of us that the car will be washed at his house instead of at the customer's residence.

This essentially extends our original car washing process to incorporate a sub-process that only kicks in when certain conditions prevent us from proceeding with the initial plan. This special sub-process is classified as a compensation task or compensation process, a primary feature of business activities.

Note that the use of this compensation process does not affect the atomic transaction-like system we applied to adding soap to the bucket full of warm water. This mirrors the relationship between business activities and atomic transactions in real life; each business activity can contain one or more individual atomic transactions.

6.5.1 Business activity protocols

As with WS-AtomicTransaction, WS-BusinessActivity is a coordination type designed to leverage the WS-Coordination context management framework. It provides two very similar protocols, each of which dictates how a participant may behave within the overall business activity.

- The *BusinessAgreementWithParticipantCompletion* protocol, which allows a participant to determine when it has completed its part in the business activity.

- The *BusinessAgreementWithCoordinatorCompletion* protocol, which requires that a participant rely on the business activity coordinator to notify it that it has no further processing responsibilities.

Business activity participants interact with the standard WS-Coordination coordinator composition to register for a protocol, as was explained in the previous *Coordination* section.

6.5.2   The business activity coordinator

When its protocols are used, the WS-Coordination controller service assumes a role specific to the coordination type—in this case it becomes a *business activity coordinator* (Figure 6.28). As explained in the previous section, this coordinator has varying degrees of control in the overall activity, based on the coordination protocols used by the participants.

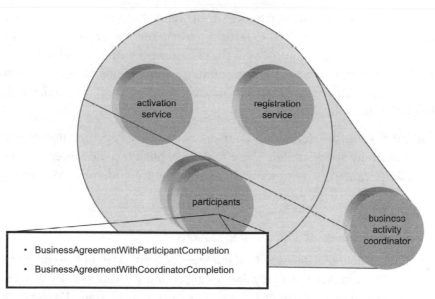

Figure 6.28
The business activity coordinator service model.

6.5.3   Business activity states

During the lifecycle of a business activity, the business activity coordinator and the activity participants transition through a series of states. The actual point of transition occurs when special notification messages are passed between these services.

For example, a participant can indicate that it has completed the processing it was required to perform as part of the activity by issuing a *completed notification*. This moves the participant from an *active state* to a *completed state*. The coordinator may respond with a *close* message to let the participant know that the business activity is being successfully completed.

However, if things don't go as planned during the course of a business activity, one of a number of options are available. Participants can enter a *compensation state* during which they attempt to perform some measure of exception handling. This generally invokes a separate compensation process that could involve a series of additional processing steps. A compensation is different from an atomic transaction in that it is not expected to rollback any changes performed by the participating services; its purpose is generally to execute plan B when plan A fails.

Alternatively, a *cancelled state* can be entered. This typically results in the termination of any further processing outside of the *cancellation notifications* that need to be distributed.

What also distinguishes business activities from atomic transactions is the fact that participating services are not required to remain participants for the duration of the activity. Because there is no tight control over the changes performed by services, they may leave the business activity after their individual contributions have been performed. When doing so, participants enter an *exit* state by issuing an *exit notification* message to the business activity coordinator.

These and other states are defined in a series of state tables documented as part of the WS-BusinessActivity specification. These tables establish the fundamental rules of the business activity protocols by determining the sequence and conditions of allowable states.

6.5.4 Business activities and atomic transactions

It is important to note that the use of a business activity does not exclude the use of atomic transactions. In fact, it is likely that a long-running business activity will encompass the execution of several atomic transactions during its lifetime (Figure 6.29).

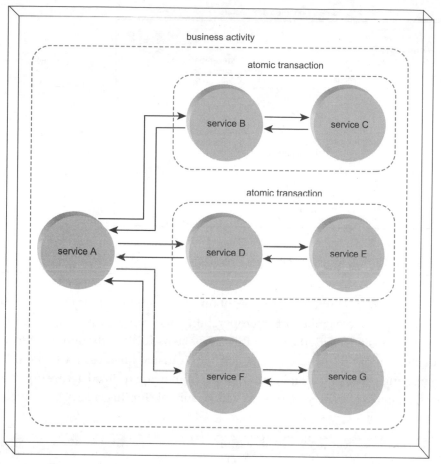

Figure 6.29
Two atomic transactions residing within the scope of a business activity.

6.5.5   Business activities and SOA

Business activities fully complement the composable nature of SOA (Figure 6.30) by tracking and regulating complex activities while also allowing them to carry on for long periods of time. Service autonomy and statelessness are preserved by permitting services to participate within an activity for only the duration they are absolutely required to. This also allows for the design of highly adaptive business activities wherein the participants can augment activity or process logic to accommodate changes in the business tasks being automated. Through the use of the compensation process, business activities increase SOA's quality of service by providing built-in fault handling logic.

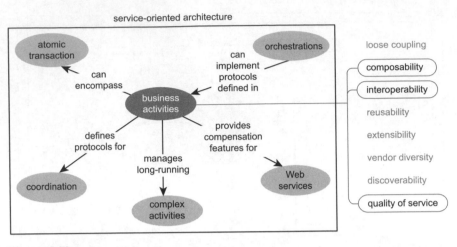

Figure 6.30
A business activity relating to other parts of SOA.

As with WS-AtomicTransaction, support of the WS-BusinessActivity extension by multiple solutions promotes inherent interoperability and can greatly simplify integration architectures. Business activities take this a few steps further, though, by allowing the scope of the activity to include interaction with outside business partners. (Note that there is nothing restricting atomic transactions from being utilized across organizations. However, business activities are typically more suitable for this type of communication.)

CASE STUDY

The TLS Purchase Order Submission Process (illustrated in Figure 6.31) involves the TLS Purchase Order Service acting as the initial sender, responsible for transmitting a SOAP message containing PO details to the RailCo Order Fulfillment Service (Step 2). Further complicating this process is the fact that purchase orders for amounts exceeding $100,000 require a separate approval step by a TLS manager (Step 1).

Vendors are given a period of 48 hours during which they are expected to check for the availability of the requested inventory and respond with either an acknowledgement message indicating that the order will be shipped or a message explaining that an order cannot be filled (or only partially filled), along with any relevant back-order information (Step 3).

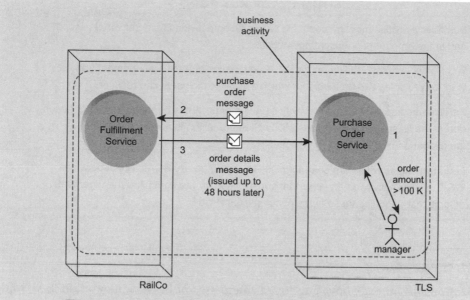

Figure 6.31

The TLS Purchase Order Submission Process wrapped in a long-running business activity and spanning two organizations (two participants).

Even though the PO Submission Process also can be classified as a complex activity, it is different from our previous case study example, as follows:

- It can take a long time for this activity to complete.
- It includes a manual review step (which can result in an approval or a rejection of the purchase order request).

To best manage this complex activity, TLS has used the same WS-Coordination context management framework applied in the previous case study example, only this time the WS-BusinessActivity coordination type is chosen instead.

SUMMARY OF KEY POINTS

- Business activities manage complex, long-running activities that can vary in scope and in the amount of participating services.

- WS-BusinessActivity builds on the WS-Coordination context management framework by providing two protocols for which activity participants can register.

- Participants and the business activity coordinator progress through a series of states during the lifespan of a business activity. State transition is accomplished through the exchange of notification messages.

- Long-running activities are commonplace in contemporary SOAs, which positions WS-BusinessActivity as an important specification for the controlled management of logic that underlies these types of complex activities.

6.6 Orchestration

Organizations that already have employed enterprise application integration (EAI) middleware products to automate business processes or to integrate various legacy environments will likely already be familiar with the concept of *orchestration*. In these systems, a centrally controlled set of workflow logic facilitates interoperability between two or more different applications. A common implementation of orchestration is the hub-and-spoke model that allows multiple external participants to interface with a central orchestration engine.

One of the driving requirements behind the creation of these solutions was to accommodate the merging of large business processes. With orchestration, different processes can be connected without having to redevelop the solutions that originally automated the processes individually. Orchestration bridges this gap by introducing new workflow logic. Further, the use of orchestration can significantly reduce the complexity of solution environments. Workflow logic is abstracted and more easily maintained than when embedded within individual solution components.

The role of orchestration broadens in service-oriented environments. Through the use of extensions that allow for business process logic to be expressed via services, orchestration can represent and express business logic in a standardized, services-based venue. When building service-oriented solutions, this provides an extremely attractive means of housing and controlling the logic representing the process being automated.

Orchestration further leverages the intrinsic interoperability sought by service designs by providing potential integration endpoints into processes. A key aspect to how orchestration is positioned within SOA is the fact that orchestrations themselves exist as services. Therefore, building upon orchestration logic standardizes process representation across an organization, while addressing the goal of enterprise federation and promoting service-orientation.

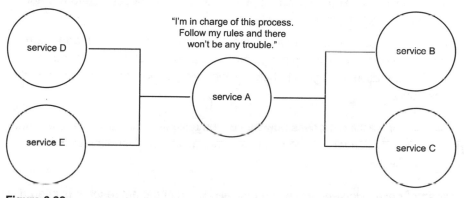

Figure 6.32
An orchestration controls almost every facet of a complex activity.

A primary industry specification that standardizes orchestration is the Web services Business Process Execution Language (WS-BPEL). This book recognizes WS-BPEL as a key second-generation extension and therefore uses its concepts and terminology as the basis for a number of discussions relating to business process modeling.

NOTE

WS-BPEL is the most recent name given to this specification, which also is known as *BPEL4WS* and just *BPEL*. For an overview of the primary parts of the WS-BPEL language and a discussion of how the name change came about, see Chapter 16.

IN PLAIN ENGLISH

After successfully washing several cars together, Chuck, Bob, Jim, and I decide to start our own company. We formalize the steps in our car washing process so that we can handle different types of cars with different cleaning requirements.

Our process is therefore affected by the following new requirements:

- We decide to hire extra help during peak hours. This introduces up to two additional members that join our team.

- Because we have no venture capital for this business, we make an arrangement with a local gas station. In exchange for using a portion of their lot for our car washing operation, we agree to help out with the gas pumping duties during their peak hours.

Our simple car washing process now has become significantly more complicated. The process is no longer fixed in that it can change at any given time as a result of various conditions and events.

- When our extra workers arrive, the task allocation of the entire team is altered.

- When gas station personnel need extra help, we are obligated to send one or more of our car washing team members to assist them.

These examples relate to predictable conditions that occur on a daily basis. Our operation is further affected by some constraints:

- If our cash flow falls below a certain amount, we are unable to afford part-time workers.

- If it rains, all work is suspended (also leading to reduced cash flow).

These constraints introduce conditions that are less common, but which we always need to take into consideration. To accommodate these potential situations, we come up with a plan that maps out our expanded process and provides alternative processes for dealing with both common and uncommon conditions.

This plan is essentially a workflow that joins individual steps with processes and subprocesses partitioned by decision points. This elaborate workflow incorporates our original process with the gas station's process and the extended process resulting from the arrival of our part-time workers. This workflow is essentially an orchestration that manages the individual process requirements and related resources, participants, events, business rules, and activities.

6.6.1 Business protocols and process definition

The workflow logic that comprises an orchestration can consist of numerous business rules, conditions, and events. Collectively, these parts of an orchestration establish a *business protocol* that defines how participants can interoperate to achieve the completion of a business task. The details of the workflow logic encapsulated and expressed by an orchestration are contained within a *process definition*.

6.6.2 Process services and partner services

Identified and described within a process definition are the allowable process participants. First, the process itself is represented as a service, resulting in a *process service* (which happens to be another one of our service models, as shown in Figure 6.33).

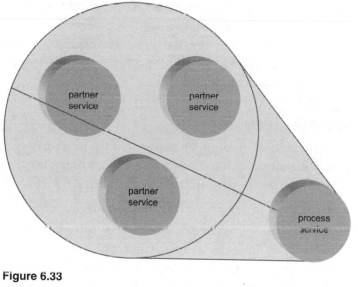

Figure 6.33
A process service coordinating and exposing functionality from three partner services.

Other services allowed to interact with the process service are identified as *partner services* or *partner links*. Depending on the workflow logic, the process service can be invoked by an external partner service, or it can invoke other partner services (Figure 6.34).

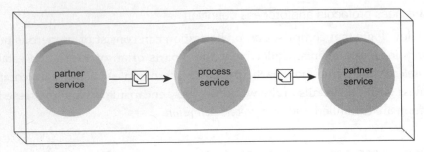

Figure 6.34

The process service, after first being invoked by a partner service, then invokes another partner service.

6.6.3   Basic activities and structured activities

WS-BPEL breaks down workflow logic into a series of predefined primitive activities. *Basic activities* (receive, invoke, reply, throw, wait) represent fundamental workflow actions which can be assembled using the logic supplied by *structured activities* (sequence, switch, while, flow, pick). How these activities can be used to express actual business process logic is explored in Chapter 16.

6.6.4   Sequences, flows, and links

Basic and structured activities can be organized so that the order in which they execute is predefined. A *sequence* aligns groups of related activities into a list that determines a sequential execution order. Sequences are especially useful when one piece of application logic is dependent on the outcome of another.

Flows also contain groups of related activities, but they introduce different execution requirements. Pieces of application logic can execute concurrently within a flow, meaning that there is not necessarily a requirement for one set of activities to wait before another finishes. However, the flow itself does not finish until all encapsulated activities have completed processing. This ensures a form of synchronization among application logic residing in individual flows.

Links are used to establish formal dependencies between activities that are part of flows. Before an activity fully can complete, it must ensure that any requirements established in outgoing links first are met. Similarly, before any linked activity can begin, requirements contained within any incoming links first must be satisfied. Rules provided by links are also referred to as *synchronization dependencies*.

6.6.5   Orchestrations and activities

As we defined earlier, an activity is a generic term that can be applied to any logical unit of work completed by a service-oriented solution. The scope of a single orchestration, therefore, can be classified as a complex, and most likely, long-running activity.

6.6.6   Orchestration and coordination

Orchestration, as represented by WS-BPEL, can fully utilize the WS-Coordination context management framework by incorporating the WS-BusinessActivity coordination type. This specification defines coordination protocols designed to support complex, long-running activities.

6.6.7   Orchestration and SOA

Business process logic is at the root of automation solutions. Orchestration provides an automation model where process logic is centralized yet still extensible and composable (Figure 6.35). Through the use of orchestrations, service-oriented solution environments become inherently extensible and adaptive. Orchestrations themselves typically establish a common point of integration for other applications, which makes an implemented orchestration a key integration enabler.

These qualities lead to increased organizational agility because:

- The workflow logic encapsulated by an orchestration can be modified or extended in a central location.
- Positioning an orchestration centrally can significantly ease the merging of business processes by abstracting the glue that ties the corresponding automation solutions together.
- By establishing potentially large-scale service-oriented integration architectures, orchestration, on a fundamental level, can support the evolution of a diversely federated enterprise.

Orchestration is a key ingredient to achieving a state of federation within an organization that contains various applications based on disparate computing platforms. Advancements in middleware allow orchestration engines themselves to become fully integrated in service-oriented environments.

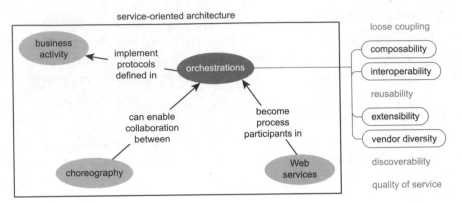

Figure 6.35
Orchestration relating to other parts of SOA.

The concept of service-oriented orchestration fully leverages all of the concepts we've discussed so far in this chapter. For many environments, orchestrations become the heart of SOA.

CASE STUDY

The series of steps we wrapped into a business activity in the previous case study example demonstrated how TLS used the WS-BusinessActivity protocol to add context management and exception handling to a long-running, complex activity. Even though the scope of a business activity can constitute a business process, it does not provide TLS with a standard means of expressing the underlying work-flow logic. For that, TLS employs a WS-BPEL orchestration (Figure 6.36).

The orchestration establishes comprehensive process logic that encompasses the business activity and extends it even further to govern additional interaction scenarios with multiple vendor services. For example, when one vendor cannot fulfill an order, the next vendor in line is sent the same purchase order. This cycle is repeated until either one vendor can complete the order in its entirety (within certain price limitations) or until all vendors have been queried. In the latter situation, the system simply assesses the best deal on the table by applying a formula that takes into account the price, percentage of order to be filled, and backorder terms.

The orchestration logic manages all aspects of the process, including the involvement of multiple vendor partner services, as well as the business activity that kicks in when a PO is processed.

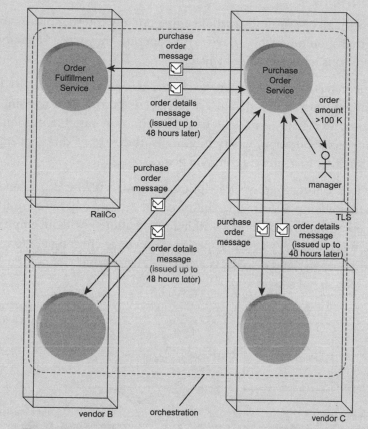

Figure 6.36

The extended TLS Purchase Order Submission Process managed by an orchestration and involving numerous potential partner organizations.

SUMMARY OF KEY POINTS

- An orchestration expresses a body of business process logic that is typically owned by a single organization.

- An orchestration establishes a business protocol that formally defines a business process definition.

- The workflow logic within an orchestration is broken down into a series of basic and structured activities that can be organized into sequences and flows.

- Orchestration has been called the "heart of SOA," as it establishes a means of centralizing and controlling a great deal of inter and intra-application logic through a standardized service model.

6.7 Choreography

In a perfect world, all organizations would agree on how internal processes should be structured, so that should they ever have to interoperate, they would already have their automation solutions in perfect alignment.

Though this vision has about a zero percent chance of ever becoming reality, the requirement for organizations to interoperate via services is becoming increasingly real and increasingly complex. This is especially true when interoperation requirements extend into the realm of collaboration, where multiple services from different organizations need to work together to achieve a common goal.

The Web Services Choreography Description Language (WS-CDL) is one of several specifications that attempts to organize information exchange between multiple organizations (or even multiple applications within organizations), with an emphasis on public collaboration (Figure 6.37). It is the specification we've chosen here to represent the concept of choreography and also the specification from which many of the terms discussed in this section have been derived.

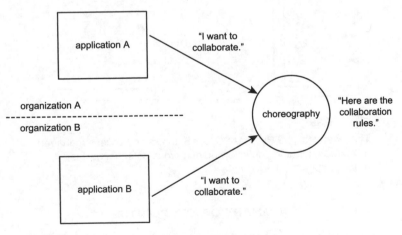

Figure 6.37
A choreography enables collaboration between its participants.

IN PLAIN ENGLISH

After a few months in operation, our little car washing enterprise achieves some success. With our flexible and adaptive system, we have been able to efficiently wash enough cars to make some profit. Once word in the car washing circles gets around, we are contacted by a nearby car washing company.

Even though this team of car washers is located only a kilometer away, they are not considered competitors. We positioned ourselves at a gas station located at the off ramp of a highway, and they are on the other side. Our customers originate from North-bound traffic, whereas theirs come from cars heading South. As a result, we have different peak hours corresponding directly to the traffic patterns of the highway. Our volume peaks during the morning rush hours, whereas theirs peaks in the afternoon.

It is suggested to us that we could form a partnership whereby we pool our respective resources (workers) to allow each of our companies to maximize the potential of each rush hour period. This form of collaboration appeals to us, as so far we've never been able to wash as many cars as we could at peak times. When customers entering the gas station grounds see a line up to our car wash, they often change their minds and drive away.

We decide to join forces with the other team. However, this arrangement soon affects our original business process. We now have to introduce a process that imposes new conditions and constraints. At the same time, though, we want to protect our existing system because it has been successful. After discussing these issues with our new partner, we come to an agreement that results in a flexible collaboration process.

A choreography is essentially a collaboration process designed to allow organizations to interact in an environment that is not owned by any one partner.

6.7.1 Collaboration

An important characteristic of choreographies is that they are intended for public message exchanges. The goal is to establish a kind of organized collaboration between services representing different service entities, only no one entity (organization) necessarily controls the collaboration logic. Choreographies therefore provide the potential for establishing universal interoperability patterns for common inter-organization business tasks.

> **NOTE**
>
> While the emphasis on choreography is B2B interaction, it also can be applied to enable collaboration between applications belonging to a single organization. The use of orchestration, though, is far more common for this requirement.

6.7.2   Roles and participants

Within any given choreography, a Web service assumes one of a number of predefined *roles*. This establishes what the service does and what the service can do within the context of a particular business task. Roles can be bound to WSDL definitions, and those related are grouped accordingly, categorized as *participants* (services).

6.7.3   Relationships and channels

Every action that is mapped out within a choreography can be broken down into a series of message exchanges between two services. Each potential exchange between two roles in a choreography is therefore defined individually as a *relationship*. Every relationship consequently consists of exactly two roles.

Now that we've defined who can talk with each other, we require a means of establishing the nature of the conversation. *Channels* do exactly that by defining the characteristics of the message exchange between two specific roles.

Further, to facilitate more complex exchanges involving multiple participants, channel information can actually be passed around in a message. This allows one service to send another the information required for it to be communicated with by other services. This is a significant feature of the WS-CDL specification, as it fosters dynamic discovery and increases the number of potential participants within large-scale collaborative tasks.

6.7.4   Interactions and work units

Finally, the actual logic behind a message exchange is encapsulated within an *interaction*. Interactions are the fundamental building blocks of choreographies because the completion of an interaction represents actual progress within a choreography. Related to interactions are *work units*. These impose rules and constraints that must be adhered to for an interaction to successfully complete.

6.7.5   Reusability, composability, and modularity

Each choreography can be designed in a reusable manner, allowing it to be applied to different business tasks comprised of the same fundamental actions. Further, using an import facility, a choreography can be assembled from independent *modules*. These modules can represent distinct sub-tasks and can be reused by numerous different parent choreographies (Figure 6.38).

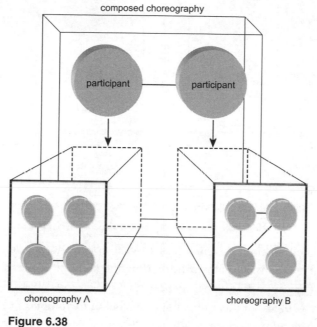

Figure 6.38
A choreography composed of two smaller choreographies.

Finally, even though a choreography in effect composes a set of non-specific services to accomplish a task, choreographies themselves can be assembled into larger compositions.

6.7.6   Orchestrations and choreographies

While both represent complex message interchange patterns, there is a common distinction that separates the terms "orchestration" and "choreography." An orchestration expresses organization-specific business workflow. This means that an organization owns and controls the logic behind an orchestration, even if that logic involves interaction with external business partners. A choreography, on the other hand, is not necessarily owned by a single entity. It acts as a community interchange pattern used for collaborative purposes by services from different provider entities (Figure 6.39).

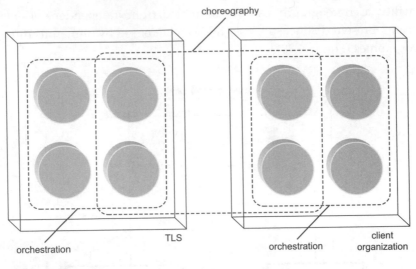

Figure 6.39
A choreography enabling collaboration between two different orchestrations.

One can view an orchestration as a business-specific application of a choreography. This view is somewhat accurate, only it is muddled by the fact that some of the functionality provided by the corresponding specifications (WS-CDL and WS-BPEL) actually overlaps. This is a consequence of these specifications being developed in isolation and submitted to separate standards organizations (W3C and OASIS, respectively).

An orchestration is based on a model where the composition logic is executed and controlled in a centralized manner. A choreography typically assumes that there is no single owner of collaboration logic. However, one area of overlap between the current orchestration and choreography extensions is the fact that orchestrations can be designed to include multi-organization participants. An orchestration can therefore effectively establish cross-enterprise activities in a similar manner as a choreography. Again, though, a primary distinction is the fact that an orchestration is generally owned and operated by a single organization.

6.7.7 Choreography and SOA

The fundamental concept of exposing business logic through autonomous services can be applied to just about any implementation scope. Two services within a single organization, each exposing a simple function, can interact via a basic MEP to complete a simple task. Two services belonging to different organizations, each exposing functionality from entire enterprise business solutions, can interact via a basic choreography to complete a more complex task. Both scenarios involve two services, and both scenarios support SOA implementations.

Choreography therefore can assist in the realization of SOA across organization boundaries (Figure 6.40). While it natively supports composability, reusability, and extensibility, choreography also can increase organizational agility and discovery. Organizations are able to join into multiple online collaborations, which can dynamically extend or even alter related business processes that integrate with the choreographies. By being able to pass around channel information, participating services can make third-party organizations aware of other organizations with which they already have had contact.

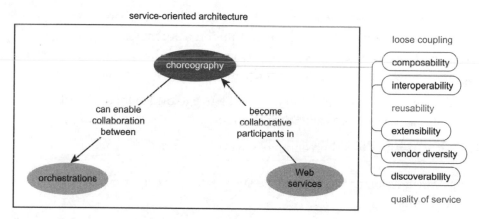

Figure 6.40
Choreography relating to other parts of SOA.

TLS owns the Sampson Steel manufacturing plant, a factory that originally produced various metal parts for automobile and airline companies. TLS uses this factory to build parts for its own railways but also continues to support the manufacture of custom parts for other clients.

A relatively significant client has surfaced over the past year, requiring specific types of steel parts for its line of products. To determine the exact design specifications of a single part, the client needs to collaborate with the manufacturing specialists that were formerly employed by Sampson Steel and that now work for TLS.

To achieve the design specification of a single part, numerous factors are taken into consideration, including:

- the complexity of the design
- the cost of materials
- the quantity of parts required
- the availability of the necessary machines within the plant
- the durability requirements of the part
- environmental conditions to which the part may be exposed

As a result, many drafts of a specification go back and forth between the client and the TLS specialists. These documents undergo automated processing steps during each review cycle, relating to privacy, patents, chemical composition, and the processing of mathematical formulas that pertain to the actual part design.

To facilitate this process, TLS and the client agree to bridge their respective automation environments with a choreography.

The participants of this choreography govern:

- the transmission and routing of the messages containing the part specification documents
- the automatic validation of specification data
- the processing of privacy and security-related policies
- the calculation of complex mathematical formulas

The choreography achieves a cross-organization process that automates the collaboration cycle required by TLS and its client to negotiate and finalize specifications for custom manufactured steel parts.

SUMMARY OF KEY POINTS

- A choreography is a complex activity comprised of a service composition and a series of MEPs.

- Choreographies consist of multiple participants that can assume different roles and that have different relationships.

- Choreographies are reusable, composable, and can be modularized.

- The concept of choreography extends the SOA vision to standardize cross-organization collaboration.

Chapter 7

Web Services and Contemporary SOA (Part II: Advanced Messaging, Metadata, and Security)

In Chapter 6 we established a series of composition and activity management concepts, each with a different scope and purpose, but all somewhat related within the context of composable SOA. Those initial concepts are complemented by additional WS-* extensions that govern specific areas of the SOAP messaging framework, the creation and exchange of metadata, and the introduction of message-level security. (Figure 7.1 introduces the individual concepts and shows how they typically inter-relate.)

As we explore the various extensions in this chapter, it becomes increasingly clear that SOAP messaging is the lifeblood of contemporary service-oriented architecture. It realizes not only the delivery of application data, but also the composable nature of SOA. The innovation of SOAP headers accounts for almost all of the features covered in Chapters 6 and 7.

To demonstrate common concepts, this chapter borrows terms provided by the following current Web services specifications:

- WS-Addressing
- WS-ReliableMessaging
- WS-Policy Framework (including WS-PolicyAttachments and WS-PolicyAssertions)
- WS-MetadataExchange
- WS-Security (including XML-Encryption, XML-Signature, and SAML)
- WS-Notification Framework (including WS-BaseNotification, WS-Topics, and WS-BrokeredNotification)
- WS-Eventing

As with Chapter 6, we only explore concepts related to WS-* extensions in this chapter. Language element descriptions and examples for the first five specifications in the preceding list are provided in Chapter 17.

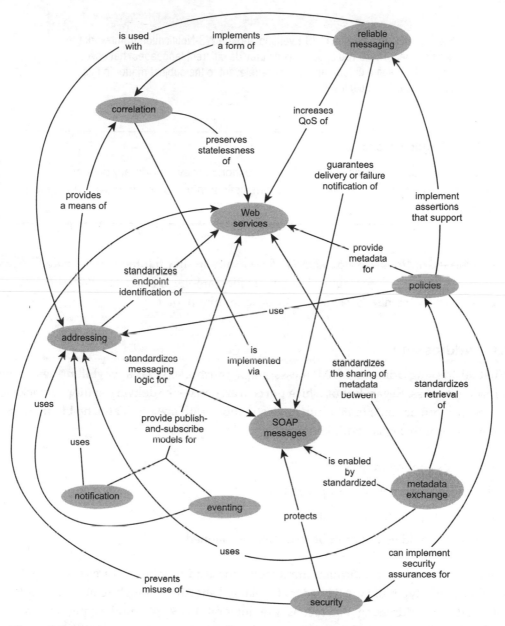

Figure 7.1
Specifications and concepts covered in this chapter.

NOTE
Markup code examples for WS-Eventing and the WS-Notification framework are not provided. These two specifications provide different languages that cover much of the same ground and are more relevant to the subject matter in this book on a conceptual level.

In Plain English sections

This chapter also contains *In Plain English* sections for every primary concept discussed. Note that these intentionally simplistic analogies continue where they left off in Chapter 6.

How case studies are used: Several of the examples in Chapter 6 are revisited here as we take a closer look at how interaction among specific TLS Web services is affected by the new concepts introduced in this chapter.

7.1 Addressing

What addressing brings to SOAP messaging is much like what a waybill brings to the shipping process. Regardless of which ports, warehouses, or delivery stations a package passes through en route to its ultimate destination, with a waybill attached to it, everyone it comes into contact with knows:

- where it's coming from
- the address of where it's supposed to go
- the specific person at the address who is supposed to receive it
- where it should go if it can't be delivered as planned

The WS-Addressing specification implements these addressing features (Figure 7.2) by providing two types of SOAP headers (explained shortly). Though relatively simple in nature, these addressing extensions are integral to SOA's underlying messaging mechanics. Many other WS-* specifications implicitly rely on the use of WS-Addressing.

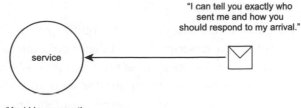

Figure 7.2
Addressing turns messages into autonomous units of communication.

NOTE

For an overview of the WS-Addressing language, see the *WS-Addressing language basics* section in Chapter 17.

IN PLAIN ENGLISH

As our car washing company grows, so do the administration duties. Every week Chuck reviews the mail and takes care of necessary paperwork. This week he receives two letters: one from our insurance company and the other from the tax office.

The first letter includes our renewed insurance policy statement, along with an invoice for another year of coverage. The "from" address on this letter is simply the name and location of the insurance company's head office. The enclosed statement contains a letter written by our account representative, outlining some of the changes in this year's policy and requesting that we mail our check directly to him. Chuck therefore encloses our payment in an envelope with a "to" address that includes an "attention" line stating that this letter should be delivered directly to the account representative.

The next letter contains another bill. This time, it's a tax statement accompanied by a letter of instruction and two return envelopes. According to the instructions, we are to use the first envelope (addressed to the A/R office) to mail a check if we are paying the full amount owing. If we cannot make a full payment, we need to use the second envelope (addressed to the collections department) to send whatever funds we have.

These scenarios, in their own crude way, demonstrate the fundamental concepts of endpoint references and message information headers, which are explained in the following sections.

7.1.1 Endpoint references

Early on in this book we established that the loosely coupled nature of SOA was implemented through the use of service descriptions. In other words, all that is required for a service requestor to contact a service provider is the provider's WSDL definition. This document, among other things, supplies the requestor with an address at which the provider can be contacted. What if, though, the service requestor needs to send a message to a specific instance of a service provider? In this case, the address provided by the WSDL is not sufficient.

Traditional Web applications had different ways of managing and communicating session identifiers. The most common approach was to append the identifier as a query string parameter to the end of a URL. While easy to develop, this technique resulted in application designs that lacked security and were non-standardized.

The concept of addressing introduces the *endpoint reference*, an extension used primarily to provide identifiers that pinpoint a particular instance of a service (as well as supplementary service metadata). The endpoint reference is expected to be almost always dynamically generated and can contain a set of supplementary properties.

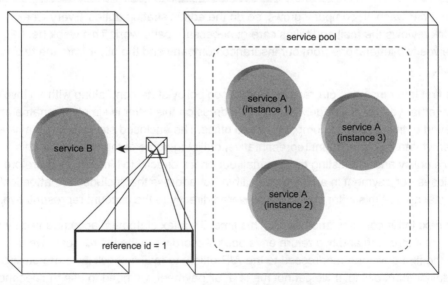

Figure 7.3
A SOAP message containing a reference to the instance of the service that sent it.

An endpoint reference consists of the following parts:

- *address*—The URL of the Web service.
- *reference properties*—A set of property values associated with the Web service instance. (In our previous *In Plain English* example, the "attention" line used in the first scenario is representative of the reference ID property.)
- *reference parameters*—A set of parameter values that can be used to further interact with a specific service instance.
- *service port type and port type*—Specific service interface information giving the recipient of the message the exact location of service description details required for a reply.
- *policy*—A WS-Policy compliant policy that provides rules and behavior information relevant to the current service interaction (policies are explained later in this chapter).

Additional parts exist, which mostly identify corresponding WSDL information. With the exception of the address, all parts are optional.

7.1.2 Message information headers

In the previous chapter we covered the various primitive message exchange patterns of which complex activities are comprised. These MEPs have predictable characteristics that can ease the manner in which Web services are designed but also can limit the service interaction scenarios within which they participate.

In sophisticated service-oriented solutions, services often require the flexibility to break a fixed pattern. For example, they may want to dynamically determine the nature of a message exchange. The extensions provided by WS-Addressing were broadened to include new SOAP headers that establish message exchange-related characteristics within the messages themselves. This collection of standardized headers is known as the *message information* (or *MI*) headers (Figure 7.4).

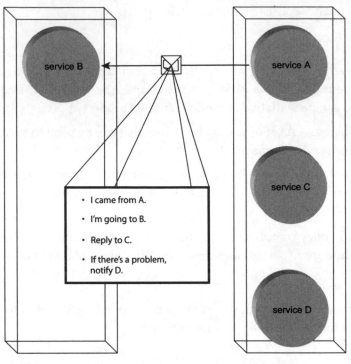

Figure 7.4
A SOAP message with message information headers specifying
exactly how the recipient service should respond to its arrival.

The MI headers provided by WS-Addressing include:

- *destination*—The address to which the message is being sent.
- *source endpoint*—An endpoint reference to the Web service that generated the message.
- *reply endpoint*—This important header allows a message to dictate to which address its reply should be sent.
- *fault endpoint*—Further extending the messaging flexibility is this header, which gives a message the ability to set the address to which a fault notification should be sent.
- *message id*—A value that uniquely identifies the message or the retransmission of the message (this header is required when using the reply endpoint header).

- *relationship*—Most commonly used in request-response scenarios, this header contains the message id of the related message to which a message is replying (this header also is required within the reply message).

- *action*—A URI value that indicates the message's overall purpose (the equivalent of the standard SOAP HTTP action value).

(Also of interest is the fact that the WS-Addressing specification provides an anonymous URI that allows MI headers to intentionally contain an invalid address.)

Outfitting a SOAP message with these headers further increases its position as an independent unit of communication. Using MI headers, SOAP messages now can contain detailed information that defines the messaging interaction behavior of the service in receipt of the message. The net result is standardized support for the use of unpredictable and highly flexible message exchanges, dynamically creatable and therefore adaptive and responsive to runtime conditions.

7.1.3 Addressing and transport protocol independence

Historically, many of the details pertaining to how a unit of communication arrives at point B after it is transmitted from point A was left up to the individual protocols that controlled the transportation layer. While this level of technology-based abstraction is convenient for developers, it also leads to restrictions as to how communication between two units of processing logic can be achieved.

The standardized SOAP headers introduced by WS-Addressing remove much of this protocol-level dependence. These headers put the SOAP message itself in charge of its own destiny by further increasing its ability to act as a standalone unit of communication.

7.1.4 Addressing and SOA

Addressing achieves an important low-level, transport standardization within SOA, further promoting open standards that establish a level of transport technology independence (Figure 7.5). The use of endpoint references and MI headers deepens the intelligence embedded into SOAP messages, increasing message-level autonomy.

Empowering a message with the ability to self-direct its payload, as well as the ability to dictate how services receiving the message should behave, significantly increases the potential for Web services to be intrinsically interoperable. It places the task-specific logic into the message and promotes a highly reusable and generic service design standard that also facilitates the discovery of additional service metadata.

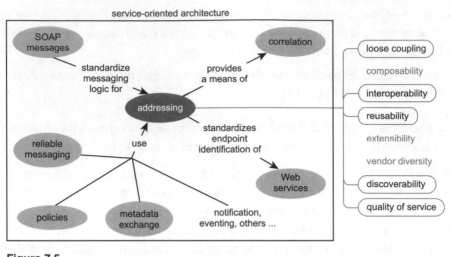

Figure 7.5

Addressing relating to other parts of SOA.

Further, the use of MI headers increases the range of interaction logic within complex activities and even encourages this logic to be dynamically determined. This, however, can be a double-edged sword. Even though MI headers can further increase the sophistication of service-oriented applications, their misuse (or overuse) can lead to some wildly creative and complex service activities.

Finally, by supporting the referencing of service instances, SOAs can be scaled in a standardized manner, without the need to resort to custom or proprietary application designs (scalability is a key QoS contribution). Having stated that, it should be pointed out that by providing functionality that enables communication with service instances, WS-Addressing indirectly supports the creation of stateful services. This runs contrary to the common service-orientation principle of statelessness (as explained in Chapter 8) and emphasizes the need for this feature to be applied in moderation.

CASE STUDY

In the previous chapter we provided several examples that explained the steps behind the vendor invoice submission process. One of these steps required that, upon receiving an invoice from a vendor, the TLS Accounts Payable Service interacts with the TLS Vendor Profile Service to have the received invoice validated against vendor account information already on file.

Due to the volume of invoice submissions received by TLS, there can be, at any given time, multiple active instances of the Accounts Payable Service. Therefore, as part of the message issued by the Accounts Payable Service to the Vendor Profile Service, a SOAP header providing a reference id is included. This identifier represents the current instance of the Accounts Payable Service and is used by the Vendor Profile Service to locate this instance when it is ready to respond with the validation information (Figure 7.6).

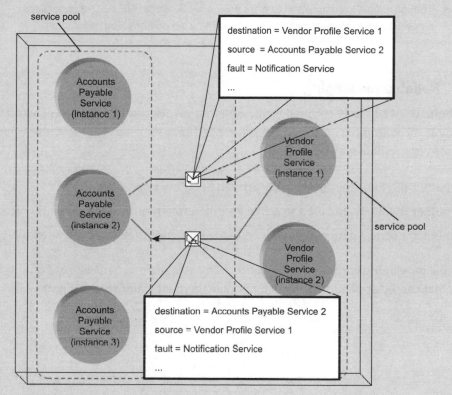

Figure 7.6

Separate service instances communicating using endpoint references and MI headers across two pools of Web services within TLS.

SUMMARY OF KEY POINTS

- Addressing extensions, as implemented by the WS-Addressing specification, introduce two important concepts: endpoint references and message information headers.

- Endpoint references provide a standardized means of identifying a specific instance of a Web service.

- Message information headers add message exchange properties to a specific message, conveying interaction semantics to recipient services.

- Though simple in comparison to other WS-* specifications, WS-Addressing inserts a powerful layer of messaging autonomy within a service-oriented architecture.

7.2 Reliable messaging

The benefits of a loosely coupled messaging framework come at the cost of a loss of control over the actual communications process. After a Web service transmits a message, it has no immediate way of knowing:

- whether the message successfully arrived at its intended destination
- whether the message failed to arrive and therefore requires a retransmission
- whether a series of messages arrived in the sequence they were intended to

Reliable messaging addresses these concerns by establishing a measure of quality assurance that can be applied to other activity management frameworks (Figure 7.7).

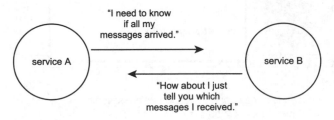

Figure 7.7
Reliable messaging provides a guaranteed notification of delivery success or failure.

WS-ReliableMessaging provides a framework capable of guaranteeing:

- that service providers will be notified of the success or failure of message transmissions
- that messages sent with specific sequence-related rules will arrive as intended (or generate a failure condition)

Although the extensions introduced by reliable messaging govern aspects of service activities, the WS-ReliableMessaging specification is different from the activity management specifications we discussed in Chapter 6. Reliable messaging does not employ a coordinator service to keep track of the state of an activity; instead, all reliability rules are implemented as SOAP headers within the messages themselves.

NOTE

Chapter 17 provides an introduction to the WS-ReliableMessaging language in the *WS-ReliableMessaging language basics* section.

IN PLAIN ENGLISH

In the last chapter's *Choreography* section we explained how our car wash had formed an alliance with the car wash located on the other side of the highway. Part of our arrangement was to share part-time workers during peak hours.

One of the workers that joined our team is named George. Though good at his job, George has a bad memory. When we request that workers from the other side walk over to help us out, we always are warned when one of those workers is George.

The walk from the other gas station is about one kilometer. Sometimes George forgets the way and gets lost. We therefore put a system in place where we agree to call the other company to tell them how many workers have arrived. If it's not equal to the number of workers they actually sent, it's usually because George has gone missing again.

Our system of calling the other company to acknowledge the receipt of the workers and to report any missing workers builds an element of reliability into our resource sharing arrangement.

7.2.1   RM Source, RM Destination, Application Source, and Application Destination

WS-ReliableMessaging makes a distinction between the parts of a solution that are responsible for initiating a message transmission and those that actually perform the transmission. It further assigns specific descriptions to the terms "send," "transmit," "receive," and "deliver," as they relate differently to these solution parts. These differentiations are necessary to abstract the reliable messaging framework from the overall SOA.

An *application source* is the service or application logic that *sends* the message to the *RM source*, the physical processor or node that performs the actual wire *transmission*. Similarly, the *RM destination* represents the target processor or node that *receives* the message and subsequently *delivers* it to the *application destination* (Figure 7.8).

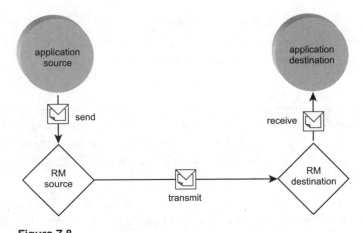

Figure 7.8
An application source, RM source, RM destination, and application destination.

7.2.2   Sequences

A *sequence* establishes the order in which messages should be delivered. Each message that is part of a sequence is labeled with a *message number* that identifies the position of the message within the sequence. The final message in a sequence is further tagged with a *last message* identifier.

7.2.3 Acknowledgements

A core part of the reliable messaging framework is a notification system used to communicate conditions from the RM destination to the RM source. Upon receipt of the message containing the last message identifier, the RM destination issues a *sequence acknowledgement* (Figure 7.9). The acknowledgement message indicates to the RM source which messages were received. It is up to the RM source to determine if the messages received are equal to the original messages transmitted. The RM source may retransmit any of the missing messages, depending on the delivery assurance used (see following section).

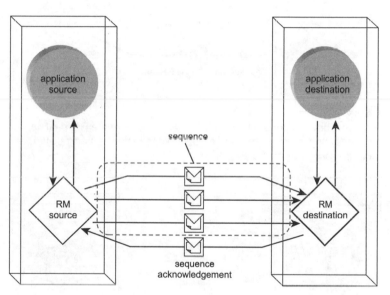

Figure 7.9

A sequence acknowledgement sent by the RM destination after the successful delivery of a sequence of messages.

An RM source does not need to wait until the RM destination receives the last message before receiving an acknowledgement. RM sources can request that additional acknowledgements be transmitted at any time by issuing *request acknowledgements* to RM destinations (Figure 7.10). Additionally, RM destinations have the option of transmitting *negative acknowledgements* that immediately indicate to the RM source that a failure condition has occurred (Figure 7.11).

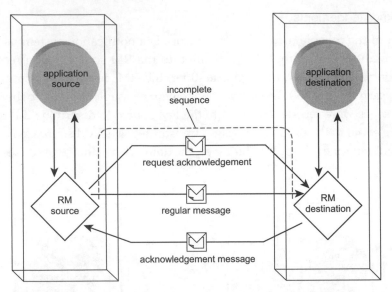

Figure 7.10

A request acknowledgement sent by the RM source to the RM destination, indicating that the RM source would like to receive an acknowledgement message before the sequence completes.

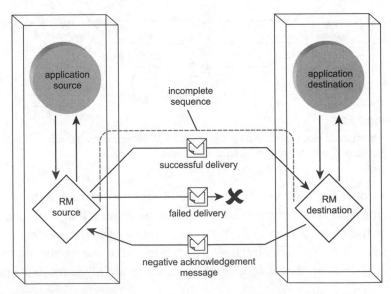

Figure 7.11

A negative acknowledgement sent by the RM destination to the RM source, indicating a failed delivery prior to the completion of the sequence.

7.2.4 Delivery assurances

The nature of a sequence is determined by a set of reliability rules known as *delivery assurances*. Delivery assurances are predefined message delivery patterns that establish a set of reliability policies.

The following delivery assurances are supported:

The *AtMostOnce* delivery assurance promises the delivery of one or zero messages. If more than one of the same message is delivered, an error condition occurs (Figure 7.12).

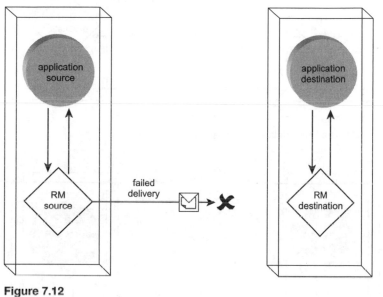

Figure 7.12
The AtMostOnce delivery assurance

The *AtLeastOnce* delivery assurance allows a message to be delivered once or several times. The delivery of zero messages creates an error condition (Figure 7.13).

The *ExactlyOnce* delivery assurance guarantees that a message only will be delivered once. An error is raised if zero or duplicate messages are delivered (Figure 7.14).

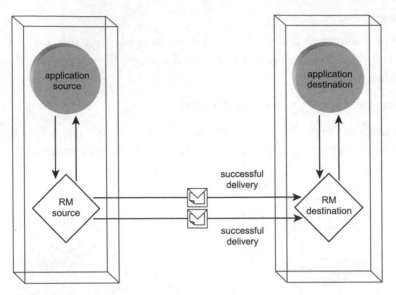

Figure 7.13
The AtLeastOnce delivery assurance.

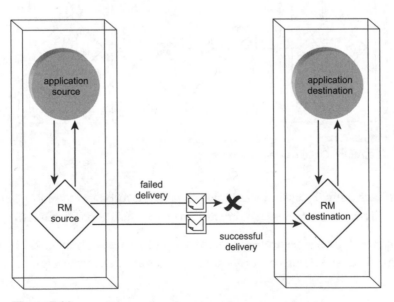

Figure 7.14
The ExactlyOnce delivery assurance.

The *InOrder* delivery assurance is used to ensure that messages are delivered in a specific sequence (Figure 7.15). The delivery of messages out of sequence triggers an error. Note that this delivery assurance can be combined with any of the previously described assurances.

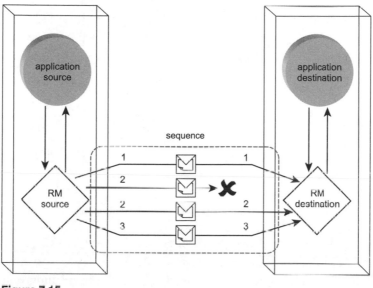

Figure 7.15
The InOrder delivery assurance.

7.2.5   Reliable messaging and addressing

WS-Addressing is closely tied to the WS-ReliableMessaging framework. In fact, it's interesting to note that the rules around the use of the WS-Addressing message id header were altered specifically to accommodate the WS-ReliableMessaging specification. Originally, message id values always had to be unique, regardless of the circumstance. However, the delivery assurances supported by WS-ReliableMessaging required the ability for services to retransmit identical messages in response to communication errors. The subsequent release of WS-Addressing, therefore, allowed retransmissions to use the same message ID.

7.2.6   Reliable messaging and SOA

Reliable messaging brings to service-oriented solutions a tangible quality of service (Figure 7.16). It introduces a flexible system that guarantees the delivery of message sequences supported by comprehensive fault reporting. This elevates the robustness of

SOAP messaging implementations and eliminates the reliability concerns most often associated with any messaging frameworks.

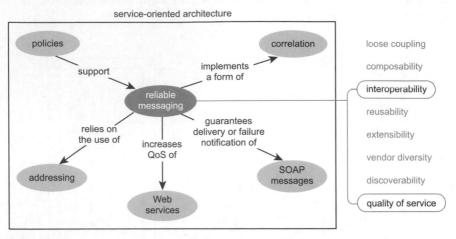

Figure 7.16
Reliable messaging relating to other parts of SOA.

By increasing the delivery quality of SOAP messages, reliable messaging increases the quality of cross-application communication channels as well. The limitations of a messaging framework no longer inhibit the potential of establishing enterprise-level integration.

CASE STUDY

To accommodate their existing accounting practices, RailCo sometimes prefers to issue bulk, month-end invoice submissions. TLS has other vendors that require this option and therefore accepts these forms of bulk submissions—but under the condition that they must be transmitted as part of the same sequence. This gives TLS the ability to issue an acknowledgement that communicates which of the invoice messages were successfully received.

RailCo complies with this requirement and enhances its existing Invoice Submission Service to package invoices in SOAP messages that support reliable messaging extensions (Figure 7.17).

The first submitted batch consists of 15 invoices. Much to RailCo's dismay, upon transmitting the last message in the sequence, TLS issues an acknowledgement message indicating that only 11 of the 15 invoice messages were actually received. In preparation for subsequent bulk submissions, RailCo extends its

Invoice Submission Service to issue an acknowledgement request message after every second invoice message sent as part of a sequence. This allows RailCo to better monitor and respond to failed delivery attempts.

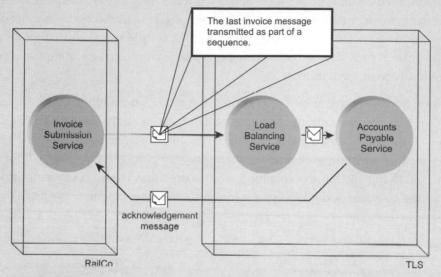

Figure 7.17
After transmitting a series of invoice messages, the last message within the sequence triggers the issuance of an acknowledgement message by TLS.

NOTE
The passive Load Balancing Service displayed in Figure 7.17 does not verify or process reliability conditions. Messages are simply passed through to the destination Accounts Payable Service.

SUMMARY OF KEY POINTS

- WS-ReliableMessaging establishes a framework that guarantees the delivery of a SOAP message or the reporting of a failure condition.

- The key parts of this framework are a notification system based on the delivery of acknowledgement messages and a series of delivery assurances that provide policies comprised of reliability rules.

- WS-ReliableMessaging is closely associated with the WS-Addressing and WS-Policy specifications.

- Reliable messaging significantly increases SOA's quality of service level and broadens its interoperability potential.

7.3   Correlation

One of the fundamental requirements for exchanging information via Web services is the ability to persist context and state across the delivery of multiple messages. Because a service-oriented communications framework is inherently loosely coupled, there is no intrinsic mechanism for associating messages exchanged under a common context or as part of a common activity. Even the execution of a simple request-response message exchange pattern provides no built-in means of automatically associating the response message with the original request.

Correlation addresses this issue by requiring that related messages contain some common value that services can identify to establish their relationship with each other or with the overall task they are participating in (Figure 7.18). The specifications that realize this simple concept provide different manners of implementation. We therefore dedicate the following section to explaining what correlation is and comparing how it is implemented by some of the WS-* extensions we've covered so far.

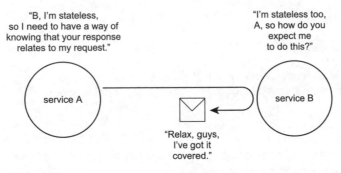

Figure 7.18

Correlation places the association of message exchanges into the hands of the message itself.

NOTE
For a look at how correlation typically is implemented as part of SOAP headers, see the examples provided in the *WS-Addressing language basics* section in Chapter 17.

IN PLAIN ENGLISH
To encourage repeat business, we introduce a promotion where, after ten visits to our car wash, your eleventh visit is free. We implement this promotion through the use of a punch card. Every time a customer drives in, we punch the driver's card. This card associates the current visit with all of the previous visits. Essentially, the punch card provides us with a form of correlation. Without it we would have a very hard time remembering which customers had visited us before.

7.3.1   Correlation in abstract

To establish a neutral point of reference, let's start with a very basic description of correlation without any reference to its implementation. In tightly bound communication frameworks the issue of correlated units of communication (individual transmissions) rarely arose. The technology that enabled tightly bound communication between components, databases, and legacy applications typically established an active connection that persisted for the duration of a given business activity (or longer). Because the connection remained active, context was inherently present, and correlation between individual transmissions of data was intrinsically managed by the technology protocol itself.

Things change dramatically when you fiddle with the coupling, however. When one stateless service sends a message to another, it loses control of the message and preserves no context of the activity in which the message is participating. It is up to the message to introduce the concept of correlation to provide services with the ability to associate a message with others.

This is achieved by embedding a value in the message that is propagated to all related messages. When a service processes a message and locates this value, it can establish a form of context, in that it can be used to associate this message with others. The nature of the context can vary. For example, a message could be part of a simple exchange activity, an atomic transaction, or a long running orchestration.

Let's now take a look at how correlation is achieved within some of the composition environments we covered in Chapter 6 and the messaging extensions discussed so far in this chapter.

7.3.2   Correlation in MEPs and activities

Because they are generic and non-business-specific in nature, MEPs and activities have no predefined notion of correlation. They are simple, conceptual building blocks incorporated and assembled by either custom-developed solutions that employ custom correlation identifiers and related processing logic or by specifications that impose proprietary forms of correlation (as described next).

7.3.3 Correlation in coordination

The context management framework provided by WS-Coordination establishes a sophisticated mechanism for propagating identifiers and context information between services. A separate activation service is responsible for creating new activities and subsequently generating and distributing corresponding context data. Services can forward this information to others that can use it to register for participation in the activity.

While context management uses a correlation-type identifier to uniquely represent a specific activity context, it goes well beyond correlation features to provide a comprehensive context management framework that can be leveraged through activity protocols, such as those supplied by the WS-AtomicTransaction and WS-BusinessActivity extensions.

7.3.4 Correlation in orchestration

WS-BPEL orchestrations need to concern themselves with the correlation of messages between process and partner services. This involves the added complexity of representing specific process instances within the correlation data. Further complicating this scenario is the fact that a single message may participate in multiple contexts, each identified by a separate correlation value.

To facilitate these requirements, the WS-BPEL specification defines specific syntax that allows for the creation of extensible *correlation sets*. These message properties can be dynamically added, deleted, and altered to reflect a wide variety of message exchange scenarios and environments.

7.3.5 Correlation in addressing

WS-Addressing's message id and relationship MI headers provide inherent correlation abilities, which can be leveraged by many composition and messaging extensions.

7.3.6 Correlation in reliable messaging

Every message that participates in a WS-ReliableMessaging sequence carries sequence information with it. This data consists of a sequence identifier that represents the series of messages required to follow the messaging rules of the sequence, along with a message identifier that identifies how the current message fits into the overall sequence. As a whole, this information can be considered correlation-related. However, its primary purpose is to support the enforcement of reliability rules.

7.3.7   Correlation and SOA

Correlation is a key contributor to preserving service autonomy and statelessness. Though simple by nature, the ability to tie messages together without requiring that services somehow manage this association is an important function of correlation, primarily because of how common message associations are in enterprise SOAs.

CASE STUDY

The PO Submission Process we described in Chapter 6 consists of a complex activity involving the TLS Purchase Order and the RailCo Order Fulfillment Services. In our previous examples we explained how the path of the PO message can be determined and extended dynamically at runtime and how it spans multiple services.

For each service that receives the PO message to understand the context under which it should process the message contents, it needs to be able to differentiate the message from others. It accomplishes this by associating a unique value with the message. In this case, the message identifier used is a value partially auto-generated and partially derived from the message PO number.

SUMMARY OF KEY POINTS

- Correlation is a required part of any SOA, as it enables the persistence of activity context across multiple message exchanges, while preserving the loosely coupled nature of service-oriented solutions.

- WS-* specifications implement correlation in different ways, but many specifications increasingly are relying on WS-Addressing for a form of standardized correlation.

- Even though values from a message's content can be used for correlation purposes, SOAP headers are the most common location for correlation identifiers.

- Correlation is an essential part of messaging within SOA, as it preserves service statelessness and (to an extent) supports message autonomy.

7.4 Policies

We now take a bit of a leap from the advanced messaging part of this chapter over to the WS-* extensions that provide enhanced metadata features for Web services.

Every automated business task is subject to rules and constraints. These characteristics trickle down to govern the behavior of the underlying services that automate the task.

The source of these restrictions could be:

- actual business-level requirements
- the nature of the data being exchanged
- organizational security measures

Further, every service and message has unique characteristics that may be of interest to other services that cross its path.

Examples include:

- behavioral characteristics
- preferences
- technical limitations
- quality of service (QoS) characteristics

Services can be outfitted with publicly accessible metadata that describes properties such as the ones listed here. This information is housed in a *policy* (Figure 7.19).

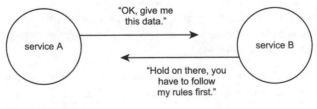

Figure 7.19
Policies can express a variety of service properties, including rules.

The use of policies allows a service to express various characteristics and preferences and keeps it from having to implement and enforce rules and constraints in a custom manner. It adds an important layer of abstraction that allows service properties to be independently managed.

NOTE

This section focuses on the design of policies for use with Web services. It is worth noting that polices can be attached to additional types of Web resources.

IN PLAIN ENGLISH

The first thing drivers see when they pull up to our operation is a sign that explains a few things about the car wash.

The sign lists three specific points:

- After driving to the car washing area, turn the engine off and exit the car.
- Our power washing equipment can be very loud. Beware.
- We recommend that you wait inside the gas station until the car wash has completed.

The first point is a rule that customers must follow before the car washing process can begin. The second is an informational statement explaining a behavioral characteristic of the car wash. The final point indicates a preference of ours (it is safer for customers and easier for us if they stay out of the way of the workers). Each of these items expresses part of an overall policy.

7.4.1 The WS-Policy framework

The WS-Policy framework establishes extensions that govern the assembly and structure of policy description documents (Figure 7.20), as well as the association of policies to Web resources. This framework is comprised of the following three specifications:

- WS-Policy
- WS-PolicyAttachments
- WS-PolicyAssertions

Note also that the WS-Policy framework forms part of the WS-Security framework. Specifically, the WS-SecurityPolicy specification defines a set of policy assertions intended for use with WS-Security (introduced later in this chapter).

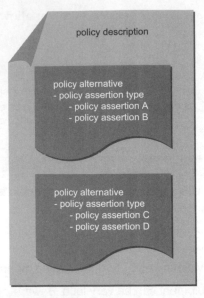

Figure 7.20

The basic structure of a policy description.

Policies can be programmatically accessed to provide service requestors with an understanding of the requirements and restrictions of service providers at runtime. Alternatively, policies can be studied by humans at design time to develop service requestors designed to interact with specific service providers.

Recent revisions to the WS-Policy framework have extended the structure of a policy description and its associated terminology. The sections below provide a brief overview.

NOTE
The *WS-Policy language basics* section in Chapter 17 provides examples of how policies are developed using the set of languages provided by WS-Policy specifications.

7.4.2 Policy assertions and policy alternatives

The service properties expressed by a policy description are represented individually by *policy assertions*. A policy description therefore is comprised of one or more policy assertions. Examples of policy assertions include service characteristics, preferences, capabilities, requirements, and rules. Each assertion can be marked as optional or required.

Policy assertions can be grouped into *policy alternatives*. Each policy alternative represents one acceptable (or allowable) combination of policy assertions. This gives a service provider the ability to offer service requestors a choice of policies. (Each of the bullet points in our last *In Plain English* analogy, for example, would warrant a policy assertion.)

7.4.3   Policy assertion types and policy vocabularies

Policy assertions can be further categorized through *policy assertion types*. Policy assertion types associate policy assertions with specific XSD schemas. In the same manner as XML vocabularies are defined in XSD schemas, *policy vocabularies* simply represent the collection of policy types within a given policy. Similarly, a *policy alternative vocabulary* refers to the policy types contained within a specific policy alternative.

7.4.4   Policy subjects and policy scopes

A policy can be associated with a Web service, a message, or another resource. Whatever a policy is intended for is called a *policy subject*. Because a single policy can have more than one subject, the collection of a policy's subjects is referred to as the *policy scope*.

7.4.5   Policy expressions and policy attachments

Policy assertions that are physically implemented using the WS-Policy language are referred to as *policy expressions*. In other words, a policy expression is simply the XML statement used to express a policy assertion in a manner so that it can be programmatically processed. Policy expressions are physically bound to policy scopes using *policy attachments*.

7.4.6   What you really need to know

If your head is spinning at this point, don't worry. Of the many concepts we just introduced, you only need to retain the following key terms to maintain a conceptual understanding of polices:

- policy
- policy alternative
- policy assertion
- policy attachment

Let's now finish this section with a look at how policies are used by other WS-* extensions and SOA as a whole.

7.4.7 Policies in coordination

When the WS-Coordination context coordination service generates context information for participating services, it can make the distribution of context data subject to the validation of security credentials and other forms of policy information. To enforce these requirements, WS-Coordination can incorporate rules established in policies.

7.4.8 Policies in orchestration and choreography

Policies can be applied to just about any subjects that are part of orchestrations or choreographies. For example, a policy can establish various requirements for orchestration partner services and choreography participants to interact.

7.4.9 Policies in reliable messaging

The WS-ReliableMessaging specification depends on the use of the WS-Policy framework to enable some of its most fundamental features. Policies are used to implement delivery assurances through the attachment of policy assurances to the messages that take part in reliable messaging exchanges. A further set of policy assertions is provided to add various supplemental rules, constraints and reliability requirements.

7.4.10 Policies and SOA

If an SOA is a city, then policies are certainly the laws, regulations, and guidelines that exist to maintain order among inhabitants. Policies are a necessary requirement to building enterprise-level service-oriented environments, as they provide a means of communicating constraints, rules, and guidelines for just about any facet of service interaction. As a result, they improve the overall quality of the loosely coupled arrangement services are required to maintain (Figure 7.21).

Policies allow services to express so much more about themselves beyond the fundamental data format and message exchange requirements established by WSDL definitions. And policies enable services to broaden the range of available metadata while still allowing them to retain their respective independence.

The use of policies increases SOA's quality of service level by restricting valid message transmissions to those that conform to policy rules and requirements. A side benefit of inserting endpoint level constraints is that the application logic underlying services is not required to perform as much custom exception handling to deal with invalid message submissions.

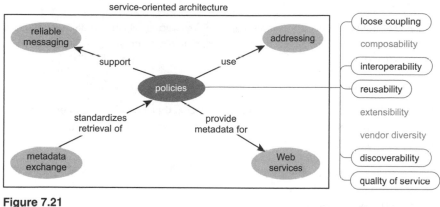

Figure 7.21
Policies relating to other parts of SOA.

Polices naturally improve the ability for services to achieve better levels of interoperation because so much more information about service endpoints can be expressed and published. Finally, because they increase the richness of service contracts, they open the door to dynamic discovery and binding.

CASE STUDY

TLS recently upgraded some of its middleware, which now provides support for the most recent version of the WS-ReliableMessaging specification. TLS wants to utilize this support but realizes that its partners still may need to continue using the previous version of WS-ReliableMessaging for some time. As a result, it chooses to support both versions by issuing a policy document containing a policy alternative.

This policy alternative states that its Vendor Profile Service will accept invoice submission sequence headers that conform to both versions of WS-ReliableMessaging, but it also expresses the fact that the newer version is preferred by TLS.

Later, TLS expands these policy assertions to include a requirement for a specific message encoding type. Regardless of which alternative is chosen by a service requestor, the same text encoding format is required.

SUMMARY OF KEY POINTS

- The WS-Policy framework provides a means of attaching properties (such as rules, behaviors, requirements, and preferences) to Web resources, most notably Web services.

- Individual properties are represented by policy assertions, which can be marked as optional or required. This allows a service to communicate non-negotiable and preferred policies.

- WS-Policy can be incorporated within the majority of WS-* extensions.

- Polices add an important layer of metadata to SOAs that increases the interoperability and discovery potential for services, while also elevating the overall quality of messaging within SOA.

7.5 Metadata exchange

When we first introduced the concept of loose coupling in Chapter 3, we explained that the sole requirement for a service requestor to interact with a service provider acting as the ultimate receiver is that the service requestor be in possession of the service provider's service description. The WSDL definition, along with any associated XSD schemas, provides the basic set of metadata required to send valid SOAP messages for consumption by the service provider.

Having just covered policies in the previous section, it is clear that, when used, policies add another important layer to the metadata stack. Using policies, our service requestor now can send SOAP messages that comply with both the WSDL interface requirements and the associated policy assertions.

Again, though, regardless of how much metadata a service makes available, the fact is that we still need to retrieve this information by either:

- manually locating it by searching for published documents
- manually requesting it by contacting the service provider entity (the service owner)
- programmatically retrieving it via a public service registry
- programmatically retrieving it by interacting with proprietary interfaces made available by the service provider entity

With the exception of using the public service registry, none of these options are particularly attractive or efficient. It would be ideal if we could simply send a standardized request such as, "give me all of the information I need to evaluate and interact with your service provider." This is exactly what *metadata exchange* accomplishes (Figure 7.22).

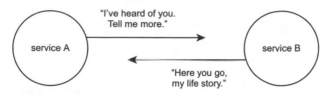

Figure 7.22
Metadata exchanges let service requestors ask what they want to know about service providers.

IN PLAIN ENGLISH

As the workload at our car wash increases, we get to the point where we are ready to hire a new worker on a full-time basis. Instead of posting an advertisement, we decide to approach a number of people we already know.

Our first request of interested candidates is that they provide us with a résumé. Because we want to check references, we always look through the résumé to see if references are attached. Sometimes they are, but most of the time it simply states that references are available upon a separate request. As a result, we contact the candidate again to request the references document.

This analogy demonstrates the simplicity of the metadata exchange concept. We first issue a request from a resource for (meta) information about that resource. If the information we receive is not sufficiently complete, we issue a second request for the remaining (meta) information.

7.5.1   The WS-MetadataExchange specification

This specification essentially allows for a service requestor to issue a standardized request message that asks for some or all of the meta information relating to a specific endpoint address.

In other words, if a service requestor knows where a service provider is located, it can use metadata exchange to request all service description documents that comprise the service contract by sending a metadata exchange request to the service provider.

Originally the WS-MetadataExchange specification specified the following three types of request messages:

- Get WSDL
- Get Schema
- Get Policy

Even though these represent the three most common types of meta information currently attached to Web services, the specification authors realized that future metadata documents would likely emerge. A subsequent revision therefore resulted in a single type of request message:

- Get Metadata

This message is further supplemented by the Get request message. Both are explained in the following sections.

> **NOTE**
>
> To see examples of WS-MetadataExchange request and response messages, see the *WS-MetadataExchange language basics* section in Chapter 17.

7.5.2   Get Metadata request and response messages

As previously mentioned, a service requestor can use metadata exchange to programmatically request available metadata documents associated with a Web service. To do so, it must issue a *Get Metadata request* message. This kicks off a standardized request and response MEP resulting in the delivery of a *Get Metadata response* message.

Here's what happens for a metadata retrieval activity to successfully complete:

1. A service requestor issues the Get Metadata request message. This message can request a specific type of service description document (WSDL, XSD schema, policy), or it can simply request that all available metadata be delivered.

2. The Get Metadata request message is received at the endpoint to which it is delivered. The requested meta information is documented in a Get Metadata response message.

3. The Get Metadata response message is delivered to the service requestor. The contents of this message can consist of the actual metadata documents, address references to the documents, or a combination of both.

Figure 7.23 illustrates these steps.

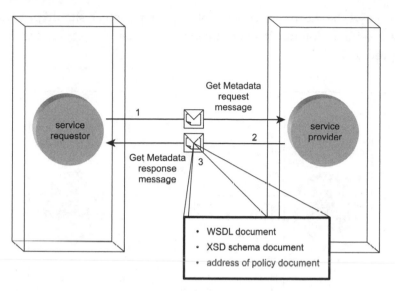

Figure 7.23
Contents of a sample Get Metadata response message.

7.5.3   Get request and response messages

In Step 3 of the preceding scenario, we explained how the Get Metadata response message does not need to actually contain all of the requested metadata. It can simply provide a list of URIs that point to the separate documents.

To allow the retrieval of *all* meta information to be fully automated, the WS-MetadataExchange specification provides a means for the service requestor to explicitly request the document content for any references that were provided as part of the original Get Metadata response message. It achieves this through the use of the *Get request* and *Get response* messages.

Here's a brief description of the steps involved in this sub-process:

1. Upon receiving the Get Metadata response message, the service requestor determines that it would like to receive the actual content of the metadata documents for which it only received references. As a result, the service requestor issues a Get request message indicating which metadata information it would like retrieved.

2. The Get request message is received at the endpoint to which it was delivered. The requested data is placed into a Get response message.

3. The Get response message is delivered to the service requestor.

Figure 7.24 shows the execution sequence of these steps, which should provide the service requestor with all the information it needs (and therefore concludes the metadata exchange process).

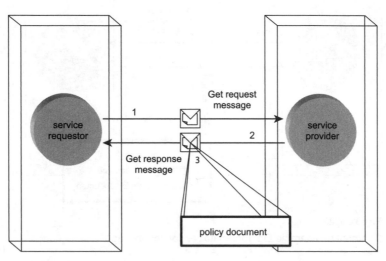

Figure 7.24
Contents of a sample Get response message.

7.5.4   Selective retrieval of metadata

Meta documents describing services with comprehensive interfaces and features can be large in size, especially when assembled into one mega-description. Use of the selective Get request message type therefore reduces the chances of unnecessary information being transported.

The Get Metadata response message first sends along what is considered the essential piece of service meta information. It is then up to the service requestor to determine what further metadata it requires. (Note that the endpoint to which a Get Metadata request message is sent can represent multiple WSDL, XSD schema, and policy documents.)

7.5.5   Metadata exchange and service description discovery

It also is important to note that metadata exchange does not really help service requestors discover service providers. Service registries, such as those implemented using the UDDI standard, can be used to discover service descriptions that meet certain search criteria. While service registries also provide location information for the actual WSDL definition of a service, they can be used in conjunction with metadata exchange messages.

Essentially, a service requestor could first query a public registry to retrieve the endpoint addresses of any Web service candidates that appear to provide the sought-after features. The same requestor could then employ metadata exchange to contact each candidate and request associated metadata documents. This would give the service requestor more information to better assess which service provider it should be working with. It also would provide the service requestor with all of the details it needs to begin interacting with the chosen service. So while it may not further the cause of attaining discoverable services, it does support discovery by rounding out the overall dynamic discovery process.

7.5.6   Metadata exchange and version control

So far we've focused on the ability of metadata exchange to enable service requestors to retrieve any necessary meta information for them to begin interacting with service providers. Another important aspect of this WS-* extension is its potential to automate the administration of service contracts.

As services evolve, the nature and scope of the functionality they deliver can undergo alterations. This can result in changes trickling down to the service meta layer, which, in turn, can lead to new versions of a service's WSDL, XSD schema, or policy documents.

This raises the age-old version control challenges. Service requestors already interacting with a service provider either need to be notified ahead of time of upcoming changes, or they need to be supported with an outdated service description.

Some services-based solutions have dealt with this problem by building custom operations that can be used to retrieve the latest service description (metadata) information. While the same functionality is essentially provided by metadata exchange, the main benefit of its use is that it implements this feature in a standardized manner. Now any service-oriented application that supports metadata exchange can allow service requestors to retrieve the latest service contract as often as they like.

When changes to meta information are expected to occur frequently, a service requestor could be programmed to periodically retrieve available metadata documents to compare them to the documents already in use. In fact, service requestors could even build metadata exchange features into their exception handling. If a standard SOAP request is rejected by the service provider as a result of an interface, schema, or policy incompatibility error, the service requestor's exception handling routine could respond by retrieving and checking the latest metadata documents.

7.5.7 Metadata exchange and SOA

The simple concepts behind metadata exchange support some key aspects of SOA (Figure 7.25). Its ability to automate the retrieval of meta information reinforces loose coupling between services, and increases the ability for service requestors to learn more about available service providers. By standardizing access to and retrieval of metadata, service requestors can programmatically query a multitude of candidate providers. Because enough service provider metadata can more easily be retrieved and evaluated, the overall discovery process is improved, and the likelihood for services to be reused is increased.

By establishing a standardized means of service description exchange, this extension can vastly improve interoperability when broadly applied to volatile environments. By being able to query service providers prior to attempting access, requestors can verify that the correct metadata is in fact being used for their planned message exchanges. This can increase the QoS factor of SOA, as it tends to avoid a multitude of maintenance problems associated with service contract changes.

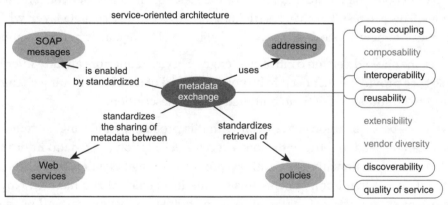

Figure 7.25
Metadata exchange relating to other parts of SOA.

It is also worth mentioning that metadata exchange reduces the need for developers to attain meta information at design time and eliminates the need for custom-developed metadata retrieval extensions. Finally, the dynamic exchange of service descriptions can lead to the potential of automating version control and other metadata-related functions.

As TLS continues to evolve its B2B solution, new features are added and some existing functionality is modified. This can, occasionally, result in changes to the WSDL interface definitions of TLS services, as well as revisions to service policies. Any of these changes can obviously affect the online partners that regularly connect to TLS.

Therefore, all public TLS services support the processing of WS-MetadataExchange requests. At the onset, partners who register for the TLS B2B solution are strongly encouraged to issue Get Metadata request messages frequently to receive the latest service contracts.

RailCo learned about this the hard way. To date they never bothered incorporating metadata exchange functionality within their services, as they were not required to do so. After a change to the TLS Accounts Payable Service WSDL, though, the RailCo Invoice Submission Service submitted an invoice message that was rejected by TLS.

The resulting error description was unclear, and exception handling logic within the RailCo service assumed this condition was the result of the TLS service being unavailable. It was therefore designed to periodically retry the message submission on a daily basis. Only after three days did someone at RailCo notice that an acknowledgement had not been received from TLS. A lengthy investigation led to the eventual discovery that the failed submissions were the result of a change to the TLS WSDL definition.

As a result of this experience, RailCo revised their Invoice Submission Service to interact with the metadata exchange functionality offered by TLS (Figure 7.26). The service now issues a periodic Get Metadata message to the TLS Accounts Payable Service.

The Accounts Payable Service responds with a Get Metadata response message containing its current WSDL, XSD schema, and policy information. The RailCo Invoice Submission Service verifies that the service description documents used by RailCo match those currently published by the TLS service.

If the verification succeeds, it's business as usual, and RailCo proceeds to issue invoice submission messages. If the metadata does not match, a special error condition is raised at RailCo's end, and no further invoices are sent until it is addressed by an administrator.

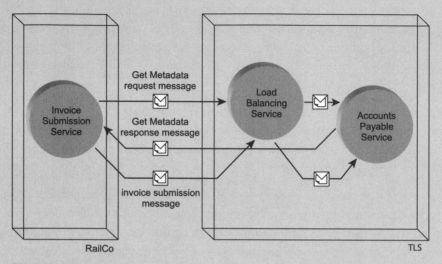

Figure 7.26

The revised RailCo Invoice Submission Process now includes a periodic metadata exchange with TLS.

SUMMARY OF KEY POINTS

- Metadata exchange allows service requestors to issue request messages to retrieve metadata for service providers.

- The WS-MetadataExchange specification standardizes two types of request messages: the Get Metadata request (which returns metadata content and/or references) and the Get request (which returns the content of a previously returned reference).

- Metadata exchange assists in improving the service description discovery process and in alleviating version control issues related to service meta information.

- Automated metadata retrieval leads to several standardized improvements within SOA and reinforces the loosely coupled nature of autonomous services.

7.6   Security

Security requirements for automation solutions are nothing new to the world of IT. Similarly, service-oriented applications need to be outfitted to handle many of the traditional security demands of protecting information and ensuring that access to logic is only granted to those permitted.

However, the SOAP messaging communications framework, upon which contemporary SOA is built, emphasizes particular aspects of security that need to be accommodated by a security framework designed specifically for Web services.

A family of security extensions parented by the WS-Security specification comprise such a framework, further broadened by a series of supplementary specifications with specialized feature sets. Sidebar 7.1 provides a list of current security-related specifications. While we clearly cannot discuss concepts for all of them, it is worth spending some time looking at the basic functions performed by the following three core specifications:

- WS-Security

- XML-Signature

- XML-Encryption

Additionally, we'll briefly explore the fundamental concepts behind *single sign-on*, a form of centralized security that complements these WS-Security extensions.

Sidebar 7.1   A list of security specifications that may be used as part of SOA. For more information regarding these specifications, visit: www.soaspecs.com.

- WS-Security
- WS-SecurityPolicy
- WS-Trust
- WS-SecureConversation
- WS-Federation
- Extensible Access Control Markup Language (XACML)
- Extensible Rights Markup Language (XrML)
- XML Key Management (XKMS)
- XML-Signature
- XML-Encryption
- Security Assertion Markup Language (SAML)
- .NET Passport
- Secure Sockets Layer (SSL)
- WS-I Basic Security Profile

Before we begin, it is worth noting that this section organizes security concepts as they pertain to and support the following five common security requirements: identification, authentication, authorization, confidentiality, and integrity.

> **NOTE**
>
> For an overview of the core language elements from the WS-Security, XML-Encryption, and XML-Signature languages, see the *WS-Security language basics* section in Chapter 17.

IN PLAIN ENGLISH

Toward the end of a working day, Jim leaves the car wash early. He has an appointment with someone selling a used power washer that we are interested in buying. Before he can meet this person, Jim must stop by the bank to withdraw a fair amount of money for the potential purchase (the seller has stated that this must be a cash sale). I also ask Jim to do me a favor and pick up a package that's waiting for me at a postal outlet near the bank.

Jim agrees and proceeds on his errand trip. Upon entering the bank, Jim must fill out a withdrawal slip on which he is asked to identify himself by writing his full name. Jim then comes face-to-face with a bank teller who, upon seeing that he wants to make a withdrawal, requests that he produce a bank card and one piece of photo ID.

Jim shows the teller his business account card and his driver's license, which the teller subsequently verifies. After it is confirmed that Jim is who he stated he was on the withdrawal slip, the teller asks Jim to enter his bank card pass code. This further ensures that he is an individual allowed to make this type of withdrawal.

With the money in hand, Jim proceeds to the postal outlet. There he presents the notification card I received in the mail indicating that a parcel is being held for me. Jim states his name (and therefore does not claim to be the same person whose name is on the notification card) and also states that he is here to pick up the parcel for someone else. The employee at the postal outlet asks Jim for ID, so he pulls out his driver's license again. Upon reviewing the information on the driver's license and the notification card, the employee informs Jim that he cannot pick up this package.

Jim's experience at the bank required that he go through three levels of clearance: identification (withdrawal slip), authentication (bank card and photo ID), and authorization (pass code and bank record). While no security was really applied to the identification part of this process, it did kick off the remaining two security phases for which Jim satisfied requirements (and for which reason he subsequently received the requested money).

At the post office, though, Jim did not pass the authorization stage. Only individuals that share the last name or reside at the same address of the person identified on the notification card are allowed to pick up deliveries on their behalf. Jim's claimed identity was authenticated by the driver's license, but because Jim is not a relative of mine and does not live at the same address as I do, he did not meet the requirement that would have authorized him to pick up the parcel.

7.6.1 Identification, authentication, and authorization

For a service requestor to access a secured service provider, it must first provide information that expresses its origin or owner. This is referred to as making a *claim* (Figure 7.27). Claims are represented by identification information stored in the SOAP header. WS-Security establishes a standardized header block that stores this information, at which point it is referred to as a *token*.

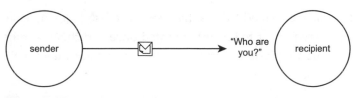

Figure 7.27
An identity is a claim made regarding the origin of a message.

Authentication requires that a message being delivered to a recipient prove that the message is in fact from the sender that it claims to be (Figure 7.28). In other words, the service must provide proof that its claimed identity is true.

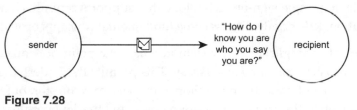

Figure 7.28
Authentication means proving an identity.

Once authenticated, the recipient of a message may need to determine what the requestor is allowed to do. This is called *authorization* (Figure 7.29).

Figure 7.29
Authorization means determining to what extent authentication applies.

7.6.2   Single sign-on

A challenge facing the enablement of authentication and authorization within SOA is propagating the authentication and authorization information for a service requestor across multiple services behind the initial service provider. Because services are autonomous and independent from each other, a mechanism is required to persist the security context established after a requestor has been authenticated. Otherwise, the requestor would need to re-authenticate itself with every subsequent request.

The concept of single sign-on addresses this issue. The use of a single sign-on technology allows a service requestor to be authenticated once and then have its security context information shared with other services that the requestor may then access without further authentication.

There are three primary extensions that support the implementation of the single sign-on concept:

- SAML (Security Assertion Markup Language)
- .NET Passport
- XACML (XML Access Control Markup Language)

As an example of a single sign-on technology that supports centralized authentication and authorization, let's briefly discuss some fundamental concepts provided by SAML.

SAML implements a single sign-on system in which the point of contact for a service requestor can also act as an *issuing authority*. This permits the underlying logic of that service not only to authenticate and authorize the service requestor, but also to assure the other services that the service requestor has attained this level of clearance.

Other services that the service requestor contacts, therefore, do not need to perform authentication and authorization steps. Instead, upon receiving a request, they simply contact the issuing authority to ask for the authentication and authorization clearance it originally obtained. The issuing authority provides this information in the form of *assertions* that communicate the security details. (The two types of assertions that contain authentication and authorization information are simply called *authentication assertions* and *authorization assertions*.)

In Figure 7.30 we illustrate some of the mechanics behind SAML.

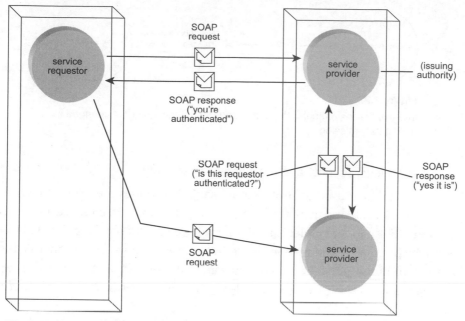

Figure 7.30

A basic message exchange demonstrating single sign-on (in this case, as implemented by SAML).

7.6.3   Confidentiality and integrity

Confidentiality is concerned with protecting the privacy of the message contents (Figure 7.31). A message is considered to have remained confidential if no service or agent in its message path not authorized to do so viewed its contents.

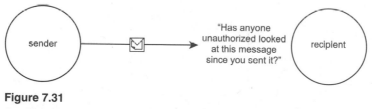

Figure 7.31

Confidentiality means that the privacy of the message has been protected throughout its message path.

Integrity ensures that a message has not been altered since its departure from the original sender (Figure 7.32). This guarantees that the state of the message contents remained intact from the time of transmission to the point of delivery.

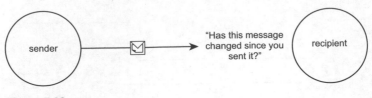

Figure 7.32

Integrity means ensuring that a message's contents have not changed during transmission.

7.6.4 Transport-level security and message-level security

The type of technology used to protect a message determines the extent to which the message remains protected while making its way through its message path. Secure Sockets Layer (SSL), for example, is a very popular means of securing the HTTP channel upon which requests and responses are transmitted. However, within a Web services-based communications framework, it can only protect a message during the transmission between service endpoints. Hence, SSL only affords us *transport-level* security (Figure 7.33).

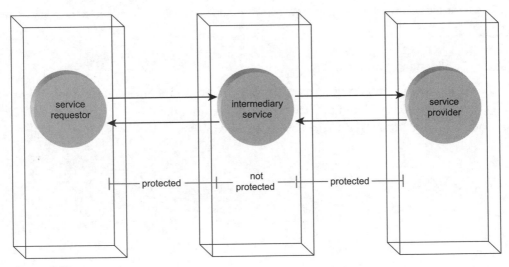

Figure 7.33

Transport-level security only protects the message during transit between service endpoints.

If, for example, a service intermediary takes possession of a message, it still may have the ability to alter its contents. To ensure that a message is fully protected along its entire message path, *message-level security* is required (Figure 7.34). In this case, security measures are applied to the message itself (not to the transport channel on which the message travels). Now, regardless of where the message may travel, the security measures applied go with it.

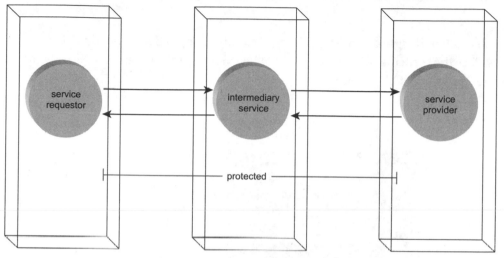

Figure 7.34
Message-level security guarantees end-to-end message protection.

7.6.5   Encryption and digital signatures

Message-level confidentiality for an XML-based messaging format, such as SOAP, can be realized through the use of specifications that comprise the WS-Security framework. In this section we focus on XML-Encryption and XML-Signature, two of the more important WS-Security extensions that provide security controls that ensure the confidentiality and integrity of a message.

XML-Encryption, an encryption technology designed for use with XML, is a cornerstone part of the WS-Security framework. It provides features with which encryption can be applied to an entire message or only to specific parts of the message (such as the password).

To ensure message integrity, a technology is required that is capable of verifying that the message received by a service is authentic in that it has not been altered in any manner since it first was sent. XML-Signature provides features that allow for an XML document to be accompanied by a special algorithm-driven piece of information that represents a digital signature. This signature is tied to the content of the document so that verification of the signature by the receiving service only will succeed if the content has remained unaltered since it first was sent.

> **NOTE**
>
> Digital signatures also support the concept of non-repudiation, which can prove that a message containing a (usually legally binding) document was sent by a specific requestor and delivered to a specific provider.

As illustrated in Figure 7.35, XML-Encryption can be applied to parts of a SOAP header, as well as the contents of the SOAP body. When signing a document, the XML-Signature can reside in the SOAP header.

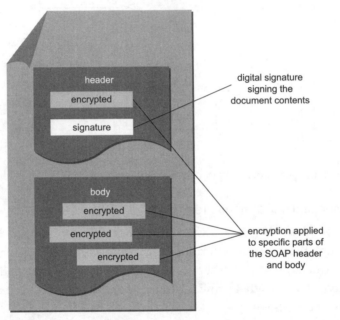

Figure 7.35
A digitally signed SOAP message containing encrypted data.

> **NOTE**
>
> Both encryption and digital signature technologies rely on the use of *keys*. These are special values used to unlock the algorithm upon which encryption and digital signatures are based. *Shared keys* are typically used by encryption technologies and require that both the sender and receiver of a message use the same key. *Public/private key pairs* are commonly used by digital signature technologies, where the message sender signs the document with a key that is different from the one used by the recipient. (One of the keys is public, but the other is private.)

7.6.6   Security and SOA

Message-level security can clearly become a core component of service-oriented solutions. Security measures can be layered over any message transmissions to either protect the message content or the message recipient. The WS-Security framework and its accompanying specifications therefore fulfill fundamental QoS requirements that enable enterprises to:

- utilize service-oriented solutions for the processing of sensitive and private data

- restrict service access as required

As shown in Figure 7.36, the security framework provided by WS-Security also makes use of the WS-Policy framework explained earlier (a separate specification called WS-SecurityPolicy provides a series of supporting policy assertions).

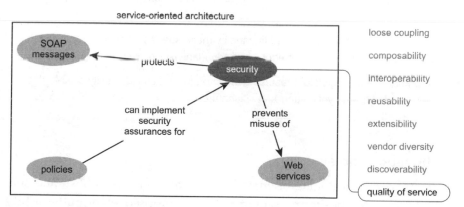

Figure 7.36

Security, as it relates to policies, SOAP messages, and Web services.

CASE STUDY

TLS has a message-level security policy that applies to any business documents sent to its B2B solution.

The policy has the following rules:

- Any dollar values residing in documents sent via SOAP messages must be encrypted.

- Any invoice submitted to TLS with a total dollar value of over $30,000 must also be digitally signed.

To comply with this policy, RailCo is required to apply XML-Encryption to the parts of the invoice message sent by the Invoice Submission Service that contain monetary values.

It further embeds a business rule into the Invoice Submission Service's underlying logic that checks for invoice totals that exceed the $30,000 mark. Those that do, have their corresponding SOAP message documents digitally signed using XML-Signature.

SUMMARY OF KEY POINTS

- Security within SOA is a multi-faceted subject matter that encompasses the feature set of numerous specifications. The WS-Security framework governs a subset of these specifications, and establishes a cohesive and composable security architecture.

- The primary aspects of security addressed by these specifications are identification, authentication, authorization, integrity, and confidentiality, as well as non-repudiation.

- Two primary technologies for preserving the integrity and confidentiality of XML documents are XML-Encryption and XML-Signature.

7.7   Notification and eventing

With its roots in the messaging-oriented middleware era, the publish-and-subscribe MEP introduces a composite messaging model, comprised of primitive MEPs that implement a push delivery pattern. It establishes a unique relationship between service providers and service requestors where information is exchanged (often blindly) to achieve a form of dynamic *notification* (Figure 7.37).

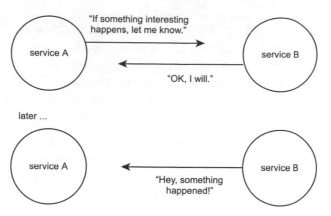

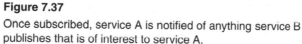

Figure 7.37

Once subscribed, service A is notified of anything service B
publishes that is of interest to service A.

While notification itself can be applied to different types of MEPs, the focus of this
section is a discussion of notification within the context of the publish-and-subscribe
pattern.

7.7.1 Publish-and-subscribe in abstract

As explained in Chapter 6, this messaging pattern can be classified as a complex MEP
assembled from a series of primitive MEPs. It involves a *publisher* service that makes
information categorized by different *topics* available to registered *subscriber* services.
Subscribers can choose which topics they want to register for, either by interacting with
the publisher directly or by communicating with a separate *broker* service. A topic is an
item of interest and often is tied to the occurrence of an event.

When a new piece of information on a given topic becomes available, a publisher broadcasts this information to all those services that have subscribed to that topic. Alternatively, a *broker* service can be used to perform the broadcast on the publisher's behalf.
This decouples the publisher from the subscriber, allowing each to act independently
and without knowledge of each other.

IN PLAIN ENGLISH

Both our car wash company and our partner's are members of the World-Wide Car Washing Consortium (W3CC), an international organization dedicated to the advancement of the field of car washing. This organization issues weekly bulletins on a number of different topics. Members can sign up for the bulletins that are of most interest to them.

Our partner wants to stay informed with most of what occurs in the car washing industry, so they are registered to receive almost all of the bulletins. We are more interested in advancements relating to soap technology and sponging techniques. Our company, therefore, only subscribes to bulletins that discuss these topics.

Whenever industry developments (events) occur that we have expressed an interest in and for as long as our subscriptions are valid, bulletins (notifications) are sent to us (the subscribers).

7.7.2 One concept, two specifications

Two major implementations of the publish-and-subscribe pattern exist:

- The WS-Notification framework
- The WS-Eventing specification

Spearheaded by IBM and Microsoft respectively, these use different approaches and terminology to cover much of the same ground. It is expected that a single publish-and-subscribe specification eventually will emerge as an industry standard. The remainder of this section is dedicated to exploring features of both specifications.

7.7.3 The WS-Notification Framework

As with other WS-* frameworks, what is represented by WS-Notification is a family of related extensions that have been designed with composability in mind.

- WS-BaseNotification—Establishes the standardized interfaces used by services involved on either end of a notification exchange.
- WS-Topics—Governs the structuring and categorization of topics.
- WS-BrokeredNotification—Standardizes the broker intermediary used to send and receive messages on behalf of publishers and subscribers.

> **NOTE**
>
> To improve clarity, we take the liberty of breaking up some of the large concatenated terms provided in the WS-Notification specifications. For example, the term "NotificationMessage" in the WS-BaseNotification specification is expressed as "notification message" in this section.

Situations, notification messages, and topics

The notification process typically is tied to an event that is reported on by the publisher. This event is referred to as a *situation*. Situations can result in the generation of one or more *notification messages*. These messages contain information about (or relating to) the situation, and are categorized according to an available set of *topics*. Through this categorization, notification messages can be delivered to services that have subscribed to corresponding topics.

Notification producers and publishers

So far we've been using the familiar "publisher" and "subscriber" terms to describe the roles services assume when they participate in the publish-and-subscribe pattern. Within WS-Notification, however, these terms have more distinct definitions.

The term *publisher* represents the part of the solution that responds to situations and is responsible for generating notification messages. However, a publisher is not necessarily required to distribute these messages. Distribution of notification messages is the task of the *notification producer*. This service keeps track of subscriptions and corresponds directly with subscribers. It ensures that notification messages are organized by topic and delivered accordingly.

Note that:

- A publisher may or may not be a Web service, whereas the notification producer is always a Web service.
- A single Web service can assume both publisher and notification producer roles.
- The notification producer is considered the service provider.

Notification consumers and subscribers

A *subscriber* is the part of the application that submits the subscribe request message to the notification producer. This means that the subscriber is not necessarily the recipient of the notification messages transmitted by the notification producer. The recipient is the *notification consumer*, the service to which the notification messages are delivered (Figure 7.38).

Note that:

- A subscriber does not need to exist as a Web service, but the notification consumer is a Web service.
- Both the subscriber and notification consumer roles can be assumed by a single Web service.
- The subscriber is considered the service requestor.

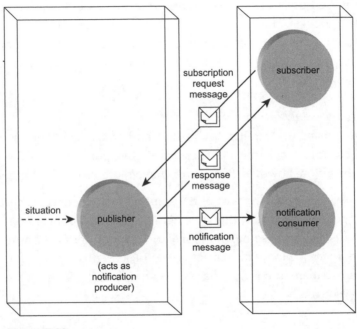

Figure 7.38
A basic notification architecture.

Notification broker, publisher registration manager, and subscription manager
To alleviate the need for direct contact between the two groups of services we described in the previous two sections, a set of supplementary services is available (Figure 7.39).

- The *notification broker*—A Web service that acts on behalf of the publisher to perform the role of the notification producer. This isolates the publisher from any contact with subscribers. Note that when a notification broker receives notification messages from the publisher, it temporarily assumes the role of notification consumer.

- The *publisher registration manager*—A Web service that provides an interface for subscribers to search through and locate items available for registration. This role may be assumed by the notification broker, or it may be implemented as a separate service to establish a further layer of abstraction.

- The *subscription manager*—A Web service that allows notification producers to access and retrieve required subscriber information for a given notification message broadcast. This role also can be assumed by either the notification producer or a dedicated service.

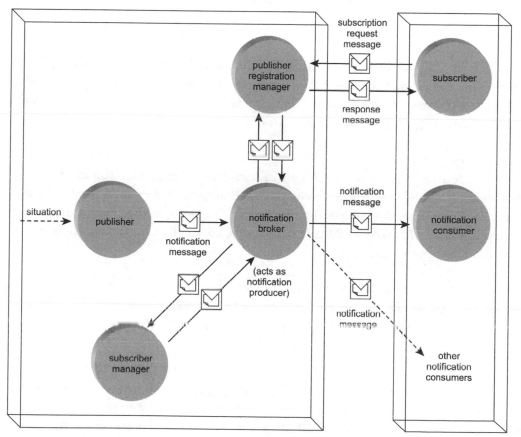

Figure 7.39

A notification architecture including a middle tier.

7.7.4   The WS-Eventing specification

As its name implies, WS-Eventing addresses publish-and-subscribe requirements by focusing on an event-oriented messaging model. When an event related to one Web service occurs, any other services that have expressed interest in the event are subsequently notified. Following are brief explanations of the terms and concepts expressed by the WS-Eventing specification.

Event sources

The term "publisher" is never actually mentioned in the WS-Eventing specification. Instead, its role is assumed by a broader-scoped Web service, known as the *event source*. This part of the eventing architecture is responsible for both receiving subscription requests and for issuing corresponding notification messages that report information about occurred events.

Event sinks and subscribers

On the subscription end of the eventing model, separate Web services manage the processing of notification and subscription messages. An *event sink* is a service designed to consume (receive) notification messages from the event source. *Subscribers* are services capable of issuing various types of subscription requests.

Subscription managers

An event source, by default, assumes the responsibility of managing subscriptions and transmitting notifications. In high volume environments it may be desirable to split these roles into separate services. To alleviate the demands on the event source, intermediate services, known as *subscription managers*, optionally can be used to distribute publisher-side processing duties.

Notification messages and subscription end messages

When an event occurs, it is reported by the event source via the issuance of a *notification message* (also called an *event message*). These are standard SOAP messages that contain WS-Eventing-compliant headers to convey event details.

WS-Eventing allows for an expiry date to be attached to subscriptions. This requires that subscribers issue renewal requests for the subscription to continue (as discussed in the next section). If a subscription is left to expire, though, it is the event source that often is expected to send a special type of notification to the corresponding event sink, called a *subscription end message*.

Subscription messages and subscription filters

Subscribers issue *subscription messages* directly to the event source or to an intermediate subscription manager. Different types of subscription-related requests can be transmitted via subscription messages.

The following specific requests are supported:

- *Subscribe*—Requests that a new subscription be created. (Note that this message also contains the filter details, as well as the endpoint destination to which a subscription end message is to be delivered. Filters are described shortly.)
- *Unsubscribe*—Requests that an existing subscription be canceled.
- *Renew*—Requests that an existing subscription scheduled to expire be renewed.
- *GetStatus*—Requests that the status of a subscription be retrieved.

For a subscriber to communicate that the event sink (on behalf of whom it is submitting the subscription request) is only interested in certain types of events, it can issue a subscription message containing a *subscription filter*. If the event source does not support filtering (or if it cannot accommodate the requested filter), the subscription request is denied.

The relationships between the subscription manager, event source, subscriber, and event sink are shown in Figure 7.40.

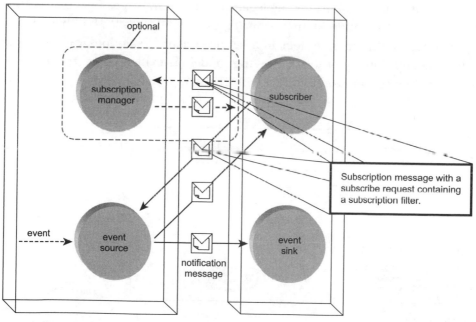

Figure 7.40
A basic eventing architecture.

7.7.5 WS-Notification and WS-Eventing

The fact that these two specifications currently provide overlapping feature sets is no indication that this will remain so in the future. It has been speculated that the reason these specifications were created separately was because the individual sponsors had diverging requirements. One of IBM's goals is to incorporate WS-Notification with its grid computing initiatives. Microsoft, on the other hand, is expected to utilize WS-Eventing within its system administration platform.

In an effort to continue promoting interoperability across proprietary platforms, IBM recently joined the WS-Eventing effort. It is entirely within the realm of possibilities that either specification will be modified to align with the other—or that the vendors involved will come to an agreement on how to establish a single notification extension that will meet their collective requirements. Language descriptions for these two specifications are therefore not currently provided in this book. (If you are interested in viewing the individual specifications, visit www.soaspecs.com.)

7.7.6 Notification, eventing, and SOA

By implementing a messaging model capable of supporting traditional publish-and-subscribe functionality, corresponding legacy features now can be fully realized within service-oriented application environments (Figure 7.41). Moreover, the ability to weave a sophisticated notification system into service-oriented solutions can significantly broaden the applicability of this messaging model (as evidenced by the before mentioned plans to incorporate notification with grid computing).

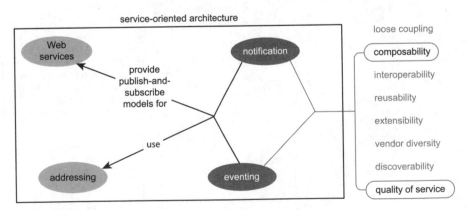

Figure 7.41
Notification and eventing establishing standardized publish-and-subscribe models within SOA.

Service-oriented solutions can increase QoS characteristics by leveraging notification mechanisms to perform various types of event reporting. For example, performance and exception management related events can trigger notification broadcasts to potential service requestors (subscribers), informing them of a variety of conditions.

CASE STUDY

In response to a series of complaints from vendors who experienced message transmission problems that resulted from changes to TLS service descriptions, TLS has decided to supplement their existing metadata exchange support by implementing a notification system. Now, business partners will be forewarned of any upcoming changes that might impact their systems.

There are many services that comprise the TLS B2B solution. Each performs a specific function that involves one or more types of partners. Not all partners need to interact with every TLS service. As a result, the notification system is set up in such a manner that partners are able to subscribe to notifications relating to specific TLS services or groups of services.

For this, TLS has provided a dedicated System Notification Service that acts as the publisher of notification messages. Partners are consequently required to implement their own subscriber services. Each notification message essentially requests that the recipient initiate a WS MetadataExchange against the provided TLS endpoint(s).

RailCo creates a separate subscription service to interact with the TLS System Notification Service. Unfortunately, RailCo calls its new service the "TLS Subscription Service," which is sure to lead to confusion in the future. Regardless, RailCo uses its service to subscribe to and receive notifications relating to the two primary services with which it interacts on a regular basis: the TLS Accounts Payable and Purchase Order Services (Figure 7.42).

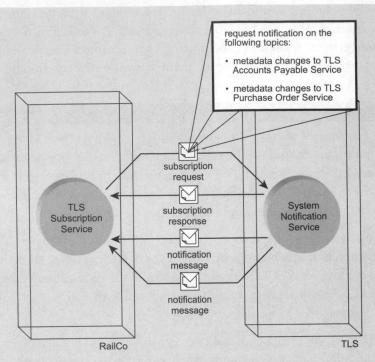

request notification on the
following topics:

• metadata changes to TLS
Accounts Payable Service

• metadata changes to TLS
Purchase Order Service

subscription
request

subscription
response

notification
message

notification
message

TLS
Subscription
Service

System
Notification
Service

RailCo

TLS

Figure 7.42

The new RailCo subscription service allows RailCo to receive notifications from the TLS System Notification Service.

SUMMARY OF KEY POINTS

- The traditional publish-and-subscribe messaging model can be implemented with
  the WS-Notification framework or the WS-Eventing specification.

- WS-Notification consists of the WS-BaseNotification, WS-Topics, and WS-Brokered-
  Notification specifications that collectively establish a subscription and notification
  system.

- The WS-Eventing specification provides similar functionality but is based on a
  moderately different architecture.

- Notification and eventing realize the popular publish-and-subscribe messaging
  model within SOA. The sophisticated messaging environment provided by SOA, in
  turn, introduces new opportunities to leverage these notification mechanisms.

Part III

SOA and Service-Orientation

So far the focus has been on the aspects of SOA as a whole. We have discussed the numerous extensions available to SOA as well as its fundamental concepts. We now turn our attention to the underlying paradigm primarily responsible for defining SOA and distinguishing it as an architectural model.

The principles and concepts covered in the next two chapters discuss the spectrum of service-orientation in detail. This establishes necessary theory that applies to the rudimentary components of primitive SOA, but also provides concepts that can be propagated and leveraged throughout service-oriented environments. For example, topics covered in these chapters form the basis for the service modeling and design processes provided in the subsequent *Building SOA* parts of this book.

Chapter 8

Principles of Service-Orientation

Before we can begin building a service-oriented solution, we need to understand what makes a service suitable for SOA. In other words, how can we build Web services that are truly service-oriented?

The answer lies in service-orientation. This approach to modeling business automation logic has resulted in a set of commonly accepted principles applied to each unit of logic that constitutes a service within an SOA. It is through the application of these principles that the primitive components of an SOA (services, descriptions, messages) are shaped in support of service-orientation.

This chapter begins with a look at how service-orientation applies to the enterprise as a whole and then discusses individual principles in-depth.

In Plain English sections

A knowledge of the principles of service-orientation is perhaps even more important than concepts covered in past chapters. They are core to the design of services regardless of what underlying technology is used to implement them. Therefore, our *In Plain English* sections return to supplement the descriptions of individual principles.

How case studies are used: As you might recall from the case study background information provided in Chapter 2, one of RailCo's business goals was to improve their existing automation processes by moving toward SOA.

In this chapter we examine the services built so far as part of RailCo's technical environment and discuss how they comply to or diverge from individual principles of service-orientation. Existing TLS services that already possess service-orientation characteristics are used for comparison purposes.

8.1 Service-orientation and the enterprise

The collective logic that defines and drives an enterprise is an ever-evolving entity constantly changing in response to external and internal influences. From an IT perspective, this *enterprise logic* can be divided into two important halves: business logic and application logic (Figure 8.1).

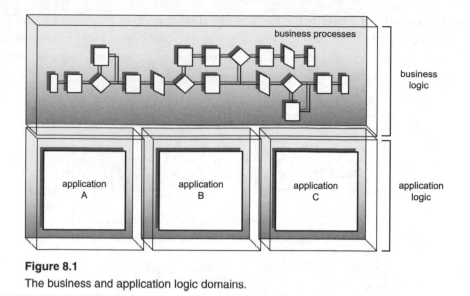

Figure 8.1

The business and application logic domains.

Each exists in a world of its own, and each represents a necessary part of contemporary organization structure. Business logic is a documented implementation of the business requirements that originate from an enterprise's business areas. Business logic is generally structured into processes that express these requirements, along with any associated constraints, dependencies, and outside influences.

Application logic is an automated implementation of business logic organized into various technology solutions. Application logic expresses business process workflows through purchased or custom-developed systems within the confines of an organization's IT infrastructure, security constraints, technical capabilities, and vendor dependencies.

Service-orientation applies to enterprise logic. It introduces new concepts that augment the manner in which this logic is represented, viewed, modeled, and shared. While the principles behind service-orientation exist in a vacuous realm of abstraction and theory, they are a necessary counterpart to the real world environments that require their guidance and structure.

The concepts introduced by service-orientation are realized through the introduction of services. Let's have a look at where services are located within the overall structure of an automated organization. As Figure 8.2 illustrates, services establish a high form of abstraction wedged between traditional business and application layers. When positioned here, services can encapsulate physical application logic as well as business process logic.

Services modularize the enterprise, forming standalone units of logic that exist within a common connectivity layer. Services can be layered so that parent services can encapsulate child services. This allows for the service layer to consist of multiple layers of abstraction (as explained later in Chapter 9).

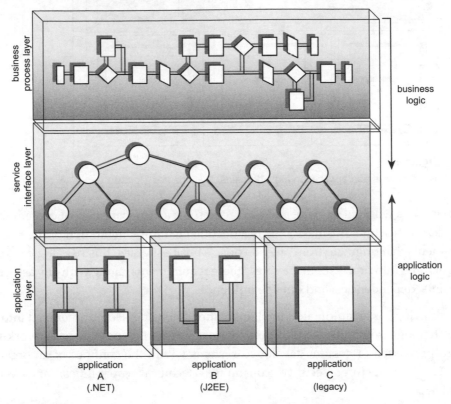

Figure 8.2

The service interface layer positioned between enterprise layers that promote application and business logic.

In Figure 8.2 we display a fragmented application layer, where individual applications are confined to the boundaries that represent their respective proprietary platform environments. Though we show services as existing in a single, continuous layer, this only illustrates the open connectivity that exists among service interfaces. Freed from proprietary ties, services can communicate via open protocols.

On a physical level, services are developed and deployed in proprietary environments, wherein they are individually responsible for the encapsulation of specific application logic. Figure 8.3 shows how individual services, represented as service interfaces within the service interface layer, represent application logic originating from different platforms.

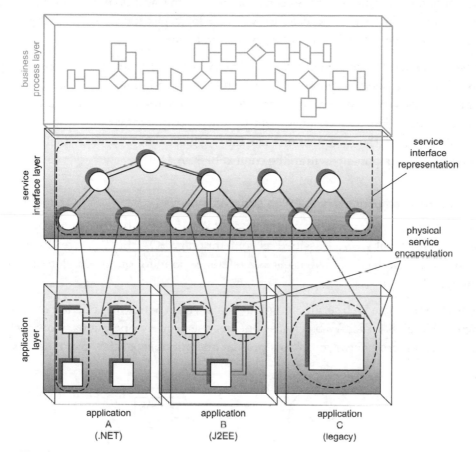

Figure 8.3

The service interface layer abstracts connectivity from service deployment environments.

SUMMARY OF KEY POINTS

- Enterprise logic can be divided into two domains: business logic and application logic. Service-oriented principles can be applied to both.

- The service interface layer positions services to represent business logic and abstract application logic.

8.2   Anatomy of a service-oriented architecture

Chapter 5 established the components of the basic (first-generation) Web services framework. This framework can be applied to implement services in just about any environment. For example, services can be appended to traditional distributed applications or used as wrappers to expose legacy system logic. However, neither of these environments resembles a "real" service-oriented architecture.

To best understand what constitutes a true SOA, we need to abstract the key components of the Web services framework and study their relationships more closely. To accomplish this, we begin by revisiting these familiar components and altering our perspective of them. First, we re-label them to reflect terminology more associated with service-orientation. Then we position them into a logical view wherein we subsequently re-examine our components within the context of SOA.

8.2.1   Logical components of the Web services framework

The communications framework established by Web services brings us the foundation technology for what we've classified as contemporary SOA. Because we covered this framework in Chapter 5, we will use it as a reference point for our discussion of service-orientation.

Let's first recap some Web services fundamentals within a logical modeling context. As shown in Figure 8.4, each Web service contains one or more operations. Note that this diagram introduces a new symbol to represent operations separately from the service.

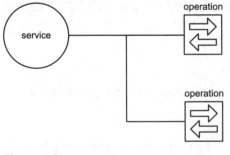

Figure 8.4
A Web service sporting two operations.

Each operation governs the processing of a specific function the Web service is capable of performing. The processing consists of sending and receiving SOAP messages, as shown in Figure 8.5.

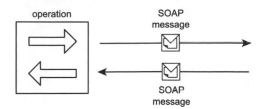

Figure 8.5
An operation processing outgoing and incoming SOAP messages.

By composing these parts, Web services form an activity through which they can collectively automate a task (Figure 8.6).

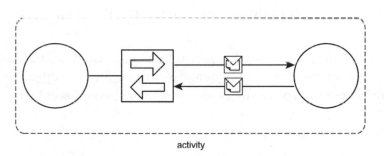

Figure 8.6
A basic communications scenario between Web services.

8.2.2   Logical components of automation logic

The Web services framework provides us not only with a technology base for enabling connectivity, it also establishes a modularized perspective of how automation logic, as a whole, can be comprised of independent units. To illustrate the inherent modularity of Web services, let's abstract the following fundamental parts of the framework:

- SOAP messages
- Web service operations
- Web services
- activities

The latter three items represent units of logic that perform work and communicate using SOAP messages. To better illustrate this in a service-oriented perspective, let's replace these terms with new ones, as follows:

- messages
- operations
- services
- processes (and process instances)

You'll notice that these are quite similar to the terms we used before. The one exception is the use of "process" instead of "activity." In later chapters we actually use the word "activity" in different contexts when modeling service-oriented business processes.

For now, the one discrepancy to be aware of is that while a Web service activity is typically used to represent the temporary interaction of a group of Web services, a process is a static definition of interaction logic. An activity is best compared to an instance of a process wherein a group of services follow a particular path through the process logic to complete a task.

Regardless, for the purposes of our discussion of service-orientation, we'll continue with our look at how automation logic is comprised of the four identified parts. We can further qualify these parts by relating each to different sized units of logic, as follows:

- messages = units of communication
- operations = units of work
- services = units of processing logic (collections of units of work)
- processes = units of automation logic (coordinated aggregation of units of work)

Figure 8.7 provides us with a primitive view of how operations and services represent units of logic that can be assembled to comprise a unit of automation logic.

Next, in Figure 8.8, we establish that messages are a suitable means by which all units of processing logic (services) communicate. This illustrates that regardless of the scope of logic a service represents, no actual processing of that logic can be performed without issuing units of communication (in this case, messages).

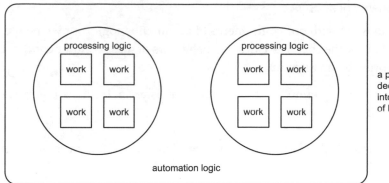

Figure 8.7
A primitive view of how SOA modularizes automation logic into units.

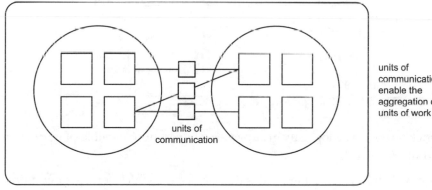

Figure 8.8
A primitive view of how units of communication enable interaction between units of logic.

The purpose of these views is simply to express that processes, services, and operations, on the most fundamental level, provide a flexible means of partitioning and modularizing logic. Regardless of the technology platform used, this remains the most basic concept that underlies service-orientation. In being able to derive this view from the Web services framework, we also have demonstrated the suitability of the Web services platform as a means of implementation for SOA.

8.2.3 Components of an SOA

We'll continue to work with our components of automation logic, but we now broaden our discussion to how the characteristics and behaviors of these components are formed within service-oriented architecture.

Each of the previously defined components establishes a level of enterprise logic abstraction, as follows:

- A message represents the data required to complete some or all parts of a unit of work.

- An operation represents the logic required to process messages in order to complete a unit of work (Figure 8.9).

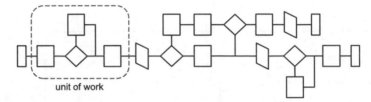

Figure 8.9
The scope of an operation within a process.

- A service represents a logically grouped set of operations capable of performing related units of work.

- A process contains the business rules that determine which service operations are used to complete a unit of automation. In other words, a process represents a large piece of work that requires the completion of smaller units of work (Figure 8.10).

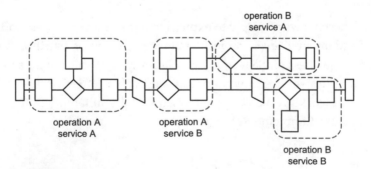

Figure 8.10
Operations belonging to different services representing various parts of process logic.

8.2.4   How components in an SOA inter-relate

Having established the core characteristics of our SOA components, let's now look at how these components are required to relate to each other:

- An operation sends and receives messages to perform work.
- An operation is therefore mostly defined by the messages it processes.
- A service groups a collection of related operations.
- A service is therefore mostly defined by the operations that comprise it.
- A process instance can compose services.
- A process instance is not necessarily defined by its services because it may only require a subset of the functionality offered by the services.
- A process instance invokes a unique series of operations to complete its automation.
- Every process instance is therefore partially defined by the service operations it uses.

Figures 8.11 and 8.12 further illustrate these relationships.

A service-oriented architecture is an environment standardized according to the principles of service-orientation in which a process that uses services (a service-oriented process) can execute. Next, we'll take a closer look at what exactly the principles of service-orientation consist of.

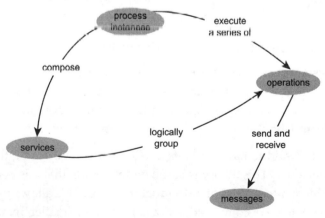

Figure 8.11
How the components of a service-oriented architecture relate.

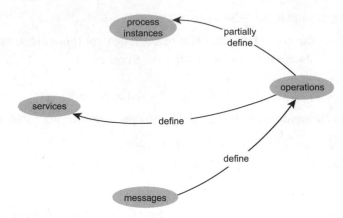

Figure 8.12
How the components of a service-oriented architecture can
define each other.

SUMMARY OF KEY POINTS

- The logical parts of an SOA can be mapped to corresponding components in the
  basic Web services framework.

- By viewing a service-oriented solution as a unit of automation logic, we establish
  that SOA consists of a sophisticated environment that supports a highly modularized
  separation of logic into differently scoped units.

- SOA further establishes specific characteristics, behaviors, and relationships among
  these components that provide a predictable environment in support of service-
  orientation.

8.3   Common principles of service-orientation

In Chapter 3 we established that there is no single definition of SOA. There is also no single governing standards body that defines the principles behind service-orientation.
Instead, there are many opinions, originating from public IT organizations to vendors
and consulting firms, about what constitutes service-orientation.

Service-orientation is said to have its roots in a software engineering theory known as
"separation of concerns." This theory is based on the notion that it is beneficial to break
down a large problem into a series of individual concerns. This allows the logic required
to solve the problem to be decomposed into a collection of smaller, related pieces. Each
piece of logic addresses a specific concern.

This theory has been implemented in different ways with different development platforms. Object-oriented programming and component-based programming approaches, for example, achieve a separation of concerns through the use of objects, classes, and components.

Service-orientation can be viewed as a distinct manner in which to realize a separation of concerns. The principles of service-orientation provide a means of supporting this theory while achieving a foundation paradigm upon which many contemporary SOA characteristics can be built. In fact, if you study these characteristics again, you will notice that several are (directly or indirectly) linked to the separation of concerns theory.

As previously mentioned, there is no official set of service-orientation principles. There are, however, a common set of principles most associated with service-orientation. These are listed below and described further in this section.

- **Services are reusable** Regardless of whether immediate reuse opportunities exist, services are designed to support potential reuse.

- **Services share a formal contract**—For services to interact, they need not share any thing but a formal contract that describes each service and defines the terms of information exchange.

- **Services are loosely coupled**—Services must be designed to interact without the need for tight, cross-service dependencies.

- **Services abstract underlying logic**—The only part of a service that is visible to the outside world is what is exposed via the service contract. Underlying logic, beyond what is expressed in the descriptions that comprise the contract, is invisible and irrelevant to service requestors.

- **Services are composable**—Services may compose other services. This allows logic to be represented at different levels of granularity and promotes reusability and the creation of abstraction layers.

- **Services are autonomous**—The logic governed by a service resides within an explicit boundary. The service has control within this boundary and is not dependent on other services for it to execute its governance.

- **Services are stateless**—Services should not be required to manage state information, as that can impede their ability to remain loosely coupled. Services should be designed to maximize statelessness even if that means deferring state management elsewhere.

- **Services are discoverable**—Services should allow their descriptions to be discovered and understood by humans and service requestors that may be able to make use of their logic.

Of these eight, autonomy, loose coupling, abstraction, and the need for a formal contract can be considered the core principles that form the baseline foundation for SOA. As explained in the *How service-orientation principles inter-relate* section later in this chapter, these four principles directly support the realization of other principles (as well as each other).

There are other qualities commonly associated with services and service-orientation. Examples include self-descriptive and coarse-grained interface design characteristics. We classify these more as service design guidelines, and they are therefore discussed as part of the design guidelines provided in Chapter 15.

NOTE

You may have noticed that the reusability and autonomy principles also were mentioned as part of the contemporary SOA characteristics described in Chapter 3. This overlap is intentional, as we simply are identifying qualities commonly associated with SOA as a whole as well as services designed for use in SOA. We further clarify the relationship between contemporary SOA characteristics and service-orientation principles in Chapter 9.

To fully understand how service-orientation principles shape service-oriented architecture, we need to explore the implications their application will have on all of the primary parts that comprise SOA. Let's take a closer look at each of the principles.

8.3.1 Services are reusable

Service-orientation encourages reuse in all services, regardless if immediate requirements for reuse exist. By applying design standards that make each service potentially reusable, the chances of being able to accommodate future requirements with less development effort are increased. Inherently reusable services also reduce the need for creating wrapper services that expose a generic interface over top of less reusable services.

This principle facilitates all forms of reuse, including inter-application interoperability, composition, and the creation of cross-cutting or utility services. As we established earlier in this chapter, a service is simply a collection of related operations. It is therefore the logic encapsulated by the individual operations that must be deemed reusable to warrant representation as a reusable service (Figure 8.13).

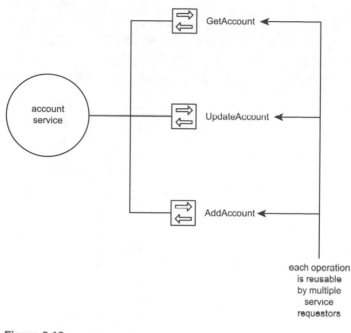

Figure 8.13
A reusable service exposes reusable operations.

Messaging also indirectly supports service reusability through the use of SOAP headers. These allow for messages to become increasingly self-reliant by grouping metadata details with message content into a single package (the SOAP envelope). Messages can be equipped with processing instructions and business rules that allow them to dictate to recipient services how they should be processed.

The processing-specific logic embedded in a message alleviates the need for a service to contain this logic. More importantly, it imposes a requirement that service operations become less activity-specific—in other words, more generic. The more generic a service's operations are, the more reusable the service.

RailCo delivered the Invoice Submission Service for the sole purpose of being able to connect to TLS's new B2B system. This Web service's primary function therefore is to send electronic invoice documents to the TLS Accounts Payable Service. The service contains the following two operations: SubmitInvoice and GetTLSMetadata (Figure 8.14).

The SubmitInvoice operation simply initiates the transmission of the invoice document. You might recall in the *Metadata exchange* section of Chapter 7 that an operation was added to periodically check the TLS Accounts Payable Service for changes to its service description. This new operation is GetTLSMetadata.

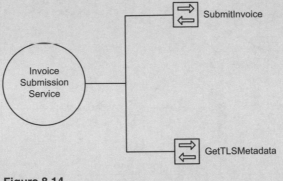

Figure 8.14
The RailCo Invoice Submission Service and its operations.

Because they were built to meet immediate and specific business requirements, these operations have no real reuse potential. The SubmitInvoice operation is designed to forward SOAP messages containing specific headers required by TLS and containing an invoice XML document structured according to a schema also defined by TLS. By its very name, the GetTLSMetadata operation identifies itself as existing for one reason: to query a specific endpoint for new metadata information.

The TLS Accounts Payable Service, on the other hand, provides a series of generic operations related to the processing of accounts payable transactions. This service is therefore used by different TLS systems, one of which is the aforementioned B2B solution.

In Chapters 11 and 12 we will submit the RailCo Invoice Submission Service to a modeling exercise in an attempt to reshape it into a service that implements actual service-orientation principles, including reusability.

> **IN PLAIN ENGLISH**
>
> One day, a government inspector stops by our car washing operation. Not knowing who he is, I ask if he would like his car washed and waxed or just washed. He responds by asking a question of his own. "Do you have a business license for this operation?"
>
> A subsequent conversation between the inspector and our team results in the revelation that we have indeed been operating without a business license. We are therefore ordered to cease all work until we obtain one. We scramble to find out what needs to be done. This leads us to visit the local Business License Office to start the process of acquiring a license.
>
> The Business License Office provides a distinct service: issuing and renewing business licenses. It is not there to service just our car washing company; it is there to provide this service to anyone requesting it. Because its service is designed to facilitate multiple service requestors, the logic that enables the service can be classified as being reusable.

8.3.2   Services share a formal contract

Service contracts provide a formal definition of:

- the service endpoint
- each service operation
- every input and output message supported by each operation
- rules and characteristics of the service and its operations

Service contracts therefore define almost all of the primary parts of an SOA (Figure 8.15). Good service contracts also may provide semantic information that explains how a service may go about accomplishing a particular task. Either way, this information establishes the agreement made by a service provider and its service requestors.

Because this contract is shared among services, its design is extremely important. Service requestors that agree to this contract can become dependent on its definition. Therefore, contracts need to be carefully maintained and versioned after their initial release.

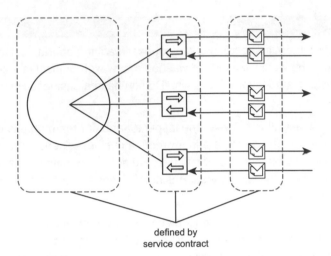

defined by
service contract

Figure 8.15
Service contracts formally define the service, operation,
and message components of a service-oriented
architecture.

As explained in Chapter 5, service description documents, such as the WSDL definition, XSD schemas, and policies, can be viewed collectively as a communications contract that expresses exactly how a service can be programmatically accessed.

CASE STUDY

From the onset, RailCo and TLS agreed to each other's service contracts, which enabled these two companies to interact via the TLS B2B system. The rules of the contract and the definition of associated service description documents all are provided by TLS to ensure a standardized level of conformance that applies to each of its online vendors.

One day, RailCo is informed that TLS has revised the policy published with the Accounts Payable Service. A new rule has been added where TLS is offering better payment terms to vendors in exchange for larger discounts. RailCo has the choice to continue pricing their products at the regular amounts and face a payment term of 60 days for their invoices or reduce their prices to get a payment term of 30 days.

Both of these options are acceptable contract conditions published by TLS. After some evaluation, RailCo decides not to take advantage of the reduced payment terms and therefore does not adjust its product prices.

IN PLAIN ENGLISH

For us to get a business license, we must fill out an application form. This process essentially formalizes our request in a format required and expected by the Business License Office.

The completed application form is much like a contract between the service provider and the requestor of the service. Upon accepting the form, the service provider agrees to act on the request.

8.3.3 Services are loosely coupled

No one can predict how an IT environment will evolve. How automation solutions grow, integrate, or are replaced over time can never be accurately planned out because the requirements that drive these changes are almost always external to the IT environment. Being able to ultimately respond to unforeseen changes in an efficient manner is a key goal of applying service-orientation. Realizing this form of agility is directly supported by establishing a loosely coupled relationship between services (Figure 8.16).

Loose coupling is a condition wherein a service acquires knowledge of another service while still remaining independent of that service. Loose coupling is achieved through the use of service contracts that allow services to interact within predefined parameters.

It is interesting to note that within a loosely coupled architecture, service contracts actually tightly couple operations to services. When a service is formally described as being the location of an operation, other services will depend on that operation-to-service association.

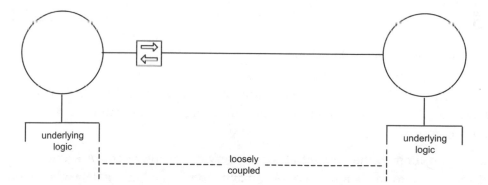

Figure 8.16

Services limit dependencies to the service contract, allowing underlying provider and requestor logic to remain loosely coupled.

CASE STUDY

Through the use of service contracts, RailCo and TLS services are naturally loosely coupled. However, one could say that the extent of loose coupling between the two service provider entities is significantly different.

TLS services are designed to facilitate multiple B2B partners, as well as internal reuse and composition requirements. This makes TLS services *very* loosely coupled from any of its service requestors.

RailCo's services, on the other hand, are designed specifically to interact with designated TLS services that are part of the overall TLS B2B solution. No attempt was made to make these services useful for any other service requestors. RailCo services are therefore considered *less* loosely coupled than TLS services.

IN PLAIN ENGLISH

After we have submitted our form, we are not required to remain at the Business License Office, nor do we need to stay in touch with them. We only need to wait until the application is processed and a license is (hopefully) issued.

This is much like an asynchronous message exchange, but it is also a demonstration of a loosely coupled relationship between services or between service provider and requestor. All we need to interact with the Business License Office is an application form that defines the information the office requires to process our request. Prior to and subsequent to the submission of that request, our car washing team (service requestor) and the Business License Office (service provider) remain independent of each other.

8.3.4   Services abstract underlying logic

Also referred to as *service interface-level abstraction*, it is this principle that allows services to act as black boxes, hiding their details from the outside world. The scope of logic represented by a service significantly influences the design of its operations and its position within a process.

There is no limit to the amount of logic a service can represent. A service may be designed to perform a simple task, or it may be positioned as a gateway to an entire automation solution. There is also no restriction as to the source of application logic a service can draw upon. For example, a single service can, technically, expose application logic from two different systems (Figure 8.17).

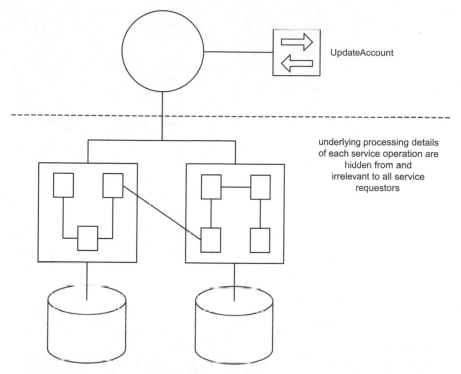

UpdateAccount

underlying processing details of each service operation are hidden from and irrelevant to all service requestors

Figure 8.17
Service operations abstract the underlying details of the functionality they expose.

Operation granularity is therefore a primary design consideration that is directly related to the range and nature of functionality being exposed by the service. Again, it is the individual operations that collectively abstract the underlying logic. Services simply act as containers for these operations.

Service interface-level abstraction is one of the inherent qualities provided by Web services. The loosely coupled communications structure requires that the only piece of knowledge services need to interact is each others' service descriptions.

CASE STUDY

Because both RailCo and TLS employ Web services to communicate, each environment successfully implements service interface-level abstraction. On RailCo's end, this abstraction hides the legacy systems involved with generating electronic invoice documents and processing incoming purchase orders. On the TLS side, services hide service compositions wherein processing duties are delegated to specialized services as part of single activities (Figure 8.18).

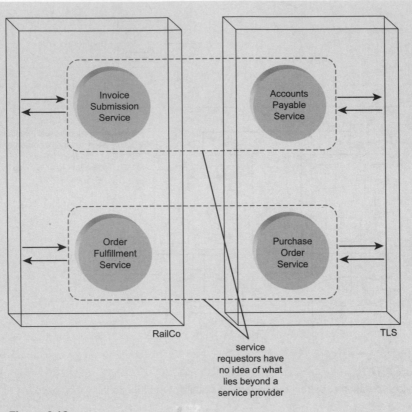

Figure 8.18
Neither of RailCo's or TLS's service requestors require any knowledge of what
lies behind the other's service providers.

IN PLAIN ENGLISH

The tasks required for the Business License Office to process our request include:

- A name check to ensure that the name of our company "Oasis Car Wash" isn't already taken.

- A background check of the company principals to ensure that none of us have had past bankruptcies.

- A verification of our sub-lease agreement to ensure that we are, in fact, allowed to operate at the gas station we have been using.

These and other tasks are performed completely unbeknownst to us. We don't know or necessarily care what the Business License Office needs to do to process our application. We are just interested in the expected outcome: the issuance of our license.

8.3.5   Services are composable

A service can represent any range of logic from any types of sources, including other services. The main reason to implement this principle is to ensure that services are designed so that they can participate as effective members of other service compositions if ever required. This requirement is irrespective of whether the service itself composes others to accomplish its work (Figure 8.19).

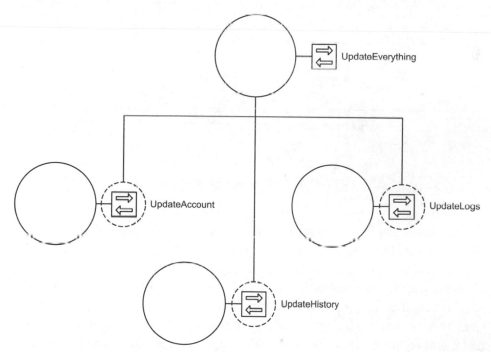

Figure 8.19
The UpdateEverything operation encapsulating a service composition.

A common SOA extension that underlines composability is the concept of orchestration. Here, a service-oriented process (which essentially can be classified as a service composition) is controlled by a parent process service that composes process participants.

The requirement for any service to be composable also places an emphasis on the design of service operations. Composability is simply another form of reuse, and therefore operations need to be designed in a standardized manner and with an appropriate level of granularity to maximize composition opportunities.

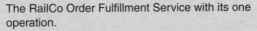
CASE STUDY

As with RailCo's Invoice Submission Service, its Order Fulfillment Service was created to meet a specific requirement in support of communication with TLS's B2B solution.

The Order Fulfillment Service contains just one public operation called ProcessTLSPO (Figure 8.20). This operation is designed in compliance with TLS vendor service specifications so that it is fully capable of receiving POs submitted by the TLS Purchase Order Service. Part of this compliance requires the operation to be able to process custom SOAP headers containing proprietary security tokens.

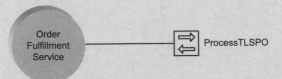

Figure 8.20
The RailCo Order Fulfillment Service with its one operation.

Though the Order Fulfillment Service is capable of acting as a composition member, its potential for being useful to any future compositions is limited. Composition support is similar to reusability in that generic functionality exposed by operations make a service more composable. This RailCo service provides one operation that performs a very specialized function, customized to processing a specific document from a specific source. It will likely not be a suitable composition member, but it can act as a controller service, composing other services to complete its PO processing tasks.

The TLS Accounts Payable Service already establishes a well-defined composition, wherein it acts as a controller service that composes the Vendor Profile and Ledger Services (Figure 8.21). Because they each expose a complete set of generic operations, all three of these services are capable of participating in other composition configurations.

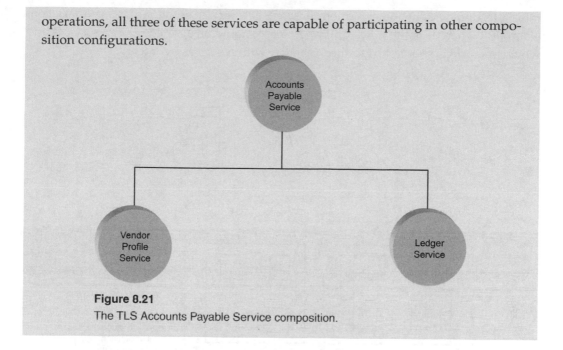

Figure 8.21
The TLS Accounts Payable Service composition.

IN PLAIN ENGLISH

Given that the services provided by the Business License Office are distinct and reusable, it can be asked to assist other government offices to participate in the completion of other services. For example, the Business Relocation Office manages all administrative paperwork for businesses that need to be moved when their location is scheduled for demolition.

As part of its many tasks, this office takes care of revising the business license information for the affected company. It does so by enlisting the Business License Office and requesting that they issue a new business license for a particular organization.

By reusing the services offered by the Business License Office, the Business Relocation Office has effectively composed services, much like a controller service reuses and composes other service providers.

8.3.6 Services are autonomous

Autonomy requires that the range of logic exposed by a service exist within an explicit boundary. This allows the service to execute self-governance of all its processing. It also eliminates dependencies on other services, which frees a service from ties that could inhibit its deployment and evolution (Figure 8.22). Service autonomy is a primary consideration when deciding how application logic should be divided up into services and which operations should be grouped together within a service context.

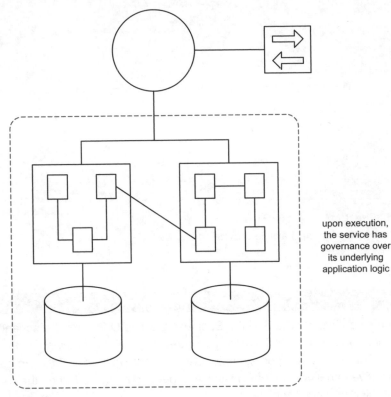

upon execution, the service has governance over its underlying application logic

Figure 8.22
Autonomous services have control over underlying resources.

Deferring the location of business rules is one way to strengthen autonomy and keep services more generic. Processes generally assume this role by owning the business rules that determine how the process is structured and, subsequently, how services are composed to automate the process logic. This is another aspect of orchestration explored in the *Orchestration service layer* section in Chapter 9.

Note that autonomy does not necessarily grant a service exclusive ownership of the logic it encapsulates. It only guarantees that at the time of execution, the service has control over whatever logic it represents. We therefore can make a distinction between two types of autonomy.

- *Service-level autonomy*—Service boundaries are distinct from each other, but the service may share underlying resources. For example, a wrapper service that encapsulates a legacy environment that also is used independently from the service has service-level autonomy. It governs the legacy system but also shares resources with other legacy clients.

- *Pure autonomy*—The underlying logic is under complete control and ownership of the service. This is typically the case when the underlying logic is built from the ground up in support of the service.

CASE STUDY

Given the distinct tasks they perform, the following three RailCo services all are autonomous:

- Invoice Submission Service
- Order Fulfillment Service
- TLS Subscription Service

Each represents a specific boundary of application logic that does not overlap with the boundary of any other services.

Autonomy in RailCo's services was achieved inadvertently. No conscious effort was made to avoid application overlap, as the services were delivered to simply meet specific connectivity requirements.

As shown in Figure 8.23, the Invoice Processing and Order Fulfillment Services encapsulate legacy logic. The legacy accounting system also is used by clients independently from the services, which makes this service-level autonomy. The TLS Notification Service achieves pure autonomy, as it represents a set of custom components created only in support of this service.

In environments where a larger number of services exist and new services are built on a regular basis, it is more common to introduce dedicated modeling processes so pure service autonomy is preserved among individual services. At TLS, for example, services undergo a service-oriented analysis to guarantee autonomy and avoid encapsulation overlap. (Service-oriented analysis is explained in Chapters 11 and 12.)

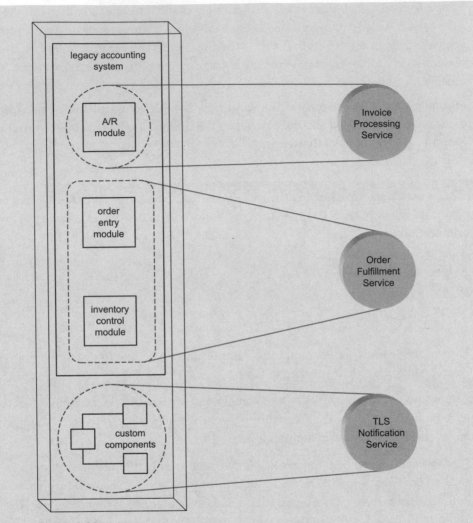

Figure 8.23
RailCo's services luckily encapsulate explicit portions of legacy and newly
added application logic.

IN PLAIN ENGLISH

Let's revisit the three tasks performed by the Business License Office when processing an application for a new business license:

- name check

- background check

- location verification

The Business License Office owns the corporate name database required to perform a name check. Also the office has personnel dedicated to visiting and verifying business site locations. When completing these two tasks, the Business License Office therefore has complete self-governance. However, when having to perform a background check, the office must share a database system with the Revenue Office. When it gets access, it can retrieve an abbreviated credit history for each of the company principals listed on the application.

The Business License Office's reliance on the shared database reduces its independence somewhat. However, its overall ability to perform the tasks within its own boundary give it a degree of autonomy.

8.3.7   Services are stateless

Services should minimize the amount of state information they manage and the duration for which they hold it. State information is data-specific to a current activity. While a service is processing a message, for example, it is temporarily stateful (Figure 8.24). If a service is responsible for retaining state for longer periods of time, its ability to remain available to other requestors will be impeded.

Statelessness is a preferred condition for services and one that promotes reusability and scalability. For a service to retain as little state as possible, its individual operations need to be designed with stateless processing considerations.

A primary quality of SOA that supports statelessness is the use of document-style messages. The more intelligence added to a message, the more independent and self-sufficient it remains. Chapters 6 and 7 explore various WS-* extensions that rely on the use of SOAP headers to carry different types of state data.

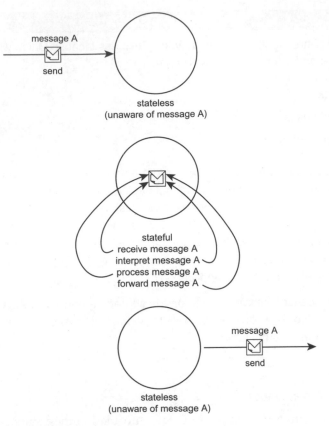

message A

send

stateless
(unaware of message A)

stateful
receive message A
interpret message A
process message A
forward message A

message A

send

stateless
(unaware of message A)

Figure 8.24
Stateless and stateful stages a service passes through while
processing a message.

As with loose coupling, statelessness is a quality that can be measured in
degrees. The RailCo Order Fulfillment Service is required to perform extra runtime parsing and processing of various standard SOAP header blocks to successfully receive a purchase order document submitted by the TLS Purchase Order
Service. This processing ties up the Order Fulfillment Service longer than, say,
the Invoice Submission Service, which simply forwards a predefined SOAP message to the TLS Accounting Service.

8.3.8   Services are discoverable

Discovery helps avoid the accidental creation of redundant services or services that implement redundant logic. Because each operation provides a potentially reusable piece of processing logic, metadata attached to a service needs to sufficiently describe not only the service's overall purpose, but also the functionality offered by its operations.

Note that this service-orientation principle is related to but distinct from the contemporary SOA characteristic of discoverability. On an SOA level, discoverability refers to the architecture's ability to provide a discovery mechanism, such as a service registry or directory. This effectively becomes part of the IT infrastructure and can support numerous implementations of SOA. On a service level, the principle of discoverability refers to the design of an individual service so that it can be as discoverable as possible.

Due to the reusable nature of TLS services and because of the volume of services that are expected to exist in TLS technical environments, an internal service registry was established (as shown in Figure 8.25 and originally explained in Chapter 5). This piece of TLS infrastructure promotes discoverability and prevents accidental redundancy. It further leverages the existing design standards used by TLS that promote the creation of descriptive metadata documents in support of service discoverability.

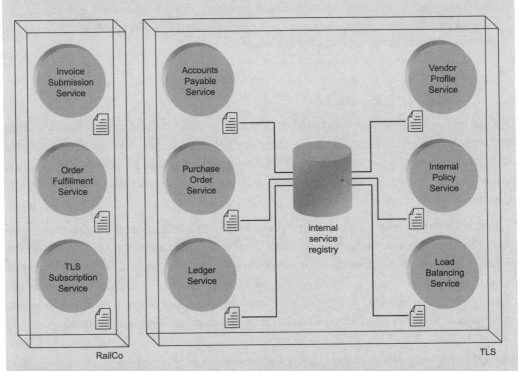

Figure 8.25
RailCo's services are not discoverable, but TLS's inventory of services are stored in an internal registry.

TLS is not interested in making its services publicly discoverable, which is why it does not register them with a public service registry. Vendors that participate in the TLS B2B system only are allowed to do so after a separate negotiation, review, and registration process.

IN PLAIN ENGLISH

After some time, our business license is finally issued. Upon receiving the certificate in the mail, we are back in business. Looking back at how this whole process began, though, there is one step we did not discuss. When we first learned that we were required to get a business license, we had to find out where the Business License Office was located. This required us to search through the phone book and locate a listing with contact information.

A service registry provides a discovery mechanism very much like a phone book, allowing potential requestors to query and check candidate service providers. In the same manner in which a registry points to service descriptions, the phone book listing led us to the location at which we were able to obtain the original business license application form.

More relevant to the principle of service discoverability is the fact that steps were taken to make the Business License Office itself discoverable. Examples include signs in the lobby of the high-rise in which the office is located, a sign on the office entrance door, brochures located at other offices, and so on.

SUMMARY OF KEY POINTS

- Different organizations have published their own versions of service-oriented principles. As a result, many variations exist.

- The most common principles relate to loose coupling, autonomy, discoverability, composability, reuse, service contracts, abstraction, and statelessness.

8.4   How service-orientation principles inter-relate

When reading through the previous descriptions, a number of questions might come to mind, such as:

- What's the difference between reusability and composability? (Aren't you reusing a service when you compose it?)

- What's the difference between autonomy and statelessness? (Aren't both a representation of service independence?)

- What's the difference between loose coupling and the use of a service contract? (Doesn't a service contract automatically implement loose coupling?)

To answer these and other questions, this section revisits our service-orientation principles to explore how each relates to, supports, or is affected by others. To accomplish this, we abbreviate the original names we assigned each principle, as follows:

- Services are reusable = service reusability
- Services share a formal contract = service contract
- Services are loosely coupled = service loose coupling
- Services abstract underlying logic = service abstraction
- Services are composable = service composability
- Services are autonomous = service autonomy
- Services are stateless = service statelessness
- Services are discoverable = service discoverability

We intentionally prefix each principle with the word "service" to emphasize that the principle applies to the design of a service only, as opposed to our SOA characteristics, which apply to the design of SOA as a whole.

NOTE
Each relationship is essentially described twice within these sections. This repetitiveness is intentional, as this part of the chapter is provided more for reference purposes. Feel free to skip ahead if you are not interested in learning about each individual principle-to-principle relationship at this point.

8.4.1   Service reusability

When a service encapsulates logic that is useful to more than one service requestor, it can be considered reusable. The concept of reuse is supported by a number of complementary service principles, as follows.

- Service autonomy establishes an execution environment that facilitates reuse because the service has independence and self-governance. The less dependencies a service has, the broader the applicability of its reusable functionality.

- Service statelessness supports reuse because it maximizes the availability of a service and typically promotes a generic service design that defers activity-specific processing outside of service logic boundaries.

- Service abstraction fosters reuse because it establishes the black box concept, where processing details are completely hidden from requestors. This allows a service to simply express a generic public interface.

- Service discoverability promotes reuse, as it allows requestors (and those that build requestors) to search for and discover reusable services.

- Service loose coupling establishes an inherent independence that frees a service from immediate ties to others. This makes it a great deal easier to realize reuse.

Additionally, the principle of service reuse itself enables the following related principle:

- Service composability is primarily possible because of reuse. The ability for one service to compose an activity around the utilization of a collection of services is feasible when those services being composed are built for reuse. (It is technically possible to build a service so that its sole purpose is to be composed by another, but reuse is generally emphasized.)

Figure 8.26 provides a diagram showing how the principle of service reusability relates to others.

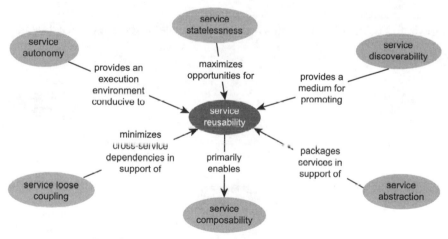

Figure 8.26
Service reusability and its relationship with other service-orientation principles.

8.4.2 Service contract

A service contract is a representation of a service's collective metadata. It standardizes the expression of rules and conditions that need to be fulfilled by any requestor wanting to interact with the service.

Service contracts represent a cornerstone principle in service-orientation and therefore support other principles in various ways, as follows:

- Service abstraction is realized through a service contract, as it is the metadata expressed in the contract that defines the only information made available to service requestors. All additional design, processing, and implementation details are hidden behind this contract.

- Service loose coupling is made possible through the use of service contracts. Processing logic from different services do not need to form tight dependencies; they simply need an awareness of each other's communication requirements, as expressed by the service description documents that comprise the service contract.

- Service composability is indirectly enabled through the use of service contracts. It is via the contract that a controller service enlists and uses services that act as composition members.

- Service discoverability is based on the use of service contracts. While some registries provide information supplemental to that expressed through the contract, it is the service description documents that are primarily searched for in the service discovery process.

The diagram in Figure 8.27 illustrates how the principle of service contract usage relates to others.

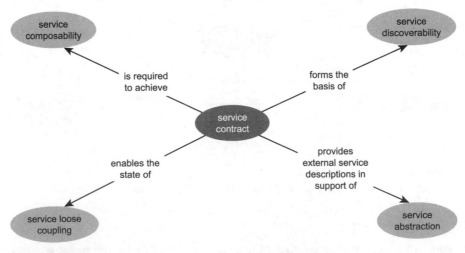

Figure 8.27
The service contract and its relationship with other service-orientation principles.

8.4.3   Service loose coupling

Loose coupling is a state that supports a level of independence between services (or between service providers and requestors). As you may have already noticed, independence or non-dependency is a fundamental aspect of services and SOA as a whole. Therefore, the principle of persisting loose coupling across services supports the following other service-orientation principles:

- Service reusability is supported through loose coupling because services are freed from tight dependencies on others. This increases their availability for reuse opportunities.

- Service composability is fostered by the loose coupling of services, especially when services are dynamically composed.

- Service statelessness is directly supported through the loosely coupled communications framework established by this principle.

- Service autonomy is made possible through this principle, as it is the nature of loose coupling that minimizes cross-service dependencies.

Additionally, service loose coupling is directly implemented through the application of a related service-orientation principle:

- Service contracts are what enable loose coupling between services, as the contract is the only piece of information required for services to interact.

Figure 8.28 demonstrates these relationships.

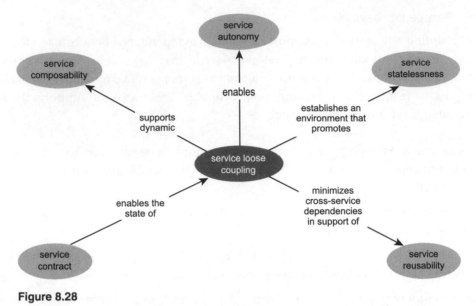

Figure 8.28
Service loose coupling and its relationship with other service-orientation principles.

8.4.4   Service abstraction

Part of building solutions with independent services is allowing those services to encapsulate potentially complex processing logic and exposing that logic through a generic and descriptive interface. This is the primary benefit of service abstraction, a principle that is related to others, as explained here:

- Service contracts, in a manner, implement service abstraction by providing the official description information that is made public to external service requestors.

- Service reusability is supported by abstraction, as long as what is being abstracted is actually reusable.

These relationships are shown in Figure 8.29.

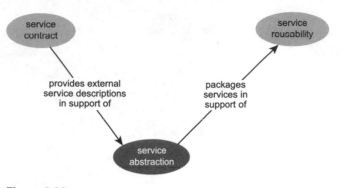

Figure 8.29
Service abstraction and its relationship with other service-orientation principles.

8.4.5   Service composability

Designing services so that they support composition by others is fundamental to building service-oriented solutions. Service composability therefore is tied to service-orientation principles that support the concept of service composition, as follows:

- Service reusability is what enables one service to be composed by numerous others. It is expected that reusable services can be incorporated within different compositions or reused independently by other service requestors.

- Service loose coupling establishes a communications framework that supports the concept of dynamic service composition. Because services are freed from many dependencies, they are more available to be reused via composition.

- Service statelessness supports service composability, especially in larger compositions. A service composition is reliant on the design quality and commonality of its collective parts. If all services are stateless (by, for example, deferring activity-specific logic to messages), the overall composition executes more harmoniously.

- Service autonomy held by composition members strengthens the overall composition, but the autonomy of the controller service itself actually is decreased due to the dependencies on its composition members.

- Service contracts enable service composition by formalizing the runtime agreement between composition members.

Figure 8.30 further illustrates these relationships.

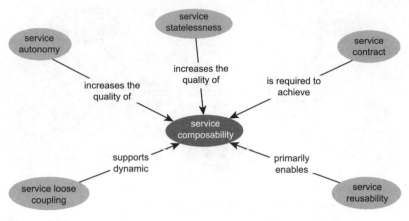

Figure 8.30
Service composability and its relationship with other service-orientation
principles.

8.4.6   Service autonomy

This principle applies to a service's underlying logic. By providing an execution environment over which a service has complete control, service autonomy relates to several other principles, as explained here:

- Service reusability is more easily achieved when the service offering reusable logic has self-governance over its own logic. Service Level Agreement (SLA) type requirements that come to the forefront for utility services with multiple requestors, such as availability and scalability, are fulfilled more easily by an autonomous service.

- Service composability is also supported by service autonomy—for much of the same reasons autonomy supports service reusability. A service composition consisting of autonomous services is much more robust and collectively independent.

- Service statelessness is best implemented by a service that can execute independently. Autonomy indirectly supports service statelessness. (However, it is very easy to create a stateful service that is also fully autonomous.)

- Service autonomy is a quality that is realized by leveraging the loosely coupled relationship between services. Therefore service loose coupling is a primary enabler of this principle.

The diagram in Figure 8.31 shows how service autonomy relates to these other principles.

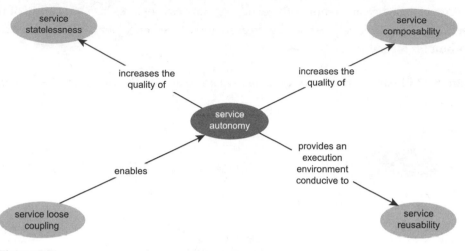

Figure 8.31
Service autonomy and its relationship with other service-orientation principles.

8.4.7   Service statelessness

To successfully design services not to manage state requires the availability of resources surrounding the service to which state management responsibilities can be delegated. However, the principle of statelessness is also indirectly supported by the following service-orientation principles:

- Service autonomy provides the ability for a service to control its own execution environment. By removing or reducing dependencies it becomes easier to build statelessness into services, primarily because the service logic can be fully customized to defer state management outside of the service logic boundary.

- Service loose coupling and the overall concept of loose coupling establishes a communication paradigm that is fully realized through messaging. This, in turn, supports service statelessness, as state information can be carried and persisted by the messages that pass through the services.

Service statelessness further supports the following principles:

- Service composability benefits from stateless composition members, as they reduce dependencies and minimize the overhead of the composition as a whole.

- Service reuse becomes more of a reality for stateless services, as availability of the service to multiple requestors is increased and the absence of activity-specific logic promotes a generic service design.

Figure 8.32 illustrates how service statelessness relates to the other service-orientation principles.

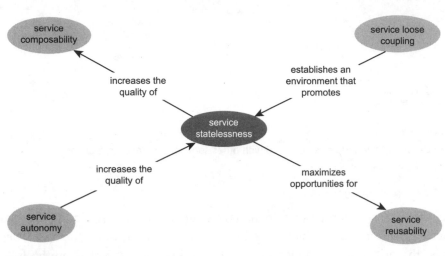

Figure 8.32
Service statelessness and its relationship with other service-orientation principles.

8.4.8   Service discoverability

Designing services so that they are naturally discoverable enables an environment whereby service logic becomes accessible to new potential service requestors. This is why service discoverability is tied closely to the following service-orientation principles:

- Service contracts are what service requestors (or those that create them) actually discover and subsequently assess for suitability. Therefore, the extent of a service's discoverability can typically be associated with the quality or descriptiveness of its service contract.

- Service reusability is what requestors are looking for when searching for services and it is what makes a service potentially useful once it has been discovered. A service that isn't reusable would likely never need to be discovered because it would probably have been built for a specific service requestor in the first place.

The diagram in Figure 8.33 shows how service discoverability fits in with the other service-orientation principles.

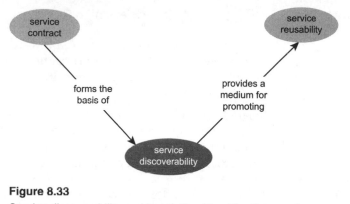

Figure 8.33
Service discoverability and its relationship with other service-orientation principles.

SUMMARY OF KEY POINTS

- Service-orientation principles are not realized in isolation; principles relate to and support other principles in different ways.

- Principles, such as service reusability and service composability, benefit from the support of other implemented principles.

- Principles, such as service loose coupling, service contract, and service autonomy, provide significant support for the realization of other principles.

8.5 Service-orientation and object-orientation (Part II)

Having now covered the fundamentals behind service-orientation principles, we can continue the discussion we began in the *Service-orientation and object-orientation (Part I)* section from Chapter 4.

Those of you familiar with object-oriented analysis and design probably will have recognized a similarity between a number of the service-orientation principles discussed and the more established principles of object-orientation.

Indeed, service-orientation owes much of its existence to object-oriented concepts and theory. Table 8.1 provides a look at which common object-orientation principles are related to the service-orientation principles we've been discussing.

Table 8.1   An overview of how service-orientation principles relate to object-orientation principles.

Service-Orientation Principle	Related Object-Orientation Principles
service reusability	Much of object-orientation is geared toward the creation of reusable classes. The object-orientation principle of modularity standardized decomposition as a means of application design. Related principles, such as abstraction and encapsulation, further support reuse by requiring a distinct separation of interface and implementation logic. Service reusability is therefore a continuation of this goal.
service contract	The requirement for a service contract is very comparable to the use of interfaces when building object-oriented applications. Much like WSDL definitions, interfaces provide a means of abstracting the description of a class. And, much like the "WSDL first" approach encouraged within SOA, the "interface first" approach also is considered an object-orientation best practice.
service loose coupling	Although the creation of interfaces somewhat decouples a class from its consumers, coupling in general is one of the primary qualities of service-orientation that deviates from object-orientation. The use of inheritance and other object-orientation principles encourages a much more tightly coupled relationship between units of processing logic when compared to the service-oriented design approach.
service abstraction	The object-orientation principle of abstraction requires that a class provide an interface to the external world and that it be accessible via this interface. Encapsulation supports this by establishing the concept of information hiding, where any logic within the class outside of what is exposed via the interface is not accessible to the external world. Service abstraction accomplishes much of the same as object abstraction and encapsulation. Its purpose is to hide the underlying details of the service so that only the service contract is available and of concern to service requestors.

Service-Orientation Principle	Related Object-Orientation Principles
service composability	Object-orientation supports association concepts, such as aggregation and composition. These, within a loosely coupled context, also are supported by service-orientation. For example, the same way a hierarchy of objects can be composed, a hierarchy of services can be assembled through service composability.
service autonomy	The quality of autonomy is more emphasized in service-oriented design than it has been with object-oriented approaches. Achieving a level of independence between units of processing logic is possible through service-orientation, by leveraging the loosely coupled relationship between services. Cross-object references and inheritance-related dependencies within object-oriented designs support a lower degree of object-level autonomy.
service statelessness	Objects consist of a combination of class and data and are naturally stateful. Promoting statelessness within services therefore tends to deviate from typical object-oriented design. Although it is possible to create stateful services and stateless objects, the principle of statelessness is generally more emphasized with service-orientation.
service discoverability	Designing class interfaces to be consistent and self-descriptive is another object-orientation best practice that improves a means of identifying and distinguishing units of processing logic. These qualities also support reuse by allowing classes to be more easily discovered. Discoverability is another principle more emphasized by the service-orientation paradigm. It is encouraged that service contracts be as communicative as possible to support discoverability at design time and runtime.

As it stands today, object-orientation and service-orientation are not necessarily competitive paradigms. Service-orientation clearly has several roots in object-orientation, and typical contemporary service-oriented solutions will consist of a mixture of services (that adhere to service-orientation principles) and object-oriented components. With a balanced design, each set of principles can be properly positioned and leveraged to complement and support each other.

SUMMARY OF KEY POINTS

- Several principles of service-orientation are related to and derived from object-orientation principles.

- Some object-orientation principles, such as inheritance, do not fit into the service-oriented world.

- Some service-orientation principles, such as loose coupling and autonomy, are not directly promoted by object-orientation.

8.6   Native Web service support for service-orientation principles

Having now worked through the individual principles of service-orientation in some detail, it becomes evident that Web services provide inherent support for some of these principles. It is important to recognize specifically which principles are built into the structure of common Web services because this allows us to place an emphasis on those that require a conscious effort to realize.

Table 8.2 recaps the principles of service-orientation and explains to what extent they are natively supported by Web services.

Table 8.2   A look at which service-orientation principles are automatically supported by Web services.

Service-Orientation Principle	Web Service Support
service reusability	Web services are not automatically reusable. This quality is related to the nature of the logic encapsulated and exposed via the Web service.
service contract	Web services require the use of service descriptions, making service contracts a fundamental part of Web services communication.
service loose coupling	Web services are naturally loosely coupled through the use of service descriptions.

Service-Orientation Principle	Web Service Support
service abstraction	Web services automatically emulate the black box model within the Web services communications framework, hiding all of the details of their underlying logic.
service composability	Web services are naturally composable. The extent to which a service can be composed, though, generally is determined by the service design and the reusability of represented logic.
service autonomy	To ensure an autonomous processing environment requires design effort. Autonomy is therefore not automatically provided by a Web service.
service statelessness	Statelessness is a preferred condition for Web services, strongly supported by many WS-* specifications and the document-style SOAP messaging model.
service discoverability	Discoverability must be implemented by the architecture and even can be considered an extension to IT infrastructure. It is therefore not natively supported by Web services.

It turns out that half of the principles of service-orientation are natural characteristics of common Web services. This underlines the synergy of the marriage between SOA and the Web services technology platform and gives us a good indication as to why Web services have been so successful in realizing SOA.

It also highlights the principles that require special attention when building service-oriented solutions. The four principles identified as *not* being automatically provided by Web services are:

- service reusability
- service autonomy
- service statelessness
- service discoverability

Chapters 11 through 15 discuss service modeling and design in detail and provide guidelines to ensure that these important principles are taken into consideration when building services for use within SOA.

These processes further emphasize the other four principles as well—though they may be automatically implemented through the use of Web services, that does not mean they will necessarily be properly realized. For example, the fact that Web services require the use of service contracts has no bearing on how well individual service descriptions are designed.

SUMMARY OF KEY POINTS

- Service abstraction, composability, loose coupling, and the need for service contracts are native characteristics of Web services that are in full alignment with the corresponding principles of service-orientation.

- Service reusability, autonomy, statelessness, and discoverability are not automatically provided by Web services. Realizing these qualities requires a conscious modeling and design effort.

NOTE

More detailed information about service-orientation design principles is available in *SOA: Principles of Service Design*, another book in the *Prentice Hall Service-Oriented Computing Series from Thomas Erl*. Visit www.soaprinciples.com and www.soabooks.com for more details. A color principles reference poster is also available at www.soaposters.com. Finally, be sure to study the SOA design patterns published at www.soapatterns.org.

Service Layers

hile the service-orientation concepts we covered in the previous chapter are what fundamentally define SOA and distinguish it from other architectural platforms, they are still just theory. To bring service-orientation into a real-life automation solution, we need to provide an environment capable of supporting its fundamental principles.

As we've already established, the Web services framework provides us with the technology and the design paradigm with which these principles can be realized. To then implement service-orientation in support of manifesting the contemporary SOA characteristics and benefits we identified back in Chapter 3, we need a means of coordinating and propagating service-orientation throughout an enterprise. This can be accomplished by service layer abstraction.

This chapter forms an approach to structuring and delivering specialized service layers around the delivery of key contemporary SOA characteristics.

How case studies are used: Both RailCo and TLS environments are revisited to identify which of the existing services correspond to the service layers discussed in this chapter.

9.1 Service-orientation and contemporary SOA

Contemporary SOA is a complex and sophisticated architectural platform that offers significant potential to solve many historic and current IT problems. In part, it achieves this potential by leveraging existing paradigms and technologies that support its overall vision. However, the majority of what it has to offer only can be harnessed thorough analysis and targeted design.

Listed here (and shown in Figure 9.1) are three of the primary influences of contemporary SOA discussed so far in this book:

- first-generation Web services concepts (explained in Chapter 5)
- second-generation (WS-*) Web Services concepts (explained in Chapters 6 and 7)
- principles of service-orientation (explained in Chapter 8)

There are, of course, many other influences. Fundamental XML concepts, for example, have driven and shaped SOA and Web services on a fundamental level. For now, though, let's focus on these three.

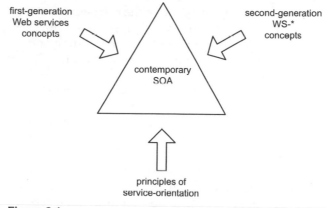

Figure 9.1

External influences that form and support contemporary SOA.

As previously stated, to fulfill the potential of this architecture, we need to understand the origins of its characteristics. This understanding equips us with a healthy knowledge of what intrinsically drives fundamental aspects of SOA. More importantly, though, it allows us to pinpoint exactly which parts of contemporary SOA must be manually bolted on to this architecture. This allows us to focus on analysis and design efforts that ensure that these parts of SOA are properly implemented and their benefits realized.

9.1.1 Mapping the origins and supporting sources of concrete SOA characteristics

In Chapter 3 we created a list of concrete characteristics commonly associated with contemporary SOA. These qualities represent the current state and expectations surrounding this architectural platform and are also a reflection of the technology being developed in its support.

We've reached a stage in this book where we've discussed each of the three contemporary SOA influences identified in the previous section as being either responsible for or that in some way relating to a number of these characteristics.

We want to ensure that we identify those characteristics not supported by these external influences so that we can discuss how they also can be realized. So let's take this opportunity to revisit our original list, with the intention of striking off the ones that already have been addressed.

Table 9.1   A review of how contemporary SOA characteristics are influenced by Web services specifications and service-orientation principles.

Characteristic	Origin and/or Supporting Source
fundamentally autonomous	Autonomy is one of the core service-orientation principles that can be applied to numerous parts of SOA. Pursuing autonomy when building and assembling service logic supports other SOA characteristics.
based on open standards	This is a natural by-product of basing SOA on the Web services technology platform and its ever-growing collection of WS-* specifications. The majority of Web services specifications are open and vendor-neutral.
QoS capable	The quality of service improvements provided by contemporary SOA are, for the most part, realized via vendor implementations of individual WS-* extensions.
architecturally composable	While composability, on a service level, is one of our service-orientation principles, for an architecture to be considered composable requires that the technology from which the architecture is built support this notion. For the most part, the specifications that comprise the WS-* landscape fully enable architectural composability by allowing a given SOA to only implement extensions it actually requires.
vendor diversity	This is really more of a benefit of SOA than an actual characteristic. Regardless, it is primarily realized through the use of the open standards provided by the Web services platform.
intrinsic interoperability	The standardized communications framework provided by Web services establishes the potential to foster limitless interoperability between services. This is no big secret. To foster intrinsic interoperability among services, though, requires forethought and good design standards. Although supported by a number of WS-* specifications, this characteristic is not directly enabled by our identified influences.

Characteristic	Origin and/or Supporting Source
discoverability	Service-level discoverability is one of our fundamental principles of service-orientation. Implementing discoverability on an SOA level typically requires the use of directory technologies, such as UDDI (one of the first-generation Web services specifications).
promotes federation	Federation is a state achieved by extending SOA into the realm of service-oriented integration. A number of key WS-* extensions provide feature-sets that support the attainment of federation. Most notable among these are the specifications that implement the concepts of orchestration and choreography.
inherent reusability	Reusability is one of the primary principles of service-orientation and one that can be applied across service-oriented solution environments. SOA promotes the creation of inherently reusable service logic within individual services and across service compositions—a benefit attainable through quality service design.
extensibility	Given that Web services are composable and based on open standards, extensibility is a natural benefit of this platform. Several WS-* extensions introduce architectural mechanisms that build extensibility into a solution. However, for the most part, this is a characteristic that must be intentionally designed into services individually and into SOA as a whole.
service-oriented business modeling	This key characteristic is supported by orchestration, although not automatically. WS-* specifications, such as WS-BPEL, provide a dialect capable of expressing business process logic in an operational syntax resulting in a process definition. Only through deliberate design, though, can these types of process definitions actually be utilized to support service-oriented business modeling.
layers of abstraction	Service-orientation principles fully promote black box-type abstraction on a service interface level. However, to coordinate logic abstraction into layers, services must be designed and organized according to specific design standards.

Table 9.1   A review of how contemporary SOA characteristics are influenced by Web services specifications and service-orientation principles. (*Continued*)

Characteristic	Origin and/or Supporting Source
enterprise-wide loose coupling	Loose coupling is one of the fundamental characteristics of Web services. Achieving a loosely coupled enterprise is a benefit expected from the coordinated proliferation of SOA and abstraction layers throughout an organization's business and application domains.
organizational agility	Though the use of Web services, service-orientation principles, and WS-* specifications support the concept of increasing an organization's agility, they do not directly enable it. This important characteristic requires dedicated analysis and design and relies on the realization of other SOA characteristics.

> **NOTE**
>
> The WS-* specifications referenced in Table 9.1 are only those covered by this book. Additional specifications exist.

9.1.2   Unsupported SOA characteristics

Having removed the concrete SOA characteristics that receive support from our identified external influences, we are now left with the following six:

- intrinsic interoperability
- extensibility
- enterprise-wide loose coupling
- service-oriented business modeling
- organizational agility
- layers of abstraction

The first two are somewhat enabled by different WS-* extensions. However, realizing these characteristics within SOA is a direct result of standardized, quality service design. The design guidelines provided in Chapter 15 provide recommendations for fostering these qualities. As a result, we'll take interoperability and extensibility off our list for now.

This leaves us with four remaining characteristics of contemporary SOA that are not directly supported or provided by the external influences we identified. These characteristics have been numbered here only to allow for easier referencing in later sections.

1. enterprise-wide loose coupling
2. support for service-oriented business modeling
3. organizational agility
4. layers of abstraction

What is most interesting about our brief study is that these four characteristics actually provide some of the most crucial benefits of this architecture. The caveat, though, is that they require a conscious effort for us to realize. This translates into extra up-front work that simply comes with the territory of building contemporary SOA.

Incorporating these key qualities into SOA requires that some very fundamental decisions be made, long before the building process of individual services actually can commence. The remaining sections in this chapter explore how structuring SOA around the creation of specialized service layers directly determines the extent to which these characteristics can be manifested.

SUMMARY OF KEY POINTS

- The primary external influences that shape and affect contemporary SOA are first- and second-generation Web services specifications and the principles of service-orientation.

- Many of the characteristics that define contemporary SOA are, in fact, provided by these external influences.

- Those characteristics not directly supplied by these influences must be realized through dedicated modeling and design effort.

- These unique characteristics represent some of SOA's most important features and its broadest benefit potential.

9.2 Service layer abstraction

In our familiar enterprise model, the service interface layer is located between the business process and application layers. This is where service connectivity resides and is therefore the area of our enterprise wherein the characteristics of SOA are most prevalent. To implement the characteristics we just identified in an effective manner, some larger issues need to be addressed.

Specifically, we need to answer the following questions:

- What logic should be represented by services?
- How should services relate to existing application logic?
- How can services best represent business process logic?
- How can services be built and positioned to promote agility?

Typically, these questions are studied and eventually answered during the service-oriented analysis phase, where services are carefully modeled in accordance with and in response to external business and project drivers. Before we delve into specific recommendations on how to succeed at the art of service modeling (as explained in Chapters 11 and 12), let's first provide some preliminary answers to these questions.

9.2.1   Problems solved by layering services

What logic should be represented by services?
In the previous chapter we established that enterprise logic can be divided into two primary domains: business logic and application logic. Services can be modeled to represent either or both types of logic, as long as the principles of service-orientation can be applied.

However, to achieve enterprise-wide loose coupling (the first of our four outstanding SOA characteristics) physically separate layers of services are, in fact, required. When individual collections of services represent corporate business logic and technology-specific application logic, each domain of the enterprise is freed of direct dependencies on the other.

This allows the automated representation of business process logic to evolve independently from the technology-level application logic responsible for its execution. In other words, this establishes a loosely coupled relationship between business and application logic.

How should services relate to existing application logic?
Much of this depends on whether existing legacy application logic needs to be exposed via services or whether new logic is being developed in support of services. Existing

systems can impose any number of constraints, limitations, and environmental require-ments that need to be taken into consideration during service design.

Applying a service layer on top of legacy application environments may even require that some service-orientation principles be compromised. This is less likely when build-ing solutions from the ground up with service layers in mind, as this affords a level of control with which service-orientation can be directly incorporated into application logic.

Either way, services designed specifically to represent application logic should exist in a separate layer. We'll therefore simply refer to this group of services as belonging to the *application service layer*.

How can services best represent business logic?

Business logic is defined within an organization's business models and business processes. When modeling services to represent business logic, it is most important to ensure that the service representation of this logic is in alignment with existing business models.

It is also useful to separately categorize services that are designed in this manner. There-fore, we'll refer to services that have been modeled to represent business logic as belong-ing to the *business service layer*. By adding a business service layer, we also implement the second of our four SOA characteristics, which is support for service-oriented business modeling.

How can services be built and positioned to promote agility?

The key to building an agile SOA is in minimizing the dependencies each service has within its own processing logic. Services that contain business rules are required to enforce and act upon these rules at runtime. This limits the service's ability to be utilized outside of environments that require these rules. Similarly, controller services that are embedded with the logic required to compose other services can develop dependencies on the composition structure.

Introducing a parent controller layer on top of more specialized service layers would allow us to establish a centralized location for business rules and composition logic related to the sequence in which services are executed. Orchestration is designed specif-ically for this purpose. It introduces the concept of a process service, capable of com-posing other services to complete a business process according to predefined workflow logic. Process services establish what we refer to as the *orchestration service layer*.

While the addition of an orchestration service layer significantly increases organizational agility (number three on our list of SOA characteristics), it is not alone in realizing this quality. All forms of organized service abstraction contribute to establishing an agile enterprise, which means that the creation of separate application, business, and orchestration layers collectively fulfill this characteristic.

Abstraction is the key

Though we addressed each of the preceding questions individually, the one common element to all of the answers also happens to be the last of our four outstanding SOA characteristics: layers of abstraction.

We have established how, by leveraging the concept of composition, we can build specialized layers of services. Each layer can abstract a specific aspect of our solution, addressing one of the issues we identified. This alleviates us from having to build services that accommodate business, application, and agility considerations all at once.

The three layers of abstraction we identified for SOA are:

- the application service layer
- the business service layer
- the orchestration service layer

Each of these layers (also shown in Figure 9.2) is introduced individually in the following sections.

NOTE

The next three sections reference service models established in previous chapters and also introduce several new service models. Appendix B provides a reference table for all service models covered in this book, including information as to where individual models are discussed.

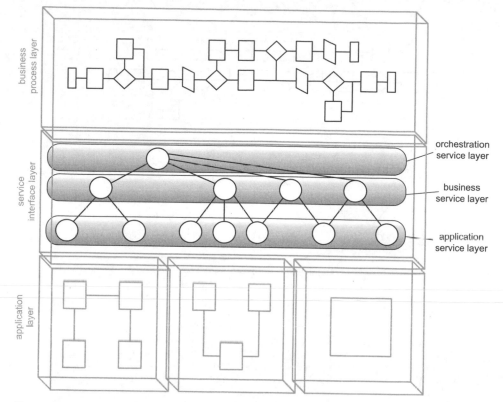

Figure 9.2
The three primary service layers.

SUMMARY OF KEY POINTS

- Through abstraction implemented via distinct service layers, key contemporary SOA characteristics can be realized—most notably, increased organizational agility.

- The three common layers of SOA are the application service layer, the business service layer, and the orchestration service layer.

9.3   Application service layer

The application service layer intentionally abstracts non-business-related logic (logic that is not derived from an organization's business models) into a set of services that can simply be referred to as *application services* (or utility services). Their purpose is to provide reusable functions that address cross-cutting concerns by representing common enterprise resources and capabilities.

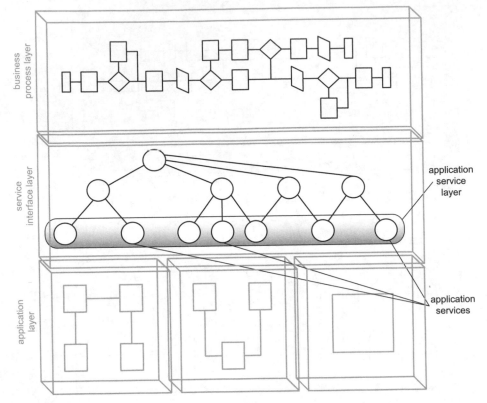

Figure 9.3
The application service layer.

Application services commonly have the following characteristics:

- they expose functionality within a specific processing context
- they draw upon available resources within a given platform
- they are solution-agnostic
- they are generic and reusable
- they can be used to achieve point-to-point integration with other application services
- they are often inconsistent in terms of the interface granularity they expose
- they may consist of a mixture of custom-developed services and third-party services that have been purchased or leased

When a separate business service layer exists (as explained in the *Business service layer* section), there is a strong motivation to turn all application services into generic utility services. This way they are implemented in a solution-agnostic manner, providing reusable operations that can be composed by business services to fulfill business-centric processing requirements.

Alternatively, if business logic does not reside in a separate layer, application services may be required to implement service models more associated with the business service layer. For example, a single application service also can be classified as a business service if it interacts directly with application logic and contains embedded business rules.

Services that contain both application and business logic can be referred to as *hybrid application services* or just *hybrid services*. This service model is commonly found within traditional distributed architectures. It is not a recommended design when building service abstraction layers. Because it is so common, though, it is discussed and referenced throughout this book.

Finally, an application service also can compose other, smaller-grained application services (such as proxy services) into a unit of coarse grained application logic. Aggregating application services is frequently done to accommodate integration requirements. Application services that exist solely to enable integration between systems often are referred to as *application integration services* or simply *integration services*.

You may have noticed that application services are very similar to the utility service model we explained in Chapter 5. In fact, you can easily rename the application service layer as the *utility service layer*. Another common term that is also used is *infrastructure services* (or the *infrastructure service layer*). You are encouraged to use whatever term best suits your naming conventions.

Because they are common residents of the application service layer, now is a good time to introduce the *wrapper service* model. Wrapper services most often are utilized for integration purposes. They consist of services that encapsulate ("wrap") some or all parts of a legacy environment to expose legacy functionality to service requestors. The most frequent form of wrapper service is a service adapter provided by legacy vendors. This type of out-of-the-box Web service simply establishes a vendor-defined service interface that expresses an underlying API to legacy logic.

Another variation of the wrapper service model not discussed in this book is the *proxy service*, also known as an *auto-generated WSDL*. This simply provides a WSDL definition that mirrors an existing component interface. It establishes an endpoint on the component's behalf, essentially allowing it to participate in SOAP communication. The proxy service should not be confused with a *service proxy*, which is used by service requestors to contact service providers (as explained in Chapter 18).

CASE STUDY

TLS has a well-defined application services layer. Of the TLS services we've discussed so far in our case study, the following are considered application services:

- Load Balancing Service
- Internal Policy Service
- System Notification Service

Each is a utility service that provides a set of generic, reusable features, and each is capable of acting as a composition member, fulfilling a specific task within a larger unit of automation.

All of the following RailCo services incorporate processing akin to application services:

- Invoice Submission Service
- Order Fulfillment Service
- TLS Subscription Service

Both the Invoice Submission and Order Fulfillment Services are somewhat hybrid, in that each also contains embedded business logic (as described further in the *Business service layer* example). The TLS Subscription Service can be classified as a pure application service, as it performs a simple, application-centric task. It's questionable whether any RailCo services would be considered utility services because none were designed with any real reusability in mind.

9.4 Business service layer

The business service layer represents a collection of services based on the business service model called *business services*.

It is through this service layer that we can achieve a close alignment between an organization's business and technology domains. Analysts, architects, and other IT professionals collaboratively complete a special analysis process through which each business service is assigned a functional context derived from one or more existing organizational business models or specifications. (For more information regarding service-oriented analysis, see Chapter 11.)

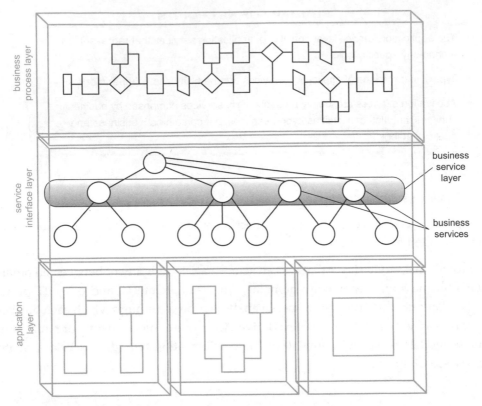

Figure 9.4
The business service layer.

In most enterprises, designing a business service layer leads to the creation of two common business service models, each of which establishes its own sub-layer.

- *Task-centric business service*—A service that encapsulates business logic specific to a task or business process that involves two or more business entities. Task-centric business services generally have limited reuse potential and can be simply referred to as *task services*.

- *Entity-centric business service*—A service that encapsulates processing logic associated with a specific business entity (such as an invoice or timesheet). Entity-centric services are useful for creating highly reusable and business process-agnostic services. Entity-centric business services can also be called *business entity services* or just *entity services*.

When a separate application service layer exists, these two types of business services can be positioned to compose application services to carry out their business logic. Task and entity-centric business services are explained in more detail in the *Deriving business services* section in Chapter 11.

Note that the hybrid service we introduced previously is actually a service that contains both business and application logic. It is therefore often referred to as a type of business service. For the purpose of establishing specialized service layers, we consider the business service layer reserved for services that abstract business logic only. We therefore classify the hybrid service as a variation of an application service, making it a resident of the application service layer.

CASE STUDY

Of the TLS services we've discussed so far in our case study examples, the following are true business services:

- Accounts Payable Service
- Purchase Order Service
- Ledger Service
- Vendor Profile Service

Each represents a well-defined boundary of business logic, and whenever one of these service's operations needs to perform a task outside of this boundary, it reuses functionality provided in another business or application service.

As we mentioned earlier, RailCo's Invoice Submission and Order Fulfillment Services are hybrid in that they contain both business rules and application-related processing. This type of service is very common in organizations that only incorporate services peripherally. Either way, for modeling purposes, these two services are classified as hybrid application services. Because business logic is not explicitly abstracted, only an application services layer exists within RailCo.

9.5   Orchestration service layer

In Chapter 6 we introduced a concept that ties into and actually extends the reach of service-orientation. This concept is orchestration. When incorporated as part of a service-oriented architecture, orchestration assumes the role of the process part we established in the *Anatomy of a service-oriented architecture* section.

Orchestration is more valuable to us than a standard business process, as it allows us to directly link process logic to service interaction within our workflow logic. This combines business process modeling with service-oriented modeling and design. And, because orchestration languages (such as WS-BPEL) realize workflow management through a process service model, orchestration brings the business process into the service layer, positioning it as a master composition controller.

The orchestration service layer introduces a parent level of abstraction that alleviates the need for other services to manage interaction details required to ensure that service operations are executed in a specific sequence (Figure 9.5). Within the orchestration service layer, *process services* compose other services that provide specific sets of functions, independent of the business rules and scenario-specific logic required to execute a process instance.

These are the same process services for which we defined the process service model described in Chapter 6. Therefore, all process services are also controller services by their very nature, as they are required to compose other services to execute business process logic.

Note that process services can also be referred to as *orchestrated task services*. This additional qualification simply communicates the nature of the task services implementation environment and also tends to imply that the service is capable of composing larger, long-running service activities. The orchestration service layer can also be called the *parent business process layer* (which may be easier for business analysts to understand). Feel free to use whatever terminology fits best with your current conventions.

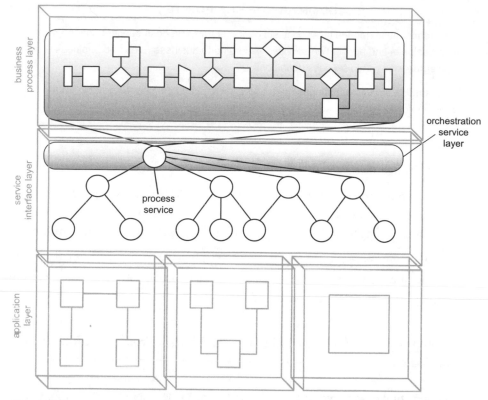

Figure 9.5

The orchestration service layer.

Also worth noting is that, as explained in Chapter 6, the introduction of an orchestration layer typically brings with it the requirement to introduce new middleware into the IT infrastructure. Orchestration servers are by no means a trivial addition and can impose significant expense and complexity.

CASE STUDY

Neither TLS or RailCo employ process services or a separate orchestration layer. As with many organizations, TLS is interested in orchestration but is uncertain as to the technology that supports it and the impact it would have on their current service architecture. By the time we reach Chapter 16, TLS will have decided to give orchestration a try. As a result, our case study will progress in that chapter to the point where we build a WS-BPEL business process definition for TLS that establishes an official orchestration service layer.

SUMMARY OF KEY POINTS

- The orchestration service layer consists of one or more process services that compose business and application services according to business rules and business logic embedded within process definitions.

- Orchestration abstracts business rules and service execution sequence logic from other services, promoting agility and reusability.

9.6   Agnostic services

A key aspect of delivering reusable services is that they introduce service layers that are not limited to a single processs or solution environment. It is important to highlight this one point, as it can blur the architectural boundary of a service-oriented solution.

An application-level SOA containing solution-agnostic services does, in fact, extend beyond the application. And, in the same manner, an application-level SOA that depends on the use of existing solution-agnostic services also does not have a well defined application boundary.

To expand on this point, let's take another look at those services more prone to providing reusable logic.

- Entity-centric business services are designed to provide a set of features that provide data management related only to their corresponding entities. They are therefore business process-agnostic. The same entity-centric business services can (and should) be reused by different process or task-centric business services.

- Application services ideally are built according to the utility service model. This makes them highly generic, reusable, and very much solution-agnostic. Different service-oriented solutions can (and should) reuse the same application services.

As shown in Figure 9.6, services can be process- and solution-agnostic while still being used as part of a service layer that connects different processes and solutions.

If the services you are delivering collectively represent the logic of an entire solution, then the architectural scope is essentially that of an application-level SOA. However, if you are building services that only extend an existing solution (or are being deployed with immediate reuse in mind), then the architectural scope can vary.

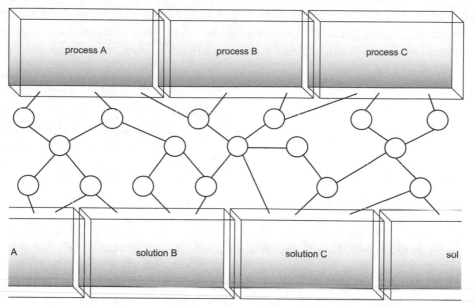

Figure 9.6

Services uniting previously isolated business processes and solution environments.

An enterprise that invests heavily in agnostic services easily can end up with an environment in which a great deal of reuse is leveraged. This is the point at which building service-oriented solutions can become more of a modeling exercise and less of an actual development project.

SUMMARY OF KEY POINTS

- Solution-agnostic service layers relate to and tie together multiple business processes and automation solutions.

- These service layers promote reuse but also blur the architectural boundaries of individual solutions.

9.7 Service layer configuration scenarios

So far we've established a relatively clean service layer model for SOA, in which logic is clearly abstracted through three distinct layers that establish a well-defined composition hierarchy. Unfortunately, real SOAs rarely resemble this state.

Many variations can exist, as the various types of services we've discussed so far can be combined to create different SOA configurations. We provide here some sample configuration scenarios and briefly discuss the characteristics of each.

Just to recap, we will explore scenarios based on the use of the following types of services:

- hybrid application services (services containing both business process and application logic)
- utility application services (services containing reusable application logic)
- task-centric business services (services containing business process logic)
- entity-centric business services (services containing entity business logic)
- process services (services representing the orchestration service layer)

<table>
<tr><td align="center">NOTE</td></tr>
<tr><td>In this section we qualify application services with the terms "hybrid" and "utility." However, in future chapters, utility application services simply are referred to as application services.</td></tr>
</table>

9.7.1   Scenario #1: Hybrid application services only

When Web services simply are appended to existing distributed application environments, or when a Web services-based solution is built without any emphasis on reuse or service-oriented business modeling, the resulting architecture tends to consist of a set of hybrid application services (Figure 9.7).

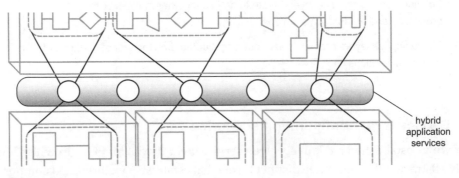

hybrid
application
services

Figure 9.7
Hybrid services encapsulating both business and application logic.

9.7.2   Scenario #2: Hybrid and utility application services

A variation of the previous configuration establishes a Web services-based architecture consisting of hybrid services and reusable application services. In this case, the hybrid services may compose some of the reusable application services. This configuration achieves an extent of abstraction, as the utility services establish a solution-agnostic application layer (Figure 9.8).

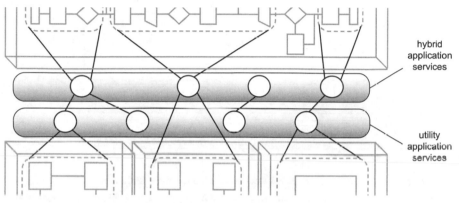

Figure 9.8
Hybrid services composing available utility application services.

9.7.3   Scenario #3: Task-centric business services and utility application services

This approach results in a more coordinated level of abstraction, given that business process logic is entirely represented by a layer of task-centric business services. These services rely on a layer of application services for the execution of all their business logic (Figure 9.9).

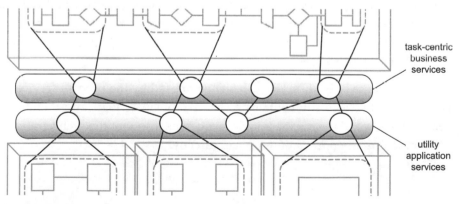

Figure 9.9
Task-centric business services and utility application services cleanly abstracting business and application logic.

9.7.4 Scenario #4: Task-centric business services, entity-centric business services, and utility application services

Here we've added a further layer of abstraction through the introduction of entity-centric business services. This positions task-centric services as parent controllers that may compose both entity-centric and application services to carry out business process logic (Figure 9.10).

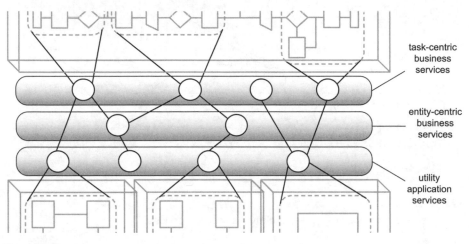

task-centric
business
services

entity-centric
business
services

utility
application
services

Figure 9.10
Two types of business services composing application services.

9.7.5 Scenario #5: Process services, hybrid application services, and utility application services

In this scenario, a parent process service composes available hybrid and application services to automate a business process. This is a common configuration when adding an orchestration layer over the top of an older distributed computing architecture that uses Web services (Figure 9.11).

Note that although the hybrid service is being composed by the process service in Figure 9.11, the hybrid service still contains embedded business logic and therefore indirectly represents some of the business logic layer. Note also that the orchestration layer also may compose utility application services directly.

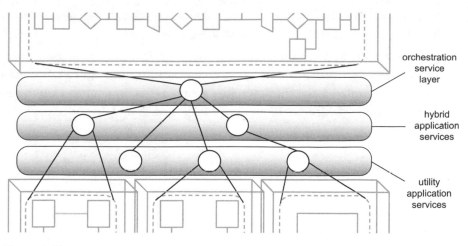

Figure 9.11

An orchestration layer providing a process service that composes different types of application services.

9.7.6 Scenario #6: Process services, task-centric business services, and utility application services

Even though task-centric services also contain business process logic, a parent process service can still be positioned to compose both task-centric and utility application services. Though only partial abstraction is achieved via task-centric services, when combined with the centralized business process logic represented by the process services, business logic as a whole is still abstracted (Figure 9.12).

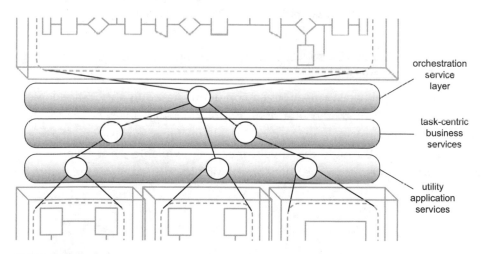

Figure 9.12

A process service composing task-centric and utility application services.

9.7.7 Scenario #7: Process services, task-centric business services, entity-centric business services, and utility application services

This variation also introduces entity-centric business services, which can result in a configuration that actually consists of four service layers. Sub-processes can be composed by strategically positioned task-centric services, whereas the parent process is managed by the process service, which composes both task-centric and entity-centric services (Figure 9.13).

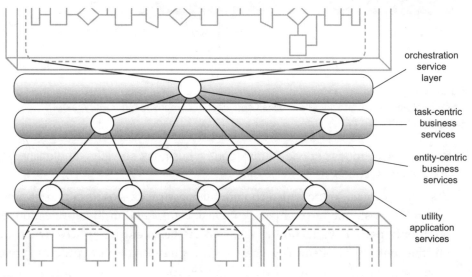

Figure 9.13
Process and business services composing utility application services.

9.7.8 Scenario #8: Process services, entity-centric business services, and utility application services

This SOA model establishes a clean separation of business and application logic, while maximizing reuse through the utilization of solution and business process-agnostic service layers. The process service contains all business process-specific logic and executes this logic through the involvement of available entity-centric business services, which, in turn, compose utility application logic to carry out the required tasks (Figure 9.14).

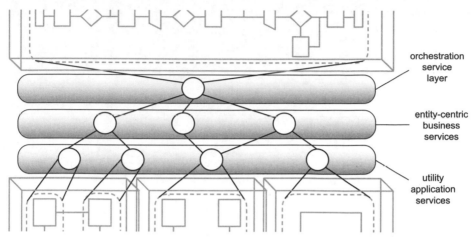

Figure 9.14

A process service composing entity-centric services, which compose utility application services.

SUMMARY OF KEY POINTS

- SOAs are configured in different shapes and sizes, depending primarily on the types of services from which they are comprised.

- Hybrid application services are found more commonly when service-oriented environments include legacy distributed application logic.

- By strategically positioning business and process services, an enterprise's business logic can be abstracted successfully from the underlying application logic.

Part IV

Building SOA
(Planning and Analysis)

The separation of business analysis and solution design and construction are quite distinct in most custom development projects. Analysts typically gather and document business requirements that are handed over to architects and developers who design and build corresponding automation logic.

A project delivering a contemporary service-oriented solution changes this approach somewhat by blurring the lines that divide the initial project phases. SOA emphasizes a direct relationship between business analysis intelligence and the services that end up representing and implementing business logic.

This results in the requirement for a unique form of analysis that needs to be completed prior to the design of individual services, as explained in Chapters 11 and 12. Before we begin this stage, Chapter 10 helps us make some decisions around how a project delivering services intended for SOA should be organized.

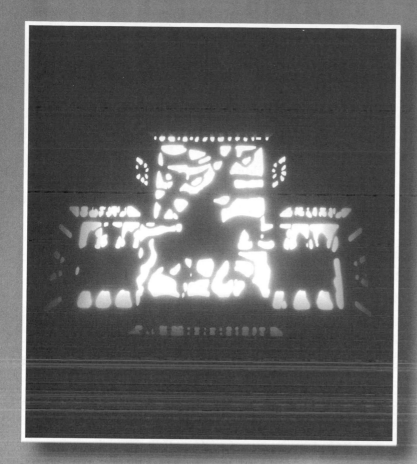

SOA Delivery Strategies

Common project phases associated with building and delivering services are established in this chapter, along with delivery strategies that arrange these stages into different sequences based on organizational priorities.

> **How case studies are used:** Examples that demonstrate different delivery strategies are provided, as TLS uses a very different approach to building their services than RailCo.

10.1   SOA delivery lifecycle phases

The lifecycle of an SOA delivery project is simply comprised of a series of steps that need to be completed to construct the services for a given service-oriented solution.

10.1.1   Basic phases of the SOA delivery lifecycle

Development projects for service-oriented solutions are, on the surface, much like other custom development projects for distributed applications. Web services are designed, developed, and deployed alongside standard components and the usual supporting cast of front- and back-end technologies. When we dig a bit deeper under the layers of service-orientation, though, we'll find that to properly construct and position services as part of SOA, traditional project cycles require some adjustments.

Looking at Figure 10.1, you may wonder why the first two phase names are prefixed with "service-oriented" when the remaining phases have names that begin with just "service." The main reason we make this distinction is because it is during the analysis and design stages that the SOA characteristics and service-orientation principles we've been discussing actually are incorporated into the solution being built. So much so, that they warrant unique analysis and design processes that are distinctly "service-oriented." The service phases are primarily concerned with the delivery of services that implement the results of service-oriented analysis and design efforts.

Let's now explain each of these lifecycle phases.

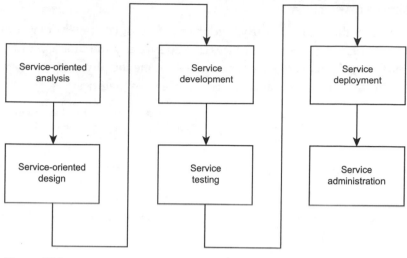

Figure 10.1
Common phases of an SOA delivery lifecycle.

10.1.2 Service-oriented analysis

It is in this initial stage that we determine the potential scope of our SOA. Service layers are mapped out, and individual services are modeled as service candidates that comprise a preliminary SOA.

A formal step-by-step service modeling process is provided as part of the two chapters (11 and 12) dedicated to the service-oriented analysis phase.

10.1.3 Service-oriented design

When we know what it is we want to build, we need to determine how it should be constructed. Service-oriented design is a heavily standards-driven phase that incorporates industry conventions and service-orientation principles into the service design process.

This phase, therefore, confronts service designers with key decisions that establish the hard logic boundaries encapsulated by services. The service layers designed during this stage can include the orchestration layer, which results in a formal business process definition.

Four formal step-by-step design processes are provided within the four chapters (13 to 16) dedicated to the service-oriented design phase.

10.1.4 Service development

Next, of course, is the actual construction phase. Here development platform-specific issues come into play, regardless of service type. Specifically, the choice of programming language and development environment will determine the physical form services and orchestrated business processes take, in accordance with their designs.

As part of our coverage of SOA platforms, we explore development and runtime technologies associated with the .NET and J2EE platforms in Chapter 18.

10.1.5 Service testing

Given their generic nature and potential to be reused and composed in unforeseeable situations, services are required to undergo rigorous testing prior to deployment into a production environment.

Below is a sampling of some of the key issues facing service testers:

- What types of service requestors could potentially access a service?
- Can all service policy assertions be successfully met?
- What types of exception conditions could a service be potentially subjected to?
- How well do service descriptions communicate service semantics?
- Do revised service descriptions alter or extend previous versions?
- How easily can the services be composed?
- How easily can the service descriptions be discovered?
- Is compliance to WS-I profiles required?
- What data typing-related issues might arise?
- Have all possible service activities and service compositions been mapped out?
- Have all compensation processes been fully tested?
- What happens if exceptions occur within compensation processes?
- Do all new services comply with existing design standards?
- Do new services introduce custom SOAP headers? And, if yes, are all potential requestors (including intermediaries) required to do so, capable of understanding and processing them?
- Do new services introduce functional or QoS requirements that the current architecture does not support?

10.1.6   Service deployment

The implementation stage brings with it the joys of installing and configuring distributed components, service interfaces, and any associated middleware products onto production servers.

Typical issues that arise during this phase include:

- How will services be distributed?

- Is the infrastructure adequate to fulfill the processing requirements of all services?

- How will the introduction of new services affect existing services and applications?

- How should services used by multiple solutions be positioned and deployed?

- How will the introduction of any required middleware affect the existing environment?

- Do these services introduce new versions of service descriptions that will need to be deployed alongside existing versions?

- What security settings and accounts are required?

- How will service pools be maintained to accommodate planned or unforeseen scalability requirements?

- How will encapsulated legacy systems with performance or reliability limitations be maintained and monitored?

> **NOTE**
>
> Service deployment is specific to the technology platform for which services are developed. Chapter 18 provides various details regarding the physical implementation of services within J2EE and .NET environments.

10.1.7   Service administration

After services are deployed, standard application management issues come to the forefront. These are similar in nature to the administration concerns for distributed, component-based applications, except that they also may apply to services as a whole (as opposed to services belonging to a specific application environment).

Issues frequently include:

- How will service usage be monitored?

- What form of version control will be used to manage service description documents?

- How will messages be traced and managed?
- How will performance bottlenecks be detected?

> **NOTE**
>
> Service testing and administration are beyond the scope of this book.

10.1.8   SOA delivery strategies

The lifecycle stages identified in the previous sections represent a simple, sequential path to building individual services.

We now need to organize these stages into a process that can:

- accommodate our preferences with regards to which types of service layers we want to deliver
- coordinate the delivery of application, business, and process services
- support a transition toward a standardized SOA while helping us fulfill immediate, project-specific requirements

The last item on this list poses the greatest challenge. The success of SOA within an enterprise is generally dependent on the extent to which it is standardized when it is phased into business and application domains. However, the success of a project delivering a service-oriented solution generally is measured by the extent to which the solution fulfills expected requirements within a given budget and timeline.

To address this problem, we need a strategy. This strategy must be based on an organization's priorities to establish the correct balance between the delivery of long-term migration goals with the fulfillment of short-term requirements. Three common strategies have emerged, each addressing this problem in a different manner.

- top-down
- bottom-up
- agile (or meet-in-the-middle)

These paths differ in priorities and practical considerations. The following three sections provide process descriptions and explore the pros and cons of each approach.

How you approach the creation of a service-oriented environment ultimately determines what you will end up with. The strategies discussed here, therefore, will confront you with some important decision-making. Choosing the right approach will determine the extent to which your service-oriented modeling and design efforts can realize the full potential of SOA.

NOTE

If you're not interested in learning about the individual steps that comprise each of the following processes at this point, feel free to skip ahead to the *Pros and cons* part of each section. Knowledge of individual process steps is not required for subsequent reading.

SUMMARY OF KEY POINTS

- The basic SOA lifecycle consists of a series of phases similar to those used for regular development projects.

- SOA introduces unique considerations in every phase of service construction and delivery.

- Different strategies exist for how to organize lifecycle stages to enable delivery of specialized service layers.

10.2 The top-down strategy

This strategy is very much an "analysis first" approach that requires not only business processes to become service-oriented, but also promotes the creation (or realignment) of an organization's overall business model. This process is therefore closely tied to or derived from an organization's existing business logic.

The top-down strategy supports the creation of all three of the service layers we discussed in the previous chapter. It is common for this approach to result in the creation of numerous reusable business and application services.

10.2.1 Process

The top-down approach will typically contain some or all of the steps illustrated and described in Figure 10.2. Note that this process assumes that business requirements have already been collected and defined.

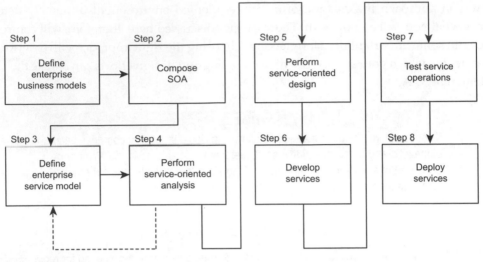

Figure 10.2
Common top-down strategy process steps.

Step 1: Define enterprise business models

The format of enterprise business models tends to vary across different organizations, each of which will have models that are unique to its business domains. Common types of enterprise business model documents include a formal ontology, an enterprise entity model, an enterprise-wide logical data model, a standardized data representation architecture (often realized through a collection of standardized XML Schemas), and other forms of models generally associated with enterprise information architecture.

Some of these models provide business-centric perspectives of an organization that prove extremely valuable sources for deriving business services. Business entity models especially tie directly into the subsequent definition of entity-centric business services.

Although listed as just a single step in our high-level process, the requirements to properly define enterprise business models can easily result in the need for one or more separate processes, each of which may require its own project and working group. On the other hand, if the required enterprise business models already exist, then this step may simply consist of their identification.

Step 2: Compose SOA

Step 2 corresponds to the Compose SOA process described in the *Steps to composing SOA* section in Chapter 14. When a top-down strategy is employed, this step is often considered part of the up-front analysis effort required prior to the delivery of services, and is therefore not associated with the service-oriented design phase.

Step 3: Define enterprise service model

This step represents the creation of a specific type of enterprise business model known as the *enterprise service model*. This specification provides a formal documentation of a planned service inventory where numerous (and sometimes all) service candidates are defined ahead of time, prior to entering delivery stages. The enterprise service model implements the service layers chosen in Step 2 and thereby establishes a standardized, layered view of an enterprise-wide service portfolio.

You will notice on Figure 10.2 that there is a optional iterative relationship between this step and the service-oriented analysis process. A recommended strategy for creating an enterprise service model is to cycle through the service-oriented analysis process once for every known business process, thereby defining and constantly refining service candidates (especially agnostic candidates) prior to actual design and development.

Step 4: Perform service-oriented analysis

A service-oriented analysis phase, such as the one described in Chapters 11 and 12, is completed.

Step 5: Perform service-oriented design

The service layers are formally defined as part of a service-oriented design process, such as the one described in Chapters 13 through 16.

Step 6: Develop the required services

Services are developed according to their respective design specifications and the service descriptions created in Step 4.

Step 7: Test the services and all service operations

The testing stage requires that all service operations undergo necessary quality assurance checks. This typically exceeds the amount of testing required for the automation logic being implemented because reusable services will likely need to be subjected to testing beyond the immediate scope of the solution.

Step 8: Deploy the services

The solution is finally deployed into production. An implementation consideration beyond those we originally identified as part of this step is the future reuse potential of the service. To facilitate multiple service requestors, highly reusable services may require extra processing power and may have special security and accessibility requirements that will need to be accommodated.

10.2.2 Pros and cons

The top-down approach to building SOA generally results in a high quality service architecture. The design and parameters around each service are thoroughly analyzed, maximizing reusability potential and opportunities for streamlined compositions. All of this lays the groundwork for a standardized and federated enterprise where services maintain a state of adaptability, while continuing to unify existing heterogeneity.

The obstacles to following a top-down approach usually are associated with time and money. Organizations are required to invest significantly in up-front analysis projects that can take a great deal of time (proportional to the size of the organization and the immediate solution), without showing any immediate results.

CASE STUDY

A variation of the top-down approach (limited to a specific business domain) was used by TLS when they first ventured into building services for their B2B solution. The result was a set of business and application services, highly standardized and very reusable. TLS enjoyed a great deal of success with this initial collection of services, as they have been able to recompose them into different configurations to accommodate changing business requirements.

The time it took to carry through the top-down analysis, though, was significant. Now that the services have proven themselves as important members of the TLS technical environment, numerous new requirements are emerging, demanding the creation of new services and even new, entirely service-driven solutions. TLS's IT department is under a great deal of pressure to deliver. Despite the success of the top-down strategy, IT managers are hesitant to undergo this process again.

SUMMARY OF KEY POINTS

- The top-down strategy promotes the formal definition of corporate business models prior to modeling service boundaries.

- It can result in the highest quality level of SOA, but it also imposes a significant volume of up-front analysis work.

10.3 The bottom-up strategy

This approach essentially encourages the creation of services as a means of fulfilling application-centric requirements. Web services are built on an "as needed" basis and modeled to encapsulate application logic to best serve the immediate requirements of the solution. Integration is the primary motivator for bottom-up designs, where the need to take advantage of the open SOAP communications framework can be met by simply appending services as wrappers to legacy systems.

10.3.1 Process

A typical bottom-up approach follows a process similar to the one explained in Figure 10.3. Note that this process assumes that business requirements have already been collected and defined.

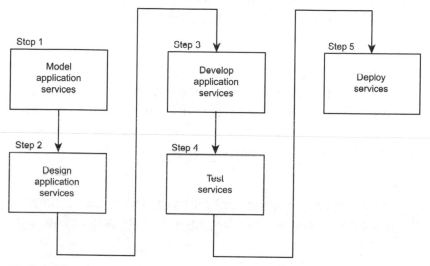

Figure 10.3
Common bottom-up strategy process steps.

Step 1: Model required application services

This step results in the definition of application requirements that can be fulfilled through the use of Web services. Typical requirements include the need to establish point-to-point integration channels between legacy systems or B2B solutions. Other common requirements emerge out of the desire to replace traditional remote communication technology with the SOAP messaging communications framework.

For solutions that employ the bottom-up strategy to deliver highly service-centric solutions, application services also will be modeled to include specific business logic and rules. In this case, it is likely that two application service layers will emerge, consisting of hybrid and utility services. Those services classified as reusable may act as generic application endpoints for integration purposes, or they may be composed by parent hybrid services.

Step 2: Design the required application services

Some of the application services modeled in Step 1 may be delivered by purchasing or leasing third-party wrapper services or perhaps through the creation of auto-generated proxy services. These services may provide little opportunity for additional design. Custom application services, though, will need to undergo a design process wherein existing design standards are applied to ensure a level of consistency. Chapter 15 provides a design process specifically for reusable application services.

Step 3: Develop the required application services

Application services are developed according to their respective service descriptions and applicable design specifications.

Step 4: Test the services

Services, their associated solution environment, and underlying legacy logic are tested to ensure that processing requirements can be met. Performance and stress testing measures often are used to set the processing parameters of legacy systems exposed via wrapper services. Security testing is also an important part of this stage.

Step 5: Deploy the services

The solution and its application services are deployed into production. Implementation considerations for application services frequently include performance and security requirements.

10.3.2   Pros and cons

The majority of organizations that currently are building Web services apply the bottom-up approach. The primary reason behind this is that organizations simply add Web services to their existing application environments to leverage the Web services technology set. The architecture within which Web services are added remains unchanged, and service-orientation principles are therefore rarely considered.

As a result, the term that is used to refer to this approach—"the bottom-up strategy"—is somewhat of a misnomer. The bottom-up strategy is really not a strategy at all. Nor is it a valid approach to achieving contemporary SOA. This is a realization that will hit many organizations as they begin to take service-orientation, as an architectural model, more seriously. Although the bottom-up design allows for the efficient creation of Web services as required by applications, implementing a proper SOA at a later point can result in a great deal of retro-fitting or even the introduction of new standardized service layers positioned over the top of the non-standardized services produced by this approach.

RailCo did not use any particular strategy when building the services they required to connect to the TLS B2B solution. They simply retrieved a set of published specifications from the TLS partner Web site and built the required services following the traditional development lifecycle they were already accustomed to.

RailCo was unaware that they were in fact following a very common approach to service construction known as the bottom-up strategy simply because this delivery approach consists of stages that closely mirror typical phases in traditional development methodology.

The result of building their Web services in this manner was predictable. The services were delivered to accommodate a specific need and therefore fulfilled immediate business requirements. Their construction was completed efficiently and cost-effectively, and the project was initially considered successful.

Some time later, though, new requirements surfaced. TLS implemented a new policy that affected some of the purchase order business logic on RailCo's end. Additionally, RailCo's own internal business process underwent a change as a result of a module upgrade within its legacy accounting system. This change carried over to affect low-level data access parameters processed by the RailCo Invoice Submission Service.

Both of these changes were an indication of things to come. Various adjustments needed to be made to the RailCo legacy systems that interfaced with their Web services, and numerous changes were made to existing automation processes as part of a company-wide initiative to improve responsiveness and efficiency.

Following are descriptions of the primary problems encountered by RailCo:

- Each change, regardless of origin, required a significant redevelopment effort that typically affected multiple services. Because there was no separation of business and application logic, change impacted a broader part of their solution environment. Also because none of the services were reusable, there was less chance that new requirements could be even partially fulfilled by existing services.

- With each programming modification came the overhead associated with the subsequent testing and deployment phases (for all services affected). This not only increased the ownership cost of each service, it also began morphing the services so that their underlying logic now exceeded the scope and context originally defined in their initial design.

SUMMARY OF KEY POINTS

- The bottom-up strategy simply is based on the delivery of application services on an "as needed" basis.

- This common approach is easy to follow but does not result in the advancement of service-orientation or contemporary SOA.

10.4 The agile strategy

The challenge remains to find an acceptable balance between incorporating service-oriented design principles into business analysis environments without having to wait before integrating Web services technologies into technical environments. For many organizations it is therefore useful to view these two approaches as extremes and to find a suitable middle ground.

This is possible by defining a new process that allows for the business-level analysis to occur concurrently with service design and development. Also known as the *meet-in-the-middle* approach, the *agile strategy* is more complex than the previous two simply because it needs to fulfill two opposing sets of requirements.

10.4.1 Process

The process steps shown in Figure 10.4 demonstrate an example of how an agile strategy can be used to reach the respective goals of the top-down and bottom-up approaches.

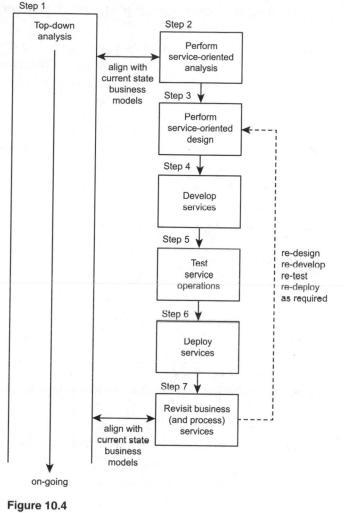

Figure 10.4

A sample agile strategy process.

Step 1: Perform a top-down analysis

This step essentially encompasses Steps 1, 2, and 3 from the top-down strategy described earlier in this chapter, except that areas of the enterprise for which service delivery is a priority are given immediate attention. After Step 2 has begun, Step 1 continues as an on-going effort to further achieve the enterprise-wide analysis goals generally associated with the top-down approach.

Step 2: When the top-down analysis has sufficiently progressed, perform service-oriented analysis

While Step 1 is still in progress, this step initiates a service-oriented analysis phase, such as the one described in Chapters 11 and 12. Depending on the magnitude of analysis required to complete Step 1, it is advisable to give that step a good head start. The further along it progresses, the more service designs will benefit.

After the top-down analysis has sufficiently progressed, model business services to best represent the business model with whatever analysis results are available. This is a key decision point in this process. It may require an educated judgment call to determine whether the on-going top-down analysis is sufficiently mature to proceed with the creation of business service models. This consideration must then be weighed against the importance and urgency of pending project requirements.

Step 3: Perform service-oriented design

The chosen service layers are defined, and individual services are designed as part of a service-oriented design process, such as the one described in Chapters 13 to 16. The extent to which the Compose SOA part of this process is required depends on the extent to which it was already addressed in Step 1.

Steps 4, 5, and 6: Develop, test, and deploy the services

Develop the services and submit them to the standard testing and deployment procedures.

Step 7: As the top-down analysis continues to progress, revisit business services

Perform periodic reviews of all business services to compare their design against the current state of the business models. Make a note of discrepancies and schedule a redesign for those services most out of alignment. This typically will require an extension to an existing service for it to better provide the full range of required capabilities. When redesigned, a service will need to again undergo standard development, testing, and deployment steps.

To preserve the integrity of services produced by this approach, the concept of *immutable service contracts* needs to be strictly enforced. After a contract is published, it cannot be altered. Unless revisions to services result in extensions that impose no restrictions on an existing contract (such as the addition of new operations to a WSDL definition), Step 7 of this process likely will result in the need to publish new contract versions and the requirement for a version management system.

10.4.2   Pros and cons

This strategy takes the best of both worlds and combines it into an approach for realizing SOA that meets immediate requirements without jeopardizing the integrity of an organization's business model and the service-oriented qualities of the architecture.

While it fulfills both short and long-term needs, the net result of employing this strategy is increased effort associated with the delivery of every service. The fact that services may need to be revisited, redesigned, redeveloped, and redeployed will add up proportionally to the amount of services subjected to this retasking step.

Additionally, this approach imposes maintenance tasks that are required to ensure that existing services are actually kept in alignment with revised business models. Even with a maintenance process in place, services still run the risk of misalignment with a constantly changing business model.

CASE STUDY

In response to new business requirements, TLS identifies the need for five, possibly six new services. These must be delivered relatively soon to address a major problem TLS is facing, resulting from glaring discrepancies between outsourced employee timesheets and corresponding customer invoices.

In Chapter 12 we walk through a step-by-step process during which we model these services as part of a new extension to our existing TLS case study. The approach taken to eventually build and deliver these new services will be based on the agile strategy.

SUMMARY OF KEY POINTS

- The agile strategy proposes a combination of top-down and bottom-up approaches.
- On-going analysis is supported, while still allowing the immediate delivery of services.
- As analysis progresses, existing services are revisited and revised as required.

NOTE

Visit www.soamethodology.com for more information about SOA project delivery strategies and processes.

Chapter 11

Service-Oriented Analysis
(Part I: Introduction)

The first and perhaps most important step along our SOA lifecycle is an analysis of what exactly the services in our SOA should consist of. This and the next chapter introduce the fundamental aspects of this project phase by establishing a formal service modeling process and raising a series of concerns that need to be addressed before we proceed to the design stage.

"Service-oriented architecture" vs. "Service-oriented environment"
As we established in Chapter 4, a service-oriented architecture represents a technical view of a business automation solution based on service-orientation principles. Because much of the discussion in this chapter is focused on business analysis in preparation for the service modeling process, we frequently use the broader term *service-oriented environment* to refer to the logical enterprise domain in which service-oriented principles are being applied. For the purposes of this chapter, therefore, a service-oriented environment can encompass business processes as well as the technology that automates them.

NOTE

Another term commonly used instead of service-oriented environment is the *SOA ecosystem*.

How case studies are used: Most of the examples in this chapter center around the RailCo environment as it prepares to proceed with a service-oriented analysis. (It is recommended that you read through these examples prior to commencing with the service modeling process in Chapter 12.)

The TLS SOA also is reviewed to highlight examples of existing entity-centric services. The last example states TLS's intention also to undergo a service-oriented analysis as the first step of a project required to deliver a new Timesheet Submission solution. This analysis phase is explored in detail at the end of Chapter 12.

11.1   Introduction to service-oriented analysis

The process of determining how business automation requirements can be represented through service-orientation is the domain of the service-oriented analysis.

11.1.1   Objectives of service-oriented analysis

Different organizations have adopted different approaches to analyzing business automation problems and developing corresponding solutions. Years of effort and documentation will often have been invested into well-established processes and modeling deliverables.

The process described in this section is not intended to supplant existing procedures. Instead, it proposes a set of supplementary steps that help shape the organization of automation logic in preparation for the service-oriented design processes. These steps raise issues that tie the use of service models, service-orientation principles, and other key considerations into a preliminary definition of services.

It is important to note that the process provided here is generic and high-level. It establishes a starting point from which an organization is expected to customize a variation of service-oriented analysis that is most suitable to its goals in relation to an SOA transition and most compatible with its existing approaches to business analysis.

The primary questions addressed during this phase are:

* What services need to be built?
* What logic should be encapsulated by each service?

The extent to which these questions are answered is directly related to the amount of effort invested in the analysis. Many of the issues we discussed in the past two chapters can be part of this stage.

The overall goals of performing a service-oriented analysis are as follows:

* Define a preliminary set of service operation candidates.
* Group service operation candidates into logical contexts. These contexts represent service candidates.
* Define preliminary service boundaries.
* Identify encapsulated logic with reuse potential.
* Ensure that the context of encapsulated logic is appropriate for its intended use.
* Identify preliminary issues that may challenge required service autonomy.
* Define any known preliminary composition models.

11.1.2 Service-oriented analysis and the enterprise service model

Service-oriented analysis can be applied at different levels, depending on which of the SOA delivery strategies are used to produce services. As explained in the previous chapter, the chosen strategy will determine whether some form of enterprise service model has been established and to what extent its detail has been defined.

It is technically possible to follow a strict top-down approach during which service-oriented analysis is iteratively applied to the enterprise service model to such an extent that all possible services have been defined with the required detail to allow service contracts for any service to be derived. However, top-down SOA efforts frequently succeed in only producing a high-level enterprise service model that establishes standardized service models, service layers, and a set of proposed service contexts, without a significantly detailed definition of what functionality is actually encapsulated by each service.

It is with this perspective of an enterprise SOA that the service-oriented analysis process described here is commonly applied. Using whatever has been established within the enterprise service model as its guide, this process addresses the definition of preliminary services within a predefined scope.

11.1.3 The service-oriented analysis process

The service-oriented analysis process is a sub-process of the overall SOA delivery lifecycle. The steps shown in Figure 11.1 represent common tasks associated with this phase and are described further in the following sections.

Note that Steps 1 and 2 are essentially information gathering tasks that are carried out in preparation for the modeling process described in Step 3.

Step 1: Define the scope of the analysis

It's always a good idea to clearly determine the scope of automation logic before you actually get into the delivery lifecycle. With traditional development projects, scope was often tied to the business process requiring automation or to some extension or enhancement to an existing solution (which usually also tied back to a change in the business process).

Service delivery projects can also have a scope that is defined by a unit of business process logic. However, it is not uncommon to only deliver a single process-agnostic service that will establish itself as a part of the overall service portfolio for use by future automated business processes. In this case, the scope is not as much a specific business task as it is the delivery of a series of tasks (operations) associated with a generic service context.

For example, a larger business process that will involve the composition of multiple services will require a scope that involves the definition of several new services and/or

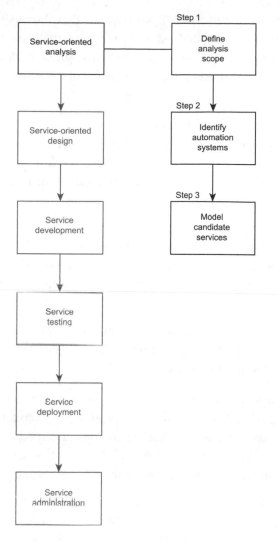

Figure 11.1
A high-level service-oriented analysis process.

the involvement of several existing services. The parent process logic itself may or may not end up residing in a service (depending on the service layers in use).

The delivery of an entity-centric business service, though, will introduce a series of processes, each tied to a generic task that represents a piece of functionality the service is required to encapsulate. Even though only a single service is being delivered, the scope may still be substantial, as each operation of the service can ultimately contain process logic that requires the composition of further services.

To properly establish the scope of the analysis requires that the business requirements we are intending to fulfill be fully defined and mature so that one or more high-level automation processes can be clearly documented with sufficient detail. This business process documentation will be used as the starting point of the service modeling process described in Step 3.

Step 2: Identify existing automation systems

Existing application logic that is already, to whatever extent, automating any of the requirements identified in Step 1 needs to be identified. While a service-oriented analysis will not determine how exactly services will encapsulate or replace legacy application logic, it does assist us in scoping the potential systems affected.

The details of how services relate to existing systems are ironed out in the service-oriented design phase. For now, this information will be used to help identify some of the more immediately recognizable constraints that can affect the definition of service candidates during the service modeling process described in Step 3.

Note that this step is more geared to supporting the modeling efforts of larger scaled service-oriented solutions. An understanding of affected legacy environments is still useful when modeling a smaller amount of services, but a great deal of research effort would generally not be required in this case.

Step 3: Model candidate services

A service-oriented analysis introduces the concept of service modeling—a process by which service operation candidates are identified and then grouped into a logical context. These groups eventually take shape as service candidates are then further assembled into a tentative composite model representing the combined logic of the planned service(s).

This process is explained in detail in the Service modeling (a step-by-step process) section of Chapter 12. Its purpose is to produce an ideal representation of business automation logic through service-orientation. The service candidates defined as a result of service modeling eventually become input for the service-oriented design processes described in Chapter 15.

CASE STUDY

Back in Chapter 2 we established that RailCo's ultimate goal is to standardize on SOA to solve its current automation problems and increase its online clientele. Subsequent chapters have talked at length about the various services RailCo has built that allow it to take part in online commerce exchanges with TLS's B2B solution.

Here is the familiar list of RailCo services:

- Invoice Submission Service
- Order Fulfillment Service
- TLS Subscription Service

Although their use has allowed RailCo to establish a Web services extension to their legacy solution environment, these three services do not constitute a true SOA. In the previous chapter we identified that the construction of these services was based purely on a bottom-up approach, resulting in the creation of what we've termed "hybrid" application services (application services that also contain business logic, intended for narrowly focused business tasks).

These services were assembled quickly to accommodate a single client. However, because that client has now formed a partnership with another air brake vendor, RailCo is only receiving a subset of its original revenue stream. This new reality has turned into a driving motivation for RailCo to commit to and invest in the standardization of a service-oriented architecture.

After a preliminary analysis of its existing Web services, it is quickly determined that there is little benefit in trying to build upon the services produced so far. Instead, it is decided to start from scratch and build a set of new services.

The agile delivery strategy (described in the previous chapter) is chosen as the approach by which these new services will be delivered. It is further determined that only application and business service layers will be modeled because RailCo is not in a position to invest in the middleware required to implement an orchestration layer.

As RailCo proceeds with its service-oriented analysis, it is able to identify some tangible benefits that an SOA can realize. These benefits appear to provide the potential to fulfill key business goals of the organization.

Specifically, preliminary analysis results indicate that:

- The application of service-orientation principles and the standardization introduced by SOA will allow a single set of services to accommodate interaction with different online partners. This would free RailCo from its ties to TLS and allow it to pursue new customers without necessarily having to build a new set of services each time.

- SOA facilitates the integration of internal legacy systems by establishing standardized application endpoints. In particular, the abstraction provided by service layers will enable RailCo to create integration channels that do not need to be removed if underlying legacy technology is replaced. This gives RailCo the ability to connect its accounting and contact management solutions knowing full well that the latter will likely need to be replaced in the future.

Because RailCo is focusing on overhauling its existing set of services, it has not yet identified any specific reusability requirements. However, it has been decided that, where feasible, services should be designed to support potential reuse. We explore the details of RailCo's analysis effort in the *Service modeling (a step-by-step process)* section in Chapter 12.

SUMMARY OF KEY POINTS

- The service-oriented analysis phase of an SOA delivery project requires that critical decisions be made that affect the shape and form of individual services as well as the overall service layers.

- Service modeling is the process of identifying candidate service operations and grouping them in candidate services.

11.2 Benefits of a business-centric SOA

The advent of Web services has publicized the importance of an open communications framework. As a result, most IT professionals are at a stage where they acknowledge the relevance of Web services technologies.

As we've established previously, the majority of Web services currently being built are, more or less, a mixture of application and business services. These types of hybrid services are attractive because, with minimal effort, they fulfill immediate requirements with clear ROI benefits. The proliferation of hybrid services is the result of the bottom-up approach having become so commonplace. They provide an immediate means for all past forms of application architecture to take part in the open Web services communications framework.

Business services, on the other hand, often need some justification. Many still resist—or are even unaware of—the benefits of introducing service-oriented principles into the domain of business analysis. It is easy to ignore service-oriented business modeling and simply focus on service-orientation as it applies to technology and technical architecture. The common rationale for this approach is that whatever business processes need to be automated can be divided up into physical Web services as required.

Many of the characteristics of contemporary SOA we listed in Chapter 3 can still be attained without the use of business services. Though it may appear that you are saving yourself a load of work by taking this path, the apparent benefits are superficial. There are very good reasons for taking the time to model and build business services. In this section we list a series of benefits for incorporating service-orientation into the business process level.

11.2.1   Business services build agility into business models

Service-orientation brings to business process models a structure that can significantly improve the flexibility and agility with which processes can be remodeled in response to changes. When properly designed, business services can establish a highly responsive information technology environment; responsive in that changes in an organization's business areas can be efficiently accommodated through re-composition of both a business process and its supporting technology architecture (as expressed by the application services layer).

As business-driven as SOAs are, there are often real world restrictions (infrastructure, security constraints, budget constraints) that require the technology side to push back. This can shift the burden of adaptation over to the business process models. This type of agility requirement can be met by the business service layer, as it allows business services to adjust to requirement changes originating from an organization's technical environments.

In other words, applying service layer abstraction to both business and technology ends establishes the potential for an enterprise to achieve a form of two-way agility (Figure 11.2).

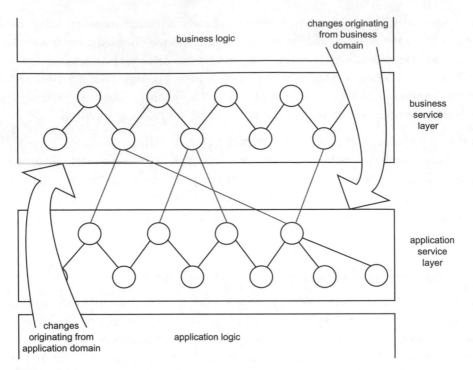

Figure 11.2

Changes originating in the business logic domain are accommodated by the application logic domain and vice versa.

11.2.2 Business services prepare a process for orchestration

Whether or not you will be moving to an orchestration-based service-oriented environment anytime soon, it is becoming increasingly important to be ready for this transition. Orchestration brings with it concepts that, when implemented, lie at the core of SOA. Therefore, modeling current processes so that they eventually can be more easily migrated to an orchestration-driven environment is recommended.

11.2.3 Business services enable reuse

The creation of a business service layer promotes reuse in both business and application services, as follows:

- By modeling business logic as distinct services with explicit boundaries, business process-level reuse can be achieved. Atomic sub-process logic or even entire processes can be reused as part of other process logic or as part of a compound process (which translates into a service composition in its own right).

- By taking the time to properly align business models with business service representation, the resulting business service layer ends up freeing the entire application service layer from assuming task or activity-specific processing functions. This allows application services to be positioned as and to evolve into pure, reusable utility services that facilitate business services across solution boundaries.

11.2.4   Only business services can realize the service-oriented enterprise

Business service modeling marries the principles of service-orientation with an organization's business model. The resulting perspective can clearly express how services relate to and embody the fulfillment of business requirements.

Applying business services forces an organization to view and reinterpret business knowledge in a service-oriented manner. Altering the perspective of how business processes can be structured, partitioned, and modeled is an essential step to achieving an environment in which service-orientation is standardized, successfully consistent, and naturally commonplace.

Though the business services layer may accurately represent a corporate business model upon implementation, it will become outdated once new and revised business requirements emerge. As long as it is kept in relative alignment with the current state of business models, it will continue to serve as a valuable view of the enterprise—valuable because it does not exist in abstract but in an implemented and operational form.

CASE STUDY

As mentioned earlier, RailCo has decided to structure its SOA around a services layer consisting of separate business and application sub-layers. Given that it does not have extensive business requirements, these layers will not contain many services. However, the important aspect of this initial project is that it will define an architecture that accommodates additional services and solutions.

As part of its analysis, RailCo has identified the following benefits of investing in extensible business services:

- Business services can be modeled in such a manner that they perform common functions for non-specific service requestors. This will allow RailCo to fulfill its first requirement of making its services available for online transactions with multiple customers.

- A separation of business and application logic will allow RailCo to wrap its legacy accounting system in one or more services. This will allow it to establish an application services layer initially consisting of an application service that will be reusable to task-specific business services.

- RailCo's second requirement also can be fulfilled by adding a service to represent the contact management system. Integration can then be achieved by again reusing the service that encapsulates the accounting service.

At this stage, RailCo simply is listing potential benefits that can be met by introducing services it has not yet even modeled.

SUMMARY OF KEY POINTS

- Investing in a separate business service layer builds agility into an SOA by abstracting business and application logic domains, allowing them to evolve independently, and adapting to each other's changes.

- Business services prepare an SOA for orchestration and promote reuse of both business process and application logic through careful encapsulation and abstraction.

- Business services are key to fulfilling an enterprise-wide standardization of service-orientation.

11.3   Deriving business services

As much as no industry-standard definition of SOA exists and as much as service-orientation principles have not been globally standardized, there is also no standardized means of modeling business services. As with all other aspects of SOA, there are plenty of opinions, and though many have ideas, few concrete methodologies have emerged. Instead, there are a select set of approaches, some of which have been more accepted than others.

Perhaps there should be no single approach to deriving services. It is not unusual for the business model behind a typical enterprise to have undergone thousands of revisions, shaped through years of adapting to the organization's surrounding business climate. Organizations employ different methodologies, business entity relationships, and vocabularies, resulting in vastly diverging business model structures. Further, there are cultural preferences and vendor platform influences that result in expression of the business models through different sets of modeling tools and languages.

The bottom line is that every business model is unique. Therefore, up-front analysis cannot be avoided to properly derive business services that best represent an organization as a cohesive business entity.

11.3.1   Sources from which business services can be derived

The inner workings of any organization, regardless of structure or size, can be decomposed into a collection of business services. This is because a business service simply represents a logical unit of work, and pretty much anything any organization does consists of units of work.

What differs, though, is how organizations structure and document the work they perform. At the beginning of this section we stressed the fact that every corporate environment is unique in the shape and size of its business models and in how it implements and maintains them. It is therefore up to the service-orientation-aware analyst to determine how to best map existing logic to services.

Below are some examples of common business analysis approaches used by many organizations. For each we briefly discuss how services can be derived.

Business Process Management (BPM) models

The advent of BPM has resulted in an industry-wide flurry of process modeling and re-modeling activity. Process models have therefore become a central form of business analysis documentation in many organizations. Business services can be derived from process workflow logic.

In Chapter 3 we established how the scope of a business service can vary. Specifically, we discussed how a service can represent a step within a process, a sub-process part of a larger process, or even an entire process (Figure 11.3).

Deriving a business service from a business process requires a thorough knowledge of the underlying workflow logic. This is because defining the scope of the business logic to be represented is a judgment call that can have significant implications when the business service is implemented as part of solution environments; hence, the better the judgment, the better the quality of the service. And, of course, the better quality services you end up with, the better quality your service-oriented environment will be.

NOTE

It is worth recalling that even though business logic encapsulation typically is illustrated using services, it is actually the service operations that represent and execute the logic in the service layer. Therefore, it is critical to ensure that when identifying logic suitable for service encapsulation, it be broken down into individual operations. Services are then determined by the proposed grouping of these operations.

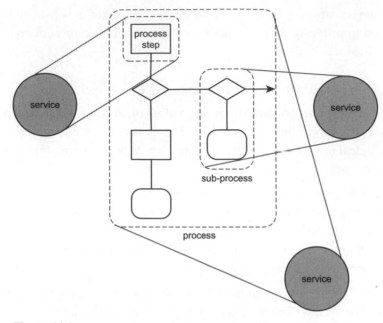

Figure 11.3
Parts of a process that can be encapsulated by a business service.

Following are descriptions of two existing RailCo processes that are currently
being partially automated by its services. In past chapters, we focused solely on
service interaction and therefore only described the involvement of RailCo's
Invoice Submission and Order Fulfillment Services as part of interaction scenarios with the TLS B2B solution. The descriptions provided here document the
steps that comprise *internal* RailCo processes because these are the processes that
eventually will be affected by the introduction of SOA.

First, we'll explore the existing Invoice Submission Process. It consists of a series
of steps that describe how invoices are generated specifically for TLS, as follows:

1. Accounting clerk creates and issues an electronic invoice using the legacy
   accounting system.

2. The save event triggers a custom script that exports an electronic copy of the
   invoice to a network folder.

3. A custom developed component, which polls this folder at ten-minute inter-
   vals, picks up the document and transforms it into an XML document.

4. The invoice XML document is then validated. If it is deemed valid, it is forwarded to the Invoice Submission Service. If validation fails, the document is rejected, and the process ends.

5. Depending on when the last metadata check was performed, the service may issue a Get Metadata request to the TLS B2B solution.

6. If the Get Metadata request is issued and if it determines that no changes were made to the relevant TLS service descriptions, the Invoice Submission Service transmits the invoice document to the TLS B2B solution using the ExactlyOnce delivery assurance. If the Get Metadata request identifies a change to the TLS service descriptions, the invoice is not submitted, and the process ends.

The internal Order Fulfillment Process is similar in that it establishes the same type of relationship between the accounting system and a Web service—only this time, the data flow is reversed, as described here:

1. The RailCo Order Fulfillment Service receives a SOAP message from TLS, containing a payload consisting of a TLS purchase order document.

2. The service validates the incoming document. If valid, the document is passed to a custom component. If the TLS PO fails validation, a rejection notification message is sent to TLS, and the process ends.

3. The component has the XML document transformed into a purchase order that conforms to the accounting system's native document format.

4. The PO then is submitted to the accounting system using its import extension.

5. The PO ends up in the work queue of an accounting clerk who then processes the document.

Note that both of these processes are intentionally incomplete. The Invoice Submission Process contains additional steps related to an acknowledgement it receives from TLS upon the successful delivery of the invoice submission. The complete Order Fulfillment Process consists of several additional steps that are required to formulate a response to TLS containing back-order information, if required. The process steps that are provided are those most relevant to our study of how implementing SOA leads to improvements for RailCo.

Note that these two process descriptions form the basis of the examples used to demonstrate the service modeling process in Chapter 12.

Entity models

Primary entities represent the main business documents and transaction areas of an enterprise. For example, Invoice, Purchase Order, Customer, and Claim are all milestone entities within different types of businesses. Further, organizations model entities according to proprietary rules and business policies. This results in entities having relationships with each other.

Entity-centric services (explained shortly) mirror the entity model by containing a set of generic operations that facilitate the different types of functions associated to the processing of the entity. Communication between different entity-centric services also can be governed by constraints relating to the inherent relationship between entities.

NOTE

These types of services often follow the OOP naming convention where a noun is used to label an object and verbs are used to name methods. Because entity-centric services represent data entities, the services can be named with nouns and the operations with verbs.

CASE STUDY

RailCo has decided to build services centered around specific tasks and is therefore not using entity models as a source for deriving business services. However, to demonstrate the concept of entities, let's briefly look at what entities exist within the RailCo business areas we've been exploring so far.

Based on the business processes we described earlier, RailCo entities of relevance are:

- Invoice
- Purchase Order

Additional entities involved with these processes could include:

- Employee
- Order
- Back Order
- Customer

Here are some examples of how the entities described above could relate to each other:

- A Purchase Order can be related to zero or more Invoices.
- A Purchase Order can only be related to one Customer.
- An Order can be related to one or more Purchase Orders.
- A Back Order can be related to one or more Purchase Orders.
- An Invoice can only be related to one Customer.
- An Employee can be related to zero or more Invoices, Purchase Orders, Orders, Back Orders, or Customers.

Figure 11.4 illustrates this series of one-to-one and one-to-many relationships.

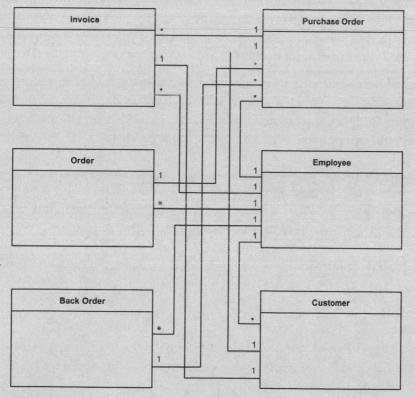

Figure 11.4

Relationships between RailCo entities (normally these entity symbols would contain attributes as well).

11.3.2   Types of derived business services

Deriving services from the two sources we just identified results in the creation of distinct types of business services.

Task-centric business services

These are Web services that have been modeled to accommodate a specific business process. Operations are grouped according to their relevance to the execution of a task in support of a process.

Typical examples of task-centric business services are:

- VerifyInvoice

- GetHistoryReport

Each of these services contains operations that relate to a particular task within the context of a process. Task-centric services usually result from modeling exercises that are focused on meeting immediate business requirements. Typical sources include use-case models and BPM process definitions.

While they require less analysis effort to produce, these types of business services have limited reusability potential. Modeling reusable task-centric business services often requires that multiple use-cases and business process models first be analyzed to identify commonality, prior to the actual modeling of the services.

CASE STUDY

Although they are hybrid (application + business) in design, the following RailCo services follow a task-centric model:

- Invoice Submission Service
- Order Fulfillment Service
- TLS Subscription Service

Note that the TLS Subscription Service displayed in the preceding list does not actually belong to TLS. It is just a poorly named service produced by RailCo for communication with TLS.

Entity-centric business services

Entity-centric business services generally are produced as part of a long-term or on-going analysis effort to align business services with existing corporate business models. Their inherent generic nature makes them highly reusable by numerous business processes. Even though entity-centric business services often are built as part of application development projects centered around a particular business process, they differ from task-centric services in that they do not provide an interface specific to that process. Instead, the source of inspiration for these types of services is entity models.

When compared to task-centric services, entity-centric services significantly increase the agility with which service-oriented processes can be remodeled. This is because task-centric services often are built to help automate one business process and can therefore get tied to that process. When the process logic changes, the context under which the services are used and composed may change as well. This may invalidate the original grouping of service operations and could result in the requirement for a redesign and redevelopment effort.

Entity-centric services do require more up-front analysis, increasing both the cost of each service and the time required to produce it. Additionally, they can be so generic in nature that they are delivered with no concept of business process logic. Their use may therefore become dependent on parent business controllers, such as process services or task-centric controller services. As we established in Chapter 9, building a business service layer consisting of a series of entity-centric services composed by a parent orchestration service layer establishes a desirable SOA, promoting a high degree of agility and accurate business model representation.

CASE STUDY

Although we have identified logical entities within RailCo, no entity-centric business services currently exist. Having followed the top-down SOA delivery strategy, though, TLS already has a set of entity-centric business services in place (Figure 11.5).

These are:

- Accounts Payable Service
- Purchase Order Service
- Ledger Service
- Vendor Profile Service

When utilized within the B2B solution, these services actually do not need to be composed by a separate task-centric or process service. The reason this parent controller layer is not required is because the Accounts Payable and Purchase Order Services are not part of a solution-specific business process. They are simply fulfilling their respective document processing roles for the accounting system, receiving valid invoices and issuing valid purchase orders. Therefore, no further workflow logic is required.

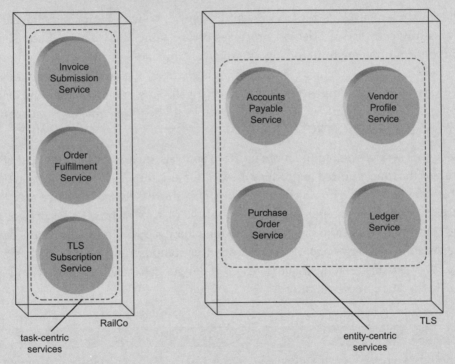

Figure 11.5
Different organizations, different approaches to building services.

TLS is planning to continue building entity-centric services. But, as decided in Chapter 10, they will deliver future business services according to the agile delivery strategy. RailCo does not have the time or budget to outfit each new business service with additional functionality for future reuse opportunities. No entity-centric services are therefore planned for RailCo.

11.3.3 Business services and orchestration

The process service, an implementation of orchestration, also can be classified as a form of business service. It is very much "business-centric," as it resides at the top of the service layer hierarchy and is responsible for composing business services according to the rules specified in the orchestration workflow logic.

Details regarding the process service are described in the *Orchestration* section of Chapter 6, the *Orchestration services layer* section of Chapter 9, as well as the service-oriented business process design portions of Chapter 16. An orchestration can compose a combination of task-centric and entity-centric business services. The core business model is represented by the entity-centric services, while business logic-related tasks can be implemented in task-centric services that are designed specifically to supplement the process service.

Essentially, the use of orchestration establishes the following structure in the services layer:

1. Workflow logic and process-specific business rules are embedded in a process definition. Orchestration composes business services (and possibly application services) according to this definition.

2. Business services compose application services to execute business logic.

3. Application services interact with underlying systems to process the required functions.

Orchestration abstracts workflow logic, positioning it outside of service boundaries. This increases agility by allowing changes to business rules to be made without affecting business or application services. This is a critical aspect of orchestration, as business process logic is subject to many factors that can result in change. These include human intervention, changes to corporate policies and business rules, and unforeseeable exception conditions.

CASE STUDY

TLS has decided that as part of its plans to expand its existing SOA, it will introduce an orchestration service layer. It begins by introducing a process service that abstracts business rules and workflow logic from the business services already in use.

Although this requires a significant modeling effort, it is anticipated that the existing service structures and service interfaces will remain unaffected. After the workflow logic represented by the process service is finalized in the service-oriented design phase, the true impact of the orchestration service layer on the existing business services will be determined.

This example is continued in the *Contrasting service modeling approaches (an example)* section at the end of Chapter 12.

SUMMARY OF KEY POINTS

- Business services are derived from common business model documents, including use-case models, business process definitions, and entity models.

- There are two distinct types of business services that are commonly derived: task-centric and entity-centric. Each has pros and cons, and each approaches encapsulation in a different manner.

Chapter 12

Service-Oriented Analysis
(Part II: Service Modeling)

This chapter continues where Chapter 11 left off, providing a detailed service modeling process that steps us through the individual tasks required to produce service and operation candidates.

> **How case studies are used:** The RailCo environment is revisited with the intention of replacing its current set of services with well-defined business and application service layers. As we progress through the service modeling process at the beginning of this chapter, these new services take form while we assemble a series of service candidates that establish preliminary service layers.
>
> Toward the end of this chapter, we join the TLS project team in a lengthy case study example that steps us through another modeling process during which we contrast different types of approaches to modeling service layers in response to new business requirements for the creation of a new SOA.

12.1 Service modeling (a step-by-step process)

A service modeling process is essentially an exercise in organizing the information we gathered in Steps 1 and 2 of the parent service-oriented analysis process. Sources of the information required can be diverse, ranging from various existing business model documents to verbally interviewing key personnel that may have the required knowledge of a relevant business area. This process can therefore be structured in many different ways. As with the parent service-oriented analysis process, the steps described in this section are best considered a starting point from which you can design your own process to fit within your organization's existing business analysis conventions and procedures.

12.1.1 "Services" versus "Service Candidates"

Before we begin, let's first introduce an important modeling term: *candidate*. The primary goal of the service-oriented analysis stage is to figure out how services are ideally defined on a logical level, so that we know what to design and build in subsequent project phases.

It is therefore helpful to continually remind ourselves that we are not actually implementing a design at this stage. We are only performing an analysis that results in a proposed separation of logic used as input for consideration during the service-oriented design phase. In other words, we are producing abstract candidates that may or may not be realized as part of the eventual concrete design.

The reason this distinction is so relevant is because once our candidates are submitted to the design process, they are subjected to the realities of the technical architecture in which they are expected to reside. Once constraints, requirements, and limitations specific to the implementation environment are factored in, the end design of a service may be a significant departure from the corresponding original candidate.

So, at this stage, we do not produce services; we create *service candidates*. Similarly, we do not define service operations; we propose *service operation candidates*. Finally, service candidates and service operation candidates are the end-result of a process called *service modeling*.

12.1.2 Process description

Up next is a series of twelve steps that comprise a proposed service modeling process, as illustrated in Figure 12.1.

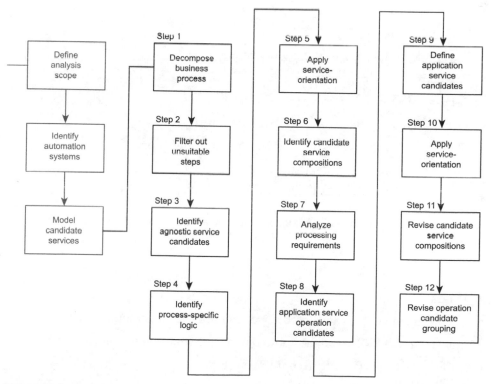

Figure 12.1
A sample service modeling process.

Step 1: Decompose the business process

Take a documented business process and break it down into a series of steps. It is important that the process workflow logic be decomposed into the most granular representation of processing steps, which may differ from the level of granularity at which the process steps were originally documented. (The *Classifying service model logic* section at the end of this chapter introduces new terms that help distinguish the scope of individual process steps.)

CASE STUDY

The scope of RailCo's service-oriented analysis includes both of the business processes we described in the *Business Process Management (BPM) models* section in Chapter 11.

Let's begin by decomposing the Invoice Submission Process (displayed in Figure 12.2) into a series of granular steps:

- Create electronic invoice.
- Issue electronic invoice.
- Export electronic invoice to network folder.
- Poll network folder.
- Retrieve electronic invoice.
- Transform electronic invoice to XML document.
- Check validity of invoice document. If invalid, end process.
- Check if it is time to verify TLS metadata.
- If required, perform metadata check. If metadata check fails, end process.

Next are the process steps of a decomposed Order Fulfillment Process (Figure 12.3):

- Receive PO document.
- Validate PO document.
- If PO document is invalid, send rejection notification and end process.
- Transform PO XML document into native electronic PO format.
- Import electronic PO into accounting system.
- Send PO to accounting clerk's work queue.

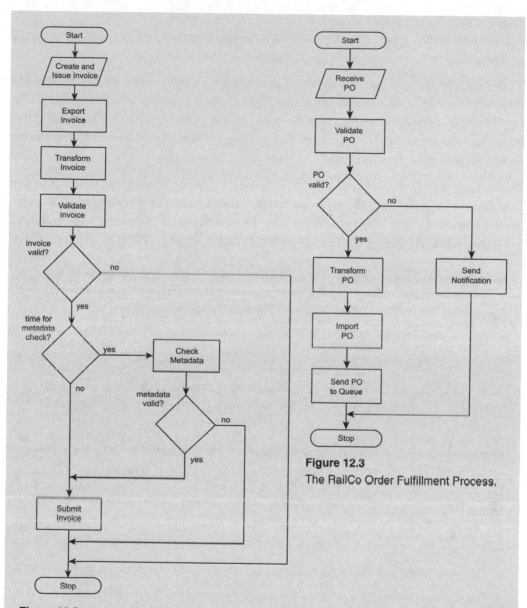

Figure 12.2
The RailCo Invoice Submission Process.

Figure 12.3
The RailCo Order Fulfillment Process.

Step 2: Filter out steps not suitable for service encapsulation

Some steps within a business process can be easily identified as not belonging to the potential logic that should be encapsulated by a service candidate.

Examples include manual process steps that cannot or should not be automated and process steps performed by existing legacy logic for which service candidate encapsulation is not an option. (The latter type of logic will often be recognizable with the information gathered as part of *Step 2: Identify existing automation systems* from the parent service-oriented analysis process.)

By filtering out these parts we are left with the processing steps most relevant to our service modeling process. The steps we remove at this stage are simply placed on a separate list and revisited when we define how the parent business process logic will need to be implemented during the service-oriented design stage.

> **NOTE**
>
> While going looking through the individual process steps you are encouraged to annotate them with initial thoughts about how they could potentially be grouped and utilized.

CASE STUDY

After reviewing each of the previously identified processing steps, we remove those that we either cannot or do not want to make part of our service-oriented solution.

Here, again, are the steps of our two processes. Those that are no longer part of our solution environment have been crossed out. Each step is further supplemented with a brief note that explains either why we have decided to remove it from our list or what we have planned for it.

Invoice Submission Process:

- ~~Create electronic invoice~~. (A manual step performed by the accounting clerk.)
- ~~Issue electronic invoice~~. (A manual step performed by the accounting clerk.)
- Export electronic invoice to network folder. (Currently a custom developed extension of the legacy system. Could be made part of a generic service candidate.)
- Poll network folder. (Currently performed by a custom developed component. Could be made part of a service candidate.)
- Retrieve electronic invoice. (Same as previous.)

- Transform electronic invoice to XML document. (Same as previous.)

- Check validity of invoice document. If invalid, end process. (Is currently being performed as part of the Invoice Submission Service's parsing routine. No foreseeable need to change this.)

- Check if it is time to verify TLS metadata. (Is currently being performed as part of the Invoice Submission Service's parsing routine. Looks like a potentially reusable operation candidate. Could be moved to a separate service candidate.)

- If required, perform metadata check. If metadata check fails, end process. (Same as previous.)

And here are the process steps of the decomposed Order Fulfillment Process:

- Receive PO document. (Is currently being performed by the Order Fulfillment Service. No foreseeable need to change this.)

- Validate PO document. (Same as previous.)

- If PO document is invalid, send rejection notification and end process. (Same as previous.)

- Transform PO XML document into native electronic PO format. (Currently performed by a custom developed component. Could be made part of a service candidate.)

- Import electronic PO into accounting system. (Currently a custom developed extension of the legacy system. Could be made part of a generic service candidate.)

- Send PO to accounting clerk's work queue. (Same as previous.)

The result of this review is that only two processing steps were removed from the Invoice Submission Process and none from the Order Fulfillment Process.

Step 3: Identify agnostic service candidates

Using any available enterprise business models from the top-down analysis (see Chapter 10, *The top-down strategy* section) as a starting point, identify or create a set of logical contexts that are agnostic to the business process but still relevant to the business process steps defined in Steps 1 and 2. Each context represents an agnostic service candidate. Group the steps for potential encapsulation within these service candidates. Each step represents a potential service operation candidate.

If the scope of the analysis is the delivery of a single agnostic service, then simply group together all actions that appear to belong to this service's context. Next, look to the enterprise service model (or corresponding documentation of the service inventory) for agnostic services (existing or new) that the remaining actions may belong to.

It is important that you do not concern yourself with how many steps belong to each group. The primary purpose of this exercise is to establish an initial set of contexts.

CASE STUDY

Going through the steps listed from in RailCo processes, the following preliminary agnostic service candidates are defined along with corresponding groups of potential operation candidates.

Legacy System Service

- Export electronic invoice to network folder.
- Import electronic PO into accounting system.
- Send PO to accounting clerk's work queue.

Metadata Checking Service

- Check if it is time to verify TLS metadata.
- If required, perform metadata check. If metadata check fails, end process.

Figure 12.4.1 provides another view of the same operation candidates being grouped according to contexts that represent service candidates.

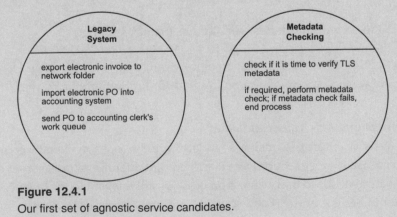

Figure 12.4.1
Our first set of agnostic service candidates.

Step 4: Identify process-specific logic

The actions that remain after completing Step 4 should represent logic that is specific to the task or business process. Common examples include process-specific business rules, conditional logic, exception logic, and logic that dictates the sequence in which other actions should be carried out.

Note that these forms of process logic may or may not be represented accurately by a step description. For example, some processing step descriptions consist of a condition and an action (if condition x occurs, then perform action y). In this case, focus on the action.

Depending on which service layers have been standardized, this type of logic will likely comprise a context for a business process definition as part of an orchestration environment or as part of one or more task-centric business services. In the latter case, be sure to clearly define the context of the task-centric business services by labeling them according to the scope of their tasks. More often than not, only one task-centric business service will be defined at this stage. This service will then be positioned as the parent controller for the service composition.

If you are only delivering a single agnostic service, then this step should not be required. Parent processes within the scope of a single service are typically implemented within one or more operations of the service. If actions should remain after completing Step 3, then revisit the wording of each action and see how it could or should be associated with the context of the service. If, for some reason, it can't, then that may indicate the need for a new service or perhaps a reduction in the original analysis scope.

Also note that regardless of where the actions will ultimately reside, it is likely that some of the identified workflow logic will eventually be dropped. This is because not all processing steps necessarily become service operations.

CASE STUDY

Based on what is remaining from the two RailCo process descriptions, two groups of operation candidates are defined, each of which comprises a potential task-centric business service candidate.

Invoice Processing Service

- Poll network folder for invoice.
- Retrieve electronic invoice.
- Transform electronic invoice to XML document.
- Check validity of invoice document. If invalid, end process.

PO Processing Service

- Receive PO document.
- Validate PO document.
- If PO document is invalid, send rejection notification and end process.
- Transform PO XML document into native electronic PO format.

Figure 12.4.2 shows how these service candidates would be drawn to represent their respective groups of operation candidates.

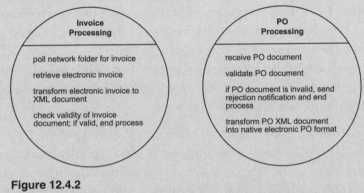

Figure 12.4.2
The first versions of two task-centric business service candidates.

Furthermore, the following conditional and sequence workflow logic is identified and kept on separate lists associated with the service candidates.

- If the invoice document is valid, proceed with the metadata check step.
- If the invoice document is invalid, end process.
- If the interval period for performing a metadata check has completed, proceed to the perform metadata check step.
- If the interval period has not completed, skip the perform metadata check step.
- If the PO document is valid, proceed with the transform PO document step.
- If the PO document is invalid, end process.

This type of business process logic does not represent operation candidates, but instead will be incorporated into the underlying logic for the corresponding task-centric business services.

Step 5: Apply service-orientation principles

So far we have just grouped processing steps derived from an existing business process. To make our service candidates truly worthy of an SOA, we must take a closer look at the underlying logic of each proposed service operation candidate. This step gives us a chance to make adjustments and apply key service-orientation principles.

Two principles that have special significance during the service modeling stage are reusability and autonomy. (The other principles are addressed in the service-oriented design process, at which point reuse and autonomy are also revisited.)

For example, it is encouraged that application and entity-centric business service candidates be equipped with additional operation candidates that facilitate future reuse. Therefore, the scope of this step can be expanded to include an analysis of additional service operation candidates not required by the current business process, but added to round out agnostic services with a more complete set of reusable operations. For business services especially, we can take advantage of the involvement of business analysts who are expected to participate in the service modeling process (but not in the subsequent service-oriented design process).

NOTE

It is recommended that newly added operation candidates be somehow tagged or labeled differently so that should the scope of the service need to be scaled down in the design phase, those operations that are required for the automation of the business process are easily distinguished from those that aren't.

With regards to autonomy, it may be possible to get a sense of the underlying processing environments for the identified service operation candidates. This is where technology architects can provide a foreknowledge of any potential legacy system functionality the operations may be required to encapsulate (again relating back to Step 2 of the parent service-oriented analysis process). Even though we are focused more on a logical definition of services at this stage, it can be beneficial to take legacy logic encapsulation requirements into account.

NOTE

Service discoverability can also be addressed at this stage. Although it may not directly influence the structure of a service candidate, it can be beneficial to take advantage of the involvement of business analysts and other subject matter experts. These professionals can contribute clear and concise descriptions that express the purpose and capabilities of a service. These statements can then be incorporated into the physical service contract during the service-oriented design phase (at which point business analysts may no longer be actively involved).

In reviewing the operation candidates within our service candidates, we make a series of adjustments, as follows.

Within the Legacy System Service, the "Send PO to accounting clerk's work queue" action can be performed only upon the receipt of a document. This operation candidate is therefore directly dependent on the "Import electronic PO into accounting system" step. We therefore decide to combine these two steps into one.

Further the "Export electronic invoice to network folder" action is performed automatically by a macro added to the legacy accounting system. It is therefore not required as part of our service candidate. This leaves us with a single operation candidate that we would like to make more reusable by allowing it to handle different types of documents.

The revised Legacy System Service list contains the following steps:

• Export document to network folder.

• Import and forward document to work queue.

Upon reviewing the Invoice Processing Service, a number of refinement opportunities arise. We determine that the "Poll network folder for invoice" action can be made more generic by turning it into an operation candidate that simply polls a given folder for different types of documents. We also decide that this action should be made part of a service candidate capable of notifying subscribers of the arrival of new documents.

Next, we decide to combine the "Retrieve electronic invoice," "Transform electronic invoice to XML document," and "Check validity of invoice document" operation candidates into a single service operation candidate called "Retrieve and transform invoice document." We don't mention the validation aspect of this action because the XML document automatically is assigned a corresponding schema. The validation of the document is therefore an intrinsic part of the transformation process.

The result of our analysis is a new context (a new service candidate), established to represent generic notification actions, as follows:

Polling Notification Service:

• Poll folder for new documents.

- If documents arrive for which there are subscribers, issue notifications.

The revised Invoice Processing Service list is left with just one step:

- Retrieve and transform invoice document.

Next, we tackle the operation candidates in the PO processing group. Though listed as such, the "Receive PO document" is not a suitable service operation candidate, as receiving a message is a natural part of service operations (and therefore not generally explicitly accounted for). We therefore remove this action from our list.

We then detect a direct dependency between the "If PO document is invalid, send rejection notification and end process" and "Validate PO document" actions. As a result we decide to combine these into a single operation candidate called "Validate PO document and send rejection notification, if required."

We move on to discover commonality between the "Transform PO XML document into native electronic PO format" action and the "Retrieve and transform invoice document" action from our Invoice Processing Service list. Both operation candidates transform accounting documents. We therefore decide to create a new service candidate that provides generic transformation. The result is a new grouping category:

Transform Accounting Documents Service:

- Transform XML documents to native format.
- Transform native documents to XML.

The revised PO Processing Service list is left with just one step:

- Validate PO document and send rejection notification, if required.

Finally, our last group of operation candidates is reviewed. The candidates themselves are still relatively suitable for what we intended. However, because we've abstracted these into a generic service candidate, we need to revise the wording to better reflect this. Specifically, we add a notification feature to our Metadata Checking Service candidate.

The revised Metadata Checking Service list contains the following steps:

- Check if it is time to verify TLS metadata. If required, perform metadata check.
- If metadata check fails, issue notification.

In this step we performed some major revisions to our original business process logic. The result is the creation of additional service candidates that succeed in abstracting logic in support of key service-orientation principles (Figure 12.5).

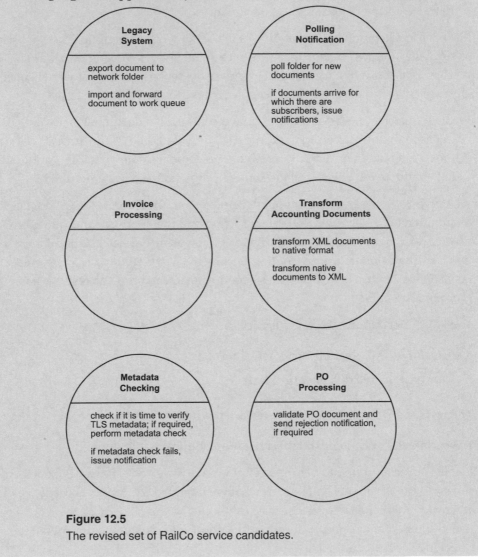

Figure 12.5
The revised set of RailCo service candidates.

Step 6: Identify candidate service compositions

Here we need to document a set of the most common scenarios that can take place within the boundaries of the business process. For each scenario, follow the required processing steps as they exist now. Don't be too concerned with the specific type of data that is being processed and passed between service candidates. Focus on the flow of action across service candidates and through service operation candidates. Also, ensure that as part of your chosen scenarios you include failure conditions that involve exception handling logic.

By identifying potential service compositions, this exercise can help determine how appropriate the grouping of service operation candidates is, while also demonstrating the potential relationships between service layers. Additionally, it will often indicate where missing workflow logic or processing steps exists. This may result in the need to define new service candidate operations and perhaps even new service candidates.

It is advisable to revisit the original grouping of service operation candidates and make any necessary refinements as part of completing this step.

CASE STUDY

In Step 4 we identified a series of service candidates that form preliminary business and application service layers.

Let's recap some of the service candidates established so far.

- Legacy System Service
- Polling Notification Service
- Transform Accounting Documents Service
- Metadata Checking Service

Each of these service candidates represents generic, reusable, and business-agnostic logic. In other words, these can all be classified as application service candidates. Collectively they establish a preliminary application service layer.

But what about our business service candidates? Well, the PO Processing Service candidate still had one action associated with it, but our Invoice Processing Service operation candidates disappeared after we abstracted all of the associated process actions into separate application service candidates.

The fact that we've reduced the processing requirements of these two service candidates does not mean that we don't have a need for them. Remember that the primary role of task-centric business services is to act as controllers, composing application services to carry out the required business logic. Both the PO Processing and Invoice Processing Service candidates establish a preliminary parent business service layer and contain all of the process logic required to compose the underlying application service candidates (Figures 12.6 and 12.7).

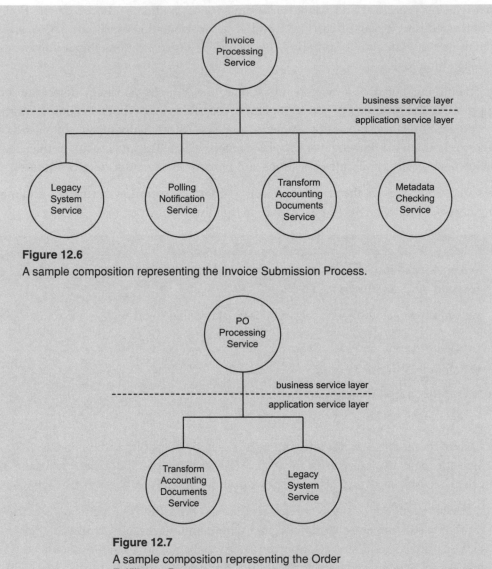

Figure 12.6
A sample composition representing the Invoice Submission Process.

Figure 12.7
A sample composition representing the Order
Fulfillment Process.

Note that to apply process instance scenarios to candidate service compositions, more detail is required than what is depicted in Figures 12.6 and 12.7. The relationships between service candidates need to be mapped to the service operation candidate level.

Step 7: Analyze application processing requirements

Because our focus so far has been on business process logic, there is a natural tendency to emphasize the definition of business service candidates over application service candidates.

This step requires that we more closely study the underlying processing requirements of each service operation candidate to abstract any further processing logic that could potentially be added to the preliminary application services layer. To accomplish this, each operation candidate is required to undergo a mini-analysis.

Specifically, what needs to be determined is:

- What underlying application logic needs to be executed to process the action described by the operation candidate.

- Whether the required application logic already exists or whether it needs to be newly developed.

- Whether the required application logic spans existing solution boundaries. In other words, is more than one system required to complete this action?

The result of this step will be a list of processing requirements that act as input for Step 8.

This and the next series of steps are especially relevant when the scope of the overall analysis is a larger, complex business process. Note that the information we gathered during Step 2 of the parent service-oriented analysis process will be referenced again during these steps.

CASE STUDY

Our business process is by no means complex, and we already have identified all of the application service candidates that represent our preliminary application logic. Therefore, the remaining steps are not required for our RailCo case study.

Step 8: Identify application service operation candidates

What Step 7 essentially leads us to do is look for an opportunity to identify more steps within our overall business process that qualify as service operation candidates for application services. This can be accomplished by breaking down each application logic processing requirement into one or more processing steps.

It is important to be explicit about how these steps are labeled so that they reference the function they are performing. Because our focus at this stage is the definition of application services, we want to avoid business-specific references. For example, when labeling the service operation candidates, you would ideally not make reference to the business process step for which this function is being identified.

Step 9: Define application service candidates

The processing steps now need to be grouped according to a logical context. Unlike with business services, application services don't have the benefit of a context predefined by existing business models and processes. The primary context therefore is *processing-centric*. This means that we are looking for a logical relationship derived from commonality between the processing functionality represented by the service operation candidates.

For example, this relationship can be based on an association with a specific legacy system, an association with one or more solution components, or (most commonly) a logical grouping according to the nature of functionality to be encapsulated by each operation candidate.

As part of this step, the current service inventory needs to be reviewed to ensure that no existing services have been defined that may already relate to any newly proposed candidate contexts.

Step 10: Apply service-orientation principles

This is essentially a repeat of Step 5 but applied specifically to the new application service candidates we have defined as a result of completing steps 7 to 9. The emphasis on reuse and autonomy is just as important when delivering application services as they are for business services.

Autonomy plays a large role in determining the functional scope of each application service operation candidate (which, in turn, influences the potential granularity of the operation candidate).

Once a suitable processing context is established for the operation candidates identified so far, it may lead to opportunities to add new operation candidates or make existing ones more generic, all in support of increasing the reuse potential of the overall service candidate.

Various other issues are factored in once service candidates are subjected to the service-oriented design process. For now, the identified service and operation candidates establish a preliminary application service layer.

Step 11: Revise candidate service compositions

Revisit the original scenarios you identified in Step 6 and run through them again. Only, this time, incorporate the new application service and operation candidates as well. This will result in the mapping of elaborate activities that bring to life expanded service compositions. Be sure to keep track of how business service candidates map to underlying application service candidates during this exercise.

Step 12: Revise service operation candidate grouping

Going through the motions of mapping the activity scenarios from Step 11 will usually result in changes to the grouping and definition of service operation candidates that have been identified so far.

CASE STUDY

Our service-oriented analysis has provided us with extremely useful results that we carry over to the upcoming service-oriented design process. The modeling exercise has tentatively addressed the goals RailCo originally set for its SOA. RailCo wanted to create an environment consisting of services with processing logic that is no longer specific to one customer so that it can pursue new clients without having to develop new services for each one.

The extent to which application logic has been abstracted resulted in a purely reusable application services layer. These planned application services can facilitate a variety of requests from business services, including the processing of invoice and purchase order documents from other customers. However, because they are business-agnostic, they can be reused by additional types of business services as well.

RailCo has therefore taken the first step to producing an inventory of reusable services that can be leveraged by a variety of future solutions. This is demonstrated by the fact that we began with separate processes that shared no common logic and ended up with a set of abstracted service operation candidates that can be shared by these and other processes.

NOTE

This process description assumes that this is the first iteration through the service modeling process. During subsequent iterations, additional steps need to be incorporated to check for the existence of relevant service candidates and service operation candidates. See also www.soamethodology.com for additional information.

SUMMARY OF KEY POINTS

- Modeling services is fundamentally a process of gathering and organizing business model information.

12.2   Service modeling guidelines

Provided here is a set of guidelines that supplement the previous modeling process with some additional considerations. These guidelines help ensure that your service candidates attain a balance of proper logic encapsulation and adherence to the service-orientation principles. (Note that some of these guidelines apply to business or application service candidates only, and are so identified.)

12.2.1   Take into account potential cross-process reusability of logic being encapsulated (task-centric business service candidates)

Identifying a real opportunity for reuse is an important consideration when grouping operation candidates into service candidates. It introduces the potential of leveraging existing units of business logic and creating a modularized enterprise business model. A knowledge of other business processes in existence or in development within an enterprise is required to recognize reuse opportunities for task-centric business service candidates (Figure 12.8).

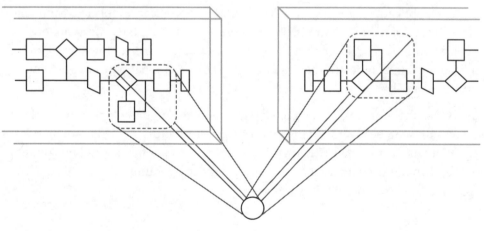

Figure 12.8
Service logic being reused across processes.

To further promote reuse, some have a tendency to model task-centric business service candidates on a granular level. The less business logic a service candidate provides, the greater the chance of it being useful to other processes. This may be true, but it is no reason not to create coarser grained service candidates that also have reuse potential. As explained later, coarse service candidates can be decomposed, providing reuse opportunities on both granular and coarse levels.

12.2.2   Consider potential intra-process reusability of logic being encapsulated (task-centric business service candidates)

Also worth mentioning is the ability for a unit of business logic to be reused within a single business process. Larger, more complex workflows sometimes repeat collections of process activities. If this redundancy is consistent and if the logic represented by these process steps is sufficiently atomic, then you can consider wrapping them into a business service candidate (Figure 12.9). Many workflow systems already accomplish this by identifying predefined processes or sub-processes.

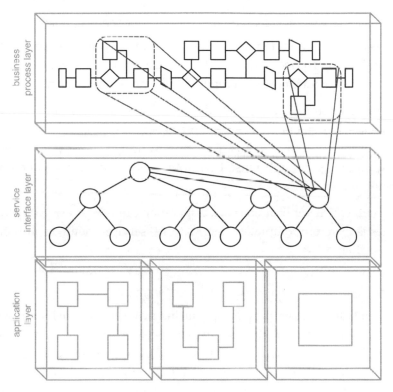

Figure 12.9
Service logic being reused within a process.

12.2.3   Factor in process-related dependencies (task-centric business service candidates)

After you've identified a set of process steps that represent the business logic you want to encapsulate, you need to ensure that you are aware of any dependencies that tie this logic to the current process or to its position within that process.

This will require a bit of analysis, in that the process will need to be broken down into granular processing steps, each of which will need to be assessed individually. What you are looking for here are any input values or parameters upon which business rules, decision points, formulas, conditional statements, or other types of workflow logic are dependent.

The extent to which a service candidate depends on external information (information external to the business service boundary) can determine its potential mobility and the degree to which it can be reused and composed.

12.2.4　Model for cross-application reuse (application service candidates)

Each business service candidate is structured to represent a specific part of the overall business model. These service candidates therefore are highly customized and carefully modeled to ensure accurate representation within a predefined business boundary.

Application service candidates typically *do not* need to be modeled to accommodate a specific business requirement. In fact, the more generic an application service candidate is, the more reusable it becomes. A business-agnostic design allows it to fulfill numerous potential requirements through reuse by multiple business service candidates across different solution boundaries.

The context with which application service operation candidates are grouped into service candidates is therefore completely neutral to the service-oriented solutions that will eventually use them.

12.2.5　Speculate on further decomposition requirements

It's useful to consider whether the part of a business process you've identified as a service candidate can exist as a potential service composition. In other words, even though immediate business requirements may be satisfied by your existing service candidates, it may be worth determining if the business logic you're encapsulating can be broken down into additional, more granular service candidates.

If decomposition is possible, then you can perform a speculative analysis to determine the likelihood that it may actually be required. This should give you sufficient information to decide whether or not to model a service candidate into a service composition. It also will help you properly label a service candidate (as explained in the *Classifying service model logic* section later in this chapter).

12.2.6   Identify logical units of work with explicit boundaries

This is simply a reiteration of the service-orientation principle that dictates that services (and service candidates) need to be autonomous. We re-emphasize this principle here as a guideline because it is also the golden rule of service modeling. The logic encapsulated by a service candidate must have an explicit boundary, meaning that it must be able to exist as an atomic collection of individual tasks.

This boundary also claims a level of independence from the underlying business or application logic. It accommodates changes to business requirements by allowing service candidates without dependencies to be more easily remodeled as part of augmented business processes. It further supports the concept of reusability and service composition on a logical level.

Note that defining boundaries for application service candidates can be more difficult than for business service candidates because these boundaries often need to encompass complex legacy environments. The details of exactly how an application service accomplishes its encapsulation are dealt with in the service-oriented design process. Therefore, the boundaries defined within application service designs can sometimes end up being significantly different from what is defined in the original service candidates.

12.2.7   Prevent logic boundary creep

As more services and service candidates are created over time, it is conceivable that some may inadvertently encapsulate business logic already contained within others. This can be prevented when services are first modeled.

Boundary creep can happen in the following circumstances:

- Services in different business processes are created at different times. The logic they encapsulate is the same.

- Services in different business processes are created at different times. The logic they encapsulate overlaps but is not the same. This is the case when different process workflows incorporate similar logic in different workflow designs.

- Services are derived from the same business process at different times. This is especially common when variations of the process exist. For example, high-level and detailed-level views of a complex process may be used by different project teams.

There are a number of steps you can take to reduce the risk of this happening:

- Check available metadata documentation of existing services prior to defining new service candidates (see the *Document services with metadata* guideline in Chapter 15).

- Implement a set of standards to be used by all those that model services (see the *Create and publish service modeling standards* guideline provided later in this section).

- Raise an awareness of this issue among all of those involved with business process and service modeling.

Note that this guideline does not apply to service composition, where the encapsulation of services by parent services intentionally results in overlapping boundaries.

12.2.8   Emulate process services when not using orchestration (task-centric business service candidates)

The introduction of the orchestration service layer changes the complexion of business and application service layers, as it establishes one or more parent controller services that pretty much run the show. If you are building business services without the use of process services, you can take steps to minimize the impact of a future move to an orchestration-based model.

The best way to prepare task-centric services is to have them emulate the process service. This means creating and positioning parent business service candidates to act like the process services that would normally form the orchestration service layer (Figure 12.10). By creating a master controller business service that simulates a process service, you end up complementing this service with business and application services that fit nicely into the orchestration composition model.

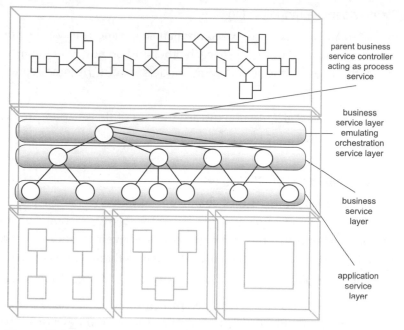

Figure 12.10
A parent business service layer acting as an orchestration layer.

12.2.9 Target a balanced model

Services rarely are modeled to perfection. And even if they are, they don't stay that way once environments around them change. It is important to accept this reality instead of wasting time and effort trying to achieve an unrealistic ideal.

A fundamental goal of any service-oriented environment is for it to be properly partitioned and represented by services modeled according to:

- business requirements
- consistent standards
- industry conventions

Often these influences will introduce conflicting modeling requirements. Therefore, it is most important to achieve a balance in your service candidates that accomplishes your goals, as you've prioritized them. The quality of a service candidate can be measured by how well its model addresses an organization's short and long-term goals.

12.2.10   Classify service modeling logic

Use a system of categorizing services based on their scope and role. Be clear on how different types of service candidates relate to each other and on how you identify and compose service candidates. Otherwise, your models could become confusing and inconsistent.

The *Classifying service model logic* section toward the end of this chapter provides a basic sample classification system.

12.2.11   Allocate appropriate modeling resources

A service-oriented enterprise is further characterized by how the business end of an organization relates to the technology responsible for its automation. Service-orientation fully supports and enforces the vision of business-driven solutions, where automation technology is designed to be inherently adaptive so that it can respond to changes in the governing business logic.

Limiting the application of service-orientation principles to technical IT staff can inhibit SOA's potential of realizing this vision. Technical architects and developers typically do not possess the depth of business knowledge required to model services with quality business logic representation. Therefore, business analysts often need to get involved in the service modeling process (Figure 12.11). Their knowledge of business models and their business process expertise usually is required to successfully model business-centric services.

12.2.12   Create and publish business service modeling standards

The guidelines supplied by this section can only provide you with a direction on how to implement service modeling within your organization. Depending on the modeling tools and methodologies already in use, you will need to incorporate those that fit within your current business modeling environments.

Regardless of which guidelines you choose to follow, it is highly recommended that you formalize them as official modeling standards. When an organization makes a move toward service-orientation, the manner in which services are modeled should ideally no longer be voluntary or open to interpretation.

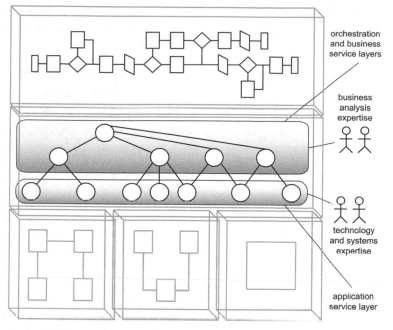

Figure 12.11

This intentionally simplistic diagram highlights the type of expertise recommended for modeling service layers.

SUMMARY OF KEY POINTS

- Keeping an eye on reuse opportunities is a key part of modeling quality service candidates. Business and application service candidates provide different types of reuse potential.

- A key requirement to effectively modeling business services is a sound knowledge of an organization's collective business process logic.

- Service candidate boundaries need to be explicit not only at the time a service is modeled, but also later, when additional services emerge.

12.3 Classifying service model logic

So far we've been classifying most of our modeling logic as service operation candidates and service candidates. As we stated earlier in the *"Services" vs. "Service Candidates"* section, the use of the term "candidate" helps us distinguish an abstract piece of logic from a concrete design. However, referring to a piece of business logic as an operation candidate or service candidate gives us no indication as to the nature of the logic being represented.

Service-oriented encapsulation allows a single operation to express a potentially broad range of logic. For example, an operation can represent a small task, such as performing a simple calculation. Or an operation can represent a large task, such as invoking four other services to perform a complex series of tasks, involving different underlying systems and processes.

When modeling business logic, it is useful to be able to understand the scope of logic represented by a candidate operation, service, or process. For this we need a system of classifying units of business logic. Provided in this section is a sample classification system wherein we refer to each level of classification as a *building block*. The term "building block" is used primarily because the composite nature of service-oriented environments lends itself well to this metaphor.

Building blocks (also known as *service modeling units*) are simply labels applied to units of business logic that assist us with the composition or decomposition of a service-oriented enterprise. You can use these labels to identify specific types of logic, distinguished primarily by scope. Additionally, as part of our classification system, we also provide some supplemental terms that help us identify other pieces of SOA models.

Feel free to use this system as a starting point, from which you can derive your own classifications or create new ones to best complement existing business analysis standards. Reading this section is recommended if you will be studying the example provided in the *Contrasting service modeling approaches* example at the end of this chapter because the terms established by this classification system are applied in this example.

12.3.1 The SOE model

Let's first introduce a master view of a service-oriented enterprise, known as the SOE model (Figure 12.12). Within this view we establish our building blocks, each increasing in scope from left to right.

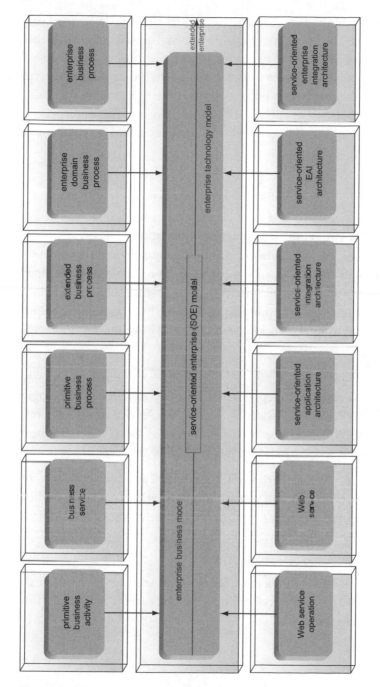

Figure 12.12
The SOE model.

Building blocks allow us to categorize distinct units of logic for both modeling and design purposes. The first layer of this view establishes the enterprise business model, a series of building blocks used to represent modeled business logic only. The third layer provides the concrete or design building blocks that comprise the enterprise technology model. The layer in between represents the core SOE model, defined collectively by abstract (business) and concrete (technology) layers. The enterprise business model layer is closely related to the service modeling process and is explained further in the following sections.

12.3.2   The enterprise business model

The building blocks in this first layer classify logic encapsulated by business service candidates only. They provide an abstract representation of a service-oriented enterprise's business intelligence, independent from the underlying technology platform with which it is implemented. Should we ever want to replace our technology platforms, we will be able to do so while still preserving our abstract, service-oriented perspective of enterprise business logic. For our purposes, these building blocks help us label and categorize logic that resides in the orchestration and business service layers.

12.3.3   "Building Blocks" versus "Service Models"

Building blocks are not an independent means of classifying service logic. They are complemented by existing classifications, such as the service models we introduced in previous chapters. While service models are useful for classifying the nature of logic encapsulated by a service, building blocks classify the *scope* of service logic.

The primary distinction is that a service model always will apply to a single service, but a building block can apply to a range of logic. In other words, a building block can also represent a subset of a service's logic or the collective logic of multiple services.

12.3.4   Basic modeling building blocks

Everything that exists within a modeled view of a service-oriented environment can be broken down into a collection of building blocks, each of which falls into one of the following three categories:

- activity
- service
- process

These terms establish an overall context. Hence, the names of our building blocks are derived from these three categories. The following represents the list of building blocks that form the enterprise business model part of the SOE model.

- primitive business activity
- primitive business service
- primitive business process
- extended business process
- enterprise domain business process
- enterprise business process

This section describes terms related to the first three (Figure 12.13), as they represent the most common and fundamental parts of our modeling environment. The remaining are more concerned with complex business process configurations beyond the scope of this book.

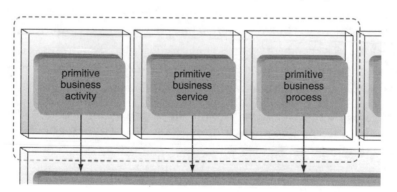

Figure 12.13
The three fundamental building blocks of the enterprise business model.

Primitive business activities
A *primitive business activity* represents the smallest piece of definable and executable business logic within a service-oriented environment. Typically this means that to whatever extent it makes sense to break down a business process, primitive business activities are the smallest parts. The assumption, therefore, is that its logic either cannot be decomposed or will not require further decomposition.

As established in the *Service modeling (a step-by-step process)* section, a recommended service modeling approach is to break down business process logic into a series of primitive business activities and to then represent each as an initial operation candidate.

The physical implementation of a primitive business activity can be compared to the functionality provided by a granular service operation. Coarse-grained operations tend to expose business logic that can be decomposed into numerous individual primitive business activities. Therefore, a granular operation exposing application logic that automates a single action of an overall business process is a suitable measure of implementation.

NOTE

Traditional business process modeling methodologies sometimes refer to a primitive business activity as an *atomic activity*.

Process activities

Related to a primitive business activity is the *process activity*. A process activity is not a building block; it is simply a term used to represent an executable step within a business process's workflow logic. Unlike primitive business activities, process activities do not have a fixed scope. The range of business logic represented by a process activity is determined by the granularity of its governing business process. Therefore, a process activity may or may not be comprised of multiple primitive business activities.

Business processes can be modeled at different levels of abstraction. A coarse-grained process will tend to include a number of coarse-grained steps. Each of these steps is a process activity within the context of a coarse-grained process. Some of the coarser process activities will likely be comprised of multiple primitive business activities.

A more detailed or fine-grained version of the same process, though, would consist of many more steps. Each of these would again be considered process activities, as they express individual steps within the context of a fine-grained process. Process activities representing more fine-grained pieces of business logic are more likely to have a one-to-one relationship with corresponding primitive business activities.

NOTE

Traditional workflow modeling conventions label a single process step that represents a collection of further process steps as a *predefined process* or *subprocess*. Also traditional business process modeling methodologies often refer to a process activity as just an *activity*.

Business services

The *business service* (or *business service candidate*) category represents the familiar business service candidate we've already been working with. Within the context of this classification system, each business service is comprised of one or more primitive business activities. These activities can reside atomically within the service, or they can interrelate. In the latter case, primitive business activities may form a logical algorithm that can establish independent workflow logic and associated business rules.

When physically implemented, the logic a business service candidate represents typically exists as a Web service. Depending on the scope of the encapsulated logic, the service candidate may be further classified under a more specialized category. Two such sub-categories are provided:

Primitive business services

A *primitive business service* (or *primitive business service candidate*) is a type of business service that encompasses functionality limited to a simple business task or function. In other words, this variation of the business service building block represents the most granular type of service within service-oriented solutions.

What distinguishes a primitive business service from others is the assumption that this service will not encapsulate functionality exposed by another service. This means that a primitive business service does not compose other services; it simply is responsible for the execution of a specific task and may or may not be a member of service compositions.

A primitive business service usually will be implemented as a granular Web service, but it also can be expressed through a coarse-grained Web service operation.

Primitive business process

A *primitive business process* represents a body of workflow logic comprised of a set of related process activities. A primitive business process is defined by a distinct functional boundary typically related to a specific business task (such as Submit Invoice or Process Purchase Order). A primitive business process can be represented by a process service or task-centric business service.

SUMMARY OF KEY POINTS

- Using a classification system allows us to label services according to the scope of logic they encapsulate.

- Business logic represented by building blocks can be decomposed into activities, services, and processes.

12.4   Contrasting service modeling approaches (an example)

The case study examples we've been exploring so far in this chapter have focused on how RailCo is transitioning toward an SOA. Let's take the time to look at another service modeling example, this time turning our attention to some new business requirements confronting TLS.

We take advantage of the fact that this scenario takes place in a different organization by altering the parameters of the service modeling exercise. Specifically, this TLS example differs from the previous RailCo examples as follows:

- TLS contrasts three separate approaches to modeling their service candidates.
- Two of the approaches considered involve establishing an orchestration layer by introducing a new process service candidate.
- One of the approaches is based on the creation of entity-centric service candidates.
- TLS employs the use of the classification system we explained in the previous section. As a result, the terms used in this example differ from the RailCo example.

Let's now take a look at how TLS attempts to address a problem with their current Timesheet Submission Process by modeling service candidates.

The problem

TLS outsources a number of its employees on a contract basis to perform various types of specialized maintenance jobs. When these employees fill out their weekly timesheets, they are required to identify what portions of their time were spent at customer sites. Currently, the amount of time for which a customer is billed is determined by an A/R clerk manually entering hours from an appointment schedule (published prior to the submission of timesheets).

Discrepancies arise when employee timesheet entries do not match the hours billed on customer invoices. To address this problem and to streamline the overall process, TLS has decided to integrate their third-party time tracking system with their large, distributed accounting solution.

The initial TLS Timesheet Submission Process

Subsequent to a business requirements analysis, TLS analysts document a simple Timesheet Submission Process. Essentially, every timesheet TLS receives from workers outsourced to clients is required to undergo a series of verification steps. If the timesheet is verified successfully, the process ends and the timesheet is accepted; whereas, a timesheet that fails verification is submitted to a separate rejection step prior to the process ending.

Here is a breakdown of the current process steps, as illustrated in Figure 12.14:

1. Receive timesheet.
2. Verify timesheet.
3. If timesheet is verified, accept timesheet submission and proceed to Step 5.
4. Reject timesheet submission.
5. Terminate process.

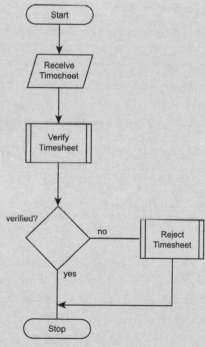

Figure 12.14
The TLS Timesheet Submission Process.

This process is self-contained and has no dependencies on any other processes. Within TLS's service-oriented environment, it therefore is considered a primitive business process.

Expanding the TLS Timesheet Submission Process

Though it only consists of five steps at this point, there is more to this process. The details are revealed as we decompose the process logic using our building blocks.

We begin with the "Verify timesheet" step, which is actually a sub-process in its own right. It therefore can be broken down into the following more granular steps:

2a. Compare hours recorded on timesheet to hours billed to clients.

2b. Confirm that authorization was given for any recorded overtime hours.

2c. Confirm that hours recorded for any particular project do not exceed a predefined limit for that project.

2d. Confirm that total hours recorded for one week do not exceed a predefined maximum for that worker.

Each of these steps is a simple action that is considered a primitive business activity. Further, upon subsequent analysis we discover that the "Reject timesheet submission" process activity can be decomposed into the following primitive business activities:

4a. Update the worker's profile record to keep track of rejected timesheets.

4b. Issue a timesheet rejection notification message to the worker.

4c. Issue a notification to the worker's manager.

Having drilled-down the original process activities, we now have a larger amount of primitive business activities. To represent our revised and more detailed process we need to show all 11 possible process activities (Figure 12.15).

1. Receive timesheet.

2. Compare hours recorded on timesheet to hours billed to clients.

3. Confirm that authorization was given for any recorded overtime hours.

4. Confirm that hours recorded for any particular project do not exceed a predefined limit for that project.

5. Confirm that total hours recorded for one week do not exceed a predefined maximum for that worker.

6. If timesheet is verified, accept timesheet submission and proceed to Step 11.

7. Reject timesheet submission.

8. Generate a message explaining the reasons for the rejection.

9. Issue a timesheet rejection notification message to the worker.

10. Issue a notification to the worker's manager.

11. Terminate the process.

As we mentioned earlier, although the initial service-oriented solution built by TLS was successful in its implementation, it has been criticized for the amount of up-front analysis effort it required. TLS therefore intends to explore alternative approaches before proceeding with larger scaled SOAs. To accomplish this, TLS analysts want to use this project to compare different service candidate configurations before proceeding to the design stage.

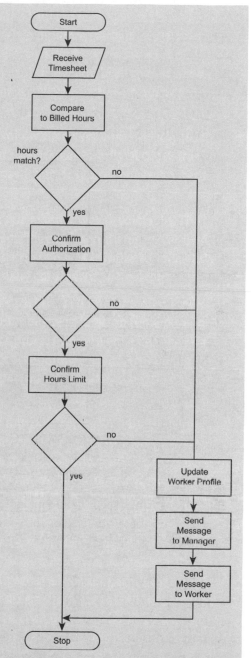

Figure 12.15
The TLS Timesheet Submission Process, where each process activity is also a primitive business activity.

Approach #1: Deriving hybrid services

TLS analysts first look at how service candidates could be derived using the most cost and time-efficient approach possible: creating hybrid, task-centric services. They are fully aware that this would not lead to a quality SOA, but they need to take practical considerations into account and therefore want to explore extremes. They begin by grouping the primitive business activities defined in their primitive business process into two categories (shown in Figure 12.16).

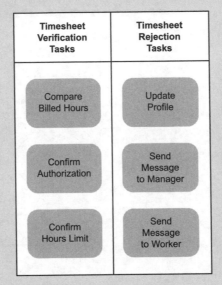

Figure 12.16
An ad-hoc grouping of primitive business activities.

These two groups seem to adequately represent the collective business process logic and are therefore used as the source from which two corresponding service candidates are derived:

- Verify Timesheet Service
- Reject Timesheet Service

As part of this process, each of the previously listed service candidates undergoes some analysis to determine exactly what would be involved with its execution. The result is a set of more granular service operation candidates, as shown in Figures 12.17 and 12.18.

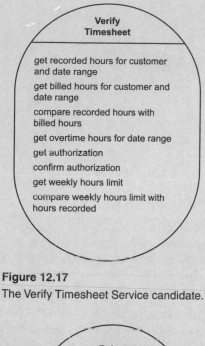

Figure 12.17

The Verify Timesheet Service candidate.

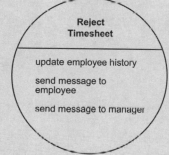

Figure 12.18

The Reject Timesheet Service candidate.

The resulting service composition (Figure 12.19) is quite simple. The Verify Timesheet Service candidate acts as a quasi-process service in that it contains the bulk of the primitive business process logic, as well as the composition logic for involving the Reject Timesheet Service, should an invalid timesheet be encountered.

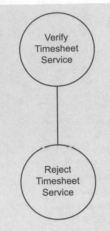

Figure 12.19

A simple service composition consisting of
two hybrid, task-centric service candidates.

Well, this analysis didn't take too long, and that is something that appealed to the
analysts. However, upon a review of their modeling efforts, some significant
drawbacks are identified with this approach. Below is a collection of pros and
cons identified with creating hybrid, task-centric services.

Pros

- Minimal analysis and modeling effort.
- Results in the creation of simple and easy-to-understand service candidates.

Cons

- No specialized service layers were created, therefore eliminating the benefit
  potential of service layer abstraction.
- No real reuse benefit is achieved, as services are very specific to a single
  process.
- No agility is achieved, as service logic is tightly coupled to process logic.

NOTE

This approach corresponds to the first of the eight scenarios covered in the
Service layer configuration scenarios section of Chapter 9.

Approach #2: Deriving entity-centric services

Next, TLS analysts revisit the familiar concept of deriving entity-centric business services. Their goal is to establish a layer of entity-centric candidates, along with a parent orchestration layer consisting of a single process service candidate.

They begin by reviewing an existing entity model relevant to the Timesheet Submission Process.

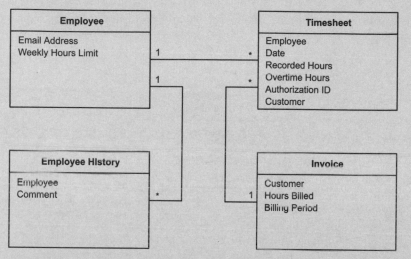

Figure 12.20
A TLS entity-model displaying entities pertinent to the Timesheet Submission Process.

TLS analysts study this model, along with the following list of granular service operation candidates identified during the previous analysis:

- get recorded hours for customer and date range
- get billed hours for customer and date range
- compare recorded hours with billed hours
- get overtime hours for date range
- get authorization
- confirm authorization
- get weekly hours limit
- compare weekly hours limit with hours recorded

- update employee history
- send message to employee
- send message to manager

Before actually putting together entity-centric business service candidates, analysts first define a preliminary process service candidate called the Timesheet Submission Process Service. They accomplish this by retrieving operation candidate descriptions that contain business rules and conditional logic, as shown in Figure 12.21.

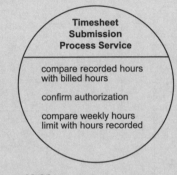

Figure 12.21
The Timesheet Submission Process Service candidate.

Next, the Timesheet entity is reviewed. It is decided that this entity warrants a corresponding entity-centric business service candidate simply called "Timesheet." Further, by analyzing its attributes, TLS determines that of the listed service operation candidates, the following should be grouped with this service candidate:

- get recorded hours for customer and date range
- get overtime hours for date range
- get authorization

However, upon subsequent analysis, it is determined that the first two operation candidates could be made more reusable by removing the requirement that a date range be the only query criteria. Although this particular business process will always provide a date range, other processes may want to request recorded or overtime hours based on other parameters. The result is a revised set of operation candidates, as shown in Figure 12.22.

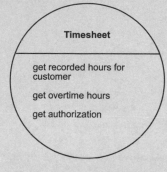

Figure 12.22
The Timesheet Service candidate.

Analysts then take a look at the Invoice entity. They again agree that this entity deserves representation as a standalone entity-centric service candidate. They name this service "Invoice" and assign it the following operation candidate:

- get billed hours for customer and date range

When the service-orientation principle of reuse is again considered, analysts decide to expand the scope of this service candidate by altering the function of the chosen operation candidate and then by adding a new one, as shown in Figure 12.23. Now service requestors can retrieve customer and billed hours information separately.

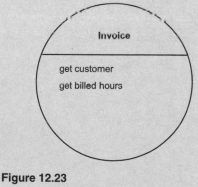

Figure 12.23
The Invoice Service candidate.

The Employee and Employee History entities are reviewed next. Because they are closely related to each other, it is decided that they can be jointly represented by a single entity-centric business service candidate, called "Employee." Two service operation candidates are assigned, resulting in the service candidate definition displayed in Figure 12.24.

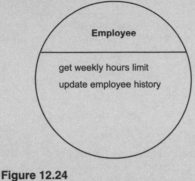

Employee

get weekly hours limit
update employee history

Figure 12.24
The Employee Service candidate.

Finally, the remaining operation candidates are grouped into a reusable application service, simply called "Notification."

- send message to employee
- send message to manager

To make the service candidate more reusable, the two operation candidates are consolidated into one, as shown in Figure 12.25.

Notification

send message

Figure 12.25
The Notification Service candidate.

Note that when normally modeling entity-centric business services, reuse would be a larger concern and many more operation candidates would be added to arrive at a series of services candidates fully equipped to manage a range of common processing requirements. In this example, most of the operation candidates we created were only related to our immediate requirements.

Figure 12.26 displays the resulting service composition, which illustrates three distinct service sub-layers: orchestration, business, and application.

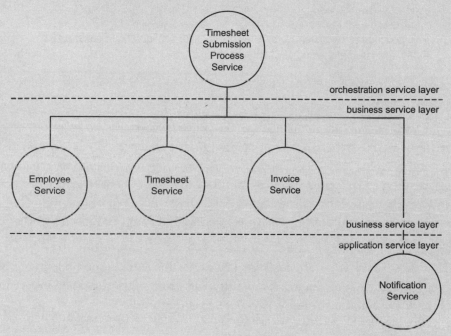

Figure 12.26
A service composition controlled by an orchestration layer.

TLS analysts conclude this modeling exercise by listing the pros and cons of their results.

Pros

- Allows for the creation of reusable service candidates.
- Establishes an extra level of abstraction via the orchestration layer.
- Highly extensible and agile.

Cons

- Requires more analysis effort.
- Results in a more complex service composition.
- Requires the creation of additional services not yet identified (application services needed to carry out processing tasks for the Employee, Timesheet, and Invoice services).

> **NOTE**
>
> This second approach corresponds to service layer configuration Scenario #8 of those discussed at the end of Chapter 9.

Approach #3: Mixing task-centric and entity-centric services

Before TLS makes a final decision, they choose to explore one more option. It has been discovered that there is reuse potential for the collection of verification tasks associated with the Timesheet Submission Process. Therefore, analysts speculate that by adding a task-centric service candidate to the set of entity-centric service candidates they just defined, they may be able to derive a reusable composition. This composition would represent a sub-process that could be reused by other master processes.

Because most of the work already has been done, this extra bit of modeling effort does not take them long. First, they identify and group the verification tasks into a new service candidate called Verify Timesheet (Figure 12.27).

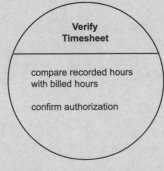

Figure 12.27
The Verify Timesheet Service candidate.

This reallocation of operation candidates does not affect any of the previously defined entity-centric candidates. It only removes some of the process workflow logic from the parent Timesheet Submission Process Service candidate. It also results in a new composition configuration (displayed in Figure 12.28) in which the task-centric service candidate adds a layer to the composition hierarchy.

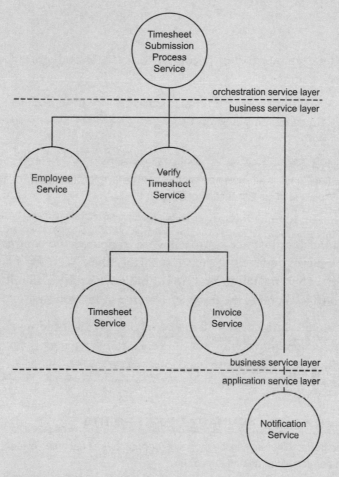

Figure 12.28
The revised service composition incorporating a task-centric service.

Pros

- Similar benefits of agility and extensibility to the entity-centric only approach.
- If the Verify Timesheet sub-process is truly reusable, there may be a benefit to abstracting it from larger process workflow logic.

Cons

- Results in an even more complex composition that introduces an additional layer of processing.
- Removal of workflow logic from the process service decentralizes control of the overall Timesheet Submission Process.

NOTE

This last approach is an implementation of service layer configuration Scenario #7, as explained in the last section of Chapter 9.

At the end of the day, the three approaches are compared and contrasted. Analysts review the pros and cons of each and balance these with short and long-term TLS goals. Their final decision is to continue with the pure entity-centric configuration (the second of the three we covered in this example).

However, as stated earlier, they will not be relying on the top-down approach any more. Pressing requirements and time constraints have motivated them to adopt the agile delivery strategy.

SUMMARY OF KEY POINTS

- When comparing different service modeling approaches, it becomes evident that there are benefits and trade-offs to each.
- The bottom line is generally that the more up-front analysis invested the greater the long-term rewards.

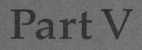

Part V

Building SOA
(Technology and Design)

Time for the rubber to hit the road, as we apply the theories, concepts, and analysis results from past chapters to real world, concrete SOA designs. The remaining chapters in this book explore numerous facets of SOA technology interspersed with detailed, step-by-step process descriptions that explain how to apply this technology to realize individual services and SOA as a whole.

Chapter 13

Service-Oriented Design
(Part I: Introduction)

At the beginning of Chapter 11 we stated that the service-oriented analysis phase is probably the most important part of our SOA delivery lifecycle. If this is the case, then the service-oriented design phase is a very close second. The service-level decisions made at this stage collectively will determine the quality and longevity of the resulting SOA.

Throughout the following four service-oriented design chapters, we emphasize the fact that custom design standards are a crucial part of this stage. We do this because their use and adherence will ultimately set the "potential barometer" for realizing many of the primary benefits of contemporary SOA.

> **How case studies are used:** Both of our fictional companies face some strategic decisions during the preparatory stage of the service-oriented design process. The choices they make with regard to how they plan to shape their respective SOAs will influence the service design processes they will undergo in the following chapters.

13.1   Introduction to service-oriented design

Service-oriented design is the process by which concrete physical service designs are derived from logical service candidates and then assembled into abstract compositions that implement a business process.

13.1.1   Objectives of service-oriented design

The primary questions answered by this phase are:

- How can physical service interface definitions be derived from the service candidates modeled during the service-oriented analysis phase?
- What SOA characteristics do we want to realize and support?
- What industry standards and extensions will be required by our SOA to implement the planned service designs and SOA characteristics?

To address these questions, the design process actually involves further analysis. This time our focus is on environmental factors and design standards that will shape our services.

The overall goals of performing a service-oriented design are as follows:

- Determine the core set of architectural extensions.
- Set the boundaries of the architecture.
- Identify required design standards.
- Define abstract service interface designs.
- Identify potential service compositions.
- Assess support for service-orientation principles.
- Explore support for characteristics of contemporary SOA.

13.1.2   "Design standards" versus "Industry standards"

The term "standards" is used frequently in this chapter. It is easy to confuse its context, so we often qualify it. *Design standards* represent custom standards created by an organization to ensure that services and SOAs are built according to a set of consistent conventions. *Industry standards* are provided by standards organizations and are published in Web services and XML specifications (as explained in the *"Standards" vs. "Specifications" vs. "Extensions"* section of Chapter 4).

13.1.3   The service-oriented design process

As with the service-oriented analysis, we first establish a parent process that begins with some preparatory work. This leads to a series of iterative processes that govern the creation of different types of service designs and, ultimately, the design of the overall solution workflow (Figure 13.1).

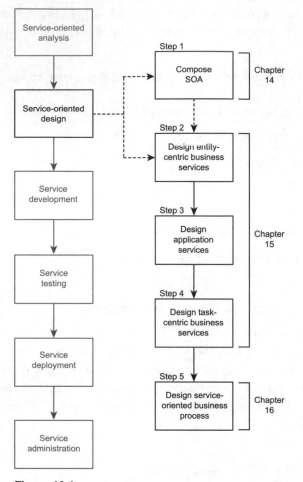

Figure 13.1
A high-level service-oriented design process.

Step 1: Compose SOA

Before services can be developed, the underlying architecture needs to be well defined. As explained in Chapter 14, this stage ask us to formally define a standard set of service layers and then choose open technologies in support of those layers.

When a top-down delivery strategy is employed, these tasks are generally completed well before service candidates are even created. However, with more tactical variations of the top-down and agile approaches being the most common forms of service delivery, technology composition of a service-oriented architecture often needs to be dealt with as part of the service-oriented design process. (The dashed lines in Figure 13.1 indicate that this step may or may not be part of the service-oriented design phase.)

Steps 2 to 4: Design services

These steps are represented by the following three separate processes provided in Chapter 15:

- Entity-centric business service design process.

- Application service design process.

- Task-centric business service design process.

Our primary input for each of these service design processes is the corresponding service candidates we produced in the service modeling process during the service-oriented analysis.

Step 5: Design service-oriented business process

Upon establishing an inventory of service designs, we proceed to create our orchestration layer—the glue that binds our services with business process logic. This step results in the formal, executable definition of workflow logic, which translates into the creation of a WS-BPEL process definition (as explained in Chapter 16).

13.1.4   Prerequisites

Before we get into the details of the service-oriented design process, we should make sure that we have a sufficient understanding of key parts of the languages required to design services.

In Chapter 5 we described concepts related to WSDL and SOAP. In the next few sections, we supply introductory descriptions of the primary elements provided by these two markup languages, in addition to a handful of key elements from the XML Schema Definition Language. (Figure 13.2 re-establishes how these three specifications relate to each other.)

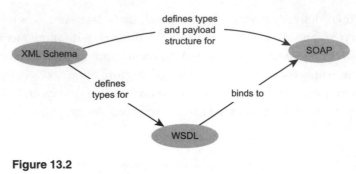

Figure 13.2
Three core specifications associated with service design.

These introductions are by no means a substitute for proper tutorials. The purpose of these sections is to provide you with enough background information so that you can better understand the following parts of the service-oriented design chapters:

• The references made to specific parts of a language in the upcoming *SOA Composition Guidelines* chapter and the service design process descriptions in Chapter 15.

• The markup code samples provided in the many case study examples interspersed throughout the three service design process descriptions in Chapter 15.

> **NOTE**
>
> If you already are comfortable with WSDL, SOAP, and XML Schema, feel free to skip ahead to the next chapter.

SUMMARY OF KEY POINTS

• Before designing services, key decision points surrounding service layers and the set of industry specifications from which SOA will be composed need to be addressed. Chapter 14 covers this step.

• The main focus of the service-oriented design phase is to transform previously modeled service candidates into physical service designs. Step-by-step service design processes are provided in Chapter 15.

• An implementation agnostic workflow definition then is required to tie all of our service designs together into a cohesive unit of process logic. Chapter 16 demonstrates the use of WS-BPEL for this purpose.

13.2 WSDL-related XML Schema language basics

The XML Schema Definition Language (XSD) has become a central and very common part of XML and Web services architectures. The hierarchical structure of XML documents can be formally defined by creating an XSD schema—hence an XML document is considered an instance of its corresponding schema. Further, the structure established within an XSD schema (Figure 13.3) contains a series of rules and constraints to which XML document instances must comply for parsers and processors to deem them valid.

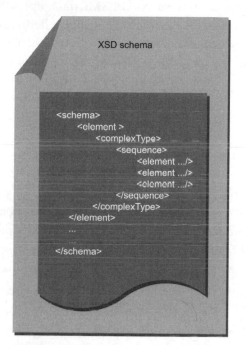

Figure 13.3
An XSD schema document.

The fundamental data representation rules provided by XSD schemas are related to representing data according to type. As with data types used in programming languages, XSD schemas provide a set of non-proprietary data types used to represent information in XML document instances.

The data types supported by XSD schemas are extensive, but they do not always map cleanly to the proprietary types used by programming languages. Therefore, many environments must go through a mapping process to select the XSD schema types best suited to represent data originating from or being delivered to proprietary application logic and data sources.

XSD schemas can exist as separate documents (typically identified by .xsd file extensions), or they may be embedded in other types of documents, such as XML document instances or WSDL definitions. XML document instances commonly link to a separate XSD schema file so that the same schema can be used to validate multiple document instances. WSDL definitions can import the contents of an XSD file, or they also can have schema content embedded inline.

Because almost all XML and Web services specifications are themselves written in XML, XSD schemas have become an intrinsic part of XML data representation and service-oriented architectures. Regardless of whether you explicitly define an XSD schema for your solution, your underlying processors will be using XSD schemas to execute many tasks related to the processing of XML documents through Web services. (The role of XSD schemas within SOA is explained further in the *XML Schema and SOA* section in Chapter 14.)

"Elements" vs. "Constructs"

Each of the specifications we explore in this and subsequent chapters provides a markup language that is expressed as an XML dialect. This means that the language itself is written in XML and is comprised of XML elements. Our focus is on describing key elements that provide features relevant to the topics discussed in this book. Sometimes we refer to language elements as *constructs*. A construct simply represents a key parent element likely to contain a set of related child elements. Therefore we use this term to communicate that the element we are discussing will contain additional elements that form a block of XML.

13.2.1   The `schema` element

The `schema` element is the root element of every XSD schema. It contains a series of common attributes used primarily to establish important namespace references. The `xmlns` attribute, for example, establishes a default namespace on its own, or can be used to declare a prefix that acts as an identifier to qualify other elements in the schema.

The `http://www.w3.org/2001/XMLSchema` namespace always is present so that it can be used to represent content in the schema that originates from the XSD specification and the elements in the schema document itself. This allows processors to distinguish native XSD schema content from user-defined content.

```
<schema xmlns="http://www.w3.org/2001/XMLSchema">
```

Example 13.1   The most basic form of schema declaration.

Other important attributes include `targetNamespace`, used to assign a namespace to the custom elements and attributes declared in the schema document, and the `element-FormDefault` attribute, which when set to a value of "qualified," requires that all elements in the XML document be associated with their corresponding namespace.

13.2.2   The `element` element

Using this element, you can declare a custom element that is then referenced by its name within an XML document instance.

For example, the following element declaration in an XSD schema:

```
<element name="InvoiceNumber" type="xsd:integer"/>
```

Example 13.2   An element declaration in an XSD schema.

…will be represented within an XML document as follows:

```
<InvoiceNumber>12345</InvoiceNumber>
```

Example 13.3   The usage of this element in an XML document instance.

…where the value in between the opening and closing `InvoiceNumber` tags is required to be an integer.

The `type` attribute of an element can be set to one of the predefined data types established by the XML Schema specification, or it can be assigned a complex type, as explained next.

13.2.3   The `complexType` and `simpleType` elements

With a `complexType` you can group elements and attributes into a composite type that can be used to represent a set of related data representations. The following example groups two elements named `ID` and `WeeklyHoursLimit` into a `complexType` named `EmployeeHours`.

```
<complexType name="EmployeeHours">
   <sequence>
      <element name="ID" type="xsd:integer"/>
      <element name="WeeklyHoursLimit" type="xsd:short"/>
   </sequence>
</complexType>
```

Example 13.4   A `complexType` containing two element declarations.

The `EmployeeHours` `complexType` can be assigned to one or more elements. This facilitates standardization and reuse of commonly grouped information and avoids redundant element declarations. Note that the `sequence` element is a type of indicator used within the `complexType` construct to establish a specific order for `element` elements.

`simpleType` elements also allow you to group related data representations, but these constructs cannot contain attributes or further child elements. (None of the examples used in this book contain `simpleType` elements.)

13.2.4   The `import` and `include` elements

XSD schemas can be modularized. This allows for one schema document to import the contents of another. Both the `import` and `include` elements are used to point to the location of the XSD schema file that will be pulled in when the schema is processed at runtime.

```
<schema xmlns="http://www.w3.org/2001/XMLSchema" ...>
   <import schemaLocation="..."
      namespace="http://www.xmltc.com/tls/schema"/>
   <include schemaLocation="..."/>
```

Example 13.5   The `import` and `include` elements.

The difference between these two elements is that `include` is used to reference schemas that use the same target namespace as the parent schema, whereas `import` is used to point to schemas that use a different target namespace. As per the previous example, a `namespace` attribute only is used with the `import` element.

13.2.5   Other important elements

The XML Schema Definition Language is large and complex and provides numerous options for structuring and validating XML document data. There are many other important parts of the language that are not used in the examples provided in this book, including:

- additional type definition elements (`attribute`, `complexContent`, `simpleContent`)
- constraint related elements (`restriction`, `enumeration`, `pattern`)
- element indicators (`maxOccurs`, `minOccurs`, `group`)
- extensibility elements (`any`, `extension`, `redefine`)
- elements for simulating relationships between elements (`unique`, `key`, `keyref`)

Entire books have been written to explain the XML Schema Definition Language. See `www.soabooks.com` for recommended reading resources.

SUMMARY OF KEY POINTS

- The XML Schema Definition Language is an intrinsic member of the XML and Web services specification landscape and is key to the service interface definition we are required to build as part of the service-oriented design process.

- XSD schemas can be embedded or imported into WSDL definitions.

13.3   WSDL language basics

The Web Services Description Language (WSDL) is the most fundamental technology standard associated with the design of services. As you will see in subsequent chapters, WSDL definitions are a central part of all aspects of service design. In Chapter 5 we introduced the WSDL document and established how it consists of separate abstract and concrete definitions.

Just to recap, the abstract definition contains a series of parts that include types, message, and port type (or interface), whereas the concrete definition is comprised of binding and service parts.

Each of these parts relates to corresponding elements (Figure 13.4) that are defined in the WSDL specification. In the following sections we describe the syntactical implementation of these elements, as they are relevant to the majority of upcoming case study examples used in Chapter 15 to demonstrate service interface design. (How WSDL relates to SOA is discussed separately in the *WSDL and SOA* section of Chapter 14.)

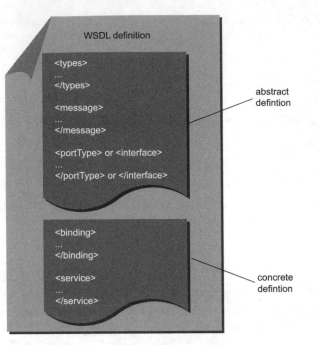

Figure 13.4
The structure of a WSDL definition.

13.3.1   The definitions element

This is the root or parent element of every WSDL document. It houses all other parts of the service definition and is also the location in which the many namespaces used within WSDL documents are established.

```
<definitions name="Employee"
   targetNamespace="http://www.xmltc.com/tls/employee/wsdl/"
   xmlns="http://schemas.xmlsoap.org/wsdl/"
   xmlns:act="http://www.xmltc.com/tls/employee/schema/accounting/"
   xmlns:hr="http://www.xmltc.com/tls/employee/schema/hr/"
   xmlns:soap="http://schemas.xmlsoap.org/wsdl/soap/"
   xmlns:tns="http://www.xmltc.com/tls/employee/wsdl/"
   xmlns:xsd="http://www.w3.org/2001/XMLSchema">
   ...
</definitions>
```

Example 13.6   A definitions element of the Employee Service, declaring a number of namespaces.

In the preceding example, the service definition is started with a `definitions` element that contains a series of attributes in which the service is assigned the name of "Employee" and in which a number of namespaces are declared.

For example, the `xmlns` attribute establishes the standard value of `http://schemas.xmlsoap.org/wsdl/` as the default namespace. This means that all of the elements that belong to the WSDL language do not need prefixes to associate them with the WSDL specification.

By defining the `xmlns:xsd` namespace declaration, all elements within the WSDL that belong to the XML Schema Definition Language need to be prefixed with the `xsd:` qualifier. Also note the use of the `xmlns:act` and `xmlns:hr` namespace declarations. These are used to distinguish between two separate schemas that are imported into the `types` construct.

The `xmlns:soap` namespace declaration establishes the `soap:` qualifier used by elements introduced later in the `bindings` construct, where the WSDL definition associates its abstract operations to concrete SOAP bindings.

13.3.2   The `types` element

The `types` construct is where XSD schema content is placed. This part of the WSDL can consist of actual XSD schema markup (an entire `schema` construct containing type definitions), or it can contain `import` elements that reference external schema definitions (or it can contain both embedded and imported XSD types).

As illustrated in Figure 13.5, the types established in this part of the WSDL definition are used to represent the XML content of message bodies. The `message` element (explained later) references these types and associates them with messages.

The SOAP message body contains XML content that can represent anything from simple parameter data to complex business documents. This content can be formally defined through types provided by the WSDL `types` area. Therefore, XSD schema `complexType` elements are commonly provided here, as they consist of groups of related types that can represent entire message body structures.

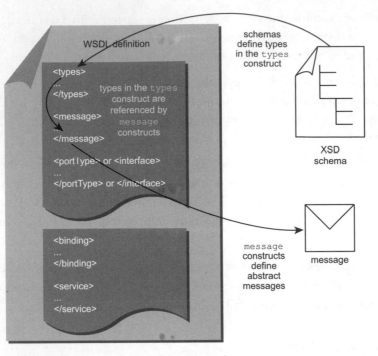

Figure 13.5
The WSDL `types` construct populated by XSD schema types used by
the `message` construct to represent the SOAP message body.

In the following example, an entire `schema` construct is embedded within the WSDL
`types` construct.

```
<types>
    <schema
        xmlns="http://www.w3.org/2001/XMLSchema"
        targetNamespace=
            "http://www.xmltc.com/railco/transform/schema/">
        <complexType name="ReturnCodeType">
            <sequence>
                <element name="Code" type="xsd:integer"/>
                <element name="Message" type="xsd:string"/>
            </sequence>
        </complexType>
    </schema>
</types>
```

Example 13.7   A `types` construct containing an XSD `schema` construct in which a `complex-
Type` is defined.

Use of the `types` construct is common in WSDL definitions with substantial content. However, it is not a required element. Native XSD schema types can be referenced directly within the `message` element, as explained next.

13.3.3   The `message` and `part` elements

For every message a service is designed to receive or transmit, a `message` construct must be added. This element assigns the message a name and contains one or more `part` child elements that each are assigned a type. `message` elements later are associated to `operation` elements to establish the input and output messages of the operation.

`part` elements use the `type` or `element` attributes to identify the data type of the message part. The `type` attribute can be assigned a simple or complex type and generally is used for RPC-style messages. `part` elements in document-style messages typically rely on the `element` attribute, which can reference an XSD `element` element. The `name` attribute is used to uniquely identify `part` elements within a `message` construct.

In the example below, we define request and response messages with two separate `message` constructs. Each message contains a `part` element that is assigned a predefined XSD element using the `element` attribute.

```
<message name="getEmployeeWeeklyHoursRequestMessage">
   <part name="RequestParameter"
      element="act:EmployeeHoursRequestType"/>
</message>
<message name="getEmployeeWeeklyHoursResponseMessage">
   <part name="ResponseParameter"
      element="act:EmployeeHoursResponseType"/>
</message>
```

Example 13.8   Two `message` constructs likely representing the input and output messages for an operation.

In the next example the `part` element is simply assigned a native XSD schema data type using the `type` attribute.

```
<message name="getID">
   <part type="xsd:integer"/>
</message>
```

Example 13.9   A simple parameter message requiring just a single integer value.

If all messages in a WSDL definition are assigned native (simple) XSD types, a separate `types` construct generally is not required.

13.3.4 The `portType`, `interface`, and `operation` elements

Service operations are defined within the `portType` area of the WSDL definition. Hence, `portType` constructs simply represent collections of operations. Individual operations are defined using the aptly named `operation` element.

```
<portType name="EmployeeInterface">
   <operation name="GetWeeklyHoursLimit">
      . . .
   </operation>
   <operation name="UpdateHistory">
      . . .
   </operation>
</portType>
```

Example 13.10   The `portType` construct hosting two `operation` constructs.

The `portType` element is defined in version 1.1 of the Web Services Description Language. Version 2.0 of this specification changes the name of this element to `interface`. The examples provided in this book are based on WSDL 1.1 and therefore continue to use the `portType` element.

13.3.5 The `input` and `output` elements (when used with `operation`)

Each `operation` construct contains `input` and/or `output` child elements that represent the request and response messages the operation is capable of processing.

In the example below, each operation has one input and one output message. The respective `input` and `output` elements are assigned messages defined in the `message` constructs (explained in the previous section) via their `message` attributes.

```
<operation name="GetWeeklyHoursLimit">
   <input message="tns:getWeeklyHoursRequestMessage"/>
   <output message="tns:getWeeklyHoursResponseMessage"/>
</operation>
<operation name="UpdateHistory">
   <input message="tns:updateHistoryRequestMessage"/>
   <output message="tns:updateHistoryResponseMessage"/>
</operation>
```

Example 13.11   `operation` elements with child `input` and `output` elements.

As explained in Chapter 6, WSDL supports predefined message exchange patterns (MEPs). The presence of input and output elements and the sequence in which they are displayed generally establishes the MEP of the operation. For instance, the two operations defined in the previous example represent the request-response MEP.

Placing a single input element within the operation construct expresses the one-way MEP, as shown in the next example.

```
<operation name="Submit">
   <input message="tns:receiveSubmitMessage"/>
</operation>
```

Example 13.12   An operation element with a single child input element.

> **NOTE**
>
> It may seem confusing to associate request-and-response with a sequence of input and then output messages because there is a tendency to think that a request requires the service to initiate communication. The reason this makes sense in the Web services world is because WSDL definitions express an interface from the perspective of the service provider. So the request-response MEP, to a WSDL, means that a requestor will send it (the service provider) a request as input, to which it (the service provider) will reply with a response as output.

13.3.6   The binding element

So far, all of the elements we've described belong to the abstract service definition. On their own, they complete the description of a service interface—but without referencing any means of messaging communication technology.

The binding element begins the concrete portion of the service definition, to assign a communications protocol that can be used to access and interact with the WSDL.

Upon first glance of the following example, the binding element appears similar in structure to the portType element. As with portType, the binding construct contains one or more operation elements. However, you'll notice the additional soap:binding and soap:operation elements interspersed within the construct syntax. These are what establish the SOAP protocol as the manner in which this WSDL can be communicated with.

```
<binding name="EmployeeBinding" type="tns:EmployeeInterface">
   <soap:binding style="document"
      transport="http://schemas.xmlsoap.org/soap/http"/>
   <operation name="GetWeeklyHoursLimit">
      <soap:operation soapAction="..."/>
      ...
   </operation>
   <operation name="UpdateHistory">
      <soap:operation soapAction="..."/>
      ...
   </operation>
</binding>
```

Example 13.13   The `binding` construct hosting concrete `operation` definitions.

Further, the `style` attribute of the `soap:binding` element defines whether the SOAP messages used to support an operation are to be formatted as document or RPC-style messages.

The value of `"document"` allows the SOAP message body to contain a fully definable XML document structure. Assigning a value of `"rpc"` to the `style` attribute requires compliance to a body structure defined within the SOAP specification, which primarily forces the root element of the body to be named after the operation name.

13.3.7   The `input` and `output` elements (when used with `binding`)

Each `operation` element within a `binding` construct mirrors the `input` and `output` message child elements defined in the abstract definition.

Within a `binding` construct, however, the `input` and `output` elements do not reference the `message` elements again. Instead, they contain protocol details that establish how the messages are going to be processed and interpreted by the chosen communication technology. In our example, the service interface has been bound to the SOAP protocol.

```
<operation name="GetWeeklyHoursLimit">
   <soap:operation soapAction="..."/>
   <input>
      <soap:body use="literal"/>
   </input>
   <output>
      <soap:body use="literal"/>
   </output>
</operation>
```

```
<operation name="UpdateHistory">
   <soap:operation soapAction="..."/>
   <input>
      <soap:body use="literal"/>
   </input>
   <output>
      <soap:body use="literal"/>
   </output>
</operation>
```

Example 13.14 input and output elements providing message processing information.

This introduces the soap:body element from the SOAP language that defines the data type system to be used by SOAP processors, via the use attribute. The use attribute can be set to "encoding" or "literal".

> **NOTE**
>
> How the style and use attributes affect the processing of messages within SOA is discussed in the *WSDL and SOA* section in Chapter 14.

13.3.8 The service, port, and endpoint elements

The service element simply provides a physical address at which the service can be accessed. It hosts the port element that contains this location information.

```
<service name="EmployeeService">
   <port binding="tns:EmployeeBinding" name="EmployeePort">
      <soap:address
         location="http://www.xmltc.com/tls/employee/"/>
   </port>
</service>
```

Example 13.15 The service and port elements establishing the physical service address.

Because we are binding to the SOAP protocol, the port element contains a child soap:address element with the physical address information. Note that the port element is replaced with the endpoint element in version 2.0 of the WSDL specification.

13.3.9 The import element

WSDL definitions support a similar form of modularity as XSD schemas do. The import element can be used to import parts of the WSDL definition as well as XSD schemas.

```
<import namespace="http://www.xmltc.com/tls/schemas/"
    location="http://www.xmltc.com/tls/schemas/employee.xsd"/>
```

Example 13.16   The `import` element referencing a schema document.

> **NOTE**
>
> See the *Consider using modular WSDL documents* guideline at the end of
> Chapter 15 for more information.

13.3.10   The `documentation` element

This optional element simply allows you to add descriptive, human-readable annota-
tions within a WSDL definition. Developers can use this information when building
service requestors or it can be programmatically retrieved through a service registry to
aid the discovery of the service.

```
<portType name="TransformInterface">
    <documentation>
        Retrieves an XML document and converts it into the
        native accounting document format.
    </documentation>
    ...
</portType>
```

Example 13.17   The `documentation` element providing a description of the overall
                    service interface.

SUMMARY OF KEY POINTS

- The Web Services Description Language is the focal point of service design, as it is
  used to design the abstract and concrete definitions of service interfaces.

- The WSDL definition hosts multiple child constructs associated with abstract and
  concrete parts of the service description.

13.4   SOAP language basics

In the previous section we established that a WSDL definition intentionally separates
abstract from concrete definition details. One of the benefits of doing so is that we can

isolate communication protocols that implement the messaging required by a service from the implementation-neutral service interface. However, given that SOAP has become the messaging format of choice for SOA, we will very likely be binding our abstract interfaces to SOAP.

Within the service-oriented design process, we place a great deal of emphasis on hand crafting the WSDL definition, along with required XSD schema types. SOAP messages generally do not require as much hands on attention. We spend more time working with SOAP syntax in Chapter 17, where we explore WS-* extensions that are implemented via SOAP headers. Still, this is as good of a time as any to introduce some basic parts of the SOAP language.

As we established in Chapter 5, the structure of SOAP messages is relatively simple. They consist of header, body, and fault sections, all encased in an envelope. Appropriately, the elements we describe in this section (Figure 13.5) are represented by the same names. (The manner in which SOA affects the utilization of SOAP is explored in the *SOAP and SOA* section in Chapter 14.)

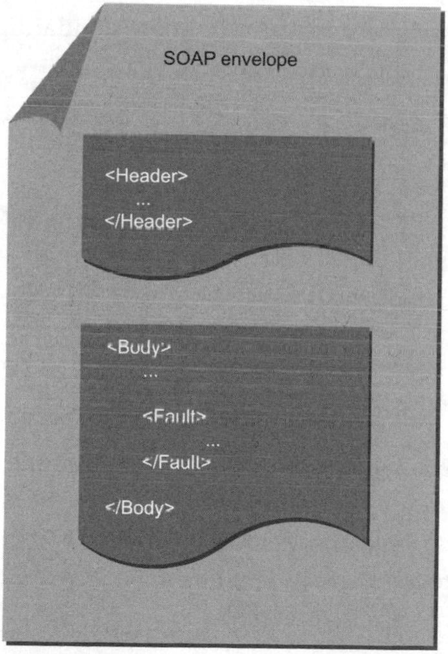

Figure 13.6
The structure of a SOAP message document.

13.4.1   The Envelope element

The Envelope element represents the root of SOAP message structures. It contains a mandatory Body construct and an optional Header construct.

```
<Envelope xmlns ="http://schemas.xmlsoap.org/soap/envelope/">
   <Header>
      . . .
   </Header>
   <Body>
      . . .
   </Body>
</Envelope>
```

Example 13.18   The root Envelope construct hosting Header and Body constructs.

13.4.2   The Header element

As explained in Chapter 5, the header portion of the SOAP message has become a key enabler of the feature set provided by WS-* specifications. Most of these extensions are implemented on a message level and introduce new standardized SOAP header blocks destined to be embedded in the Header construct.

```
<Header>
   <x:CorrelationID
      xmlns:x="http://www.xmltc.com/tls/headersample/"
      mustUnderstand="1">
         0131858580-JDJ903KD
   </x:CorrelationID>
</Header>
```

Example 13.19   The Header construct hosting a header block.

Header blocks also can be customized, as shown in Example 13.19, where the SOAP header is used to host a unique CorrelationID element. The mustUnderstand attribute indicates that the contents of the header must be understood by any receiver of the message that is required to process this header. If the mustUnderstand value is set to "0" the processing of this header becomes optional.

13.4.3   The Body element

This is the one required child element of the SOAP Envelope construct. It contains the message payload formatted as well-formed XML. The structure and naming used to define this part of the SOAP message relates to the `style` and `use` attributes discussed in the previous WSDL `binding` element description.

SOAP message `Body` constructs are defined within the WSDL `message` constructs which, as we've already established, reference XSD schema data type information from the WSDL `types` construct (Figure 13.7).

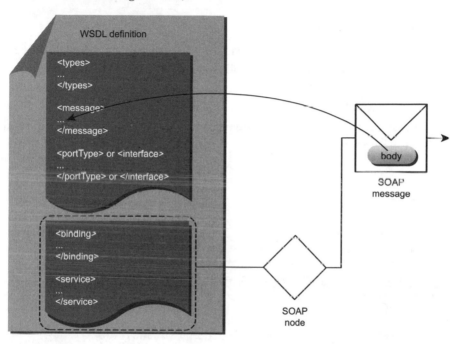

Figure 13.7
A SOAP message body defined within the WSDL `message` construct. The actual processing of the SOAP message via a wire protocol is governed by the constructs within the concrete definition.

```
<Body>
    <soa:book xmlns:soa="http://www.soabooks.com/">
        <soa:ISBN>
            0131858580
        </soa:ISBN>
        <soa:title>
            Service-Oriented Architecture
            Concepts, Technology, and Design
        </soa:title>
    </soa:book>
</Body>
```

Example 13.20   The contents of a sample `Body` construct.

While SOAP header blocks can be processed actively during the transmission of a SOAP message, the SOAP body should not be touched. However, if allowed, intermediary services can still read and derive information from body content. For example, a correlation identifier used in a SOAP header can be generated based on the ISBN value shown in the preceding example.

13.4.4   The `Fault` element

The optional `Fault` construct provides a ready made error response that is added inside the `Body` construct. In the example that follows, this fault information is further subdivided using additional child elements. The `faultcode` element contains one of a set of fault conditions predefined by the SOAP specification. Both the `faultstring` and `detail` elements provide human readable error messages, the latter of which can host an entire XML fragment containing further partitioned error details.

```
<Body>
   <Fault>
      <faultcode>
         MustUnderstand
      </faultcode>
      <faultstring>
         header was not recognized
      </faultstring>
      <detail>
         <x:appMessage
            xmlns:x="http://www.xmltc.com/tls/faults">
               The CorrelationID header was not
               processed by a recipient that was
               required to process it. Now a fault's
               been raised and it looks like this
               recipient is going to be a problem.
         </x:appMessage>
      </detail>
   </Fault>
</Body>
```

Example 13.21   The `Fault` construct residing within the `Body` construct.

In our example a `Fault` construct is provided to respond to a `MustUnderstand` violation that may occur when a service expected to process the message correlation identifier fails to do so.

SUMMARY OF KEY POINTS

- SOAP is the primary messaging standard used to define messages required for services to communicate.

- Most of the WS-* specifications rely on the use of SOAP headers to implement their features.

- A SOAP message document consists of a parent `Envelope` construct that hosts a required `Body` and optional `Header` and `Fault` constructs.

13.5   Service interface design tools

The service-oriented design phase is the first in which real technology is touched. Though we are not yet programming Web services, the primary deliverable of this stage is a physical service interface definition.

As we've already established, to design a service interface requires the use of the WSDL and XML Schema markup languages. This section discusses three common approaches to working with these languages.

13.5.1   Auto-generation

WSDL and XSD schema markup code can be auto-generated using a development utility. Typically, this program will derive the service interface from some existing source, such as a component class.

This approach is common with developers who want to efficiently generate a service interface that mirrors the interface of a distributed back-end component. The result is a Web service that follows the proxy service model and one that generally is geared to bring RPC-style communication into the SOAP messaging framework.

The use of this method is highly discouraged within SOAs. It runs contrary to the standardization required to establish a consistent series of endpoints within service-oriented environments. It also opposes the preference of WS-* specifications for a document-style (non-RPC-style) messaging model.

Although auto-generation of service interfaces is a feature promoted by several prominent development platforms, it is not one that is explored in this book. The service design processes described in Chapter 15 all are based on a "WSDL first" approach, meaning that a service interface must be designed prior to the development of the service's immediate underlying application logic.

13.5.2   Design tools

Several front-end tools providing a visual representation of the different parts of the service interface currently exist. These allow you to drag and drop elements and constructs associated with the WSDL and XML Schema languages to assemble a service interface without having to type out elaborate markup syntax.

To help ease the transition of developers more accustomed to traditional component-based solution environments, these tools provide graphical user interfaces that promote "don't worry about the WSDL" features. The end result is typically an auto-generated WSDL definition consisting of markup produced within the confines of the tool's output generation capabilities.

As development platforms begin to incorporate more and more of the Web services technology set as part of their native environments, front-end tools are becoming increasingly sophisticated.

When planning to use a design tool, take the following considerations into account:

- Does the tool allow you to take ownership of the WSDL it auto-generates? If yes, you may be able to use the tool as a starting point to create the overall structure of the WSDL definition. Then, you have the option of continuing to work with the markup independently.

- Does the tool allow you to view existing WSDL definitions accurately? If you've created your own WSDL, it may be preferable to be able to view its element hierarchy through a graphical interface. Some tools, however, cannot accurately interpret a WSDL that was not created using the tool.

- Does the tool validate accurately against the W3C WSDL specification? Some front-end tools are tied to a particular server platform and therefore may validate WSDL markup according to the constraints of the proprietary features provided by the platform's server products.

- Does the tool allow you to edit and maintain WSDL definitions without inserting unwanted markup? This is a primary concern of many development products—regardless of whether the WSDL definition initially was created with the tool or whether you are using it to make changes to an existing definition, some tools have the tendency of inserting excess markup code.

The service design processes provided in this book can be completed with the right design tool. The best types of tools are editors that allow you to seamlessly switch between a graphical view and a source code view and that supplement this with built-in WS-I Basic Profile compliance testing features.

13.5.3   Hand coding

If you are a developer or an analyst proficient with the syntax-level details of the WSDL and XSD languages, you can consider writing out the service interface designs using a simple text (or XML) editor. This approach gives you the ultimate level of control over your service design and helps you avoid issues associated with some design tools.

If you would like a visual representation of some of your larger or more complex definitions, you still can use a modeling tool as a viewer only. You simply let it read in your WSDL file and provide you with a graphical view. As long as you don't actually save your work using the tool, you will maintain your independence. Further, these tools can be helpful for validating the hand coded service definitions.

Although it is very common to use WSDL design tools, we take complete control of our service descriptions in each of the three service design processes described in Chapter 15, building them from scratch according to our design standards and preferences. As a result, all of the accompanying case study examples provide samples based on this approach. We do this to best demonstrate the use of the WSDL language within SOA.

CASE STUDY

While gearing up for the delivery of their respective SOA solutions, both RailCo and TLS give some thought to how they are going to tackle the design of service interfaces. IT staff in both organizations gained hands-on experience building Web services in past projects and are therefore relatively comfortable with the core SOA technology set.

Each project team decides to proceed by hand coding the required WSDL definitions and associated XSD schema types, using an editor with validation and WS-I compliance testing features.

SUMMARY OF KEY POINTS

- Auto-generating service interfaces by deriving them from existing component classes is not a desirable service design approach for building SOA.

- As long as modeling tools don't interfere with WSDL output, they can provide a rapid approach to the service-oriented design process.

- Hand coding WSDL service definitions and associated XSD schema content provides the highest degree of independence and can be supplemented with an editor that provides validation and testing features.

Chapter 14

Service-Oriented Design
(Part II: SOA Composition
Guidelines)

efining an architecture is a common step within the delivery lifecycle of any form of automation solution project. It establishes application boundaries, the supporting technology set, and target deployment environments. However, as we know by now, SOA brings with it unique characteristics that differ from traditional architectural models. This also leads to a unique approach to defining the architecture itself.

How case studies are used: Both of our companies face some strategic decisions during this preparatory stage of the service-oriented design process. The choices they make with regard to how they plan to shape their respective SOAs will influence the service design processes they undergo in the following chapter.

14.1   Steps to composing SOA

Regardless of the shape or size of your SOA, it will consist of a number of technology components that establish an environment in which your services will reside (Figure 14.1). The fundamental components that typically comprise an SOA include:

- an XML data representation architecture

- Web services built upon industry standards

- a platform capable of hosting and processing XML data and Web services

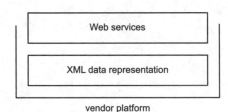

Figure 14.1
The most fundamental components of a Web services-based SOA.

However, to support and realize the principles and characteristics we've explored as being associated with both the primitive and contemporary types of SOA requires some additional design effort.

Common questions that need to be answered at this stage include:

- What types of services should be built, and how should they be organized into service layers?

- How should first-generation standards be positioned to best support SOA?
- What features provided by available extensions are required by the SOA?

These issues lead to an exercise in composition, as we make choices that determine what technologies and architectural components are required and how these parts are best assembled.

Provided in Figure 14.2 and further described in the following sections is an informal set of steps for composing a service-oriented architecture. Depending on your goals and the nature of your technical environment, additional considerations likely will be needed.

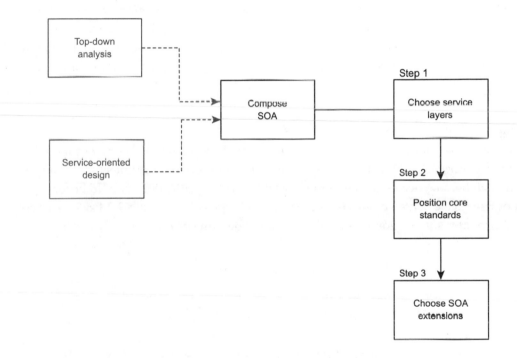

Figure 14.2
Suggested steps for composing a preliminary SOA. As explained in Chapter 13, depending on the delivery strategy employed, the Compose SOA step can be part of a top-down analysis effort or it can be positioned as a preparatory stage within a service-oriented design process.

14.1.1   Step 1: Choose service layers

Composing an SOA requires that we first decide on a design configuration for the service layers that will comprise and standardize logic representation within our architecture. This step is completed by studying the candidate service layers produced during the service-oriented analysis phase and exploring service layers and service layer configuration scenarios provided in Chapter 9. Some guidelines are provided in the *Considerations for choosing service layers* section.

14.1.2   Step 2: Position core standards

Next, we need to assess which core standards should comprise our SOA and how they should be implemented to best support the features and requirements of our service-oriented solution. The *Considerations for positioning core SOA standards* section provides an overview of how each of the core XML and Web services specifications commonly is affected by principles and characteristics unique to SOA.

14.1.3   Step 3: Choose SOA extensions

This final part of our "pre-service design process" requires that we determine which contemporary SOA characteristics we want our service-oriented architecture to support. This will help us decide which of the available WS-* specifications should become part of our service-oriented environment. The *Considerations for choosing SOA extensions* section provides some guidelines for making these determinations.

SUMMARY OF KEY POINTS

- Prior to commencing with the design of individual services, it is advisable to perform some preparatory tasks to formally define a service-oriented architecture.

- Recommended steps include finalizing a service layer configuration and choosing available extensions required to fulfill requirements associated with SOA as a whole.

- The positioning of Web services standards is also a factor, as SOA imposes distinct design principles and characteristics.

14.2   Considerations for choosing service layers

The service-oriented analysis process likely will have resulted in a preliminary identification of a suitable service layer configuration. The first step to designing SOA is deciding how you intend to configure service layers within your environment, if at all (Figure 14.3).

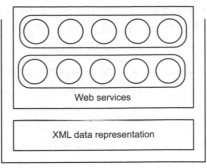

Figure 14.3
Designated service layers organize and
standardize Web services within SOA.

Depending on the scope of your planned architecture, this step may require an analysis process that is highly organization-specific. Immediate and long-term goals need to be taken into account because when you choose a configuration, you essentially are establishing a standard means of logic and data representation.

The biggest question you will be faced with is: "Should we invest in building business services?" This one decision point deserves a great deal of attention. The answer to this question will set your SOA on one of two very different paths. To assist you with making this and other decisions relating to service layers, here are some high-level guidelines:

- *Existing configurations*—If service layers already have been standardized within your enterprise, you should make every attempt to conform new service designs to these layers. The exception to this is if a need to alter the current service layer configuration has been identified. Then the scope of your project will include a change to the overall complexion of your enterprise's standard SOA.

- *Required standards*—If you are building new types of services or service layers, ensure that these are delivered along with accompanying design standards. These standards must be written so that they apply to the services as part of this and future projects.

- *Service composition performance*—Service compositions can impose a significant amount of processing overhead, especially when intermediary services are required to process the contents of SOAP messages. In this case, each hop between requestor and provider can result in validation, deserialization, and serialization steps. This can really add up, especially in environments not equipped with enterprise processors or accelerators. It is highly advisable to conduct performance tests prior to deciding on a multi-level service layer configuration.

- *Service deployment*—When designing service layers that will produce solution-agnostic services, deployment can become a concern. In a highly distributed environment, reusable services that are centrally located can impose remote messaging latency on solutions that need to connect to them. Redundant deployment of services can solve this problem, but this approach also results in an administration burden. These and other deployment issues need to be assessed prior to proceeding with solution-agnostic service layers.

- *Service versioning*—If you are planning to deliver reusable services as part of your service-oriented solution, ensure that you fully understand the extent to which future service requestors could possibly come to rely on them. After the service is deployed, extensions may be required to further complete the service's expected feature set. If these extensions result in changes to the initial interface, a versioning system will need to be in place to accommodate your solution and any other requestors that are using the service.

- *Business services and XSD schema designs*—If your enterprise already has established a comprehensive XML data representation architecture, it is worth taking a look at your existing set of XSD schemas. These should be analyzed for potential compatibility issues with planned business services. This is especially important when considering the use of entity-centric business services, as these rely on the processing of document entities that would ideally be accompanied by entity-centric schemas.

- *Business service maintenance*—If proceeding with the agile delivery strategy (as explained in Chapter 10), the on-going maintenance of business services needs to be planned for. As the top-down analysis proceeds, revisiting services to keep their business logic representation in alignment introduces a separate administration process that may need to tie into the versioning system mentioned earlier.

SUMMARY OF KEY POINTS

- Practical considerations need to be taken into account when deciding on what service layer configuration an SOA is to standardize on.

- Key factors include performance, deployment, and administration.

14.3 Considerations for positioning core SOA standards

This second step within the SOA composition sub-process requires that we establish the foundation standards that will form the basis of our architecture. On the surface, this may seem like a pretty easy task, given that the core family of standards most SOA vendors support is provided by a very commonly accepted set of XML and first-generation Web services specifications (Figure 14.4).

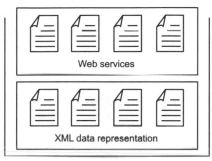

Figure 14.4

SOA can structure the manner in which common XML and Web services standards are applied.

However, this step is not limited to simply picking and choosing what we want. We are required to properly position these standards so that they end up supporting the key characteristics we need our SOA to deliver. Therefore, this section consists of a series of discussions about how the utilization of core XML and Web services standards is commonly affected when utilized within the design parameters of a service-oriented architecture.

14.3.1   Industry standards and SOA

Even though we are creating abstract service designs, they still are realized in a physical implementation through the use of specific Web services markup languages. These languages originate from published specifications of which different versions in different stages of maturity exist. New versions of a specification can alter and extend the feature set provided by previous versions.

It therefore is important to ensure that your SOA is fully standardized with respect to the specification versions that establish a fundamental layer of your technology architecture. This not only ensures standardization within an organization, it also expresses consistent metadata to any services with which external partners may need to interface. This, of course, promotes interoperability.

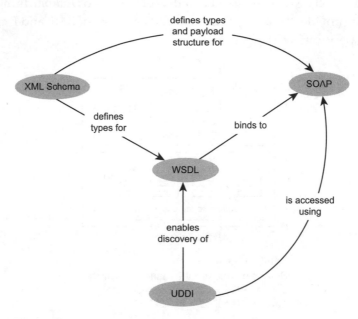

Figure 14.5
The operational relationship between core SOA specifications.

Figure 14.5 recaps the core specifications that commonly are found in SOA. Let's discuss these further to explore how they can influence our service designs and how the standards themselves are shaped by and positioned within SOA.

14.3.2   XML and SOA

Fundamental to everything that comprises a contemporary SOA is data representation via XML. Practically all of the specifications within the Web services platform are expressed through XML and natively rely on the support and management of XML documents to enable all forms of communication. Further, for any SOA to be truly successful, it must build upon and remain in alignment with the underlying XML data representation architecture. This can raise various issues worth thinking about during the service-oriented design phase, including:

RPC-style versus document-style SOAP messages

To accommodate RPC communication, traditional data representation architectures tend to shape XML documents around a parameter data exchange model. This results in a fine-grained communications framework within distributed environments that inevitably leads to the use of RPC-style SOAP messages. This further conflicts with the document-style messaging model preferred by many WS-* specifications (as also explained in the *SOAP and XML* section).

Auto-generated XML

Many development tools offer the ability to provide auto-generated XML output. XML may be derived in numerous ways resulting in an instant XML data representation of a data model or data source. While useful to fulfill immediate conversion or data sharing requirements, the persistent use of auto-generated XML can lead to the proliferation of non-standardized data representation.

For example, when XML is auto-generated from different sources, the resulting XML documents tend to become inconsistent in structure and context and often vastly differ from those custom developed according to in-house standards. This causes problems with SOA, which relies on a unified data representation to promote a vision of enterprise-wide interoperability and federation.

Fitting SOA on top of an established XML data representation architecture

Steps can be taken to marry an established XML data representation environment with SOA. For example, it is highly advisable to ensure that the existing XML data representation architecture is fully standardized prior to moving to SOA. Even if the standards are not in complete alignment with how your services will need to express corporate data, it is important that the existing data representation be consistent and predictable. After standardization has been achieved, service abstraction can be used to bridge representation disparity.

The most effective way to coordinate this type of migration is to create a transition plan. Such a plan would include transition phases that specifically address XML compatibility issues.

14.3.3   The WS-I Basic Profile

The Basic Profile is the result of WS-I efforts to assemble a set of mature, core specifications that comprise a commonly supported and well aligned Web services platform.

Specifications are evaluated individually on a version by version basis. Many organizations turn to the Basic Profile because complying to its rules guarantees a level of industry-wide conformance.

For example, versions 1.0 and 1.1 of the Basic Profile propose that organizations standardize on the following specifications:

- WSDL 1.1
- SOAP 1.1
- UDDI 2.0
- XML 1.0
- XML Schema 1.0

Further, the Basic Profile dictates how features of each specification should and should not be implemented. This document therefore introduces a series of design standards of its own, targeted primarily at resolving potential interoperability issues.

Note that WS-I profiles are themselves versioned. A requirement, therefore, to using these profiles is that your current development tools support all of the specification versions referenced by a specific profile version.

Listed here are some examples of the design standards provided by the Basic Profile:

- SOAP envelopes cannot contain Document Type Declarations or processing instructions.
- The use of the SOAP `encodingStyle` attribute within SOAP envelopes is highly discouraged.
- Required SOAP header blocks must be checked prior to proceeding with the processing of other header blocks and the message contents.
- When a WSDL `part` construct (within the `message` construct) uses the `element` attribute, it must reference a global element declaration.
- The sequence of elements within the SOAP `Body` construct must be identical to the sequence established in the corresponding WSDL `parts` construct.
- The WSDL `binding` element can only use the WSDL SOAP binding.

Use of the WS-I Basic Profile is not only recommended if you are required to deliver WS-I compliant solutions, as explained in the *Use WS-I Profiles even if WS-I compliance isn't required design* guideline in Chapter 15.

14.3.4   WSDL and SOA

The creation of WSDL definitions is an important part of the SOA delivery lifecycle. The service interface is the focal point of the service-oriented design phase and the primary deliverable of each of the service design processes. WSDL definitions are the end result of business and technology analysis efforts and establish themselves as the public endpoints that form a new layer of infrastructure within a service-oriented enterprise. Some of the key design issues that relate to WSDL design within SOA are highlighted here:

Standardized use of namespaces
WSDL documents are comprised of elements associated with different specifications, including SOAP, XML Schema, and the WSDL specification itself. These are further supplemented by user-defined elements. Namespace standardization therefore becomes a primary concern. (The *Use namespaces carefully* design guideline provided in Chapter 15 emphasizes this issue further.)

Modular service definitions
As with many XML and WS-* specifications, WSDL supports the capability for service definitions to be composed. This means that you can modularize your WSDL documents to facilitate reuse and centralized maintenance. (See the *Consider using modular WSDL documents* design guideline provided in Chapter 15.)

Compatibility of granularity
Service interface granularity ideally corresponds to XML document granularity. However, the "WSDL first" design approach often conflicts with existing XML document structures. If anticipated, these challenges can be dealt with by incorporating design-time measures, such as the use of an additional service abstraction layer.

14.3.5   XML Schema and SOA

XML Schema definitions (or XSD schemas) establish data integrity throughout service-oriented architectures. They are used intrinsically by many WS-* specifications but are most prominent in their role as defining a service's public data model. Following are some considerations as to how XSD schemas can be positioned and utilized in support of SOA.

Modular XSD schemas

XSD schemas can be broken down into individual modules that are assembled at run-time using the `include` statement (for schemas with the same target namespace) or the `import` statement (for schemas with different target namespaces). Because WSDL documents also can be modularized, the XSD schema contents of the WSDL `types` construct can reside in a separate document.

Schema modularization establishes a flexible data representation architecture that fits nicely into the composable world of SOA. XSD schema modules can provide various definitions that can be reused by different WSDL definitions that process messages with identical or similar payloads. Further, entity-centric XSD schemas can be designed to represent specific information sets that correspond to corporate entity models. This directly supports the business-centric aspects of contemporary SOA as implemented by the entity-centric business service layer.

Document-style messages and XSD schemas

The document-style SOAP messages required by SOA are increasingly intelligence-heavy and therefore place a greater emphasis on advanced validation requirements. For example, there can be a tendency to bundle groups of XML data into a single SOAP message.

The use of extensible or redefined schemas may, therefore, be required when building documents that represent multiple data contexts. However, even the advanced features of the XML Schema Definition Language may be insufficient. Supplementary technologies (XSLT, for example) may be required to implement extensions, such as conditional validation.

14.3.6   SOAP and SOA

SOAP messages are what fuel all action within contemporary SOA. They are therefore considered just as fundamental to service-oriented environments as WSDL definitions. Following are two primary areas in which SOAP messaging can be affected.

SOAP message style and data types

Probably the biggest impact SOA can have on an existing SOAP framework is in how it imposes a preferred payload structure and data type system. This relates specifically to the `style` attribute used by the `soap:binding` element and the `use` attribute assigned to the `soap:body` element, as explained in the *WSDL language basics* section in Chapter 13 and discussed in the *Use the SOAP document and literal attribute values* guideline at the end of Chapter 15.

Because introducing SOA into RPC-style distributed environments can inhibit the potential of many WS-* specifications that expect document-style payloads, changes need to be made to accommodate SOA requirements. For example, RPC-style approaches support the transmission of granular XML documents with targeted data. This leads to the creation of many granular, parameter-type XML documents. Therefore, these documents may need to be bundled to support the coarser grained, document messaging model.

The use of schema modules may be required to accommodate the assembly of unique SOAP message payloads from differently structured XML data sources. In the end, though, standardization is key. Consistent XML document structures will accommodate the runtime assembly of document-style SOAP payloads.

SOAP headers

Because a WSDL definition describes a service, it is the primary deliverable of each of our service design processes. However, it only provides a partial description of the SOAP messages required for services to communicate within contemporary SOA. While the XSD types used by WSDL definitions define and validate the contents of a SOAP message's Body construct, they do not typically supply information regarding SOAP header blocks implemented via WS-* extensions.

Metadata embedded into SOAP message headers alleviates the need for a service to contain logic specific to message exchange scenarios. The SOAP headers used by messages processed by a service depend primarily on the WS-* specifications supported by the service-oriented architecture in which the service resides. Therefore, the identification and definition of SOAP headers is tied to the establishment of our SOA and its supported WS-* specifications.

These extensions shape the overall messaging framework and determine the extent to which SOAP messages self-govern their message path and the processing they ask of services that receive them. Understanding the extent of metadata abstraction allows us to adjust service operations accordingly.

14.3.7 Namespaces and SOA

An easily overlooked part of establishing a standardized SOA is the information domain organization system provided to us through the use of namespaces. Namespaces in SOA cannot be created arbitrarily. They must be viewed as identifiers of business or technology domains and accordingly applied as qualifiers for corresponding WSDL elements.

The WS-I Basic Profile provides a set of best practices for implementing namespaces within WSDL definitions. However, additional design standards are required to ensure that namespaces are used properly in XML documents outside of WSDL definition boundaries. See the *Use namespaces carefully* guideline in Chapter 15 for some more information.

14.3.8   UDDI and SOA

UDDI provides an industry standard means of organizing service description pointers to accommodate the process of discovery through service registries. When implemented, UDDI typically represents an enterprise-wide architectural component positioned to provide a central discovery mechanism within and across SOAs.

Therefore, depending on the scope (application-level, enterprise-wide, etc.) of the service-oriented architecture being designed, UDDI may become one of the technologies established as part of the overall service-oriented environment.

While UDDI enables the discovery of service descriptions and is also one of the core specifications identified by the WS-I Basic Profile, some organizations are resorting to traditional directory-based approaches (such as LDAP) to keep track of their service descriptions. Regardless, our service design processes take potential discovery into account by promoting the creation of intuitive service interface designs and the documentation of supplementary metadata (as explained in the *Document services with metadata* guideline in Chapter 15).

CASE STUDY

In an attempt to design an environment that fosters service-orientation from the ground up, RailCo discards the architecture that hosts its existing Web services.

It then completes the following steps:

1. Existing forms of XML data representation are studied, and it is discovered that, to date, little actual XML formatted data is being utilized by RailCo solutions. This is seen as a positive development, as the XML usage that is identified has been implemented in a highly non-standardized manner. In support of this new project, XML data representation standards are established to position XSD schemas that represent key RailCo information sets using a document-style format.

2. The document + literal SOAP message type is chosen as the preferred messaging model. Existing development tools and application servers are

reviewed to ensure that support for this style of SOAP message is consistent. This, surprisingly, reveals that one of RailCo's products only provides support for RPC-style SOAP messaging. Fortunately, replacing this product is not too expensive, nor is the change disruptive, as no other Web services-based solutions exist.

3. Namespaces are standardized to reflect the creation of planned WSDL definitions and XSD schemas.

4. Finally, it is decided that there is no need for a discovery component within their planned SOA. Therefore, UDDI is excluded as part of the core standards within the RailCo SOA (Figure 14.6).

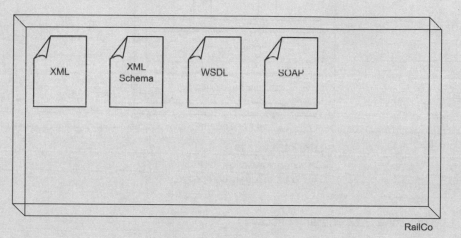

Figure 14.6
A composed view of the core standards that comprise part of RailCo's planned SOA.

TLS already underwent this process during the delivery of their first service-oriented solution. Because their existing SOA was the result of an extensive top-down delivery process, TLS architects are confident that they will be able to build upon this environment without further re-evaluation.

SUMMARY OF KEY POINTS

- The WS-I Basic Profile provides a convenient guideline by which to choose specific versions of core SOA specifications. Relevant specifications identified by the Basic Profile include XML, XML Schema, WSDL, SOAP, and UDDI.

- SOA imposes design requirements and preferences that further affect how features within these primary specifications are utilized and positioned

14.4   Considerations for choosing SOA extensions

Although by completing Steps 1 and 2 we may have assembled a basic service-oriented environment consisting of core standards and planned service layers, Step 3 is where we get to compose unique variations of SOA (Figure 14.7).

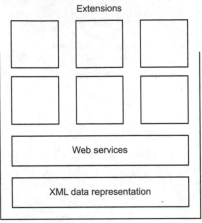

Figure 14.7
WS-* extensions allow for individual SOAs to be uniquely composed.

14.4.1   Choosing SOA characteristics

As we've already established numerous times, primitive SOA is based on the principles of service-orientation that drive at the root of the service-oriented environment we are building. However, when you begin to explore how service-oriented business processes and application environments can be extended, composed, and even reconfigured, the true power of SOA really comes to light.

In Chapter 3 we established a list of contemporary SOA characteristics. We later revisited this list in Chapter 9 to determine which of these characteristics are provided by the primary influences that shape SOA, which we identified as:

- principles of service-orientation
- first-generation Web services concepts
- WS-* concepts

In the previous section of this chapter we covered the core standards that implement some service-orientation principles through first-generation Web services (and XML) specifications. Although there is some leeway as to what standards can be chosen (UDDI, for example, is not yet that common), for the most part, the first-generation Web services standards establish a commonly accepted core architecture and therefore are considered required components of contemporary SOA.

Most of the contemporary SOA characteristics we studied in Chapter 9 are optional, which means that we only need to pursue features of the characteristics we actually require. This is in line with the composite nature of SOA. As a result, the decisions we make regarding how we define our target SOA will be influenced heavily by how our requirements can be addressed or fulfilled by specific qualities of the architecture we are building.

Therefore, it is recommended that you identify the primary SOA characteristics you want your services to inherently support and promote. If you are building an application-level SOA that is destined to reside within an existing enterprise-wide SOA, then many of the required characteristics will have already been defined for you. However, if you are delivering your first service-oriented architecture, this becomes a critical decision point and one worth mulling over *before* proceeding with the design of service interfaces.

14.4.2   Choosing WS-* specifications

It is through the use of the many available WS-* specifications that we can build upon our foundation architecture extensions that implement features specific to our automation requirements. When you understand what characteristics or features you need your service-oriented architecture to support, you can begin exploring the possibility of those characteristics being realized through the use of the extensions provided by WS-* specifications.

Unfortunately, choosing which WS-* features we want as part of our service-oriented environment is not a matter of selecting a series of checkboxes on a form and clicking the "Apply" button. While the WS-* landscape continues to evolve, vendor support for some specifications will continue to remain inconsistent. Further, until a specification is fully implemented via a vendor platform, it is not uncommon for revisions to surface. Though parts of the WS-* arena remain volatile, other parts have become more settled.

Therefore, the key considerations for adding the features of a WS-* specification to your SOA is the maturity of the specification itself, and the available support it is receiving by product vendors—specifically, vendors whose products you already are using.

14.4.3   WS-BPEL and SOA

Worth singling out at this point is the WS-BPEL specification. It is a good example of a WS-* extension for which relatively strong vendor support already exists. We first introduced concepts derived from WS-BPEL in Chapter 6 during our discussion of orchestration.

An operational business process language, such as WS-BPEL, is of immediate importance to our service design process because it enables us to create process services that establish the orchestration service layer (Figure 14.8).

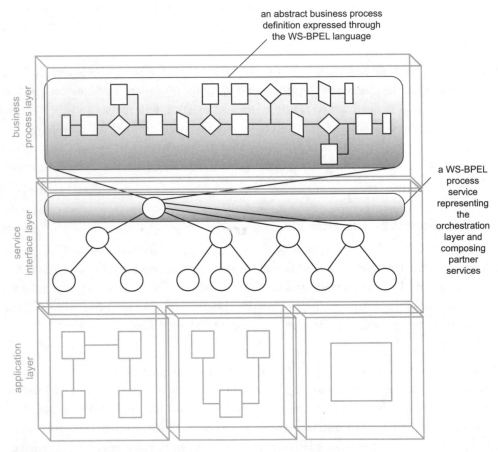

Figure 14.8
WS-BPEL realizing the orchestration service sub-layer within our service layer.

A key advantage to working with WS-BPEL is that we are able to use its markup to create a process description with no ties to a particular implementation technology. Another reason we highlight WS-BPEL is because we use its syntax as part of the examples provided in Chapter 16, to demonstrate the creation of an orchestration layer for one of our case studies.

CASE STUDY

RailCo is not in a position to invest heavily in creating the perfect SOA at this stage. Therefore, qualities such as intrinsic interoperability must take a back seat to more practical requirements. Further, none of the products that comprise RailCo's current technical environment provide any further support for WS-* specifications that RailCo was already using as part of their previous Web services solution (described in Chapters 6 and 7).

However, at the same time, architects do not want to build an environment that will need to be overhauled again in the near future. Upon reviewing the list of characteristics offered by contemporary SOA, RailCo identifies extensibility as being one that is of foremost importance to its future goals.

By focusing on the creation of extensible services, it is believed that a quality SOA can be delivered now to service immediate needs, while still capable of being extended to incorporate future requirements as they arise.

Extensibility is not one of the characteristics that is implemented automatically by a WS-* specification. Instead (as explained in Chapter 9), it is a quality that is realized through design. Therefore, as RailCo proceeds to build its service designs, it will keep extensibility in mind. (Examples in the following chapter explain design decisions made by RailCo in consideration of extensibility.)

TLS, on the other hand, already has an SOA in place, supported by a set of design standards with an emphasis on promoting a number of SOA characteristics, such as reuse, discoverability, and interoperability.

A new characteristic TLS is interested in fostering throughout its service-oriented solution environments is a service-oriented business modeling paradigm. Due to the unavailability of an adequate orchestration engine during the development of its original B2B system, this first service-oriented solution delivered by TLS did not incorporate an orchestration layer.

Since then, though, their underlying technology has significantly improved its support for key WS-* extensions. Most notably, orchestration support has been added in the form of a WS-BPEL orchestration engine. As a result, the TLS Timesheet Submission Process we introduced in Chapter 12 will be defined as a WS-BPEL process definition in Chapter 16.

Figure 14.9 displays the resulting set of specifications that comprise TLS's expanded SOA.

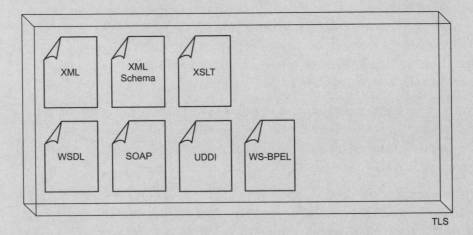

Figure 14.9
A composed view of the SOA TLS is planning for the Timesheet Submission solution.

SUMMARY OF KEY POINTS

- The extensions required for an SOA generally depend on which of the contemporary SOA characteristics need to be realized.

- The ability to implement WS-* extensions is dependent on the maturity of the specification providing the extension and available vendor support.

Chapter 15

Service-Oriented Design
(Part III: Service Design)

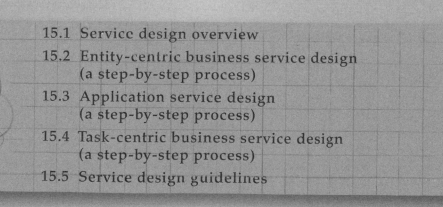

Before we can develop a service, we need to have defined the interface of that service. This is the mantra of the commonly accepted "WSDL first" approach to designing Web services, and it is also the basis for each of the three service design processes we describe in this chapter. Defining the service interface prior to development is important to establishing a highly standardized service-oriented architecture and required to realize a number of the characteristics we identified as being part of contemporary SOA.

Specifically, the following benefits can be attained by creating the service contract prior to the service logic:

- Services can be designed to accurately represent the context and function of their corresponding service candidates.

- Conventions can be applied to service operation names, which leads to standardized endpoint definitions.

- The granularity of operations can be modeled in abstract to provide consistent and predictable interface designs that also establish a message size and volume ratio suitable for the target communications infrastructure.

- Underlying applications are required to conform to the expression of the service design, not vice versa. (This often results in the need for a business façade layer to compose older components that rely on RPC-style communication.)

- The design of business services can be assisted by business analysts to ensure an accurate representation of business logic.

The process descriptions provided in this chapter are generic in nature and only *suggest* a series of steps for completing the design of service interfaces. They should be viewed as a starting point from which organizations can derive their own, custom design processes.

How case studies are used: Case studies take on a heightened significance in this chapter, as they are the means by which we introduce markup samples. Essentially, a subset of the service candidates we created in Chapter 11 are put through the design processes we establish in this chapter.

As part of these processes we create various WSDL definitions and associated XSD schemas. Complete versions of these files can be downloaded from the book's support site, at www.soabooks.com.

NOTE
The end result WSDL and XSD schema documents in these samples have been tested for compliance with the WS-I Basic Profile version 1.1.

15.1 Service design overview

The ultimate goal of these processes is to achieve a balanced service design. Typically this constitutes a Web service that accommodates real-world requirements and constraints, while still managing to:

- encapsulate the required amount of logic
- conform to service-orientation principles
- meet business requirements

You might be looking at your list of service candidates and wondering where to begin. It is good to raise this question, as there is a preferred sequence in which to create service designs. The rule of thumb is: design agnostic, reusable services first. This allows services that express logic specific to a process to compose reusable services as fixed resources (while also proving the quality of their reusability).

Given the four main types of service layers we identified previously, following is a suggested design sequence:

1. Entity-centric business services (Chapter 15)
2. Application services (Chapter 15)
3. Task-centric business services (Chapter 15)
4. Process services (Chapter 16)

This sequence is actually more of a guideline, as in reality, the service design process is not always that clear cut. For example, after creating an initial set of application service designs, you proceed to build task-centric services. Only while incorporating various operations, you realize that additional application service-level features are required to carry them out. This results in you having to revisit the application service designs to determine if you should add operations or entirely new services.

15.1.1 Design standards

It is important to note that a firm set of design standards is critical to achieving a successful SOA. Because the design we are defining as part of this phase is concrete and permanent, every service produced needs to be as consistent as possible. Otherwise, many key SOA benefits, such as reusability, composability, and especially agility, will be jeopardized. It is therefore assumed that prior to starting this phase, design standards are already in place. (The *Service design guidelines* section at the end of this chapter provides some recommendations that can help form the basis for standards.)

In our previous service-oriented analysis process, design standards were not as heavily emphasized (the need for standards was mentioned in a supporting guideline but was not made part of the process itself). This is primarily because service candidates can continue to be modified and refined after corresponding services have been developed and implemented, without significant impact. Standards are still relevant to service-oriented analysis, but not as much as they are integral to service-oriented design.

15.1.2 About the process descriptions

The sample processes in this section consist of generic sets of steps that highlight the primary considerations for creating service designs. This is our last chance to ensure a service properly expresses its purpose and capabilities.

As part of each abstract service description we create, the following parts are formally defined:

- definition of all service operations
- definition of each operation's input and output messages
- definition of associated XSD schema types used to represent message payloads

Note that individual service designs are composed later into a WS-BPEL process definition in Chapter 16.

15.1.3   Prerequisites

As explained in Chapter 13, our service design processes approach the creation of the service interface from a hand coding perspective. This means that many references to the WSDL and XSD schema markup languages are made throughout the process descriptions.

Further, to support our processes, numerous interspersed case study examples provide actual WSDL and XSD schema markup samples. Reading through the WSDL and XSD tutorials provided in Chapter 13 therefore is recommended to best understand the process descriptions and associated examples.

CASE STUDY

Both of our fictional organizations have completed the service-oriented analysis phase for their respective SOAs. In doing so, each has established a set of service candidates that will form the basis for their service-oriented design. Let's review which of the service candidates we will be incorporating into the examples interspersed throughout this chapter.

The service modeling exercise performed by TLS produced the following five new service candidates that represent its new Timesheet Submission solution:

- Timesheet Submission Process (Process)
- Employee (Entity-centric)
- Timesheet (Entity-centric)
- Invoice (Entity-centric)
- Notification (Application)

Following the suggested design sequence, TLS will be subjecting the three entity-centric services to the corresponding service design process first. Next, it will design the Notification Service, along with additional application services that are required. Finally, the business process logic itself will be defined, as the Timesheet Submission Process Service is designed through a WS-BPEL process definition.

Amidst all this activity, our examples will focus on the design of the following two services:

- The Employee Service candidate will be referenced in the examples provided as part of the *Entity-centric business service design* process description.

- The Timesheet Submission Process Service candidate will become the basis for the workflow logic we need to establish a proper service composition for the Timesheet Submission Process. (TLS achieves this in Chapter 16.)

The service candidates modeled by RailCo consist of the following four application services and two task-centric business services.

- Invoice Processing (Task-centric)

- PO Processing (Task-centric)

- Legacy System (Application)

- Polling Notification (Application)

- Transform Accounting Documents (Application)

- Metadata Checking (Application)

The two service candidates here will be referenced in our design process description examples:

- The Transform Accounting Document Service candidate will be used to demonstrate the *Application service design* process description.

- The Invoice Processing Service candidate will be used as part of the *Task-centric business service design* section.

SUMMARY OF KEY POINTS

- The three design processes described in this chapter are based on the "WSDL first" approach.

- Design standards play a critical role in shaping the service design process and in guaranteeing a consistently standard SOA.

15.2   Entity-centric business service design (a step-by-step process)

Entity-centric business services represent the one service layer that is the least influenced by others. Its purpose is to accurately represent corresponding data entities defined within an organization's business models. These services are strictly solution- and business process-agnostic, built for reuse by any application that needs to access or manage information associated with a particular entity.

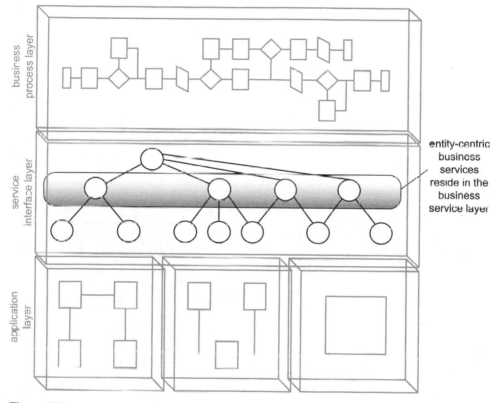

entity-centric business services reside in the business service layer

Figure 15.1
Entity-centric services establish the business service layer.

Because they exist rather atomically in relation to other service layers, it is beneficial to design entity-centric business services prior to others. This establishes an abstract service layer around which process and underlying application logic can be positioned.

15.2.1 Process description

Provided next is the step-by-step process description wherein we establish a recommended sequence of detailed steps for arriving at a quality entity-centric business service interface (Figure 15.2).

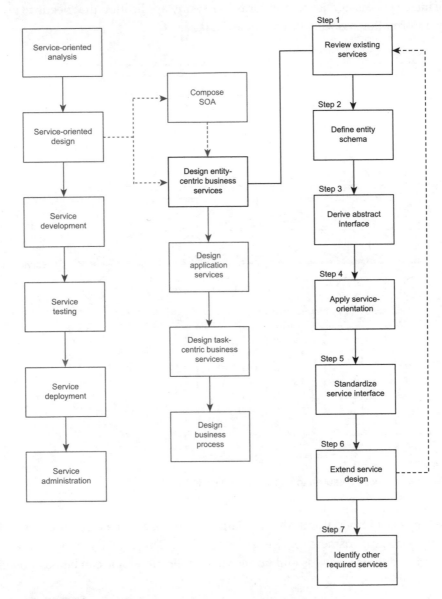

Figure 15.2
The entity-centric business service design process.

Note that the order in which these steps are provided is not set in stone. For example, you may prefer to define a preliminary service interface prior to establishing the actual data types used to represent message body content. Or perhaps you may find it more effective to perform a speculative analysis to identify possible extensions to the service before creating the first cut of the interface.

All of these can be legitimate approaches. The key is to ensure that in the end, design standards are applied equally to all service operations and that all processing requirements are accurately identified.

Let's begin now with the design of our entity-centric business service.

CASE STUDY

The examples provided alongside this process description revisit the TLS environment. Specifically, we take another look at the Employee Service candidate that was modeled at the end of Chapter 12 (Figure 15.3).

Figure 15.3
The Employee Service candidate.

The Employee Service was modeled intentionally to facilitate an entity-centric grouping of operations. As part of the Timesheet Submission Process, this service is required to contribute two specific functions.

The first requires it to execute a query against the employee record to retrieve the maximum number of hours the employee is authorized to work within a week. The other piece of functionality it needs to provide is the ability to post updates to the employee's history. As you may recall from the original Timesheet Submission Process, this action is required only when a timesheet is rejected.

The result of the TLS service modeling process was to express these two functions through the assignment of the following two operation candidates:

- get weekly hours limit
- update employee history

This service candidate now provides us with a primary input from which we derive a service design by following the steps in the following entity-centric business service design process.

NOTE

The "get weekly hours limit" operation candidate (which later becomes the getWeeklyHoursLimit operation) proposes an unusually fine-grained operation. Service operations, in general, tend to be more coarse-grained to overcome the performance overhead associated with SOAP message exchanges. For simplicity's sake, we retain the granularity of this operation, as it fulfills the functional requirements of our business process. For more information regarding service interface granularity, see the *Apply a suitable level of interface granularity* guideline at the end of this chapter.

Step 1: Review existing services

Ideally, when creating entity-centric services, the modeling effort resulting in the service candidates will have taken any existing services into account. However, because service candidates tend to consist of operation candidates relevant to the business requirements that formed the basis of the service-oriented analysis, it is always worth verifying to ensure that some or all of the processing functionality represented by operation candidates does not already exist in other services.

Therefore, the first step in designing a new service is to confirm whether it is actually even necessary. If other services exist, they may already be providing some or all of the functionality identified in the operation candidates—or—they may have already established a suitable context in which these new operation candidates can be implemented (as new operations to the existing service).

This is only TLS's second service-oriented solution. The first was created to establish an external interface with their accounting system via a B2B environment. That solution was built according to the top-down delivery strategy and therefore resulted in a collection of entity-centric business services.

Architects involved with the service design for this new Timesheet Submission application are pretty confident that the new set of services in no way overlaps with the existing ones. However, because the B2B solution was built by a completely different project team, they agree that it is worth the effort to review existing services before commencing with the design process.

Their investigation reveals that the following entity-centric business services were delivered as part of the B2B project: Accounts Payable Service, Purchase Order Service, Ledger Service, and Vendor Profile Service (Figure 15.4).

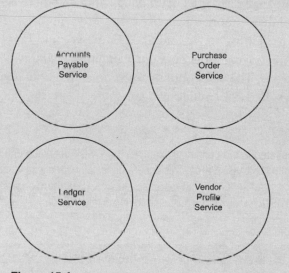

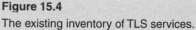

Figure 15.4
The existing inventory of TLS services.

It appears evident by the naming alone that each service represents an entity separate and distinct from the Employee entity proposed by the current service candidate. Just to be sure, though, each service description (along with any supplemental metadata) is reviewed. The project architects then conclude that no overlap exists, which gives them the green light to proceed with the design of the Employee Service.

Step 2: Define the message schema types

It is useful to begin a service interface design with a formal definition of the messages the service is required to process. To accomplish this we need to formalize the message structures that are defined within the WSDL `types` area.

SOAP messages carry payload data within the `Body` section of the SOAP envelope. This data needs to be organized and typed. For this we rely on XSD schemas. A standalone schema actually can be embedded in the `types` construct, wherein we can define each of the elements used to represent data within the SOAP body.

In the case of an entity-centric service, it is especially beneficial if the XSD schema used accurately represents the information associated with this service's entity. This "entity-centric schema" can become the basis for the service WSDL definition, as most service operations will be expected to receive or transmit the documents defined by this schema.

Note that there is not necessarily a one-to-one relationship between entity-centric services and the entities that comprise an entity model. You might recall in the service modeling example from Chapter 12, we combined Employee and EmployeeHistory entities into one Employee Service. In this case, you can either create two separate schemas or combine them into one. The latter option is recommended only if you are confident you will never want to split these entities up again.

NOTE

As demonstrated in the upcoming example, the WSDL definition can import schemas into the `types` area. This can be especially beneficial when working with standardized schemas that represent entities. (See the *Consider using modular WSDL documents* guideline for more information.)

CASE STUDY

TLS invested in creating a standardized XML data representation architecture (for their accounting environment only) some time ago. As a result, an inventory of entity-centric XSD schemas representing accounting-related information sets already exists.

At first, this appears to make this step rather simple. However, upon closer study, it is discovered that the existing XSD schema is very large and complex. After some discussion, TLS architects decide—for better or for worse—that they will not use the existing schema with this service at this point. Instead, they opt to derive a lightweight (but still fully compliant) version of the schema to accommodate the simple processing requirements of the Employee Service.

They begin by identifying the kinds of data that will need to be exchanged to fulfill the processing requirements of the "Get weekly hours limit" operation candidate. They end up defining two complex types: one containing the search criteria required for the request message received by the Employee Service and another containing the query results returned by the service. The types are deliberately named so that they are associated with the respective messages. These two types then constitute the new Employee.xsd schema file.

```xsd
<xsd:schema xmlns:xsd="http://www.w3.org/2001/XMLSchema"
   targetNamespace=
      "http://www.xmltc.com/tls/employee/schema/accounting/">
   <xsd:element name="EmployeeHoursRequestType">
      <xsd:complexType>
         <xsd:sequence>
            <xsd:element name="ID" type="xsd:integer"/>
         </xsd:sequence>
      </xsd:complexType>
   </xsd:element>
   <xsd:element name="EmployeeHoursResponseType">
      <xsd:complexType>
         <xsd:sequence>
            <xsd:element name="ID" type="xsd:integer"/>
            <xsd:element name="WeeklyHoursLimit"
               type="xsd:short"/>
         </xsd:sequence>
      </xsd:complexType>
   </xsd:element>
</xsd:schema>
```

Example 15.1   The Employee schema providing `complexType` constructs used to establish the data representation anticipated for the "Get weekly hours limit" operation candidate.

> **NOTE**
>
> The `complexType` constructs are wrapped in `element` constructs to comply with WS-I requirements for document + literal SOAP messages.

However, just as the architects attempt to derive the types required for the "Update employee history" operation candidate, another problem presents itself.

They discover that the schema from which they derived the Employee.xsd file does not represent the EmployeeHistory entity, which this service candidate also encapsulates.

Another visit to the accounting schema archive reveals that employee history information is not governed by the accounting solution. It is, instead, part of the HR environment—for which no schemas have been created.

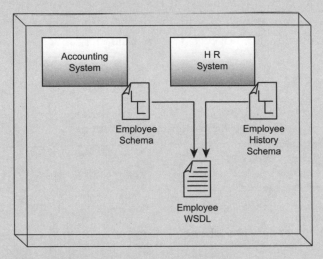

Figure 15.5
Two schemas originating from two different data sources.

Not wanting to impose on the already standardized design of the Employee schema, it is decided that a second schema definition be created (Figure 15.5). Analysts get involved and produce the following EmployeeHistory.xsd schema:

```
<xsd:schema xmlns:xsd="http://www.w3.org/2001/XMLSchema"
   targetNamespace=
      "http://www.xmltc.com/tls/employee/schema/hr/">
   <xsd:element name="EmployeeUpdateHistoryRequestType">
      <xsd:complexType>
         <xsd:sequence>
            <xsd:element name="ID" type="xsd:integer"/>
            <xsd:element name="Comment" type="xsd:string"/>
         </xsd:sequence>
      </xsd:complexType>
   </xsd:element>
   <xsd:element name="EmployeeUpdateHistoryResponseType">
```

```
              <xsd:complexType>
                 <xsd:sequence>
                    <xsd:element name="ResponseCode"
                        type="xsd:byte"/>
                 </xsd:sequence>
              </xsd:complexType>
           </xsd:element>
        </xsd:schema>
```

Example 15.2   The EmployeeHistory schema, with a different `targetNamespace` to
                   identify its distinct origin.

To promote reusability and to allow for each schema file to be maintained separately from the WSDL, the XSD schema `import` statement is used to pull the contents of both schemas into the Employee Service WSDL `types` construct.

```
<types>
   <xsd:schema targetNamespace=
       "http://www.xmltc.com/tls/employee/schema/">
       <xsd:import namespace=
           "http://www.xmltc.com/tls/employee/schema/accounting/"
           schemaLocation="Employee.xsd"/>
       <xsd:import namespace=
           "http://www.xmltc.com/tls/employee/schema/hr/"
           schemaLocation="EmployeeHistory.xsd"/>
   </xsd:schema>
</types>
```

Example 15.3   The WSDL `types` construct being populated by imported schemas.

Step 3: Derive an abstract service interface

Next, we analyze the proposed service operation candidate and follow these steps to define an initial service interface:

1. Confirm that each operation candidate is suitably generic and reusable by ensuring that the granularity of the logic encapsulated is appropriate. Study the data structures defined in Step 2 and establish a set of operation names.

2. Create the `portType` (or `interface`) area within the WSDL document and populate it with `operation` constructs that correspond to operation candidates.

3. Formalize the list of input and output values required to accommodate the processing of each operation's logic. This is accomplished by defining the appropriate message constructs that reference the XSD schema types within the child part elements.

The TLS architects decide on the following operations names: GetEmployee-WeeklyHoursLimit and UpdateEmployeeHistory (Figure 15.6).

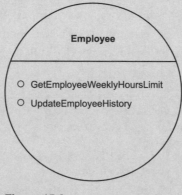

Figure 15.6
The Employee Service operations.

They subsequently proceed to define the remaining parts of the abstract definition, namely the message, and portType constructs.

```
<message name="getEmployeeWeeklyHoursRequestMessage">
   <part name="RequestParameter"
      element="act:EmployeeHoursRequestType"/>
</message>
<message name="getEmployeeWeeklyHoursResponseMessage">
   <part name="ResponseParameter"
      element="act:EmployeeHoursResponseType"/>
</message>
<message name="updateEmployeeHistoryRequestMessage">
   <part name="RequestParameter"
      element="hr:EmployeeUpdateHistoryRequestType"/>
</message>
<message name="updateEmployeeHistoryResponseMessage">
   <part name="ResponseParameter"
```

```
         element="hr:EmployeeUpdateHistoryResponseType"/>
</message>
<portType name="EmployeeInterface">
   <operation name="GetEmployeeWeeklyHoursLimit">
      <input message=
         "tns:getEmployeeWeeklyHoursRequestMessage"/>
      <output message=
         "tns:getEmployeeWeeklyHoursResponseMessage"/>
   </operation>
   <operation name="UpdateEmployeeHistory">
      <input message=
         "tns:updateEmployeeHistoryRequestMessage"/>
      <output message=
         "tns:updateEmployeeHistoryResponseMessage"/>
   </operation>
</portType>
```

Example 15.4   The `message` and `portType` parts of the Employee Service definition that implement the abstract definition details of the two service operations.

> **NOTE**
>
> TLS has standardized on the WSDL 1.1 specification because it is conforming to the requirements dictated by version 1.1 of the WS-I Basic Profile and because none of its application platforms support a newer WSDL version. WSDL 1.1 uses the `portType` element instead of the `interface` element, which is introduced by WSDL 2.0.

Step 4: Apply principles of service-orientation

Here's where we revisit the four service orientation principles we identified in Chapter 8 as being those not provided by the Web services technology set:

- service reusability
- service autonomy
- service statelessness
- service discoverability

Reusability and autonomy, the two principles we already covered in the service modeling process, are somewhat naturally part of the entity-centric design model in that the operations exposed by entity-centric business services are intended to be inherently generic and reusable (and because the use of the `import` statement is encouraged to reuse schemas and create modular WSDL definitions). Reusability is further promoted in Step 6, where we suggest that the design be extended to facilitate requirements beyond those identified as part of our service candidate.

Because entity-centric services often need to be composed by a parent service layer and because they rely on the application service layer to carry out their business logic, their immediate autonomy is generally well defined. Unless those services governed by an entity-centric controller have unusual processing requirements or impose dependencies in some manner, entity-centric services generally maintain their autonomy.

It is for similar reasons as those just mentioned that statelessness is also relatively manageable. Entity-centric services generally do not possess a great deal of workflow logic and for those cases in which multiple application or business services need to be invoked to carry out an operation, it is preferred that state management be deferred as much as possible (to, for example, document-style SOAP messages).

Discoverability is an important part of both the design of entity-centric services and their post-deployment utilization. As we mentioned in Step 1, we need to ensure that a service design does not implement logic already in existence. A discovery mechanism would make this determination much easier. Similarly, one measure we can take to make a service more discoverable to others is to supplement it with metadata details using the `documentation` element, as explained in the *Document services with metadata* guideline.

CASE STUDY

Upon a review of the initial abstract service interface, it is determined that a minor revision can be incorporated to better support fundamental service-orientation. Specifically, meta information is added to the WSDL definition to better describe the purpose and function of each of the two operations and their associated messages.

```
<portType name="EmployeeInterface">
   <documentation>
      GetEmployeeWeeklyHoursLimit uses the Employee
      ID value to retrieve the WeeklyHoursLimit value.
      UpdateEmployeeHistory uses the Employee ID value
      to update the Comment value of the EmployeeHistory.
   </documentation>
```

```
      <operation name="GetEmployeeWeeklyHoursLimit">
        <input message=
          "tns:getEmployeeWeeklyHoursRequestMessage"/>
        <output message=
          "tns:getEmployeeWeeklyHoursResponseMessage"/>
      </operation>
      <operation name="UpdateEmployeeHistory">
        <input message=
          "tns:updateEmployeeHistoryRequestMessage"/>
        <output message=
          "tns:updateEmployeeHistoryResponseMessage"/>
      </operation>
    </portType>
```

Example 15.5 The service interface, supplemented with additional metadata
documentation.

Step 5: Standardize and refine the service interface

Depending on your requirements, this can be a multi-faceted step involving a series of design tasks. Following is a list of recommended actions you can take to achieve a standardized and streamlined service design:

- Review existing design standards and guidelines and apply any that are appropriate. (Use the guidelines and proposed standards provided at the end of this chapter as a starting point.)

- In addition to achieving a standardized service interface design, this step also provides an opportunity for the service design to be revised in support of some of the contemporary SOA characteristics we identified in the *Unsupported SOA characteristics* section of Chapter 9.

- If your design requirements include WS-I Basic Profile conformance, then that can become a consideration at this stage. Although Basic Profile compliance requires that the entire WSDL be completed, what has been created so far can be verified.

CASE STUDY

The TLS architect in charge of the Employee Service design decides to make adjustments to the abstract service interface to apply current design standards. Specifically, naming conventions are incorporated to standardize operation names, as shown in Figure 15.7.

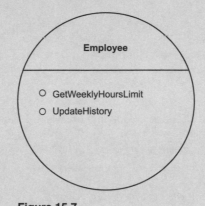

Figure 15.7
The revised Employee Service operation names.

```
<operation name="GetWeeklyHoursLimit">
  <input message="tns:getWeeklyHoursRequestMessage"/>
  <output message="tns:getWeeklyHoursResponseMessage"/>
</operation>
<operation name="UpdateHistory">
  <input message="tns:updateHistoryRequestMessage"/>
  <output message="tns:updateHistoryResponseMessage"/>
</operation>
```

Example 15.6   The two `operation` constructs with new, standardized names.

As explained in the *Apply naming standards* guideline, the use of naming standards provides native support for intrinsic interoperability, a key contemporary SOA characteristic.

Step 6: Extend the service design

The service modeling process tends to focus on evident business requirements. While promoting reuse always is encouraged, it often falls to the design process to ensure that a sufficient amount of reusable functionality will be built into each service. This is especially important for entity-centric business services, as a complete range of common operations typically is expected by their service requestors.

This step involves performing a speculative analysis as to what other types of features this service, within its predefined functional context, should offer.

There are two common ways to implement new functionality:

- add new operations
- add new parameters to existing operations

While the latter option may streamline service interfaces, it also can be counter-intuitive in that too many parameters associated with one operation may require that service requestors need to know too much about the service to effectively utilize it.

Adding operations is a straight-forward means of providing evident functions associated with the entity. The classic set of operations for an entity-centric service is:

- GetSomething
- UpdateSomething
- AddSomething
- DeleteSomething

Security requirements notwithstanding, establishing these standard operations builds a consistent level of interoperability into the business service layer, facilitating ad-hoc reusability and composition.

> **NOTE**
>
> Despite the naming suggestions listed here, when designing business services to reflect existing entity models, it is often beneficial to carry over the naming conventions already established (even if this means adjusting existing naming standards accordingly).

If entirely new tasks are defined, then they can be incorporated by new operations that follow the same design standards as the existing ones. If new functional requirements are identified that relate to existing operations, then a common method of extending these operations is to add input and output values. This allows an operation to receive and transmit a range of message combinations. Care must be taken, though, to not overly complicate operations for the sake of potential reusability. It often is advisable to subject any new proposed functionality to a separate analysis process.

Also, while it is desirable and recommended to produce entity-centric services that are completely self-sufficient at managing data associated with the corresponding entity domain, there is a key practical consideration that should be factored in. For every new operation you add, the means by which that operation completes its processing also needs to be designed and implemented. This boils down to the very probable requirement for additional or extended application services. As long as the overhead for every new operation is calculated and deemed acceptable, then this step is advisable.

Note that upon identifying new operations, Steps 1 through 5 need to be repeated to properly shape and standardize added extensions.

CASE STUDY

TLS is under time pressure to deliver the Timesheet Submission solution. It is therefore decided that they will not extend the service design at this point. The standards applied so far have guaranteed them an easily extensible service design, where additional operations can be added without breaking the original service interface.

However, to demonstrate this step, let's speculate as to the kinds of operations that *could* have been added to the Employee Service. Given that this service represents two entities, it likely will require a larger range of operations than most entity-centric services, as shown in Figure 15.8.

Following is an example that shows how the `portType` construct could be expanded with supplementary operations (`documentation` elements have been omitted to save space):

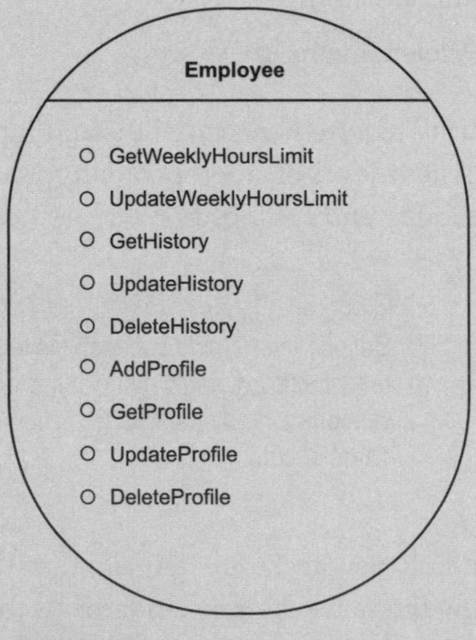

Employee

- O GetWeeklyHoursLimit
- O UpdateWeeklyHoursLimit
- O GetHistory
- O UpdateHistory
- O DeleteHistory
- O AddProfile
- O GetProfile
- O UpdateProfile
- O DeleteProfile

Figure 15.8
An Employee Service offering a full range of operations.

```
<portType name="EmployeeInterface">
   <operation name="GetWeeklyHoursLimit">
      <input message="tns:getWeeklyHoursRequestMessage"/>
      <output message="tns:getWeeklyHoursResponseMessage"/>
   </operation>
   <operation name="UpdateWeeklyHoursLimit">
      <input message=
         "tns:updateWeeklyHoursRequestMessage"/>
      <output message=
         "tns:updateWeeklyHoursResponseMessage"/>
   </operation>
   <operation name="GetHistory">
      <input message="tns:getHistoryRequestMessage"/>
      <output message="tns:getHistoryResponseMessage"/>
   </operation>
   <operation name="UpdateHistory">
      <input message="tns:updateHistoryRequestMessage"/>
      <output message="tns:updateHistoryResponseMessage"/>
   </operation>
   <operation name="DeleteHistory">
      <input message="tns:deleteHistoryRequestMessage"/>
      <output message="tns:deleteHistoryResponseMessage"/>
   </operation>
   <operation name="AddProfile">
      <input message="tns:addProfileRequestMessage"/>
      <output message="tns:addProfileResponseMessage"/>
   </operation>
   <operation name="GetProfile">
      <input message="tns:getProfileRequestMessage"/>
      <output message="tns:getProfileResponseMessage"/>
   </operation>
   <operation name="UpdateProfile">
      <input message="tns:updateProfileRequestMessage"/>
      <output message="tns:updateProfileResponseMessage"/>
   </operation>
   <operation name="DeleteProfile">
      <input message="tns:deleteProfileRequestMessage"/>
      <output message="tns:deleteProfileResponseMessage"/>
   </operation>
</portType>
```

Example 15.7 An expanded `portType` construct.

These additional operations provide a well rounded set of data processing extensions that enable the Employee Service to be reused by a variety of solutions.

Step 7: Identify other required services

While the service modeling process from our service-oriented analysis may have identified some key application services, it may not have been possible to define them all.

Now that we have an actual design for this new business service, you can study the processing requirements of each of its operations more closely. In doing so, you should be able to determine if additional application services are required to carry out each piece of exposed functionality. If you do find the need for new application services, you will have to determine if they already exist, or if they need to be added to the list of services that will be delivered as part of this solution.

CASE STUDY

Let's take another look at the two operations we designed into the Employee Service:

- GetWeeklyHoursLimit
- UpdateHistory

The first requires that we access the employee profile. At TLS, employee information is stored in two locations:

- Payroll data is kept within the accounting system repository, along with additional employee contact information.
- Employee profile information, including employee history details, is stored in the HR repository.

When an XML data representation architecture was first implemented at TLS, entity-centric XSD schemas were used to bridge some of the existing disparity that existed among the many TLS data sources. Being aware of this, the service architect investigates the origins of the Employee.xsd schema used as part of the Employee.wsdl definition to determine the processing requirements for the GetWeeklyHoursLimit operation.

It is discovered that although the schema accurately expresses a logical data entity, it represents a document structure derived from two different physical repositories. Subsequent analysis reveals that the weekly hours limit value is stored in the accounting database. The processing requirement for the GetWeeklyHoursLimit operation is then written up as follows:

Application service-level function capable of issuing the following query against the accounting database: "Return employee's weekly hour limit using the employee ID as the only search criteria."

Next, the details behind the UpdateHistory operation are studied. This time it's a bit easier, as the EmployeeHistory.xsd schema is associated with a single data source—the HR employee profile repository. Looking back at the original analysis documentation, the architect identifies the one piece of information that this particular solution will need to update within this repository. Therefore, the processing requirement definition goes beyond the immediate requirements of the solution, as follows:

Application service-level function capable of issuing an update to the "comment" column of the employee history table in the HR employee profile database, using the employee ID value as the sole criteria.

It looks like the Timesheet Submission solution may require new application services to facilitate Employee Service processing requirements, as illustrated in the expanded composition shown in Figure 15.9. Both of these newly identified requirements will need to be subjected to the service modeling process described in Chapter 12.

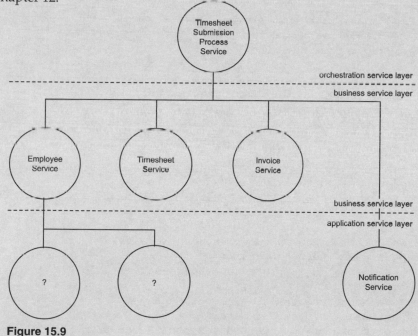

Figure 15.9
The revised composition hierarchy identifying new potential application services.

It is eventually revealed that only one new application service is required to accommodate the Employee Service—a Human Resources wrapper service that also can facilitate the Timesheet Service. Additionally, it is discovered that the processing required by the Invoice Service can be fulfilled by the existing TLS Accounts Payable Service.

CASE STUDY (PROCESS RESULTS)

Here is the final version of the Employee Service definition, incorporating the changes to element names and all of the previous revisions.

```
<definitions name="Employee"
   targetNamespace="http://www.xmltc.com/tls/employee/wsdl/"
   xmlns="http://schemas.xmlsoap.org/wsdl/"
   xmlns:act=
      "http://www.xmltc.com/tls/employee/schema/accounting/"
   xmlns:hr="http://www.xmltc.com/tls/employee/schema/hr/"
   xmlns:soap="http://schemas.xmlsoap.org/wsdl/soap/"
   xmlns:tns="http://www.xmltc.com/tls/employee/wsdl/"
   xmlns:xsd="http://www.w3.org/2001/XMLSchema">
   <types>
      <xsd:schema targetNamespace=
          "http://www.xmltc.com/tls/employee/schema/">
          <xsd:import namespace=
             "http://www.xmltc.com/tls/employee/schema/
                 accounting/"
             schemaLocation="Employee.xsd"/>
          <xsd:import namespace=
             "http://www.xmltc.com/tls/employee/schema/hr/"
             schemaLocation="EmployeeHistory.xsd"/>
      </xsd:schema>
   </types>
   <message name="getWeeklyHoursRequestMessage">
      <part name="RequestParameter"
         element="act:EmployeeHoursRequestType"/>
   </message>
   <message name="getWeeklyHoursResponseMessage">
      <part name="ResponseParameter"
         element="act:EmployeeHoursResponseType"/>
   </message>
   <message name="updateHistoryRequestMessage">
      <part name="RequestParameter"
         element="hr:EmployeeUpdateHistoryRequestType"/>
   </message>
```

```
    <message name="updateHistoryResponseMessage">
      <part name="ResponseParameter"
        element="hr:EmployeeUpdateHistoryResponseType"/>
    </message>
    <portType name="EmployeeInterface">
      <documentation>
        GetWeeklyHoursLimit uses the Employee ID value
        to retrieve the WeeklyHoursLimit value.
        UpdateHistory uses the Employee ID value to
        update the Comment value of the EmployeeHistory.
      </documentation>
      <operation name="GetWeeklyHoursLimit">
        <input message=
          "tns:getWeeklyHoursRequestMessage"/>
        <output message=
          "tns:getWeeklyHoursResponseMessage"/>
      </operation>
      <operation name="UpdateHistory">
        <input message=
          "tns:updateHistoryRequestMessage"/>
        <output message=
          "tns:updateHistoryResponseMessage"/>
      </operation>
    </portType>
    ...
</definitions>
```

Example 15.8 The final abstract service definition.

> **NOTE**
>
> This process has produced an abstract definition only. The full WSDL document, including concrete definition details, along with the imported XSD schemas, can be downloaded at www.soabooks.com.

SUMMARY OF KEY POINTS

- Entity-centric business services need to be designed to accurately represent existing business entities, while remaining business process-agnostic.

- Some speculative analysis may be required to properly outfit an entity-centric business service with the required range of generic operations.

15.3   Application service design (a step-by-step process)

Application services are the workhorses of SOA. They represent the bottom sub-layer of the composed service layer (Figure 15.10), responsible for carrying out any of the processing demands dictated to them by the business and orchestration layers.

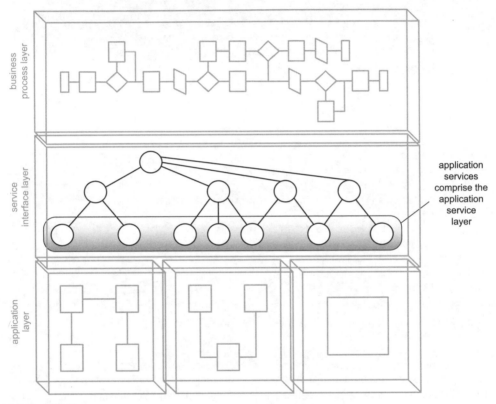

Figure 15.10
Application services establish the bottom sub-layer of the service layer.

Unlike services in business-centric layers, the design of application services does not require business analysis expertise. The application service layer is a pure, service-oriented abstraction of an organization's technical environments, best defined by those who understand these environments the most.

Because of the many real-world and technology-specific considerations that need to be taken into account, application services can be the hardest type of service to design. Further, the context established by these services can be constantly challenged, as technology is upgraded or replaced, and as related application logic is built or altered.

15.3.1   Process description

Figure 15.11 provides a proposed service design process for creating application service interfaces. Note that all references made to "application services" in this and remaining chapters imply that they are reusable utility application services.

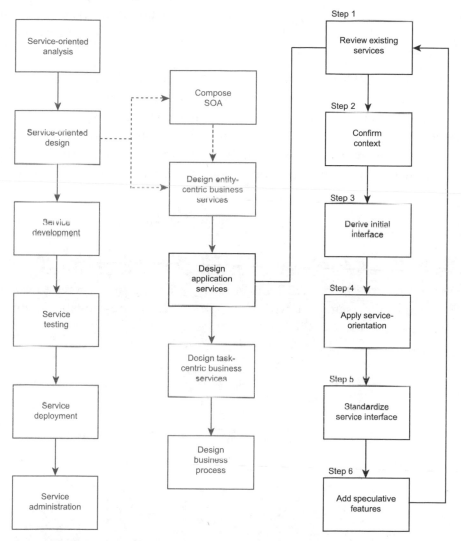

Figure 15.11
The application service design process.

When viewing Figure 15.11, you'll notice that this process shares a number of steps with the previous entity-centric business service process. This is because both application and entity-centric services establish reusable service logic and therefore rely on parent controllers to compose them into business process-specific tasks.

However, there are key aspects in how the two processes differ. Note, for example, how the confirmation of the operation grouping context is isolated into a separate step. Establishing context for application services is an important and much less clear-cut part of service design.

Further, there is no step in which processing requirements are defined. This is primarily due to the fact that application services are responsible for implementing the processing details required to carry out the business logic of their parent business services. This, of course, does not mean that processing requirements for application services do not exist. They do, only they are part of the design of the underlying service application logic. Because we are only designing a service interface at this stage, it is not considered part of the process.

Let's begin putting together the application service interface.

CASE STUDY

We now switch over to the RailCo environment, where the focus is on the design of the Transform Accounting Documents application service candidate (Figure 15.12) that was modeled in Chapter 12.

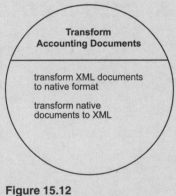

Figure 15.12
The Transform Accounting
Documents Service candidate.

This candidate establishes a "document transformation context," which justifies the grouping of its two very similar operation candidates:

- transform XML documents to native format
- transform native documents to XML

These two lines of information establish a base from which we can derive a physical service design via the steps in the upcoming design process.

Step 1: Review existing services

Avoiding redundancy within application services can be more challenging than with other types of reusable services. Business services, for example, benefit from well documented business models that already provide a clear separation of logic. These documents typically don't exist for application services, making it easy, especially in larger organizations, for redundant functionality to inadvertently emerge. Extra up-front research effort is therefore required to complete this step.

Additionally, because these services provide such generic functionality, it is worth, at this stage, investigating whether the features you require can be purchased or leased from third-party vendors. Because application services should be designed for maximum reusability, third-party Web services (which typically are built to be reusable) can make a great deal of sense, as long as required quality of service levels can be met.

CASE STUDY

RailCo is delivering this service as part of a solution that is replacing their original hybrid Invoice Submission and Order Fulfillment Services. The only other service that exists within the RailCo environment is the TLS Subscription Service, used to interact with the TLS publishing extension. Therefore, this step is completed rather quickly, as little effort is required to determine that functionality planned for the Transform Accounting Document service will not end up being redundant.

Step 2: Confirm the context

When performing a service-oriented analysis it's natural to be focused on immediate business requirements. As a result, application service candidates produced by this phase will frequently not take the contexts established by existing application services into account.

Therefore, it is important that the operation candidate grouping proposed by service candidates be re-evaluated and compared with existing application service designs. Upon reassessing the service context, you may find that one or more operations actually belong in other application services.

NOTE

This step was not required as part of the entity-centric business service design, as the context of entity-centric services is predefined by the corresponding entity models.

CASE STUDY

A review of the one existing RailCo service and the additional services planned as part of this solution confirms that the grouping context proposed for the two operation candidates of the Transform Accounting Documents service candidate is valid.

Step 3: Derive an initial service interface

Analyze the proposed service operation candidates and follow the steps below to define the first cut of the service interface:

1. Using the application service candidate as your primary input, ensure that the granularity of the logic partitions represented by the operation candidates are appropriately generic and reusable.

2. Document the input and output values required for the processing of each operation candidate and define message structures using XSD schema constructs (which essentially establishes the WSDL `types` construct).

3. Complete the abstract service definition by adding the `portType` (or `interface`) area (along with its child `operation` constructs) and the necessary `message` constructs containing the `part` elements that reference the appropriate schema types.

Note that as generic units of processing logic, application services will be used by different types of business services. Each business service will be processing a different type of business document (invoice, purchase order, claim, etc.). Therefore, application services need to be designed in such a manner that they can process multiple document types. Depending on the nature of the information being processed, there are several design options.

Examples include:

- Create a set of operations that are generic but still document specific. For example, instead of a single Add operation, you could provide separate AddInvoice, AddPO, and AddClaim operations.
- Application services can be outfitted to support SOAP attachments, allowing a generic operation to issue a generic SOAP message containing a specific business document.

CASE STUDY

RailCo begins by deriving the two operation names shown in Figure 15.13.

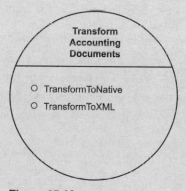

Figure 15.13
The first cut of the Transform
Accounting Documents Service.

It then moves on to define the `types` construct of its service definition to formalize the message structures. First, it tackles the request and response messages for the TransformToNative operation.

```
<xsd:schema targetNamespace=
   "http://www.xmltc.com/railco/transform/schema/">
   <xsd:element name="TransformToNativeType">
      <xsd:complexType>
         <xsd:sequence>
            <xsd:element name="SourcePath"
```

```
                    type="xsd:string"/>
              <xsd:element name="DestinationPath"
                    type="xsd:string"/>
         </xsd:sequence>
      </xsd:complexType>
   </xsd:element>
   <xsd:element name="TransformToNativeReturnCodeType">
      <xsd:complexType>
         <xsd:sequence>
            <xsd:element name="Code"
                type="xsd:integer"/>
            <xsd:element name="Message"
                type="xsd:string"/>
         </xsd:sequence>
      </xsd:complexType>
   </xsd:element>
</xsd:schema>
```

Example 15.9   The XSD schema types required by the TransformToNative operation.

Upon assessing the message requirements of the TransformToXML operation,
RailCo discovers that the required types are identical. Streamlining the schema
design with shared complex types is considered, but RailCo decides against it. It
chooses instead to create a second set of elements with redundant complex types
because it would like the freedom to change these types independently in the
future.

```
<xsd:element name="TransformToXMLType">
   <xsd:complexType>
      <xsd:sequence>
         <xsd:element name="SourcePath"
            type="xsd:string"/>
         <xsd:element name="DestinationPath"
            type="xsd:string"/>
      </xsd:sequence>
   </xsd:complexType>
</xsd:element>
<xsd:element name="TransformToXMLReturnCodeType">
   <xsd:complexType>
      <xsd:sequence>
         <xsd:element name="Code"
```

```
                     type="xsd:integer"/>
              <xsd:element name="Message"
                   type="xsd:string"/>
         </xsd:sequence>
    </xsd:complexType>
</xsd:element>
```

Example 15.10   The additional tpes for use by the TransformToXML operation.

Next, the initial version of the abstract service definition for the RailCo Transform Account Documents Service is completed by providing the remaining message and portType constructs.

```
<message name="transformToNativeRequestMessage">
   <part name="RequestParameter"
      element="trn:TransformToNativeType"/>
</message>
<message name="transformToNativeResponseMessage">
   <part name="ResponseParameter"
      element="trn:TransformToNativeReturnCodeType"/>
</message>

<message name="transformToXMLRequestMessage">
   <part name="RequestParameter"
      element="trn:TransformToXMLType"/>
</message>
<message name="transformToXMLResponseMessage">
   <part name="ResponseParameter"
      element="trn:TransformToXMLReturnCodeType"/>
</message>

<portType name="TransformInterface">
   <operation name="TransformToNative">
      <input message=
           "tns:transformToNativeRequestMessage"/>
        <output message=
           "tns:transformToNativeResponseMessage"/>
   </operation>
   <operation name="TransformToXML">
      <input message=
         "tns:transformToXMLRequestMessage"/>
      <output message=
```

```
            "tns:transformToXMLResponseMessage"/>
    </operation>
</portType>
```

Example 15.11   The `message` and `portType` constructs of the abstract Transform
Accounting Documents Service definition.

> **NOTE**
>
> RailCo is mandated by TLS to build services that are WS-I Basic Profile 1.1 com-
> pliant. This requires RailCo to use the WSDL 1.1 specification to build service
> interfaces. This suits RailCo fine, as none of its middleware supports newer ver-
> sions of WSDL anyway.

Step 4: Apply principles of service-orientation

This step highlights the four principles of service-orientation we listed in Chapter 8, as being those that are not intrinsically provided by the Web services platform (service reusability, service autonomy, service statelessness, and service discoverability).

Reuse was discussed in the service modeling process and is addressed directly in Step 5, where we look at making our application service as useful to potential service requestors as possible. However, the existing operation candidates also should be reviewed to ensure they are designed to be generic and reusable.

Autonomy is of primary concern when designing application services. We must ensure that the underlying application logic responsible for executing the service operations does not impose dependencies on the service, or itself have dependencies. This is where the information we gathered in Step 2 of the service-oriented analysis process provides us with a starting point to investigate the nature of the application logic each service operation needs to invoke. Step 6 provides an analysis that covers this and other technology-related issues.

Statelessness also may be more difficult to achieve with application services. Because they are required to interface with a variety of different application platforms, these services are subject to highly unpredictable implementation environments. Sooner or later, application services are bound to encounter challenges that impose unreasonable or inconsistent performance requirements (outdated legacy systems are known for this). Therefore, the best way to promote a stateless application service design is to carry out as much up-front analysis as possible. Knowing in advance what the performance demands will be will allow you to investigate alternatives before you commit to a particular design.

As with entity-centric services, discoverability can be an important part of evolving the application services layer. To guarantee that this design does not overlap with the logic already provided by other application services, a discoverability mechanism is useful. This becomes more of an infrastructure requirement that can be planned as part of an SOA implementation. However, the *Document services with metadata* guideline still applies, as application services should be supplemented with as much metadata as possible.

CASE STUDY

The Transform Accounting Documents Service undergoes a review to ensure that it is properly incorporating service-orientation principles.

First, the reuse potential of its two operations is assessed:

- TransformToNative
- TransformToXML

After some discussion around whether these two operations should be combined into one generic Transform operation, it is decided to leave them as they are. The descriptive nature of the operations is preferred, and RailCo would like the option of evolving each operation separately in the future.

Next, the issues of autonomy and statelessness are discussed. Autonomy is not a problem, given that the logic required to carry out its transformation functions is contained within the service's underlying application logic. In other words, there are no dependencies on other programs. Statelessness also is not considered to be a concern because this service will be responsible for its own processing.

Finally, it is agreed that to better accommodate future discoverability, the service definition be outfitted with additional metadata documentation.

```
<portType name="TransformInterface">
   <documentation>
      Retrieves an XML document and converts it
      into the native accounting document format.
   </documentation>
```

```
<operation name="TransformToNative">
   <input message=
      "tns:transformToNativeRequestMessage"/>
   <output message=
      "tns:transformToNativeResponseMessage"/>
</operation>
<documentation>
   Retrieves a native accounting document and
   converts it into an XML document.
</documentation>
<operation name="TransformToXML">
   <input message=
      "tns:transformToXMLRequestMessage"/>
   <output message=
      "tns:transformToXMLResponseMessage"/>
</operation>
</portType>
```

Example 15.12   The Transform Accounting Documents `portType` construct with supplemental metadata documentation.

Step 5: Standardize and refine the service interface

Even though the role and purpose of application services differs from other types of
services, it is important that they be designed in the same fundamental manner. We
accomplish this by ensuring that the resulting application service WSDL definition is
based on the same standards and conventions used by others.

Following is a list of recommended actions you can take to achieve a standardized and
streamlined service design:

- Apply any existing design standards relevant to the service interface. (For a list of
  suggested standards, review the guidelines provided at the end of this chapter.)

- Review any of the contemporary SOA characteristics you've chosen to have your
  services support and assess whether it is possible to build support for this characteristic into this service design.

- Optionally incorporate WS-I Basic Profile rules and best practices to whatever
  extent possible.

CASE STUDY

Some changes are made to the service as a result of the considerations taken into account as part of this step. Upon reviewing naming standards, it is determined that the chosen names for the operations are in line with existing conventions. The name given to the service itself, however, is not. Therefore, the service is renamed from "Transform Accounting Documents" to "Transform Accounting."

Then the need to support a primary contemporary SOA characteristic is raised. RailCo established early on that it wants to be able to expand its SOA in the future with a minimal amount of redevelopment effort. Therefore, the characteristic of extensibility should be built into each of its services to whatever extent feasible.

Upon a review of the service design, increased extensibility is achieved with the following adjustments:

- The service name is changed again, this time shortened to just "Transform."
- The TransformXMLToNative and TransformNativeToXML operations are renamed to something more generic. The new names are ForAccountingImport and ForAccountingExport (Figure 15.14). This naming change trickles down to the `element` and `message` names as well.

Figure 15.14
The final design of the Transform Service.

```
<types>
   <xsd:schema targetNamespace=
      "http://www.xmltc.com/railco/transform/schema/">
      <xsd:element name="ForImportType">
         <xsd:complexType>
            <xsd:sequence>
               <xsd:element name="SourcePath"
                  type="xsd:string"/>
               <xsd:element name="DestinationPath"
                  type="xsd:string"/>
            </xsd:sequence>
         </xsd:complexType>
      </xsd:element>
      <xsd:element name="ForImportReturnCodeType">
         <xsd:complexType>
            <xsd:sequence>
               <xsd:element name="Code"
                  type="xsd:integer"/>
               <xsd:element name="Message"
                  type="xsd:string"/>
            </xsd:sequence>
         </xsd:complexType>
      </xsd:element>
      <xsd:element name="ForExportType">
         <xsd:complexType>
            <xsd:sequence>
               <xsd:element name="SourcePath"
                  type="xsd:string"/>
               <xsd:element name="DestinationPath"
                  type="xsd:string"/>
            </xsd:sequence>
         </xsd:complexType>
      </xsd:element>
      <xsd:element name="ForExportReturnCodeType">
         <xsd:complexType>
            <xsd:sequence>
               <xsd:element name="Code"
                  type="xsd:integer"/>
               <xsd:element name="Message"
                  type="xsd:string"/>
            </xsd:sequence>
         </xsd:complexType>
      </xsd:element>
   </xsd:schema>
</types>
```

Example 15.13   The revised types construct.

These modifications position the service as a transformation utility that initially supports only transformation functions for use with the accounting system but that can be extended to offer additional transformation-related features.

Step 6: Outfit the service candidate with speculative features

If you are interested in delivering highly reusable application services, you can take this opportunity to add features to this service design. These new features can affect existing operations or can result in the addition of new operations. For application services, speculative extensions revolve around the type of processing that falls within the service context.

Of course, before actually adding speculative extensions to the application service, you should repeat Step 1 to confirm that no part of these new operations already exists within other services. Additionally, when adding new extensions, Steps 2 through 5 also need to be repeated to ensure that they are properly standardized and designed in alignment with the portion of the service interface we've created so far.

CASE STUDY

Although RailCo would like to build highly reusable application services, it cannot afford to do so at this time. Having designed the Transform Service to be sufficiently generic and reusable so that it can be used by both the Invoice Submission and Order Fulfillment Processes, RailCo is confident that its immediate requirements are being fulfilled. Further, because extensibility is being emphasized as well, RailCo feels that it can continue to evolve this service if future reusability opportunities present themselves.

Following is the final version of the Transform Service definition, incorporating the changes to element names and all of the previous revisions.

```
<definitions name="Transform"
   targetNamespace=
      "http://www.xmltc.com/railco/transform/wsdl/"
   xmlns="http://schemas.xmlsoap.org/wsdl/"
   xmlns:soap="http://schemas.xmlsoap.org/wsdl/soap/"
   xmlns:tns="http://www.xmltc.com/railco/transform/wsdl/"
   xmlns:trn="http://www.xmltc.com/railco/transform/schema/"
   xmlns:xsd="http://www.w3.org/2001/XMLSchema">
   <types>
      <xsd:schema targetNamespace=
         "http://www.xmltc.com/railco/transform/schema/">
         <xsd:element name="ForImportType">
            <xsd:complexType>
               <xsd:sequence>
                  <xsd:element name="SourcePath"
                     type="xsd:string"/>
                  <xsd:element name="DestinationPath"
                     type="xsd:string"/>
               </xsd:sequence>
            </xsd:complexType>
         </xsd:element>
         <xsd:element name="ForImportReturnCodeType">
            <xsd:complexType>
               <xsd:sequence>
                  <xsd:element name="Code"
                     type="xsd:integer"/>
                  <xsd:element name="Message"
                     type="xsd:string"/>
               </xsd:sequence>
            </xsd:complexType>
         </xsd:element>
         <xsd:element name="ForExportType">
            <xsd:complexType>
               <xsd:sequence>
                  <xsd:element name="SourcePath"
                     type="xsd:string"/>
                  <xsd:element name="DestinationPath"
                     type="xsd:string"/>
               </xsd:sequence>
            </xsd:complexType>
         </xsd:element>
```

```
        <xsd:element name="ForExportReturnCodeType">
           <xsd:complexType>
              <xsd:sequence>
                 <xsd:element name="Code"
                    type="xsd:integer"/>
                 <xsd:element name="Message"
                    type="xsd:string"/>
              </xsd:sequence>
           </xsd:complexType>
        </xsd:element>
     </xsd:schema>
</types>

<message name="ForAccountingImportRequestMessage">
   <part name="RequestParameter"
      element="trn:ForImportType"/>
</message>
<message name="ForAccountingImportResponseMessage">
   <part name="ResponseParameter"
      element="trn:ForImportReturnCodeType"/>
</message>
<message name="ForAccountingExportRequestMessage">
   <part name="RequestParameter"
      element="trn:ForExportType"/>
</message>
<message name="ForAccountingExportResponseMessage">
   <part name="ResponseParameter"
      element="trn:ForExportReturnCodeType"/>
</message>

<portType name="TransformInterface">
   <documentation>
      ForAccountingImport retrieves an XML
      document and converts it into the native
      accounting document format.
      ForAccountingExport retrieves a native
      accounting document and converts it into
      an XML document.
   </documentation>
   <operation name="ForAccountingImport">
     <input message=
        "tns:ForAccountingImportRequestMessage"/>
     <output message=
        "tns:ForAccountingImportResponseMessage"/>
   </operation>
   <operation name="ForAccountingExport">
     <input message=
```

```
          "tns:ForAccountingExportRequestMessage"/>
      <output message=
          "tns:ForAccountingExportResponseMessage"/>
    </operation>
  </portType>
  ...
</definitions>
```

Example 15.14   The final abstract service definition.

NOTE

This process has produced an abstract definition only. The full WSDL document, including sample concrete definition details, is available for download at `www.soabooks.com`.

SUMMARY OF KEY POINTS

- Application services need to be designed in a solution-agnostic manner, implementing the utility service model so that reuse can be maximized.

- Speculative analysis may be required to design a service interface that exposes adequately generic and reusable operations.

15.4   Task-centric business service design (a step-by-step process)

The process for designing task-centric services usually require less effort than the previous two design processes, simply because reuse is generally not a primary consideration. Therefore, only the service operation candidates identified as part of the service modeling process are addressed here.

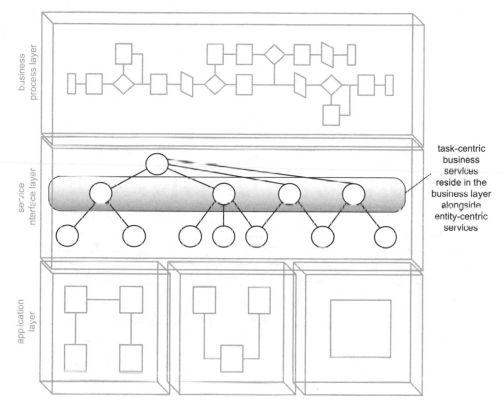

task-centric
business
services
reside in the
business layer
alongside
entity-centric
services

Figure 15.15

Task-centric business services can comprise the business service layer, along with entity-centric neighbors.

15.4.1   Process description

As shown in Figure 15.16, this process starts off with a new kind of step in which workflow logic is mapped out. This is because task-centric business services are expected to contain and govern portions of business processes.

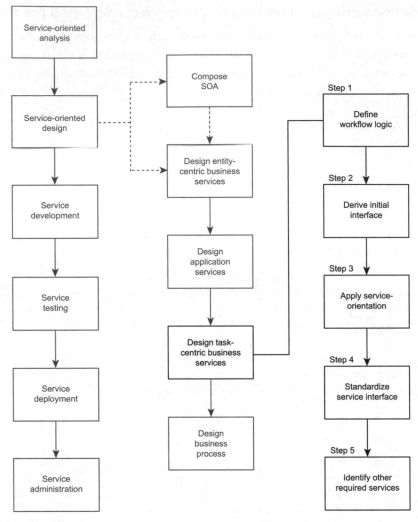

Figure 15.16
The task-centric business service design process.

Note that there is no step encouraging you to extend the service design beyond the feature set you already defined in the service modeling stage. As previously mentioned, providing a generic and reusable interface is not a priority for task-centric services.

Time now to begin our service design.

The RailCo service modeling process identified the need for a task-centric business service to govern the processing of invoices produced by the legacy accounting system. This resulted in the Invoice Processing Service candidate shown in Figure 15.17.

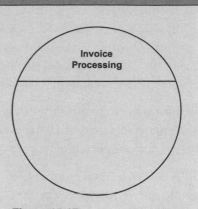

At first it appears as though this service does not contain much of anything. This is actually not unusual for smaller scale task-centric services. A service candidate with no operation candidates simply means that this service is a pure controller, solely dedicated to coordinating the underlying service composition. It also means that RailCo will need to define its service interface from scratch during this design process.

Figure 15.17
The Invoice Processing Service candidate.

Fortunately, there is a starting point, provided by the composition model (Figure 15.18) produced during Step 6 of the service modeling process from Chapter 12.

It looks like the Invoice Processing Service actually will be quite busy, as it needs to compose up to four separate services to process a single invoice submission.

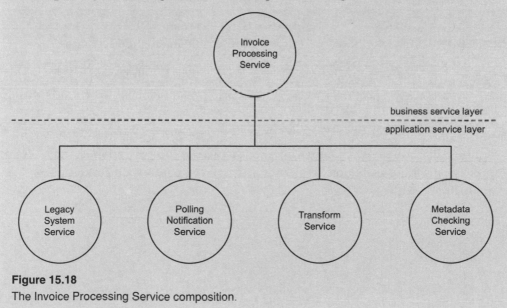

Figure 15.18
The Invoice Processing Service composition.

Step 1: Define the workflow logic

Task-centric services typically will contain embedded workflow logic used to coordinate an underlying service composition. Our first step, therefore, is to define this logic for every possible interaction scenario we can imagine. If you performed the mapping exercise in the *Identify candidate service compositions* step of the service modeling process in Chapter 12, then you will have preliminary composition details already documented.

Because we are designing our task-centric business service *after* our entity-centric and application service designs have been completed, we will need to revisit these scenario documents and turn them into concrete service interaction models.

Different traditional modeling approaches can be used to accomplish this step (we use simple activity diagrams in our case study examples). The purpose of this exercise is to document each possible execution path, including all exception conditions. The resulting diagrams also will be useful input for subsequent test cases.

NOTE

The workflow logic does not reside in the service interface we are designing in this process. We are defining workflow logic for the purpose of extracting the message exchanges with which this service will be involved. This provides us with information that helps us define types, operations, and message formats.

CASE STUDY

RailCo generates activity diagrams for all foreseeable interaction scenarios involving the Invoice Processing Service. Let's have a look at two of these diagrams.

Figure 15.19 illustrates the conditions and message exchanges required to successfully complete the invoice submission.

Figure 15.20 shows how a failure condition stops the process dead in its tracks. In this case, the Transformation Service returns an error, perhaps due to receiving an invalid document.

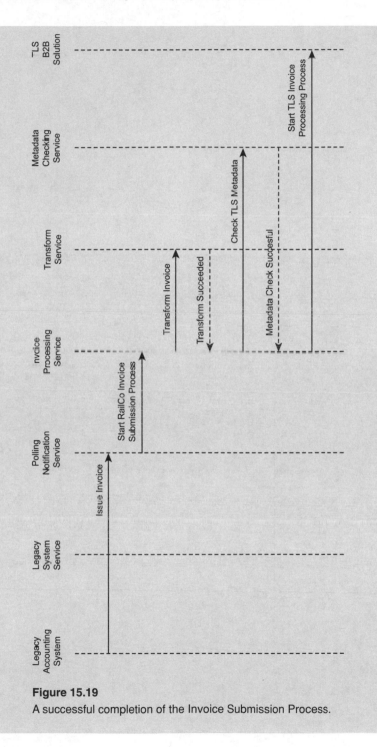

Figure 15.19

A successful completion of the Invoice Submission Process.

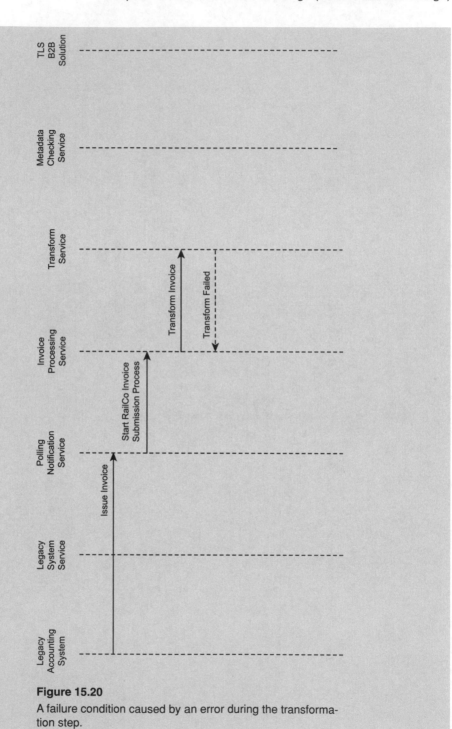

Figure 15.20

A failure condition caused by an error during the transformation step.

Step 2: Derive the service interface

Follow these suggested steps to assemble an initial service interface:

1. Use the application service operation candidates to derive a set of corresponding operations.

2. Unlike previous design processes, the source from which we derive our service interface this time also includes the activity diagrams and the workflow logic we documented in Step 1. This information gives us a good idea as to what additional operations our task-centric service may require.

3. Document the input and output values required for the processing of each operation and populate the `types` section with XSD schema types required to process the operations.

4. Build the WSDL definition by creating the `portType` (or `interface`) area, inserting the identified `operation` constructs. Then add the necessary `message` constructs containing the `part` elements that reference the appropriate schema types.

CASE STUDY

Because our service candidate provided us with no operation candidates, RailCo turns to the activity diagrams it created to derive the set of actions the service is required to perform (Figure 15.21):

- Start RailCo Invoice Processing—Receives the notification message sent by the Polling Notification Service, which kicks off the RailCo Invoice Submission Process.

- Transform Invoice—Issues a request for the Transform Service to retrieve the invoice document from the network folder and transform it into XML.

- Check TLS Metadata—Issues a request to the Metadata Checking Service for it to determine whether it's time to perform a metadata check (and then perform the metadata check, if required).

- Start TLS Invoice Processing—Forwards the invoice document to TLS, which initiates the separate TLS invoice processing process.

Of these actions, the latter three require that the service act as a requestor to initiate a message exchange with other services. These actions therefore will be implemented as part of the service's underlying business logic.

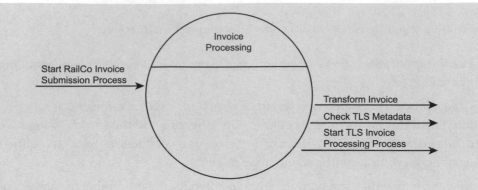

Figure 15.21
Identified requests and responses for the Invoice Processing Service.

The "Start RailCo Invoice Submission Process" action, though, is initiated by the Polling Notification Service, meaning that the Invoice Processing Service receives the request while acting as the service provider. This action therefore needs to be expressed in the service interface.

First, the naming is reconsidered to something more appropriate, as shown in Figure 15.22.

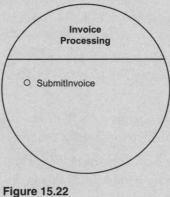

Figure 15.22
The Invoice Processing Service
with a new operation.

Carrying forward with this naming change, RailCo begins by defining the data exchange requirements for this one operation. The service interface design needed to interact with the Polling Notification Service requires an ID value, along with the location path of the invoice document file to be supplied. (This is because the Polling Notification Service does not actually physically retrieve and forward documents; it simply notifies other services of the arrival of specific types of files in a particular folder.)

RailCo starts by creating a preliminary types construct with the following complexType to match these parameter requirements:

```
<types>
   <xsd:schema targetNamespace=
      "http://www.xmltc.com/railco/invoiceservice/schema/">
      <xsd:element name="SubmitInvoiceType">
         <xsd:complexType>
            <xsd:sequence>
               <xsd:element name="ContextID"
                  type="xsd:integer"/>
               <xsd:element name="InvoiceLocation"
                  type="xsd:string"/>
            </xsd:sequence>
         </xsd:complexType>
      </xsd:element>
   </xsd:schema>
</types>
```

Example 15.15   A complexType construct designed to receive two parameters from the Polling Notification Service.

Next, it defines the operation and its associated message within the portType and message constructs:

```
<message name="receiveSubmitInvoiceMessage">
   <part name="RequestParameter"
      element="invs:SubmitInvoiceType"/>
</message>
<portType name="InvoiceProcessingInterface">
   <operation name="SubmitInvoice">
      <input message="tns:receiveSubmitInvoiceMessage"/>
   </operation>
</portType>
```

Example 15.16   The remaining parts of the abstract Invoice Processing Service definition establishing an operation with just one input message.

Note that because the message sent by the Polling Notification Service is based on the one-way MEP, the SubmitInvoice operation construct contains one input message element and no output elements.

Step 3: Apply principles of service-orientation

Before we get too far ahead in our service design, it is beneficial to take another look at the four service-orientation principles we covered in Chapter 8, which are not automatically provided to us through the use of Web services (service reusability, service autonomy, service statelessness, and service discoverability).

Reuse opportunities for task-centric services are much more rare than for entity-centric and application services. This is because task-centric services represent a portion of workflow logic specific to a business process. However, reuse still can be achieved. The *Take into account the potential cross-process reusability of the logic being encapsulated* and *Consider the potential intra-process reusability of the logic being encapsulated* modeling guidelines in Chapter 12 address this and still are applicable to this process.

Because they almost always act as parent controller services in compositions, the autonomy of task-centric services is generally dependent on the autonomy of the underlying child services. A consistent state of autonomy can therefore be challenging to maintain.

Task-centric services contain workflow logic that may impose processing dependencies in service compositions. This can lead to the need for state management. However, the use of document-style SOAP messages allows the service to delegate the persistence of some or all of this state information to the message itself.

It is always useful for services to be discoverable, but the need for task-centric services to be discovered is not as pressing as with other, more generically reusable services. Regardless, task-centric services can achieve reuse, and their existence should be known to others. Therefore, the *Document services with metadata* guideline provided at the end of this chapter also is recommended.

CASE STUDY

There is no requirement for the Invoice Processing Service to be reusable, and autonomy and statelessness are also not considered immediate concerns. As with the RailCo Transform Service that was designed previously, this service design is supplemented with additional metadata documentation to support discoverability.

```
<portType name="InvoiceProcessingInterface">
   <documentation>
      Initiates the Invoice Submission Process.
   </documentation>
   <operation name="SubmitInvoice">
      <input message="tns:receiveSubmitInvoiceMessage"/>
   </operation>
</portType>
```

Example 15.17   The portType construct with an additional documentation element.

Step 4: Standardize and refine the service interface

Although task-centric business services will tend to have more creative operation names, existing conventions still need to be applied. Here is the standard list of recommended actions you can take to achieve a standardized and streamlined service design:

- Incorporate existing design standards and guidelines. (A set of recommended guidelines is provided at the end of this chapter.)

- Ensure that any chosen contemporary SOA characteristics are fully supported by the service interface design.

- Take WS-I Basic Profile standards and best practices into account.

With regard to design standards relating to operation granularity, some leniency may be required to accommodate the processing of the service's embedded workflow sequence logic. Also, task-centric business services can benefit from reusing existing WSDL modules, in particular, XSD schema definitions.

CASE STUDY

Supporting the characteristic of extensibility is key to RailCo, as they are uncertain as to how their SOA will grow and evolve over time. In reviewing the service interface definition for the Invoice Processing Service, they realize that they are tailoring this interface to a single service requestor: the Polling Notification Service. It is foreseeable that the process logic encapsulated by this service could need to be invoked differently in the future.

For example:

- A change to the overall invoice submission process may require that this service be sent a pre-transformed XML version of the actual invoice document.

- If new services continue to be added to the RailCo technical environment, it would also be beneficial for this service to accept an invoice document so that it can participate in larger service compositions.

To address these extensibility requirements, RailCo makes an adjustment to the schema markup within the `types` construct. Because an XSD schema representing the invoice document already exists (as a result of building the underlying processing logic for the Transform Service), it is decided to incorporate this schema as part of this WSDL.

To avoid creating redundant markup, the schema is imported into the `types` construct. The original `complexType` then is extended to include a new element representing the root element of the invoice document defined in the Invoice.xsd file. Service requestors now are required to submit either a document location or the document itself. (If you are wondering why the `choice` indicator was not used with this schema, see the *Case Study* (*Process Results*) section.)

```
<types>
   <xsd:schema targetNamespace=
      "http://www.xmltc.com/railco/invoiceservice/schema/">
      <xsd:import namespace=
         "http://www.xmltc.com/railco/invoice/schema/"
         schemaLocation="Invoice.xsd"/>
      <xsd:element name="SubmitInvoiceType">
         <xsd:complexType>
            <xsd:sequence>
               <xsd:element name="ContextID"
                  type="xsd:integer"/>
               <xsd:element name="InvoiceLocation"
                  type="xsd:string"/>
               <xsd:element name="InvoiceDocument"
                  type="inv:InvoiceType"/>
            </xsd:sequence>
         </xsd:complexType>
      </xsd:element>
   </xsd:schema>
</types>
```

Example 15.18   The revised `types` construct of the Invoice Processing Service definition.

The fact that acceptable input values for this operation have been altered should be reflected in the `documentation` element contents, as follows:

```
<documentation>
   Initiates the Invoice Submission Process.
   Requires either the invoice document location
   or the document.
</documentation>
```

Example 15.19   The `documentation` element contents also have been changed.

One more change is made during this step of the service design process. The original operation name "SubmitInvoice" is reconsidered. Following an internal naming convention, the name is trimmed to just "Submit" (Figure 15.23). Because the service name already communicates the fact that its context revolves around the processing of an invoice document, there is no need to repeat the word "invoice" within operation names.

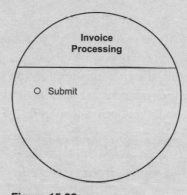

Figure 15.23
The Invoice Processing Service
with a revised operation name.

This affects both the original portType and message constructs, as follows:

```
<message name="receiveSubmitMessage">
   <part name="RequestParameter"
      element="invs:SubmitInvoiceType"/>
</message>
<portType name="InvoiceProcessingInterface">
   <documentation>
      Initiates the Invoice Submission Process.
      Requires either the invoice document location
      or the document.
   </documentation>
   <operation name="Submit">
      <input message="tns:receiveSubmitMessage"/>
   </operation>
</portType>
```

Example 15.20   The revised message and portType constructs.

Step 5: Identify other required services

To carry out their share of a solution's process logic, task-centric services can compose application and both entity-centric and additional task-centric business services. Therefore, the implementation of a task-centric service interface requires that any needed underlying service layers are in place to support the processing requirements of its operations.

Because this is the last of our three service design processes, all required supporting services need to be identified. They may consist of services that already existed and/or services we just designed during the previous application service design process. The design of process logic within the task-centric business service may also reveal the need for additional services that haven't yet been considered.

CASE STUDY

Because RailCo had already designed the previously modeled application services and because subsequent activity diagrams did not identify the need for any additional services, there are no further processing requirements involving other services. However, because the Invoice Processing Service interface was extended to support future extensibility, it now is capable of accepting a pre-transformed invoice document as an input parameter.

In our original workflow logic we established a step in the process that positioned the Transform Service as taking care of both validation and transforming tasks. The workflow logic therefore needs to be altered to make the interaction with the Transform Service optional if the Submit operation of the Invoice Processing Service receives an invoice document as part of its input (because it is already transformed and because validation of the document will occur at the time it is received). This change does not affect other services; it only requires that a new conditional processing step be added to the application logic encapsulated by the Invoice Processing Service.

CASE STUDY (PROCESS RESULTS)

Following is the final version of the InvoiceProcessing Service definition, incorporating the changes to element names and all of the previous revisions.

```
<definitions name="InvoiceProcessing"
    targetNamespace=
        "http://www.xmltc.com/railco/transform/wsdl/"
```

```
   xmlns="http://schemas.xmlsoap.org/wsdl/"
   xmlns:inv="http://www.xmltc.com/railco/invoice/schema/"
   xmlns:invs=
      "http://www.xmltc.com/railco/invoiceservice/schema/"
   xmlns:soap="http://schemas.xmlsoap.org/wsdl/soap/"
   xmlns:tns="http://www.xmltc.com/railco/transform/wsdl/"
   xmlns:xsd="http://www.w3.org/2001/XMLSchema">
   <types>
      <xsd:schema targetNamespace=
         "http://www.xmltc.com/railco/invoiceservice/
            schema/">
         <xsd:import namespace=
            "http://www.xmltc.com/railco/invoice/schema/"
            schemaLocation="Invoice.xsd"/>
         <xsd:element name="SubmitInvoiceType">
            <xsd:complexType>
               <xsd:sequence>
                  <xsd:element name="ContextID"
                     type="xsd:integer"/>
                  <xsd:element name="InvoiceLocation"
                     type="xsd:string"/>
                  <xsd:element name="InvoiceDocument"
                     type="inv:InvoiceType"/>
               </xsd:sequence>
            </xsd:complexType>
         </xsd:element>
      </xsd:schema>
   </types>
   <message name="receiveSubmitMessage">
      <part name="RequestParameter"
         element="invs:SubmitInvoiceType"/>
   </message>
   <portType name="InvoiceProcessingInterface">
      <documentation>
         Initiates the Invoice Submission Process.
         Requires either the invoice document
         location or the document.
      </documentation>
      <operation name="Submit">
         <input message="tns:receiveSubmitMessage"/>
      </operation>
   </portType>
   ...
</definitions>
```

Example 15.21   The final abstract service definition.

Those of you familiar with XSD may have noticed an opportunity to incorporate a `choice` construct within this schema. In the past, some middleware vendors have been slow to support more than the most rudimentary XSD features for use with WSDL. Schemas for externally accessible Web services therefore sometimes had to be over-simplified by avoiding key elements. Support has rapidly improved, but it is still advisable to confirm this support.

> **NOTE**
>
> This process has produced an abstract definition only. The full WSDL document, including sample concrete definition details and the imported schema, can be downloaded at `www.soabooks.com`.

SUMMARY OF KEY POINTS

- The primary design concern for task-centric business services is an accurate representation of the business process logic they are required to execute.

- Reuse and speculative design extensions are secondary concerns.

15.5   Service design guidelines

Incorporating service-oriented design principles into formal standards is critical to the success of SOA within an organization. Provided in this section is a set of guidelines that can be used as a starting point from which you can derive your own standards.

15.5.1   Identify technical constraints

It is recommended that you take the time to study and document any known processing demands of each identified service operation. First, for each operation, write a list of the processing functions required for the operation to carry out its processing. Then, for every entry on this list, find out exactly how the processing of the function will need to be executed in the existing technical environment.

The types of details we are specifically looking for are:

- The physical connection point of the particular function. (In other words, what components need to be invoked, what API functions need to be called, or which adapters need to be activated.)
- Security constraints related to any part of the processing.
- Response time of each processing function.

- Availability of the underlying system performing the processing function.
- Environmental factors relating to service deployment location.
- Technical limitations of underlying application logic (especially when exposing legacy systems).
- Administration requirements imposed by the service.
- Potential SLA requirements.

After characteristics of individual processing functions have been gathered, they need to be viewed collectively. For example, individual response times need to be added to calculate the overall estimated execution time of the operation. The result of this study is typically a series of constraints and limitations imposed by the technical environment onto our service interface. In some cases, the restrictions will be so severe that an operation may need to be significantly augmented.

Note that when transitioning an organization toward an enterprise-wide SOA, there is a tendency to want to service-orient everything. However, it is important to identify which processing requirements cannot be fulfilled by the Web services technology set. It may *not* make sense to expose some portions of underlying legacy application logic as Web services. Either way, it is worth reminding ourselves that even though this book focuses on the creation of services as Web services, SOA is in fact an implementation-neutral architectural model and service-orientation is an implementation-neutral design paradigm. Existing forms of application logic not made available through Web services can still be modeled as services. This is of particular relevance to application services, where exposing application logic through a Web service may not always be the right decision. For example, façade components are often created to encapsulate functionality from different sources and to then expose a distinct context representing a set of reusable functions. This results in a legitimate service, which may, in the future, still be expressed via a Web service.

15.5.2   Apply naming standards

Labeling services is the equivalent to labeling IT infrastructure. It is therefore essential that service interfaces be as consistently self-descriptive as possible.

Naming standards therefore need to be defined and applied to:

- service endpoint names
- service operation names
- message values

Existing naming conventions vary by organization. Some employ OO naming standards where objects are assigned nouns and methods are labeled with verbs. Others simply apply verbs to both components and their methods. Although it would be very useful, there is no perfect naming standard for all organizations. The key is that whatever standards you choose must be implemented consistently throughout all service-oriented solution environments.

Here are some suggestions:

- Service candidates with high cross-application reuse potential should always be stripped of any naming characteristics that hint at the business processes for which they were originally built. For example, instead of naming an operation GetTimesheetSubmissionID, simply reduce it to GetTimesheetID or just GetID.

- Application services need to be named according to the processing context under which their operations are grouped. Both the verb+noun or noun only conventions can be used. Simplified examples of suitable application service names are CustomerDataAccess, SalesReporting, and GetStatistics.

- Application service operations need to clearly communicate the nature of their individual functionality. Examples of suitable application service operation names are GetReport, ConvertCurrency, and VerifyData.

- Entity-centric business services need to remain representative of the entity models from which their corresponding service candidates were derived. Therefore, the naming conventions used must reflect those established in the organization's original entity models. Typically, this type of service uses the noun only naming structure. Examples of suitable entity-centric business service names are Invoice, Customer, and Employee.

- Service operations for entity-centric business services should be verb-based and should not repeat the entity name. For example, an entity-centric service called Invoice should not have an operation named AddInvoice.

15.5.3   Apply a suitable level of interface granularity

As evidenced by the case study examples in this chapter, the granularity at which services can be designed can vary. The trend to create interfaces for Web services that are coarser than those traditionally designed for RPC-based components has been encouraged by vendors as a means of overcoming some of the performance challenges associated with XML-based processing.

Performance, of course, is critical to the success and ultimate evolution of service-oriented solutions. However, other considerations also need to be taken into account. The coarser the granularity of an interface, the less reuse it may be able to offer. If multiple functions are bundled into a single operation, it may be undesirable for requestors who only require the use of one of those functions. Additionally, some coarse-grained interfaces may actually impose redundant processing or data exchange by forcing requestors to submit data not relevant to a particular activity.

Service interface granularity is a key strategic decision point that deserves a good deal of attention during the service-oriented design phase. Here are some guidelines for tackling this issue:

- Fully understand the performance limitations of the target deployment environment and explore alternative supporting technologies (such as the binary encoding extensions developed by the W3C), if required.

- Explore the possibility of providing alternate (coarse and less coarse-grained) WSDL definitions for the same Web services. Or explore the option of supplying redundant coarse and less coarse-grained operations in the same WSDL definition. These approaches de-normalize service contracts but can address performance issues and accommodate a range of requestors.

- Assign coarse-grained interfaces to services designated as solution endpoints and allow finer-grained interfaces for services confined to predefined boundaries. This, of course, runs somewhat contrary to service-orientation principles and SOA characteristics that promote reuse and interoperability in services. Interoperability is promoted in coarse-grained services, and reusability is more fostered in finer-grained services. One could standardize a composition model that requires coarse-grained services to act as controllers and endpoints for finer-grained services.

Regardless of your approach, ensure that it is consistent and predictable so that an SOA can meet performance demands while remaining standardized.

CASE STUDY

TLS chose an approach to interface granularity where services positioned for use by requestors outside of TLS would provide consistently coarse-grained interfaces. Operations on these services would accept all of the data required to process a particular activity. Further round-trips between external requestor and the service would only be required if absolutely necessary or if internal policies demanded it.

Services used within TLS could provide less coarse-grained operations to facilitate reuse and a broader range of potential (internal) requestors, as long as the processing overhead imposed by less coarse-grained operations was acceptable.

15.5.4   Design service operations to be inherently extensible

Regardless of how well services are designed when first deployed, they can never be fully prepared for what the future holds. Some types of business process changes result in the need for the scope of entities to be broadened. As a result, corresponding business services may need to be extended. While service characteristics such as reusability and composability are thought through when partitioning logic as part of the service modeling process, extensibility is more of a physical design quality that needs to be considered during design.

Depending on the nature of the change, extensibility can sometimes be achieved without breaking the existing service interface. It is important to design operations and messages to be as activity-agnostic as possible. This supports the processing of future non-specific values and functions that are still related to the operation's or message's overall purpose. Further, it is a good habit to respond to new processing requirements by first investigating the possibility of composing other available services (including services that can be purchased or leased). This may succeed in fulfilling requirements without having to touch the service interface.

Note that extensions to an existing service interface will impact the corresponding XSD schema. These extensions can be facilitated by supplying new schemas specifically for the extension. Before going down this road, though, ensure that established version control standards are firmly in place.

CASE STUDY

Due to the size of the TLS corporation, it is not uncommon for employees to be reallocated or to seek vertical or lateral position changes. The latter scenario is made further common by the "promote from within" motto encouraged by many divisional directors.

When an employee changes position or rank, the employee is expected to update his/her own profile using a form on the local intranet. Because this step is voluntary, it is often never performed. This, predictably, results in an increasingly out-of-date set of profiles. To counter this trend, the TLS Timesheet Submission Process is altered to include an employee profile verification step. Once implemented, it will verify profile information prior to accepting a timesheet. Timesheets submitted by employees with invalid profiles will simply be rejected.

To implement this new requirement, the Timesheet Service interface is not altered. Instead, the underlying service logic is extended to incorporate a separate application service that performs the profile verification.

15.5.5 Identify known and potential service requestors

Services are almost always built as part of the delivery of a specific automation solution. Therefore, they are designed to address business requirements as they pertain to that application. Limiting a service design to fulfill immediate requirements can inhibit its potential as a reusable, adaptive, and interoperable unit of processing logic.

It is therefore advisable that any existing service design process incorporate a speculative analysis of how that service may be utilized outside its initial application boundaries. In other words, it can be useful and practical to identify any potential future service requestors and to then incorporate their anticipated requirements into the current service design.

This can lead to additional functional requirements, which may or may not be desirable, depending on the current project scope, budget, and other related constraints. More importantly, though, this can lead to design refinements that may not significantly impact the current project at all. For example, it may be possible to adjust the granularity of service interfaces at the design stage without much impact to the overall project.

15.5.6 Consider using modular WSDL documents

WSDL service descriptions can be assembled dynamically at runtime through the use of import statements that link to separate files that contain parts of the service definition. This allows you to define modules for types, operations, and bindings that can be shared across WSDL documents.

It also allows you to leverage any existing XSD schema modules you may already have designed. Many organizations separate schemas into granular modules that represent individual complex types. This establishes a centralized repository of schemas that can be assembled into customized master schema definitions. By enabling you to import XSD schema modules into the types construct of a WSDL definition, you now can have your WSDL documents use those same schema modules.

> **NOTE**
>
> Incidentally, the WS-I Basic Profile requires that when designing modular WSDL definitions, the `import` statement be used to import other WSDL definitions or XSD schemas.

TLS considers importing the bindings construct so that it can be reused and perhaps even dynamically determined. However, it is later decided to leave the bindings construct as part of the WSDL document. Here is the import statement used to carry out this test:

```
<import namespace="http://.../common/wsdl/"
    location="http://.../common/wsdl/bindings.wsdl"/>
```

Example 15.22   An import element used to pull in the bindings construct residing in a separate file.

15.5.7   Use namespaces carefully

A WSDL definition consists of a collection of elements with different origins. Therefore, each definition often will involve a number of different namespaces. Following is a list of common namespaces used to represent specification-based elements:

- http://schemas.xmlsoap.org/wsdl/

- http://schemas.xmlsoap.org/wsdl/soap/

- http://www.w3.org/2001/XMLSchema/

- http://schemas.xmlsoap.org/wsdl/http/

- http://schemas.xmlsoap.org/wsdl/mime/

- http://schemas.xmlsoap.org/soap/envelope/

When assembling a WSDL from modules, additional namespaces come into play, especially when importing XSD schema definitions. Further, when defining your own elements, you can establish more namespaces to represent application-specific parts of the WSDL documents. It is not uncommon for larger WSDL documents to contain up to ten different namespaces and the qualifiers to go along with them. Therefore, it is highly recommended that you organize the use of namespaces carefully within and across WSDL documents.

The WS-I Basic Profile requires the use of the targetNamespace attribute to assign a namespace to the WSDL as a whole. If the XSD schema is embedded within the WSDL definition, then the WS-I Basic Profile requires that it also be assigned a targetNamespace value (which can be the same value used by the WSDL targetNamespace).

Some of the common namespaces identified earlier are not required by the TLS Employee Service and therefore are omitted from the list of `definitions` attributes. A `targetNamespace` is added, along with two namespaces associated with the two imported schemas.

```
<definitions name="Employee"
    targetNamespace="http://www.xmltc.com/tls/employee/wsdl/"
    xmlns="http://schemas.xmlsoap.org/wsdl/"
    xmlns:act=
        "http://www.xmltc.com/tls/employee/schema/accounting/"
    xmlns:hr="http://www.xmltc.com/tls/employee/schema/hr/"
    xmlns:soap="http://schemas.xmlsoap.org/wsdl/soap/"
    xmlns:tns="http://www.xmltc.com/tls/employee/wsdl/"
    xmlns:xsd="http://www.w3.org/2001/XMLSchema">
    ...
</definitions>
```

Example 15.23 The namespace declarations within the `definitions` element of the TLS Employee.wsdl file.

15.5.8 Use the SOAP document and literal attribute values

There are two specific attributes that establish the SOAP message payload format and the data type system used to represent payload data. These are the `style` attribute used by the `soap:binding` element and the use attribute assigned to the `soap:body` element. Both of these elements reside within the WSDL `binding` construct.

How these attributes are set is significant as it relates to the manner in which SOAP message content is structured and represented:

- The `style` attribute can be assigned a value of "document" or "rpc." The former supports the embedding of entire XML documents within the SOAP body, whereas the latter is designed more to mirror traditional RPC communication and therefore supports parameter type data.

- The use attribute can be set to a value of "literal" or "encoded." SOAP originally provided its own type system used to represent body content. Later, support for XSD data types was incorporated. This attribute value indicates which type system you want your message to use. The "literal" setting states that XSD data types will be applied.

When considering these two attributes, the following four combinations are possible and supported by SOAP:

- `style:RPC` + `use:encoded`
- `style:RPC` + `use:literal`
- `style:document` + `use:encoded`
- `style:document` + `use:literal`

The `style:document` + `use:literal` combination is preferred by SOA because it supports the notion of the document-style messaging model that is key to realizing the features of many key WS-* specifications. Further, the WS-I Basic Profile requires that the use attribute always be set to "literal."

CASE STUDY

In building the concrete part of the Employee Service interface definition, TLS architects decide to use the `style:document` + `use:literal` combination, as shown here:

```
<binding name="EmployeeBinding"
    type="tns:EmployeeInterface">
    <soap:binding style="document"
        transport="http://schemas.xmlsoap.org/soap/http"/>
    <operation name="GetWeeklyHoursLimit">
        <soap:operation
            soapAction="http://www.xmltc.com/soapaction"/>
        <input>
            <soap:body use="literal"/>
        </input>
        <output>
            <soap:body use="literal"/>
        </output>
    </operation>
    <operation name="UpdateHistory">
        <soap:operation
            soapAction="http://www.xmltc.com/soapaction"/>
        <input>
            <soap:body use="literal"/>
        </input>
        <output>
            <soap:body use="literal"/>
        </output>
    </operation>
</binding>
```

Example 15.24 The `binding` construct of the TLS Employee.wsdl document.

15.5.9 Use WS-I Profiles even if WS-I compliance isn't required

If WS-I compliance is not on your list of immediate requirements, it still is recommended that you consider using the many standards and best practices provided by the Basic Profile document. They are sound, well researched, and proven and can save you a great deal of time and effort when developing your own design standards.

> **NOTE**
>
> Another WS-I deliverable we have not covered in this book is the Basic Security Profile, which governs and standardizes the use of security-related specifications for interoperability purposes. Visit `www.ws-i.org` for more information.

15.5.10 Document services with metadata

As evidenced by the discussions we had about WS-Policy and WS-MetadataExchange in Chapter 7, the WS-* platform is placing an ever-increasing amount of emphasis on the quality and depth of service descriptions. It won't be uncommon, though, for many SOAs to exist without the benefit of a technical environment capable of supporting service description content beyond that provided by WSDL definitions.

Policies in particular represent an important metadata supplement to WSDL definitions. For example, a policy may express certain security requirements, processing preferences, and behavioral characteristics of a service provider. This allows service requestors to better assess a service provider and offers them the opportunity to be fully prepared for interaction.

Polices are formally implemented using a set of WS-* specifications described in Chapter 7. Regardless of whether these specifications actually are used in an organization, policy information should still be documented as part of any service design. This not only provides developers building service requestors for a given service provider a great deal of useful information, it also accommodates an eventual move to when policies become a common part of service-oriented architectures.

Whatever unique properties a service has, they should be documented to easily communicate a service's requirements, characteristics, or restrictions to others that may want to use it. This information can be added to a WSDL definition through the use of the `documentation` element and it could even be contained within a metadata document that is published separately and easily accessible. This promotes the discovery and reuse of services. When possible, this documentation also can be physically attached to electronic modeling diagrams.

> **NOTE**
>
> If you are designing WS-I compliant services, you can improve the quality of your service description metadata by attaching WS-I conformance claims. These advertise compliance to specific WS-I profiles. See `www.ws-i.org` for more information.

SUMMARY OF KEY POINTS

- The design of a Web service needs to achieve a balance between meeting requirements expressed in the service candidate models and those imposed by real-world considerations.

- Starting the service design with the creation of a WSDL definition is a recommended approach to building quality services that adhere to existing interface design standards.

> **NOTE**
>
> Visit `www.soamethodology.com` for more information about service design processes and how they relate to the overall SOA delivery lifecycle.

Chapter 16

Service-Oriented Design (Part IV: Business Process Design)

The orchestration service layer provides a powerful means by which contemporary service-oriented solutions can realize some key benefits. The most significant contribution this sub-layer brings to SOA is an abstraction of logic and responsibility that alleviates underlying services from a number of design constraints.

For example, by abstracting business process logic:

- Application and business services can be freely designed to be process-agnostic and reusable.
- The process service assumes a greater degree of statefulness, thus further freeing other services from having to manage state.
- The business process logic is centralized in one location, as opposed to being distributed across and embedded within multiple services.

In this chapter we tackle the design of an orchestration layer by using the WS-BPEL language to create a business process definition.

> **How case studies are used:** Our focus in this chapter is the TLS environment. We provide case study examples throughout the step-by-step process description during which TLS builds a WS-BPEL process definition for the Timesheet Submission Process. This is the same process for which service candidates were modeled in Chapter 12 and for which the Employee Service interface was designed in Chapter 15.

16.1 WS-BPEL language basics

Before we can design an orchestration layer, we need to acquire a good understanding of how the operational characteristics of the process can be formally expressed. This book uses the WS-BPEL language to demonstrate how process logic can be described as part of a concrete definition (Figure 16.1) that can be implemented and executed via a compliant orchestration engine.

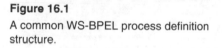

Figure 16.1
A common WS-BPEL process definition structure.

Although you likely will be using a process modeling tool and will therefore not be required to author your process definition from scratch, a knowledge of WS-BPEL elements still is useful and often required. WS-BPEL modeling tools frequently make reference to these elements and constructs, and you may be required to dig into the source code they produce to make further refinements.

> **NOTE**
>
> If you are already comfortable with the WS-BPEL language, feel free to skip ahead to the *Service-oriented business process design (a step-by-step process)* section.

16.1.1   A brief history of BPEL4WS and WS-BPEL

Before we get into the details of the WS-BPEL language, let's briefly discuss how this specification came to be. The Business Process Execution Language for Web Services (BPEL4WS) was first conceived in July, 2002, with the release of the BPEL4WS 1.0 specification, a joint effort by IBM, Microsoft, and BEA. This document proposed an orchestration language inspired by previous variations, such as IBM's Web Services Flow Language (WSFL) and Microsoft's XLANG specification.

Joined by other contributors from SAP and Siebel Systems, version 1.1 of the BPEL4WS specification was released less than a year later, in May of 2003. This version received more attention and vendor support, leading to a number of commercially available BPEL4WS-compliant orchestration engines. Just prior to this release, the BPEL4WS specification was submitted to an OASIS technical committee so that the specification could be developed into an official, open standard.

The technical committee is in the process of finalizing the release of the next version of BPEL4WS. It has been announced that the language itself has been renamed to the Web Services Business Process Execution Language, or WS-BPEL (and assigned the 2.0 version number). The changes planned for WS-BPEL have been made publicly available on the OASIS Web site at `www.oasis-open.org`.

Notes have been added to the element descriptions in this section where appropriate to indicate changes in syntax between BPEL4WS and WS-BPEL. For simplicity's sake, we refer to the Business Process Execution Language as WS-BPEL in this book.

16.1.2   Prerequisites

It's time now to learn about the WS-BPEL language. If you haven't already done so, it is recommended that you read Chapter 6 prior to proceeding with this section. Concepts relating to orchestration, coordination, atomic transactions, and business activities are covered in Chapter 6, and are therefore not repeated here. This chapter also assumes you have read through the WSDL tutorial provided in Chapter 13.

16.1.3   The `process` element

Let's begin with the root element of a WS-BPEL process definition. It is assigned a name value using the `name` attribute and is used to establish the process definition-related namespaces.

```
<process name="TimesheetSubmissionProcess"
    targetNamespace="http://www.xmltc.com/tls/process/"
    xmlns=
        "http://schemas.xmlsoap.org/ws/2003/03/
            business-process/"
    xmlns:bpl="http://www.xmltc.com/tls/process/"
    xmlns:emp="http://www.xmltc.com/tls/employee/"
    xmlns:inv="http://www.xmltc.com/tls/invoice/"
```

```
xmlns:tst="http://www.xmltc.com/tls/timesheet/"
xmlns:not="http://www.xmltc.com/tls/notification/">
<partnerLinks>
   . . .
</partnerLinks>
<variables>
   . . .
</variables>
<sequence>
   . . .
</sequence>
. . .
</process>
```

Example 16.1   A skeleton `process` definition.

The `process` construct contains a series of common child elements explained in the following sections.

16.1.4   The `partnerLinks` and `partnerLink` elements

A `partnerLink` element establishes the port type of the service (partner) that will be participating during the execution of the business process. Partner services can act as a client to the process, responsible for invoking the process service. Alternatively, partner services can be invoked by the process service itself.

The contents of a `partnerLink` element represent the communication exchange between two partners—the process service being one partner and another service being the other. Depending on the nature of the communication, the role of the process service will vary. For instance, a process service that is invoked by an external service may act in the role of "TimesheetSubmissionProcess." However, when this same process service invokes a different service to have an invoice verified, it acts within a different role, perhaps "InvoiceClient." The `partnerLink` element therefore contains the `myRole` and `partnerRole` attributes that establish the service provider role of the process service and the partner service respectively.

Put simply, the `myRole` attribute is used when the process service is invoked by a partner client service, because in this situation the process service acts as the service provider. The `partnerRole` attribute identifies the partner service that the process service will be invoking (making the partner service the service provider).

Note that both `myRole` and `partnerRole` attributes can be used by the same `partner-Link` element when it is expected that the process service will act as both service requestor and service provider with the same partner service. For example, during asynchronous communication between the process and partner services, the `myRole` setting indicates the process service's role during the callback of the partner service.

```
<partnerLinks>
    <partnerLink name="client"
        partnerLinkType="tns:TimesheetSubmissionType"
        myRole="TimesheetSubmissionServiceProvider"/>
    <partnerLink name="Invoice"
        partnerLinkType="inv:InvoiceType"
        partnerRole="InvoiceServiceProvider"/>
    <partnerLink name="Timesheet"
        partnerLinkType="tst:TimesheetType"
        partnerRole="TimesheetServiceProvider"/>
    <partnerLink name="Employee"
        partnerLinkType="emp:EmployeeType"
        partnerRole="EmployeeServiceProvider"/>
    <partnerLink name="Notification"
        partnerLinkType="not:NotificationType"
        partnerRole="NotificationServiceProvider"/>
</partnerLinks>
```

Example 16.2　The `partnerLinks` construct containing one `partnerLink` element in which the process service is invoked by an external client partner and four `partner-Link` elements that identify partner services invoked by the process service.

You'll notice that in Example 16.2, each of the `partnerLink` elements also contains a `partnerLinkType` attribute. This refers to the `partnerLinkType` construct, as explained next.

16.1.5 The `partnerLinkType` element

For each partner service involved in a process, `partnerLinkType` elements identify the WSDL `portType` elements referenced by the `partnerLink` elements within the process definition. Therefore, these constructs typically are embedded directly within the WSDL documents of every partner service (including the process service).

The `partnerLinkType` construct contains one role element for each role the service can play, as defined by the `partnerLink` `myRole` and `partnerRole` attributes. As a result, a `partnerLinkType` will have either one or two child role elements.

```
<definitions name="Employee"
   targetNamespace="http://www.xmltc.com/tls/employee/wsdl/"
   xmlns="http://schemas.xmlsoap.org/wsdl/"
   xmlns:plnk=
      "http://schemas.xmlsoap.org/ws/2003/05/partner-link/"
   ...
>
   ...
   <plnk:partnerLinkType name="EmployeeServiceType" xmlns=
      "http://schemas.xmlsoap.org/ws/2003/05/partner-link/">
      <plnk:role name="EmployeeServiceProvider">
         <portType name="emp:EmployeeInterface"/>
      </plnk:role>
   </plnk:partnerLinkType>
   ...
</definitions>
```

Example 16.3   A WSDL definitions construct containing a partnerLinkType construct.

Note that multiple partnerLink elements can reference the same partnerLinkType. This is useful for when a process service has the same relationship with multiple partner services. All of the partner services can therefore use the same process service portType elements.

> **NOTE**
>
> In version 2.0 of the WS-BPEL specification, it is being proposed that the portType element be changed so that it exists as an attribute of the role element.

16.1.6   The variables element

WS-BPEL process services commonly use the variables construct to store state information related to the immediate workflow logic. Entire messages and data sets formatted as XSD schema types can be placed into a variable and retrieved later during the course of the process. The type of data that can be assigned to a variable element needs to be predefined using one of the following three attributes: messageType, element, or type.

The messageType attribute allows for the variable to contain an entire WSDL-defined message, whereas the element attribute simply refers to an XSD element construct. The type attribute can be used to just represent an XSD simpleType, such as string or integer.

```
<variables>
   <variable name="ClientSubmission"
      messageType="bpl:receiveSubmitMessage"/>
   <variable name="EmployeeHoursRequest"
      messageType="emp:getWeeklyHoursRequestMessage"/>
   <variable name="EmployeeHoursResponse"
      messageType="emp:getWeeklyHoursResponseMessage"/>
   <variable name="EmployeeHistoryRequest"
      messageType="emp:updateHistoryRequestMessage"/>
   <variable name="EmployeeHistoryResponse"
      messageType="emp:updateHistoryResponseMessage"/>
   ...
</variables>
```

Example 16.4   The `variables` construct hosting only some of the child `variable` elements used later by the Timesheet Submission Process.

Typically, a variable with the `messageType` attribute is defined for each input and output message processed by the process definition. The value of this attribute is the message name from the partner process definition.

16.1.7   The `getVariableProperty` and `getVariableData` functions

WS-BPEL provides built-in functions that allow information stored in or associated with variables to be processed during the execution of a business process.

getVariableProperty(variable name, property name)
This function allows global property values to be retrieved from variables. It simply accepts the variable and property names as input and returns the requested value.

getVariableData(variable name, part name, location path)
Because variables commonly are used to manage state information, this function is required to provide other parts of the process logic access to this data. The `getVariableData` function has a mandatory variable name parameter and two optional arguments that can be used to specify a part of the variable data.

In our examples we use the `getVariableData` function a number of times to retrieve message data from variables.

```
getVariableData ('InvoiceHoursResponse',
                 'ResponseParameter')

getVariableData ('input','payload',
                 '/tns:TimesheetType/Hours/...')
```

Example 16.5 Two `getVariableData` functions being used to retrieve specific pieces of data from different variables.

16.1.8 The `sequence` element

The `sequence` construct allows you to organize a series of activities so that they are executed in a predefined, sequential order. WS-BPEL provides numerous activities that can be used to express the workflow logic within the process definition. The remaining element descriptions in this section explain the fundamental set of activities used as part of our upcoming case study examples.

```
<sequence>
   <receive>
      . . .
   </receive>
   <assign>
      . . .
   </assign>
   <invoke>
      . . .
   </invoke>
   <reply>
      . . .
   </reply>
</sequence>
```

Example 16.6 A skeleton `sequence` construct containing only some of the many activity elements provided by WS-BPEL.

Note that `sequence` elements can be nested, allowing you to define sequences within sequences.

16.1.9   The `invoke` element

This element identifies the operation of a partner service that the process definition intends to invoke during the course of its execution. The `invoke` element is equipped with five common attributes, which further specify the details of the invocation (Table 16.1).

Table 16.1   `invoke` element attributes

Attribute	Description
`partnerLink`	This element names the partner service via its corresponding `partnerLink`.
`portType`	The element used to identify the `portType` element of the partner service.
`operation`	The partner service operation to which the process service will need to send its request.
`inputVariable`	The input message that will be used to communicate with the partner service operation. Note that it is referred to as a variable because it is referencing a WS-BPEL `variable` element with a `messageType` attribute.
`outputVariable`	This element is used when communication is based on the request-response MEP. The return value is stored in a separate `variable` element.

```
<invoke name="ValidateWeeklyHours"
    partnerLink="Employee"
    portType="emp:EmployeeInterface"
    operation="GetWeeklyHoursLimit"
    inputVariable="EmployeeHoursRequest"
    outputVariable="EmployeeHoursResponse"/>
```

Example 16.7   The `invoke` element identifying the target partner service details.

16.1.10 The `receive` element

The `receive` element allows us to establish the information a process service expects upon receiving a request from an external client partner service. In this case, the process service is viewed as a service provider waiting to be invoked.

The `receive` element contains a set of attributes, each of which is assigned a value relating to the expected incoming communication (Table 16.2).

Table 16.2 `receive` element attributes

Attribute	Description
`partnerLink`	The client partner service identified in the corresponding `partnerLink` construct.
`portType`	The process service `portType` that will be waiting to receive the request message from the partner service.
`operation`	The process service operation that will be receiving the request.
`variable`	The process definition `variable` construct in which the incoming request message will be stored.
`createInstance`	When this attribute is set to "yes," the receipt of this particular request may be responsible for creating a new instance of the process.

Note that this element also can be used to receive callback messages during an asynchronous message exchange.

```
<receive name="receiveInput"
    partnerLink="client"
    portType="tns:TimesheetSubmissionInterface"
    operation="Submit"
    variable="ClientSubmission"
    createInstance="yes"/>
```

Example 16.8 The `receive` element used in the Timesheet Submission Process definition to indicate the client partner service responsible for launching the process with the submission of a timesheet document.

16.1.11   The `reply` element

Where there's a `receive` element, there's a `reply` element when a synchronous exchange is being mapped out. The `reply` element is responsible for establishing the details of returning a response message to the requesting client partner service. Because this element is associated with the same `partnerLink` element as its corresponding `receive` element, it repeats a number of the same attributes (Table 16.3).

Table 16.3   `reply` element attributes

Attribute	Description
partnerLink	The same `partnerLink` element established in the `receive` element.
portType	The same `portType` element displayed in the `receive` element.
operation	The same `operation` element from the `receive` element.
variable	The process service `variable` element that holds the message that is returned to the partner service.
messageExchange	It is being proposed that this optional attribute be added by the WS-BPEL 2.0 specification. It allows for the `reply` element to be explicitly associated with a message activity capable of receiving a message (such as the `receive` element).

```
<reply partnerLink="client"
    portType="tns:TimesheetSubmissionInterface"
    operation="Submit"
    variable="TimesheetSubmissionResponse"/>
```

Example 16.9   A potential companion `reply` element to the previously displayed `receive` element.

16.1.12 The `switch`, `case`, and `otherwise` elements

These three structured activity elements allow us to add conditional logic to our process definition, similar to the familiar select case/case else constructs used in traditional programming languages. The `switch` element establishes the scope of the conditional logic, wherein multiple `case` constructs can be nested to check for various conditions using a `condition` attribute. When a `condition` attribute resolves to "true," the activities defined within the corresponding `case` construct are executed.

The `otherwise` element can be added as a catch all at the end of the `switch` construct. Should all preceding `case` conditions fail, the activities within the `otherwise` construct are executed.

```
<switch>
   <case condition=
      "getVariableData('EmployeeResponseMessage',
                     'ResponseParameter')=0">
      . . .
   </case>
   <otherwise>
      . . .
   </otherwise>
</switch>
```

Example 16.10 A skeleton `case` element wherein the `condition` attribute uses the `get-VariableData` function to compare the content of the EmployeeResponseMessage variable to a zero value.

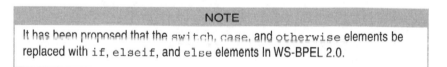

> **NOTE**
> It has been proposed that the `switch`, `case`, and `otherwise` elements be replaced with `if`, `elseif`, and `else` elements In WS-BPEL 2.0.

16.1.13 The `assign`, `copy`, `from`, and `to` elements

This set of elements simply gives us the ability to copy values between process variables, which allows us to pass around data throughout a process as information is received and modified during the process execution.

```
<assign>
  <copy>
    <from variable="TimesheetSubmissionFailedMessage"/>
    <to variable="EmployeeNotificationMessage"/>
  </copy>
  <copy>
    <from variable="TimesheetSubmissionFailedMessage"/>
    <to variable="ManagerNotificationMessage"/>
  </copy>
</assign>
```

Example 16.11 Within this `assign` construct, the contents of the `TimesheetSubmission-FailedMessage` variable are copied to two different message variables.

Note that the `copy` construct can process a variety of data transfer functions (for example, only a part of a message can be extracted and copied into a variable). `from` and `to` elements also can contain optional `part` and `query` attributes that allow for specific parts or values of the variable to be referenced.

16.1.14 `faultHandlers`, `catch`, and `catchAll` elements

This construct can contain multiple `catch` elements, each of which provides activities that perform exception handling for a specific type of error condition. Faults can be generated by the receipt of a WSDL-defined fault message, or they can be explicitly triggered through the use of the `throw` element. The `faultHandlers` construct can consist of (or end with) a `catchAll` element to house default error handling activities.

```
<faultHandlers>
   <catch faultName="SomethingBadHappened"
          faultVariable="TimesheetFault">
     ...
   </catch>
   <catchAll>
     ...
   </catchAll>
</faultHandlers>
```

Example 16.12 The `faultHandlers` construct hosting `catch` and `catchAll` child constructs.

16.1.15 Other WS-BPEL elements

The following table provides brief descriptions of other relevant parts of the WS-BPEL language.

Table 16.4 Quick reference table providing short descriptions for additional WS-BPEL elements (listed in alphabetical order).

Element	Description
compensationHandler	A WS-BPEL process definition can define a compensation process that kicks in a series of activities when certain conditions occur to justify a compensation. These activities are kept in the compensationHandler construct. (For more information about compensations, see the *Business activities* section in Chapter 6.)
correlationSets	WS-BPEL uses this element to implement correlation, primarily to associate messages with process instances. A message can belong to multiple correlationSets. Further, message properties can be defined within WSDL documents.
empty	This simple element allows you to state that no activity should occur for a particular condition.
eventHandlers	The eventHandlers element enables a process to respond to events during the execution of process logic. This construct can contain onMessage and onAlarm child elements that trigger process activity upon the arrival of specific types of messages (after a predefined period of time, or at a specific date and time, respectively).
exit	See the terminate element description that follows.
flow	A flow construct allows you to define a series of activities that can occur concurrently and are required to complete after all have finished executing. Dependencies between activities within a flow construct are defined using the child link element.
pick	Similar to the eventHandlers element, this construct also can contain child onMessage and onAlarm elements but is used more to respond to external events for which process execution is suspended.

Table 16.4   Quick reference table providing short descriptions for additional WS-BPEL elements (listed in alphabetical order) (*Continued*).

Element	Description
scope	Portions of logic within a process definition can be sub-divided into scopes using this construct. This allows you to define `variables`, `faultHandlers`, `correlationSets`, `compensationHandler`, and `eventHandlers` elements local to the scope.
terminate	This element effectively destroys the process instance. The WS-BPEL 2.0 specification proposes that this element be renamed `exit`.
throw	WS-BPEL supports numerous fault conditions. Using the `throw` element allows you to explicitly trigger a fault state in response to a specific condition.
wait	The `wait` element can be set to introduce an intentional delay within the process. Its value can be a set time or a predefined date.
while	This useful element allows you to define a loop. As with the `case` element, it contains a `condition` attribute that, as long as it continues resolving to "true," will continue to execute the activities within the `while` construct.

SUMMARY OF KEY POINTS

- A WS-BPEL process definition is represented at runtime by the process service.

- Services that participate in WS-BPEL defined processes are considered partner services and are established as part of the process definition.

- Numerous activity elements are provided by WS-BPEL to implement various types of process logic.

16.2   WS-Coordination overview

> **NOTE**
>
> Only element descriptions are provided in this section. Concepts relating to these elements are covered in Chapter 6. If you are not interested in learning about WS-Coordination syntax at this point, then feel free to skip ahead to the *Service-oriented business process design* process description. This section is not a prerequisite to continue with the remainder of the book.

Provided in this section is a brief look at WS-Coordination, which can be used to realize some of the underlying mechanics for WS-BPEL orchestrations. Specifically, we describe some of the elements from the WS-Coordination specification and look at how they are used to implement the supplementary specifications that provide coordination protocols (WS-BusinessActivity and WS-AtomicTransaction).

Note that a syntactical knowledge of these languages is generally not necessary to create WS-BPEL process definitions. We discuss these languages at this stage only to provide an insight as to how WS-Coordination can be positioned within a WS-BPEL orchestration model, and to get a glimpse at some of the syntax behind the specifications we first introduced only on a conceptual level in Chapter 6.

When we explained WS-Coordination earlier, we described the overall coordination mechanism that consists of the activation service, the registration service, a coordinator, and participants that implement specific protocols. It is likely that these underlying context management services will be automatically governed by the orchestration engine platform for which you are creating a WS-BPEL process definition.

In terms of the WS-Coordination language and its two protocol documents, what may be of interest to you is the actual `CoordinationContext` header that is inserted into SOAP messages. You may encounter this header if you are monitoring messages or if you need to perform custom development associated with the coordination context.

Also while this section briefly discusses the WS-Coordination specification within the context of the orchestration service layer, it is important to note that this specification is a standalone SOA extension in its own right. Its use is in no way dependent on WS-BPEL or an orchestration service layer.

16.2.1   The `CoordinationContext` element

This parent construct contains a series of child elements that each house a specific part of the context information being relayed by the header.

```
<Envelope
   xmlns="http://schemas.xmlsoap.org/soap/envelope/"
   xmlns:wsc=
      "http://schemas.xmlsoap.org/ws/2002/08/wscoor"
   xmlns:wsu=
      "http://schemas.xmlsoap.org/ws/2002/07/utility">
   <Header>
      <wsc:CoordinationContext>
         <wsu:Identifier>
            . . .
         </wsu:Identifier>
         <wsu:Expires>
            . . .
         </wsu:Expires>
         <wsc:CoordinationType>
            . . .
         </wsc:CoordinationType>
         <wsc:RegistrationService>
            . . .
         </wsc:RegistrationService>
      </wsc:CoordinationContext>
   </Header>
   <Body>
      . . .
   </Body>
</Envelope>
```

Example 16.13   A skeleton `CoordinationContext` construct.

The activation service returns this `CoordinationContext` header upon the creation of a new activity. As described later, it is within the `CoordinationType` child construct that the activity protocol (WS-BusinessActivity, WS-AtomicTransaction) is carried. Vendor-specific implementations of WS-Coordination can insert additional elements within the `CoordinationContext` construct that represent values related to the execution environment.

16.2.2   The `Identifier` and `Expires` elements

These two elements originate from a utility schema used to provide reusable elements. WS-Coordination uses the `Identifier` element to associate a unique ID value with the current activity. The `Expires` element sets an expiry date that establishes the extent of the activity's possible lifespan.

```
<Envelope
   ...
   xmlns:wsu=
      "http://schemas.xmlsoap.org/ws/2002/07/utility">
   ...
   <wsu:Identifier>
      http://www.xmltc.com/ids/process/33342
   </wsu:Identifier>
   <wsu:Expires>
      2008-07-30T24:00:00.000
   </wsu:Expires>
   ...
</Envelope>
```

Example 16.14   `Identifier` and `Expires` elements containing values relating to the header.

16.2.3   The `CoordinationType` element

This element is described shortly in the *WS-BusinessActivity and WS-AtomicTransaction coordination types* section.

16.2.4   The `RegistrationService` element

The `RegistrationService` construct simply hosts the endpoint address of the registration service. It uses the `Address` element also provided by the utility schema.

```
<wsc:RegistrationService>
   <wsu:Address>
      http://www.xmltc.com/bpel/req
   </wsu:Address>
</wsc:RegistrationService>
```

Example 16.15   The `RegistrationService` element containing a URL pointing to the location of the registration service.

16.2.5   Designating the WS-BusinessActivity coordination type

The specific protocol(s) that establishes the rules and constraints of the activity are identified within the `CoordinationType` element. The URI values that are placed here are predefined within the WS-BusinessActivity and WS-AtomicTransaction specifications.

This first example shows the `CoordinationType` element containing the WS-BusinessActivity coordination type identifier. This would indicate that the activity for which the header is carrying context information is a potentially long-running activity.

```
<wsc:CoordinationType>
   http://schemas.xmlsoap.org/ws/2004/01/wsba
</wsc:CoordinationType>
```

Example 16.16   The `CoordinationType` element representing the WS-BusinessActivity protocol.

16.2.6   Designating the WS-AtomicTransaction coordination type

In the next example, the `CoordinationType` element is assigned the WS-AtomicTransaction coordination type identifier, which communicates the fact that the header's context information is part of a short running transaction.

```
<wsc:CoordinationType>
   http://schemas.xmlsoap.org/ws/2003/09/wsat
</wsc:CoordinationType>
```

Example 16.17   The `CoordinationType` element representing the WS-AtomicTransaction protocol.

SUMMARY OF KEY POINTS

- WS-Coordination provides a sophisticated context management system that may be leveraged by WS-BPEL.

- WS-BusinessActivity and WS-AtomicTransaction define specific protocols for use with WS-Coordination.

16.3 Service-oriented business process design (a step-by-step process)

Designing the process of a service-oriented solution really just comes down to properly interpreting the business process requirements you have collected and then implementing them accurately. The trick, though, is to also account for all possible variations of process activity. This means understanding not just *what* can go wrong, but *how* the process will respond to unexpected or abnormal conditions.

Historically, business processes were designed by analysts using modeling tools that produced diagrams handed over to architects and developers for implementation. The workflow diagram and its accompanying documentation were the sole means of communicating how this logic should be realized within an automated solution. While diligent analysis and documentation, coupled with open minded and business-aware technical expertise, can lead to a successful collaboration of business and technical team members, this approach does leave significant room for error.

This gap is being addressed by operational business modeling languages, such as WS-BPEL. Modeling tools exist, allowing technical analysts and architects to graphically create business process diagrams that represent their workflow logic requirements, all the while auto-generating WS-BPEL syntax in the background.

These tools typically require that the user possess significant knowledge of the WS-BPEL language. However, more sophisticated tools, geared directly at business analysts, already are emerging, removing the prerequisite of having to understand WS-BPEL to create WS-BPEL process definitions.

The result is a diagram on the front-end that expresses the analysts' vision of the process and a computer executable process definition on the back-end that can be handed over to architects and developers for immediate (and not-open-to-interpretation) implementation (Figure 16.2).

When operational, the WS-BPEL process is appropriately represented and expressed through a process service within the service interface layer. This process service effectively establishes the orchestration service sub-layer, responsible for governing and composing business and application layers.

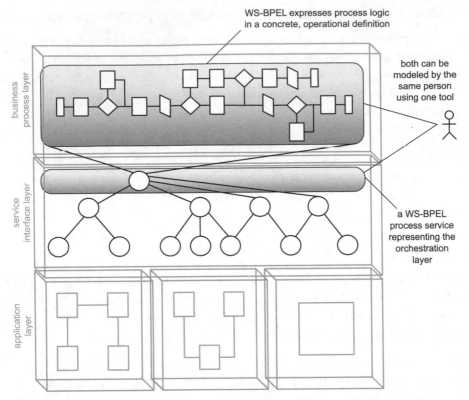

Figure 16.2

A concrete definition of a process service designed using a process modeling tool.

16.3.1 Process description

The following step-by-step design process (Figure 16.3) provides some high-level guidance for how to approach the creation of a WS-BPEL process definition. The steps are similar to those used by the *Task-centric business service design* process described in Chapter 15, except for one important detail.

When we designed a task-centric service, we simply produced a service interface capable of handling anticipated message exchanges. The details of the workflow logic were deferred to the design and development of the underlying application logic. When designing a WS-BPEL process, this workflow logic is abstracted into a separate process definition. Therefore, the design of workflow details is addressed at this stage, along with the definition of the process service interface.

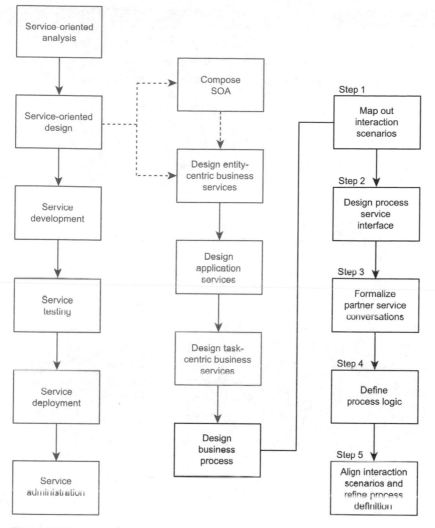

Figure 16.3

A high-level process for designing business processes.

The examples used to demonstrate each step are intentionally simple so that the basic WS-BPEL element descriptions we just covered in the previous section can be easily understood. When designing more complex workflow logic, a more detailed and elaborate design process is required.

Business process design is the last step in our overall service-oriented design process. This means that, for the most part, the application and business services required to carry out the process logic will have already been modeled and designed as we begin.

The original workflow logic for the TLS Timesheet Submission Process (Figure 16.4) that was created during the modeling exercise in Chapter 12 is revisited as TLS analysts and architects embark on designing a corresponding WS-BPEL process definition.

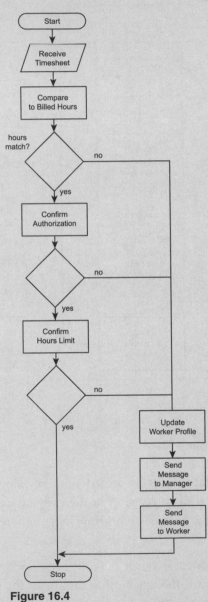

Figure 16.4
The original TLS Timesheet Submission Process.

As part of completing the previous service design processes, TLS now has the inventory of service designs displayed in Figure 16.5. In our previous case study examples, we only stepped through the creation of the Employee Service. The other service designs are provided here to help demonstrate the WS-BPEL partner links we define later on.

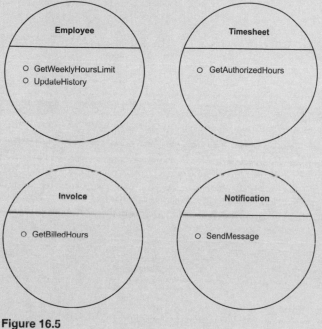

Figure 16.5
Service designs created so far.

TLS also digs out the original composition diagram (Figure 16.6) that shows how these four services form a hierarchical composition, spearheaded by the Timesheet Submission Process Service TLS plans to build.

Finally, TLS architects revive the original service candidate created for the Timesheet Submission Process Service (Figure 16.7).

With all of this information in hand, TLS proceeds with the business process design.

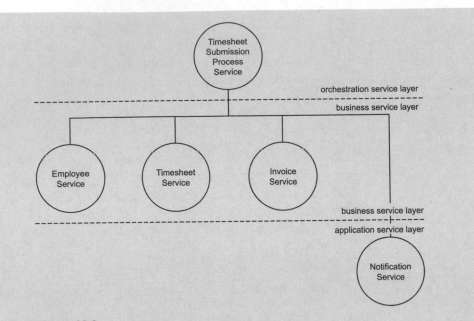

Figure 16.6

The original service composition defined during the service modeling stage.

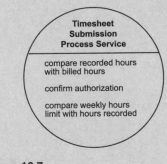

Figure 16.7

The Timesheet Submission Process Service candidate.

Step 1: Map out interaction scenarios

By using the following information gathered so far, we can define the message exchange requirements of our process service:

- Available workflow logic produced during the service modeling process in Chapter 12.

- The process service candidate created in Chapter 12.

- The existing service designs created in Chapter 15.

This information now is used to form the basis of an analysis during which all possible interaction scenarios between process and partner services are mapped out. The result is a series of processing requirements that will form the basis of the process service design we proceed to in Step 2.

CASE STUDY

TLS maps out a series of different service interaction scenarios using activity diagrams. Following are examples of two scenarios.

Figure 16.8 illustrates the interaction between services required to successfully complete the Timesheet Submission Process with a valid timesheet submission. Note that in this scenario, the Notification Service is not used.

Figure 16.9 demonstrates a scenario in which the timesheet document is rejected by the Timesheet Service. This occurs because the timesheet failed to receive proper authorization.

The result of mapping out interaction scenarios establishes that the process service has one potential client partner service and four potential partner services from which it may need to invoke up to five operations (Figure 16.10).

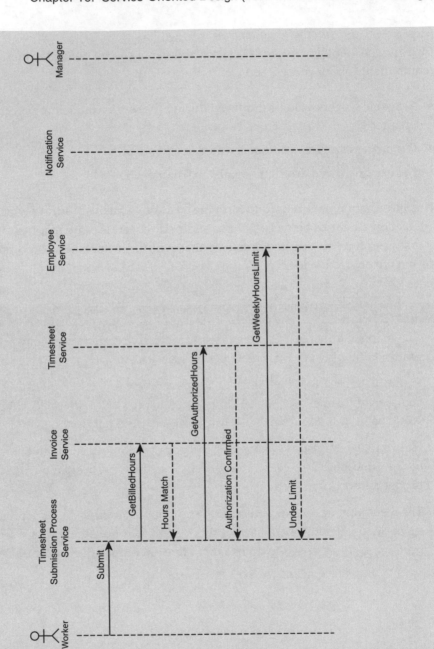

Figure 16.8

A successful completion of the Timesheet Submission Process.

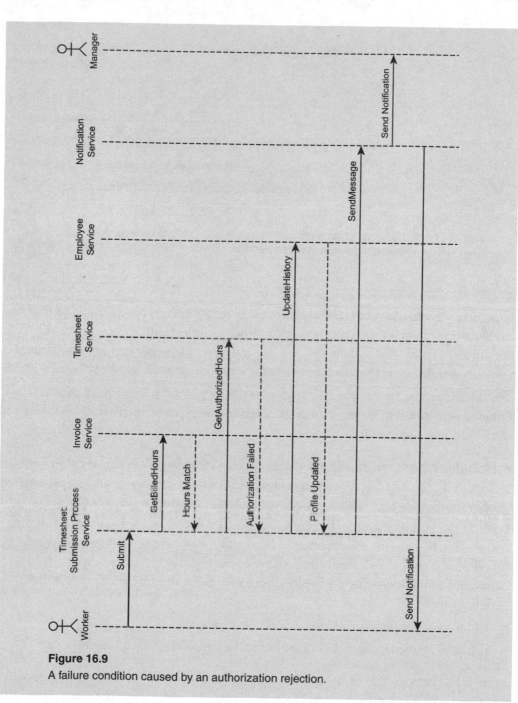

Figure 16.9

A failure condition caused by an authorization rejection.

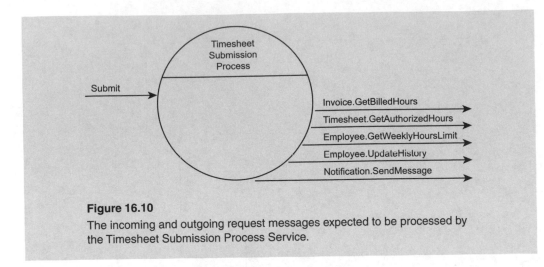

Figure 16.10

The incoming and outgoing request messages expected to be processed by
the Timesheet Submission Process Service.

Step 2: Design the process service interface

Now that we understand the message exchange requirements, we can proceed to define
a service definition for the process service. When working with process modeling tools,
the process service WSDL definition will typically be auto-generated for you. However,
you also should be able to edit the source markup code or even import your own WSDL
definition.

Either way, it is best to review the WSDL definition being used and revise it as necessary.
Here are some suggestions:

- Document the input and output values required for the processing of each operation, and populate the `types` section with XSD schema types required to process the
  operations. Move the XSD schema information to a separate file, if required.

- Build the WSDL definition by creating the `portType` (or `interface`) area, inserting
  the identified `operation` constructs. Then add the necessary `message` constructs
  containing the `part` elements that reference the appropriate schema types. Add
  naming conventions that are in alignment with those used by your other WSDL
  definitions.

- Add meta information via the `documentation` element.

- Apply additional design standards within the confines of the modeling tool.

There is less opportunity to incorporate the other steps from the service design processes
described in Chapter 15. For example, applying the service-orientation principle of
statelessness is difficult, given that process services maintain state so that other services
don't have to.

It looks like the Timesheet Submission Process Service interface will be pretty straightforward. It only requires one operation used by a client to initiate the process instance (Figure 16.11).

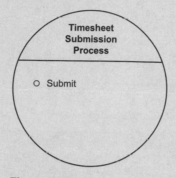

Figure 16.11
Timesheet Submission Process
Service design.

Following is the corresponding WSDL definition:

```
<definitions name="TimesheetSubmission"
   targetNamespace="http://www.xmltc.com/tls/process/wsdl/"
   xmlns="http://schemas.xmlsoap.org/wsdl/"
   xmlns:ts="http://www.xmltc.com/tls/timesheet/schema/"
   xmlns:tsd=
      "http://www.xmltc.com/tls/timesheetservice/schema/"
   xmlns:soap="http://schemas.xmlsoap.org/wsdl/soap/"
   xmlns:tns="http://www.xmltc.com/tls/timesheet/wsdl/"
   xmlns:plnk=
      "http://schemas.xmlsoap.org/ws/2003/05/partner-link/">
<types>
   <xsd:schema xmlns:xsd="http://www.w3.org/2001/XMLSchema"
      targetNamespace=
      "http://www.xmltc.com/tls/
         timesheetsubmissionservice/schema/">
      <xsd:import namespace=
         "http://www.xmltc.com/tls/timesheet/schema/"
         schemaLocation="Timesheet.xsd"/>
      <xsd:element name="Submit">
        <xsd:complexType>
          <xsd:sequence>
            <xsd:element name="ContextID"
```

```
                              type="xsd:integer"/>
                  <xsd:element name="TimesheetDocument"
                      type="ts:TimesheetType"/>
              </xsd:sequence>
          </xsd:complexType>
      </xsd:element>
    </xsd:schema>
</types>
<message name="receiveSubmitMessage">
    <part name="Payload" element="tsd:TimesheetType"/>
</message>
<portType name="TimesheetSubmissionInterface">
    <documentation>
        Initiates the Timesheet Submission Process.
    </documentation>
    <operation name="Submit">
        <input message="tns:receiveSubmitMessage"/>
    </operation>
</portType>
<plnk:partnerLinkType name="TimesheetSubmissionType">
    <plnk:role name="TimesheetSubmissionService">
        <plnk:portType
            name="tns:TimesheetSubmissionInterface"/>
    </plnk:role>
</plnk:partnerLinkType>
</definitions>
```

Example 16.18   The abstract service definition for the Timesheet Submission
                Process Service.

Note the bolded `plnk:parnterLinkType` construct at the end of this WSDL definition. This is added to every partner service.

Step 3: Formalize partner service conversations
We now begin our WS-BPEL process definition by establishing details about the services
with which our process service will be interacting.

The following steps are suggested:

1. Define the partner services that will be participating in the process and assign each
   the role it will be playing within a given message exchange.

2. Add `parterLinkType` constructs to the end of the WSDL definitions of each partner service.

3. Create `partnerLink` elements for each partner service within the process definition.

4. Define `variable` elements to represent incoming and outgoing messages exchanged with partner services.

This information essentially documents the possible conversation flows that can occur within the course of the process execution. Depending on the process modeling tool used, completing these steps may simply require interaction with the user-interface provided by the modeling tool.

CASE STUDY

Now that the Timesheet Submission Process Service has an interface, TLS can begin to work on the corresponding process definition. It begins by looking at the information it gathered in Step 1. As you may recall, TLS determined the process service as having one potential client partner service and four potential partner services from which it may need to invoke up to five operations.

Roles are assigned to each of these services, labeled according to how they relate to the process service. These roles are then formally defined by appending existing service WSDL definitions with a `partnerLinkType` construct.

Example 16.19 shows how the Employee Service definition (as designed in Chapter 15) is amended to incorporate the WS-BPEL `partnerLinkType` construct and its corresponding namespace.

```
<definitions
    name="Employee"
    targetNamespace="http://www.xmltc.com/tls/employee/wsdl/"
    xmlns="http://schemas.xmlsoap.org/wsdl/"
    xmlns:act=
        "http://www.xmltc.com/tls/employee/schema/accounting/"
    xmlns:hr="http://www.xmltc.com/tls/employee/schema/hr/"
    xmlns:soap="http://schemas.xmlsoap.org/wsdl/soap/"
    xmlns:tns="http://www.xmltc.com/tls/employee/wsdl/"
    xmlns:plnk=
        "http://schemas.xmlsoap.org/ws/2003/05/partner-link/">
    ...
    <plnk:partnerLinkType name="EmployeeType">
        <plnk:role name="EmployeeService">
            <plnk:portType name="tns:EmployeeInterface"/>
```

```
        </plnk:role>
    </plnk:partnerLinkType>
</definitions>
```

Example 16.19   The revised Employee service `definitions` construct.

This is formalized within the process definition through the creation of `partner-Link` elements that reside within the `partnerLinks` construct. TLS analysts and architects work with a process modeling tool to drag and drop `partnerLink` objects, resulting in the following code being generated.

```
<partnerLinks>
    <partnerLink name="client"
        partnerLinkType="bpl:TimesheetSubmissionProcessType"
        myRole="TimesheetSubmissionProcessServiceProvider"/>
    <partnerLink name="Invoice"
        partnerLinkType="inv:InvoiceType"
        partnerRole="InvoiceServiceProvider"/>
    <partnerLink name="Timesheet"
        partnerLinkType="tst:TimesheetType"
        partnerRole="TimesheetServiceProvider"/>
    <partnerLink name="Employee"
        partnerLinkType="emp:EmployeeType"
        partnerRole="EmployeeServiceProvider"/>
    <partnerLink name="Notification"
        partnerLinkType="not:NotificationType"
        partnerRole="NotificationServiceProvider"/>
</partnerLinks>
```

Example 16.20   The `partnerLinks` construct containing `partnerLink` elements for each of the process partner services.

Next the input and output messages of each partner service are assigned to individual `variable` elements, as part of the `variables` construct. A `variable` element also is added to represent the Timesheet Submission Process Service Submit operation that is called by the HR client application to kick off the process.

```
<variables>
  <variable name="ClientSubmission"
    messageType="bpl:receiveSubmitMessage"/>
  <variable name="EmployeeHoursRequest"
    messageType="emp:getWeeklyHoursRequestMessage"/>
  <variable name="EmployeeHoursResponse"
    messageType="emp:getWeeklyHoursResponseMessage"/>
  <variable name="EmployeeHistoryRequest"
    messageType="emp:updateHistoryRequestMessage"/>
  <variable name="EmployeeHistoryResponse"
    messageType="emp:updateHistoryResponseMessage"/>
  <variable name="InvoiceHoursRequest"
    messageType="inv:getBilledHoursRequestMessage"/>
  <variable name="InvoiceHoursResponse"
    messageType="inv:getBilledHoursResponseMessage"/>
  <variable name="TimesheetAuthorizationRequest"
    messageType="tst:getAuthorizedHoursRequestMessage"/>
  <variable name="TimesheetAuthorizationResponse"
    messageType="tst:getAuthorizedHoursResponseMessage"/>
  <variable name="NotificationRequest"
    messageType="not:sendMessage"/>
</variables>
```

Example 16.21   The `variables` construct containing individual `variable` elements representing input and output messages from all partner services and for the process service itself.

If you check back to the Employee Service definition TLS designed in Chapter 15, you'll notice that the `name` values of the `message` elements correspond to the values assigned to the `messageType` attributes in the previously displayed `variable` elements.

Step 4: Define process logic

Finally, everything is in place for us to complete the process definition. This step is a process in itself, as it requires that all existing workflow intelligence be transposed and implemented via a WS-BPEL process definition.

CASE STUDY

The TLS team now creates a process definition that expresses the original work-flow logic and processing requirements, while accounting for the two service interaction scenarios identified earlier. The remainder of this example explores the details of this process definition.

A visual representation of the process logic about to be defined in WS-BPEL syntax is displayed in Figure 16.12. (Note that this diagram illustrates the process flow that corresponds to the success condition expressed by the first of the two activity diagrams created during Step 1.)

> **NOTE**
>
> The complete process definition is several pages long and therefore is not displayed here. Instead, we highlight relevant parts of the process, such as activities and fault handling. The entire process definition is available for download at www.soabooks.com.

Established first is a `receive` element that offers the Submit operation of the Timesheet Submission Process Service to an external HR client as the means by which the process is instantiated.

```
<receive xmlns=
    "http://schemas.xmlsoap.org/ws/2003/03/business-process/"
    name="receiveInput"
    partnerLink="client"
    portType="tns:TimesheetSubmissionInterface"
    operation="Submit"
    variable="ClientSubmission"
    createInstance="yes"/>
```

Example 16.22   The `receive` element providing an entry point by which the process can be initiated.

By tracing the `receive` element's `operation` value back to the original Timesheet Submission Service WSDL, you can find out that the expected format of the input data will be a complete timesheet document, defined in a separate XSD schema document. When a document is received, it is stored in the ClientSubmission process variable.

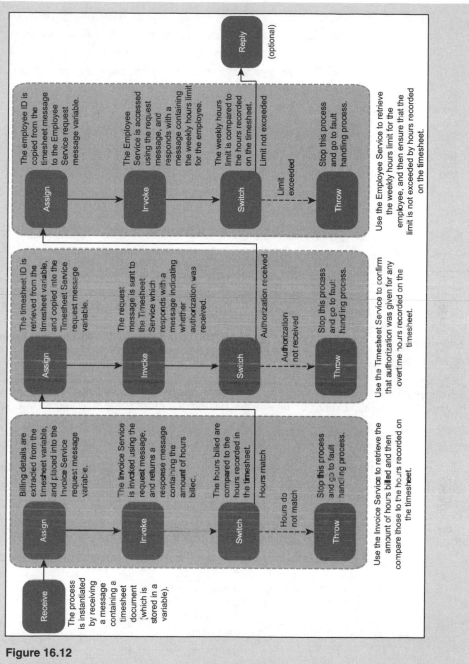

Figure 16.12

A descriptive, diagrammatic view of the process definition logic.

As per the interaction logic defined in the initial activity diagram (Step 1), the first activity the process is required to perform is to interact with the Invoice Service to compare the hours submitted on the timesheet with the hours actually billed out to the client. The Invoice Service will not perform the comparison for the process; instead, it will simply provide the amount of hours for a given invoice identified by an invoice number.

Before invoking the Invoice Service, the `assign` construct first needs to be used to extract values from the original timesheet document, which now is stored in the ClientSubmission variable. Specifically, the customer ID and date values (encapsulated in the `BillingInfo` element) are required as input for the Invoice Service's GetBilledHours operation.

```
<assign name="GetInvoiceID">
   <copy>
      <from variable="ClientSubmission" part="payload"
         query="/TimesheetType/BillingInfo"/>
      <to variable="InvoiceHoursRequest"
         part="RequestParameter"/>
   </copy>
</assign>
```

Example 16.23   The `assign` and `copy` constructs hosting a `from` element that retrieves customer billing information from the message stored in the ClientSubmission variable and a `to` element that is used to assign these values to the InvoiceHoursRequest variable.

Now that the InvoiceHoursRequest variable contains the required input values for the Invoice Service's GetBilledHours operation, the `invoke` element is added.

```
<invoke name="ValidateInvoiceHours"
   partnerLink="Invoice"
   operation="GetBilledHours"
   inputVariable="InvoiceHoursRequest"
   outputVariable="InvoiceHoursResponse"
   portType="inv:InvoiceInterface"/>
```

Example 16.24   The `invoke` element containing a series of attributes that provide all of the information necessary for the orchestration engine to locate and instantiate the Invoice Service.

Upon invoking the Invoice Service, a response message is received from the Get-BilledHours operation. As defined in the `invoke` element's `outputVariable` attribute, this message is stored in the InvoiceHoursResponse variable.

If the value in this variable matches the value in the timesheet document, then the hours have been validated. To determine this, the `switch` construct is used. A child `case` construct is added, which contains a `condition` attribute in which the conditional logic is defined.

```
<switch name="BilledHoursMatch">
   <case condition=
      "getVariableData('InvoiceHoursResponse',
                       'ResponseParameter') !=
      getVariableData('input','payload',
                      '/tns:TimesheetType/Hours/...')">
      <throw name="ValidationFailed"
         faultName="ValidateInvoiceHoursFailed"/>
   </case>
</switch>
```

Example 16.25　The `switch` construct hosting a `case` element that uses the `getVariableData` function within its `condition` attribute to compare hours billed against hours recorded.

If the condition (billed hours is not equal to invoiced hours) is not met, then the hours recorded on the submitted timesheet document are considered valid, and the process moves to the next step.

If the condition *is* met, a fault is thrown using the `throw` element. This circumstance sends the overall business activity to the `faultHandlers` construct, which resides outside of the main process flow. This is the scenario portrayed in the second of the two activity diagrams assembled by TLS in Step 1 and is explained later in this example.

What TLS has just defined is a pattern consisting of the following steps:

1. Use the `assign`, `copy`, `from`, and `to` elements to retrieve data from the ClientSubmission variable and assign it to a variable containing an outbound message.

2. Use the `invoke` element to interact with a partner service by sending it the outbound message and receiving its response message.

3. Use the `switch` and `case` elements to retrieve and validate a value from the response message.

4. Use the `throw` element to trigger a fault, if validation fails.

A good part of the remaining process logic repeats this pattern, as illustrated in the original process overview displayed back in Figure 16.12. For brevity, this part of the process is summarized here:

- Use the `assign` construct to copy the TimesheetID value from the ClientSubmission variable to the TimesheetAuthorizationRequest variable that is used via the `invoke` element as the input message for the GetAuthorizedHours operation of the Timesheet service. The authorization result is extracted from the response message within the `switch` construct, and if positive, the process proceeds to the next step. If authorization fails, a fault is raised using the `throw` element.

- Using the `assign` element, the EmployeeID value is retrieved from the ClientSubmission variable and placed in the EmployeeHoursRequest variable. This variable becomes the request message used by the `invoke` element to communicate with the Employee Service's GetWeeklyHoursLimit operation. The response message from that operation is submitted to the `condition` attribute of the `case` element within the `switch` construct. The result is a determination as to whether the employee exceeded the allowed maximum hours per week. If the value was exceeded, the process jumps to the `fault-Handlers` construct.

That pretty much sums up the primary processing logic of the TLS Timesheet Submission Process. Although the initial requirements do not call for it, the process flow could end with a `reply` element that responds to the initial client that instantiated the process.

Now it's time to turn our attention to the second scenario (portraying a failure condition) mapped out in the other activity diagram from Step 1. To accommodate this situation, TLS architects choose to implement a `faultHandlers` construct, as shown here:

```
<faultHandlers>
   <catchAll>
      <sequence>
```

```
        . . .
      </sequence>
    </catchAll>
</faultHandlers>
```

Example 16.26   The `faultHandlers` construct used in this process.

Although individual `catch` elements could be used to trap specific faults, TLS simply employs a `catchAll` construct, as all three thrown faults require the same exception handling logic.

The tasks performed by the fault handler routine are:

1. Update employee profile history.
2. Send notification to manager.
3. Send notification to employee.

To implement these three tasks, the same familiar `assign` and `invoke` elements are used. Figure 16.13 shows an overview of the fault handling process logic.

Note that the following, abbreviated markup code samples reside within the `sequence` child construct of the parent `faultHandlers` construct established in the previous example.

First up is the markup code for the "Update employee profile history" task.

```
<assign name="SetEmployeeMessage">
   <copy>
      <from variable="ClientSubmission" .../>
      <to variable="EmployeeHistoryRequest" .../>
   </copy>
   <copy>
      <from expression="..."/>
      <to variable="EmployeeHistoryRequest" .../>
   </copy>
</assign>
<invoke name="UpdateHistory"
   partnerLink="Employee"
   portType="emp:EmployeeInterface"
   operation="UpdateHistory"
   inputVariable="EmployeeHistoryRequest"
   outputVariable="EmployeeHistoryResponse"/>
```

Example 16.27   Two copy elements used to populate the EmployeeHistoryRequest
                    message.

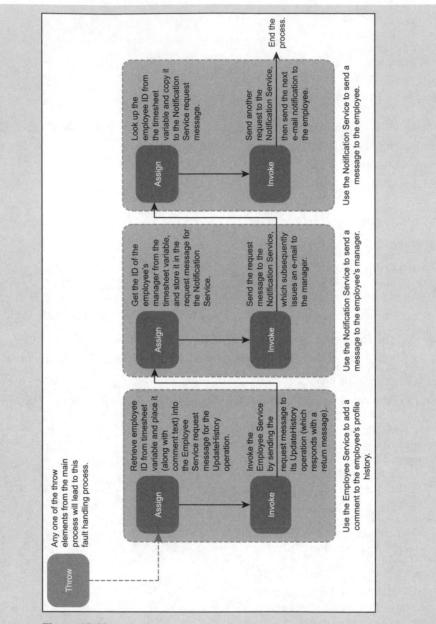

Figure 16.13

A visual representation of the process logic within the `fault-Handlers` construct.

To perform the first task of updating the employee history, the fault handler routine uses an `assign` construct with two `copy` constructs. The first retrieves the EmployeeID value from the ClientSubmission variable, while the latter adds a static employee profile history comment.

The `invoke` element then launches the Employee Service (used previously for its GetWeeklyHoursLimit operation) and submits the EmployeeHistoryRequest message to its UpdateHistory operation to log the profile history comment.

The next block of markup code takes care of both the remaining "Send notification" tasks.

```
<assign name="GetManagerID">
   <copy>
      <from expression="getVariableData(...)"/>
      <to variable="NotificationRequest" .../>
   </copy>
</assign>
<invoke name="SendNotification"
   partnerLink="Notification"
   portType="not:NotificationInterface"
   operation="SendMessage"
   inputVariable="NotificationRequest"/>
<assign name="GetEmployeeID">
   <copy>
      <from expression="getVariableData(...)"/>
      <to variable="NotificationRequest" .../>
   </copy>
</assign>
<invoke name="SendNotification"
   partnerLink="Notification"
   portType="not:NotificationInterface"
   operation="SendMessage"
   inputVariable="NotificationRequest"/>
<terminate name="EndTimesheetSubmissionProcess"/>
```

Example 16.28 The last activities in the process.

The `faultHandlers` construct contains two more `assign` + `invoke` element pairs. Both use the Notification Service's SendMessage operation, but in different ways. The first `assign` construct extracts the ManagerID value from the ClientSubmission variable, which is then passed to the Notification Service. It is

the sole parameter that the service subsequently uses to look up the corresponding e-mail address for the notification message.

Next, the second `assign` construct retrieves the EmployeeID value from the same
ClientSubmission variable, which the Notification Service ends up using to send
a message to the employee.

The very last element in the construct, `terminate`, halts all further processing.

Step 5: Align interaction scenarios and refine process (optional)
This final, optional step encourages you to perform two specific tasks: revisit the original interaction scenarios created in Step 1 and review the WS-BPEL process definition to
look for optimization opportunities.

Let's start with the first task. Bringing the interaction scenarios in alignment with the
process logic expressed in the WS-BPEL process definition provides a number of benefits, including:

- The service interaction maps (as activity diagrams or in whatever format you created them) are an important part of the solution documentation and will be useful
  for future maintenance and knowledge transfer requirements.

- The service interaction maps make for great test cases and can spare testers from
  having to perform speculative analysis.

- The implementation of the original workflow logic as a series of WS-BPEL activities
  may have introduced new or augmented process logic. Once compared to the existing interaction scenarios, the need for additional service interactions may arise,
  leading to the discovery of new fault or exception conditions that then can be
  addressed back in the WS-BPEL process definition.

Secondly, spending some extra time to review your WS-BPEL process definition is well
worth the effort. WS-BPEL is a multi-feature language that provides different
approaches for accomplishing and structuring the same overall activities. By refining
your process definition, you may be able to:

- Consolidate or restructure activities to achieve performance improvements.
- Streamline the markup code to make maintenance easier.
- Discover features that were previously not considered.

CASE STUDY

TLS analysts and architects revise their original activity diagrams so that they accurately reflect the manner in which process logic was modeled using WS-BPEL. However, in reviewing the interaction scenarios and their current process model, they recognize a key refinement that could significantly optimize the process definition they just created.

Here's a recap of the three primary tasks performed by this process:

1. Validate recorded timesheet hours with hours billed on invoice.
2. Confirm authorization of timesheet.
3. Ensure that hours submitted are equal to or less than the weekly hours limit.

As shown in Figure 16.14, the process has been designed so that these three tasks execute sequentially (one begins only after the former ends). Although this approach is useful when dependencies between tasks exist, it is determined that there are no such dependencies between these three tasks.

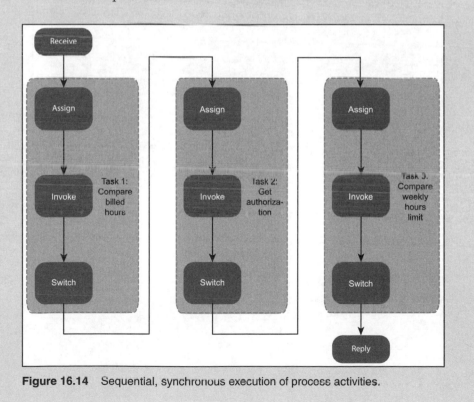

Figure 16.14   Sequential, synchronous execution of process activities.

Therefore, they all can be executed at the same time, the only condition being that the process cannot continue beyond these tasks until all have completed. This establishes a parallel processing model.

By utilizing the WS-BPEL `flow` construct, TLS can model the three activities to execute concurrently (Figure 16.15), resulting in significant performance gains. It is further determined that the same form of optimization can be applied to the process logic within the fault handling routine, as neither of those activities have inter-dependencies either.

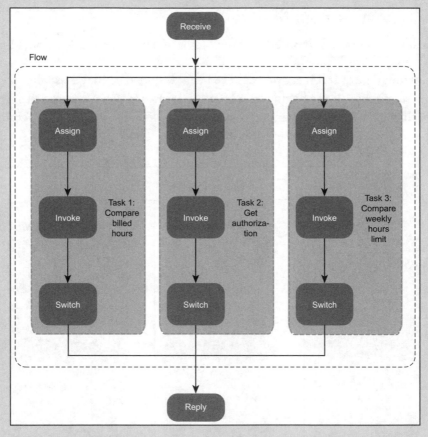

Figure 16.15   Concurrent execution of process activities using the `flow` construct.

Finally, while reviewing the structure of the fault handling routine, a further refinement is suggested. Because the last two activities invoke the same Notification Service, they can be collapsed into a `while` construct that loops twice through the `invoke` element.

SUMMARY OF KEY POINTS

- Designing a process service requires the design of the service interface and the design of the process definition.

- Process definition is typically accomplished using a graphical modeling tool, but familiarity with WS-BPEL language basics is often still required.

- There are numerous ways in which WS-BPEL process definitions can be streamlined and optimized.

Chapter 17

Fundamental WS-* Extensions

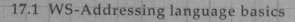

Now that we've established the primary service sub-layers of our service-oriented environment, it is a good time to consider additional means of extending the feature-set of SOA.

This chapter provides entry-level, syntactical overviews of the following five key WS-* extensions:

- WS-Addressing
- WS-ReliableMessaging
- WS-Policy Framework
- WS-MetadataExchange
- WS-Security Framework

We first introduced concepts relating to the features provided by these specifications in Chapter 7. We now round out that discussion with a series of language element descriptions that provides some technical insight into how these features are realized.

You `mustUnderstand` this

When we introduced the primary SOAP elements in Chapter 12, we also discussed the importance of the `mustUnderstand` attribute. Worth noting at this point is that this attribute can be used with the headers discussed throughout this chapter to ensure that recipient services are required to acknowledge and process key parts of the SOAP header.

> **How case studies are used:** This chapter provides a series of markup code samples that correspond to the case study examples provided in the *Addressing, Reliable messaging, Policies, Metadata exchange*, and *Security* sections of Chapter 7. Essentially, the examples explained in Chapter 7 are shown in their implemented form here.

17.1   WS-Addressing language basics

> **NOTE**
>
> Only element descriptions are provided in this section. Concepts relating to WS-Addressing are covered in Chapter 7. If you have not yet read Chapter 7, it is recommended you do so before proceeding.

The most common implementations of WS-Addressing standardize the representation of service endpoint locations and unique correlation values that tie together request and response exchanges. However, additional features are available that allow for the design of highly self-sufficient SOAP messages. Specifically, WS-Addressing includes extensions that support endpoint references for pointing messages to specific instances of Web services and message information (MI) headers that outfit messages with various types of transportation details.

WS-Addressing is a core WS-* extension providing features that can be used intrinsically or alongside features offered by other WS-* specifications. Figure 17.1 shows how WS-Addressing relates to the other extensions covered by this chapter.

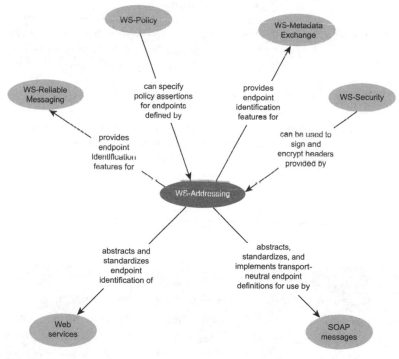

Figure 17.1

How WS-Addressing relates to the other WS-* specifications discussed in this chapter.

17.1.1 The `EndpointReference` element

The `EndpointReference` element is used by the `From`, `ReplyTo`, and `FaultTo` elements described in the *Message information header elements* section. This construct can be comprised of a set of elements that assist in providing service interface information (including supplementary metadata), as well as the identification of service instances.

The WS-Addressing elements described in Table 17.1 can be associated with an `EndpointReference` construct.

Table 17.1 WS-Addressing endpoint reference elements.

Element	Description
Address	The standard WS-Addressing `Address` element used to provide the address of the service. This is the only required child element of the `EndpointReference` element.
ReferenceProperties	This construct can contain a series of child elements that provide details of properties associated with a service instance.
ReferenceParameters	Also a construct that can supply further child elements containing parameter values used for processing service instance exchanges.
PortType	The name of the service `portType`.
ServiceName and PortName	The names of the `service` and `port` elements that are part of the destination service WSDL `definition` construct.
Policy	This element can be used to establish related WS-Policy policy assertion information.

CASE STUDY

Following is a sample `EndpointReference` construct generated to express information specific to a RailCo Accounts Payable Service instance. Note the application-specific child elements added in the `ReferenceProperties` and `ReferenceParameters` constructs.

```
<wsa:EndpointReference>
   <wsa:Address>
      http://www.xmltc.com/railco/...
   </wsa:Address>
   <wsa:ReferenceProperties>
      <app:id>
         unn:AFJK3231lws
      </app:id>
   </wsa:ReferenceProperties>
   <wsa:ReferenceParameters>
      <app:sesno>
        22322447
      </app:sesno>
   </wsa:ReferenceParameters>
</wsa:EndpointReference>
```

Example 17.1 A SOAP header containing the `EndpointReference` construct.

To see how this information is implemented within a SOAP header, skip to the next example.

17.1.2   Message information header elements

This collection of elements (first introduced as concepts in Chapter 7) can be used in various ways to assemble metadata-rich SOAP header blocks. Table 17.2 lists the primary elements and provides brief descriptions.

Table 17.2   WS-Addressing message information header elements

Element	Description
MessageID	An element used to hold a unique message identifier, most likely for correlation purposes. This element is required if the `ReplyTo` or `FaultTo` elements are used.
RelatesTo	This is also a correlation header element used to explicitly associate the current message with another. This element is required if the message is a reply to a request.
ReplyTo	The reply endpoint (of type `EndpointReference`) used to indicate which endpoint the recipient service should send a response to upon receiving the message. This element requires the use of `MessageID`.

Table 17.2   WS-Addressing message information header elements (*Continued*)

Element	Description
From	The source endpoint element (of type `EndpointReference`) that conveys the source endpoint address of the message.
FaultTo	The fault endpoint element (also of type `EndpointReference`) that provides the address to which a fault notification should be sent. `FaultTo` also requires the use of `MessageID`.
To	The destination element used to establish the endpoint address to which the current message is being delivered.
Action	This element contains a URI value that represents an action to be performed when processing the MI header.

The following case study example describes a SOAP envelope containing a header block consisting of two MI Header elements.

CASE STUDY

At the end of the *Addressing* section in Chapter 7, an example was provided in which RailCo and TLS exchanged messages across service pools. Following is a sample of the type of message issued by RailCo's Accounts Payable Service to TLS's Vendor Profile Service. The `From`, `ReplyTo`, and `FaultTo` elements contain endpoint reference information with different `Address` values.

```
<Envelope
   xmlns="http://schemas.xmlsoap.org/soap/envelope/"
   xmlns:wsa=
      "http://schemas.xmlsoap.org/ws/2004/08/addressing"
   xmlns:app="http://www.xmltc.com/railco/...">
   <Header>
      <wsa:Action>
         http://www.xmltc.com/tls/vp/submit
      </wsa:Action>
      <wsa:To>
         http://www.xmltc.com/tls/vp/...
      </wsa:To>
```

```
<wsa:From>
   <wsa:Address>
      http://www.xmltc.com/railco/ap1/...
   </wsa:Address>
   <wsa:ReferenceProperties>
      <app:id>
         unn:AFJK323llws
      </app:id>
   </wsa:ReferenceProperties>
   <wsa:ReferenceParameters>
      <app:sesno>
         22322447
      </app:sesno>
   </wsa:ReferenceParameters>
</wsa:From>
<wsa:MessageID>
   uuid:243234234-43gf433
</wsa:MessageID>
<wsa:ReplyTo>
   <wsa:Address>
      http://www.xmltc.com/railco/ap2/
   </wsa:Address>
   <wsa:ReferenceProperties>
      <app:id>
         unn:AFJK323llws
      </app:id>
   </wsa:ReferenceProperties>
   <wsa:ReferenceParameters>
      <app:sesno>
         22322447
      </app:sesno>
   </wsa:ReferenceParameters>
</wsa:ReplyTo>
<wsa:FaultTo>
   <wsa:Address>
      http://www.xmltc.com/railco/ap-err/
   </wsa:Address>
   <wsa:ReferenceProperties>
      <app:id>
         unn:AFJK323llws
      </app:id>
   </wsa:ReferenceProperties>
   <wsa:ReferenceParameters>
      <app:sesno>
         22322447
      </app:sesno>
   </wsa:ReferenceParameters>
</wsa:ReferenceParameters>
```

```
    </wsa:FaultTo>
  </Header>
  <Body>
    ...
  </Body>
</Envelope>
```

Example 17.2   A SOAP header with WS-Addressing message information header
                   elements, three of which contain Endpoint Reference elements.

Notice how in this header block, the WS-Addressing `Address` element is used,
not the `Address` element from the utility schema used in the WS-Coordination
examples from Chapter 16.

17.1.3   WS-Addressing reusability

The endpoint identification and message routing mechanisms provided by WS-
Addressing establish a generic set of extensions useful to custom service-oriented solutions but also reusable by other WS-* specifications. As such, WS-Addressing can be
viewed as a utility specification that further supports the notion of composability within
SOA.

Although we don't discuss the WS-Notification or WS-Eventing languages in any detail,
let's take a brief glimpse at their `Header` constructs for some examples of how WS-
Addressing message information header elements are reused in support of other WS-*
extensions.

CASE STUDY

At the end of Chapter 7 RailCo sets itself up to receive notification messages from
TLS's System Notification Service. If this publish-and-subscribe model had been
based on the WS-Notification framework, the SOAP `Header` construct of a notification message would look something like the following example:

```
<Header>
  <wsa:Action>
    http://www.ibm.com/xmlns/stdwip/web-services/
      WS-BaseNotification/Notify
  </wsa:Action>
```

```
   <wsa:To>
       http://www.xmltc.com/tls/endpoint1
   </wsa:To>
</Header>
<Body>
   ... Notification Details ...
</Body>
```

Example 17.3   A sample WS-Notification SOAP header for a notification message.

Alternatively, if the framework chosen had been based on the WS-Eventing specification, the SOAP `Header` area would be as follows:

```
<Header>
   <wsa:Action>
       http://www.example.org/oceanwatch/2003/WindReport
   </wsa:Action>
   <wsa:MessageID>
       uuid:568b4ff2-5bc1-4512-957c-0fa545fd8d7f
   </wsa:MessageID>
   <wsa:To>
       http://www.other.example.com/OnStormWarning
   </wsa:To>
   ... Subscription Details ...
</Header>
<Body>
   ... Notification Details ...
</Body>
```

Example 17.4   A sample WS-Eventing SOAP header for a notification message.

(WS-Addressing elements are bolded in each of the preceding examples.)

Notice how the WS-Eventing SOAP header places subscription details in the `Header` construct and notification information in the `Body` area, while the WS-Notification header structure locates the bulk of the notification information in the `Body` construct.

Examples 17.3 and 17.4 demonstrate that while WS-Notification and WS-Eventing establish the same basic messaging model using very different approaches, each relies on WS-Addressing to structure its SOAP header. This commonality is a tribute to the movement toward open standards that are universally accepted. In fact, each of the remaining specifications covered in this chapter also utilize WS-Addressing message information header elements.

SUMMARY OF KEY POINTS

- WS-Addressing provides a collection of message header elements that can supplement a message with various (mostly routing-related) meta information.

- The WS-Addressing specification defines a set of reusable extensions that are becoming intrinsically commonplace among other WS-* specifications.

- It is worth remembering that some of the message information header elements established by WS-Addressing are of type EndpointReference and can therefore contain a variety of endpoint metadata.

17.2   WS-ReliableMessaging language basics

NOTE
Only element descriptions are provided in this section. Concepts relating to WS-ReliableMessaging are covered in Chapter 7.

WS-ReliableMessaging introduces critical quality of service features for the guaranteed delivery or failure notification of SOAP messages. It also positions itself as a fundamental WS-* extension, as shown in Figure 17.2.

When message exchanges are governed by a WS-ReliableMessaging-capable communications framework, the concepts of sequences and acknowledgements become paramount to just about every message transmission.

Coming up are descriptions for the following key WS-ReliableMessaging language elements:

- `Sequence` element
- `MessageNumber` element
- `LastMessage` element
- `SequenceAcknowledgement` element
- `AcknowledgementRange` element

- `Nack` element

- `AckRequested` element

Further supplementing these descriptions is a quick reference table containing brief descriptions of the following additional elements and assertions: `SequenceRef`, `AcknowledgementInterval`, `BaseRetransmissionInterval`, `InactivityTimeout`, `Expires`, and `SequenceCreation`.

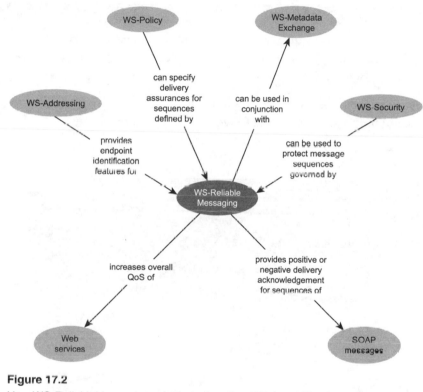

Figure 17.2
How WS-ReliableMessaging relates to the other WS-* specifications discussed in this chapter.

17.2.1 The `Sequence`, `MessageNumber`, and `LastMessage` elements

As explained in Chapter 7, the delivery of messages within a WS-ReliableMessaging framework can be guaranteed to occur in a specific order. The `Sequence` construct resides in the SOAP message header to represent the location of the current message in relation to the overall sequence of messages within which it is being delivered.

To accomplish this, the `Sequence` construct relies on a set of child elements. The `Identifier` element is used to contain an ID value associated with the sequence itself, while the `MessageNumber` element contains a number that is the position of the message within the overall sequence order.

Finally, the `LastMessage` element can be added to the `Sequence` construct to communicate the fact that the current message is the final message of the sequence.

As explained in the case study example at the end of the *Reliable messaging* section of Chapter 7, RailCo is required to use WS-ReliableMessaging to perform bulk invoice submissions.

The sample SOAP message below contains the header used by RailCo during the transmission of the last of a series of invoice message submissions.

```
<Envelope
    xmlns="http://schemas.xmlsoap.org/soap/envelope/"
    xmlns:wsu="http://schemas.xmlsoap.org/ws/2002/07/utility"
    xmlns:wsrm="http://schemas.xmlsoap.org/ws/2004/03/rm">
    <Header>
        <wsrm:Sequence>
            <wsu:Identifier>
                http://www.xmltc.com/railco/seq22231
            </wsu:Identifier>
            <wsrm:MessageNumber>
                12
            </wsrm:MessageNumber>
            <wsrm:LastMessage/>
        </wsrm:Sequence>
    </Header>
    <Body>
        . . .
    </Body>
</Envelope>
```

Example 17.5   A `Sequence` construct with a `LastMessage` element, indicating that this is the final message in the sequence.

17.2.2 The `SequenceAcknowledgement` and `AcknowledgementRange` elements

Upon the arrival of one or more messages within a sequence, the recipient service may issue a message containing the `SequenceAcknowledgement` header construct to communicate that the original delivery was successful. This construct again uses the `Identifier` element to identify the sequence, but it also needs an element to convey which of the messages within the sequence were received and which were not.

It accomplishes this through the use of the `AcknowledgementRange` element, which contains the `Upper` and `Lower` attributes that indicate a range of messages that *were* received. This range is based on the `MessageNumber` values of the messages, which, when they are first generated, are incremented. So one `AcknowledgementRange` element communicates each consecutive set of messages received. Therefore, a message that is not received is not accounted for within the ranges specified in the `AcknowledgementRange` elements.

If this sounds a bit confusing, have a look at how the SOAP header is structured in Example 17.6.

CASE STUDY

The markup code below shows the SOAP message returned from TLS after receiving the final invoice submission from RailCo.

```
<Envelope
    xmlns="http://schemas.xmlsoap.org/soap/envelope/"
    xmlns:wsu="http://schemas.xmlsoap.org/ws/2002/07/utility"
    xmlns:wsrm="http://schemas.xmlsoap.org/ws/2004/03/rm">
    <Header>
        <wsrm:SequenceAcknowledgement>
            <wsu:Identifier>
                http://www.xmltc.com/tls/seq22231
            </wsu:Identifier>
            <wsrm:AcknowledgementRange Upper="4" Lower="1"/>
            <wsrm:AcknowledgementRange Upper="8" Lower="6"/>
            <wsrm:AcknowledgementRange Upper="12" Lower="11"/>
            <wsrm:AcknowledgementRange Upper="15" Lower="14"/>
        </wsrm:SequenceAcknowledgement>
    </Header>
    <Body>
        ...
    </Body>
</Envelope>
```

Example 17.6   A `SequenceAcknowledgement` construct indicating that 11 out of a sequence of 15 messages were received.

Apparently, RailCo's bulk invoice submissions didn't go too well. The sequence acknowledgement message it receives uses four `AcknowledgementRange` elements to communicate the fact that out of the 15 messages it was expecting, only 11 were received.

Specifically, the `AcknowledgementRange` elements state that:

- messages with `MessageNumber` values 1 to 4 were received
- messages with `MessageNumber` values 6 to 8 were received
- messages with `MessageNumber` values 11 to 12 were received
- messages with `MessageNumber` values 14 to 15 were received

In other words, messages with `MessageNumber` values of 5, 9, 10, and 13 did not make it.

17.2.3   The `Nack` element

Communicating the delivery failure of a message can, alternatively, be accomplished using the `Nack` (negative acknowledgement) element. Instead of identifying which messages with `MessageNumber` values were received, it shows which were not.

CASE STUDY

TLS also could issue negative sequence acknowledgement messages such as the one that follows, where only those messages not received are indicated.

```
<Envelope
    xmlns="http://schemas.xmlsoap.org/soap/envelope/"
    xmlns:wsu="http://schemas.xmlsoap.org/ws/2002/07/utility"
    xmlns:wsrm="http://schemas.xmlsoap.org/ws/2004/03/rm">
    <Header>
        <wsrm:SequenceAcknowledgement>
            <wsu:Identifier>
                http://www.xmltc.com/tls/seq22231
            </wsu:Identifier>
            <wsrm:Nack>
                5
            </wsrm:Nack>
        </wsrm:SequenceAcknowledgement>
    </Header>
```

```
    <Body>
        ...
    </Body>
</Envelope>
```

Example 17.7   A `SequenceAcknowledgement` construct containing a `Nack` element that indicates that the fifth message was not received.

17.2.4   The `AckRequested` element

RM destinations typically issue SOAP messages with `SequenceAcknowledgement` headers at predefined times, such as upon the receipt of a message containing the `LastMessage` element. However, an RM source service can request that the RM destination send out a sequence acknowledgement message on demand by using the `AckRequested` header construct.

This construct simply contains a standard `Identifier` element to pinpoint the sequence for which it is requesting an acknowledgement message. It also can include a `MessageNumber` element that gives an indication as to which message receipt the RM source is most interested in.

CASE STUDY

RailCo tries another bulk invoice submission. Because of the poor delivery ratio experienced during the previous attempt, RailCo this time requests acknowledgement messages from TLS prior to the arrival of the last message in a sequence.

Following is an example of the acknowledgement RailCo issues after the transmission of every second invoice message within a sequence.

```
<Envelope
    xmlns="http://schemas.xmlsoap.org/soap/envelope/"
    xmlns:wsu="http://schemas.xmlsoap.org/ws/2002/07/utility"
    xmlns:wsrm="http://schemas.xmlsoap.org/ws/2004/03/rm">
    <Header>
        <wsrm:AckRequested>
            <wsu:Identifier>
                http://www.xmltc.com/tls/seq22232
            </wsu:Identifier>
        </wsrm:AckRequested>
```

```
    </Header>
    <Body>
       . . .
    </Body>
</Envelope>
```

Example 17.8   The `AckRequested` header construct indicating that the RM source
would like to receive a sequence acknowledgement message.

17.2.5   Other WS-ReliableMessaging elements

Table 17.3 provides an overview of additional elements that are part of the WS-ReliableMessaging language.

Table 17.3   Additional WS-ReliableMessaging elements.

Element	Description
SequenceRef	This construct allows you to attach policy assertions to a sequence, which introduces the ability to add various delivery rules, such as those expressed in the delivery assurances explained in Chapter 7.
AcknowledgementInterval	Specifies an interval period that an RM destination can use to automatically transmit acknowledgement messages.
BaseRetransmissionInterval	An interval period used by the RM source to retransmit messages (for example, if no acknowledgements are received).
InactivityTimeout	A period of time that indicates at what point a sequence will time out and subsequently expire.
Expires	A specific date and time at which a sequence is scheduled to expire.
SequenceCreation	Sequences are generally created by the RM Source, but the RM Destination may use this element to force the creation of its own sequence.

17.3 WS-Policy language basics

> **NOTE**
>
> Only element descriptions are provided in this section. Concepts relating to WS-Policy are covered In Chapter 7.

The WS-Policy framework establishes a means of expressing service metadata beyond the WSDL definition. Specifically, it allows services to communicate rules and preferences in relation to security, processing, or message content. Policies can be applied to a variety of Web resources, positioning this specification as another fundamental part of the WS-* extensions discussed in this chapter (Figure 17.3).

The WS-Policy framework is comprised of the following three specifications:

- WS-Policy
- WS-PolicyAssertions
- WS-PolicyAttachments

These collectively provide the following elements covered in this section, which demonstrate how policies are formulated and attached to element or document-level subjects:

- `Policy` element
- `TextEncoding`, `Language`, `SpecVersion`, and `MessagePredicate` assertions
- `ExactlyOne` element

- `All` element

- `Usage` and `Preference` attributes

- `PolicyReference` element

- `PolicyURIs` attribute

- `PolicyAttachment` element

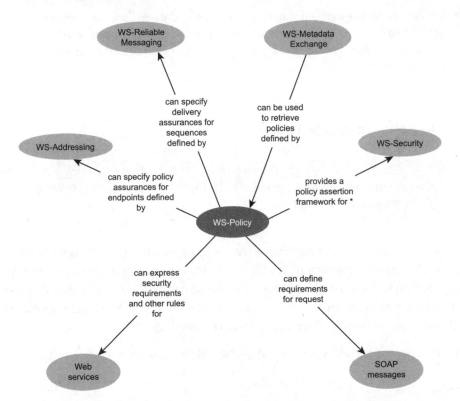

* A separate WS-SecurityPolicy specification provides a set of predefined policy assertions for WS-Security.

Figure 17.3
How WS-Policy relates to the other WS-* specifications discussed in this chapter.

17.3.1   The `Policy` element and common policy assertions

The `Policy` element establishes the root construct used to contain the various policy assertions that comprise the policy. The WS-PolicyAssertions specification supplies the following set of common, predefined assertion elements:

- `TextEncoding`—Dictates the use of a specific text encoding format.

- `Language`—Expresses the requirement or preference for a particular language.

- `SpecVersion`—Communicates the need for a specific version of a specification.

- `MessagePredicate`—Indicates message processing rules expressed using XPath statements.

These elements represent assertions that can be used to structure basic policies around common requirements. Policy assertions also can be customized, and other WS-* specifications may provide supplemental assertions.

Each assertion can indicate whether its use is required or not via the value assigned to its `Usage` attribute. A value of "Required" indicates that its conditions must be met. Additionally, the use of the `Preference` attribute allows an assertion to communicate its importance in comparison to other assertions of the same type.

Examples of policy assertions are provided in the subsequent sections.

17.3.2 The `ExactlyOne` element

This construct surrounds multiple policy assertions and indicates that there is a choice between them, but that one must be chosen.

CASE STUDY

As explained in the case study example provided at the end of the *Policies* section in Chapter 7, TLS initially produced a policy definition giving partner requestors the option of sending bulk invoice submission messages that comply to one of two versions of the WS-ReliableMessaging specifications.

Following is a sample policy definition that uses the `ExactlyOnce` construct to communicate the `SpecVersion` policy alternative. The `SpecVersion` element's `Preference` attribute expresses TLS's preferred option.

```
<wsp:Policy
    xmlns:wsp="http://schemas.xmlsoap.org/ws/2002/12/policy">
    <wsp:ExactlyOne>
        <wsp:SpecVersion wsp:Usage="wsp:Required"
            wsp:Preference="10" wsp:URI=
                "http://schemas.xmlsoap.org/ws/2004/03/rm"/>
        <wsp:SpecVersion wsp:Usage="wsp:Required"
            wsp:Preference="1" wsp:URI=
                "http://schemas.xmlsoap.org/ws/2003/02/rm"/>
    </wsp:ExactlyOne>
</wsp:Policy>
```

Example 17.9   The `ExactlyOne` construct housing two alternative policy assertions, one of which must be used.

17.3.3   The All element

The All construct introduces a rule that states that all of the policy assertions within the construct must be met. This element can be combined with the ExactlyOne element, where collections of policy assertions can each be grouped into All constructs that are then further grouped into a parent ExactlyOne construct. This indicates that the policy is offering a choice of assertions groups but that the assertions in any one of the alternative All groups must be met.

CASE STUDY

TLS later expands its original policy definition to enforce a standard text encoding format. It adds the same TextEncoding assertion to each of its policy alternatives and groups the assertions using the All construct, as shown here:

```
<wsp:Policy
    xmlns:wsp="http://schemas.xmlsoap.org/ws/2002/12/policy">
    <wsp:ExactlyOne>
        <wsp:All ID="Invoice1">
            <wsp:SpecVersion wsp:Usage="wsp:Required"
                wsp:Preference="10" wsp:URI=
                    "http://schemas.xmlsoap.org/ws/2004/03/rm"/>
            <wsp:TextEncoding wsp:Usage="wsp:Required"
                Encoding="iso-8859-5"/>
        </wsp:All>
        <wsp:All ID="Invoice2">
            <wsp:SpecVersion wsp:Usage="wsp:Required"
                wsp:Preference="1" wsp:URI=
                    "http://schemas.xmlsoap.org/ws/2003/02/rm"/>
            <wsp:TextEncoding wsp:Usage="wsp:Required"
                Encoding="iso-8859-5"/>
        </wsp:All>
    </wsp:ExactlyOne>
</wsp:Policy>
```

Example 17.10   The All and ExactlyOne constructs used together to provide two alternative policy groups.

Note that a separate OneOrMore construct can also be used to group policy assertions much like the All construct, except that one (or more) of the policy assertions must be met.

17.3.4   The Usage attribute

As you've seen in the previous examples, a number of WS-Policy assertion elements contain a Usage attribute to indicate whether a given policy assertion is required. This attribute is a key part of the WS-Policy framework as its values form part of the overall policy rules. The Usage attribute actually has a number of settings worth knowing about, as shown in Table 17.4.

Table 17.4   Possible settings for the Usage attribute.

Attribute Value	Description
Required	The assertion requirements must be met, or an error will be generated.
Optional	The assertion requirements may be met, but an error will not be generated if they are not met.
Rejected	The assertion is unsupported.
Observed	The assertion applies to all policy subjects.
Ignored	The assertion will intentionally be ignored.

17.3.5   The Preference attribute

Policy assertions can be ranked in order of preference using this attribute. This is especially relevant if a service provider is flexible enough to provide multiple policy alternatives to potential service requestors.

The Preference attribute is assigned an integer value. The higher this value, the more preferred the assertion. When this attribute is not used, a default value of "0" is assigned to the policy assertion.

17.3.6   The PolicyReference element

So far we've only been discussing the creation of policy documents. However, we have not yet established how policies are associated with the subjects to which they apply. The PolicyReference element is one way to simply link an element with one or more policies. Each PolicyReference element contains a URI attribute that points to one policy document or a specific policy assertion within the document. (The ID attribute of the policy or grouping construct is referenced via the value displayed after the "#" symbol.)

If multiple `PolicyReference` elements are used within the same element, the policy documents are merged at runtime.

NOTE

`PolicyReference` elements can reside within the `Policy` construct, allowing for the creation of reusable policy modules.

CASE STUDY

If TLS wanted to place policies relating to its Employee Service documents in separate definitions it could do so by using the `PolicyReference` elements, as shown here:

```
<Employee ...>
   <wsp:PolicyReference URI=
      "http://www.xmltc.com/tls/policy1.xml#Employee1"/>
   <wsp:PolicyReference URI=
      "http://www.xmltc.com/tls/policy2.xml#Employee2"/>
</Employee>
```

Example 17.11   Separate `PolicyReference` elements referencing two policy documents.

17.3.7   The `PolicyURIs` attribute

Alternatively, the `PolicyURIs` attribute also can be used to link to one or more policy documents. The attribute is added to an element and can be assigned multiple policy locations. As with `PolicyReference`, these policies are then merged at runtime.

CASE STUDY

TLS could also reference its employee policy definitions by using the `PolicyURIs` attribute, as shown here:

```
<Employee wsp:PolicyURIs=
   "http://www.xmltc.com/tls/policy1.xml#Employee1"
   "http://www.xmltc.com/tls/policy2.xml#Employee2"/>
```

Example 17.12   The `PolicyURIs` attribute referencing two policy documents.

17.3.8 The `PolicyAttachment` element

Another way of associating a policy with a subject is through the use of the `Policy-Attachment` construct. The approach taken here is that the child `AppliesTo` construct is positioned as the parent of the subject elements. The familiar `PolicyReference` element then follows the `AppliesTo` construct to identify the policy assertions that will be used.

CASE STUDY

Finally, TLS can embed the policy assertion reference using the `PolicyAttachment` and `AppliesTo` constructs. In the following example, the policy assertion is attached to a specific endpoint reference.

```
<wsp:PolicyAttachment>
    <wsp:AppliesTo>
        <wsa:EndpointReference
            xmlns:emp="http://www.xmltc.com/tls/employee">
            <wsa:Address>
                http://www.xmltc.com/tls/ep1
            </wsa:Address>
            <wsa:PortType>
                emp:EmployeeInterface
            </wsa:PortType>
            <wsa:ServiceName>
                emp:Employee
            </wsa:ServiceName>
        </wsa:EndpointReference>
    </wsp:AppliesTo>
    <wsp:PolicyReference URI=
        "http://www.xmltc.com/EmployeePolicy.xml"/>
</wsp:PolicyAttachment>
```

Example 17.13 The `PolicyAttachment` construct using the child `AppliesTo` construct to associate a policy with a WS-Addressing `Endpoint-Reference` construct.

17.3.9 Additional types of policy assertions

It is important to note that policy assertions can be utilized and customized beyond the conventional manner in which they are displayed in the preceding examples.

For example:

- Policy assertions can be incorporated into WSDL definitions through the use of a special set of policy subjects that target specific parts of the definition structure. A separate `UsingPolicy` element is provided for use as a WSDL extension.

- WS-ReliableMessaging defines and relies on WS-Policy assertions to enforce some of its delivery and acknowledgement rules.

- WS-Policy assertions can be created to communicate that a Web service is capable of participating in a business activity or an atomic transaction.

- A policy assertion can be designed to express a service's processing requirements in relation to other WS-* specifications.

- WS-Policy assertions commonly are utilized within the WS-Security framework to express security requirements.

SUMMARY OF KEY POINTS

- WS-Policy specifications establish an extensible policy definition framework that can be used to add a layer of messaging integrity to SOAs.

- Policies can consist of one or more policy assertions, which can further be grouped and offered as alternatives using the `ExactlyOne`, `All`, or `OneOrMore` constructs.

- There are different options as to how policies can be attached to the resources they govern, as provided by the `PolicyAttachment` and `PolicyReference` elements and the `PolicyURIs` attribute.

17.4 WS-MetadataExchange language basics

> **NOTE**
>
> Only element descriptions are provided in this section. Concepts relating to WS-MetadataExchange are covered in Chapter 7.

WS-MetadataExchange provides a standardized means by which service description documents can be requested and supplied. This specification establishes a set of features that supports important SOA characteristics, such as interoperability and quality of service (Figure 17.4).

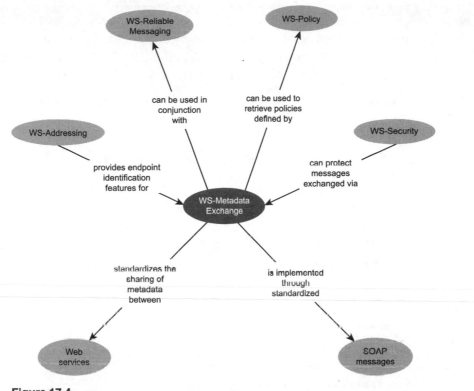

Figure 17.4
How WS-MetadataExchange relates to the other WS-* specifications discussed in this chapter.

The scope of the WS-MetadataExchange language is fairly small in comparison to other WS-* specifications. As we established in Chapter 7, the following two forms of metadata requests are standardized:

- GetMetadata
- Get

The descriptions that follow discuss the primary elements used to compose these two types of request messages.

17.4.1   The GetMetadata element

This element can be placed on its own in the Body area of a SOAP message, or it can be turned into a construct that hosts child Dialect and Identifier elements (explained next).

In the scenario described as part of the case study example at the end of the *Metadata exchange* section in Chapter 7, RailCo designed its Invoice Processing Service to perform a periodic metadata check against TLS's Accounts Payable Service.

Here is a sample of RailCo's first cut of the GetMetadata request message.

```
<Envelope
    xmlns="http://www.w3.org/2003/05/soap-envelope"
    xmlns:wsa=
        "http://schemas.xmlsoap.org/ws/2004/08/addressing"
    xmlns:wsx="http://schemas.xmlsoap.org/ws/2004/09/mex">
    <Header>
        <wsa:Action>
            http://schemas.xmlsoap.org/ws/2004/09/mex/
                GetMetadata/Request
        </wsa:Action>
        <wsa:To>
            http://www.xmltc.com/tls/ap1/
        </wsa:To>
        <wsa:MessageID>
            uuid:23492372938
        </wsa:MessageID>
        <wsa:ReplyTo>
            <wsa:Address>
                http://www.xmltc.com/railco/inv1/
            </wsa:Address>
        </wsa:ReplyTo>
    </Header>
    <Body>
        <wsx:GetMetadata/>
        ...
    </Body>
</Envelope>
```

Example 17.14   A SOAP request message containing the `GetMetadata` element in the
`Body` construct. Note the use of the WS-Addressing message information header elements in the SOAP header.

17.4.2   The `Dialect` element

This element specifies the type and version of the metadata specification requested. The use of the `Dialect` element guarantees that the metadata returned to the service requesting it will be understood.

RailCo refines its original GetMetadata request message by adding a `Dialect` construct to specify that an XSD schema conforming to the 2001 specification is required, as shown here:

```
<Body>
   <wsx:GetMetadata>
      <wsx:Dialect>
         http://www.w3.org/2001/XMLSchema
      </wsx:Dialect>
   </wsx:GetMetadata>
</Body>
```

Example 17.15 The `Dialect` element being used to indicate that the XSD schema requested should comply to version 1.0 of the XML Schema Definition Language.

17.4.3   The `Identifier` element

While the `Dialect` element specifies the type of metadata being requested, this element further narrows the criteria by asking for a specific part of the metadata.

Finally, RailCo adds the `Identifier` construct to pinpoint exactly which XSD schema it wants TLS to return.

```
<Body>
   <wsx:GetMetadata>
      <wsx:Dialect>
         http://www.w3.org/2001/XMLSchema
      </wsx:Dialect>
      <wsx:Identifier>
         http://www.www.xmltc.com/tls/schemas/ap1/schemas
      </wsx:Identifier>
   </wsx:GetMetadata>
</Body>
```

Example 17.16 The `Identifier` element added to specify the XSD schema's target namespace.

17.4.4 The `Metadata`, `MetadataSection`, and `MetadataReference` elements

These three elements are used to organize the content of the message sent in response to a GetMetadata request. The parent `Metadata` construct resides in the SOAP message `Body` area and houses one or more child `MetadataSection` constructs that each represent a part of the returned metadata.

If the contents of the metadata document are returned, they are placed within the `MetadataSection` construct. However, if only a pointer to the document is returned, its location is found in the `MetadataReference` construct (further qualified by a regular WS-Addressing `Address` element).

CASE STUDY

TLS responds to RailCo's GetMetadata request with the following message containing the entire WSDL definition of the Accounts Payable Service, along with a pointer to the associated XSD schema.

```
<Envelope
    xmlns="http://www.w3.org/2003/05/soap-envelope"
    xmlns:wsa=
      "http://schemas.xmlsoap.org/ws/2004/08/addressing"
    xmlns:wsx="http://schemas.xmlsoap.org/ws/2004/09/mex">
    <Header>
      <wsa:Action>
          http://schemas.xmlsoap.org/ws/2004/09/
              mex/GetMetadata/Response
      </wsa:Action>
      <wsa:RelatesTo>
          23492372938
      </wsa:RelatesTo>
      <wsa:To>
          http://www.xmltc.com/railco/inv1
      </wsa:To>
    </Header>
    <Body>
      <wsx:Metadata>
          <wsx:MetadataSection ...>
              <wsdl:definitions>
                  ... the entire WSDL definition ...
              </wsdl:definitions>
          </wsx:MetadataSection>
          <wsx:MetadataSection ...>
              <wsx:MetadataReference>
                  <wsa:Address>
```

```
                    http://www.www.xmltc.com/tls/ap1/schemas
                </wsa:Address>
            </wsx:MetadataReference>
        </wsx:MetadataSection>
    </wsx:Metadata>
    </Body>
</Envelope>
```

Example 17.17   A `GetMetadata` response message returning the contents of an entire WSDL definition, along with a pointer to the associated XSD schema.

Note that the `MetadataSection` element can contain `Dialect` and `Identifier` attributes that correspond to the `Dialect` and `Identifier` elements explained previously.

17.4.5   The Get message

As previously mentioned, the response to a GetMetadata request message can include a `MetadataReference` construct that contains the location of metadata documents not returned in this initial message. To explicitly request one of these documents, a separate Get message is issued.

While this message does not contain a specific Get element, it does adhere to a standardized SOAP header format, as follows.

CASE STUDY

RailCo wants to take no chances and therefore designs its Invoice Processing Service to always request full copies of supplementary service description documents. Below is the Get message issued by RailCo, requesting the XSD schema identified in TLS's previous GetMessage response message.

```
<Header>
    <wsa:Action>
        http://schemas.xmlsoap.org/ws/2004/09/mex/Get/Request
    </wsa:Action>
    <wsa:MessageID>
        23492372938
    </wsa:MessageID>
    <wsa:ReplyTo>
        <wsa:Address>
            http://www.xmltc.com/railco/sub1
```

```
      </wsa:Address>
    </wsa:ReplyTo>
    <wsa:To>
       http://www.www.xmltc.com/tls/schemas/not1
    </wsa:To>
</Header>
```

Example 17.18 A Get message SOAP header identified by the `Action` element value. The resource being requested is targeted in the `To` element.

SUMMARY OF KEY POINTS

- WS-GetMetadata provides the `GetMetadata` construct that houses the contents of the message used to request metadata from a service provider.

- The `Dialect` and `Identifier` elements can be applied to further narrow request criteria.

- The response to a GetMetadata request message organizes the retrieved metadata information using the `Metadata` and `MetadataSection` constructs.

17.5   WS-Security language basics

> **NOTE**
>
> Only element descriptions are provided in this section. Concepts relating to WS-Security are covered in Chapter 7.

The WS-Security framework provides extensions that can be used to implement message-level security measures. These protect message contents during transport and during processing by service intermediaries. Additional extensions implement authentication and authorization control, which protect service providers from malicious requestors. WS-Security is designed to work with any of the WS-* specifications we discuss in this chapter, as shown in Figure 17.5.

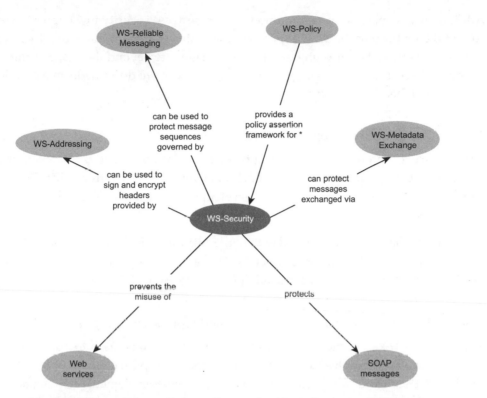

* A separate WS-SecurityPolicy specification provides a set of predefined policy assertions for WS-Security.

Figure 17.5
How WS-Security relates to the other WS-* specifications discussed in this chapter.

The WS-Security framework is comprised of numerous specifications, many in different stages of acceptance and maturation. In this book we've concentrated on some of the more established ones, namely.

- WS-Security
- XML-Encryption
- XML-Signature

Note that WS-Security represents a framework but also a specification that defines language elements. Because the language element descriptions provided in this chapter originate from three separate specifications, we qualify each element name with its origin.

Additionally, as part of our exploration of Web services security in Chapter 7, we discussed the features of the SAML specification, which enable centralized authentication and authorization. Because single sign-on languages are beyond the scope of this book, we don't discuss SAML language elements. (However, we do provide an example of a SAML SOAP header later on.)

17.5.1   The `Security` element (WS-Security)

This construct represents the fundamental header block provided by WS-Security. The `Security` element can have a variety of child elements, ranging from XML-Encryption and XML-Signature constructs to the token elements provided by the WS-Security specification itself.

`Security` elements can be outfitted with `actor` attributes that correspond to SOAP actor roles (explained at the end of Chapter 5). This allows you to add multiple `Security` blocks to a SOAP message, each intended for a different recipient.

17.5.2   The `UsernameToken`, `Username`, and `Password` elements (WS-Security)

The `UsernameToken` element provides a construct that can be used to host token information for authentication and authorization purposes. Typical children of this construct are the `Username` and `Password` child elements, but custom elements also can be added.

17.5.3   The `BinarySecurityToken` element (WS-Security)

Tokens stored as binary data, such as certificates, can be represented in an encoded format within the `BinarySecurityToken` element.

17.5.4   The `SecurityTokenReference` element (WS-Security)

This element allows you to provide a pointer to a token that exists outside of the SOAP message document.

For each invoice generated by RailCo's Invoice Submission Service, it must provide a standard `Username` and `Password` token pair in the SOAP message header, as shown here:

```
<Envelope
    xmlns="http://schemas.xmlsoap.org/soap/envelope/">
    <Header>
        <wsse:Security xmlns:wsse=
            "http://schemas.xmlsoap.org/ws/2002/12/secext">
            <wsse:UsernameToken>
                <wsse:Username>
                    rco-3342
                </wsse:Username>
                <wsse:Password Type="wsse:PasswordDigest">
                    93292348347
                </wsse:Password>
            </wsse:UsernameToken>
        </wsse:Security>
    </Header>
    <Body>
        . . .
    </Body>
</Envelope>
```

Example 17.19 The `Security` SOAP header used by RailCo to provide user name and password values.

17.5.6 Composing `Security` element contents (WS-Security)

As previously mentioned, the WS-Security specification positions the `security` element as a standardized container for header blocks originating from other security extensions. The following example illustrates this by showing how a SAML block is located within the `Security` construct. (As previously mentioned, single sign-on languages are beyond the scope of this book. The SAML-specific elements shown in this example therefore are not explained.)

CASE STUDY

After RailCo's Invoice Submission Service has been authenticated by the TLS Accounts Payable Service (acting as the issuing authority), RailCo's service is automatically granted access to other TLS services.

Should RailCo want its Invoice Submission Service to then invoke any one of these TLS services, the TLS service would not need to re-authenticate or re-authorize the RailCo service requestor. Instead, the TLS service would request security information from the issuing authority, which would respond with assertion information, such as the authorization assertion shown here:

```
<Envelope
    xmlns="http://schemas.xmlsoap.org/soap/envelope/">
    <Header>
        <wsse:Security xmlns:wsse=
            "http://schemas.xmlsoap.org/ws/2002/12/secext">
            <saml:Assertion xmlns:saml="..."...>
            <saml:Conditions ...>
            <saml:AuthorizationDecisionStatement
                Decision="Permit"
                Resource="http://www.xmltc.com/tls/...">
                <saml:Actions>
                    ...
                    <saml:Action>
                        Execute
                    </saml:Action>
                </saml:Actions>
                ...
            </saml:AuthorizationDecisionStatement>
        </wsse:Security>
    </Header>
    <Body>
        ...
    </Body>
</Envelope>
```

Example 17.20   The WS-Security SOAP header hosting a SAML authorization assertion.

17.5.6   The `EncryptedData` element (XML-Encryption)

This is the parent construct that hosts the encrypted portion of an XML document. If located at the root of an XML document, the entire document contents are encrypted.

The `EncryptedData` element's `Type` attribute indicates what is included in the encrypted content. For example, a value of `http://www.w3.org/2001/04/xmlenc#Element` indicates that the element and its contents will be encrypted, whereas the value of `http://www.w3.org/2001/04/xmlenc#Content` states that encryption will only be applied to the content within the opening and closing tags.

17.5.7 The `CipherData`, `CipherValue`, and `CipherReference` elements (XML-Encryption)

The `CipherData` construct is required and must contain either a `CipherValue` element hosting the characters representing the encrypted text or a `CipherReference` element that provides a pointer to the encrypted values.

CASE STUDY

In Chapter 15 RailCo designed a task-centric business service that uses an XSD schema to represent a small, custom invoice document as part of its transmission. This schema was imported and established a construct with a root `InvoiceType` element.

Following is an example of an XML document instance of this schema.

```
<InvoiceType>
    <Number>
        2322
    </Number>
    <Total>
        $32,322.73
    </Total>
    <Date>
        07.16.05
    </Date>
</InvoiceType>
```

To comply with TLS's security requirements, RailCo is required to apply encryption to any dollar amounts in business documents exchanged via the TLS B2B system. Shown in the following code example is the same XML fragment but with XML-Encryption elements representing the `Total` element and value.

```
<InvoiceType>
    <Number>
        2322
```

```
  </Number>
  <EncryptedData
      xmlns="http://www.w3.org/2001/04/xmlenc#"
      Type="http://www.w3.org/2001/04/xmlenc#Element">
      <CipherData>
          <CipherValue>
              R5J7UUI78
          </CipherValue>
      </CipherData>
  </EncryptedData>
  <Date>
      07.16.05
  </Date>
</InvoiceType>
```

Example 17.21   An XML document within a SOAP message containing an encrypted element.

17.5.8   XML-Signature elements

A digital signature is a complex piece of information comprised of specific parts that each represent an aspect of the document being signed. Therefore, numerous elements can be involved when defining the construct that hosts the digital signature information. Table 17.5 provides brief descriptions of some of the main elements.

Table 17.5   XML-Signature elements

Element	Description
`CanonicalizationMethod`	This element identifies the type of "canonicalization algorithm" used to detect and represent subtle variances in the document content (such as the location of white space).
`DigestMethod`	Identifies the algorithm used to create the signature.
`DigestValue`	Contains a value that represents the document being signed. This value is generated by applying the `DigestMethod` algorithm to the XML document.

Element	Description
KeyInfo	This optional construct contains the public key information of the message sender.
Signature	The root element, housing all of the information for the digital signature.
SignatureMethod	The algorithm used to produce the digital signature. The digest and canonicalization algorithms are taken into account when creating the signature.
SignatureValue	The actual value of the digital signature.
SignedInfo	A construct that hosts elements with information relevant to the SignatureValue element, which resides outside of this construct.
Reference	Each document that is signed by the same digital signature is represented by a Reference construct that hosts digest and optional transformation details.

CASE STUDY

TLS further requires that all invoices submitted with a total of over $30,000 must also be digitally signed. RailCo therefore inserts an XML-Signature compliant signature in the SOAP header of its invoice submission message, as shown here:

```
<Envelope ...>
   <Header>
      <wsse:Security xmlns:wsse=
         "http://schemas.xmlsoap.org/ws/2002/12/secext">
         <Signature Id="RailCo333" xmlns=
            "http://www.w3.org/2000/09/xmldsig#">
         <SignedInfo>
            <CanonicalizationMethod Algorithm=
               "http://www.w3.org/TR/2001/
                REC-xml-c14n-20010315"/>
            <SignatureMethod Algorithm=
               "http://www.w3.org/2000/09/
                xmldsig#dsa-sha1"/>
```

```
               <Reference URI=
                  "http://www.w3.org/TR/2000/
                     REC-xhtml1-20000126/">
                  <DigestMethod Algorithm=
                     "http://www.w3.org/2000/09/
                        xmldsig#sha1"/>
                  <DigestValue>
                     LLSFK032093548=
                  </DigestValue>
               </Reference>
            </SignedInfo>
            <SignatureValue>
               9879DFSS3=
            </SignatureValue>
            <KeyInfo>
               ...
            </KeyInfo>
         </Signature>
      </wsse:Security>
   </Header>
   <Body>
      ...invoice document with total exceeding $30,000...
   </Body>
</Envelope>
```

Example 17.22   A SOAP message header containing a digital signature.

SUMMARY OF KEY POINTS

- WS-Security establishes the standardized `Security` SOAP header block container that can be used for WS-Security defined token information or to host security blocks from other specifications.

- XML-Encryption provides a construct that replaces XML content with language-specific elements that represent encryption information.

- XML-Signature establishes the `Signature` block comprised of various algorithm pointers and parts from which the digital signature is derived.

SOA Platforms

All of the concepts and open technologies and specifications we discussed so far in this book require the support of a vendor platform for us to build a functional service-oriented architecture. It is therefore worth taking a look at the current technology offerings provided by the two primary development and runtime platforms used to build both traditional distributed solutions, and now, our primitive and contemporary SOA models.

This chapter begins with an overview of some development and architecture platform basics that explain the common parts of the development and runtime ends of a distributed technology platform. This section establishes a neutral reference point from which we then launch into our coverage of SOA support provided by J2EE and .NET.

Note that sections 18.2 and 18.3 in this chapter are structured identically. This is intentional so as to allow you to cross-reference topics covered between the two platforms. Note also that this chapter draws no comparisons between J2EE and .NET; it only provides a high-level documentation of the platforms' respective support for SOA.

NOTE

Both the J2EE and .NET platforms support the WSDL-first design approach through features that allow for the import of WSDL definitions or the auto-generation of classes derived from WSDL documents. Covering the Java language and the various .NET programming languages is beyond the scope of this book. Code samples are therefore not provided in this chapter. However, a number of recommended books on building Web services are listed at www.soabooks.com.

How case studies are used: TLS and RailCo proceed to develop their new service-oriented applications with .NET and J2EE platform technology, respectively. While RailCo makes their platform choice out of necessity, TLS decides to change platforms as an exercise to prove enterprise-wide service interoperability.

18.1   SOA platform basics

Before we begin to look at the specifics of the J2EE and .NET platforms, let's first establish some of the common aspects of the physical development and runtime environments required to build and implement SOA-compliant services.

18.1.1 Basic platform building blocks

Taking a step back from SOA for a moment, let's start by defining the rudimentary building blocks of a software technology platform. The realization of a software program puts forth some basic requirements, mainly:

- We need a development environment with which to program and assemble the software program. This environment must provide us with a development tool that supports a programming language.

- We need a runtime for which we will be designing our software (because it provides the environment that will eventually host the software).

- We need APIs that expose features and functions offered by the runtime so that we can build our software program to interact with and take advantage of these features and functions.

- Finally, we need an operating system on which to deploy the runtime, APIs, and the software program. The operating system interfaces with the underlying hardware and likely will provide additional services that can be used by the software program (through the use of additional APIs).

Each of these requirements can be represented as a layer that establishes a base architecture model (Figure 18.1).

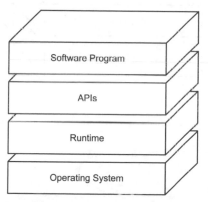

Figure 18.1
Fundamental software technology
architecture layers.

18.1.2 Common SOA platform layers

As we established early on in this book, contemporary SOA is a distributed architectural model, built using Web services. Therefore, an SOA-capable development and runtime platform will be geared toward a distributed programming architecture that provides support for the Web services technology set.

As a result, we have two new requirements:

- We need the ability to partition software programs into self-contained and composable units of processing logic (components) capable of communicating with each other within and across instances of the runtime.

- We need the ability to encapsulate and expose application logic through industry standard Web services technologies.

To upgrade our fundamental architecture model so that we can build service-oriented solutions, we need to add new layers to represent the requirements we just identified (Figure 18.2).

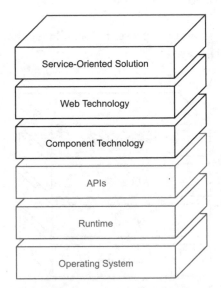

Figure 18.2

The common layers required by a development and runtime platform for building SOA.

18.1.3   Relationship between SOA layers and technologies

When we introduce components and Web services to our architecture model, we end up with a number of different relationships forged between the fundamental architecture layers and the specific technologies introduced by the Web services framework (namely, WSDL, SOAP, UDDI, and the WS-* specifications).

To better understand these dynamics, let's briefly review the requirements for each of the primary relationships.

- The Web Technology layer needs to provide support for the first-generation Web services technology set to enable us to build a primitive SOA.

- The Web Technology layer needs to provide support for WS-* specifications for us to fulfill some of the contemporary SOA characteristics.

- The Web Technology layer needs to provide a means of assembling and implementing its technology support into Web services.

- The Component Technology layer needs to support encapsulation by Web services.

- The Runtime layer needs to be capable of hosting components and Web services.

- The Runtime layer needs to provide a series of APIs in support of components and Web services.

- The APIs layer needs to provide functions that support the development and processing of components and Web services technologies.

Figure 18.3 illustrates these relationships.

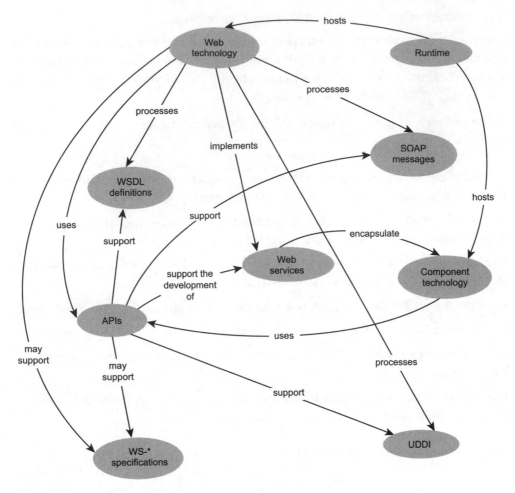

Figure 18.3
A logical view of the basic relationships between the core parts of a service-oriented
architecture.

18.1.4   Fundamental service technology architecture

So far we've established the overall pieces that comprise a fundamental, abstract service-oriented architecture. What is of further interest to us are the specifics behind the
relationship between the Web Technology and Component Technology layers.

By studying this relationship, we can learn how service providers and service requestors
within an SOA can be designed, leading us to define a service-level architecture.

Service processing tasks

As we've established in previous chapters, service providers are commonly expected to perform the following tasks:

- Supply a public interface (WSDL definition) that allows it to be accessed and invoked by a service requestor.
- Receive a SOAP message sent to it by a service requestor.
- Process the header blocks within the SOAP message.
- Validate and parse the payload of the SOAP message.
- Transform the message payload contents into a different format.
- Encapsulate business processing logic that will do something with the received SOAP message contents.
- Assemble a SOAP message containing the response to the original request SOAP message from the service requestor.
- Transform the contents of the message back into the format expected by the service requestor.
- Transmit the response SOAP message back to the service requestor.

Service providers are designed to facilitate service requestors. A service requestor can be any piece of software capable of communicating with a service provider. Service requestors are commonly expected to:

- Contain business processing logic that calls a service provider for a particular reason.
- Interpret (and possibly discover) a service provider's WSDL definition.
- Assemble a SOAP request message (including any required headers) in compliance with the service provider WSDL definition.
- Transform the contents of the SOAP message so that they comply with the format expected by the service provider.
- Transmit the SOAP request message to the service provider.
- Receive a SOAP response message from the service provider.
- Validate and parse the payload of the SOAP response message received by the service provider.
- Transform the SOAP payload into a different format.
- Process SOAP header blocks within the message.

Service processing logic

Looking at these tasks, it appears that the majority of them require the use of Web technologies. The only task that does not fall into this category is the processing of business logic, where the contents of the SOAP request are used to perform some function that may result in a response. Let's therefore group our service provider and requestor tasks into two distinct categories.

- *Message Processing Logic*—The part of a Web service and its surrounding environment that executes a variety of SOAP message processing tasks. Message processing logic is performed by a combination of runtime services, service agents, as well as service logic related to the processing of the WSDL definition.

- *Business Logic*—The back-end part of a Web service that performs tasks in response to the receipt of SOAP message contents. Business logic is application-specific and can range dramatically in scope, depending on the functionality exposed by the WSDL definition. For example, business logic can consist of a single component providing service-specific functions, or it can be represented by a legacy application that offers only some of its functions via the Web service.

NOTE
There is no association between the terms "business logic" and "business service." Every type of Web service (application service, business service) has underlying business logic.

Viewing a service provider in this manner allows us to logically partition the service logic, as shown in Figure 18.4.

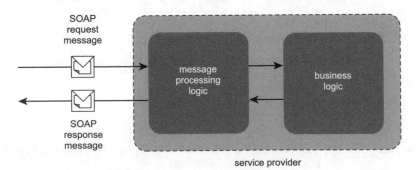

Figure 18.4
A service provider consisting of message processing and business logic.

We now can divide the original service provider tasks into these two categories, as shown in Table 18.1.

Table 18.1   Service provider logic categorization.

Message Processing Logic	Business Logic
SOAP message receipt and transmission.	Application-specific business processing logic.
SOAP message header processing.	
SOAP message payload validation and parsing.	
SOAP message payload transformation.	

These groups represent logic only, including the messaging logic required to process the WSDL definition. But what about the WSDL itself? This critical piece of a service needs to be distinctly identified, as it relates to and affects a great deal of the surrounding messaging processing logic. To keep things simple we will group the WSDL with other metadata documents (such as policies and schemas) and classify them collectively as the *endpoint*.

NOTE

What is represented by the term "endpoint" often varies in different vendor platforms. For the purposes of this book, an endpoint is an implementation of the metadata that comprises the technical service contract. Also note that we only identify the endpoint with a service provider. Although a service requestor may be a Web service in its own right (and therefore also classifiable as a service provider), the endpoint is of most interest to us when a service acts as a service provider.

As shown in Figure 18.5, the endpoint is not located in front of the service message processing logic. Instead, it is wedged within the message processing logic block because some of the runtime components that comprise the message processing logic may be executed prior to the endpoint being contacted by an incoming message. (Examples of this are provided later in this section.)

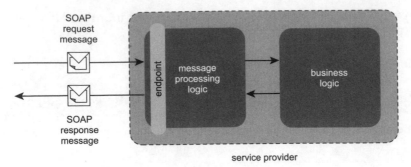

Figure 18.5
A revised service provider model now including an endpoint within the
message processing logic.

Let's move on to the service requestor. As shown in Figure 18.6, the primary difference
between how service logic is used in requestors and providers is related to the role of
business logic. The business logic part of a service requestor is responsible for initiating
an activity (and the resulting SOAP message exchange), whereas the business logic
within a service provider responds to an already initiated activity.

Table 18.2 revisits the original service requestor tasks and displays abbreviated versions,
categorized into two groups.

Table 18.2   Service requestor logic categorization.

Message Processing Logic	Business Logic
WSDL interpretation (and discovery).	Application-specific business processing logic.
SOAP message transmission and receipt.	
SOAP message header processing.	
SOAP message payload validation and parsing.	
SOAP message payload transformation.	

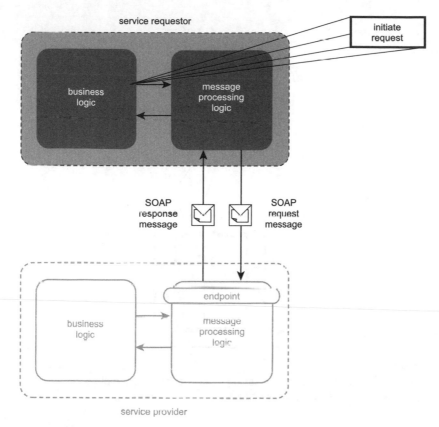

Figure 18.6

A service requestor consisting of message processing and business logic.

Message processing logic

Let's now take a closer look at the typical characteristics of the message processing logic of a service provider and service requestor. This part consists of functions or tasks performed by a combination of runtime services and application-specific extensions. It is therefore not easy to nail down which elements of the message processing logic belong exclusively to the service.

For example, Figure 18.7 shows some common processing layers represented by the message processing logic of a service provider. Among these layers are tasks, such as header processing, that are generic and applied to all service providers. Validation or transformation tasks, on the other hand, may involve service-specific XSD schemas and XSLT stylesheets and therefore may be considered exclusive to the service provider (even though validation and transformation tasks themselves are executed by generic runtime processors).

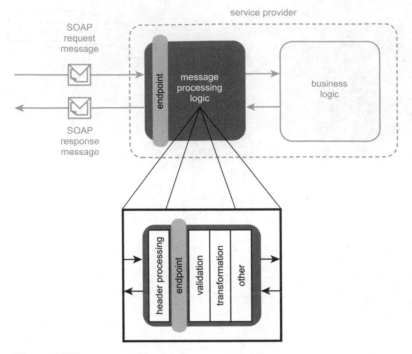

Figure 18.7

An example of the types of processing functions that can comprise the
message processing logic of a service.

Although the message processing logic for service requestors and service providers may
be similar, there is an important implementation-level difference. The service provider
supplies an endpoint that expresses an interface and associated constraints with which
all service requestors must comply.

Vendor platforms accomplish this by supporting the creation of proxy components.
These components exist as part of the message processing logic (Figure 18.8) and are
commonly auto-generated from the service provider WSDL definition (and associated
service description documents). They end up providing a programmatic interface that
mirrors the WSDL definition but complies to the native vendor runtime environment.

Proxies accept method calls issued from the regular vendor platform components that
contain the service requestor business logic. The proxies then use vendor runtime services to translate these method calls and associated parameters into SOAP request messages. When the SOAP request is transmitted, the proxy is further able to receive the
corresponding SOAP response from the service provider. It then performs the same type
of translation, but in reverse.

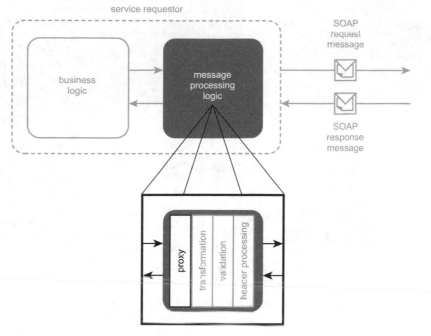

Figure 18.8

The message processing logic part of a service requestor includes a proxy component.

NOTE
Proxies can exist as static components or they can be dynamically created. Vendor-specific proxy components are discussed further in the J2EE and .NET sections.

Business logic

As we previously established, business logic can exist as a standalone component, housing the intelligence required to either invoke a service provider as part of a business activity or to respond to a request in order to participate in such an activity.

As an independent unit of logic, it is free to act in different roles. For example, Figure 18.9 shows a unit of business logic being encapsulated as part of a service provider but also acting as a service requestor.

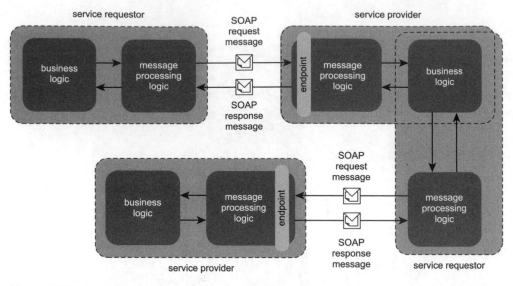

Figure 18.9
The same unit of business logic participating within a service provider and a service requestor.

If units of business logic exist as physically separate components, the same business logic can be encapsulated by different service providers, as illustrated in Figure 18.10.

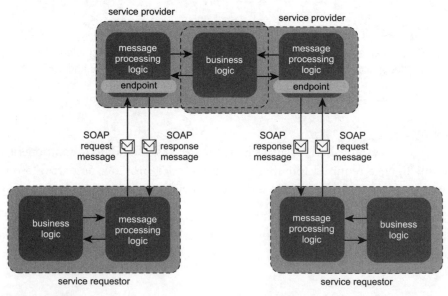

Figure 18.10
One unit of business logic being encapsulated by two different service providers.

Because units of business logic can exist in their native distributed component format, they also can interact with other components that may not necessarily be part of the SOA, as shown in Figure 18.11. This, in fact, is a very common model in distributed environments where components (as opposed to services) are composed to execute specific tasks on behalf of the service provider.

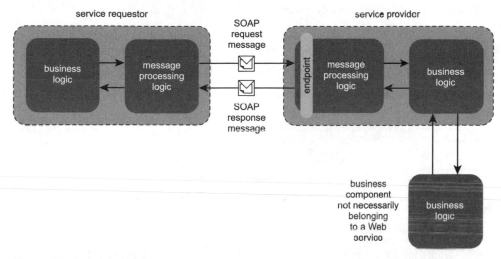

Figure 18.11

The same unit of business logic facilitating a service provider and acting on its own by communicating independently with a separate component.

Note that the service business logic shown in Figure 18.11 may be interacting with a separate native component to complete the processing requested by the service requestor. In this case the second component can be considered as belonging to the overall automation logic encapsulated by the service provider.

Service agents

A type of software program commonly found within the message processing logic of SOA platforms is the *service agent*. Its primary role is to perform some form of automated processing prior to the transmission and receipt of SOAP messages. As such, service agents are a form of intermediary service.

For example, service agents that reside alongside the service requestor will be engaged after a SOAP message request is issued by the service requestor and before it actually is transmitted to the service provider. Similarly, requestor agents generally kick in upon the initial receipt of a SOAP response, prior to the SOAP message being received by the remaining service requestor logic.

The same goes for service agents that act on the service provider's behalf. They typically pre-process SOAP request messages and intercept SOAP response messages prior to transmission.

Service agents usually address cross-cutting concerns, providing generic functions to alleviate the processing responsibilities of core Web service logic. Examples of the types of tasks performed by service agents include:

* SOAP header processing (Figure 18.12)
* filtering (based on SOAP header or payload content)
* authentication and content-based validation
* logging and auditing
* routing

An agent program usually exists as a lightweight application with a small memory footprint. It typically is provided by the runtime but also can be custom developed.

NOTE
What's the difference between a service agent intermediary and an intermediary Web service? The determining factor is typically the availability of a WSDL endpoint. Service agents don't generally have or require one, as they are designed to intercept message traffic automatically. An intermediary that is also a Web service will supply a published WSDL definition, establishing itself as a legitimate endpoint along the message path. Note that a service agent intermediary can be designed to also be a Web service intermediary.

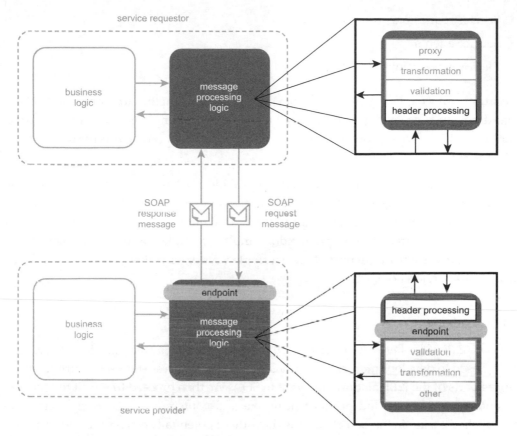

Figure 18.12

Service agents processing incoming and outgoing SOAP message headers.

18.1.5 Vendor platforms

Let's now explore SOA support provided by both J2EE and .NET platforms. The next two sections consist of the following sub-sections through which each platform is discussed:

- Architecture components
- Runtime environments
- Programming languages
- APIs
- Service providers

- Service requestors
- Service agents
- Platform extensions

Because we are exploring platforms from the perspective that they are comprised of both standards and the vendor manufactured technology that implements and builds upon these standards, we mention example vendor products that can be used to realize parts of a platform.

Even though every effort has been made to provide a balanced and equal documentation of each platform, it should be noted that the difference in vendor support required that some of the documentation be approached differently. For example, because J2EE is a platform supported by multiple vendors, multiple vendor products are mentioned. Because .NET is a platform provided by a single vendor, only that vendor's supporting products are referenced.

18.2   SOA support in J2EE

The *Java 2 Platform Enterprise Edition (J2EE)* is one of the two primary platforms currently being used to develop enterprise solutions using Web services. This section briefly introduces parts of the J2EE platform relevant to SOA. We then proceed to revisit the service-orientation principles and primary primitive and contemporary SOA characteristics established earlier in this book to discuss how these potentially can be realized using the previously explained parts of J2EE.

It is important to note that this section does not provide an in-depth explanation of the J2EE platform, nor do we get into how to program Web services using Java. There are already many comprehensive books that cover this vast subject area (see www.soabooks.com for recommended reading). The purpose of this section is simply to continue our exploration of SOA realization. In doing so, we highlight some of the main areas of interest within the J2EE platform.

18.2.1   Platform overview

The Java 2 Platform is a development and runtime environment based on the Java programming language. It is a standardized platform that is supported by many vendors that provide development tools, server runtimes, and middleware products for the creation and deployment of Java solutions.

The Java 2 Platform is divided into three major development and runtime platforms, each addressing a different type of solution. The *Java 2 Platform Standard Edition (J2SE)* is designed to support the creation of desktop applications, while the *Micro Edition (J2ME)* is geared toward applications that run on mobile devices. The Java 2 Platform Enterprise Edition (J2EE) is built to support large-scale, distributed solutions. J2EE has been in existence for over five years and has been used extensively to build traditional n-tier applications with and without Web technologies.

The J2EE development platform consists of numerous composable pieces that can be assembled into full-fledged Web solutions. Let's take a look at some of the technologies more relevant to Web services.

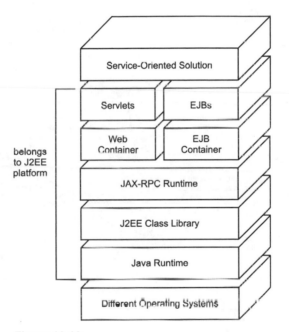

Figure 18.13
Relevant layers of the J2EE platform as they relate
to SOA.

Figure 18.13 does not illustrate the relationship between J2EE platform components. It only shows the underlying layers provided by the J2EE platform that support a J2EE service-oriented solution.

The Servlets + EJBs and Web + EJB Container layers (as well as the JAX-RPC Runtime) relate to the Web and Component Technology layers established earlier in the *SOA platform basics* section. They do not map cleanly to these layers because to what extent component and Web technology is incorporated is largely dependent on how a vendor chooses to implement this part of a J2EE architecture.

The components shown in Figure 18.13 inter-relate with other parts of the overall J2EE environment (as shown in Figure 18.14) to provide a platform capable of realizing SOA.

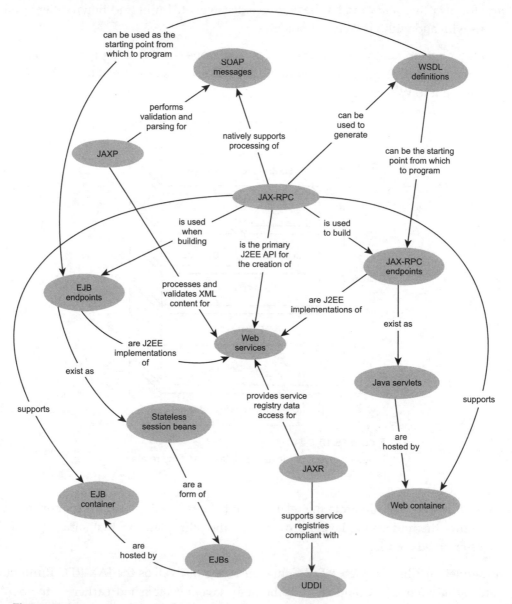

Figure 18.14

How parts of the J2EE platform inter-relate.

Before we discuss each of these components individually, let's begin with an overview of some key J2EE specifications. There are many J2EE standards published by Sun Microsystems that establish the parts of the J2EE architecture to which vendors that implement and build products around this environment must conform. Three of the more significant specifications that pertain to SOA are listed here:

- *Java 2 Platform Enterprise Edition Specification*—This important specification establishes the distributed J2EE component architecture and provides foundation standards that J2EE product vendors are required to fulfill in order to claim J2EE compliance.

- *Java API for XML-based RPC (JAX-RPC)*—This document defines the JAX-RPC environment and associated core APIs. It also establishes the Service Endpoint Model used to realize the JAX-RPC Service Endpoint, one of the primary types of J2EE Web services (explained later).

- *Web Services for J2EE*—The specification that defines the vanilla J2EE service architecture and clearly lays out what parts of the service environment can be built by the developer, implemented in a vendor-specific manner, and which parts must be delivered according to J2EE standards.

The latter specification establishes the important *Port Component Model* introduced later in the *Service providers* section.

Architecture components

J2EE solutions inherently are distributed and therefore componentized. The following types of components can be used to build J2EE Web applications:

- *Java Server Pages (JSPs)*—Dynamically generated Web pages hosted by the Web server. JSPs exist as text files comprised of code interspersed with HTML.

- *Struts*—An extension to J2EE that allows for the development of Web applications with sophisticated user-interfaces and navigation.

- *Java Servlets*—These components also reside on the Web server and are used to process HTTP request and response exchanges. Unlike JSPs, servlets are compiled programs.

- *Enterprise JavaBeans (EJBs)*—The business components that perform the bulk of the processing within enterprise solution environments. They are deployed on dedicated application servers and can therefore leverage middleware features, such as transaction support.

While the first two components are of more relevance to establishing the presentation layer of a service-oriented solution, the latter two commonly are used to realize Web services.

Runtime environments

The J2EE environment relies on a foundation Java runtime to process the core Java parts of any J2EE solution. In support of Web services, J2EE provides additional runtime layers that, in turn, supply additional Web services specific APIs (explained later). Most notable is the JAX-RPC runtime, which establishes fundamental services, including support for SOAP communication and WSDL processing.

Additionally, implementations of J2EE supply two types of component containers that provide hosting environments geared toward Web services-centric applications that are generally EJB or servlet-based.

- *EJB container*—This container is designed specifically to host EJB components, and it provides a series of enterprise-level services that can be used collectively by EJBs participating in the distributed execution of a business task. Examples of these services include transaction management, concurrency management, operation-level security, and object pooling.

- *Web container*—A Web container can be considered an extension to a Web server and is used to host Java Web applications consisting of JSP or Java servlet components. Web containers provide runtime services geared toward the processing of JSP requests and servlet instances.

As explained in the *Service providers* section, EJB and Web containers can host EJB-based or servlet-based J2EE Web services. Web service execution on both containers is supported by JAX-RPC runtime services. However, it is the vendor-specific container logic that generally determines the shape and form of the system-level message processing logic provided in support of Web services.

NOTE

J2EE vendors provide containers as part of their server products. A container then establishes the runtime that hosts an instance of the vendor's server software. Examples of currently available containers are Sun ONE (Open Network Environment) Application Server, IBM WebSphere, and Oracle Application Server Containers for J2EE (OC4J).

Programming languages

As its name implies, the Java 2 Platform Enterprise Edition is centered around the Java programming language. Different vendors offer proprietary development products that provide an environment in which the standard Java language can be used to build Web services.

> **NOTE**
>
> Examples of currently available development tools are Rational Application Developer from IBM, Java Studio from Sun Microsystems, and JDeveloper from Oracle.

APIs

J2EE contains several APIs for programming functions in support of Web services. The classes that support these APIs are organized into a series of *packages*. Here are some of the APIs relevant to building SOA.

- *Java API for XML Processing (JAXP)*—This API is used to process XML document content using a number of available parsers. Both Document Object Model (DOM) and Simple API for XML (SAX) compliant models are supported, as well as the ability to transform and validate XML documents using XSLT stylesheets and XSD schemas. Example packages include:
  - ~ `javax.xml.parsers`—A package containing classes for different vendor-specific DOM and SAX parsers.
  - ~ `org.w3c.dom` and `org.xml.sax`—These packages expose the industry standard DOM and SAX document models.
  - ~ `javax.xml.transform`—A package providing classes that expose XSLT transformation functions.
- *Java API for XML-based RPC (JAX-RPC)*—The most established and popular SOAP processing API, supporting both RPC-literal and document-literal request-response exchanges and one-way transmissions. Example packages that support this API include:
  - ~ `javax.xml.rpc` and `javax.xml.rpc.server`—These packages contain a series of core functions for the JAX-RPC API.
  - ~ `javax.xml.rpc.handler` and `javax.xml.rpc.handler.soap`—API functions for runtime message handlers are provided by these collections of classes. (Handlers are discussed shortly in the *Service agents* section.)

- ~ `javax.xml.soap` and `javax.xml.rpc.soap`—API functions for processing SOAP message content and bindings.
- *Java API for XML Registries (JAXR)*—An API that offers a standard interface for accessing business and service registries. Originally developed for ebXML directories, JAXR now includes support for UDDI.
  - ~ `javax.xml.registry`—A series of registry access functions that support the JAXR API.
  - ~ `javax.xml.registry.infomodel`— Classes that represent objects within a registry.
- *Java API for XML Messaging (JAXM)*—An asynchronous, document-style SOAP messaging API that can be used for one-way and broadcast message transmissions (but can still facilitate synchronous exchanges as well).
- *SOAP with Attachments API for Java (SAAJ)*—Provides an API specifically for managing SOAP messages requiring attachments. The SAAJ API is an implementation of the SOAP with Attachments (SwA) specification.
- *Java Architecture for XML Binding API (JAXB)*—This API provides a means of generating Java classes from XSD schemas and further abstracting XML-level development.
- *Java Message Service API (JMS)*—A Java-centric messaging protocol used for traditional messaging middleware solutions and providing reliable delivery features not found in typical HTTP communication.

Of these APIs, the two most commonly used for SOA are JAX-RPC to govern SOAP messaging and JAXP for XML document processing. The two other packages relevant to building the business logic for J2EE Web services are `javax.ejb` and `javax.servlet`, which provide fundamental APIs for the development of EJBs and servlets.

Note that we do not discuss these APIs any further. They are mentioned here only to demonstrate the grouping of API functions in J2EE packages.

Service providers

As previously mentioned, J2EE Web services are typically implemented as servlets or EJB components. Each option is suitable to meet different requirements but also results in different deployment configurations, as explained here:

- *JAX-RPC Service Endpoint*—When building Web services for use within a Web container, a JAX-RPC Service Endpoint is developed that frequently is implemented as a servlet by the underlying Web container logic. Servlets are a common incarnation of Web services within J2EE and most suitable for services not requiring the features of the EJB container.

- *EJB Service Endpoint*—The alternative is to expose an EJB as a Web service through an EJB Service Endpoint. This approach is appropriate when wanting to encapsulate existing legacy logic or when runtime features only available within an EJB container are required. To build an EJB Service Endpoint requires that the underlying EJB component be a specific type of EJB called a *Stateless Session Bean*.

Regardless of vendor platform, both types of J2EE Web services are dependent on the JAX-RPC runtime and associated APIs.

> **NOTE**
>
> A frequent point of confusion is the naming of the JAX-RPC Service Endpoint and the JAX-RPC runtime. Many initially assume that the JAX-RPC runtime is associated only with the JAX-RPC Service Endpoint and the Web container. However, because JAX-RPC establishes a standardized service processing layer that spans both Web and EJB containers, its runtime applies to both JAX-RPC Service Endpoints and EJB Service Endpoints.

Also a key part of either service architecture is an underlying model that defines its implementation, called the *Port Component Model*. As described in the Web Services for J2EE specification, it establishes a series of components that comprise the implementation of a J2EE service provider, including:

- *Service Endpoint Interface (SEI)*—A Java-based interpretation of the WSDL definition that is required to follow the JAX-RPC WSDL-to-Java mapping rules to ensure consistent representation.

- *Service Implementation Bean*—A class that is built by a developer to house the custom business logic of a Web service. The Service Implementation Bean can be implemented as an EJB Endpoint (Stateless Session Bean) or a JAX-RPC Endpoint (servlet). For an EJB Endpoint, it is referred to as an *EJB Service Implementation Bean* and therefore resides in the EJB container. For the JAX-RPC Endpoint, it is called a *JAX-RPC Service Implementation Bean* and is deployed in the Web container.

Figure 18.15 illustrates how the J2EE components fit into our familiar service provider model.

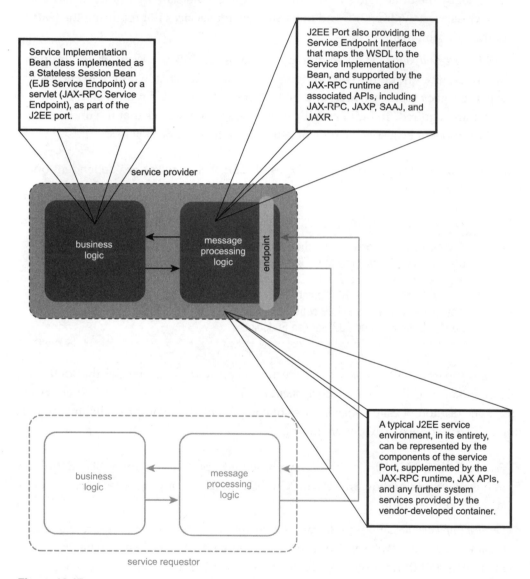

Service Implementation Bean class implemented as a Stateless Session Bean (EJB Service Endpoint) or a servlet (JAX-RPC Service Endpoint), as part of the J2EE port.

J2EE Port also providing the Service Endpoint Interface that maps the WSDL to the Service Implementation Bean, and supported by the JAX-RPC runtime and associated APIs, including JAX-RPC, JAXP, SAAJ, and JAXR.

service provider

business logic

message processing logic

endpoint

A typical J2EE service environment, in its entirety, can be represented by the components of the service Port, supplemented by the JAX-RPC runtime, JAX APIs, and any further system services provided by the vendor-developed container.

business logic

message processing logic

service requestor

Figure 18.15
A typical J2EE service provider.

Service requestors

The JAX-RPC API also can be used to develop service requestors. It provides the ability to create three types of client proxies, as explained here:

- *Generated stub*—The generated stub (or just "stub") is the most common form of service client. It is auto-generated by the JAX-RPC compiler (at design time) by consuming the service provider WSDL, and producing a Java-equivalent proxy component. Specifically, the compiler creates a Java remote interface for every WSDL portType which exposes methods that mirror WSDL operations. It further creates a stub based on the WSDL port and binding constructs. The result is a proxy component that can be invoked as any other Java component. JAX-RPC takes care of translating communication between the proxy and the requesting business logic component into SOAP messages transmitted to and received from the service provider represented by the WSDL.

- *Dynamic proxy* and *dynamic invocation interface*—Two variations of the generated stub are also supported. The dynamic proxy is similar in concept, except that the actual stub is not created until its methods are invoked at runtime. Secondly, the dynamic invocation interface bypasses the need for a physical stub altogether and allows for fully dynamic interaction between a Java component and a WSDL definition at runtime.

The latter options are more suited for environments in which service interfaces are more likely to change or for which component interaction needs to be dynamically determined. For example, because a generated stub produces a static proxy interface, it can be rendered useless when the corresponding WSDL definition changes. Dynamic proxy generation avoids this situation.

Figure 18.16 explains how J2EE technologies work together within the service requestor model.

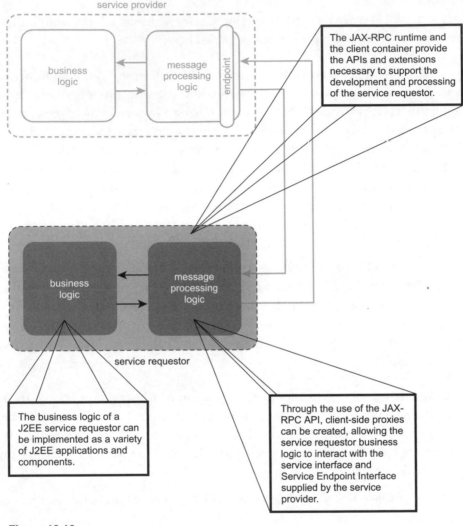

Figure 18.16
A typical J2EE service requestor.

Service agents

Vendor implementations of J2EE platforms often employ numerous service agents to perform a variety of runtime filtering, processing, and routing tasks. A common example is the use of service agents to process SOAP headers.

To support SOAP header processing, the JAX-RPC API allows for the creation of specialized service agents called *handlers* (Figure 18.17)—runtime filters that exist as extensions to the J2EE container environments. Handlers can process SOAP header blocks for messages sent by J2EE service requestors or for messages received by EJB Endpoints and JAX-RPC Service Endpoints.

Multiple handlers can be used to process different header blocks in the same SOAP message. In this case the handlers are chained in a predetermined sequence (appropriately called a *handler chain*).

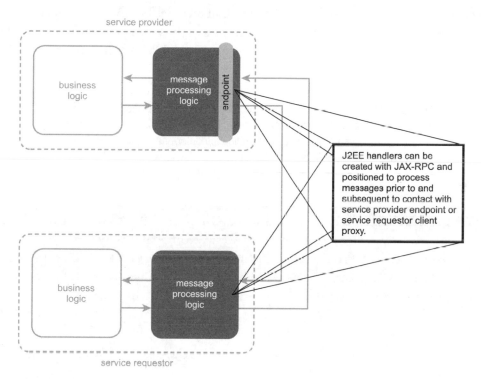

Figure 18.17
J2EE handlers as service agents.

Platform extensions
Different vendors that implement and build around the J2EE platform offer various platform extensions in the form of SDKs that extend their development tool offering. The technologies supported by these toolkits, when sufficiently mature, can further

support contemporary SOA. Following are two examples of currently available platform extensions.

- *IBM Emerging Technologies Toolkit*—A collection of extensions that provide prototype implementations of a number of fundamental WS-* extensions, including WS-Addressing, WS-ReliableMessaging, WS-MetadataExchange, and WS-Resource Framework.
- *Java Web Services Developer Pack*—A toolkit that includes both WS-* support as well as the introduction of new Java APIs. Examples of the types of extensions provided include WS-Security (along with XML-Signature), and WS-I Attachments.

NOTE

The WS-Resource Framework consists of a collection of specifications (WS-ResourceProperties, WS-ResourceLifetime, WS-BaseFaults, and WS-ServiceGroup) that establish a means of managing state information associated with Web services. For more information, visit www.soaspecs.com.

CASE STUDY

As explained throughout earlier chapters, RailCo originally delivered a set of Web services so that it could register as an online vendor for TLS's B2B solution. A recent change in strategy prompted RailCo to broaden the scope and potential of their Web services so that they could achieve the following two goals:

- Qualify as vendors for other online client solutions.
- Reengineer the architecture hosting the services so that it can become fully SOA-compliant.

The initial Web services-based application was developed using the .NET framework. At first RailCo planned to replace this solution with a set of redesigned .NET services. However, a recent corporate reorganization trimmed its IT budget to such an extent that it was not able to renew the contracts of the four consultant project team that delivered the original .NET solution.

To continue with its plan, RailCo had to draw upon in-house resources. The small group of Java programmers responsible for maintaining the Java-based accounting system were identified as potential candidates for the job. Because they had not yet worked with any of the Web services-related APIs, they needed to undergo training to get up to speed on JAX-RPC and JAXP.

Though this delayed the original plan, an SOA eventually was realized, hosting the new Invoice Processing and Order Fulfillment applications, built as J2EE solutions consisting of a set of JAX-RPC Service Endpoints.

18.2.2 Primitive SOA support

The J2EE platform provides a development and runtime environment through which all primitive SOA characteristics can be realized, as follows.

Service encapsulation

The distributed nature of the J2EE platform allows for the creation of independent units of processing logic through Enterprise Java Beans or servlets. EJBs or servlets can contain small or large amounts of application logic and can be composed so that individual units comprise the processing requirements of a specific business task or an entire solution.

Both EJBs and servlets can be encapsulated using Web services. This turns them into EJB and JAX-RPC Service Endpoints, respectively. The underlying business logic of an endpoint can further compose and interact with non-endpoint EJB and servlet components. As a result, well-defined services can be created in support of SOA.

Loose coupling

The use of interfaces within the J2EE platform allows for the abstraction of metadata from a component's actual logic. When complemented with an open or proprietary messaging technology, loose coupling can be realized. EJB and JAX-RPC Endpoints further establish a standard WSDL definition, supported by J2EE HTTP and SOAP runtime services. Therefore, loose coupling is a characteristic that can be achieved in support of SOA.

Messaging

Prior to the acceptance of Web services, the J2EE platform supported messaging via the JMS standard, allowing for the exchange of messages between both servlets and EJB components. With the arrival of Web services support, the JAX-RPC API provides the means of enabling SOAP messaging over HTTP.

Also worth noting is the availability of the SOAP over JMS extension, which supports the delivery of SOAP messages via the JMS protocol as an alternative to HTTP. The primary benefit here is that this approach to data exchange leverages the reliability features provided by the JMS framework. Within SOA this extension can be used by the business logic of a Web service, allowing SOAP messages to be passed through from the message process logic (which generally will rely on HTTP as the transport protocol). Either way, the J2EE platform provides the required messaging support for primitive SOA.

18.2.3   Support for service-orientation principles

We've established that the J2EE platform supports and implements the first-generation Web services technology set. It is now time to revisit the four principles of service-orientation not automatically provided by Web services and briefly discuss how each can be realized through J2EE.

Autonomy

For a service to be fully autonomous, it must be able to independently govern the processing of its underlying application logic. A high level of autonomy is more easily achieved when building Web services that do not need to encapsulate legacy logic. JAX-RPC Service Endpoints exist as standalone servlets deployed within the Web container and are generally built in support of newer SOA environments.

It may therefore be easier for JAX-RPC Service Endpoints to retain complete autonomy, especially when they are only required to execute a small amount of business logic. EJB Service Endpoints are required to exist as Stateless Session Beans, which supports autonomy within the immediate endpoint logic. However, because EJB Service Endpoints are more likely to represent existing legacy logic (or a combination of new and legacy EJB components), retaining a high level of autonomy can be challenging.

Reusability

The advent of Enterprise Java Beans during the rise of distributed solutions over the past decade established a componentized application design model that, along with the Java programming language, natively supports object-orientation. As a result, reusability is achievable on a component level. Because service-orientation encourages services to be reusable and because a service can encapsulate one or more new or existing EJB components, reusability on a service level comes down to the design of a service's business logic and endpoint.

Statelessness

JAX-RPC Service Endpoints can be designed to exist as stateless servlets, but the JAX-RPC API does provide the means for the servlet to manage state information through the use of the `HTTPSession` object. It is therefore up to the service designer to ensure that statelessness is maximized and session information is only persisted in this manner when absolutely necessary.

As previously mentioned, one of the requirements for adapting an EJB component into an EJB Service Endpoint is that it be completely stateless. In the J2EE world, this means that it must be designed as a Stateless Session Bean, a type of EJB that does not manage state but that may still defer state management to other types of EJB components (such as *Stateful Session Beans* or *Entity Beans*).

Discoverability

As with reuse, service discoverability requires deliberate design. To make a service discoverable, the emphasis is on the endpoint design, in that it must be as descriptive as possible.

Service discovery as part of a J2EE SOA is directly supported through JAXR, an API that provides a programmatic interface to XML-based registries, including UDDI repositories. The JAXR library consists of two separate APIs for publishing and issuing searches against registries.

Note that even if JAXR is used to represent a UDDI registry, it does so by exposing an interface that differs from the standard UDDI API. (For example, a UDDI `Business-Entity` is a JAXR `Organization`, and a UDDI `BusinessService` is a JAXR `Service`.)

18.2.4   Contemporary SOA support

Extending an SOA beyond the primitive boundary requires a combination of design and available technology in support of the design. Because WS-* extensions have not yet been standardized by the vendor-neutral J2EE platform, they require the help of vendor-specific tools and features.

We now take another look at some of the characteristics we associated with contemporary SOA in Chapter 9. How J2EE standards either automatically support these characteristics or how they can be fulfilled through deliberate application of J2EE technologies is explained.

Based on open standards

The Web services subset of the J2EE platform supports industry standard Web services specifications, including WSDL, SOAP, and UDDI. As explained later in the *Intrinsically interoperable* section, support for the WS-I Basic Profile also has been provided. Further, the API specifications that comprise the J2EE platform are themselves open standards, which further promotes vendor diversity, as described in the next section.

> **NOTE**
>
> It should also be mentioned that some J2EE vendors have provided significant contributions to the actual creation of Web services specifications.

Supports vendor diversity

Adherence to the vanilla J2EE API standards has allowed for a diverse vendor marketplace to emerge. Java application logic can be developed with one tool and then ported over to another. Similarly, Java components can be designed for deployment mobility across different J2EE server products.

Further, by designing services to be WS-I Basic Profile compliant, vendor diversity beyond J2EE platforms is supported. For example, an organization that has built an SOA based on J2EE technology may choose to build another using the .NET framework. Both environments can interoperate if their respective services conform to the same open standards. This also represents vendor diversity.

Intrinsically interoperable

Interoperability is, to a large extent, a quality deliberately designed into a Web service. Aside from service interface design characteristics, conformance to industry-standard Web services specifications is critical to achieving interoperable SOAs, especially when interoperability is required across enterprise domains.

As of version 1.1, the JAX-RPC API is fully capable of creating WS-I Basic Profile-compliant Web services. This furthers the vision of producing services that are intrinsically interoperable. Care must be taken, though, to prevent the use of handlers from performing runtime processing actions that could jeopardize this compliance.

> **NOTE**
>
> IBM's Rational Application Developer provides built-in support for building WS-I compliant Web services. Further, the Wscompile tool, which is part of the J2EE SDK from Sun Microsystems, allows for the auto-generation of WS-I Basic Profile compliant WSDL definitions.

Promotes federation

Strategically positioned services coupled with adapters that expose legacy application logic can establish a degree of federation. Building an integration architecture with custom business services and legacy wrapper services can be achieved using basic J2EE APIs and features. Supplementing such an architecture with an orchestration server (and an accompanying orchestration service layer) further increases the potential of unifying and standardizing integrated logic. (This is discussed in the *Supports service-oriented business modeling* section as well.)

Also worth taking into consideration is the *J2EE Connector Architecture (JCA)*, a structured, adapter-centric integration architecture through which *resource adapters* are used to bridge gaps between J2EE platforms and other environments. As with JMS, JCA is traditionally centered around the use of proprietary messaging protocols and platform-specific adapters. Recently, however, support for asynchronous and SOAP messaging has been introduced. Further, service adapters have been made available to tie JCA environments into service-oriented solutions.

Numerous integration server platforms also are available to support and implement the overall concept of enterprise-wide federation. Depending on the nature of the integration architecture, service-oriented integration environments are built around orchestration servers or enterprise service bus offerings (or both).

> **NOTE**
>
> The Sun ONE Connector Builder product is an example of a vendor implementation of JCA that supports the creation of a SOAP messaging layer. Also a number of J2EE vendors provide orchestration servers with native WS-BPEL support, including IBM's WebSphere Business Integration Server Foundation product and Oracle's BPEL Process Manager.

Architecturally composable

Given the modular nature of supporting API packages and classes and the choice of service-specific containers, the J2EE platform is intrinsically composable. This allows solution designers to use only the parts of the platform required for a particular application. For example, a Web services solution that only consists of JAX-RPC Service Endpoints will likely not have a need for the JMS class packages—or—a J2EE SOA that does not require a service registry will not implement any part of the JAXR API.

With regards to taking advantage of the composable contemporary SOA landscape, the J2EE platform, in its current incarnation, does not yet provide native support for WS-* specifications. Instead, extensions are supplied by product vendors that implement and build upon J2EE standards. The extent to which the WS-* features of an SOA based on the J2EE platform can be composed is therefore currently dependent upon the vendor-specific platform used.

Extensibility

As with any service-oriented solution, those based on the J2EE platform can be designed with services that support the notion of future extensibility. This comes down to fundamental design characteristics that impose conventions and structure on the service interface level.

Because J2EE environments are implemented by different vendors, extensibility can sometimes lead to the use of proprietary extensions. While still achieving extensibility within the vendor environment, this can limit the portability and openness of Java solutions.

Supports service-oriented business modeling

Beyond consistent and standardized design approaches to building service layers along the lines of the application, entity, and task-centric services we've established in previous chapters, there is no inherent support for service-oriented business modeling within J2EE.

This is primarily because the concept of orchestration is not a native part of the J2EE platform. Instead, orchestration services and design tools are provided by vendors to supplement the J2EE Web services development and runtime environment. Service-oriented business modeling and the service layers we've discussed in this book can therefore be created with the right vendor tools.

Logic-level abstraction

JAX-RPC Service Endpoints and EJB Service Endpoints can be designed into service layers that abstract application-specific or reusable logic. Further, entire J2EE solutions can be exposed through these types of services, when appropriate.

Depending on the vendor server platform used, some limitations may be encountered when building service compositions that require message-level security measures. These limitations may inhibit the extent of feasible logic-level abstraction.

Organizational agility and enterprise-wide loose coupling

In past chapters we explored the enablement of enterprise-wide agility through the implementation of abstraction via service sub-layers. As discussed in the previous section, the creation of these service layers is possible with the help of a vendor-specific orchestration server. Although the orchestration offering is proprietary, the fact that other Web services are J2EE standardized further promotes an aspect of agility realized through the vendor diverse nature of the J2EE marketplace.

For example, if a vendor server platform is not satisfying current business needs and requires replacement, application, entity-centric, and task-centric services likely will be sufficiently mobile so that they can be used in the replacement environment. The orchestration logic may or may not be portable, depending on whether a common orchestration language, such as WS-BPEL, was used to express the process logic.

To attain a state where business and technology domains of an enterprise are loosely coupled and achieve full, two-way agility, requires the fulfillment of a number of contemporary SOA characteristics identified in this book. The J2EE platform provides a foundation upon which to build a standardized and extensible SOA. Enterprise features offered by vendor platforms need to be incorporated to add layers on top of this foundation necessary to driving service-orientation across the enterprise.

SUMMARY OF KEY POINTS

- The J2EE platform is comprised of many APIs (JAXP, JAX-RPC, JAXR, etc.), supports the creation of two primary types of service providers (JAX-RPC Service Endpoints, EJB Service Endpoints) and the generation of three types of service requestor proxies (generated stub, dynamic proxy, and dynamic invocation interface).

- J2EE provides native support for the creation of primitive SOAs.

- Of the four primitive service-orientation principles not automatically realized through first-generation Web services technologies, all can be fulfilled with proper design and the use of appropriate J2EE APIs.

- Some contemporary SOA characteristics are supported by native J2EE platform features, while others require the involvement of vendor-specific products and extensions. The fact that J2EE supports the development of WS-I Basic Profile compliant services promotes several key contemporary SOA characteristics, such as intrinsic interoperability, federation, open standards, and vendor diversity.

- Much like the Web services specification landscape, the J2EE platform consists of a series of technologies that are based on open standards. This allows vendors to build proprietary tools and server platforms around a standardized foundation. It also establishes a marketplace allowing organizations to pick and choose J2EE products.

18.3   SOA support in .NET

The .NET framework is the second of the two platforms for which we discuss SOA support in this book. As with the previous section, we first introduce the primary parts of the .NET platform and then delve into our familiar primitive SOA characteristics, service-orientation principles, and contemporary SOA characteristics. For each we explore .NET features that provide direct or indirect support.

We also need to repeat our disclaimer about how this chapter does not provide any detailed explanation of the .NET framework. A number of books exist dedicated to describing the various parts of the .NET development and runtime platform, and several are mentioned in the recommended reading page at www.soabooks.com.

18.3.1   Platform overview

The .NET framework is a proprietary solution runtime and development platform designed for use with Windows operating systems and server products. The .NET platform can be used to deliver a variety of applications, ranging from desktop and mobile systems to distributed Web solutions and Web services.

A primary part of .NET relevant to SOA is the *ASP.NET* environment, used to deliver the Web Technology layer within SOA (and further supplemented by the *Web Services Enhancements (WSE)* extension).

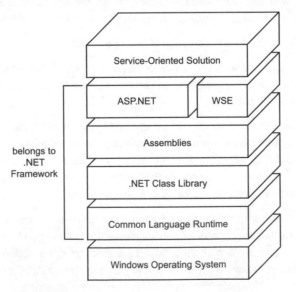

Figure 18.18
Relevant layers of the .NET framework, as they relate to SOA.

> **NOTE**
>
> Version 2.0 of the .NET framework introduces some new features to and changes
> some aspects of the ASP.NET architecture. Where appropriate, these changes
> are pointed out in the sections that follow.

Figure 18.18 does not provide a model that represents the .NET framework in its entirety. Instead, it simply shows the typical layers upon which .NET service-oriented solutions are built. In this diagram the ASP.NET + WSE and Assemblies layers correspond to the Web and Component Technology layers in our original, vendor-neutral model we established at the beginning of this chapter. As shown in Figure 18.19, these and the other parts of the .NET framework inter-relate to provide a platform through which services can be created in support of SOA.

Architecture components

The .NET framework provides an environment designed for the delivery of different types of distributed solutions. Listed here are the components most associated with Web-based .NET applications:

- *ASP.NET Web Forms*—These are dynamically built Web pages that reside on the Web server and support the creation of interactive online forms through the use of a series of server-side controls responsible for auto-generating Web page content.

- *ASP.NET Web Services*—An ASP.NET application designed as a service provider that also resides on the Web server.

- *Assemblies*—An assembly is the standard unit of processing logic within the .NET environment. An assembly can contain multiple classes that further partition code using object-oriented principles. The application logic behind a .NET Web service is typically contained within an assembly (but does not need to be).

ASP.NET Web Forms can be used to build the presentation layer of a service-oriented solution, but it is the latter two components that are of immediate relevance to building Web services.

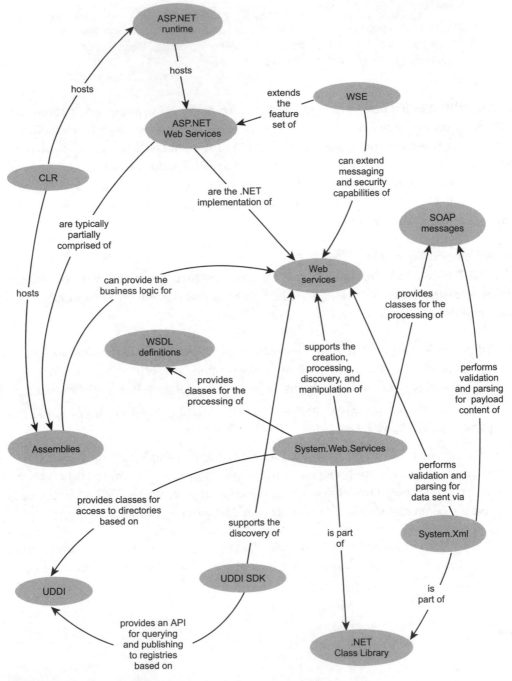

Figure 18.19
How parts of the .NET framework inter-relate.

Runtime environments

The architecture components previously described rely on the *Common Language Runtime (CLR)* provided by the .NET framework. CLR supplies a collection of runtime agents that provide a number of services for managing .NET applications, including cross-language support, central data typing, and object lifecycle and memory management.

Various supplementary runtime layers can be added to the CLR. ASP.NET itself provides a set of runtime services that establish the *HTTP Pipeline*, an environment comprised of system service agents that include HTTP modules and HTTP handlers (see the *Service agents* section for more information). Also worth noting is that the established COM+ runtime provides a further set of services (including object pooling, transactions, queued components, and just-in-time activation) that are made available to .NET applications.

Programming languages

The .NET framework provides unified support for a set of programming languages, including Visual Basic, C++, and the more recent C#. The .NET versions of these languages have been designed in alignment with the CLR. This means that regardless of the .NET language used, programming code is converted into a standardized format known as the *Microsoft Intermediate Language (MSIL)*. It is the MSIL code that eventually is executed within the CLR.

NOTE
Visual Studio establishes a standardized development environment through which .NET programming languages can be applied.

APIs

.NET provides programmatic access to numerous framework (operating system) level functions via the *.NET Class Library*, a large set of APIs organized into namespaces. Each namespace must be explicitly referenced for application programming logic to utilize its underlying features.

Following are examples of the primary namespaces that provide APIs relevant to Web services development:

- *System.Xml*—Parsing and processing functions related to XML documents are provided by this collection of classes. Examples include:

  ~ The `XmlReader` and `XmlWriter` classes that provide functionality for retrieving and generating XML document content.

~ Fine-grained classes that represent specific parts of XML documents, such as the `XmlNode`, `XmlElement`, and `XmlAttribute` classes.

- *System.Web.Services*—This library contains a family of classes that break down the various documents that comprise and support the Web service interface and inter-action layer on the Web server into more granular classes. For example:

  ~ WSDL documents are represented by a series of classes that fall under the `System.Web.Services.Description` namespace.

  ~ Communication protocol-related functionality (including SOAP message documents) are expressed through a number of classes as part of the `System.Web.Services.Protocols` namespace.

  ~ The parent `System.Web.Services` class that establishes the root namespace also represents a set of classes that express the primary parts of ASP.NET Web service objects (most notably, the `System.Web.Services.WebService` class).

  ~ Also worth noting is the `SoapHeader` class provided by the `System.Web.Services.Protocols` namespace, which allows for the processing of standard SOAP header blocks.

In support of Web services and related XML document processing, a number of additional namespaces provide class families, including:

- `System.Xml.Xsl`—Supplies documentation transformation functions via classes that expose XSLT-compliant features.

- `System.Xml.Schema`—A set of classes that represent XML Schema Definition Language (XSD)-compliant features.

- `System.Web.Services.Discovery`—Allows for the programmatic discovery of Web service metadata.

Note that we do not discuss these class libraries any further. They are only provided here to demonstrate the organization of .NET APIs into the .NET class hierarchy.

Service providers

.NET service providers are Web services that exist as a special variation of ASP.NET applications, called *ASP.NET Web Services*. You can recognize a URL pointing to an ASP.NET Web Service by the ".asmx" extension used to identify the part of the service that acts as the endpoint. ASP.NET Web Services can exist solely of an ASMX file containing inline code and special directives, but they are more commonly comprised of an ASMX endpoint and a compiled assembly separately housing the business logic.

Figure 18.20 shows how the pieces of a .NET Web service are positioned within our service provider model.

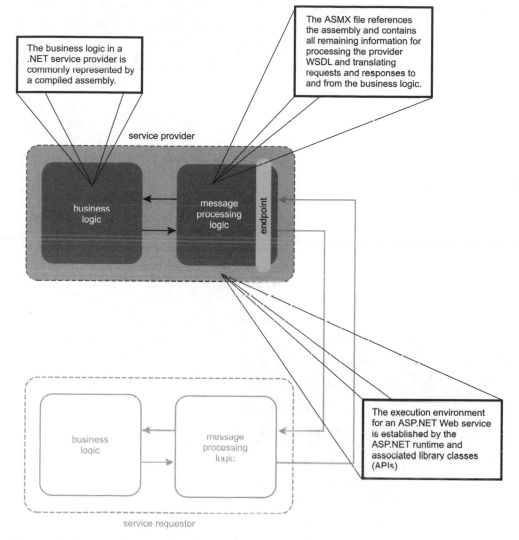

The business logic in a .NET service provider is commonly represented by a compiled assembly.

The ASMX file references the assembly and contains all remaining information for processing the provider WSDL and translating requests and responses to and from the business logic.

The execution environment for an ASP.NET Web service is established by the ASP.NET runtime and associated library classes (APIs)

Figure 18.20

A typical .NET service provider.

Service requestors

To support the creation of service requestors, .NET provides a proxy class that resides alongside the service requestor's application logic and duplicates the service provider interface. This allows the service requestor to interact with the proxy class locally, while delegating all remote processing and message marshalling activities to the proxy logic.

The .NET proxy translates method calls into HTTP requests and subsequently converts the response messages issued by the service provider back into native method return calls.

The code behind a proxy class is auto-generated using Visual Studio or the WSDL.exe command line utility. Either option derives the class interface from the service provider WSDL definition and then compiles the proxy class into a DLL.

Figure 18.21 explains how .NET proxies behave within the standard service requestor model.

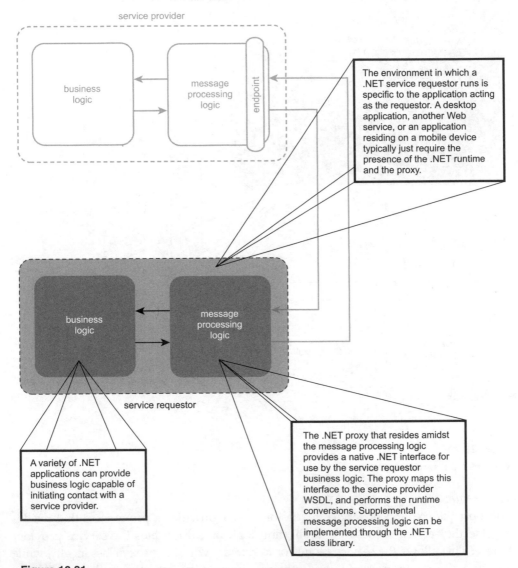

Figure 18.21
A typical .NET service requestor.

Service agents

The ASP.NET environment utilizes many system-level agents that perform various run-time processing tasks. As mentioned earlier, the ASP.NET runtime outfits the HTTP Pipeline with a series of *HTTP Modules* (Figure 18.22). These service agents are capable of performing system tasks such as authentication, authorization, and state management. Custom HTTP Modules also can be created to perform various processing tasks prior and subsequent to endpoint contact.

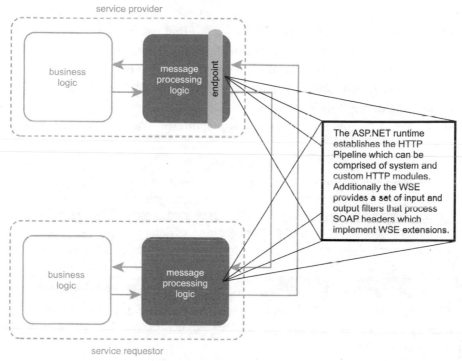

The ASP.NET runtime establishes the HTTP Pipeline which can be comprised of system and custom HTTP modules. Additionally the WSE provides a set of input and output filters that process SOAP headers which implement WSE extensions.

Figure 18.22
Types of .NET service agents.

Also worth noting are *HTTP Handlers,* which primarily are responsible for acting as run-time endpoints that provide request processing according to message type. As with HTTP Modules, HTTP Handlers can also be customized. (Other parts of the HTTP Pipeline not discussed here include the *HTTP Context, HTTP Runtime,* and *HTTP Application* components.)

Another example of service agents used to process SOAP headers are the filter agents provided by the WSE toolkit (officially called *WSE filters*). The feature set of the WSE is explained in the next section (*Platform extensions*), but let's first briefly discuss how these extensions exist as service agents.

WSE provides a number of extensions that perform runtime processing on SOAP headers. WSE therefore can be implemented through input and output filters that are responsible for reading and writing SOAP headers in conjunction with ASP.NET Web proxies and Web services. Much like the pre-processing scenarios we established in the *Service agents* sub-section of the *SOA platforms* section at the beginning of this chapter, WSE filters position themselves to intercept SOAP messages after submission on the service provider's end and prior to receipt on the service requestor's side.

Platform extensions

The Web Services Enhancements (WSE) is a toolkit that establishes an extension to the .NET framework providing a set of supplementary classes geared specifically to support key WS-* specification features. It is designed for use with Visual Studio and currently promotes support for the following WS-* specifications: WS-Addressing, WS-Policy, WS-Security (including WS-SecurityPolicy, WS-SecureConversation, WS-Trust), WS-Referral, and WS-Attachments and DIME (Direct Internet Message Encapsulation).

NOTE

We have not discussed WS-Referral or WS-Attachments in this book. The first is a Microsoft specification intended specifically to govern the use of SOAP routers. WS-Attachments uses the DIME encoding format used to send SOAP messages with attachments. For more information, see www.soaspecs.com.

CASE STUDY

Many of TLS's Web systems historically have been Java-based. In fact, the B2B solution explained throughout previous chapters was developed as a series of EJB Endpoints.

The original plan was for the upcoming Timesheet Submission project also to be delivered as part of the existing J2EE environment. However, the senior TLS architect in charge of overseeing the project was made aware of the recent availability of a team of four .NET consultants proficient in the delivery of ASP.NET Web Services.

This sparks the idea that this next solution could be based on the .NET framework instead. Subsequent to a meeting with management and peers, it is decided to hire these consultants to build the Timesheet Submission application as a .NET solution.

This decision is made for two reasons:

- TLS is curious to deliver an application based on the .NET framework and ASP.NET Web Services so that it can compare characteristics of the Timesheet Submission application (such as performance, stability, extensibility) with the existing J2EE B2B solution. In other words, TLS wants to use this opportunity to contrast vendor platforms.

- TLS made an effort to make all Web services part of the B2B solution fully WS-I Basic Profile-compliant. Though these services passed the criteria imposed on them by automated testing tools, TLS has not yet been able to prove real world compliance for those services that only perform internal tasks (public endpoint services, such as the Accounts Payable Service, are accessed by service requestors from different platforms every day and have therefore proven their cross-platform interoperability). By building ASP.NET Web Services in-house, TLS can test intrinsic interoperability characteristics for services from both solutions. Though not the primary reason for making this decision, this secondary benefit still is considered notable.

Given the freedom in vendor diversity provided by building service-oriented solutions, TLS can invest relatively safely in an application based on a different technology platform, knowing full well that .NET services should be fully interoperable with J2EE services (especially because TLS will be subjecting the .NET Web services to the same design standards used for their B2B solution).

Though it is technically safe, another consideration that factored into this decision was the maintenance commitment imposed by having to support both J2EE and .NET programming logic. Because TLS's IT environment is volatile and ever-growing, the risks and expenses associated with this consideration were deemed acceptable. The justification being that bringing a .NET solution within organizational boundaries will eventually lead to the development of in-house .NET expertise. It is hoped that this, in turn, will result in a more balanced skill-set that can accommodate the technology-related impact of future corporate mergers and acquisitions.

18.3.2   Primitive SOA support

The .NET framework natively supports primitive SOA characteristics through its runtime environment and development tools, as explained here.

Service encapsulation
Through the creation of independent assemblies and ASP.NET applications, the .NET framework supports the notion of partitioning application logic into atomic units. This promotes the componentization of solutions, which has been a milestone design quality of traditional distributed applications for some time. Through the introduction of Web services support, .NET assemblies can be composed and encapsulated through ASP.NET Web Services. Therefore, the creation of independent services via .NET supports the service encapsulation required by primitive SOA.

Loose coupling
The .NET environment allows components to publish a public interface that can be discovered and accessed by potential clients. When used in conjunction with a messaging framework, such as the one provided by Microsoft Messaging Queue (MSMQ), a loosely coupled relationship between application units can be achieved.

Further, the use of ASP.NET Web Services establishes service interfaces represented as WSDL descriptions, supported by a SOAP messaging framework. This provides the foremost option for achieving loose coupling in support of SOA.

Messaging
When the .NET framework first was introduced, it essentially overhauled Microsoft's previous distributed platform known as the Distributed Internet Architecture (DNA). As part of both the DNA and .NET platforms, the MSMQ extension (and associated APIs) supports a messaging framework that allows for the exchange of messages between components.

MSMQ messaging offers a proprietary alternative to the native SOAP messaging capabilities provided by the .NET framework. SOAP, however, is the primary messaging format used within contemporary .NET SOAs, as much of the ASP.NET environment and supporting .NET class libraries are centered around SOAP message communication and processing.

18.3.3   Support for service-orientation principles

The four principles we identified in Chapter 8 as being those not automatically provided by first-generation Web services technologies are the focus of this section, as we briefly highlight relevant parts of the .NET framework that directly or indirectly provide support for their fulfillment.

Autonomy

The .NET framework supports the creation of autonomous services to whatever extent the underlying logic permits it. When Web services are required to encapsulate application logic already residing in existing legacy COM components or assemblies designed as part of a traditional distributed solution, acquiring explicit functional boundaries and self-containment may be difficult.

However, building autonomous ASP.NET Web Services is achieved more easily when creating a new service-oriented solution, as the supporting application logic can be designed to support autonomy requirements. Further, self-contained ASP.NET Web Services that do not share processing logic with other assemblies are naturally autonomous, as they are in complete control of their logic and immediate runtime environments.

Reusability

As with autonomy, reusability is a characteristic that is easier to achieve when designing the Web service application logic from the ground up. Encapsulating legacy logic or even exposing entire applications through a service interface can facilitate reuse to whatever extent the underlying logic permits it. Therefore, reuse can be built more easily into ASP.NET Web Services and any supporting assemblies when developing services as part of newer solutions.

Statelessness

ASP.NET Web Services are stateless by default, but it is possible to create stateful variations. By setting an attribute on the service operation (referred to as the *WebMethod*) called `EnableSession`, the ASP.NET worker process creates an `HttpSessionState` object when that operation is invoked. State management therefore is permitted, and it is up to the service designer to use the session object only when necessary so that statelessness is continually emphasized.

Discoverability

Making services more discoverable is achieved through proper service endpoint design. Because WSDL definitions can be customized and used as the starting point of an ASP.NET Web Service, discoverability can be addressed, as follows:

- The programmatic discovery of service descriptions and XSD schemas is supported through the classes that reside in the `System.Web.Services.Discovery` namespace. The .NET framework also provides a separate UDDI SDK.

- .NET allows for a separate metadata pointer file to be published alongside Web services, based on the proprietary DISCO file format. This approach to discovery is further supported via the Disco.exe command line tool, typically used for locating and discovering services within a server environment.

- A UDDI Services extension is offered on newer releases of the Windows Server product, allowing for the creation of private registries.

- Also worth noting is that Visual Studio contains built-in UDDI support used primarily when adding services to development projects.

18.3.4   Contemporary SOA support

Keeping in mind that one of the contemporary SOA characteristics we identified early on in Chapter 3 was that SOA is still evolving, a number of the following characteristics are addressed by current and maturing .NET framework features and .NET technologies.

Based on open standards

The .NET Class Library that comprises a great deal of the .NET framework provides a number of namespaces containing collections of classes that support industry standard, first-generation Web services specifications.

As mentioned earlier, the WSE extension to .NET provides additional support for a distinct set of WS-* specifications. Finally, as described later in the *Intrinsically interoperable* section, version 2.0 of the .NET framework and Visual Studio 2005 provide native support for the WS-I Basic Profile.

Also worth noting is that Microsoft itself has provided significant contributions to the development of several key open Web services specifications.

Supports vendor diversity

Because ASP.NET Web Services are created to conform to industry standards, their use supports vendor diversity on an enterprise level. Other non-.NET SOAs can be built around a .NET SOA, and interoperability will still be a reality as long as all exposed Web services comply to common standards (as dictated by the Basic Profile, for example).

The .NET framework provides limited vendor diversity with regard to its development or implementation. This is because it is a proprietary technology that belongs to a single vendor (Microsoft). However, a third-party marketplace exists, providing numerous add-on products. Additionally, several server product vendors support the deployment and hosting of .NET Web Services and assemblies.

Intrinsically interoperable

Version 2.0 of the .NET framework, along with Visual Studio 2005, provides native support for the WS-I Basic Profile. This means that Web services developed using Visual Studio 2005 are Basic Profile compliant by default. (Previous versions of Visual Studio can be used to develop Basic Profile compliant Web services, but they require the use of third-party testing tools to ensure compliance.) Additional design efforts to increase generic interoperability also can be implemented using standard .NET first-generation Web services features.

Promotes federation

Although technically not part of the .NET framework, the BizTalk server platform can be considered an extension used to achieve a level of federation across disparate enterprise environments. It supplies a series of native adapters and is further supplemented by a third-party adapter marketplace. BizTalk also provides an orchestration engine with import and export support for BPEL process definitions.

Architecturally composable

The .NET Class Library is an example of a composable programming model, as classes provided are functionally granular. Therefore, only those functions actually required by a Web service are imported by and used within its underlying business logic.

With regard to providing support for composable Web specifications, the WSE supplies its own associated class library, allowing only those parts required of the WSE (and corresponding WS-* specifications) to be pulled into service-oriented solutions.

Extensibility

ASP.NET Web Services subjected to design standards and related best practices will benefit from providing extensible service interfaces and extensible application logic (implemented via assemblies with service-oriented class designs). Therefore, extensibility is not a direct feature of the .NET framework, but more a common sense design approach to utilizing .NET technology.

Functional extensibility also can be achieved by extending .NET SOAs through compliant platform products, such as the aforementioned BizTalk server.

Supports service-oriented business modeling

Service-oriented business modeling concepts can be implemented with .NET by creating the standard application, entity-centric, and task-centric service layers described earlier in this book.

The orchestration layer requires the use of an orchestration engine, capable of executing the process definition that centralizes business workflow logic. Orchestration features are not a native part of the .NET framework. However, they can be implemented by extending a .NET solution environment with the BizTalk server platform.

Logic-level abstraction

.NET SOAs can position ASP.NET Web Services and service layers to abstract logic on different levels. Legacy and net-new application logic can be encapsulated and wholly abstracted through proper service interface design. Service compositions can be built to an extent through the use of custom SOAP headers and correlation identifiers or by taking advantage of WSE extensions, such as the support provided for WS-Addressing and WS-Referral. (WSE also provides fundamental support for message-level security through extensions that implement portions of the WS-Security framework.)

Organizational agility and enterprise-wide loose coupling

Because the .NET framework supports the development of industry-standard Web services, the proper positioning and application of service layers allows for the creation of the required layers of abstraction that promote fundamental agility. The use of an orchestration layer can further increase corporate responsiveness by alleviating services from business process-specific logic and reducing the need for task-centric services.

The ultimate state of a service-oriented enterprise is to attain a level of bi-directional agility between business and technology domains. This can be achieved through contemporary SOA and requires that many of the discussed characteristics be fully realized. The .NET framework provides a foundation for SOA, capable of fully manifesting the primitive SOA characteristics and select qualities associated with contemporary SOA. Microsoft extensions to the .NET framework and third-party products are required to implement enterprise-wide loose coupling and realize the benefits associated with organizational agility.

SUMMARY OF KEY POINTS

- Building service-oriented solutions with .NET typically involves creating service providers as ASP.NET Web Services (supported by processing logic in business components implemented as assemblies) and service requestors that use auto-generated proxy classes.

- The Common Language Runtime and the .NET Class Library are cornerstones of the .NET framework.

- .NET provides the necessary environment and tools to build primitive SOAs.

- The four outstanding principles of service-orientation can be realized by applying design conventions to ASP.NET Web Services. Principles such as autonomy and reusability are achieved more easily when adding new service logic (as opposed to encapsulating legacy logic), whereas discovery requires explicit design.

- A subset of the contemporary SOA characteristics can be fulfilled with native .NET features, while others can be realized through product extensions.

- The .NET framework provides industry-compliant support for Web services and the WS-I Basic Profile. Further, it supports the limited implementation of select WS-* specifications, via the WSE toolkit.

18.4   Integration considerations

Every automation solution, regardless of platform, represents a collection of features and functions designed to execute some form of business process in support of one or more related tasks. The requirements for which such a system is built are generally well-defined and relevant at the time of construction. But, as with anything in life, they are eventually subject to change.

There are many drivers of change in contemporary corporations. Here are some of the more common examples:

- The expansion of an organization's business areas. When organizations undergo periods of growth, their business interests often broaden. This can include the incorporation of ancillary business operations that supplement their primary line of business, or it can go as far as the assimilation of entirely new business areas. These may or may not be related to the organization's primary goals but will almost always end up impacting the underlying technology environments responsible for automating the original business processes.

- The contraction of an organization's business areas. Corporations sometimes are forced to cut back on the scope of their operation. This may be a required response to changes in the general economic climate or changes in an organization's immediate business environment (such as the arrival of a new competitor or the loss of a primary client). Regardless, a reduction in business scope will require significant adjustments to existing business processes. These, in turn, can result in major changes to underlying automation logic. It is important to note that business area contraction is not always synonymous with a reduction in an organization's size. Sometimes, organizations simply eliminate some business areas to increase the focus on others.

- The acquisition of one organization by another. This situation obviously brings with it a multitude of issues, as the incorporation of a company's assets into an existing environment requires coordinated integration on a number of levels. Affected business processes typically are augmented or remodeled entirely, as is the supporting automation logic. Most integration issues arise from the introduction of foreign data models disparate in design and content.

- The merging of two organizations. This situation may require different integration requirements than the acquisition scenario. A corporate merger may not result in a clear cut relationship between two organizations, in that every merger is based on some form of operational agreement. The resulting requirements can include direct integration or even assimilation of automation solutions, but they also will very likely introduce the need for some form of cross-organization collaboration.

As the business arena becomes increasingly "global," these events are expected to become more common. Because of their magnitude, they can impose a great deal of change onto existing business automation environments. This is the primary reason that organizational agility has become so important.

When the extent of change is so broad that it affects multiple processes and application environments, it tests an organization's ability to adapt, for example:

- *Cross-platform interoperability*—The ability of previously standalone applications to be integrated with other applications that reside on and were developed with different vendor platforms.

- *Changes to cross-platform interoperability requirements*—The ability of existing integration channels to be augmented or replaced entirely in response to technical or business-related changes.

- *Application logic abstraction*—The ability for existing application logic to be re-engineered or even replaced entirely (often with new underlying technology).

The agility contemporary SOA brings to an organization can be fully leveraged when building integration architectures. The many benefits and characteristics we identified in this book as being attainable via SOA outfit the enterprise with the ability to meet the challenges we just explained. Service-oriented integration therefore empowers organizations to become highly responsive to change, all the while building on the service foundation established by SOA. (Service-oriented integration is explored in the companion guide to this book, *Service-Oriented Architecture: A Field Guide to Integrating XML and Web Services*.)

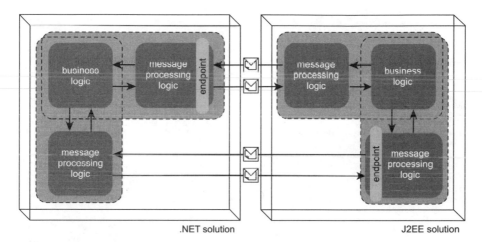

.NET solution   J2EE solution

Figure 18.23

Disparate solutions communicating freely across an open communications platform. A testament to the inherent interoperability established by SOA

Case Studies: Conclusion

A.1 RailCo Ltd.

RailCo's original goals were to upgrade its automation systems so that it could remain competitive and continue its business relationship with its primary client, TLS. RailCo had lost TLS as a customer when a competitor managed to provide air brake parts at a lower price while also interfacing with TLS's B2B system. RailCo rushed to catch up, producing a pair of Web services designed only for use with the TLS system. This allowed RailCo to regain its position as a TLS vendor.

These two initial Web services were

- Invoice Submission Service
- Order Fulfillment Service

(Another service was added later to interact with the TLS Notification Service.)

However, even though RailCo had successfully reconnected with TLS, it had lost its exclusive relationship. It now found itself in a position where it had to bid against an aggressive competitor for every purchase order issued; therefore, it was still losing revenue.

The only way RailCo could avoid significant downsizing was by finding new clients. To accomplish this, RailCo needed to continue pursuing the online vendor marketplace with other transit companies providing B2B solutions. It then became evident that RailCo's current set of Web services was insufficient for this purpose. Because they had been designed solely for use with TLS, they were not useful for interacting with other customers that dictated different business and transaction requirements.

RailCo was then faced with an important decision—either develop a custom set of services for each new client or start from scratch and build a standardized set of services generic enough to facilitate multiple clients. It chose the latter option and decided that the best way to achieve this goal was to overhaul its existing environment in favor of an SOA.

RailCo's two primary business processes are:

- Order Fulfillment (accepting and processing purchase orders from a client) and
- Invoice Submission (sending an invoice to a client).

RailCo proceeded with a service-oriented analysis that decomposed its business process logic into a series of service candidates. This revealed the need for the following potential services and service layers:

- A business service layer consisting of two task-centric business services.
- An application service layer comprised of four application services.

RailCo did not have the technology or the budget to invest in middleware capable of providing orchestration. It therefore chose not to pursue centralizing its business logic in an orchestration service layer.

Instead, it was decided to represent each business process with a task-centric business service that would act as a controller for a layer of application services. The following services were modeled and then designed:

- Invoice Processing Service (task-centric)
- PO Processing Service (task-centric)
- Legacy System Service (application)
- Polling Notification Service (application)
- Transform Service (application)
- Metadata Checking Service (application)

Reusability and extensibility in particular were emphasized during the design of its application services. RailCo wanted its initial SOA to consist of services that supported both of its current business processes, while being sufficiently extensible to accommodate future requirements without too much impact.

To realize the Invoice Submission Process, RailCo was able to compose these services into a two-level hierarchy, where the parent Invoice Processing Service coordinates the execution of all application services (Figure A.1).

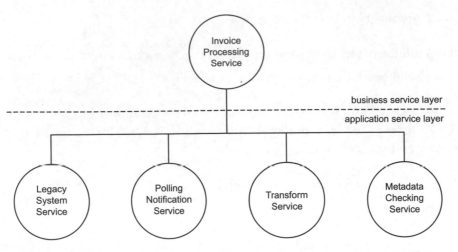

Figure A.1   RailCo's service composition that automates its Invoice Submission Process.

The Order Fulfillment Process can now be automated via the PO Processing Service, which reuses two of the same application services used by the Invoice Submission Process (Figure A.2).

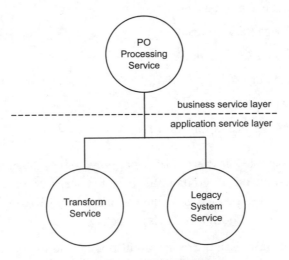

Figure A.2   The Order Fulfillment Process is automated by a PO Processing Service that composes two reusable application services.

In the face of some bad news involving the departure of the .NET consultants responsible for delivering their original Web services, RailCo was able to put internal resources to good use. Subsequent to a training effort, the new SOA was created as a J2EE solution.

RailCo has fulfilled its original goals by producing an SOA that supports two service-oriented solutions. RailCo can now continue its online transactions with TLS while confidently seeking new customers. Additional clients introducing new requirements can be accommodated with minimal impact. Its standardized application service layer will likely continue to offer reusable functionality to accommodate the fulfillment of new requirements. And any functional gaps will likely be addressed by extending the services without significantly disrupting existing implementations.

Further, should RailCo decide to replace its task-centric business services with an orchestration service layer in the future, the abstraction established by the existing application service layer will protect the application services from having to undergo redevelopment.

Upon completing this project, RailCo discovers a side benefit to its new solution environment. By having established the Legacy System Service (which is essentially a wrapper service for its accounting system) as part of its application service layer, it has opened up a generic endpoint that can facilitate integration.

This provides the potential for RailCo to enable interoperability between its accounting system and its contact management application (first introduced in Chapter 2). By allowing these two environments to share data, RailCo can more efficiently take on and service new clients with coordinated contact and financial history profiles.

A.2 Transit Line Systems Inc.

TLS had already built a service-oriented solution when we began our timeline in this book. It successfully established a B2B environment that facilitated online transactions with multiple vendors.

The application was comprised of business and application service layers that consisted of the following services:

- Accounts Payable Service
- Purchase Order Service
- Vendor Profile Service
- Ledger Service

- Load Balancing Service
- Internal Policy Service
- Notification Service (added later)

As you may recall, TLS did not actually require the use of a task-centric or process service. Its Accounts Payable and Purchase Order Services already contained the necessary business logic to receive invoices and issue purchase orders.

TLS decided to continue investing in SOA to address two critical business goals:

- The need to increase the responsiveness of its IT environments so that changes to its business models (which occur relatively frequently) can be accommodated without major disruptions.
- The need to establish a federated environment to standardize the many different systems it has accumulated through acquisitions and partnerships.

As part of TLS's SOA initiative, it chose to proceed with a second service-oriented solution: the automation and validation of timesheet submissions. This next project was also tasked with some extra analysis to study different service layer configurations. Because of recent technology upgrades, TLS is in a position to explore options that were not available when they built their first solution.

TLS proceeded through an elaborate service-oriented analysis phase during which it modeled a series of service candidates that collectively represented the business process logic identified in the required Timesheet Submission Process. It then went on to compare three different service layer configurations. It finally decided to proceed with the following configuration:

- An orchestration service layer establishing a single process service.
- A business service layer consisting of three entity-centric business services.
- An application service layer consisting of one application service (and two additional services that were added later).

The use of an orchestration service layer was new to TLS, as its previous platform did not provide support for an orchestration engine. After going through the service-oriented design process, interfaces for the following individual services were built:

- Employee Service (entity-centric)
- Timesheet Service (entity-centric)

- Invoice Service (entity-centric)
- Notification Service (application)
- Human Resources Service (application)

Additionally, it was discovered that the existing Accounts Payable Service created for the B2B solution would be able to facilitate the processing requirements of the planned Invoice Service. This reuse opportunity was leveraged, and the Accounts Payable Service was enlisted to support this process as well.

Next, TLS carried its existing process workflow logic over to the service-oriented business process design stage. It established a WS-BPEL process definition to encapsulate the workflow logic for the Timesheet Submission Process. This process definition coordinated the activities of all services and successfully realized the planned orchestration service layer (Figure A.3).

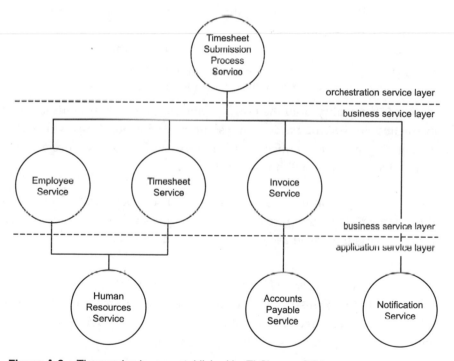

Figure A.3   The service layers established by TLS's new SOA.

TLS proceeded to build this solution but for various reasons decided to create it using a different development platform from the one used to deliver the original B2B system. It took advantage of the availability of a group of .NET consultants and chose to develop the Timesheet Submission solution as a .NET application. The rationale was that it would prove interoperability with its existing J2EE services and eventually increase the diversity of its internal skill-set.

By building this second service-oriented solution, TLS has taken small but important steps toward realizing its primary goals, as follows:

- By successfully establishing an orchestration service layer, TLS can now utilize this layer for future solutions. Because orchestration was introduced early on, TLS can standardize on centralized business process abstraction without any real retrofitting.

- By continuing to add to its initial set of entity-centric business services, TLS furthers its goal of increasing organizational agility. An orchestration layer, coupled with a layer of entity-centric business services, establishes a solid foundation for business logic abstraction. This also results in a loosely coupled relationship with the expanding application services layer. Future response times are expected to decrease as these two abstraction layers continue to grow.

- By exposing functionality from their legacy timesheet and HR systems and by further abstracting parts of their accounting solution, TLS is building an increasingly federated environment. It is anticipated that the cost of integration projects involving federated applications will drop significantly.

A subsequent corporate planning session results in a list of new strategic goals for TLS, one of which happens to be the purchase of an air brake supplier. This would give TLS all the air brake parts they need at wholesale cost and would also open up a potential new business area.

Upon subsequent investigation, TLS identifies a number of acquisition candidates. RailCo Ltd. ranks high on this list. One of the benefits documented in the evaluation report on RailCo is the fact that its automation solution environment contains standardized, service-oriented applications and legacy endpoints.

This appealed to the TLS architects who were asked to assess the IT environments of each candidate. Inspired by the success of their second service-oriented solution, TLS IT managers asked architects to favor candidates with standardized service-oriented environments. With RailCo they recognized an opportunity to leverage existing SOAs for an easier and more cost-effective integration effort.

A.3   The Oasis Car Wash

What ever happened to our car wash venture? Soon after receiving our business license, we were approached by Ron, the straight-laced owner of the car washing company with whom we partnered and shared resources during each other's peak hours. Ron presented us with a buy-out offer which, after some discussion, we decided to accept. Bob, Jim, and I left our soaps and buckets behind to seek new opportunities. Chuck, though, was asked by Ron to continue working at the car wash. Chuck took care of all the administration, and Ron recognized him as a valuable resource for the upcoming integration effort of merging the two companies into a single (hopefully service-oriented) car washing enterprise.

Appendix B

Service Models Reference

Services can be categorized based on the nature of the logic they encapsulate and the manner in which they are typically utilized within SOA. This book introduces a series of these categories and calls them service models.

Because service model descriptions are interspersed in various chapters, we provide a master list in this Appendix for quick reference purposes. Note that services can (and often do) belong to more than one service model.

Table B-1 An overview of service models.

Service Model	Description	Chapters
Application service	A generic category used to represent services that contain logic derived from a solution or technology platform. Services are generally distinguished as application services when creating service abstraction layers.	9, 11, 12, 15
Business service	A generic category used to represent services that contain business logic. When establishing specialized service layers, services that fall into the business service layer are collectively referred to as business services. However, individually these services are classified as entity-centric or task-centric business services.	5, 9, 11, 12, 15
Controller service	A service that composes others. Variations of this model exist, depending on the position of the controller in the composition hierarchy. The parent controller service can be classified as the master controller and a service that composes a subset of a larger composition can be labeled a sub-controller.	5

Service Model	Description	Chapters
Coordinator services	Three service models are derived from the concept of coordination: the coordinator, the atomic transaction coordinator, and the business activity coordinator. All three models are specific to the WS-Coordination specification and related protocols.	6
Entity-centric business service	A business process-agnostic variation of the business service that represents one or more related business entities. This type of service is created when establishing a business service layer.	9, 11, 12, 15
Hybrid service	A service that contains both business and application logic. Most services created as part of traditional distributed solutions fall into this category. When organizing services into abstraction layers, hybrid services are considered part of the application service layer.	9
Integration service	An application service that also acts as an endpoint to a solution environment for cross-application integration purposes.	9
Process service	A service that represents a business process as implemented by an orchestration platform and described by a process definition. Process services reside in the orchestration service layer.	6, 9, 11, 12, 16
Task-centric business service	A business process-specific variation of the business service that represents an atomic unit of process logic. Task-centric services are different from process services in that the process logic is provided by the underlying service logic, not by a separate process definition.	9, 11, 12, 15

Table B-1　An overview of service models (*Continued*).

Service Model	Description	Chapters
Utility service	A service that offers reusable logic. This category is primarily intended for the classification of solution-agnostic application services. However, it also can be used to refer to reusable business services.	5, 9
Wrapper service	A type of integration service that encapsulates and exposes logic residing within a legacy system. Wrapper services are commonly provided by legacy system vendors and therefore frequently introduce non-standardized interfaces.	9

Glossary

An on-line master glossary for all titles in the *Prentice Hall Service-Oriented Computing Series from Thomas Erl* is provided at www.soaglossary.com.

About the Author

Thomas Erl is the world's top-selling SOA author, the Series Editor of the *Prentice Hall Service-Oriented Computing Series from Thomas Erl*, and Editor of *The SOA Magazine*.

With over 80,000 copies in print world-wide, his books have become international best-sellers and have been formally endorsed by senior members of major software organizations, such as IBM, Microsoft, Oracle, BEA, Sun, Intel, SAP, and HP. His most recent titles are *SOA: Principles of Service Design* and *SOA Design Patterns* (www.soabooks.com).

Thomas is also the founder of SOA Systems Inc. (www.soasystems.com), a company specializing in SOA training and strategic consulting services with a vendor-agnostic focus. Through his work with standards organizations and independent research efforts, Thomas has made significant contributions to the SOA industry, most notably in the areas of service-orientation and SOA methodology.

Thomas is a speaker and instructor for private and public events, and has delivered many workshops and keynote speeches. He has also developed an industry-recognized SOA training and certification program. For more information, see www.soaschool.com and www.soatraining.com.

Papers and articles written by Thomas have been published in numerous industry trade magazines and Web sites, and he has delivered Webcasts and interviews for many publications, including the *Wall Street Journal*.

For more information, visit www.thomaserl.com.

About the Photographs

I hope you enjoy the collection of photos used for the book cover and divider pages. I took these recently while visiting various cities, including Bratislava, Prague, Vienna, and Washington. Some introduce a degree of symbolism related to a particular subject matter, while others just seem to embody a topic in an indefinable manner. Incorporating these photographs made me realize that they, much like services, uniquely abstract and express distinct parts of our world.

Index

BOOKS ONLINE

ENABLED

THIS BOOK IS SAFARI ENABLED

INCLUDES FREE 45-DAY ACCESS TO THE ONLINE EDITION

The Safari® Enabled icon on the cover of your favorite technology book means the book is available through Safari Bookshelf. When you buy this book, you get free access to the online edition for 45 days.

Safari Bookshelf is an electronic reference library that lets you easily search thousands of technical books, find code samples, download chapters, and access technical information whenever and wherever you need it.

TO GAIN 45-DAY SAFARI ENABLED ACCESS TO THIS BOOK:

- Go to www.informit.com/safarifree
- Enter the coupon code: MXJN-1GUK-1BJ4-NTKT-DFHQ
- New Safari users, complete the brief registration form. Safari subscribers, just log in.

If you have difficulty registering on Safari Bookshelf or accessing the online edition, please e-mail customer-service@safaribooksonline.com.

PRENTICE
HALL

The SOA Magazine

The SOA Magazine is a monthly online publication provided by
SOA Systems Inc. and Prentice Hall, and is officially associated with
the *Prentice Hall Service-Oriented Computing Series from Thomas Erl*.

The SOA Magazine is dedicated to publishing specialized SOA articles,
case studies, and papers by industry experts and professionals. The
common criteria for contributions is that each explore a distinct aspect
of service-oriented computing.

Visit The SOA Magazine at **www.soamag.com** or www.soamagazine.com.
If you are interested in contributing, use the online form. If you would like
to be automatically notified when new issues are published, send a blank
e-mail to: notify@soasystems.com

The International SOA Symposium

The International SOA Symposium is the world's most comprehensive SOA event for practitioners,
showcasing the leading SOA experts and speakers from around the world. The theme of the event
is "substance only", with an emphasis on ensuring that each session provides in-depth coverage
and true educational value for the most important SOA-related topics, including:

- SOA Architecture & Design
- Service Modeling & BPM
- SOA & Business
- SOA & REST
- SOA & Web 2.0

- SOA Governance
- SOA Programming
- SOA Innovations
- SOA Infrastructure & Technology
- SOA Project Delivery & Methodology

Additionally, the SOA Symposium regularly includes:

- Book Launch Ceremonies
- Expert Panels

- Hundreds of Free Books for Contests & Giveaways
- Exclusive Content

The International SOA Symposium attracts the world's leading SOA experts, including many of the
authors of the *Prentice Hall Service-Oriented Computing Series from Thomas Erl*.

For more information, visit **www.soasymposium.com**. To be notified of the latest event information,
send a blank e-mail to: notify@soasymposium.com